Political Parties, Interest Groups, and Public Policy

Political Parties, Interest Groups, and Public Policy

Group Influence in American Politics

DENNIS S. IPPOLITO
THOMAS G. WALKER

Emory University

PRENTICE-HALL, INC., *Englewood Cliffs, New Jersey 07632*

Library of Congress Cataloging in Publication Data

Ippolito, Dennis S.
    Political parties, interest groups, and public policy.

    Includes bibliographical references and index.
    1. Political parties—United States.
2. Pressure groups—United States.   I. Walker, Thomas G., joint author.   II. Title.
JK2261.I66   329'.02   79-16057
ISBN 0-13-684357-3

©1980 by Prentice-Hall, Inc., Englewood Cliffs, N.J. 07632

All rights reserved. No part of this book may be reproduced in any form or by any means without permission in writing from the publisher.

Printed in the United States of America

10 9 8 7 6 5 4 3 2 1

Editorial/production supervision
   by Colette Conboy and Penny Linskey
Manufacturing buyer: Harry P. Baisley

Prentice-Hall International, Inc., *London*
Prentice-Hall of Australia Pty. Limited, *Sydney*
Prentice-Hall of Canada, Ltd., *Toronto*
Prentice-Hall of India Private Limited, *New Delhi*
Prentice-Hall of Japan, Inc., *Tokyo*
Prentice-Hall of Southeast Asia Pte. Ltd., *Singapore*
Whitehall Books Limited, *Wellington, New Zealand*

Contents

Preface ix

one
Parties, Interest Groups, and Democratic Politics 1

Institutional Linkages and Democratic Government *2*
Contemporary Trends—Political Parties *11*
Contemporary Trends—Interest Groups *16*
Summary *20*

part one
POLITICAL PARTIES 23

two
The Party System in the United States 25

Origin and Development of the Party System *26*
Party Competition *35*
Third Parties *46*
Summary *58*

three
The Political Party Organization   60

The National Organizations   *62*
State and Local Organizations   *75*
Maintaining the Organization   *83*
Summary   *91*

four
Parties and the Electorate   93

Political Interest and Involvement   *95*
Partisan Indentification: The Weakening of Party Loyalties   *99*
Partisan Identification: Interparty Differences   *105*
Independents and Partisans   *123*
The Impact of Partisan Change   *130*
Summary   *132*

five
The Party Elites: Inter-Party Differences   134

Official Policy Differences   *136*
Attitudinal Differences   *153*
Summary   *168*

six
The Party in Politics: Nominations and Elections   170

Nominating Practices: An Overview   *171*
Elections: An Overview   *178*
Presidential Nominations and Elections   *192*
Nonpresidential Elections   *200*
Summary   *207*

seven
The Party in Politics: Governing 209

Political Parties and the Legislature *210*
Political Parties and the Executive Branch *234*
Political Parties and the Judiciary *243*
Summary *249*

eight
Party Conflicts and the Future of the Party System 251

Party Structure *251*
Party Goals *258*
Conflict and Change *265*

part two
INTEREST GROUPS 267

nine
Interest Groups as Political Organizations 268

The Nature and Function of Interest Groups *269*
Contemporary American Interest Groups *281*
The Internal Structure of Interest Groups *310*
Summary *318*

ten
Indirect Lobbying: Interest Groups and the Public 320

Interest Groups and Public Opinion *321*
Interest Groups and Elections *339*
Summary *362*

eleven
Direct Lobbying: Interest Groups and Government 364

Lobbying the Legislative Branch *365*
Lobbying the Executive Branch *386*
Lobbying the Judicial Branch *399*
Summary *409*

twelve
Parties, Interest Groups, and American Politics 411

Political Parties *412*
Interest Groups *414*
Recent Trends and Future Prospects *416*

Index 423

Preface

The voting age population of the United States now includes approximately 150 million individuals. The interests of a large and diverse electorate are not easily or automatically represented in government. In order to facilitate popular control of government, we must necessarily depend, in part, upon groups that can organize societal interests and bring these interests to bear upon those who must ultimately decide governmental policy. This book examines two types of political organizations—parties and interested groups—that perform this crucial function.

The general organization of this book reflects reasonably distinct treatments of these groups. *Part One* (chapters 2-8) deals with the historical development, structure, and functions of the American party system. It also devotes considerable attention to interparty differences, analyzing the attitudes and beliefs of the party electorates and of the competing party leaderships, as well as the policies advanced in recent years by the Democratic and Republican parties. We hope that this will provide students with an objective approach for understanding the behavior and evaluating the performance of the two major parties. *Part Two* (chapters 9-11) discusses the organization and politically-relevant activities of various types of interest groups. The emphasis within this section is on the ways in which interest groups attempt to influence government policy.

We have also described the growing similarities between political parties and interest groups and how these affect contemporary American politics. Over the past two decades, the lines of demarcation between these organizations have become rather blurred. This reflects, to a considerable extent, the demise of parties as predominant political organizations. Many of the functions traditionally monopolized by the parties are now shared among competing types of political organizations, including, of course, interest groups. This is certainly the case with electoral politics, and it appears to be increasingly characteristic of representative functions as well. While one cannot confidently predict the long-term results of these and related changes, it is likely that they will materially affect the conduct of democratic politics. We have, therefore, dealt at some length with the implications of party decline and the corresponding rise of interest group politics.

Dennis S. Ippolito
Thomas G. Walker

Political Parties,
Interest Groups,
and Public Policy

one

Parties, Interest Groups, and Democratic Politics

Political parties and interest groups are important institutional components of democratic politics. They serve as intermediaries between the public and government, providing stable organizational mechanisms through which public interests and preferences can be communicated to policymakers and can thereby influence decisions on public policy. For many individuals, parties or interest groups can help make government understandable and, by uniting individuals, political participation meaningful.

It is also apparent, however, that public attitudes toward parties and interest groups are usually negative.[1] The merits of partisan and special interest politics find few public defenders. This may reflect society's distaste for the open pursuit of influence and power, or perhaps the public shares James Madison's concern that partisanship and factions threaten the public good and private rights. Madison, however, soon reconciled himself to the practical benefits of party, even if his philo-

---

[1] For an examination of the public's confidence in parties, see Arthur H. Miller, "Rejoinder," *American Political Science Review,* 68 (September 1974), 989-1001. Miller also reports that public perceptions of the influence of special interests changed during the 1960s. The percentage of a national sample agreeing that government was "pretty much run by *a few big interests* looking out for themselves" as opposed to being run "for the *benefit of all* the people" increased from 29.0 percent to 49.6 percent. Arthur H. Miller, "Political Issues and Trust in Government: 1964-1970," *American Political Science Review,* 68 (September 1974), 953.

sophical anxieties persisted. And government, in Madison's time as today, has exercised power that directly and intentionally affects the objectives and ambitions of competing groups. Whether one likes it or not, group interests are dominant forces in the political process, and democratic politics inevitably involves bargaining, negotiation, and compromise in order to reconcile legitimate interests. Political organizations such as parties and interest groups are therefore necessary instrumentalities of group action and democratic politics.

The purpose of this book, then, is to examine the roles, functions, and performance of parties and interest groups within the context of representative democratic government. Such an examination must necessarily analyze the changes in the party system and in interest group politics during the past decade. While it is still too early to judge the full impact of many of these changes, it is our view that certain "reforms" at least reflect serious misconceptions about the political interests and capacities of most citizens and the actual operations of government. Reforms that are democratizing in intent, for example, are not necessarily democratizing in practice. The politics of change in our most basic intermediate institutions provides a useful focus for analyzing this disjunction and assessing its consequences.

INSTITUTIONAL LINKAGES AND DEMOCRATIC GOVERNMENT

A democratic political system is based on certain assumptions about the acquisition and exercise of authority. One key assumption is that the preferences or opinions of the governed should be taken into account as public officials make their decisions. In a system of direct democracy, the public would act as decision maker, and interests would be immediately represented. A representative democracy, however, requires that the public choose representatives—such as legislators and executives—to act in its behalf. The relationship between the public and its representatives is therefore a crucial one, for it affects the congruence between public preferences and government policy. Democratic theory provides some guidance in the form of ethical prescriptions defining the responsibilities of leaders and citizens, but it is less helpful in dealing with the actual processes through which public policy is decided. How are decision makers apprised of public interests and preferences; how is public influence transmitted; how is accountability enforced? Moreover, how is each of these to be accomplished on a continuing basis?

Some of the answers are found in the formalized means that democracies have developed for structuring the interaction between the public and political leaders. These include institutional linkages such as elections, political parties and interest groups, and representative institutions. While these linkages often complement or supplement each other, there are important distinctions among them.

Elections

A system of free, competitive, and relatively frequent elections provides for the peaceful acquisition and transfer of power. It also serves to promote popular control of government. As Madison explained in *Federalist* No. 52, "Frequent elections are unquestionably the only policy" that can secure a government's "immediate dependence on, and necessary sympathy with, the people."[2]

The electoral linkage posits a direct relationship between voters and public officials. The public has certain preferences that it wishes to see translated into government action. Candidates have a clear interest in being elected or returned to office; their electoral appeals and, for the successful candidates, subsequent decisions in office will therefore attempt to satisfy electorate preferences. Since its votes can be used as rewards or sanctions, the electorate has a readily available and potent means for disciplining its leaders.

There are, however, certain practical limits on the degree of popular control provided by elections. The electoral linkage presupposes that the voters will be presented with real policy choices during campaigns. However, it is necessary for the voters to have sufficient interest and information in order to respond intelligently to these choices. They must be knowledgeable about the issues, aware of the differences between opposing candidates, and willing to make electoral judgments on the basis of policy. The electorate, in sum, must satisfy certain requirements about activity, information, and rationality.

These requirements are not always met. Voter turnout in the United States, for example, is relatively low in comparison to other industrial democracies; more important, turnout varies significantly among various segments of the population, as well as by type of election. For those who do vote, awareness of candidates' issue positions is often quite limited, as is familiarity with many important policy issues.[3] And, of course, election campaigns typically focus attention on a very limited range of policy issues. It is not always clear how opposing candidates differ even on these issues, nor is it necessarily the case that their systematic differences correspond to issue patterns within the electorate.[4]

As a result of these and related factors, elections do not usually provide clear public majorities or mandates on which to base future policy initiatives. More often, they constitute a retrospective judgment of past governmental performance.[5] And while this does not severely restrict the discretion of public officials,

---

[2] *The Federalist Papers* (New York: New American Library, 1961), p. 327.

[3] There is considerable literature on this point. For an examination of possible changes in issue awareness, see Norman H. Nie, Sidney Verba, and John R. Petrocik, *The Changing American Voter* (Cambridge, Mass.: Harvard University Press, 1976).

[4] See John L. Sullivan and Robert E. O'Connor, "Electoral Choice and Popular Control of Public Policy: The Case of the 1966 House Elections," *American Political Science Review,* 66 (December 1972), 1256-68.

[5] See Gerald M. Pomper, *Elections in America* (New York: Dodd, Mead & Company, 1968), especially chap. 4; and V. O. Key, Jr., *The Responsible Electorate* (Cambridge, Mass.: The Belknap Press of Harvard University Press, 1966).

it does provide a clear incentive for them to act in anticipation of future judgment at the polls. The electoral linkage, then, provides the electorate with potent rewards and sanctions that it can employ in order to achieve policy objectives. At the same time, however, a degree of organization and coherence is necessary if this linkage involves a mass electorate and substantial numbers of candidates. Majorities must be built, for example, to elect a president or to pass legislation in Congress. This can only be accomplished through the mobilization of large numbers of voters with similar policy interests or candidate preferences. It is this mobilization that parties traditionally have provided.

Political Parties and Interest Groups

A second type of linkage is based upon the activities of stable, organized groups that serve as intermediaries between their members (or supporters) and government. An intermediate institution allows individuals with common interests or preferences to join in a collective effort to influence government policy. It also serves to oversee the actions of government officials and to hold them accountable. Parties and interest groups, however, differ in how they perform these functions.

Political Parties. Many political organizations seek to influence government policy, but the political party is distinctive in several important respects. First, it pursues influence by attempting to elect its candidates to office. The major American parties are even considered to be somewhat atypical in their electoral emphasis when compared to the more ideological democratic parties in Western Europe, for example. Democratic and Republican dominance of national elections is obvious, and their control at the state and local level is only slightly less pervasive. Nonparty organizations also recruit and support candidates, of course, but their electoral involvement is usually limited and sporadic when compared to the party. In order to achieve any policy goals, the party must be able to contest elections effectively. This is the key to its political influence.

Second, the party differs from other political organizations in its mobilizing capability. During a presidential campaign, the party tries to bring together tens of millions of individual voters. Here again, nonparty organizations can perform an analogous function, but the number and diversity of voters involved are typically limited when viewed in the context of the truly mass mobilization achieved by a major party. Despite the increasing number of political independents in the electorate, approximately two-thirds of the adult population continues to express an identification with either the Democratic or Republican party. Thus, the party still represents the most important vehicle for electorate mobilization; no other organization can match its capacity to aggregate masses of individuals and a diversity of groups.

Third, the range of policy interests with which the parties must deal is extremely broad. Most political organizations have specific and fairly narrow policy concerns. As a result, their attempts to influence policy are sharply focused. Few issues, however, lack a partisan dimension, and the parties must therefore handle a formidable array of foreign and domestic policies. Of course, a party's commitments to various policy goals are not necessarily equal and are not always clearly defined. Similarly, the parties may try to avoid taking positions on certain controversial issues or, failing that, may attempt to blur their differences. Nevertheless, the major parties usually do respond to widespread expectations that they stake out positions across the broad range of governmental programs; such expectations are not characteristic of other political organizations.

These party characteristics provide much of the complementarity between the party and electoral linkages. The party is subject to the electorate's rewards and sanctions. If it hopes to elect its nominees, it must support policies and provide candidates that have voter appeal. At the same time, the electorate depends upon the party to order and simplify the choices it must make in an election. For the individual voter, this involves a trade-off. A limited number of candidates and choices is less likely to produce that single candidate who embodies all the interests and preferences of a particular voter. However, even if such a candidate existed, his appeal would be limited to voters with virtually identical interests and preferences, and this in turn would reduce the possibility of any candidate receiving widespread support, much less an electoral majority. Therefore, the ultimate effect of an individual's vote would be quite minimal. With a reduced number of choices, the "perfect mirroring" between candidate and voter is unlikely, but by aggregating individuals whose interests and preferences are similar or at least not in conflict, electoral majorities are possible, and the practical effect of the individual's vote is enhanced. As the party groups together citizens and links them to candidates willing to support their interests, it provides coherence for the electoral linkage.

If the party is successful in its electoral bid, it must continue to satisfy voters if it wishes to retain control of government in future elections. This means that it must implement those policies and programs that constituted its electoral appeal and must respond to new issues or problems in a manner that the electorate will find acceptable. Sufficient organization and discipline must therefore be achieved among the party's officeholders to convince the electorate that the party can govern effectively. Just as it attempts to organize the electorate to attain electoral majorities, the party also works to build legislative majorities in order to achieve policy goals.

There are, of course, shortcomings in the actual operation of the party linkage. Some of these are a result of voter capabilities. If the party linkage is to translate voter preferences into public policy, voters must be able to understand the policy differences between the parties and to monitor a party's performance in office. The electorate's perception of interparty differences has perhaps sharpened over the past two decades, but there has not been a corresponding increase in its ability to judge party performance on the basis of issues.[6] There is considerable evidence to indicate that the parties provide meaningful policy choices for the voter, although these are perhaps more evident in certain issue areas than in others.[7] The parties, however, often encounter problems in implementing their programs. Cohesion within the congressional parties, for example, is limited; a substantial bloc of legislators within each party tends to be rather lukewarm in supporting programs that their fellow party members consider to be party policy. Indeed, some Democrats and some Republicans vote with the opposition party more frequently than with their own.[8]

Despite these limitations, the party linkage is helpful in facilitating the kinds of retrospective judgments that voters are capable of making. Voters can assess what has occurred while one party controlled the White House, for example, weigh the criticisms and competing claims of the opposition party, and decide whether to maintain or to transfer power. Again, a limitation and simplification of choices occurs, but the party is at least accountable to the electorate in a realistic fashion.

There is, then, a delicate balance that a party must maintain between its electoral goals and its beliefs. If its candidates or programs lack voter appeal, it cannot achieve its basic objective. Given the diversity of interests and groups in the United States, a party that is decidedly ideological in its appeal will find it difficult to elect candidates. At the same time, a party must have sufficient ideological coherence to determine its policy goals and to appeal to the electorate on the basis of and govern in accordance with those goals.

Interest Groups. Private associations representing numerous groups and interests in society play a major role in American politics. Like the political party, with which it is sometimes allied, the interest group seeks to influence government policy. While it may support candidates, however, its efforts are not primarily directed toward contesting elections, nor do interest groups seek the responsibility for managing the government. Rather, the interest group attempts to use various resources—information, expertise, publicity, and, of course, campaign or electoral assistance of different types—to influence the policy decisions of government officials. The political role of the interest group, then, is to provide a link between its members and those in government who are responsible for policies and programs that directly affect those members.[9]

---

[6] Stanley R. Freedman, "The Salience of Party and Candidate in Congressional Elections: A Comparison of 1958 and 1970," in *Public Opinion and Public Policy,* rev. ed., ed. N. Luttbeg (Homewood, Ill.: The Dorsey Press, 1974), pp. 126-31.

[7] In addition, it may be that while candidates' attitudes follow a fairly consistent liberal-conservative division, mass attitudes may be ordered along a different dimension. Sullivan and O'Connor, "Electoral Choice and Popular Control of Public Policy," pp. 1264-65.

[8] For an examination of congressional voting behavior, see chapter 7.

[9] On the nonpolitical functions of interest groups, see Mancur Olson, *The Logic of Collective Action: Public Goods and the Theory of Groups* (Cambridge, Mass.: Harvard University Press, 1965).

The members of an interest group may be individuals or institutions, such as corporations and other organizations. What ties these members together is a common interest, frequently (though not always) economic, that they wish to have represented before government. It is this "special interest" that defines the composition and policy objectives of the typical interest group.

Interest group politics involves communication and methods of persuasion. The membership of an interest group has a defined interest in a specific policy area, and it is the interest group's responsibility to keep members informed about what the government is doing or proposing to do. A corresponding responsibility is to inform those in government about the preferences or opinions of the group's members. But interest group activities do not usually stop at this point. Because it has political resources—votes, endorsements, money, and other campaign assistance—the interest group can attempt to bargain or negotiate with government officials in order to advance the political interests of its members. Lobbying efforts aimed at legislators and administrators, then, are a continuing form of interest group activity. The interest group is not simply a spokesman for an interest; it actively represents that interest by utilizing persuasion and pressure to achieve group objectives.

The interest group linkage is rarely criticized for being ineffective. Indeed, most of the prominent economic interest groups are attacked for being too effective and successful in dealing with government. There are, however, interesting questions concerning the representativeness of interest group politics. For example, substantial segments of the population, particularly those at lower socioeconomic levels, are not organized and hence are outside the interest group system.[10] In addition, there is evidence to indicate that interest group leaders do not always represent the preferences of their members accurately.[11] These and related critiques will be examined in detail later in the book. At this point, however, it should simply be emphasized that the interest group linkage is extremely important in American politics and supplements parties or the formal institutions of government as a mechanism for transmitting popular influence to government. This does not mean that all interests are represented or that those represented are equally effective. It does mean that group interests are basic to the political process, and the interest group linkage aggregates and articulates those interests through private organizations. Moreover, there is accountability in interest group politics. Just as parties must garner popular support if they are to survive, interest groups must satisfy their members if they are to remain viable organizations. This is, to be sure, a limited form of accountability, but it is not an unimportant one.

---

[10] In addition, activity within organizations also varies with social status. See Gabriel A. Almond and Sidney Verba, *The Civic Culture* (Princeton, N.J.: Princeton University Press, 1963), p. 315.

[11] See, for example, Norman R. Luttbeg and Harmon Zeigler, "Attitude Consensus and Conflict in an Interest Group: An Assessment of Cohesion," *American Political Science Review*, 60 (September 1966), 655-66.

Representative Institutions

Other linkages between the public and government can occur through the operation of formal governmental institutions, such as legislatures, that perform representative functions. One such linkage arises from the representative role that requires a legislator to act in accordance with his constituents' preferences regardless of his personal beliefs. This type of representation, known as the *instructed delegate,* asserts as a matter of principle that the representative is bound to defer to the wishes of those he represents.

A substantial portion of the public expects representatives to act as instructed delegates.[12] Not surprisingly, this type of representation also finds acceptance in Congress. One study of the House, for example, found that approximately one-fourth of the members interviewed considered themselves to be delegates and almost one-third agreed that "a Representative ought to work for what his constituents want even though this may not always agree with his personal views."[13] Although it is difficult to distinguish between principle and electoral pragmatism when a representative follows his constituents' lead, it is apparent that certain issues arouse constituency feelings to the point that a representative's behavior is constrained. The debate over the Panama Canal treaties in early 1978 indicated that some senators were acutely sensitive to public opinion in their states and were willing to cast their votes in accordance with their perception of majority opinion. Similarly emotional and controversial issues such as public funding of abortions, school busing, or gun control may be so salient and public opinion so clear-cut in a given district or state that legislators are forced into a position, regardless of their personal preferences.

In order for this linkage to work, then, certain conditions must be fulfilled. The representative must first accept an obligation to subordinate his own beliefs and judgments to the opinion of his constituency. Once he accepts this obligation, he must accurately assess that opinion, and this presents problems. A member of Congress, for example, must vote on hundreds of issues each session. His constituents are unlikely to have clearly defined attitudes on a great many of these, either because they are unaware of or are unconcerned with them. Further, on those issues where constituency attitudes do exist, majority opinion may not be readily apparent. Additional complications are introduced when the representative must assess the intensity and stability of opinion on an issue. These factors suggest the difficulties that an instructed delegate faces in trying to evaluate constituency opinion, and previous studies indicate that accurate perceptions are rare on foreign policy issues, somewhat more frequent on social welfare issues, and most likely on civil rights issues.[14] This suggests that the effectiveness of representative roles as linkages is highly variable also.

---

[12] See, for example, Roger H. Davidson, *The Role of the Congressman* (New York: Pegasus, 1969), p. 115.

[13] Ibid., pp. 118-19.

[14] Warren E. Miller and Donald E. Stokes, "Constituency Influence in Congress," *American Political Science Review,* 57 (March 1963), 45-56.

A second representative linkage is established when the representative shares his constituency's views. The basic assumption here is that because the representative and his constituents share a common background, they develop similar political attitudes and beliefs that shape their views about specific issues. There is no need for communication between the representative and his constituency. Simply by voting his own preferences, he votes his constituents' preferences as well. Moreover, the constituency need not even have information or preferences on an issue. The representative in effect responds to a new issue the way his constituents would if they were confronted with it.

It is possible for shared attitudes and beliefs to develop in issue areas that dominate the politics of a community for a sustained period of time, and for representatives and constituents to share a background that does influence their response to new or emerging policy issues. Numerous studies indicate, however, that on a broad range of issues, the mass public and political elites have different attitudes and issue positions.[15] More limited evidence on Congress suggests that there is considerable variation in the sharing of attitudes from one issue area to another.[16]

The linkages provided by representative institutions, then, do transmit popular influence, and they may be particularly important on those occasions when public opinion is stimulated by dramatic, emotional policy issues. The representative as agent or advocate for his constituency is not simply a theoretical prescription; it describes with a degree of accuracy how certain issues are handled by public officials. But there are also a great many issues where officials respond to other pressures. Just as there are limits on the effectiveness of other linkages, the representative models are limited by what the public and its representatives know and can be expected to know about each other's issue positions.

Linkages and Policy

The formal linkages discussed here are not the only forms of interaction between the public and government. Officials concerned about public attitudes have a variety of means to assess public opinion—letters from private citizens, informal contacts with individuals and groups, and, on some issues at least, public opinion polls. Some members of Congress supplement these with their own constituency polls in order to evaluate district or state opinion.[17] Information is also transmitted from officials to the public, in forms ranging from presidential news conferences or speeches to congressional newsletters to the more specialized publications of executive agencies and congressional committees. The public is also not limited to com-

---

[15] For an influential discussion of how and why these differences occur, see Philip E. Converse, "The Nature of Belief Systems in Mass Publics," in *Ideology and Discontent*, ed. D. Apter (New York: The Free Press, 1964).

[16] Miller and Stokes, "Constituency Influence in Congress," p. 52.

[17] On the weaknesses of congressional polls, see Dennis S. Ippolito, Thomas G. Walker, and Kenneth R. Kolson, *Public Opinion and Responsible Democracy* (Englewood Cliffs, N.J.: Prentice-Hall, Inc., 1976), pp. 290-91.

municating its preferences through formal channels; direct action techniques such as petitions, demonstrations, and ad hoc protest organizations may be quite valuable in bringing issues or popular discontent to the attention of those in government. As has been noted, parties may sometimes be reluctant to deal with controversial issues, and existing interest groups may not adequately represent important societal interests.

One cannot realistically expect the formal linkages of national politics to provide a perfect translation of public preferences into government policy. The linkages do not produce policy. Rather, they define a relationship between government decision makers and the public, thereby providing a mechanism for transmitting popular influence to those decision makers and, not incidentally, for transmitting communications from decision makers to the public. Moreover, public preferences are not the only criterion that officials use in making their decisions. Representative democracy does not require that public opinion be the sole determining factor of an issue; it does require that officials act in good faith in taking legitimate public preferences and interests into account.

It is in this context that intermediate institutions perform valuable functions. The party system, for example, simplifies and orders the choices that the voter must make. The electoral linkage is usually a crude indicator of the public's policy preferences, since electoral choices are limited in number and general in nature. Therefore, elections as programmatic mandates—clearly defined issues, clearly differentiated candidate positions, and firm electorate judgments—are rare. More frequently, an election provides the voter with the opportunity to judge government's past performance. The party serves as a focus for such retrospective judgments and allows a mass electorate to issue a relatively coherent verdict about the actions that government is taking or proposing to take. The party linkage may provide only limited information about the policy preferences of individual voters, but through periodic elections, it can bring a high degree of pressure to bear upon officials.[18]

The interest group linkage is not geared to serving the mass electorate as such, nor is interest group pressure confined to elections. What the linkage can do, however, is communicate to government decision makers detailed information about the policy preferences of organized interests in society. By concentrating its activities upon a narrow range of issues and upon key decision makers, the interest group can exert considerable pressure on decisions that affect its "special interest." Moreover, since interest groups are typically active throughout the policy process, they can serve to hold officials accountable between elections and also to extend the reach of popular influence to administrative as well as elected officials.

---

[18] For an examination of the pressure and information characteristics of various forms of participation, see Sidney Verba and Norman H. Nie, *Participation in America: Political Democracy and Social Equality* (New York: Harper & Row, Publishers, 1972), pp. 47-48.

The contribution of intermediate institutions lies in the structuring of relationships between the public and government. Parties allow the mass electorate to influence policy by providing relatively coherent choices about who will govern. Interest groups allow a diverse and pluralist society to bring more detailed policy preferences and more focused pressure to bear on those who govern. The politics of parties and interest groups is heavily biased, of course, toward self-interest. These groups are, after all, directly and intimately involved in the competition for advantage. Partisanship or special interests, however, are not incompatible with democratic politics. On the contrary, the competition between parties is vital to democratic politics, as is the competition among various centers of power that expresses itself as interest group politics.

It is also clear, however, that parties and interest groups do not function independently of the political and social environment. As we have noted, there are alternatives to party or interest group linkages. The connections between various linkages, as well as the relative influence and importance of each, can change significantly over time. It may be useful, then, to discuss briefly some major trends in party and interest group politics, since these might alter the effectiveness of intermediate political linkages.

CONTEMPORARY TRENDS—POLITICAL PARTIES

During the past decade, there have been numerous analyses of the future of the American party system, few of which have suggested that the party system of the future will closely resemble that of the past.[19] Most analysts have argued that electoral realignments are either taking place or about to occur and that these will produce new majority coalitions in national politics. There has been, however, considerable disagreement about which party and what ideology would be advanced by a new majority.[20] Finally, some analysts have concluded that the party system is dying if not dead, although here again there has been some question about the implications and desirability of its demise.[21]

What these predictions have in common is the perception that the parties face serious and unresolved problems in dealing with the electorate, with candidates

---

[19] Perhaps the most persuasive argument of this position is contained in James L. Sundquist, *Dynamics of the Party System: Alignment and Realignment of Political Parties in the United States* (Washington, D.C.: Brookings Institution, 1973).

[20] The view from the conservative perspective was set forth by Kevin Phillips, *The Emerging Republican Majority* (New Rochelle, N.Y.: Arlington House, 1969); the "moderate" or centrist approach was advanced by Richard M. Scammon and Ben J. Wattenberg, *The Real Majority* (New York: Coward-McGann Geoghegan, 1970); the liberal realignment or potential realignment was discerned by Louis Harris, *The Anguish of Change* (New York: W. W. Norton, 1973).

[21] The most interesting and provocative interpretation of "partisan decomposition" is Walter Dean Burnham, *Critical Elections and the Mainsprings of American Politics* (New York: W. W. Norton, 1970).

and officeholders, and even with their own activists. These problems may also be cumulative—as a party loses its influence with voters and its control of electoral politics, it also loses its ability to bargain effectively with candidates and elected officials. Unable to mobilize voters, it cannot coordinate government. There is a great deal of evidence to suggest party decline in each of these areas.

Electorate Partisanship

Perhaps the single most important change in the party system has been the decline in party loyalties. Voters today are less likely to identify themselves as Democrats or Republicans, and more likely to see themselves as Independents, than they were 15 or 20 years ago. From the early 1940s through the mid-1960s, for example, Independent identification was in the 20-25 percent range. Since that time, it has increased substantially until more than one-third of the electorate now classifies itself as Independent.[22]

A weakening of party loyalties has been evident even among partisan identifiers. The proportion of strong identifiers in the electorate—that is, those who say they are strong Democrats or strong Republicans—was fairly stable for over a decade but then dropped sharply after the mid-1960s.[23] Moreover, the voting behavior of partisans has changed; split-ticket voting has increased dramatically in recent periods.[24]

A more general example of the electorate's changing response to parties involves "party images"—voters' responses to questions concerning what they like and dislike about the parties. A recent study reports that the party images "are less well defined and less rich than they once had been," suggesting that the parties have become less meaningful to the voters.[25]

These changes describe an electorate less committed to parties, less susceptible to party appeals and loyalties, and therefore more responsive to short-term factors such as issues and candidate images during elections. This is also an electorate that is potentially more volatile in its voting behavior, at least during presidential elections when candidates and issues have relatively high electoral visibility. As evidence of this, the electoral swings between recent presidential elections have been unusual; from 1960 through 1976, "cliffhangers" and "landslides" alternated regularly, as did party fortunes.

---

[22] Moreover, there have been changes in the political information and activity of Independents as compared to partisan identifiers. See Gerald M. Pomper, *Voters' Choice* (New York: Dodd, Mead & Company, 1975), pp. 31-35.

[23] See Paul R. Abramson, "Generational Change and the Decline of Party Identification in America," *American Political Science Review,* 70 (June 1976), 469-78.

[24] Arthur H. Miller et al., "A Majority Party in Disarray: Policy Polarization in the 1972 Election" (Ann Arbor, Mich.: Center for Political Studies, 1973), p. 90.

[25] Richard J. Trilling, *Party Image and Electoral Behavior* (New York: John Wiley & Sons, 1976), p. 211.

At the congressional level, however, there has been an equally remarkable degree of stability. The Democratic edge in national party identification that has existed for the past several decades has regularly been translated into Democratic congressional majorities. Only twice in the post-World War II era have the Republicans gained control of Congress, in 1947-48 and in 1953-54. But the partisan integration of the vote—the party's ability to persuade voters to support the party ticket, including its presidential and congressional candidates—has also decreased during this period, making it much more difficult for even the majority party to mobilize the electorate on a stable basis and to coordinate government.[26]

Electoral Politics

Party decline is also evident in electoral politics. The parties are no longer the sole suppliers of the resources and expertise that win elections, just as they no longer monopolize voter cues. There is a new technology in electoral politics that allows candidates to deal directly with voters. As this technology has developed over the past several decades, it has reduced the incentives and rewards that parties can employ in bargaining with candidates and officeholders.

Candidates can now raise their own funds through public appeals, using direct-mail or other sophisticated techniques to supplement their own funds or contributions from "traditional sources." Consultants can be employed to design and manage campaigns, thus taking advantage of modern advertising and polling methods and providing the appropriate "media mix." And, of course, television can be used to reach large numbers of voters directly and immediately.

Candidate independence is further enhanced by the direct primary system of nominations. This system is firmly entrenched in the states and is used to nominate candidates for most local and state offices and for virtually all House and Senate seats. As of 1976, a majority of states also used presidential preference primaries to choose delegates to the national nominating conventions. While the specific features of primary systems vary from state to state, the central fact is that primaries make it more difficult for party organizations to name the party's candidates. Since the right to wear the party label is determined by the primary elections, the party's ability to screen out candidates, based on ideology or other considerations, is reduced. And of course the same techniques that are employed in general election campaigns can be employed in primaries. Indeed, candidates sometimes find it expedient to run as antiparty candidates in order to demonstrate their independence to the electorate.

If candidates can secure nominations and run successful campaigns while at the same time bypassing or ignoring their party organization, they obviously are not heavily indebted to the party once they are in office. This makes it difficult for the

---

[26] On split results for U.S. House and presidential voting, see Burnham, *Critical Elections*, pp. 108-9.

party to achieve the necessary unity among its officeholders to implement the program that it supposedly represents. Independence while running means independence in office, at least independence as it relates to the party. Officeholders can still be indebted to other interests. (And even if all of their funds come from the electorate, thus making them "independent" of all interests except the public's, one might well wonder what that interest is and whether the public will be capable of enforcing accountability.)

The "new politics" of recent years is an amalgam—part ideology and programmatic appeals, part personal image of the candidate, and part political style. It emphasizes direct communication between the candidate and voter, and its proponents often claim that this is desirable and necessary because the modern voter is more sophisticated. Whatever else may be true about the "new politics," however, it does deny the need for active intermediaries between the voters and the candidates.

Campaign consultants, pollsters, media experts, and the like have changed campaign politics and affected the party's role in electoral politics. Parties still spend money, supply volunteers, and turn out the vote, but they are frequently not central actors in major campaigns. And this limits partisan controls over candidates and officeholders.

Organizational Politics

The parties today are also facing serious internal problems that threaten their organizational strength. The so-called "new politics" that we have discussed is candidate-oriented, and this means that the parties often must compete with their own candidates for the money and volunteers that are required to run the organiation. Similarly, the proliferation of political organizations in recent years provides the politically interested with almost unlimited choice in terms of organizational outlets for advancing issues or causes. The party is not, therefore, the only type of political organization available to the political activist, nor is it the most attractive alternative as far as many activists are concerned.

It is important to recognize that the American parties have traditionally depended on volunteers. There are, of course, organization leaders and officials that are paid by the party, but the party's manpower needs are filled largely by volunteers. In order to attract and keep these individuals, the party must offer appropriate incentives or rewards. Numerous studies of party activists indicate that their motivations differ significantly—some are primarily concerned with tangible, personal benefits such as patronage positions, government contacts, and political careers that party work might provide; some enjoy the social aspects of party work, the camaraderie of political activity; and some are motivated by issue concerns or personal loyalties to candidates or causes.[27] Party organizations reflect

---

[27] This categorization follows the general distinctions among material, solidary, and purposive incentives discussed in Peter Clark and James Q. Wilson, "Incentive Systems: A Theory of Organization," *Administrative Science Quarterly*, 6 (1961), 129-66.

these differences in the incentives they offer. While a degree of diversity usually characterizes an organization, a predominant incentive pattern may be evident. A general trend in incentive patterns appears to exist among party organizations, with tangible, personal benefits becoming less important and ideological or issue incentives more important.

It appears, for example, that not only the availability but also the attractiveness of patronage has diminished. The party's usefulness in achieving social mobility has also declined as the numerous ethnic groups for which it performed this function have moved into the "mainstream" of American life. Political ambitions are still important motivations, but these can now be successfully pursued outside the party framework and without the apprenticeship ethic that the party has often tried to enforce.

An increasing number of activists, however, are being drawn to party work, because they wish to pursue public policy goals. At first glance, this type of activism may appear more commendable than the traditional type with its emphasis on personal, material benefits. It may also appear very helpful to the party, since issue-motivated activists bring considerable energy and skills to their party work. There is some evidence, however, that the issue-motivated activist often has a political approach or style that has negative implications for party politics.[28] This style is characterized as "amateur" or "purist," and it describes activists who are less concerned with winning elections than with seeing the party and its candidates express a particular political philosophy. Their allegiance to the party is limited or nonexistent, so they may decide to leave the party whenever they are dissatisfied with the issue positions or candidates it supports. They are insistent on intraparty democracy, even at the expense of organizational unity and effectiveness. Political compromise or bargaining is viewed as distasteful, if not immoral; indeed, the purist's approach to politics is usually moralistic.

For this type of activist, the parties must be clearly differentiated in terms of issues and must base their appeals to voters on these differences. Party leaders and candidates, moreover, should do what is "right" rather than what is popular. In addition, the party should be willing to sacrifice victory if necessary in order to maintain its ideological purity and integrity.

The extent of this political style is not clear. Thus far, it has been identified in some local party reform movements and also in recent presidential campaigns. The outstanding examples of the latter are probably the McGovern campaign of 1972 and the Goldwater campaign of 1964. The purist approach apparently characterized a substantial proportion of McGovern and Goldwater supporters, although they were of course quite different ideologically. Indeed, the 1972 Democratic convention appears to have been a triumph of amateur activism. Based on their

---

[28] James Q. Wilson, for example, suggests that the amateur forces rigidity upon the party by emphasizing policy goals rather than electoral success. *The Amateur Democrat* (Chicago: University of Chicago Press, 1962), especially chap. 12. See also Nelson W. Polsby and Aaron Wildavsky, *Presidential Elections*, 4th ed. (New York: Charles Scribner's Sons, 1976), pp. 29-40.

attitudes concerning the importance of party unity, winning elections, and party loyalty, one study classified over one-half of the delegates as amateurs.[29] A similar study found that 83 percent of the McGovern delegates were purists or amateurs.[30] Indeed, among Democratic delegates in 1972 less than one-half identified themselves as strong partisans, as compared to almost three-fourths of the delegates at the Republican convention.[31]

For the parties, the long-term impact of the amateur or purist activist may be quite serious. These activists are not, after all, much concerned with the party electorates, and the results are predictable. Goldwater and McGovern each lost an extraordinary proportion of his party's traditional supporters; both were, as the saying goes, buried in landslides. If its activists function as advocates for narrow ideological interests, a party courts electoral disaster. But the weakness of contemporary party organization, its inability to attract loyalists, and the institutionalization of intraparty democracy have served to strengthen the purists. They are educated and committed, willing to attend party conferences and meetings and to vote in primaries; the party's rank-and-file members simply do not participate at a comparable level. As a consequence, the party continually risks being captured by those who have no interest in its role as an active intermediary between the mass public and government.

CONTEMPORARY TRENDS—INTEREST GROUPS

The general decline of political parties as a linkage institution in national politics has been at least partially offset by the increased viability of American interest groups. In decades past America's "special interests" were generally confined to business associations and corporations which held vast economic resources and used the political process to maintain their favorable status. Since the New Deal period in the 1940s corporate political power has been somewhat balanced by the rise in political influence of the large labor unions. These economic interests along with the traditional agricultural organizations were the major special interest participants in the public policy-making process. Fledgling organizations that did not agree with the dominant economic interest groups were periodically born, but usually did not survive many political seasons. During the 1950s and early 1960s there was very little alteration in the arena of interest group politics. However, in recent years there have been major changes in the form and substance of pressure group activities. Today there are more interest organizations representing a wider variety of causes

---

[29] John W. Soule and Wilma E. McGrath, "A Comparative Study of Presidential Nominating Conventions: The Democrats 1968 and 1972," *American Journal of Political Science,* 19 (August 1975), 511.

[30] Dennis G. Sullivan et al., *The Politics of Representation: The Democratic Convention 1972* (New York: St. Martin's Press, 1974), p. 124.

[31] Joseph H. Boyett, "Background Characteristics of Delegates to the 1972 Conventions: A Summary Report of Findings from a National Sample," *Western Political Quarterly,* 27 (September 1974), 477.

and employing a more complete arsenal of political weapons than ever before. Contemporary evidence and political events indicate a greater role for organized interests than had previously been assumed.[32]

The Development of Public Interest and Countervailing Interest Groups

Pressure groups active in today's politics represent many interests not championed by organizations a decade or two ago. Most notable among the varieties of new interest groups are the public interest groups. Traditionally, pressure organizations were concerned primarily with private interests, working to improve the fortunes of group members. Today's public interest groups, however, are committed to policies which they believe to be for the good of society generally, rather than group members exclusively. The advent of the successful public interest group is a relatively new development in the history of pressure group politics.

The phenomenon of the public interest group is clearly exemplified by the citizen lobbies, Common Cause and Public Citizen.[33] Common Cause grew from the efforts of John Gardner beginning in 1968 when Gardner resigned as Secretary of Health, Education, and Welfare. Common Cause is devoted to a wide range of public policy reforms designed to make government more responsive, accessible, and accountable to the citizenry. Backed by a membership of more than a quarter million individuals, Common Cause has enjoyed notable successes in the area of election campaign reform. Public Citizen is the umbrella organization that coordinates and finances the various Ralph Nader-inspired lobby groups. Nader's first organization, the Center for the Study of Responsive Law, was begun in 1969. Additional units, concentrating on tax reform, health policy, Congress, the administrative agencies and other governmental matters, have been added to the organization over the years. The purpose of the Nader organizations is to conduct research and lobbying activities to bring about public policies that will enhance what the group sees as the common good. Public Citizen is involved in numerous projects, most of which have a reform or consumer orientation.

Common Cause and Public Citizen are significant developments in interest group politics because they represent successful, relatively well-financed public interest organizations which have received considerable public support. They are part of a movement toward the development of pressure organizations which are willing to challenge the traditional economic interest groups. Public interest efforts had been launched several times in the past but few remained viable for any period of time; none of these past attempts gained the prominence or strength necessary to provide effective opposition to the well-established economic lobbies. However,

---

[32] For an interesting discussion of this point see Michael T. Hayes, "The Semi-Sovereign Pressure Groups: A Critique of Current Theory and an Alternative Typology," *Journal of Politics*, 40 (February 1978), 134-161.

[33] For a discussion of these groups see *Congressional Quarterly Weekly Report*, 34 (May 15, 1976), 1197-1205.

the 1970s saw the development of numerous groups devoted to using the political process to improve the public interest and the strengthening of several already existing noneconomic lobby organizations which had experienced marginal effectiveness in years past.

Many of the newer lobbying organizations represent special interests which previously had been represented inadequately, if at all. Pressure groups are successfully working on behalf of the environment, welfare recipients, the aged, various ethnic and racial groups, women, the mentally ill, convicts, consumers, and a host of other causes. Many of these groups constitute a countervailing force against certain established economic interest groups. For example, in years past business interest groups enjoyed relative success in interest group politics because they met opposition only from organized labor. Today business is faced with opponents from the organized labor movement, environmentalists, consumer groups, and other newly formed pressure organizations. The development of these countervailing interest groups has improved the representativeness of interest group politics. Persons previously ignored in this process now have organizations devoted to the promotion of their own special interests. Pressure group politics remains distinctly tipped in favor of the traditional economic interests, but the public interest groups and the countervailing interest groups have significantly opened the lobbying process to previously unheard voices.

Public interest lobbies have not only formed in relatively large numbers over the past decade, but they have become increasingly effective and adept at using the political process. Such groups have made skillful use of publicity, developed research capabilities and expertise, and shown impressive command of political strategy. Senator Abraham Ribicoff of Connecticut noted in 1976 that "instead of the big lobbyists of the major corporations dominating the hearings process, you have had practically every committee in Congress according 'equal time' to public interest people."[34]

The rise of the public interest group movement has accelerated the efforts of corporate, labor and other traditional economic groups. This has prompted a general increase in pressure group activities designed to influence the making of public policy. Nevertheless, these lobbying efforts are generally much more balanced than in previous years.[35]

Interest Group Targets

Historically, lobbying has been associated with the legislative branch. Congress has been the focus of interest group attention because it traditionally controls much of the nation's policy-making authority and also offers multiple points of access for interest group participation. However, the policy-making authority of the executive and judicial branches of government has increased since the days of the

[34] Quoted in *Congressional Quarterly Weekly Report,* 34 (May 15, 1976), 1197.
[35] *Congressional Quarterly Weekly Report,* 34 (June 12, 1976), 1511-1512.

New Deal. Interest groups have responded to this shift in power by allocating greater portions of their lobbying resources to attempts directed at influencing the administrative and adjudicative departments.

The executive branch now offers three relatively distinct levels of policy-making authority which have become the targets of pressure group influence attempts. The president has become the primary source of important legislative proposals and, while access to the president's inner circle is necessarily limited, interest groups attempt to approach this level of the executive branch with their demands. The administrative agencies also wield a good deal of public policy power by executing the policy decisions of Congress and the president. The lobbying effort aimed at this bureaucratic level has increased in recent years and has been so successful that critics of the interest group role in politics have claimed that many such agencies have become captured by the special interests that courted their favor. Finally, the regulatory agencies have offered opportunities for interest group access to the executive branch. With more than 100 agencies possessing regulatory power at the federal level, pressure groups have found these commissions fertile ground for efforts to promote favorable public policy choices.

The judiciary in recent decades has assumed an ever-increasing role in the making of national public policy. Traditionally, civil rights groups used the courts extensively to attain governmental outcomes which were not forthcoming from the legislative or executive branches. Today, more interest groups than ever before are turning to the courts in order to attain group objectives. Environmental groups, consumer organizations, "good government" associations, civil rights groups, and religious organizations have become regular users of the remedies available from the judiciary.

Today's successful interest group is likely to have multiple governmental targets for its lobbying efforts. Strategies are often devised which call for influence attempts directed at all three branches. No longer does the legislative department command the nearly exclusive attention of pressure organizations.

Lobbying Tactics

Traditionally, lobbying efforts on behalf of interest organizations have taken the form of direct contact with governmental officials. This strategy was generally an effective one, particularly for groups like labor unions, which represent large numbers of voters, and corporations, which represent significant economic power. Direct contact lobbying is still used extensively today and remains an effective interest group tactic.

However, interest groups have been increasingly involved in attempts to influence public opinion as well. Shaping the contours of mass opinion has two important consequences. First, the interest group can influence the general political climate. By promoting the interest group itself and the general cause it represents, the pressure organization is able to create a feeling of good will among the citizenry and lay the foundation for public support should the group's fortunes later be jeopardized by proposed public policy alternatives. Second, an interest group is able to mobilize the citizenry to contact their representatives in Congress concerning pending public policy decisions. This form of grassroots lobbying has become an exceptionally effective lobbying tactic for those groups that are capable of convincing members of the public to call or write their governmental representatives. These indirect, grassroots lobbying campaigns, conducted via mass media advertising and computerized mass mailing techniques, have been called "the major growth area of organized lobbying today."[36]

Interest Group Regulation

At the national level the legal regulation of interest group influence attempts is substantially contained in the 1946 Federal Regulation of Lobbying Act. In addition, laws governing the internal revenue system place certain limitations on lobbying by voluntary associations. Most knowledgeable observers of the governmental process have concluded that the existing regulations are inadequate. The 1946 law imposes registration and disclosure requirements on those persons whose principle purpose is the influencing of legislation in Congress. The law has numerous loopholes which make its effectiveness suspect. While most realize the need for reforming the lobbying regulations, there has been general disagreement regarding the specific reforms to enact. Obviously nothing encourages interest group activity more than proposals to regulate lobbying. Not only are pressure organizations interested in such legislation generally, but specific groups are fearful of any change that might give an advantage to natural political rivals.

One of the major deficiencies with the present legislation is that it governs lobbying as it existed when the law was passed in 1946. It therefore fails to take into account some of the fundamental changes in interest group politics that have occurred in recent years. For example, the current legislation has no provision for the regulation of indirect, grassroots lobbying campaigns, nor does the present statute cover executive branch lobbying. Lobby law reforms currently pending before Congress and having substantial support would be significant advances in bringing the regulation of interest group activity up to date. Such regulations would not restrict or prohibit lobbying, which is a protected right under the freedom of association, petition, and speech provisions of the First Amendment, but would impose greater registration and disclosure requirements to allow the public to be more fully informed of the activities of America's special interests.

SUMMARY

Recent trends in American politics indicate that significant changes in the party and interest group systems have occurred. Many of these changes appear to have weakened the parties as intermediaries between the governed and the govern-

---

[36] See *Congressional Quarterly Weekly Report*, 36 (April 22, 1978), 955.

ment. Certainly the parties are less important to voters, candidates, and activists than they have been in the past. On the other hand, interest groups have become increasingly visible in recent years. Participants in pressure group politics are more numerous and represent a greater diversity of interests than ever before. The tactics and targets of interest group influence attempts have also experienced substantial innovations. In subsequent chapters, we will deal more fully with these changes and their implications, not only for political parties and interest groups but for democratic politics as well.

part ONE

POLITICAL PARTIES

two

The Party System in the United States

The American two-party system is an old and remarkably durable institution. For more than a century, the Democratic and Republican parties have managed to dominate electoral politics in the United States. And for almost three-quarters of a century prior to the Democratic-Republican division, national politics was similarly shaped by the confrontations first between the Federalists and the Republicans and later between the Democrats and the Whigs. Even within its earliest stages of development, the American party system not only provided an organizational model for parties elsewhere but also established precedents for the peaceful transfer of power and for the acceptance of a "loyal opposition" in government.

Despite important continuities, there have been substantial changes in the American party system. The major parties have been both the agents and the victims of great political and social upheavals—the establishment of nationhood and emergence of democratic institutions, the struggle over slavery, industrialization and economic collapse, as well as the civil rights and antiwar movements of the 1960s. In some cases, the existing parties were unable to contain the forces of change, with the result that new electoral alignments and party systems were formed. There has been some recent speculation, as we noted earlier, that the two-party system is now giving way to a period of no-party politics. Without discounting important evidence of party decline, it is also apparent that the party system has survived periods that were far more challenging than our current travail.

It should be helpful, then, to gain historical perspective on American party politics before directing our attention to the state of our contemporary two-party system. This chapter, therefore, will be devoted to the origin and development of the party system, the competitive characteristics of the two-party system, and the role of third parties in American politics.

ORIGIN AND DEVELOPMENT OF THE PARTY SYSTEM

The rapid emergence of political parties in the new American republic was something of an anomaly. Among the founding fathers, the prevailing view of parties was decidedly negative, a reflection of the antiparty theme that marked European political philosophy during the seventeenth and eighteenth centuries. David Hume, an eighteenth century Scottish historian and philosopher, expressed the widespread antipathy toward parties in his essay "Of Parties in General." Unlike many of his contemporaries, Hume believed that parties were inevitable in a free society but nonetheless concluded that "factions subvert government, render laws impotent, and beget the fiercest animosities among men of the same nation who ought to give mutual assistance and protection to each other."[1]

Indeed, the only consistent defender of political parties during this period was Edmund Burke, the Irish theorist and statesman. It was Burke who argued that political parties could provide positive benefits and who provided a classic definition of the party as "a body of men united for promoting by their joint endeavors the national interest upon some particular principle in which they are all agreed."[2] According to Burke, the cause of good government could be advanced by such groups, bound together by loyalty and principle and engaged in open opposition and competition.

In America, however, the Burkean conception of parties was rejected, at least in theory. There was particular concern that parties would be especially divisive in the early stages of national development and might therefore endanger political stability. While the Constitution did not prohibit parties, it was hoped that the separation of powers and the system of checks and balances would create institutionally-based rivalries that would limit the growth of permanent, organized parties. The constitutional division between the president and Congress, for example, was aimed at providing each branch with the motives, powers, and opportunities necessary to maintain its independence from the other and thus to avoid a mutual dependence on parties. As Madison's defense of pluralism and liberty in Number 10 of *The Federalist* argued, parties would undoubtedly emerge, but constitutional safeguards and the size of the republic would mitigate "against the event of any one party being able to outnumber and oppress the rest."[3]

---

[1] Quoted in Richard Hofstadter, *The Idea of a Party System* (Berkeley, Cal.: University of California Press, 1969), p. 25.

[2] Quoted ibid., p. 32.

[3] *The Federalist Papers* (New York: New American Library, 1961), p. 84.

While Madison and others were wary of parties, there were specific conditions that appear to have facilitated, and perhaps even necessitated, the emergence of parties. The social and economic structure of the republic was becoming more complex and differentiated, resulting in a growing variety of groups and interests that the political system had to represent. Cultural change, especially the decline of aristocratic politics and its replacement by more democratic and popular views of government and society, was proceeding inexorably, if somewhat unevenly, throughout the states. The new Constitution had created a "common political arena" in which basic issues of national authority and policy had to be decided. Finally, the historical explanation of the origin of American parties includes what "appears to have been some sense of felt need on the part of political elites for structures by means of which they could conduct political business in a reasonably predictable manner."[4] As William Chambers, a party historian, further explains:

> Neither Hamilton, James Madison, nor Jefferson in the 1790's, nor many of the working politicians who gathered around Andrew Jackson in the late 1820's and early 1830's, were necessarily conscious that they were building political parties. Yet as they went about the business of trying to influence voters, win elections, satisfy diverse group interests, or conduct public affairs, this is in effect what they did.[5]

The First Party System: Party in the Government

Liberty and freedom, then, were the primary concerns of Madison and the other framers, but effective and stable government was also an important consideration. In practice, this meant a government that could make and execute policy, and party soon became the agency through which the executive and legislative branches spanned the constitutional division that had been established between them. The first major party developments took place within the government as the two central figures in Washington's cabinet—Alexander Hamilton, Secretary of the Treasury, and Thomas Jefferson, Secretary of State—competed for support for their policies in Congress. The Federalists, as Hamilton's followers were known, and the Jeffersonian Republicans were divided over a variety of domestic and foreign policy issues: the relative powers of the central government and the states, commercial and financial policies, and support of England versus France (see Table 2.1). The divisions were deep and sometimes bitter, with the efforts of each side directed toward keeping the "dangerous and disloyal partisans" of the other from gaining control of government. Hamilton's forceful sponsorship of a federal economic program soon stimulated the emergence of defined and fairly stable

---

[4] William N. Chambers, "Party Development and the American Mainstream," in *The American Party Systems: Stages of Political Development*, ed. W. N. Chambers and W. D. Burnham (New York: Oxford University Press, 1967), p. 10.

[5] Ibid., p. 10.

TABLE 2.1 Party Systems in the United States

Developmental Stage	Period	Major Parties	Key Figures	Partisan Issues
I. Establishment of Party Legitimacy and Initial Development	1790s–1820s	Republicans Federalists	Jefferson, Madison Hamilton, Adams	Commercial Policy Financial Policy Power of Central Government French Revolution
II. Party Organization and Mass Electorates	1820s–1850s	Democrats Whigs	Jackson Clay, Webster	National Bank Commercial Policy Internal Improvements Slavery Tariff
III. Sectional Parties and Electoral Realignment	1860s–1890s	Republicans Democrats	Lincoln	Reconstruction Industrialization Tariff Monetary Policy
IV. Electoral Realignment	1890s–1920s	Republicans Democrats		Gold Standard Tariff Regulatory Policy Agrarian–Urban
V. Electoral Realignment	1930s–present	Democrats Republicans	Roosevelt	Social Welfare Policy Economic Management Civil Rights Social Change

proadministration and antiadministration forces in Congress which became even more sharply defined with subsequent policy decisions.

Within the first decade, the intragovernmental party system evidenced a number of significant developments: the establishment of congressional caucuses to decide party policy and to nominate presidential and vice-presidential candidates; the emergence of party organization in the legislature to select floor leaders and committee memberships; and the use of party to link administration leaders with a stable base of support in Congress.[6] By necessitating the formation of legislative majorities to pass laws, the Constitution provided an important impetus to the emergence of an intragovernmental party organization.

Party Outside the Government. If party was a central agency in organizing the government, it also was a means for organizing public opinion and for controlling the selection of political leaders. The Federalists, for example, sought to mobilize public support for their policies through public meetings, county committees, and petition campaigns. Similar tactics were employed by the "Democratic Societies" that formed during the early 1790s. These were local political organizations that were chiefly concerned with U.S. policy toward France and England. Pro-French, and therefore pro-Jeffersonian Republican, the Democratic Societies spread quickly after Washington's Proclamation of Neutrality in the Anglo-French war. In addition to sponsoring petitions and resolutions directed toward Congress, the Democratic Societies soon became active in organizing election campaigns against the Federalists. This included nominating candidates for all levels of elective offices as well as the electioneering activities that became characteristic of party organizations.

The Republican-Federalist conflict over foreign policy was the most dramatic in a series of policy differences and personal rivalries that divided political leadership and the electorate. Moreover, once Washington announced his refusal to run for a third term, the need for political organization at the electoral level was reinforced. In order to gain a majority of the electoral college, the parties were forced to contest state legislative elections in those states where the legislature was empowered to choose electors, while in others they were forced to organize popular support behind party electors.[7] And, of course, the state legislatures also chose U.S. Senators. Thus, the electoral scope of the parties during the 1790s was unusually broad, extending to state and local as well as national offices. With the growing number of elective offices and the expansion of the electorate that occurred during the early nineteenth century, the opportunities and rewards for effective grassroots party organization increased substantially.

[6] On the emergence of voting blocs in Congress, see Mary P. Ryan, "Party Formation in the United States Congress, 1789-1796: A Quantitative Analysis," *William and Mary Quarterly,* 28 (October 1971), 523-42.

[7] An interesting account of the early presidential races and the building of party organization is presented in James MacGregor Burns, *The Deadlock of Democracy* (Englewood Cliffs, N.J.: Prentice-Hall, Inc., 1963), chap. 2.

The Transfer of Power. The first party system also made possible a momentous event with the election of 1800 and Jefferson's selection as president in 1801—the peaceful transfer of power from one party to the other. The rhetoric of the 1790s, along with a number of government actions, such as the Alien and Sedition Acts of 1798, suggested that the idea of a loyal opposition party was not widely accepted or understood. As one noted historian concluded, "Federalist leaders made no secret of their hope of destroying opposition."[8] Jefferson's view of the Federalist "Monocrats" was hardly more tolerant.

Nevertheless, it was the Federalists who finally elected Jefferson as president. The pledged electors of the Republican party inadvertently threw the election into the House of Representatives by casting equal numbers of votes for Jefferson, their acknowledged choice for president, and for Aaron Burr, their candidate for vice president. The Constitution was not written with party tickets in mind and did not specify separate ballots for the two offices.[9] The results of the election were close; Jefferson and Burr each had 73 electoral votes while John Adams, the incumbent president, had 65 votes, and his running mate, Charles Pinckney, had 64. At first, Hamilton sought to reverse the result by having Gov. John Jay of New York call a special session of the outgoing Federalist-controlled state legislature in order to name Federalist presidential electors. Jay refused, and the new Republican legislature accordingly chose electors to support Jefferson and Burr.[10]

The Federalists still held a 58-48 majority in the lame-duck Congress, however, and many of them favored Burr. Hamilton, recovering from his unbecoming conduct in the New York case, intervened on behalf of Jefferson:

> I trust the Federalists will not finally be so mad as to vote for Burr. I speak with intimate and accurate knowledge of his character. His elevation can only promote the purposes of the desperate and the profligate. If there be a man in the world I ought to hate, it is Jefferson. With Burr I have always been personally well. But the public good must be paramount to every private consideration.[11]

---

[8] Hofstadter, *The Idea of a Party System,* p. 106.

[9] This was, of course, altered by the adoption of the Twelfth Amendment that was ratified in July 1804. The amendment requires electors to cast separate ballots for president and vice president. In the event that no candidate receives a majority of electoral votes for president, the House chooses the president from among the three persons with the greatest number of electoral votes. Votes are taken by state, with each state having one vote. A majority of states is necessary for election, and a quorum consists of a member or members from two-thirds of the states. Selection of the vice president if no candidate receives a majority of electoral votes is by the Senate, which picks from the top two candidates. A majority of the entire Senate is required for election, with a quorum requirement of two-thirds of the members.

[10] Linda K. Kerber, "The Federalist Party," in *History of U.S. Political Parties, Vol. I, 1789-1860,* ed. A. M. Schlesinger, Jr. (New York: Chelsea House Publishers, 1973), p. 16.

[11] Quoted in *Congressional Quarterly's Guide to U.S. Elections* (Washington, D.C.: Congressional Quarterly, Inc., 1975), p. 206.

Despite Hamilton's plea, a majority of Federalists still supported Burr. If the votes had been cast individually, it is probable that Burr would have been chosen, but since each state had a single vote, Jefferson was finally elected after 36 ballots. One Federalist who helped to break the deadlock was James A. Bayard of Delaware. He supported Jefferson's election "so . . . as not to hazard the Constitution,"[12] and later wrote to Hamilton that "the means existed of electing Burr, but this required his cooperation. By deceiving one man (a great blockhead) and tempting two (not incorruptible), he might have secured a majority of the states."[13] The election of 1800 showed that the Constitution could withstand the rigors of transferring power, and it established a precedent which, although now taken for granted, in reality constitutes the acid test of a free, competitive party system.

Party Politics. Jefferson came into office with a large Republican majority in the House and proceeded to strengthen his party's organization in Congress in order to implement administration programs. Steps were taken to consolidate power by using federal patronage to reward party supporters, assisting the Republican party newspapers, and extending and reorganizing the party's electoral machinery. In addition, the congressional nominating caucus, which had previously operated in secret, became the open and accepted means of choosing presidential and vice-presidential candidates. The 1804 election also saw the establishment of a fledgling national committee, composed of Republican representatives and senators from the various states, to supervise the elections and plan electoral strategy.[14]

Despite these structural advances, the first party system did not endure. For a variety of reasons—an increasingly unpopular ideology, the lack of ingrained party loyalties, the absence of professional party leadership—the Federalists declined as an electoral force after Jefferson's election.[15] After the War of 1812, there was no serious possibility of a Federalist revival. Without the spur of interparty competition, the Republicans became increasingly susceptible to factional warfare, and by the election of 1824, the party could no longer resolve its internal tensions. There was a four-way contest for the presidency that destroyed the congressional nominating caucus. Subsequently, Andrew Jackson led in electoral votes, but since no candidate received a majority, the election was thrown into the House of Representatives which chose John Quincy Adams. The first party system was in disarray, but it had established a number of organizational precedents and shown that parties could provide positive benefits in a republican government.

---

[12] Quoted in Hofstadter, *The Idea of a Party System*, p. 129.

[13] Quoted in *Guide to Elections*, p. 207.

[14] Noble E. Cunningham, Jr., "The Jeffersonian Republican Party," in *History of U.S. Political Parties, Vol. I, 1789-1860*, ed. A. M. Schlesinger, Jr. (New York: Chelsea House Publishers, 1973), p. 264.

[15] See Paul Goodman, "The First American Party System," in *The American Party System: Stages of Political Development*, ed. W. N. Chambers and W. D. Burnham (New York: Oxford University Press, 1967), pp. 85-89.

The Second Party System: Democratizing the Parties

The 1820s represented a transitional period for the party system. The importance of electoral organization increased as the suffrage was expanded and as states shifted to the selection of electors by popular vote. By 1828, only two states still retained election by the state legislatures, and most states used the at-large, winner-take-all system to choose electors. In the 1824 presidential election, the total popular vote was approximately 366,000; this more than tripled, to 1.15 million, in 1828.

The followers of Andrew Jackson were the first to capitalize on these electoral changes, organizing a new Democratic party structure that could deal effectively with a mass electorate. Local, county, and state Jackson organizations were built and coordinated by central committees. Newspapers were established across the country to publicize Jackson and his programs, and a variety of techniques were employed to reach the new "mass" electorate, including torchlight parades and mass rallies.[16]

The Jacksonian innovations were expanded and institutionalized in the 1830s with the establishment of national, state, and local party committees along with official party leadership positions, such as the national chairman. In addition, the national convention system quickly became the accepted method of nominating presidential candidates and with it came the national party platform. This was a rather extraordinary period in party politics, with unusually intense involvement on the part of the electorate. The aristocratic parties of the first party system were replaced by the electoral parties of the second, and if the antiparty sentiments of the first had not entirely disappeared, they were gradually being superseded by the democratization of politics. The Democratic-Whig division was based on significant issues—the tariff, internal improvements, and financial policy—which reflected a more general conflict over the distribution of wealth and power in society. And, at least until slavery eclipsed these issues and led to sectional parties, the second party system showed that national, competitive parties could mobilize a mass electorate, maintain stable organizations, and organize the government. However, the second party system, while more fully developed than the first, was unable to survive the sectional strains arising from the slavery issue, and it disintegrated during the 1850s.

The Third Party System: Democrats vs. Republicans

The Democratic and Republican parties that developed during the third party system continued the process of electorate mobilization, directing their efforts toward developing party loyalties and stimulating turnout in a large and

---

[16] Michael F. Holt, "The Democratic Party 1828-1860," in *History of U.S. Political Parties, Vol. I, 1789-1860*, ed. A. M. Schlesinger, Jr. (New York: Chelsea House Publishers, 1973), pp. 503-04.

growing electorate. In 1866, for example, the Republicans and Democrats in Congress each established congressional campaign committees to assist in their election campaigns. This period is considered in certain respects to be a high-point in party politics: party loyalty and party voting were unusually high, the parties were organizationally strong, and the partisan press reached enormous numbers of voters.[17] Massive numbers of immigrants were mobilized by the urban political machines, which also served as social welfare and employment agencies. At the same time, political corruption flourished at all levels of government, and while it is not at all clear that the parties were in this regard exceptional among the political institutions of that era, the resulting stain has never been erased.

The electoral alignments of the third party system were in large part sectional, reflecting the divisiveness of the Civil War. While the Republicans were able to maintain their majority party status, there was strong interparty competition, particularly in presidential elections. However, the existing alignments did not correspond to and could not incorporate the developing social and economic divisions that accompanied the rapid industrialization of American society. These divisions resulted in the first major realignment of the Democratic-Republican two-party system, a realignment reflecting party adaptation to sociopolitical change.

The Fourth Party System:
The Impact of Progressivism

The election of 1896 established a period of strong Republican dominance that was to last, with only slight interruptions, for the next three decades. Against the unsuccessful efforts of the Democrats under William Jennings Bryan to forge a coalition of small farmers and the urban working class, the Republicans were able to identify themselves as the party of the new industrial order. By the turn of the century, urbanization and industrialization were profoundly changing American society, and the Republican party was able to consolidate its strength among the newly dominant social groups. In the battle between agrarianism and industrialism, the parties of 1896 provided a choice, and the Democrats came out the loser.

The fourth party system was thus characterized by a general decline in party competition when compared to the Democratic-Republican contests of earlier years or to the Democratic-Whig divisions of the 1830s and 1840s. The lack of party competition, moreover, was particularly evident among the state party systems. The moderate sectionalism of the third party system had thus become the sharp and dramatic sectionalism of the fourth, typified by the Democratic Solid South and the Republican Northeast.

This was a period, too, of sustained attacks on the party organizations, spearheaded by the Progressive movement. The Progressive movement was not opposed to industrialization, but it was committed to limiting if not eliminating the perceived

[17]Walter Dean Burnham, *Critical Elections and the Mainsprings of American Politics* (New York: W. W. Norton & Co., Inc., 1970), chap. 4.

excesses of partisan politics and party bosses. Its guiding assumption was that an enlightened citizenry could achieve "good government" directly, without the aid of intermediate institutions such as parties. As a consequence, it sponsored reforms that would allow citizens to propose and adopt legislation (the initiative and referendum), nominate candidates (the direct primary), discipline officeholders (the recall), and elect judges and U.S. senators. Patronage was attacked through civil service reform. Party organization was made subject to extensive legislative regulation by the states, and election laws were changed to require personal registration and secret ballots. In some states, the Progressives achieved the ultimate success of abolishing partisan elections altogether, at least for municipal offices.

The attacks of Progressivism were not confined to the parties. Social reform was an important objective, and it took the form of regulatory laws, child labor legislation, and similar efforts to curb the excesses of "unbridled capitalism." The focus of the Progressive effort, however, was state and local politics. Although many of the issues that it raised about economic and social equality did not mobilize a national reform effort until the New Deal, the Progressive movement had an enormous impact on the state and local parties and hence on the national party system. As one study of party reform concludes, "Few would dispute that the progressive reforms contributed more than those of any other epoch to make our parties what they are today."[18]

The fourth party system, which appeared to be stable during the early 1920s, was transformed by a massive electoral realignment during the 1930s. The character of the Democratic party changed dramatically during the 1920s as representatives of the rural and urban underprivileged gained increasing influence, and the shock of the Great Depression created a new and dominant coalition under Franklin Roosevelt. This fifth party system has had a continuing profound effect upon the national political agenda.

The Fifth Party System: New Deal Politics

The period following the early 1930s has been characterized both by major electoral realignments and by important institutional changes in the party system. The Roosevelt coalition was constructed of diverse new groups—such as organized labor, blacks, Jews—added to the traditionally Democratic white South and urban Catholics. It was, of course, constructed in the midst of the Great Depression and primarily based on the proposition that government intervention was necessary to assure economic prosperity and stability and to provide a more equitable distribution of economic resources. For the next several decades, the politics of economic regulation and the welfare state remained at or near the top of the national political agenda. But since the early 1960s, other potent social and cultural issues have

[18] Austin Ranney, *Curing the Mischiefs of Faction, Party Reform in America* (Berkeley, Cal.: University of California Press, 1975), p. 19.

emerged to strain seriously the party coalitions. In terms of electoral alignments and realignments, the future of the fifth party system is still in doubt.

The institutional changes of the fifth party system have primarily involved presidential politics. In 1936, the Democratic party abolished the two-thirds rule, which gave the South a potential veto of presidential nominees, and replaced it with majority nomination by delegates to the national convention. In the 1950s, both parties began to establish greater control over their state and local affiliates. At first, this was aimed at discouraging open opposition to the party's national nominees. This gradually accelerated, however, to cover how convention delegates should be chosen and, at least in the case of the 1972 Democratic rules, what kinds of persons could be selected. There has been, as might be expected, considerable controversy over the specific rules regarding delegate selection, but the parties have succeeded in pressing their claims for substantial centralization of authority with respect to presidential politics.

At the same time, the party organizations have, as we noted in chapter 1, been buffeted by social and technological changes. Television and public opinion polls allow politicians and the public to deal directly with each other and thus minimize the need for active intermediaries such as the party. The city machines are gone. The stable, committed electorates have shrunk. Under these circumstances, it is not at all clear what future institutional innovations or changes will occur within the two parties.

Just as the previous systems succeeded in achieving major objectives—nationhood, democratization, industrialization—the fifth party system has been a period of unprecedented governmental intervention in the economy and society. The lines of partisan division, however, are no longer clearly defined, at least within the mass electorate. Two-party competition is limited, and neither party has developed especially strong leadership. All of this suggests that the two-party system, which has survived some rude shocks, is in for some more. The development of the party system is still in progress.

PARTY COMPETITION

While the U.S. party system's development has conformed to the broad outlines of a two-party system, there have been significant variations in the degree of interparty competition at different electoral levels. In addition to the cycles of dominance in national party politics, there have also been major realignments in many states over the past century. The purpose of this section is to examine these patterns of change and assess their implications for the future of two-party politics.

It might be helpful, however, first to review the criteria used to analyze interparty competition. According to the classification scheme generally used in studying party systems, American state party systems are categorized as two-party competitive, modified or predominantly one-party, or one-party, depending on the level of competition (measured by actual election results) for a particular office or set of offices over a period of time. In addition to the actual votes received by the competing parties, such factors as turnover in party control of offices or the proportions of legislative seats held by the parties are sometimes considered as well.

For example, requirements for a genuinely competitive two-party system might include the following: (1) the two major parties must receive most of the votes and control most of the offices, so that third parties or minor parties are usually inconsequential; (2) either major party must be capable of capturing a majority of votes—that is, there are no large (perhaps 10 percent or greater) and consistent differentials between the two parties' shares of the votes; and (3) party control of offices changes with some frequency from election to election.

In a modified one-party state system, the vote share differentials are large and persistent, and there is very limited turnover in party control of offices. While the minority party may receive perhaps 40-45 percent of the vote on the average, it lacks the electoral strength to mount serious challenges for most statewide offices. Similarly, it may have an electoral base sufficiently concentrated to insure a number of state legislative seats, but it cannot realistically compete for control of the legislature. The minority party in a modified one-party system, then, may be organized and important, but it is definitely subordinate to the majority party.

The one-party state may have two parties on the ballot, but the electoral results are well known in advance. The majority party has an overwhelming electoral advantage for virtually all offices. Since nomination by the majority party is tantamount to election, the serious competition in one-party states usually takes place between factions and personalities within the majority party during the primaries. Until recently, the southern states exhibited this one-party pattern at all electoral levels. The Solid South was Democratic in presidential and congressional elections, governors and other officials elected statewide were invariably Democratic, there were huge Democratic majorities in the state legislatures, and most county and local offices were also controlled by Democrats. At the same time, there were intense factional conflicts within the Democratic party in most southern states.[19] Over the past two decades, however, the Solid South has largely disappeared in presidential politics, and Democratic hegemony has also eroded at the state level, although to a lesser extent. This change in the South reflects the general decline of one-partyism in the United States.[20]

Because there are so many schemes for classifying the states within these broad categories, it is extremely important to clarify such variables as the time period covered, the specific offices involved, and the standards used to distinguish between competitive and noncompetitive elections.[21] Table 2.2, for example,

---

[19] See, for example, V. O. Key, Jr., *Southern Politics* (New York: Alfred A. Knopf, 1949).

[20] See Paul T. David, *Party Strength in the United States, 1872-1970* (Charlottesville, Va.: University Press of Virginia, 1972).

[21] For a method of also incorporating turnover in office, see Joseph C. Schlesinger, "A Two-Dimensional Scheme for Classifying the States According to Degree of Inter-Party Competition," *American Political Science Review*, 49 (December 1955), 1120-28.

TABLE 2.2 Classification of States by Interparty Competition, Hypothetical Cases, 1946-1978

	Years Held Governorship[a]		Average Percentage Gubernatorial Vote		Years Controlled State Legislature[b]		Average Percentage State Legislative Seats	
	Dem	Rep	Dem	Rep	Dem	Rep	Dem	Rep
State A	12	20	48.5	51.5	16	16	52.3	47.7
State B	28	4	60.5	39.5	30	2	64.2	35.8
State C	32	0	82.5	17.5	32	0	92.5	7.5

[a]Four-year term.
[b]Lower-house, two-year term.

presents some hypothetical cases that might be used to illustrate competition at the state level during the post-World War II period. The classification here, of course, would be quite simple. In State A, the two parties share control of the governorship and state legislature, their average vote shares are within several percentage points of each other, and their relative strengths in the legislature are, on the average, similarly close. State A is, for these offices and time period, two-party competitive.

State B is less competitive. The Republican party has significant electoral strength, but it has only managed to win one gubernatorial election out of eight and to gain control of the state legislature once in sixteen elections. Its average vote share and proportion of legislative seats are not in the strongly competitive range, but they are substantial enough to provide a continuous and organized opposition. State B, then, would be a modified one-party state that is predominantly Democratic for these offices. It may well be that the state is much more competitive in presidential elections and would therefore be classified differently if we were focusing on the presidency. State C, of course, is clearly a one-party state, since the Democrats confront a negligible Republican opposition.

Unfortunately, many states are not so readily classified, and it becomes necessary to specify precisely how competition will be defined in order to handle these cases. Is, for example, a competitive share of the vote within the 55-45 percent range or a 60-40 percent range? Is it a noncompetitive election when a party receives two-thirds or more of the vote, or is an even higher level required? For much of the following discussion, we will be dealing with fairly general patterns that do not require such definite answers, but as state party systems are discussed, it should be remembered that the extraordinary variety among the American states makes classification complex and difficult.

National Elections

If we take the first criterion of a two-party system—that the electoral prospects of third parties are minimal—we find that the appropriate level of major party dominance is clearly achieved in national politics. The Democratic and Republican parties have shared exclusive control of the presidency and Congress since the Civil War. The relative strengths of the two parties, however, have shifted markedly during this time.

The overall pattern is shown in Table 2.3. The chronological periods used here correspond to the preceding discussion of the third, fourth, and fifth party systems, and the shifts in party strength reflect the realignments that occurred in 1896 and 1932. While the Republicans have an edge in both presidential and senatorial control over the entire period, this is a result of Republican dominance prior to 1932. Since that time, the Democratic party has won 8 of 12 presidential contests and has controlled Congress (that is, held a majority of seats in the House and Senate) for all but four years. Except for a two-year period at the beginning of

TABLE 2.3 Party Control of the Presidency and Congress, 1869-1981

	Years Controlled Presidency		Years Controlled House		Years Controlled Senate*	
Period:	Dem	Rep	Dem	Rep	Dem	Rep
1869-1897	8	20	16	12	4	24
1897-1933	8	28	10	26	6	30
1933-1981	32	16	44	4	44	4
	48	64	70	42	54	58

*U.S. Senators were elected by state legislatures during the entire first period (1869-1897) and almost half of the second. The Seventeenth Amendment ratified in 1913 established popular election of the Senate.

President Eisenhower's first term in 1953, the Republican party has not had simultaneous control of the executive and legislative branches in almost five decades.

Presidential Elections. The changes in party strength and interparty competition at the presidential level are somewhat more complex than these general patterns indicate. Table 2.4 illustrates this by showing the Republican percentage of the two-party vote for president over the past century. In the post-Civil War period, the Republicans captured five of seven presidential contests, but their popular vote margins were extremely small in most instances. Indeed, in 1876 and 1888, the Republican candidates received fewer votes than did the Democratic nominees but still gained a majority of electoral votes. This was, then, a highly competitive period in which each party's vote usually remained within a fairly narrow range around 50 percent. The only exception was Grant's reelection in 1872, and Grant was the only president during this period to be elected to consecutive terms.

The second electoral period, 1896-1928, again shows the Republicans winning most elections, but the races have become much less competitive. The average percentage that the Republicans received in their successful races was 58.2 percent compared to 51.3 percent during the earlier period. The Democrats captured only two elections, 1912 and 1916 (the first was in large part the result of a bitter split in the Republican party), and their performance in other races was well below that prior to the 1896 realignment.

The most recent period covers presidential elections since the beginning of the New Deal. Here, the Democrats gain ascendancy, winning all but four elections. Although the Democratic victories in 1932 and 1936 were huge, the Republican party has subsequently and steadily improved its position. With the significant exception of 1964, the party has been competitive in every post-World War II election and has actually split the elections evenly with the Democrats since the late 1940s. And the Democratic party, despite its majority status, has lost by very large margins in three of its four defeats (1952, 1956, and 1972). At the presidential level, then, the party system is still highly competitive.

TABLE 2.4 Party Competition in Presidential Elections

	Winning Party/Candidate	Republican Percentage of Major Party Vote
Period: 1868-1892		
1868	Republican (Grant)	52.7
1872	Republican (Grant)	55.9
1876	Republican (Hayes)	48.4
1880	Republican (Garfield)	50.1
1884	Democratic (Cleveland)	49.9
1888	Republican (Harrison)	49.5
1892	Democratic (Cleveland)	48.2
Period: 1896-1928		
1896	Republican (McKinley)	52.2
1900	Republican (McKinley)	53.1
1904	Republican (Roosevelt)	60.0
1908	Republican (Taft)	54.5
1912	Democratic (Wilson)	35.6
1916	Democratic (Wilson)	48.3
1920	Republican (Harding)	63.8
1924	Republican (Coolidge)	65.2
1928	Republican (Hoover)	58.8
Period: 1932-1976		
1932	Democratic (Roosevelt)	40.9
1936	Democratic (Roosevelt)	37.5
1940	Democratic (Roosevelt)	45.0
1944	Democratic (Roosevelt)	46.2
1948	Democratic (Truman)	47.7
1952	Republican (Eisenhower)	55.4
1956	Republican (Eisenhower)	57.8
1960	Democratic (Kennedy)	49.9
1964	Democratic (Johnson)	38.7
1968	Republican (Nixon)	50.4
1972	Republican (Nixon)	61.8
1976	Democratic (Carter)	48.9

Congressional Elections. The electoral strength of the Democratic party has been much more visible at the congressional level than at the presidential level. Over the past two decades, for example, the Democratic congressional majorities have been unusually large, averaging approximately 60 percent of the seats in the House and Senate (see Table 2.5). While the limited cohesion of the congressional parties means that numerical majorities are not as formidable as they might appear, the fact remains that the Republicans have not been able to compete effectively for the benefits and advantages that accrue to the party that organizes the House or Senate—selecting the committee and floor leaders, holding committee majorities, hiring committee staff, and determining the legislative agenda and schedule. The period of uninterrupted Democratic control of both chambers that began in 1955 is by far the longest by either party in over a century.

TABLE 2.5 Party Control in the House and Senate, 1933-1979

		Percentage of Seats Held by Democratic Party*	
Congress	Year	House	Senate
96th Congress	1979-1981	63.4	59.0
95th Congress	1977-1979	67.9	61.0
94th Congress	1975-1977	66.9	60.6
93rd Congress	1973-1975	55.2	56.0
92nd Congress	1971-1973	58.5	54.0
91st Congress	1969-1971	55.9	57.0
90th Congress	1967-1969	56.9	64.0
89th Congress	1965-1967	67.8	68.0
88th Congress	1963-1965	59.3	67.0
87th Congress	1961-1963	60.2	65.0
86th Congress	1959-1961	64.9	65.3
85th Congress	1957-1959	53.8	51.0
84th Congress	1955-1957	53.3	50.0
83rd Congress	1953-1955	48.7	50.0
82nd Congress	1951-1953	53.9	51.0
81st Congress	1949-1951	60.5	56.3
80th Congress	1947-1949	43.3	46.7
79th Congress	1945-1947	55.8	58.9
78th Congress	1943-1945	50.7	60.4
77th Congress	1941-1943	61.6	68.8
76th Congress	1939-1941	60.8	71.9
75th Congress	1937-1939	76.4	79.1
74th Congress	1935-1937	73.8	71.9
73rd Congress	1933-1935	71.8	62.5

*As of the beginning of the first session of each Congress. The percentage figure is for the total number of seats filled and excludes vacancies.

The variations in party strength since the Civil War are shown in Table 2.6, which lists the Democratic percentage of the two-party vote for the U.S. House during the three electoral periods that we have been using. (This measure is calculated by adding the votes that each party receives in all of the individual congressional districts in a given year. It does not necessarily correspond to the proportion of seats that the party receives.) From 1868-1894, interparty competition was

TABLE 2.6 Two-Party Vote for the U.S. House, 1868-1976

	Democratic Percentage		
	High	Low	Average
1868-1894	54.2 (1890)	44.5 (1894)	50.1
1896-1930	57.1 (1912)	37.7 (1920)	46.7
1932-1976	58.6 (1974)	45.3 (1946)	55.1

extremely high in House elections (as it was in presidential elections), with only 0.2 percent separating the parties' average percentages of the national vote over the entire time span. Moreover, the variation in the Democratic vote percentage is less than 10 percentage points, with both the high and low points (1890 and 1894, respectively) coming just before the 1896 realignment.

After 1896, Democratic strength dropped significantly. The party's average share of the national House vote dropped to less than 47 percent, and the range of variation—a low of 37.7 percent and a high of 57.1 percent—is double that of the preceding electoral period. From 1896-1930, then, the Republicans held a decided if not overwhelming edge at the congressional level.

The most recent period has been the least competitive. The average Democratic percentage of the House vote is 55.1 percent for the period 1932-1976, the highest level reached by either party during the electoral eras shown. Figure 2.1 clearly shows the development of this dominance from 1932 to 1976. The Republicans were able to recover fairly quickly from losses suffered during the Depression so that by 1938 the Democratic share of the House vote dropped to less than 51 percent. From then until the late 1950s, the Democrats were kept well below 55 percent, and on three occasions (1942, 1946, and 1952), the Republicans received a majority of the popular vote for the House. The 1958 election, which took place

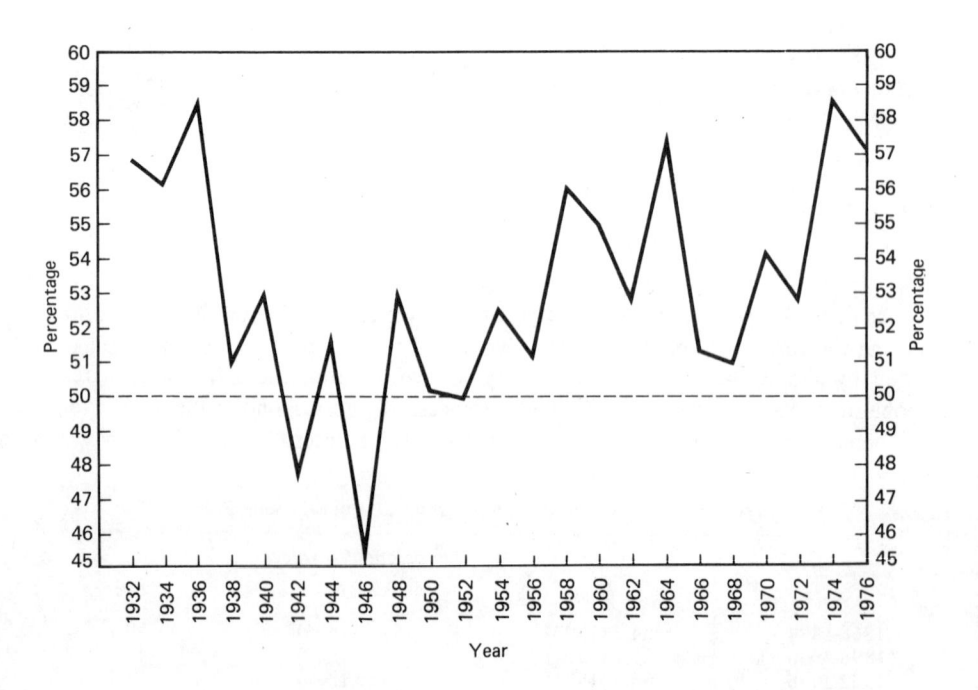

FIGURE 2.1 The Democratic Party Share of the Two-Party Vote for the U.S. House, 1932-1976

during a recession, saw a dramatic increase in Democratic strength, and the differentials between the parties have been substantial in most elections since that time.

Thus, while the Republican party holds a substantial number of congressional seats and is capable of fielding serious candidates in all sections of the country, it is not sufficiently strong to challenge the Democrats' congressional supremacy. Moreover, there is no evidence to suggest that Republican strength will increase enough to change this situation markedly in the foreseeable future. Two-party competition, then, is much greater at the presidential level than at the congressional level.

State Party Systems

The outcome of presidential and congressional elections depends, of course, on party strength within the states. The state parties, moreover, must also contest a large number of state and local elections. There are now more than a half-million elected officials in the states, and while the parties are not involved in many of the local and special district elections for these officials, they are frequently much more interested in and affected by state races than national races.

As discussed previously, it is difficult to find a method for classifying state party systems that will satisfy everyone. Nevertheless, it is necessary to have a general understanding of state-to-state variations in competition in order to analyze electoral trends in the party system.[22] Our first assessment of these variations concerns presidential elections. Because of the presidency's unusual visibility, it is advisable to examine presidential contests separately from other elections in a state. Some states, for example, are competitive in presidential elections but not in congressional or gubernatorial elections.[23]

Figure 2.2 a-c illustrates how competition in the states has changed over the past century. The classification scheme used here is quite simple: (1) a state is classified as competitive if neither party carries it 75 percent or more of the time during an electoral period—for example, California has gone Democratic six times and Republican six times in the last twelve elections, so it is classified as competitive for 1932-1976; (2) if either party carries a state's electoral vote 75 percent or more of the time, that state is classified as predominantly Democratic or predominantly Republican.

The most obvious and significant change in presidential voting has been the sharp increase in the number of competitive states since 1932. Approximately two-thirds of the states are now in the competitive category, as compared to less than one-third in each of the preceding electoral periods. However, while the number of

---

[22] See Burnham, *Critical Elections*, chap. 2.

[23] Also, there is a weaker relationship between voting for president and voting for other offices, such as governor, U.S. House, or U.S. Senate, than there is between voting for other of these paired offices. David, *Party Strength in the United States*, pp. 21-24.

12 - ☐ Competitive
16 - ▨ Predominantly Republican
10 - ▨ Predominantly Democratic

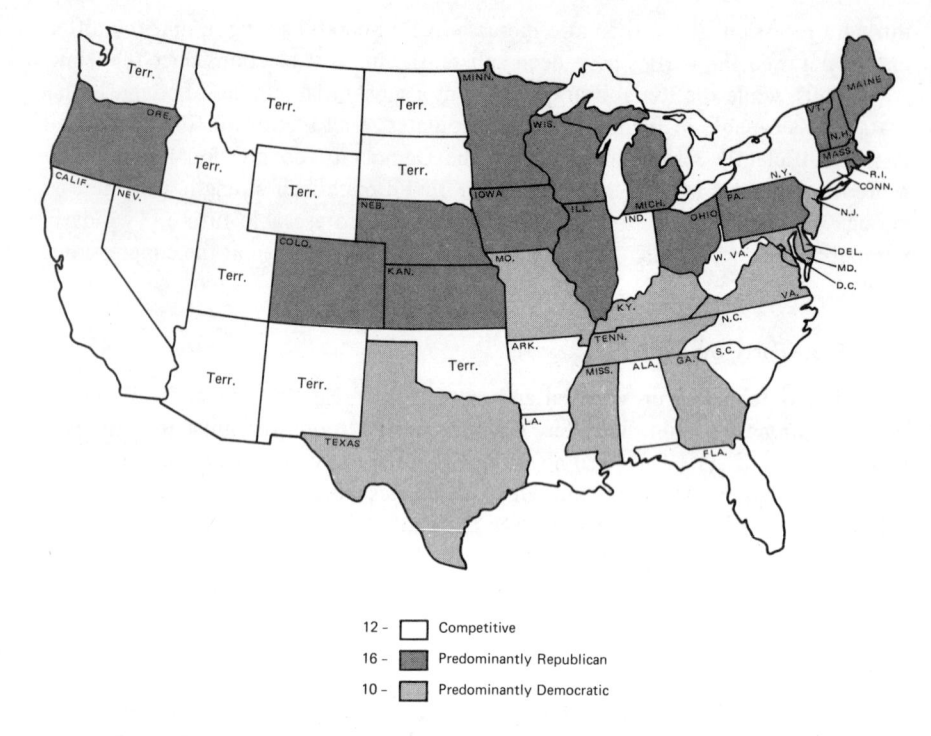

FIGURE 2.2a State Party Strength in Presidential Elections, 1868-1892. Six of the designated territories became states in time to participate in the 1892 election, but did not participate in prior elections. The remaining four (Arizona, New Mexico, Oklahoma, and Utah) held territorial status during this entire period.

predominantly Democratic and predominantly Republican states is roughly equal, the Democratic states in this group account for more than 100 electoral votes, some two and one-half times as many as their Republican counterparts.

The patterns here complement our earlier observations about national presidential voting. The Republican electoral base has eroded substantially since its high point from 1896 to 1928. Several formerly Republican states have shifted over to the Democratic side (Massachusetts, Minnesota, Rhode Island, and West Virginia), but most have simply become competitive. At the same time, the Democratic party actually has fewer committed states than it had previously, in large part because of the breakup of the Solid South. Therefore, while the Republicans face an uphill fight in presidential races, they are competitive in most states.

Below the presidential level, however, the movement in the direction of the Democratic party has been stronger. Perhaps the most comprehensive study of long-term party strength in the states was completed in 1972 by Paul T. David.[24]

[24] Ibid., pp. 19-61.

14 - ☐ Competitive
23 - ▓ Predominantly Republican
11 - ░ Predominantly Democratic

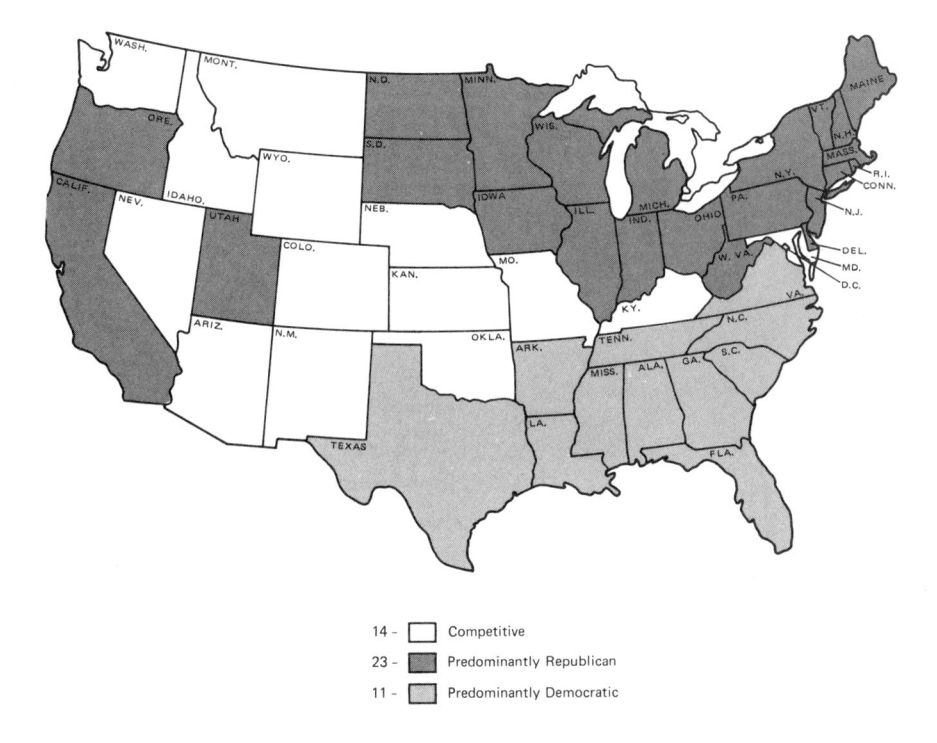

FIGURE 2.2b State Party Strength in Presidential Elections, 1896-1928

Professor David used a composite measure of party strength that included gubernatorial, U.S. Senate, and U.S. House races. His analysis found that within the party system following the 1896 realignment, 18 states were predominantly Republican, 12 states predominantly Democratic, and 18 states competitive (see Figure 2.3). For the Republican states, the combined average percentage of the two-party vote was over 60 percent Republican.[25] The Democratic states, which included the eleven states of the Confederacy and Arizona, had a combined average of over 80 percent of the two-party vote in the Democratic column. The competitive states had an almost even split—50.8 percent Republican and 49.2 percent Democratic. The sharp, sectional character of politics during the fourth party system is clearly shown in Figure 2.3; the Democrats held an overwhelming advantage in the South, while the Republicans had broader if less overwhelming strength throughout the rest of the nation.

Since 1932, however, a number of states, including some very large, industrialized ones, have shifted away from the Republican side (See Figure 2.4). All of these, however, have become competitive. The only states to move firmly into the Democratic column are six that were formerly classified as competitive; most of

---

[25] For the weighting procedure used in this calculation, see ibid., pp. 41-50.

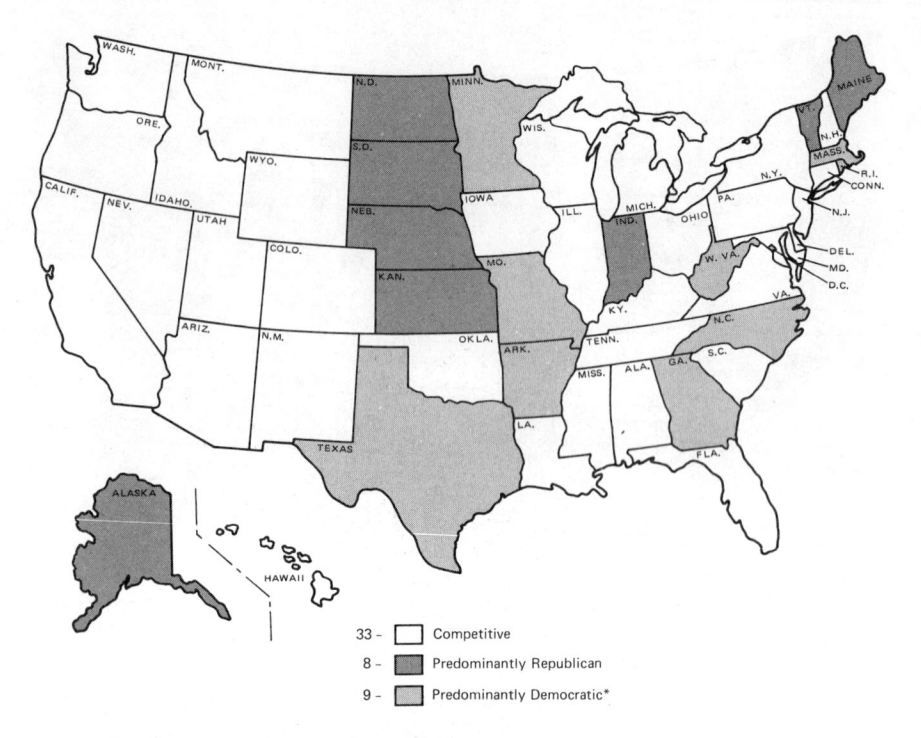

FIGURE 2.2c State Party Strength in Presidential Elections, 1932-1976, excludes District of Columbia

33 - Competitive
8 - Predominantly Republican
9 - Predominantly Democratic*

these are fairly small. The trend, then, is in the direction of greater competition within more states. If the South also continues its gradual movement toward two-party politics (and follows the pattern of the formerly Republican states), the result would be the most advanced nationalization of two-party competition since the Civil War.

Despite the obvious weaknesses of the Republican party, then, there is at the present time unusual potential for developing competitive two-party politics in most states. Whether the Republicans will be able to benefit from this potential is problematic. But at least from these perspectives on party competition, it does not appear that the more pessimistic assessments of the party system's future are correct.

THIRD PARTIES

The term *third parties* is frequently misleading in that it both overstates the importance of most minor parties and understates their diversity. Minor or third parties differ along several important dimensions—geographical focus, scope of ideological concern, purpose, and significance. Most minor parties have no electoral

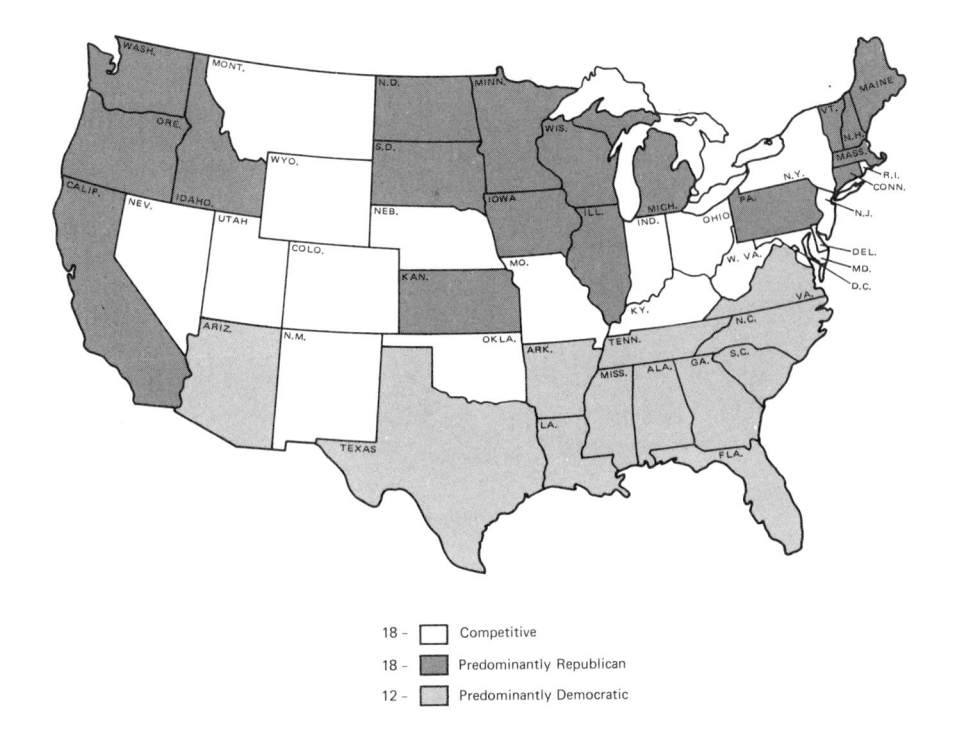

FIGURE 2.3 Partisanship in the United States, 1896-1930. *Source:* Paul T. David, *Party Strength in the United States, 1872-1970* (Charlottesville, Va.: University Press of Virginia, 1972), p. 40.

Legend:
- 18 — Competitive
- 18 — Predominantly Republican
- 12 — Predominantly Democratic

or programmatic impact in terms of the party system. They exist to promote, rather forlornly in most instances, an exotic cause or doctrine. Occasionally, however, a minor or third-party movement does have a substantial and lasting effect on party politics.

In 1976, numerous third parties actively promoted candidates, with rather poor results. As shown in Table 2.7, some three dozen parties (in addition to the Democratic and Republican parties) entered candidates in the presidential, congressional, and gubernatorial races that year. (The party labels are, in most cases, self-explanatory. Some, such as the Owl Party, are somewhat elusive.)[26] Their *combined* votes, however, amounted to less than two percent of the total popular vote for

---

[26] The Owl Party was founded in 1976 by Olympia, Washington nightclub owner Red Kelly. Its slogan is, naturally enough, "We Don't Give a Hoot," and its platform promises to heal the continental divide. In 1976, the party's nominees for state office were nightclub patrons and musicians. When the rent on Kelly's nightclub was raised in 1978, he threatened to move the party headquarters to Seattle. The Owl Party is unusual in that humor, however strained, is not characteristic of very many third parties.

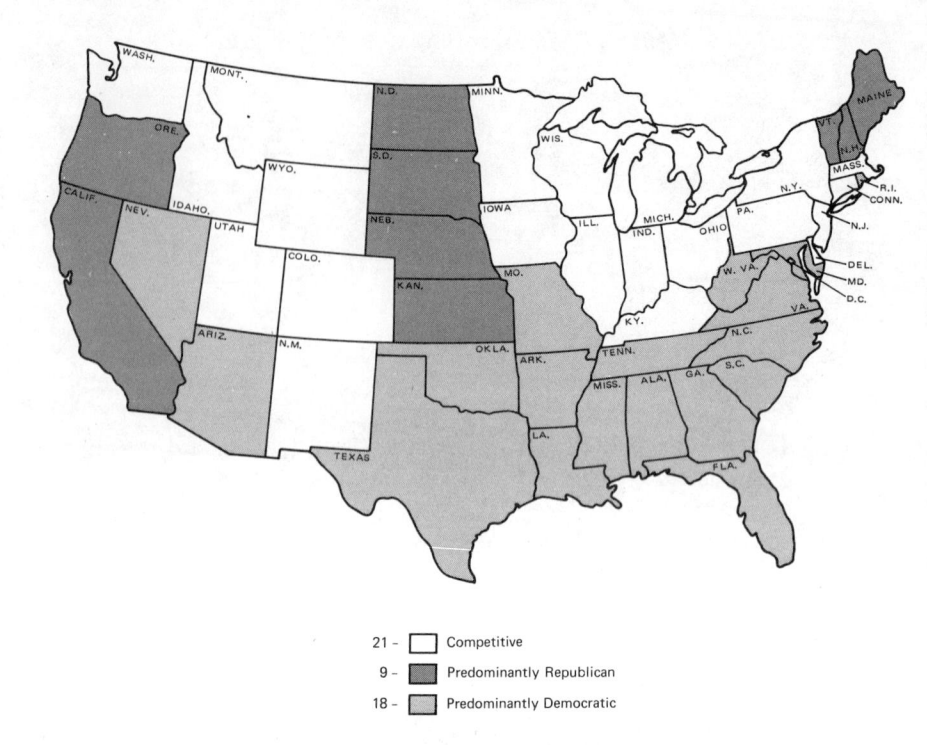

21 - ☐ Competitive
9 - ▓ Predominantly Republican
18 - ▒ Predominantly Democratic

FIGURE 2.4 Partisanship in the United States, 1932-1970. *Source:* Adapted from Paul T. David, *Party Strength in the United States, 1872-1970* (Charlottesville, Va.: University of Virginia, 1972), p. 53.

TABLE 2.7 Third Parties in the 1976 Elections

American	Liberal
American Constitution	Libertarian
American Independent	Labor Party
Conservative	La Raza Unida
Concerned Citizens	Liberty Union
Co-Equal Citizens	Mayflower Party
Communist	Nonpartisan
Constitutional	National Democratic Party of Alabama
Democratic Socialist	Owl Party
Free Libertarian	Prohibition
George Wallace Party	Peace and Freedom
Human Rights	People's Party
Independent American	Revolutionary Workers
Independent Conservative	Socialist Labor
Independents for Godly Government	Socialist Workers
Independent	United States Labor Party
Independent Party	Workers
	White Power Party

Source: *Congressional Quarterly Weekly Report*, 35, No. 12 (March 19, 1977), 491.

TABLE 2.8 Major and Third Party Voting, 1976[a]

	Democratic Vote	Per Cent	Republican Vote	Per Cent	Others Vote	Per Cent
President	40,828,587	50.1	39,147,613	48.0	1,575,748	1.9
U.S. House	41,749,411	56.2	31,244,059	42.1	1,277,975	1.7
U.S. Senate	31,574,275	54.4	24,552,689	42.3	1,958,069	3.4
Governor	7,677,751	48.8	7,929,153	50.4	137,020	0.9

[a]U.S. House vote excludes six districts where candidates ran unopposed. The U.S. Senate and gubernatorial votes are aggregates of the 32 Senate and 14 governorship races in 1976.
Source: *Congressional Quarterly Weekly Report*, 35, No. 12 (March 19, 1977), 491.

president and for the U.S. House and to less than one percent of the votes for governor (see Table 2.8). Moreover, the best showing—3.4 percent in U.S. Senate races—was largely attributable to Sen. Harry F. Byrd, Jr., who won his Virginia race as an Independent. It should be mentioned that Senator Byrd's designation is somewhat unusual. He actually inherited the famous Byrd Democratic machine in Virginia and took on the Independent label after a primary split in the party. In any case, his was the only third-party victory; none of the other genuine third-party candidacies was seriously competitive.

National Third Parties

If the third-party showing in 1976 was rather dismal, it was not unrepresentative of previous efforts. With the significant exceptions of 1948 and 1968, for example, third-party presidential voting has been relatively low since the early 1940s (see Table 2.9). Prior to 1968, some interpreted this as signaling the end of minor

TABLE 2.9 Minor Parties in Presidential Elections, 1868-1976

	Combined Percentage of Total Popular Vote		Combined Percentage of Total Popular Vote
1868		1924	17.11
1872	.54	1928	1.02
1876	.26	1932	2.93
1880	3.47	1936	2.67
1884	3.25	1940	.48
1888	3.55	1944	.73
1892	11.0	1948	5.38
1896	2.27	1952	.49
1900	2.82	1956	.66
1904	5.99	1960	.72
1908	5.37	1964	.48
1912	34.99	1968	13.86
1916	4.65	1972	1.78
1920	5.54	1976	1.9

TABLE 2.10 Third Party Presidential Voting, Leading Post-Civil War Candidacies[a]

Year	Party	Candidate	Electoral Votes	Percentage of Popular Vote
1892	Populist	Weaver	22 (of 444)	8.5
1912	Progressive	Theodore Roosevelt	88 (of 531)	27.39
1924	Progressive	La Follette	13 (of 531)	16.56
1948	States' Rights Democrat	Thurmond	39 (of 531)[b]	2.40
1968	American Independent	Wallace	46 (of 538)[c]	13.5

[a] Excludes electoral votes cast by "faithless electors" in 1956, 1960, 1968 and 1972, as well as the split in electoral votes that occurred when the Democratic presidential nominee in 1872 died after election day but before the electors met.
[b] Includes one electoral vote cast by a "faithless elector"—a Truman elector in Tennessee.
[c] Includes one electoral vote cast by a "faithless elector"—a Nixon elector in North Carolina.

party influence in presidential politics, but the Wallace candidacy that year dampened such speculation. Now there is renewed interest in the electoral potential of third-party presidential movements, and it may well be that an especially appealing candidate could achieve some success outside the major parties. Below the presidential level, however, third-party prospects appear to be poor.

The 1948 and 1968 cases, moreover, are atypical. In the post-Civil War period, third-party candidates have been able to win electoral votes in only five elections (see Table 2.10). The number of electoral votes involved has usually been under 10 percent (the only exception being 1912), while the percentage of the popular vote has exceeded 10 percent on three occasions—1912, 1924, and 1968. At this point, then, it might be helpful to review briefly these third-party "successes."

The Populist Party. The Populist or People's Party of 1892 was the first post-Civil War third party to gain a significant presidential vote. Its strength was concentrated in the West and the South, reflecting its essential character as a party of agrarian protest. The Populist party included several elements—the Granger movement, the earlier Greenback party, the Farmer's Alliance, and related agricultural groups. It supported a wide range of economic and political reforms. Among the former, its platform emphasized inflating the money supply (symbolized by the gold versus silver debate), nationalization of the railroads, expanded credit for farmers, and a graduated income tax. The party also declared itself in favor of the direct election of U.S. Senators, the initiative and referendum, direct primaries, a one-term limit for the president, and women's suffrage. Something of the tone of the Populist platform is reflected in its long preamble denouncing both major parties as tools of "capitalists, corporations, national banks, rings, trusts, watered stock, ... and userers. ... They propose to sacrifice our homes, lives, and children on the altar of mammon; to destroy the multitude in order to secure corruption funds from the millionaires."

In the 1892 elections, the Populists did well at all levels, winning several governorships, nearly a dozen House seats, and numerous local offices in addition to their 22 electoral votes and 8.5 percent of the popular vote in the presidential contest. Their impact was considerable within the Democratic party, since they drew from a similar electoral base, and the parties soon merged in some western states. By 1896, the extent of Populist influence became apparent with the nomination of William Jennings Bryan by the Democrats, and the adoption of a platform advocating the unlimited coinage of silver and other populist-sponsored policies. Conservative Democrats were even unable to gain convention approval of a resolution commending the incumbent Cleveland administration.

The fusion of the Populist and Democratic parties had electoral and programmatic effects. The Populists forced a widening of the policy division between the Republican and Democratic parties over economic policy and social reform. The strong element of class-based politics that characterized the 1896 realignment had the effect of cementing Republican strength in the Northeast and consolidating Democratic and Populist strength in the South and West (see Figure 2.5). A shift of conservative Democrats to the Republican party in 1896 (and a less pronounced movement of progressive Republicans to the Democratic party) was therefore a major result of the Populist movement.

The Progressives, 1912 and 1924. If the Populists were an indication of the strains within the Democratic coalition, the significant third-party movements in the following decades arose within the dominant Republican party. The Progressive party that emerged in 1912 was a Republican faction that coalesced around Theodore Roosevelt. Roosevelt had supported Taft as his successor to the presidency in 1908, but his growing dissatisfaction over the Taft administration's policies and performance led him to challenge Taft for the Republican nomination in 1912. When Taft was renominated, Roosevelt and his followers left the party to run under the Progressive banner. The Progressive party's agitation for governmental reform was accompanied by a heavy emphasis on federal regulation of business interests and social welfare policy, including a national health service and social insurance system. Like the Populists in 1892, the Progressives denounced the Democratic and Republican parties as "tools of corrupt interests which use them impartially to serve their selfish purposes." According to the Progressive platform, this "unholy alliance" created "an invisible government owing no allegiance and acknowledging no responsibility to the people."

If Roosevelt was unable to prevail within his old party, he still retained a formidable popular base, and his candidacy destroyed whatever prospects Taft might have had to gain reelection. Indeed, Roosevelt outdistanced Taft in both electoral votes—88 to 8—and popular votes—27.4 percent to 23.2 percent. And whatever chance Taft or Roosevelt might have had if running alone, the Republican

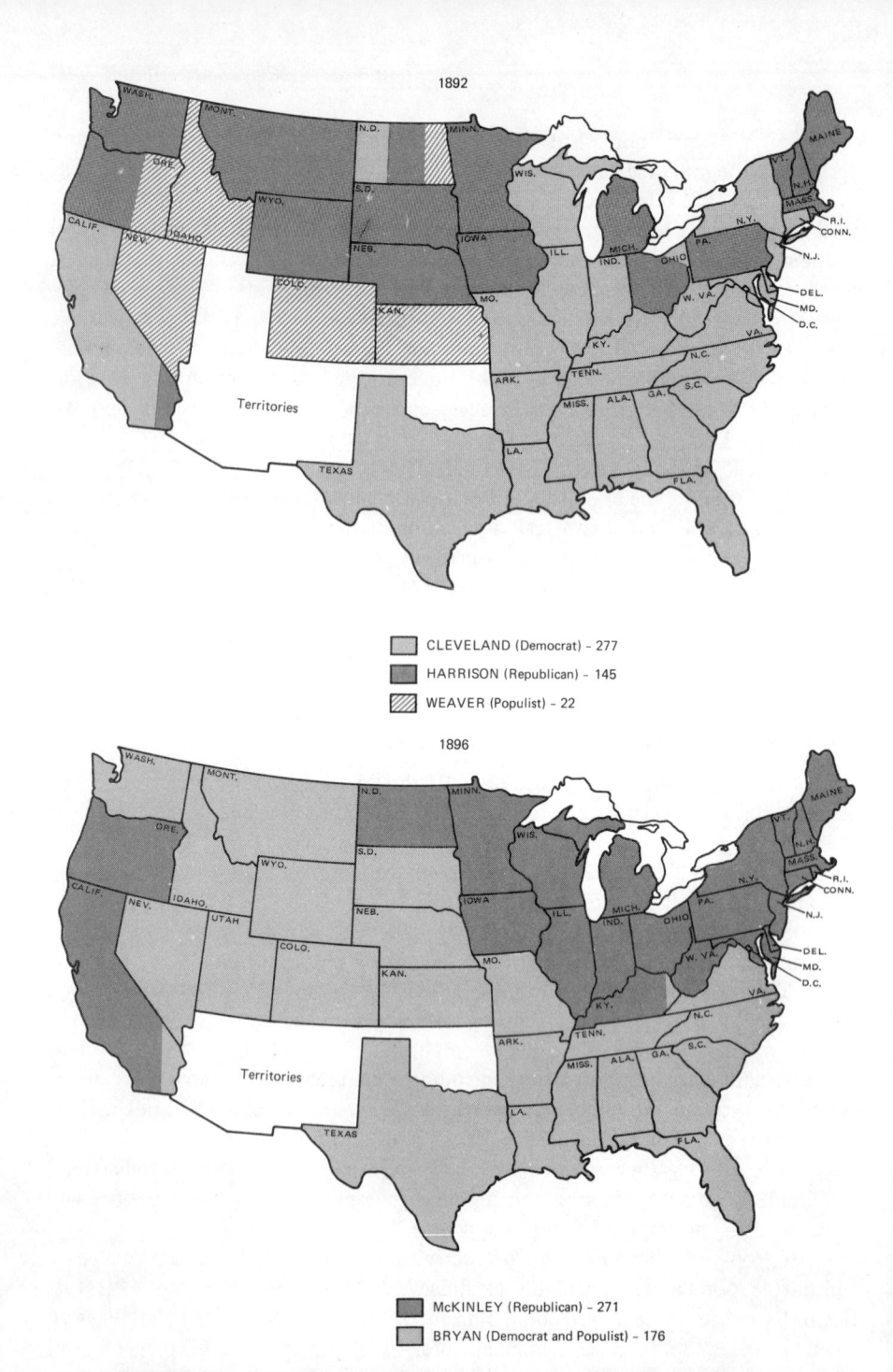

FIGURE 2.5 The 1892 and 1896 Electoral Votes, by State. *Source: Congressional Quarterly's Guide to U.S. Elections* (Washington, D.C.: Congressional Quarterly, Inc., 1975), pp. 240, 241.

split allowed Woodrow Wilson to sweep 435 electoral votes with less than 42 percent of the popular vote (see Figure 2.6). The long-term effect of the 1912 split, in any case, was probably to strengthen the conservative wing within the Republican party. The Republicans and Progressives met in separate conventions in 1916, but the Progressives finally accepted Charles Evans Hughes, a Supreme Court justice and former governor of New York, who was the leading candidate at the Republican convention. By 1920, with the nomination of Harding, the conservatives had regained firm control of the party.

The Progressive party that was launched in 1924 was not a secessionist movement along the lines of 1912, although the Progressive's presidential nominee, Sen. Robert M. La Follette of Wisconsin, had earlier been nominated at the 1924 Republican convention. La Follette's strength was minimal, however, amounting to only 34 votes out of over 1100 and concentrated largely within his own state delegation. Like its 1912 predecessor, however, the Progressive movement of 1924 was a response to the dominant conservatism within the Republican party. The Progressive convention was called by the Conference for Progressive Political Action and included groups opposed to the economic, agricultural, and labor policies of the

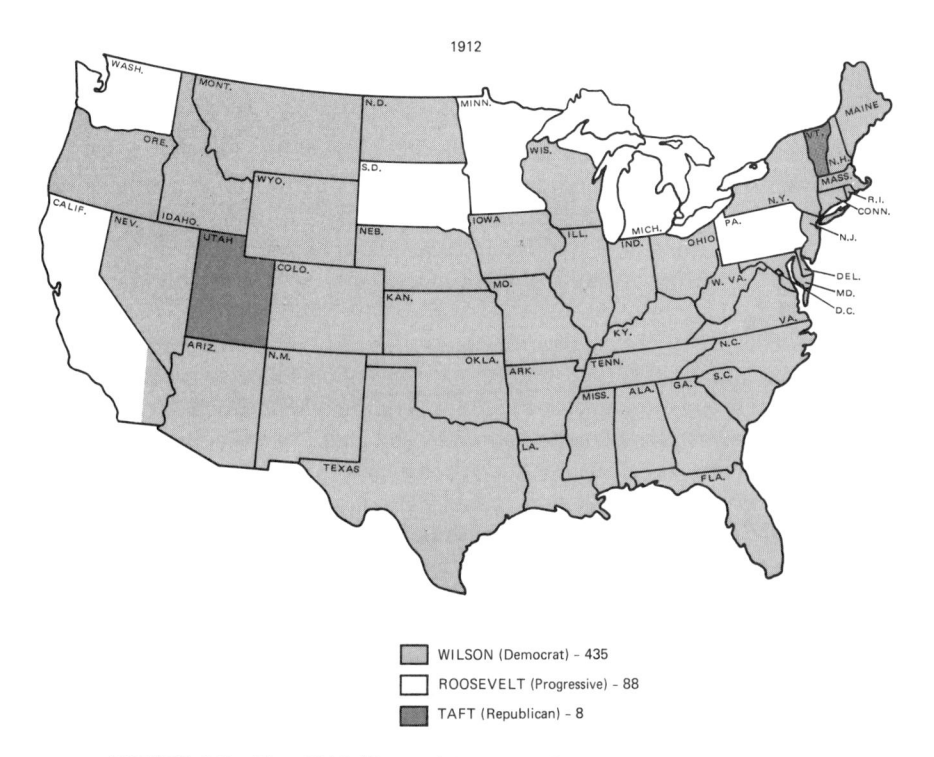

WILSON (Democrat) - 435
ROOSEVELT (Progressive) - 88
TAFT (Republican) - 8

FIGURE 2.6 The 1912 Electoral Vote, by State. *Source: Congressional Quarterly's Guide to U.S. Elections* (Washington, D.C.: Congressional Quarterly, Inc., 1975), p. 245.

Harding-Coolidge administration. The party platform called for government action to control business interests and break up monopolies, to protect labor's right to organize, to reduce tariffs, and to assist farmers. The Progressives also advocated some unusual governmental reforms, including elections of federal judges for fixed terms, a national referendum and initiative, and an amendment giving Congress the power to veto Supreme Court decisions.

La Follette's candidacy, unlike Roosevelt's, did not appreciably hurt the Republican's presidential nominee. La Follette carried only one state, Wisconsin, although he did run well in the Midwest and West, finishing second in 11 states. But Coolidge was overwhelmingly elected, carrying 35 states and finishing with over 54 percent of the vote despite the three-man race. The Democrats meanwhile were embroiled in a blood-letting convention marred by controversies over the Ku Klux Klan, prohibition, Catholicism, and the morality of urban civilization. After a series of platform fights, it took 103 ballots to nominate a presidential candidate, John W. Davis of West Virginia.

La Follette died in 1925, and the Progressive party did not enter a nominee in 1928. Instead, the Wisconsin delegation to the Republican convention sponsored a minority platform that was presented by La Follette's son who had succeeded to his father's Senate seat. As in every convention since 1908, the Republicans rejected the Progressives' platform proposals, in this case without a vote being taken. If the Progressive party effort of 1924, then, had any impact, it was likely the foreshadowing of the Republican breakup that occurred in 1932.

The South Secedes, 1948, 1968. If the Progressive parties of 1912 and 1924 resulted from strains within the majority party coalition, the southern insurgencies of 1948 and 1968 were similar indications of dissension. In these latter instances, however, the majority party was Democratic, the split was between the liberal northern and conservative southern wings of the party, and the catalyst was civil rights.

The Dixiecrat, or States' Rights Democratic, party of 1948 was formed after southern delegates to the 1948 Democratic convention failed to block a strong civil rights plank and were unable to prevent Truman's nomination. A number of southern delegates walked out of the convention and later met with other disaffected southern Democrats to challenge the national party. The States' Rights party nominated two southern governors, Strom Thurmond of South Carolina and Fielding Wright of Mississippi, as its presidential and vice-presidential nominees and adopted a platform that denounced the national party's policies on civil rights and affirmed the delegates' support of "segregation of the races and the racial integrity of each race."

What followed were battles within the southern states between the "loyalists" supporting the national party and the Dixiecrats over which candidates would run as official Democratic party nominees. The Dixiecrats were successful in controlling the party label in four states, Alabama, Louisiana, Mississippi, and South Carolina,

1948

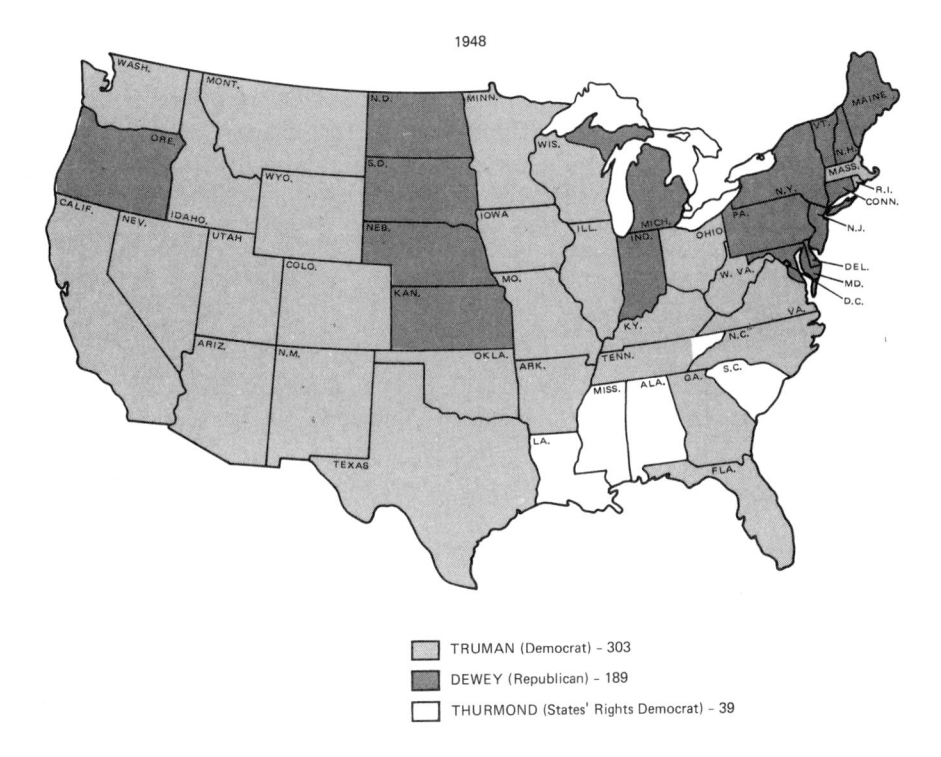

☐ TRUMAN (Democrat) - 303
■ DEWEY (Republican) - 189
☐ THURMOND (States' Rights Democrat) - 39

FIGURE 2.7 The 1948 Electoral Vote, by State. *Source: Congressional Quarterly's Guide to U.S. Elections* (Washington, D.C.: Congressional Quarterly, Inc., 1975), p. 254.

all of which were carried by the Thurmond-Fielding ticket. The States' Rights Democrats failed, however, to deny Truman other southern states and had no appreciable effect outside the South (see Figure 2.7).[27]

The 1948 split did not cost the Democratic party the election, but it served notice that the issue of southern influence was serious. During the next two decades, the Democratic party struggled to preserve its unity. Despite occasional bolts by some southern leaders and sporadic unpledged elector efforts, a third-party movement did not recur until 1968. By that time, however, the long-term forces of

---

[27] There actually was a three-way split among the Democrats in 1948, with a left-wing insurgency mounted by Henry A. Wallace under the Progressive party label. Wallace had been Secretary of Agriculture, Vice President, and Secretary of Commerce under Roosevelt, and he managed to attract almost as many votes as Thurmond. Wallace's strength, however, was concentrated largely in New York and California, which provided some 60 percent of all his votes and where he managed to draw 8.3 percent and 4.7 percent, respectively, of the total vote.

social and economic change had effectively destroyed the "Solid South" in presidential politics.

The 1968 third-party movement was announced by Alabama Governor George C. Wallace on February 8, 1968. This time it was not simply a regional splinter movement but a presidential third party that eventually gained official ballot status in all 50 states. The American Independent party, like its Dixiecrat predecessor, was upset about civil rights, accusing the federal government of "flagrant violation" of the Tenth Amendment guarantee that "the powers not delegated to the United States by the Constitution, nor prohibited by it to the states, are reserved to the states respectively, or to the people." The platform also included broad attacks on the federal judiciary, calls for strict law enforcement, and a promise to bring the war in Vietnam to "a military conclusion" if good-faith negotiating efforts failed. The Wallace movement sought to capitalize, moreover, on the economic policy resentments of working class Democrats and farmers, promising tax relief and reform, social security increases, and increases in agricultural support prices.

Wallace did not succeed in deadlocking the electoral college, but he nevertheless did remarkably well, carrying five states, gaining 46 electoral votes, and receiving more than 13 percent of the total popular vote. Although Wallace's strength was concentrated in the South (see Figure 2.8), he managed to pull 10 percent or more of the vote in a dozen northern states, including such large, industrialized states as Michigan, Ohio, and Indiana. Whether the Wallace candidacy doomed the Democrat's chances in 1968 is problematical. The party also suffered from a severe internal split over Vietnam and a destructive convention in Chicago that was accompanied by street riots. The voting behavior analyses of the 1968 election indicate that while Wallace voters were predominately Democrats, many of them would probably have defected to Nixon if Wallace had not run.[28]

In 1972, Wallace challenged for the Democratic nomination, but his campaign was aborted by an assassination attempt that left him paralyzed. The Democrats then nominated Sen. George McGovern, who was unacceptable both to the Wallace forces in the party and to much of the party outside the South. The South's total desertion of the Democratic party in the presidential election was overshadowed by an overwhelming national rejection of the McGovern candidacy. The split between the northern and southern wings of the party, however, was still unresolved. In 1976, Wallace again challenged for the nomination, only to lose to a fellow southerner, Jimmy Carter. The Carter nomination did a great deal to heal the regional split within the party, and Carter's election probably ended George Wallace's presidential ambitions. If this interpretation is correct, the likelihood of a southern bolt of any consequence appears remote in the near future, since there is no central figure around whom a southern protest could coalesce.

---

[28] See Philip E. Converse, Warren E. Miller, Jerrold G. Rusk, and Arthur C. Wolfe, "Continuity and Change in American Politics: Parties and Issues in the 1968 Elections," *American Political Science Review,* 63 (December 1969), 1083-1105.

1968

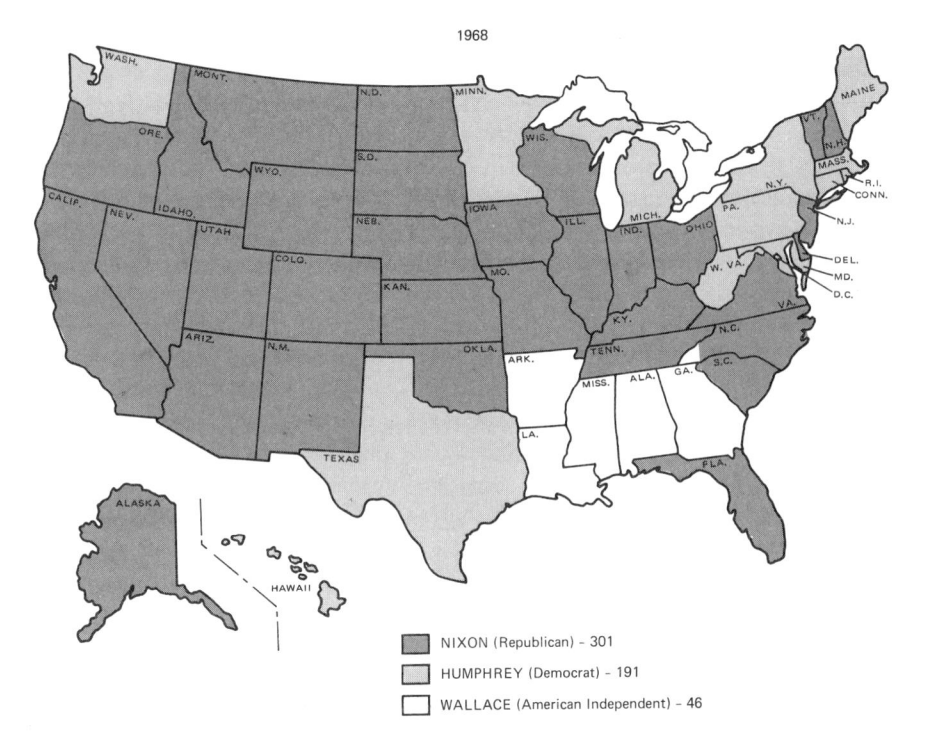

NIXON (Republican) - 301
HUMPHREY (Democrat) - 191
WALLACE (American Independent) - 46

FIGURE 2.8 The 1968 Electoral Vote, by State. *Source: Congressional Quarterly's Guide to U.S. Elections* (Washington, D.C.: Congressional Quarterly, Inc., 1975), p. 259.

If Wallace did not force any long-term programmatic or electoral realignments, his movement did have important implications for the party system. He was able to get on the ballot in all 50 states, and in the process he forced the elimination of state laws that made it difficult, if not impossible, for a new third party to place its national nominees on the ballot.[29] Wallace also succeeded in raising large amounts of funds from small contributors despite the lack of an established national base. His success in mounting a national campaign with limited resources in a short period of time could therefore encourage future efforts by politicians with an appreciable national following but insufficient strength to gain a party nomination.

Other Minor Parties

In addition to the temporary national third parties, there are two other types that should be noted, at least for curiosity's sake. First, there are those parties that nominate national candidates every four years with no realistic hope of influencing

[29] *Williams v. Rhodes,* 393 U.S. 23 (1968).

the election outcome; instead, their goal is to bring certain issues or principles to the public's attention. These are doctrinal or propagandizing parties, in effect. For many decades, the Prohibition and Socialist parties operated in this fashion. The Socialists, who espoused an American variant of democratic socialism, offered candidates in all but one election from 1900 through the mid-1950s. Under their more prominent leaders, such as Eugene Debs and Norman Thomas, the Socialists managed to gain some 3-6 percent of the vote between 1904 and 1920. After 1932, when it won slightly over 2 percent, the party went into a decline from which it never recovered. The Prohibition party began in 1892, earlier than the Socialists, and offered candidates through 1972, but their first year—in which they gathered 2.25 percent of the vote—was their best. After that came a slow but steady decline to lows of .02 percent in 1968 and 1972. With the disappearance of these not-so-hardy perennials, the record for perseverance goes to the Socialist Labor party which has been intermittently nominating national candidates since the 1890s. Other Marxist parties occasionally enter the fray and may display some staying power. In addition, conservative parties, such as the Libertarian party, have recently been established and may be able to sustain their activities over several elections. Whatever their ideological differences, however, these types of parties are essentially outside the party system and are of interest primarily to their small groups of dedicated followers.

A second type of party that should be mentioned is one that has had some lasting influence on state politics. At the present time, there are few third-party movements that significantly affect state party systems. In the past, however, third parties such as the Farmer-Labor party in Minnesota (which eventually merged with the Democratic party) and the Progressive party in Wisconsin were important electoral forces. The Liberal and Conservative parties in New York are rather lonely survivors among state parties. Aided by a state law that allows them to endorse nominees of the major parties and to have votes under their labels added to a candidate's other votes, these two parties are occasionally able to exercise some leverage in state elections and New York city elections. With these exceptions, however, there are no signs at present of serious third-party movements within the states.

SUMMARY

Since its establishment, the American party system has been dominated by two-party politics. States and even regions have succumbed to one-partyism, often for considerable periods of time. National parties have split and, in the case of the Federalists and Whigs, eventually disappeared. Electoral realignments have periodically occurred, resulting in changes in party competition and party strength. But overall there has been a remarkable and, compared to party systems elsewhere, atypical adherence to competitive two-party politics through much of American history.

When the United States initiated its experiment in self-government, there was widespread opposition to politics based on parties. This reflected an antiparty theme, popular among many political theorists, which charged that parties subverted political stability and order. In spite of philosophical objections, however, the political party soon became the institutional means for organizing government, mobilizing public opinion, and controlling the selection of political leadership. In little more than a decade, the first American party system was able to accomplish the peaceful transfer of power. By the 1830s, when the second party system was firmly established, parties had become recognized as legitimate, effective, and *necessary* features of democratic politics.

Since the Civil War, electoral competition in the United States has been monopolized by the Democratic and Republican parties. Upon occasion, third parties have challenged this dominance, but no third-party movement has had a long-term electoral impact. While the two major parties have usually been able, therefore, to contain virtually all partisan conflict, their relative strengths have fluctuated in response to social and economic changes in society.

In the post-Civil War period, for example, each party had a definite sectional base of support, but there was a high degree of competition in national elections. During the 1890s, the Republican party established itself as the party of the newly ascendant industrial, urban order. The sectional bases of party strength became sharper, interparty competition in national elections declined, and the Republicans enjoyed majority party status for three decades. The Great Depression, however, produced another electoral realignment, and this time the Democrats, led by Franklin Roosevelt, built a majority coalition based on federal intervention in the economy and domestic social welfare programs.

The Democratic party's majority status has continued since the 1930s, but there have been important recent changes in interparty competition. While the Republican party remains competitive in presidential elections, it is unable to challenge the Democratic party's congressional supremacy. At the state level, one-partyism has declined, although the Republican party has not fully exploited the potential for two-party politics. At present, the party system is not highly competitive, and this suggests that it is in a transitional phase. Whether that transition is toward electoral realignment or toward the demise of two-party politics is the subject of considerable debate, but the two-party system has in the past shown great resilience and durability.

three

The Political Party Organization

Political party structure in the United States includes three fairly distinct elements: (1) the party's electoral supporters, usually characterized as the party in the electorate; (2) public officials, primarily executive and legislative, who have gained office under the party label and are designated as the party in government; and (3) the formal machinery of party committees and party officials that is empowered to carry out the tasks and responsibilities, chiefly electoral, assigned to the parties by law and custom. This last group, the formal party organization, consists of national, state, and local party groups and officials.

Traditionally, the influence of the two national parties over their state affiliates has been limited at best. A strict party hierarchy with clear lines of authority between superior and subordinate party units does not correspond to the reality of American politics. Similarly, the disciplined and effective party machine that plays such a large (and usually sinister) part in our political folklore is not characteristic of party organization today, and indeed probably never was characteristic of party activity in many areas of the country. Party work is not the kind of vocation to which many people aspire today, and the American parties have neither the resources nor the talent to develop the organizational strength and continuity that we associate with the "well-oiled machine."

It is also essential to point out the extensive variations among the party organizations of the 50 states. Part of this results from the differences in state regulation. Constitutional and statutory provisions affecting the parties differ substantially from state to state. In some, the statutes set out in bewildering detail the organizational form the party must follow as well as the procedural requirements it must meet in selecting its officials and carrying out its functions. In a few states, statutory regulation is minimal. While most states fall between these extremes, there is no simple and convenient way to classify the states according to the substance and intent of their legislative regulations. The only rule is that parties in different states are subject to varying legal requirements.

In addition, party organizations reflect the history and sociopolitical environments of the states. In most southern states, for example, the long period of one-party dominance was characterized by weak and undeveloped formal party structures. Electoral politics was dominated not by the party but rather by candidates and factions within the party competing for control of various offices. The Democratic party consisted, in reality, of its officeholders and their followers. In some of the large, industrialized states of the Northeast and Midwest, however, party organization has long played a significant role in nominating and electing candidates to public office. Indiana, for example, has a very powerful Democratic state organization sustained by a substantial patronage base. While few state organizations can match this organization model, there are county and city organizations in some states that enjoy comparable reputations.

There are, then, several distinctive features of party organization in the United States. First, the parties continue to be affected by the decentralizing tendencies of federalism. State parties enjoy an exceptionally high degree of autonomy with respect to national party units. Second, the organizational structures that the parties have developed within the states are based upon geographical divisions that in turn provide a framework for elections. Each layer of the party organization from wards and districts to city and county committees to state central committees—has a number of offices for which it is chiefly responsible. This generally means that races for local offices (town, city, and county) and for the state legislature are handled by party committees at or below the county level. Statewide offices, such as U.S. senator and governor, fall within the purview of the state committee. Third, the influence of various party organizations and party officials within the states depends ultimately upon electoral effectiveness. Formal organizational lines do not insure any hierarchy of authority. A strong party organization is one that can successfully mobilize the electorate behind candidates who will, in turn, show loyalty and allegiance to the organization. In this context, it must be acknowledged that party organization in the United States at all levels has suffered a long-term decline in its influence on the electoral process. Direct primaries and presidential preference primaries have weakened if not eliminated the party organization's role in the recruitment and nomination of major candidates. Modern candidates are also less dependent upon the parties for mobilizing voters, since they can readily employ the available technology for direct, mass appeals. Party organizations are not dead, but their future role and influence are not especially promising.

THE NATIONAL ORGANIZATIONS

On December 7, 1974, delegates to the Democratic party's first midterm conference (indeed, the first such meeting for either party) made history of a sort by ratifying the first formal charter to be adopted by a major American party. (A second midterm conference was held in December 1978, but it was, as expected, fairly well controlled by President Carter's supporters.) Adoption of the charter was the culmination of several years of effort and controversy, and it represented an important reconciliation between party "regulars" and party "reformers." The charter's provisions fall into several broad categories.

First, the charter delineates the powers and responsibilities of the traditional national party institutions—the national convention and national committee. Second, it establishes new organizational units—a judicial council, finance council, and education and training council—under the national committee. Third, the charter provides for future midterm conferences, subject to decisions by the national committee. With the possible exception of the judicial council which was given limited authority over state plans for selecting national convention delegates, these provisions did not represent significant changes in national party affairs or control.

Most of the controversy prior to and during the conference was centered around Article Ten, which covers group representation in party organization and in delegate selection procedures. The key issue was one which had split the party for years: whether quotas should be established to insure representation for minority groups, women, and young voters. The draft provision that was presented to the conference outlawed quotas and stated that as long as states operated within an approved affirmative action plan, their convention delegations could not be challenged as discriminatory based on composition alone. Moreover, the burden of proof to sustain a charge of discrimination under such circumstances would be upon those bringing the challenge. Under pressure from the Black Caucus and the Women's Caucus, Section 6 was altered to make affirmative action challenges easier.[1] The fight over this change, which for a time threatened to destroy the conference, reflected the extraordinary preoccupation with group representation that has altered, at least for some activists, the purposes and goals of party politics and national conventions.

The midterm conference and adoption of the charter were considered by some observers to be milestones in American party politics, for these changes had long been urged by those who espoused more centralized and programmatic parties. Needless to say, there was also opposition to reforms designed to reduce the autonomy of state and local parties. In reviewing the current standing of national-state party relations, although it is possible to ascertain centralizing tendencies, there is

---

[1] Jeffrey L. Pressman, Denis G. Sullivan, and F. Christopher Arterton, "Cleavages, Decisions, and Legitimation: The Democrats' Mid-Term Conference, 1974," *Political Science Quarterly*, 91 (Spring 1976), 100.

little to suggest that these tendencies have or will markedly change the long-standing weaknesses in national party organization.

The National Conventions

Since the 1830s, the major American parties have nominated their presidential and vice presidential candidates through national delegate conventions. In addition to its nominating function, the national convention is also the highest governing body within both the Democratic and Republican parties. Since it is in session for only a few days every four years, however, the convention obviously cannot supervise day-to-day party operations. Specifically, the convention settles credentials disputes, establishes the party's rules, adopts a platform, and designates the national ticket. Such decisions have not ordinarily raised major issues concerning national-state party relations, but there have been exceptions, especially in recent years.

Delegate Apportionment. First, the national conventions decide the allocation formulas to be used in apportioning delegate votes among the states. During the nineteenth and early twentieth centuries, both parties allocated delegate votes based upon state population. Then, in 1924, the Republicans instituted a bonus system that provided additional votes to states supporting the Republican presidential candidate. The Democrats followed this procedure two decades later, and since that time, both parties have employed various apportionment rules that take into account a state's electoral support for party candidates as well as its population.

The constitutionality of these procedures has been challenged in several court cases. The Democrats' 1972 formula, which established the nearly equal weighting of population and support for past Democratic presidential candidates, was attacked in two different suits which charged a violation of the one-man, one-vote principle established by the Supreme Court in the legislative reapportionment cases. The first suit, which also challenged the Republican party's formula, contended that only the population criterion was constitutionally valid. This claim was rejected by a federal district court and by the Court of Appeals for the District of Columbia. The second suit, which was initiated by liberal Democratic groups, maintained that the one-man, one-vote principle should apply but that only party voters should be counted. While a federal district court accepted this claim and ordered that the party allocate its delegate votes solely on the basis of previous presidential voting in the states, the Court of Appeals for the District of Columbia overruled this decision.[2] In 1976, the Supreme Court refused to hear a challenge by

---

[2] The Court of Appeals for the District of Columbia has suggested, however, that the matter of delegate allocation is subject to judicial review. *Bode v. National Democratic Party,* 452 F. 2d 1302 (1971). The Supreme Court took a more restrained view of judicial intervention in party affairs when it reversed a 1972 D.C. Court of Appeals ruling on California's winner-take-all primary. *O'Brien v. Brown,* 401 U.S. 1 (1972).

the Ripon Society, a liberal Republican organization, of the Republican party's allocation formula. Thus far, then, the courts have found the parties' apportionment formulas to be acceptable under the Constitution, although there has been considerable enthusiasm in the lower federal courts for extending judicial supervision over these procedures.

Allocation formulas as such do not directly affect the operations of state parties, but they have an obvious impact on a state's relative influence on presidential politics. In addition, there is an important issue involved in how the bonus system works—whether it should be based exclusively on presidential voting or should also take into account gubernatorial and congressional elections. The latter would benefit state parties that can effectively contest a variety of offices and would therefore recognize the state party's continuing role in mobilizing electoral support for the party. In recent years, however, the Democrats and Republicans have decided to include only presidential voting.[3]

Party Rules and Procedures. A second and potentially more significant area in which the national conventions can attempt to regulate state parties is through rules and procedures affecting delegate selection. Prior to the 1950s, the conventions of both parties were generally cautious in challenging state delegate selection procedures, especially in those instances where state law was involved. The state parties were considered responsible for choosing their national convention delegates, and in the absence of serious credentials challenges, the conventions did not become involved in who was chosen or how they were chosen.

Beginning in the 1950s, however, Democratic conventions gradually established stronger control over state party procedures relating to delegate selection. Initially, this effort was limited to insuring that state parties would not abridge party loyalty by appropriating the party label for candidates not nominated by the conveniton. The "loyalty pledge" provisions in 1952 and 1956 were aimed at the southern states which had supported or acquiesced in the Dixiecrat takeover of the Democratic label in 1948 or which might be considering future bolts. Thus, the 1952 convention rules required delegates to pledge their good faith to insure that the nominees of the convention would be placed on their state ballots under the Democratic party label. In 1956, the pledge was dropped but additional rules were adopted to strengthen party loyalty. During the 1960s, the Democrats were confronted with civil rights issues relating to party practices in the South. In 1964, several southern delegations were challenged on the grounds of racial discrimination in delegate selection procedures. Black voters were not allowed in most southern

---

[3] In 1972, for example, the Republican convention rejected by more than 2-1 a proposal to revise delegate allocation formulas to take into account gubernatorial and congressional contests. Party conservatives, especially from the South, opposed this change. On the Democratic side, it has been the liberals who have favored increased reliance on presidential results in allocating delegates.

jurisdictions to participate in party affairs or to vote in elections. The convention therefore adopted a rule prohibiting racial discrimination in state party affairs and requiring each state party—as a precondition for sending delegates to future conventions—"to assure that voters in the State, regardless of race, color, creed, or national origin, will have the opportunity to participate fully in party affairs."[4] This rule was the basis for the 1968 Democratic convention's refusal to seat the entire "regular" Mississippi delegation. While the Mississippi party had followed state law in choosing its delegation, the convention's decision clearly signaled the national Democratic party's intention to enforce nondiscrimination requirements for state parties.

The 1968 Democratic convention took other steps that had an even greater impact on the state Democratic parties. First, it ended use of the unit rule for convention proceedings and voted to eliminate it from all levels of the party by 1972. The unit rule procedure allowed the entire vote of a state delegation to be controlled by a majority of its delegates if so instructed by the state party. In some states, party leaders used the delegation control provided by the unit rule as the key element in their convention bargaining. By abolishing the unit rule, the convention sought to eliminate "bossed delegations," although this also meant that negotiations and bargaining among the various state delegations would be much more difficult.

The convention also responded to criticisms that state delegate selection procedures were not sufficiently open and democratic by ordering the Democratic National Committee to establish a special commission to investigate and make recommendations concerning the broadening of citizen participation in party affairs. The Democratic National Committee subsequently appointed a Commission on Party Structure and Delegate Selection, whose first chairman (1969-1971) was Senator George McGovern of South Dakota. McGovern was, of course, the party's presidential nominee in 1972, and there was considerable speculation that his quest for the nomination was greatly aided by the rules he had sponsored.[5]

In any case, the Commission on Party Structure and Delegate Selection recommended far-reaching alterations in state party practices, including the extraordinary requirement that each state's delegation bear "a reasonable relationship" to the composition of the state's population in terms of the proportions of women, young people, and minority groups. It also proposed guidelines to insure that delegate selection processes would be open and accessible to all party members. State committees were to be prohibited from naming more than 10 percent of the

---

[4] Austin Ranney, *Curing the Mischiefs of Faction* (Berkeley: University of California Press, 1975), pp. 183-84.

[5] McGovern resigned as chairman in June 1971 and was replaced by Rep. Donald Fraser of Minnesota. Hence, the commission is usually called the McGovern-Fraser Commission.

state's delegation; secret caucuses and proxy voting were to be eliminated, along with the unit rule; and, of course, the delegations so chosen had to meet the representation quotas for women, blacks, and young voters. In all, 18 guidelines were formulated and submitted to the Democratic National Committee.[6] When these were approved, states had to be in compliance with the new rules if they were to be seated at the 1972 convention.

Whatever the merit of individual guidelines, it is clear that they represented an unprecedented attack on the autonomy of state parties. The national party was asserting its right to regulate how states chose delegates, regardless of party rules or even laws within the states. At the 1972 Democratic National Convention, this assertion went even further, as the party adopted new rules barring the future use of winner-take-all primaries (as used in California) and open primaries (as used in Wisconsin). More recently, a Commission on Presidential Nominations and Party Structure has recommended further regulation of when states hold primaries, where candidates may enter primaries, and what representational requirements the state delegations must meet (see chapter 6 for a full discussion of these points).[7]

The Republican party has also implemented changes designed to prohibit racial discrimination in delegate selection and to promote greater popular participation in delegate selection processes. These were largely the result of recommendations made by a Committee on Delegates and Organization that was appointed in 1969 and issued its report in 1971. Proposals to set group representation requirements for minorities and women were rejected by the 1972 Republican convention. The Republican party has not attempted to regulate state parties as strictly or as extensively as have the Democrats.

The traditional conception of the national parties as loose confederations of autonomous state parties that come together every four years is no longer completely accurate. The Democratic party has undertaken a sustained effort to centralize authority at the national level. Its adoption of a charter, however marginal its immediate effects, was a victory for those seeking to build a strong, national party organization. The continuing changes in delegate selection rules are another reflection of the urge to monitor and supervise state party activities between elections. The midterm party conference that meets between conventions has long been advocated by those seeking more "responsible" national parties. Whether these changes will actually strengthen party organization, however, is unclear. Their effects thus

---

[6] See Commission on Party Structure and Delegate Selection, *Mandate for Reform* (Washington, D.C.: Democratic National Committee, 1970).

[7] After the 1972 convention, there was another Commission on Delegate Selection and Party Structure (headed by Barbara Mikulski, then a member of the Baltimore City Council) that presented recommended changes for the 1974 midterm conference. Subsequent to the 1976 convention, another commission (headed by Morley Winograd, a Michigan party official) was set up to study the delegate selection process and make recommendations to the 1978 midterm conference.

far have been largely confined to presidential politics, and there is very little evidence that popular participation or interest in party affairs has been stimulated to any significant extent. Indeed, there are some party professionals who contend that the Democratic "reforms" have made it much more difficult to select convention delegates who truly represent the interests and beliefs of rank-and-file Democrats. As a result, it is possible that continued factional and ideological conflicts within the party will continue to divert attention away from the primary purpose of a convention—to unite behind a candidate who can win. This, in turn, may lead to a further widening of the not inconsiderable gap between presidential politics and party politics at other levels.

The National Committees

Between the quadrennial party conventions, the responsibility for national party activities and operations rests with the national committees. Although state party leaders and officials have gained direct representation on the national committees of each party, the responsibilities and attention of the national committees continue to be largely oriented toward presidential politics. Thus, their activities include planning and organizing the national convention (and, for the Democrats, the midterm conference), fund raising, campaign management, publicizing party programs and policy, and general party administration. Under current federal laws regulating campaign finance, the national committees are authorized to receive and spend supplementary funds for presidential and congressional candidates during general elections. In the case of presidential candidates, national committee expenditures now add some $3-4 million over and above the expenditure limits set by law, representing a significant financial involvement in the presidential campaign. Finally, the national committees are empowered to fill vacancies on the national ticket that occur after the convention. In 1972, for example, the Democratic National Committee chose Sargent Shriver as the party's vice-presidential candidate after Senator Thomas Eagleton's resignation.

While the functions of the national committees are wide-ranging, their authority is usually quite modest. In particular, the national committee of the president's party has virtually no independent power. It either functions as an extension of the White House, or it is simply bypassed and ignored. Most presidents do not pay much attention to party organization once they are elected, and this lack of concern limits what the national committee can accomplish. Moreover, even the out-party national committee has never been able to establish a clear position as opposition party spokesman or party leader. Indeed, its activities are dominated by the goal of recapturing the White House. If it is successful, then the perennial problems of the in-party national committee must be faced. As the statements below indicate, views on what the national committees should do (and can do) vary widely.

*The President and the National Committee:
The View from the White House*

"I do think that we have a great role out there to help the President in knowing what the people are thinking. We . . . want to try and create some kind of a two-way communications system, utilizing the state party, local organizations, members of the national committee, and the special constituencies that make up the Democratic party . . . ."

President Carter to the Democratic National Committee, January, 1977.[8]

"I don't think you have had the support that was needed from the White House. . . . This year there will be a much closer allegiance between the White House and the DNC."

President Carter to the Democratic National Committee, February, 1978.[9]

*The President and the National Committee:
The View from the Party Leaders*

"The DNC should be the political extension of the White House."

Paul Tipps, Ohio State Democratic Party Chairman.[10]

"The national committee in supporting the President ought not to be just a clerk. . . . If we got in another position like Southeast Asia, the party ought to say we go just so far in support."

Kenneth M. Curtis, Democratic National Committee Chairman (announcing his resignation after one year as party chairman).[11]

The National Committee: The Out-Party View

"The Republican National Committee doesn't represent a hell of a lot except itself."

Lyn Nofziger, Political Adviser to Ronald Reagan.[12]

The Democratic and Republican National Committees now differ substantially in size and composition. The Democratic National Committee has approximately 350 members representing a variety of party groups. Over 300 are chosen within the states: the chairman and next highest ranking officer of the opposite sex from

[8] *Congressional Quarterly Weekly Report*, 35, no. 5 (January 29, 1977), 178.
[9] *Congressional Quarterly Weekly Report*, 36, no. 5 (February 4, 1978), 278.
[10] *Congressional Quarterly Weekly Report*, 36, no. 2 (January 14, 1978), 61.
[11] Ibid.
[12] Ibid., p. 63.

each state party are members of the DNC, and an additional 200 positions are apportioned among the states on the same basis as national convention delegates. The states have some latitude as to how these latter positions are filled (existing procedures include selection by primaries, party groups, or party conventions), subject of course to the party charter's requirements about public participation and balance between men and women. In addition, the DNC includes congressional party leaders (4), Democratic mayors and governors (6), leaders of the National Young Democrats (3), and, in case anyone is still left out, up to 25 additional members to be added by the national committee membership.

The Republican National Committee is about half the size of the DNC, and its membership is confined to state party officials. Each state (as well as the District of Columbia, Guam, Puerto Rico, and the Virgin Islands) is represented by its party chairman and also by a national committeeman and national committeewoman. These last two officials are chosen by different methods in the states, although the predominant selection procedure in the past has been by state party convention.

Since even these groups are too large and diverse to supervise party affairs on a continuing basis, each national committee operates through an executive committee and other special committees. In fact, however, the direction and extent of national committee activity are determined largely by the national chairman. Because there are clear limits on what even the most imaginative and energetic chairman can do when his party controls the presidency, there are opportunities for more substantial contributions under out-party status.

The National Chairman. The national committees formally elect the national chairman. In practice, the party's presidential nominee chooses the chairman who will serve during his campaign and, if he is elected, throughout his tenure as president. The person who serves as national chairman for the losing candidate is invariably replaced. In this case, the national committee controls the replacement, although it must usually contend with pressures from the defeated presidential candidate and from opponents seeking to wrest control of the party away from the "losers." For example, after George McGovern's defeat in 1972, the party replaced Jean Westwood with Robert Strauss who was considered better able to resolve the ideological and organizational tensions generated by McGovern's nomination. Strauss's tenure as chairman, which lasted four years, reinforced his reputation as a skilled party professional. He was able to mediate effectively among the party's major constituencies, raise funds to assist Democratic candidates, and strengthen party unit and organization for the 1976 campaign. Of course, Strauss benefited considerably from the Republican misfortunes stemming from the Watergate scandal. With the Democratic party's overwhelming victory in the 1974 congressional election and an appointed Republican president, there was growing confidence within the party that victory in 1976 was probable and should therefore be given the highest priority.

After the Republicans lost in 1976, there was agreement among most Republican leaders that a "technician" should be chosen as chairman in order to rebuild the party at all levels and also to avoid an ideological confrontation between Ford and Reagan supporters on the national committee. However, the Republicans were also concerned with a need to improve their party's image through a much more active and aggressive party leadership. Finally, in January 1977, the Republican National Committee chose former Senator Bill Brock of Tennessee, who had been defeated for reelection in November, as its new chairman. Brock was reputed to be a skilled organizer and effective party spokesman. Probably more to the point, he was perceived as neutral in the Ford-Reagan struggle and was accordingly each side's second choice.

With Carter's election, Strauss moved into the administration. His successor, Kenneth Curtis, former governor of Maine, soon ran into serious difficulties with both the White House and state party leaders. Administration officials were reportedly displeased with Curtis for not using the national committee as a vehicle for developing grassroots support for administration initiatives. When he named Curtis, President Carter announced that he wanted to strengthen and expand the responsibilities of the national committee, particularly to provide better communication between the White House and the public. If this suggestion was serious, little was done to implement it, and Curtis wound up concentrating his efforts on retiring the party debt (which had lingered since the mid-1960s) and improving the technical and professional services—such as polling, research, campaign management, and media utilization—the committee could offer to party candidates in 1978. In December 1977, a frustrated Curtis announced his resignation and was replaced by John C. White of Texas, who had served as deputy agriculture secretary in the Carter administration.

The criticisms from outside were familiar and equally illuminating. State party officials attacked the White House for bypassing them on patronage, undercutting their fundraising efforts, and most important, for ignoring the regular party organizations and concentrating instead on the personal organizations that the Carter campaign had established in the states. In April 1977, the protests grew so strong that the Democratic National Committee passed a resolution calling for the president to consult state party leaders before making appointments and before holding fundraising activities in their states.

The Democratic party's problems early in Carter's term paralleled the Republican National Committee's dismal experience under the Nixon administration. In both instances, the White House was interested in reelecting the president, not strengthening the party.[13] The party chairman under such circumstances can do little beyond carrying complaints back and forth. It is also worth noting that the Democratic Charter now calls for the national committee to "formulate and disseminate statements of party policy." Since this is widely considered to be the sole

---

[13]Things have not been appreciably different in other administrations, according to David Broder. See *The Party's Over* (New York: Harper & Row, Publishers, 1972).

prerogative of the White House, it is unlikely that any independent attempts to articulate policy would be tolerated.

For the opposition party, the opportunities for leadership by the national chairman are somewhat greater, although not unlimited. In 1956, for example, the Democratic chairman, Paul Butler, had the national committee establish a Democratic Advisory Council. Its membership of about 25 included nationally prominent Democrats such as former president Harry Truman and twice-presidential candidate Adlai Stevenson, and its purpose was to issue statements and interpretations of party policy. While Democratic congressional leaders refused to serve on the advisory council, it was able to command substantial media attention in speaking for the "presidential wing" of the party. During their period as the out party in the early 1960s, the Republicans followed this Democratic example by establishing an "All-Republican Conference." This group included Eisenhower administration officials, Republican governors, and other party notables. It too ran into conflict with both the party's congressional leadership and its 1964 presidential candidate, Senator Barry Goldwater. After losing the presidency to Richard Nixon in 1968, the Democratic National Committee established a 66-member Democratic Policy Council that was supposed to represent diverse elements and different levels of the party. Like earlier experiments, this attempt at institutionalizing an opposition voice was soon caught in the crossfire between presidential hopefuls, congressional leaders, and party ideologues.

Some national chairmen have been able to provide needed assistance to state and local party organizations. Ray Bliss, who served as Republican chairman from 1965 to 1969, took the lead in providing state organizations with technical services such as electronic data-processing systems for handling voting analyses, surveys, and financial data.[14] His concentration on organization building rather than policy pronouncements was widely credited with helping the party to recover from its 1964 electoral disaster. Despite his accomplishments and standing in the party, however, he was quickly replaced after Richard Nixon took office.

There has been very little continuity in the goals of party chairmen. To a certain extent, this reflects the differing political conditions that lead to their selection. It is also a result of the varying backgrounds, interests, and capabilities of recent chairmen. The increasing tendency of both parties to choose current or former elected officials, particularly members of Congress, rather than persons with substantial party organizational experience reduces the likelihood that the national committees will provide leadership in modernizing the state and local organizations. And with recent presidents, with the possible exception of Gerald Ford, treating the national committees as annoyances, it is unlikely that the role of these national organizations and their leaders will be substantially enhanced.

---

[14] Robert J. Huckshorn, *Party Leadership in the States* (University of Massachusetts Press, 1976), pp. 136-38.

The Congressional Campaign Committees

Democrats and Republicans in Congress have each established a number of party committees to handle party organizational tasks (such as leadership selection and committee assignments), to develop party policy and strategy on legislative matters, and to provide assistance in congressional election campaigns. In the House, the Democratic National Congressional Committee and the National Republican Congressional Committee are responsible for helping their party's incumbents to win reelection. The same responsibility falls to the Republican and Democratic Senatorial Campaign Committees. Occasionally, the campaign committees give aid to congressional candidates in districts or states where the party has no incumbent, but their first priority is protecting those already in office.

The campaign committees are allowed to provide direct financial assistance to candidates. The federal election law allows the senatorial campaign committees, for example, to provide up to $17,500 to a candidate for the general election.[15] In addition, the committees provide various forms of indirect assistance—research services, campaign literature, advice on media use and campaign management, and the scheduling of personal appearances by party leaders and notables at fundraisers and speeches.

There are some general rules that the campaign committees normally follow. Their efforts are confined to general elections; intervention in party primaries is avoided. The committees also do not serve to enforce party discipline. While party leaders may obviously intervene to help favored members, there are few instances of the campaign committees withholding assistance from those who do not vote with their party colleagues or who do not support the party leaders. Party support, in other words, is not a precondition for campaign assistance.

The campaign committees, then, are solely concerned with congressional elections. They are independent of the national committees as well as state and local party organizations. There have been sporadic attempts to coordinate fundraising activities, for example, between the congressional committees and national committees. And in recent years, the Republican National Committee has allocated substantial funds to the party's congressional campaign committees.[16] However, the campaign committees have shown little enthusiasm for formal cooperation over a broad range of activities. Members of Congress perceive, probably accurately, the national committees as competitors if not antagonists, and they have been reluctant to subordinate their immediate reelection interests to other party interests.

---

[15] Under the Federal Election Campaign Act Amendments of 1974, this limit was $5000. This was raised to $17,500 by the 1976 amendments.

[16] The Democratic National Committee also budgeted $2 million for congressional races in 1978. This was the first time it was able to do so since the mid-1960s, because of the enormous debt it had carried since the 1968 election. The Republican National Committee's financial assistance for the 1978 congressional elections was spurred by the party's dismal showing in 1976, when its House and Senate candidates were outspent by their Democratic opponents.

The congressional parties and their campaign committees reflect some of the basic weaknesses of the American parties. Members of Congress are not bound, of course, to the national party platform. Their connections with the national committees are informal and weak, and their lack of influence within the national conventions is almost shocking.[17] On an individual basis, they may be closely tied to state and local organizations, although the direct primary system of nominations tends to weaken even these ties. In national politics, the presidential party and the congressional party have rarely been closely allied. Since there is little likelihood that this will change substantially in future years, the ability of national party organizations to coordinate, much less direct, national party affairs will no doubt continue to be quite limited.

Other National Groups

Additional national organizations have developed over the years. Each party has a national association of state party chairmen, and party governors and mayors are also organized. These groups are independent of the national committees, although there are overlapping memberships. The Democratic and Republican state party chairmen are now automatically members of their respective national committees. The Democratic National Committee also assigns a small number of positions to representatives of the Democratic Governor's Conference and Democratic Mayor's Conference.

Relations between the national committees and the organizations of party leaders and elected officials are not always harmonious. State chairmen in both parties had to overcome considerable opposition to gain representation on the national committees, and many continue to feel that the national committees consciously neglect the interests and needs of the state parties.[18] There is also disagreement among state party leaders over the wisdom of adopting policy positions either independently or in concert with other national organizations.[19] Among chairmen of both parties, there is the sentiment that party organizational needs are neglected by the national committees and, when their party controls the presidency, by the White House.

The state governors have also pressed for greater collective influence within their respective parties. The national committees have provided limited financial and other assistance and, in the case of the Democratic party, have set aside three seats on the DNC for the chairman and two additional members of the Democratic Governors Conference. The Republican governors enjoyed a brief surge of publicity

---

[17]This has led to suggestions that convention positions be reserved for members of Congress. The Winograd Commission recommended this to the Democratic National Committee in 1978.

[18]See Huckshorn, *Party Leadership in the States*, pp. 169-91.

[19]Ibid., p. 178.

during the mid-1960s, but their attempt to speak for the party was ended with the Republican capture of the White House in 1968. More recently, their dwindling numbers have hindered them from moving strongly into the opportunities created by out-party status.

The national committees have also established affiliated women's and youth groups. There are women's divisions within each national committee, and the Republicans have a National Federation of Republican Women that is nominally independent of the national committee. The youth groups—the Young Republican National Federation and the Young Democratic Clubs of America—are made up of state and local organizations and have financial and organizational ties to the national committees. They have recruited a significant number of officials and activists for the parties; one recent study of state party chairmen found that one in six started as an officer in a Young Democrat or Young Republican organization.[20] Given the recent attempts to integrate women and young voters into regular party channels, however, the future of these special divisions and groups appears rather uncertain.

Attempts have been made to establish regional organizations as intermediaries between the state parties and the national organizations. The Republican party's state chairmen are organized into four regional groups as well as a national association, and the chairmen of the regional associations are represented on the executive committee of the Republican National Committee. The Republicans have also used these regional groups as forums to discuss party policy and strategy with national party leaders and elected officials. Despite efforts to institutionalize a formal regional system within the Democratic party, the Democrats rejected at their charter conference a plan for regional associations tied directly to the national committee and national conventions. It is possible, however, that the parties will eventually move to develop formal regional organizations that can provide technical and professional electoral services to the state parties.

National Party Control and Power

The lines of authority between the national party organizations and the state and local parties have traditionally been weak, but there have been important changes in recent years, at least with respect to the national conventions. The conventions, especially within the Democratic party, have strengthened their control over state party structure and procedure relating to delegate selection. To this extent, there has been a centralization of authority that is quite unusual in American party politics. At the same time, however, the national committees remain relatively powerless. The Democratic Charter, for example, does not alter the national committee's functions or powers in any significant fashion, and it is unlikely that any attempt to do so could succeed against the determined opposition of state party leaders.

[20] Ibid., p. 35.

The national committees thus remain in a state of limbo. When a party loses the White House, interest in the national committee as a party imagebuilder and vehicle to recapture the presidency increases. Once a candidate is nominated, the national committee becomes a campaign auxiliary at best; if that candidate is elected, the national committee finds itself with little autonomy or importance. The kinds of organizational development assistance and expertise that the national committees might provide to the state and local parties have simply not commanded the continued attention of national party leaders.

Moreover, the national committees have not been able to assert their supremacy over other national party groups, most notably the congressional campaign committees. Not only do the national committees find it difficult to coordinate the state parties in any meaningful fashion, but their focus on national politics is restricted almost exclusively to presidential politics. The national committees do not play a meaningful role in bringing together presidential and congressional interests within the party.

STATE AND LOCAL ORGANIZATIONS

The structure and activities of party organization differ greatly from state to state. There may also be substantial variations within a state or between the parties in a particular jurisdiction. State law, party rules, historical and demographic factors, as well as individual leaders and activists can all have an impact on the shape and authority of state and local party organizations.

Where parties are considered to be private associations, as they were in the United States prior to the Civil War and still are in most western democracies, legal regulation of their internal operations is minimal or nonexistent.[21] Over the past century, however, legal regulation of the state parties has become increasingly extensive and elaborate. In all but a few southern states, the parties today are subject to statutory controls over their membership, structure, procedure, duties, and authority.

The states usually determine, for example, all or most of the following: (1) how an organization qualifies as a party and can have its candidates placed on the ballot; (2) how nominations for elected, public offices are made; (3) how membership in the party is defined—that is, who is allowed to vote in party primaries; (4) how the party is organized, its officials chosen, and its responsibilities defined; and (5) how the party raises, reports, and spends its campaign funds.[22] While the specifics and enforcement of such regulations differ among the states, the underlying purpose of many regulatory efforts has been to weaken the party's powers. Frequently, this has been accomplished by providing the public with

---

[21] The major exception is the Federal Republic of Germany. See Lewis J. Edinger, *Politics in Germany* (Boston: Little, Brown and Company, 1968).

[22] Austin Ranney, "Parties in State Politics," in *Politics in the American States,* 2nd ed., ed. H. Jacob and K. Vines (Boston: Little, Brown and Company, 1971), p. 83.

greater access to party affairs and more control over party decisions. The direct primary method of nominations is perhaps the best single example of an antiparty "reform" that finds its proponents arguing its democratizing effects. It is also worth noting that attacks on the parties' autonomy have at times been led by elected officials anxious to gain independence from organizational control, as well as to respond to popular concerns over corruption and bossism in the parties.

Described by one critic as "mere jousting grounds for embattled politicians," the state parties have suffered a long-term decline.[23] Well-organized, professionally-led, and independent state party organizations have become rather rare in recent decades, although some analyses suggest that the parties are making a comeback in many states.[24] In any case, the state and local "machines" have disappeared almost everywhere, only to be replaced by poorly-organized, unstable, and ineffective organizations in most instances rather than strong, democratized parties.

Legal Structure

With the exception of a few southern states, the structure of party organization is usually defined in some detail by statute. This typically includes the specific units or levels of organization that must be established, as well as their composition, method of selection, and duties and responsibilities. Since there is a uniform emphasis among most states on the nominating and electoral functions of parties, the levels of party organization parallel the geographical jurisdictions of electoral offices. This means a progression from very small electoral units that are primarily responsible for local candidates to county committees and finally to state committees whose electoral jurisdictions are broader (see Figure 3.1). A number of intermediate organizations are frequently provided for townships, cities, and state legislative districts, and also for congressional districts whose boundaries are not coterminous with a single county. Where and how these fit depend on the population size of counties. Heavily populated counties, for example, may include several congressional districts, as well as numerous state legislative seats. More often, congressional districts include two or more counties, and the congressional district organization is thus an intermediate level between the county and state organizations. In most areas, however, this kind of congressional district organization does not play a significant role in party affairs.[25]

In addition to the party committees, there are also party conventions and party caucuses held at various levels. In some states, rank-and-file voters can attend precinct or district caucuses that select delegates to county, state, and national party conventions. Party voters also usually choose, either in the party primary or

---

[23] James MacGregor Burns, *The Deadlock of Democracy* (Englewood Cliffs, N.J.: Prentice-Hall, Inc., 1963), pp. 236-41.

[24] Huckshorn, *Party Leadership in the States.*

[25] V. O. Key, Jr., *Politics, Parties, and Pressure Groups,* 5th ed. (New York: Thomas Y. Crowell Company, 1964), pp. 327-28.

```
                Electoral Responsibility                    Party Units
    ┌─────────────────────────────┐      ┌──────────────────┐
    │ Governor, U.S. Senator,     │─────▶│ State Central    │
    │ Other Statewide Offices     │      │ Committee        │
    └─────────────────────────────┘      └──────────────────┘
    ┌─────────────┐                                            ┌──────────────┐
    │ U.S. House  │───────────────────────────────────────────▶│ Congressional│
    └─────────────┘                                            │ District     │
    ┌─────────────────────────────┐      ┌──────────────────┐  │ Committee    │
    │ County Commissioners,       │      │ County Party     │  │              │
    │ County Executive, Other     │─────▶│ Committee        │  └──────────────┘
    │ County Officials            │      │                  │
    └─────────────────────────────┘      └──────────────────┘
    ┌─────────────────────────────┐      ┌──────────────────┐
    │ Mayor, City Council,        │      │ Intermediate Party│
    │ Other Local Officials;      │─────▶│ Committees       │
    │ State House and Senate      │      │ (City, State Legislative)│
    └─────────────────────────────┘      └──────────────────┘
                                         ┌──────────────────┐
                                         │ Lower Echelon Party│
                                         │ Units            │
                                         │ (Zone, Area, Ward)│
                                         └──────────────────┘
                                         ┌──────────────────────────────┐
                                         │ Precinct Committeemen, Committeewomen│
                                         └──────────────────────────────┘
```

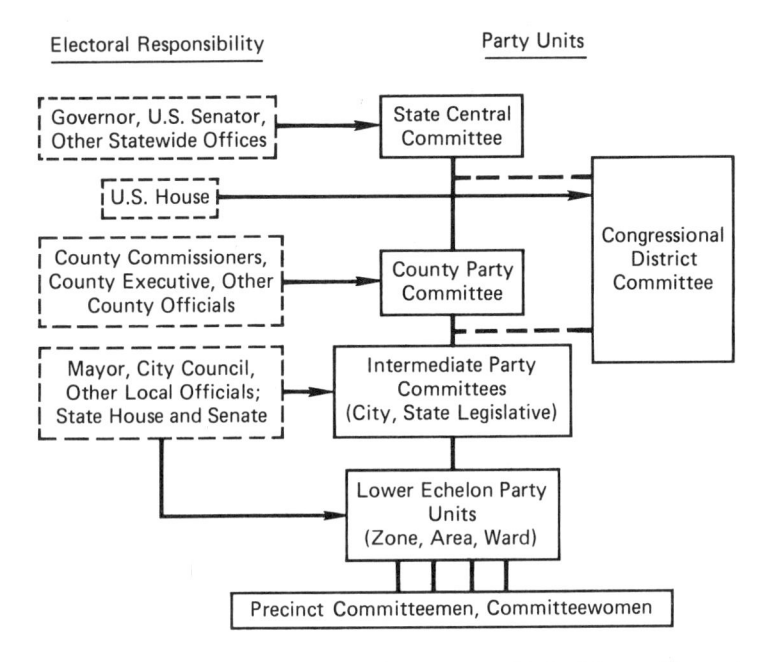

FIGURE 3.1 Units of Party Organization and Their Primary Electoral Responsibilities

in precinct caucuses, the precinct committeemen and committeewomen (certain states specify one male and one female committee member from each precinct) that constitute the base of the party organization. Above this level, it is difficult to generalize about the composition of party committees and the selection process for members and officials of these committees. State central committees, for example, are sometimes comprised of representatives from counties; elsewhere the representation may be by congressional district or by state legislative district. These representatives, in turn, are selected in several ways:

(1) by party voters in primaries;
(2) by other party officials in conventions or caucuses; and
(3) by virtue of holding designated status on lower party committees (ex officio membership).[26]

There is, then, a formal organizational hierarchy that proceeds upward from the more than 100,000 precincts or electoral districts to the approximately 3,000 counties and then to the 50 state committees. Despite this pyramidlike setup, there is no guarantee that clear lines of authority will connect the organizational units at different levels. A number of states have at least some county parties that are well

---

[26] Ranney, "Parties in State Politics," p. 92.

organized and fairly autonomous in their dealings with the state party. In other states, the lack of discipline and control within one level of the party may simply reflect the absence of serious organization at any level. Occasionally, city and ward organizations may dominate politics in an area. As one scholar recently concluded about state party organizations:

> Lines of authority and responsibility do not flow in the party hierarchy as they do in business, labor, military, or educational organizations. The man at the top of the party pyramid may not really be the top man. The party structure is ill defined and obscure. The people who run it often do not have a wide public identification, and the chairman's relatively short term often does not grant him time to broaden his following.[27]

State Committees. The state party organizations are capped by legally-established state central or state executive committees. As mentioned earlier, the state party committees are far from uniform in their composition, selection processes, and duties. At one extreme, the authority of state committees may amount to effective control of nominations for statewide offices, state party platforms, and party finances; at the other, the state committee may be restricted to carrying out trivial duties spelled out by state statutes. In between fall the majority of state committees that are attempting to retain some independent authority in dealing with candidates, elected officials, and other party groups.

The state committee's primary responsibilities are electoral and organizational. It can be active in recruiting candidates, raising funds, and managing campaigns. It can also assist local organizations by providing technical services and information. This might include centralizing polling and voter analysis operations, maintaining voting records of opposition party officials, providing campaign literature and speech materials, and keeping local organizations and candidates up to date on campaign finance laws, party rules, and so forth. Since the early 1960s, many states have centralized these and other related services in an attempt to professionalize party operations and to respond to the growing formalism in party rules and state regulation.[28]

Despite these moves toward professionalization of state party operations, many state committees exhibit some of the same weaknesses as the national committees. They are sometimes dominated by elected officials, usually governors but sometimes U.S. senators, in much the same way that the national committee is overshadowed once the party wins the presidency. For example, during his four consecutive terms as governor of New York, Nelson Rockefeller was able to dominate completely his state's Republican party; and Senator Edward Kennedy of Massachusetts has long exercised substantial, if less pervasive, control over that state's Democratic party.

---

[27] Huckshorn, *Party Leadership in the States*, p. 2.
[28] Ibid., pp. 254-57.

The state parties must also compete with the personal electoral organizations that candidates sometimes establish, as well as with the extraparty organizations that have been active in states like California and Wisconsin. These Democratic and Republican club organizations have for several decades provided a forum for intraparty ideological battles that have easily overshadowed the closely regulated and largely perfunctory activities of the regular party organizations.[29] Wisconsin's volunteer organizations have played a prominent role in party politics since the 1920s and have gradually usurped the duties and authority of the statutory party organizations.[30]

As if the difficulties of competing with candidate and volunteer organizations were not enough, the state parties have also been challenged by the national parties. The Democratic party's new rules and delegate selection procedures have eliminated state party control of convention delegations, and both national parties have shown signs of attempting to prescribe uniform state party structures and procedures. Moreover, recent presidents have not been supportive of state party organizations. The White House has even occasionally undercut the efforts of the state parties by tacitly supporting the reelection of opposition party congressional incumbents. President Nixon, for example, once made it clear that he would not be upset if Democratic Senators Eastland and Jackson were reelected, much to the chagrin of the Mississippi and Washington Republican parties. In the 1970 New York senatorial election, Nixon administration officials made no secret of their preference for Conservative party nominee James Buckley over the Republican incumbent, Charles Goodell; Buckley won a narrow victory in a three-man race. Nixon's Democratic predecessors had also occasionally shown an appreciation of the loyal opposition, particularly in the case of the late Senator Everett Dirksen of Illinois, who served as minority leader for Senate Republicans during the Kennedy and Johnson administrations.

Along these same lines, few administrations have shown any enthusiasm for helping to strengthen state party organizations. The state parties are expected to mobilize grassroots support for administration programs and to assist presidential reelection efforts, but there has been little in the way of reciprocity. Organizational and fundraising efforts have been centralized in the White House, and the amount of patronage channeled through the state parties seems to have declined sharply over the past two decades.[31]

---

[29] See Robert L. Morlan and Leroy C. Hardy, *Politics in California* (Belmont, Calif.: Dickinson Publishing Co., 1968).

[30] See Leon D. Epstein, *Politics in Wisconsin* (Madison: University of Wisconsin Press, 1958).

[31] According to Carter administration spokesmen, the amount of available patronage has declined by two-thirds. In addition, appointments have been increasingly centralized in the White House or cabinet. *Congressional Quarterly Weekly Report*, 36, no. 2 (January 14, 1978), 59.

The State Chairman. The chairman of the state party occupies at least a potentially important position as spokesman for the state organization and its representative in national party affairs. Some of the highly respected professional party chairmen, such as Ray Bliss of Ohio and the late John Bailey of Connecticut, have not only been effective state leaders but have also been influential national party chairmen.[32] More often, however, the position of state party chairman has been characterized by high turnover, meager staff resources, and, in general, a low degree of professionalization.

The formal authority delegated to the state chairman is usually quite modest. In addition, the state chairman is sometimes little more than the agent of a governor or other high elected official who wants to insure that the party organization stays friendly, in much the same way that the president perceives the chairman of the national committee. The roles of the contemporary state party chairmen were described in a major study as falling into three categories:

1. The Political Agent serves as the partisan arm of an incumbent governor or, in a few cases, some other elected official who ... is able to exercise party control. The Political Agent ... serves, in effect, as the governor's deputy for political affairs. He seldom exercises real control over the party apparatus, usually deferring to the governor whom he serves.[33]
2. The In-Party Independent Chairman has considerably more flexibility in the exercise of his powers than does the Political Agent. He is not bound by the personal wishes of his governor, although he obviously must be interested in them. He operates at a different level and his power derives from sources within the party organization itself.... His fortune is tied to the success of the party and his goal is for *party* success. He is party oriented rather than candidate oriented. He often tends to be a "nuts and bolts" chairman who devotes many hours to organizational matters, candidate recruitment, and the efforts to influence the nominating process.[34]
3. The Out-Party Independent ... presides over a party that does not control the governor's office. He usually emerges from a personal power base or is elected as the choice of an unsuccessful gubernatorial candidate....[35]
Most of the Out-Party Independent Chairmen view themselves as *the* party leader. As such they assume a greater burden of responsibilities as party spokesmen, mediators between party factions, and campaign strategists.[36]

The responsibilities of the state chairman, then, have more to do with situational and personal factors than with formal authority. In general, most chairmen emphasize their organizational and electoral duties as being the most important aspect of their work. Table 3.1 shows how state chairmen in each party rate their various responsibilities.

---

[32] Bailey served as DNC chairman from 1961-68, while remaining as Connecticut state party chairman. Bliss was RNC chairman from 1965-69.

[33] Huckshorn, *Party Leadership in the States*, p. 77.

[34] Ibid., pp. 88-89.

[35] Ibid., p. 89.

[36] Ibid., p. 95.

TABLE 3.1   Responsibilities Rated "Very Important" by State Chairmen

Democrats (N39)		Republicans (N41)	
Party organization builder	92.1%	Campaign strategist	90.4%
Fund raiser	92.1	Party organization builder	82.9
Campaign strategist	84.2	Campaigner	75.6
Campaigner	68.4	Fund raiser	70.7
Recruiter of candidates	65.8	Recruiter of candidates	68.3
Mediator between factions	63.2	Patronage dispenser	51.2
Spokesman for party	57.9	Morale builder	46.3
Morale builder	50.0	Mediator between factions	42.5
Policy maker	50.0	Spokesman for party	41.5
Patronage dispenser	34.2	Policy maker	34.0
Liaison with private interests	31.6	Link between national and local	22.0
Spokesman for governor	18.4	Spokesman for governor	21.9
Link between national and local	15.8	Liaison with private interests	19.5

Note: During the course of a pilot study, interviews with selected state chairmen identified the above party responsibilities as the most important ones from the point of view of the chairmen. During the full study each chairman was asked to indicate his estimation of the importance of each item by designating it as "very important," "important," or "unimportant."

Source: Robert J. Huckshorn, *Party Leadership in the States* (University of Massachusetts Press, 1976), p. 100.

The study from which the data on chairmen's responsibilities were taken also suggests that the position of state party chairman may be assuming greater importance in state politics. There has been an influx of energetic and talented chairmen who have substantially improved the technical expertise and organizational effectiveness of their state parties. If this trend toward greater professionalization continues, it might help to reverse the decline in state party organization.[37]

The County Committees. The more than 3,000 counties in the United States are an important organizational level for each of the parties. The chairmen of the county party organizations are frequently local political leaders of some note. Some may even exercise considerable authority within their state parties, and a select few may achieve national prominence. This is especially true when the local organization has some of the attributes of a powerful "party machine."

The significance of the county organization is partly a reflection of the sheer number of offices that are elected at or below the county level. These include county officials (executive, legislative, judicial and law enforcement); town, city, or village officeholders; special district officials; state legislators; and, in very populous counties, members of the U.S. House.

In addition, the local party organization is responsible for actually getting out the vote. It is at this level that electorate mobilization can occur on a continuing basis. While the local organization is inevitably involved in state and national

[37] Ibid., pp. 259-74.

electioneering, its efforts are concentrated on candidates elected solely within its jurisdiction. A study of Democratic and Republican party officials in a large suburban county (Nassau County, New York) found that fewer than five percent directed their efforts primarily toward statewide or presidential elections. The overwhelming majority concentrated on candidates who were elected within the county.[38] The local organization is responsible for these candidates in terms of recruitment and nomination, campaign management, and fundraising. Moreover, these local races usually require substantial organizational efforts in order to stimulate voter interest. The electoral focus of the local party, then, is based on conditions that are not easily changed and that reinforce the localist orientation of party politics.[39]

The primary responsibilities of the county organization and of the intermediate party levels beneath it are generally campaign-related or organizational. They include voter drives and registration efforts, fundraising, campaign management and campaign operations, recruiting party activists and party officials, and general organizational supervision and leadership. The local parties may also be active in providing constituent services for local residents, distributing patronage, recruiting and nominating candidates, and in some areas, attempting to inform party members and voters about both national and local policy issues.[40]

The counties were, of course, the setting in which many of the most fabled urban and rural machines operated. The decline of virtually all of these organizations reflects a number of factors—the lessening availability and attractiveness of patronage, broadened and more accessible social welfare services provided by government, and changes in public attitudes, among others. There are, however, local parties today that are well organized, strongly led, and highly influential in terms of local politics. Whether they exercise the political monopoly characteristic of the "machines," however, is doubtful.

Interrelationships. There are links between the national and state parties and among the different organizational levels within the states. Even with the recent efforts of the national parties to regulate certain state and local practices, however, the national party system remains highly decentralized. At the same time, the state and local parties are rarely organizational monoliths. Independence and decentralization are also evident within most, if not all, state party systems:

> County, state, and national party organs are each to a degree autonomous.... Though the levels of party organization are intimately interrelated, the linkage is from the bottom up rather than from the top down.... Members of party committees, no matter what the committee's level, usually

---

[38] Dennis S. Ippolito and Lewis Bowman, "Goals and Activities of Party Officials in a Suburban Community," *Western Political Quarterly,* 22 (September 1969), 577.

[39] Ibid.

[40] Dennis S. Ippolito, "Political Perspectives of Suburban Party Leaders," *Social Science Quarterly,* 49 (March 1969), 810-11.

have a base of power in some geographical area smaller than the jurisdiction of the committee on which they sit. An influential county committeeman is apt to be a power in his precinct, township, or election district. A member of the state committee to be reckoned with is usually a leader of note in his county.... Advancement in the political organization tends to be an expansion of influence from a geographical base rather than an ascent up a ladder.[41]

With variations along so many dimensions, it becomes quite difficult to move beyond fairly limited generalizations and comparisons of state (or local) party organizations. One study, for example, attempted to rank the states in terms of "party organization authority" by using three factors: (1) the size of the permanent party staff; (2) the party's legal authority over nominations; and (3) the party's effective control over nominations as reflected by the degree of competition within the nomination process.[42] The study found that the states fell into five groups, from low to high, with a plurality (16 states) falling in the middle. The eight states that ranked highest were Connecticut, Delaware, Indiana, Michigan, Minnesota, New Jersey, New York, and South Dakota. At the other end of the scale were seven states: Alabama, California, Kansas, Maryland, Nevada, Oklahoma, and Tennessee. However, the state party rankings based on this measure were found to be unrelated to other factors generally thought to affect organizational strength, such as the availability of patronage.

The national, state, and local party organizations, then, do exhibit the differentiation and decentralization commonly associated with American party politics. There are no simple or easy explanations for this phenomenon. Historical and legal factors are certainly important, as is the primacy of the electoral function that characterizes many party organizations. It is also apparent that the two parties must attempt to operate within an extraordinarily diverse and pluralistic society, and this imposes obligations and constraints on a party that wishes to remain competitive.

MAINTAINING THE ORGANIZATION

Parties in the United States are considered to be "cadre" parties as distinguished from the mass-membership parties in some western democracies.[43] This designation reflects the relative weaknesses of the American parties in terms of personnel and resources. The major parties have few members in any formal sense; "card-carrying" Democrats or Republicans who pay membership dues, participate in party affairs,

---

[41] Key, *Politics, Parties and Pressure Groups*, p. 328.

[42] Ronald E. Weber, "Competitive and Organizational Dimensions of American State Party Systems." Paper prepared for 1969 annual meeting of the Northeastern Political Science Association.

[43] See Leon D. Epstein, *Political Parties in Western Democracies* (New York: Frederick A. Praeger, Publishers, 1967), chap. 6. He cites the British parties as prototypes of mass-membership organizations.

and work for the *party* at election time represent a very small fraction of the adult population.[44] Organizational activities, which often tend to be minimal except during election campaigns, are usually carried out by small groups of part-time officials and volunteers. More often than not, this is by necessity not choice.

The party organization must contend with more than legal regulations and restrictions. It must also compete for resources and personnel with a rapidly expanding number of nonparty groups, ranging from candidates' personal organizations to various interest groups. In order to compete successfully, the party must provide the incentives necessary to attract and keep its officials and workers. It must also take positive steps to recruit these activists.

Incentives and the Party Organization

There have been many studies of why individuals become involved and stay involved in party work. Because of the various locales, organizational levels, and time periods in which these studies have been conducted, clear comparisons are not always possible. There appears to have been, however, a significant shift over time in the kinds of incentives that activists seek and the parties can provide. A classic study of Chicago ward politics during the 1930s, for example, found that "the most common motive for entering politics given by the precinct captains interviewed was that they hoped to obtain some concrete reward."[45] (In years to come, the Daley machine in Chicago would become the most famous of the "patronage armies.") Other studies conducted during the 1930s and 1940s tended to find a similar emphasis on economic rewards in other locales, although factors such as prestige, friendship, and party loyalty were also found to be important.[46] For much of this period, as well as for the earlier eras of party history, personal rewards were considered to be the dominant incentives offered by the party organization.

Starting in the 1950s, however, some analysts detected the emergence of new types of activists "who viewed the party organization as an instrument for effectuating policies rather than as a source of personal gain."[47] In New York and California, this phenomenon was especially evident, leading to "club movements" that challenged or replaced the regular party organizations.[48] These new activists soon came to be known as "amateurs," not as a pejorative assessment of their skills, but rather to distinguish them from conventional politicians or "professionals."[49] The

[44] See Burns, *Deadlock of Democracy*, pp. 236-37.

[45] Harold Gosnell, *Machine Politics: Chicago Model* (Chicago: University of Chicago Press, 1937), p. 67.

[46] Sonya Forthal, *Cogwheels of Democracy: A Study of the Precinct Captain* (New York: The Williams-Frederick Press, 1946).

[47] Robert S. Hirschfield, Bert E. Swanson, and Blanche D. Blank, "A Profile of Political Activists in Manhattan," *Western Political Quarterly*, 15 (September 1962), 491.

[48] James Q. Wilson, *The Amateur Democrat* (Chicago: University of Chicago Press, 1962).

[49] Ibid. The following distinctions are drawn primarily from pp. 1-31.

amateur and professional differed in their outlook on politics and the style of politics they practiced. The amateur focused on policy issues which he felt should be decided on their "merits"; he felt an obligation to participate and was uncomfortable with the personal rewards of politics; and he was convinced that the party should serve as the vehicle for articulating and defending issue positions. The professional was constrained by a different political ethic. Parties were supposed to win elections, since only elections provided the rewards (economic or social) needed to sustain the organization. To the professional, according to Wilson:

> Politics . . . consists of concrete questions and specific persons who must be dealt with in a manner that will "keep everybody happy" and thus minimize the possibility of defeat at the next election. The professional politician rarely broods about his function in society, the larger significance of the issues with which he deals, or the consistency of his procedures with some well-worked out theory of democracy. Although he is not oblivious to the ends implied by political outcomes, he sees . . . the good of society as the by-product of efforts that are aimed, not at producing the good society, but at gaining power and place for one's self and one's party.[50]

Of course, these distinctions cannot always be clearly drawn. Amateurs are not found everywhere, nor are they necessarily represented equally at the various levels of a party organization. Patronage continues to be a staple of many rural as well as urban organizations.[51] Elsewhere, party loyalties, social contacts, and ethnic solidarity account for the participation of numerous activists in party work.[52] And within the same community, the competing parties sometimes can be clearly differentiated in terms of amateur as opposed to professional incentives.[53] Nevertheless, incentive systems are frequently thought to affect the party organization's operations and electoral effectiveness, so these changes may be important.

In some instances, the linkage between incentives and organization behavior is quite strong. The late Richard Daley, for example, was perhaps our most famous contemporary politician "boss."[54] As chairman of the Cook County Democratic Central Committee for almost a quarter of a century and as mayor of Chicago, Daley presided over a classic machine. His ward and township committeemen

---

[50] Ibid., p. 4.

[51] Phillip Althoff and Samuel C. Patterson, "Political Activism in a Rural County," *Midwest Journal of Political Science,* 10 (February 1966), 39-51.

[52] See, for example, Robert H. Salisbury, "The Urban Party Organization Member," *Public Opinion Quarterly,* 29 (Winter 1965-1966), 550-64. Salisbury reports that "much political behavior is to be explained as habitual." People who work for the parties tend to come from family backgrounds in which similar political activities were carried on.

[53] Ippolito, "Political Perspectives of Suburban Party Leaders."

[54] See, for example, William F. Gleason, *Daley of Chicago* (New York: Simon and Schuster, 1970); Milton L. Rakove, *Don't Make No Waves—Don't Back No Losers: An Insider's Analysis of the Daley Machine* (Bloomington: Indiana University Press, 1975); and Mike Royko, *Boss: Richard J. Daley of Chicago* (New York: New American Library, 1971).

supervised several thousand precinct captains who in turn were responsible for thousands of party workers. Many of these party officials and workers were on the public payroll and also controlled the distribution of additional patronage. This patronage army, variously estimated at between 20,000 and 35,000, was responsible for getting out the vote, providing services within neighborhoods, and giving the party financial support. Additional funds came from economic interests that benefited from government contracts, franchises and licenses, or other favors. According to one source:

> Contractors may be the biggest of all contributors. Daley's public works program has poured billions into their pockets, and they in turn have given millions back to the party in contributions.... Even Republican businessmen contribute money to the Machine, more than they give to Republican candidates. Republicans can't do anything for them, but Daley can.[55]

The Daley machine combined elective offices and jobs with services and favors to fill the financial and personnel needs of a large urban machine, and it did so with such effectiveness that Daley was for a very long time a powerful figure in not only state but also national Democratic party politics. There are many other jurisdictions, however, in which patronage and preferment incentives have been widely available but where the party organizations have been weak or nonexistent.[56] Patronage is often controlled by individual officeholders rather than by the party, and it may be used in these instances to strengthen the personal organizations of elected officials. In addition, the benefits of patronage utilization are not always clear. Some studies have found that many patronage employees do not participate even in election campaigns.[57] Thus, even where material incentives are available and can be utilized by the party, there is no guarantee of effective, centralized organization.

The fact is that although the debate over political spoils—patronage and preferment—has been going on since the early nineteenth century, there has usually been a surprising lack of hard evidence about its uses or effects. Certainly the expansion of civil service and merit systems and the introduction of competitive bidding and similar administrative requirements have removed much of the emotional fervor from the issue of spoils, but it is not at all clear that these reforms have eliminated material incentives from politics. It may well be that large-scale preferment and upper-echelon patronage have increased substantially with the growth of government spending and services. Here again, however, control over these incentives appears to lie with elected officials and nonparty groups.

The use of material incentives, then, is not easy to assess. Political jobs may

---

[55] Royko, *Boss*, p. 75.

[56] Raymond E. Wolfinger, "Why Political Machines Have Not Withered Away and Other Revisionist Thoughts," *Journal of Politics*, 34 (May 1972), 365-98.

[57] Frank J. Sorauf, "Patronage and Party," *Midwest Journal of Political Science*, 3 (May 1959), 115-26.

not be an incentive for some activists who have established careers and good incomes. As one Democrat in a suburban "amateur" organization explained, there may be other reasons behind a reluctance to use patronage:

> The problem is—does patronage produce as good a man as did the ideological, policy appeal that the party had before it got strength. This is something the party has to face as we get stronger.... We want the best leaders and workers we can get, and patronage is not a good way to get them.[58]

For a Republican party leader in the same area, the view of patronage was quite different:

> While I wouldn't say that my job depends on doing party work, there is some connection. Since I became executive committeeman..., I've been promoted twice and almost doubled my salary. I owe a lot to the party, but I've worked hard for it, so I think I deserve special consideration. I like politics, so I might be in it anyway, but it helps when you know you're getting something out of it.[59]

It may well be that material incentives alone cannot sustain political organization in the absence of effective leadership or other organizational requirements. What we do tend to accept is the idea that when these other organizational requirements are met, material incentives can provide personnel and financial resources for the party organization, and they will do so in a manner that does not seriously restrict the party leadership's autonomy.

A similar absence of restrictions may characterize an organization that uses intangible incentives such as social contacts, prestige, and personal loyalties to attract its workers. Here the party organization may be closely linked to ethnic and neighborhood groups and may be built on long-standing personal ties.[60] Under such circumstances, the party is not endangered by ideological splits, since party members are not "using" the party to achieve policy goals. Instead, the organization must contend with direct conflicts between individuals and groups. It can maintain its electoral emphasis, however, while attempting to resolve these internal matters, since the issues do not involve the nature of the party's appeal.

In contrast to these types of incentive systems, the "amateur" organization is characterized by a heavy emphasis on issues, citizen obligation, and "good government." Amateur activists are not drawn to politics by the express hope of a direct economic reward or even by the enjoyment of the personal relations and socializing within the party. They believe that political activity should be selfless, directed toward promoting policies or principles that will benefit society. Since they also insist that the party stand for the "right things," amateur activists are committed

---

[58] Dennis S. Ippolito, "Patronage and the Local Party Organization, The Case of Suburban Party Leaders," *Virginia Social Science Journal,* 3 (November 1968), 94.

[59] Ibid., p. 92.

[60] See Wilson, *The Amateur Democrat,* pp. 9-10.

to internal party procedures that are formal and democratic. The party organization of the amateur, in sum, must meet the tests of ideological consistency and organizational democracy. Whether the party passes these tests is decided not by the electorate but by its activists. Winning elections is not a sufficient goal for the party. The party must make internal decisions and articulate positions that are in accordance with the sentiments of its activists. Only then can it legitimately pursue electoral victory.

Whether activism of this type is selfless or simply indulgent is not always obvious. In addition, there is nothing to stop the politically ambitious from adopting the rhetoric of amateur politics in order to achieve their personal objectives. Our concern, however, is not with unraveling motives or measuring sincerity. Even if the amateur is seriously principled and dedicated, what are the consequences of highly ideological activism? Does it foster extremism within the party? Does it subordinate the party's essential accountability to the electorate? While it is not especially easy to answer these questions, it is apparent that amateur activists may have a decided impact on the goals and purposes of the political party. Just as "spoils politics" may lead to corruption and the debasement of politics, amateur politics may have equally negative consequences if based upon a fundamental misconception of the party system's relationship to the public. Amateur activists are not representative of the public in terms of socioeconomic characteristics. They tend to be better educated and to hold higher status occupations. More important, their interest in issues and issue-oriented parties differentiates them clearly from the party rank and file.[61] Thus the kinds of parties that the amateurs desire may not correspond to the capacities or interests of the mass electorate.

Amateur organizations, then, are member-oriented rather than electorate-oriented. Their members are attracted by the issues, principles, and occasionally the ideologues of politics rather than by the party organizations. Their loyalties are conditional and depend upon the fulfillment of their demands. As a consequence, amateur organizations are sometimes marked by high turnover, internal discord, and moralist rhetoric.[62] Indeed, the amateur organization's intraparty battles are ofttimes more important to its members than the interparty competition of electoral politics.

---

[61] Ibid., p. 343.

[62] Some studies conclude that considerable motivational change, usually toward personalized incentives, takes place among amateur activists. See Wilson, *The Amateur Democrat;* Samuel J. Eldersveld, *Political Parties: A Behavioral Analysis* (Chicago: Rand McNally and Company, 1964), chap. 11; M. Margaret Conway and Frank B. Feigert, "Motivation, Incentive Systems, and the Political Party Organization," *American Political Science Review,* 62 (December 1968), 1159-73. For a contrasting view, see Dennis S. Ippolito, "Motivational Reorientation and Change Among Party Activists," *Journal of Politics,* 31 (November 1969), 1098-1101; and Lewis Bowman, Dennis Ippolito, and William Donaldson, "Incentives for the Maintenance of Grassroots Political Activism," *Midwest Journal of Political Science,* 13 (February 1969), 126-39.

Whether they be called amateurs or purists, the issue-activists have become a significant phenomenon in party politics over the past two decades. The Goldwater candidacy of 1964, the McCarthy insurgency in 1968, and the McGovern movement of 1972 were conspicuous examples of the strength of issue-activism within both parties.[63] These candidacies also represented for many critics the ultimate effects of ideological political incentives—ruptured parties, extremist appeals, and electoral defeat.

It is possible that presidential politics has now become the dominant area of participation for amateur activists. Their interests and emphases have never been locally oriented. Instead, they have used local organizations as a vehicle for debating national issues and general political principles, not for handling local problems. Their relative lack of involvement in local party organizations today may indicate that national candidates, nonparty groups, and causes are a more attractive focus for the efforts of amateur activists. Even if this shift continues, however, it does not point to a resurgence of local organizations based on personal incentives. Moreover, to the extent that the national organizations attempt to intervene in local party affairs and procedures, the tensions between amateurs and professionals will be exacerbated.

In contrasting the traditional and the amateur activist (or organization), it is easy to slip into stereotypes and caricatures. It is helpful to remember the findings of one study that found local parties to be "motivationally complex and pluralistic...."[64] Professionals may be as interested in issues as amateurs, and amateurs do like to win. But these groups may differ in their orientation to parties and their emphasis on winning as the legitimate and principal goal for the party. Where commitment to party is a core value, as it is for professionals, the organization has the flexibility to compromise among various groups and interests. Where commitment to the party is based largely, if not exclusively, on its internal democracy and ideological consistency, the possibility of compromise is reduced.

In a similar manner, the relative emphasis placed on winning may distinguish the amateur from the professional. For the latter, the purpose of the party is to win elections, and it must respond to the voters in order to do. The amateur, however, does not tolerate ambiguities and compromises, regardless of their electoral justification.

It is in their attitudes toward *party,* then, that the amateurs and professionals differ.[65] Just as their incentives contrast, they also have different views on the importance of organizational maintenance and the pragmatism of electoral appeals.

[63] On the Goldwater and McCarthy movements, see Nelson W. Polsby and Aaron Wildavsky, *Presidential Elections,* 4th ed. (New York: Charles Scribner's Sons, 1976), pp. 29-40. On the McGovern activists, see Jeane Kirkpatrick, *The New Presidential Elite* (New York: Russell Sage Foundation and The Twentieth Century Fund, 1976).

[64] Eldersveld, *Political Parties,* p. 64.

[65] See Kirkpatrick, *The New Presidential Elite,* p. 114.

While it is impossible to predict the ultimate consequences of these competing perspectives, it is difficult to see how the highly personalized politics of amateur organizations can possibly strengthen the parties. Indeed, one might conclude that the changes in incentive systems, like changes in the electorate's response to the parties, weaken the party organizations and make it more difficult for them to serve as mediators among a broad range of interests and groups.

Recruitment and the Party Organization

The ability of amateurs and other activists to move in and out of party organizations reflects the open recruitment processes that operate at virtually all levels of American party and electoral politics. Party organizations do not usually have the luxury of choosing new activists from among great numbers of the talented and willing. More often, they have neither the internal resources nor the available pool of interested potential activists to sustain a regular recruitment operation. And with the statutory requirements that prescribe public participation in choosing party officials, the party organization may be unable to control its recruitment process even when it attempts to do so.

The studies of party recruitment show considerable variability among organizations in different locales. Eldersveld's study of the Detroit party organizations found that one-third of the precinct leaders were "self-starters," as opposed to some 56 percent who were recruited by party personnel, politically-involved nonparty groups, and relatives and friends.[66] In Nassau County, New York, over 60 percent of the Democratic party officials and a majority of the Republican officials reported that they independently decided to become involved in party work.[67] Studies of local party workers in Massachusetts and North Carolina found relatively low levels of self-recruitment.[68] As Eldersveld has noted, recruitment "strategies" may be affected by the competitive strength of the party, the demographic composition of an area, and the party's organizational effectiveness. But he also emphasizes that party recruitment is generally "fairly open, unstructured, and fluid . . . ."[69]

The recruitment process is related to the party's incentive system. Whether self-recruited or organizationally-recruited, the activist must perceive certain benefits to be gained from party work. Thus the pool of potential activists defines to a considerable degree the types of incentives the parties are expected to offer. If the parties do not or cannot offer these, the activists will join other political organizations that are better able to provide the desired benefits or rewards.[70]

---

[66] Eldersveld, *Political Parties*, pp. 127-28.

[67] Dennis S. Ippolito, "Political Perspectives and Party Leadership: A Case Study of Nassau County, New York" (Ph. D. dissertation, University of Virginia, 1967), p. 71.

[68] Lewis Bowman and G. R. Boynton, "Recruitment Patterns among Local Party Officials," *American Political Science Review*, 60 (September 1966), 667-76.

[69] Eldersveld, *Political Parties*, p. 120.

[70] See Glen Browder and Dennis S. Ippolito, "The Suburban Party Activist: The Case of Southern Amateurs," *Social Science Quarterly*, 52 (June 1972), 172-74.

One can point to a similar lack of party control over recruitment for upper-echelon leadership positions. The current methods of selecting convention delegates, for example, do not reward seniority or apprenticeship within the party. In addition, many state and local party organizations are so casual that leadership recruitment does not exist in any formal sense.

Numerous factors, therefore, affect the recruitment of party activists. It is clear, however, that few organizations have clearly defined recruitment systems designed to provide like-minded recruits. Statutory restrictions, alternative types of political organization, and limited resources limit the control available through the recruitment process. It is unlikely, for example, that the relatively weak position in which the parties find themselves in controlling nominations for elected office (because of the direct primary) helps them to maintain organizational vitality. Just as candidates may pursue independent appeals to the electorate, activists can choose from organizational alternatives to the party. Since the party cannot monopolize the avenues to elected office, it must share with other groups and candidates that portion of the population that is willing to participate in politics.

The incentive systems and recruitment processes that mark party politics today tend to reinforce our earlier emphasis on decentralization and diffusion of power. Few party organizations are able to mediate effectively between the party in government and the party electorates. They are accessible to activists whose goals may not only weaken the organization but also limit the party's electoral appeal. In some areas, the parties are so enfeebled that any activity at all is remarkable.

There is no truly "typical" party organization, but one that is adequately organized and strongly led is clearly the exception today. The conventional associations between parties and bosses are far off the mark in describing present realities (and probably historical truths). Whether the persistence of these images ultimately makes much difference is problematical, but it does suggest that symbols and myths are not totally absent from politics.

SUMMARY

The political party organization consists of party officials, committees, and conventions that carry out the functions, chiefly electoral, assigned to the parties by law and custom. Party organizations in the United States are not impressive when compared to their counterparts in other democracies. In the United States, there is little hierarchical control as one moves from local to state to national organizations. Decentralization has been and remains a distinguishing characteristic of the party system. At both the state and national levels, moreover, elected officials usually dominate the party organizations. Most organizations are dependent upon part-time leaders and volunteers. Their resources are limited, and their activities are confined primarily to election periods.

In part, the weakness of American party organization results from legal regulations and restrictions. The state parties are, in most cases, subject to extensive statutory controls over their membership, structure, procedures, activities, and authority. Most important, the party organizations do not control their own nominations. Nominations for virtually all major offices in the states (and for many local offices as well) are determined by party primaries. In only a few states have the party organizations been able to maintain control of nominations under the direct primary, and these exceptions are the result of other state laws that facilitate this control. The direct primary method of nomination accounts for a fundamental weakness in state and local party organization.

In addition, the American parties have been unable to overcome the electoral effects of federalism. The national parties have traditionally had a tenuous relationship with the state parties. Every four years, the national convention attempts to induce unity and cooperation among the state parties, but these attempts are sometimes unsuccessful and always temporary. While the recent efforts by the national parties to regulate delegate selection procedures in the states represent a degree of centralization, the effects thus far have been confined almost exclusively to presidential politics. At all levels, party organizations are responsive to the electoral fortunes of candidates within their immediate jurisdiction. Controls or sanctions from one level to another have little relevance to decentralized electoral politics.

The weakness of party organizations makes them susceptible to dominance by the party in government. The president, for example, controls his party's national committee. Recognizing the national party's presidential preoccupation, members of Congress have created their own independent party campaign organizations. In many states, governors or other elected officials exercise strict control over their state party organizations. Moreover, the meager resources and limited personnel of most party organizations make these organizations equally susceptible to domination by highly organized issue activists, who can further weaken the organization by limiting its electoral appeal.

A variety of factors can thus be identified to explain the less than impressive power of party organization in the United States. One result of this lack of authority, however, is that party organizations cannot mediate effectively between the party in government and the party electorates. Despite their emphasis on electoral politics, the party organizations do not control the avenues to elected office, and there is little likelihood that their control will increase in the future.

four

Parties and the Electorate

The American electorate's approach to political parties, as well as to politics generally, has changed in a number of important respects over the past few decades. The proportion of Independents—that is, those who do not identify with either major party—in the electorate has grown substantially, while the proportion of strong party identifiers has declined. Vote switching from election to election and split-ticket voting during a single election have risen markedly. The public's evaluations of the parties and their performance in government have become more negative. These and related developments have been interpreted by some as signaling the long-term decline of the party's role in mobilizing the electorate and serving as the primary shaper of electoral choice.

The relationship between the political party and the electorate is an undeniably crucial one. One school of democratic theory holds that there are practical justifications for parties that organize and simplify choices for voters. Since the electorate is uninformed on many issues and is generally characterized by low levels of political interest and involvement, it is unrealistic to expect "government by the people" with respect to the specifics of government policy. Moreover, there are numerous, conflicting interests in society which cannot be reduced to precise and coherent ideological choices, regardless of the numbers of parties or candidates in an election. In the light of this, the parties theoretically provide voters with single, fundamental choices in the form of competing candidates. The parties are not without ideologies or principles, but in order to remain competitive, they must be able to incorporate various interests and groups, and this inevitably drives them toward the political "center." This view of the parties sees democracy as "that institutional arrangement for arriving at political decisions in which people acquire the power to decide by means of a competitive struggle for the people's vote."[1] The parties are groups "whose members propose to act in concert in the competitive struggle for political power."[2] Democracy therefore is best served by strong, competitive parties that provide the limited types of choices that the electorate is equipped to make.

This view of democracy has been repeatedly challenged by those who assert that it unnecessarily restricts public participation in politics. In addition, the types of parties that are desirable is also a matter of dispute. Critics charge that the two major parties do not provide the distinct policy choices that the electorate wants and that would allow the public to exert greater influence over government policy. According to these analysts, most people are able to respond to issue-oriented parties.[3]

The controversy over the merits of "responsible," ideologically distinctive, issue-oriented parties has been going on, with greater or lesser intensity, for decades. In evaluating the arguments for and against ideologically based parties, however, it is helpful to consider the actual characteristics and behavior of the American electorate in addition to theories. What are the levels of participation and activity for the average voter? How do voters differ on issues and in terms of ideology? Are the parties insufficiently distinctive for many voters, or do they provide the necessary choices for a mass electorate?

The answers to these and similar questions are not always simple and clear-cut. We indicated earlier that important changes have occurred in the public's responses to parties and politics over the past several decades. Whether these signify a "new American voter" and a "new politics" is the subject of a vast and complicated debate involving political scientists, party activists, and political leaders.[4] This chapter will examine some of the important patterns and changes that define

---

[1] Joseph Schumpeter, *Capitalism, Socialism, and Democracy* (London: George Allen and Unwin, 1954), p. 269.

[2] Ibid., p. 283.

[3] For an illuminating discussion and rebuttal of these points, see James Q. Wilson, *The Amateur Democrat* (Chicago: University of Chicago Press, 1962), pp. 340-47.

[4] The thesis of electorate change is handled somewhat differently in two recent analyses: Norman H. Nie, Sidney Verba, and John R. Petrocik, *The Changing American Voter* (Cambridge: Harvard University Press, 1976); and Warren E. Miller and Teresa E. Levitin, *Leadership and Change: Presidential Elections from 1952 to 1976* (Cambridge: Winthrop Publishers, Inc., 1976). For a study that stresses the continuities in the party system, see James R. Sundquist, *Dynamics of the Party System* (Washington, D.C.: The Brookings Institution, 1973). For an excellent study that stresses the differences between issue activists and rank-and-file voters and the possibility of a new dynamic in presidential politics, see Everett Carll Ladd Jr. and Charles D. Hadley, *Transformations of the American Party System*, 2d ed. (New York: W. W. Norton and Company, Inc., 1978).

the American electorate and will analyze how they affect the fundamental relationship between people and parties.

POLITICAL INTEREST AND INVOLVEMENT

An important aspect of mass political behavior is the individual voter's involvement in political life. Several major studies of the American electorate conducted during the 1950s found that the "ordinary citizen" was only peripherally involved. Most people's major concerns were personal ones related to the daily well-being of themselves and their families. The salience of most political issues was quite low, and the level of knowledge about even the most dramatic issues was limited. Interest in politics was surprisingly modest for most people, and their participation in political activities rarely went beyond voting.[5]

The relative calm that marked the Eisenhower years, however, was abruptly transformed during the 1960s and early 1970s. Deep social and political divisions emerged with the war in Vietnam, race riots, increases in crime, campus unrest, and a mixed bag of issues commonly referred to as cultural or social—drugs, abortion, women's rights, societal permissiveness, and the like. These issues changed the political agenda radically and were accompanied by alterations in the electorate's composition. It was becoming younger, better educated, and more affluent. There was a burgeoning new middle class—college-educated and concentrated in professional and managerial positions. In addition, between 1960 and 1974, the college student population increased by 5 million to a total of almost 9 million.[6]

For some, these changes portended a "new politics" of issues rather than candidates or parties, in which the electorate would be active and involved. The available data, however, do not show any consistent changes in political participation within the mass electorate. There were some increases in involvement and activity during the 1960s, but they were not especially dramatic, and they have been reversed, if not eliminated, during the 1970s.

Voting. In the 1976 election, almost 82 million votes were cast for president. While this was the highest total in history, voting *turnout* was at its lowest rate since 1948 (see Table 4.1).[7] From 1952 to 1968, the proportion of the voting age population that actually voted was fairly consistent, with only a 3.5 percent difference separating the highest year (1960) and the lowest year (1956). In the 1972 and 1976 elections, however, the turnout rate dropped substantially.

---

[5]The definitive work on the electorate during this period is Angus Campbell et al., *The American Voter,* abr. ed. (New York: John Wiley & Sons, Inc., 1964).

[6]Ladd and Hadley, *Transformations of the American Party System,* p. 198.

[7]There are a number of methodological issues that affect turnout estimates. See, for example, U.S. Department of Commerce, Bureau of the Census, *Current Population Reports, Population Characteristics, Series P-20, no. 322, Voting and Registration in the Election of November 1976* (Washington, D.C.: Government Printing Office, March 1978), pp. 7-9. Survey data usually overstate participation rates by at least 5-10 percent.

TABLE 4.1 Voting Turnout in Presidential and Midterm Congressional Elections, 1948-1978 (Percentage of the Voting Age Population Participating)

Presidential Elections		Midterm Elections[a]	
1948	51.1	1946	37.1
1952	61.6	1950	41.1
1956	59.3	1954	41.7
1960	62.8	1958	43.0
1964	61.9	1962	45.4
1968	60.9	1966	45.4
1972	55.5	1970	43.5
1976	54.4	1974	36.1
		1978	36.1

[a]Voting for U.S. House of Representatives.

Source: U.S. Department of Commerce, Bureau of the Census, *Statistical Abstract of the United States, 1977* (Washington, D.C.: Government Printing Office, 1977), p. 508; *U.S. News and World Report*, 85, no. 24 (November 20, 1978), 23.

A similar decrease has occurred in congressional midterm elections. Here, the highest turnout rates were achieved in 1962 and 1966. Since that time, turnout has declined to its pre-1950 level. It should be noted, however, that less than a majority of the electorate voted in off-year congressional elections even during the peak years.

The decline in voter turnout is partially due to changes in the age distribution of the voting age population. The proportion of the electorate under 35 years of age increased from 28 percent in 1964 to 40 percent in 1976. A large part of this increase was a result of the Twenty-sixth Amendment that extended the right to vote to persons 18-20 years of age. Younger age groups have traditionally been characterized by poor turnout, and it has been estimated that approximately 30 percent of the decrease in overall turnout rates can be attributed to changes in the age distribution of the electorate.[8]

As shown in Table 4.2, however, there has been a general decline in turnout since the mid-1960s among men and women, blacks and whites, all age groups, and all educational levels. If the electorate was more highly politicized during the 1960s, it would appear that this was caused primarily by immediate situational factors rather than by long-term changes in the electorate's political interest and involvement. In addition to the overall trend, other interesting demographic changes took place. First, the turnout differential that had existed between men and women for more than half a century had almost disappeared by 1976. Second, the smallest decrease in turnout among the various age groups was registered by

[8]Ibid., p. 1.

TABLE 4.2 Voting Turnout in Presidential Elections, by Population Subgroup, 1964 and 1976 (Percentage Voting)

	1964	*1976*	*Difference*
Sex:			
Male	71.9	59.6	−12.3
Female	67.0	58.8	−8.2
Race:			
White	70.7	60.9	−9.8
Black	58.5	48.7	−9.8
Age:			
18-20 years	—*	38.0	—
21-34 years	60.5	52.3	−8.2
35-54 years	74.4	65.6	−8.8
55 and over	70.8	65.8	−5.0
Education:			
Elementary, 0-7 years	51.2	37.3	−13.9
8 years	67.0	51.4	−15.6
High school, 1-3 years	65.4	47.2	−18.2
4 years	76.1	59.4	−16.7
College, 1-3 years	82.1	68.1	−14.0
4 years or more	87.5	79.8	−7.7

*Only 4 states (Georgia, Kentucky, Alaska, and Hawaii) had voters in this age group in 1964. The participation rate for these states was 39.2 percent.

Source: U.S. Department of Commerce, Bureau of the Census, Population Characteristics, Series P-20, No. 322, *Voting and Registration in the Election of November 1976* (Washington, D.C.: Government Printing Office, March 1978), p. 2.

those 55 and over. By 1976, their turnout rate was essentially the same as that of the 35-54 age group and considerably above the rates for younger voters. Since these older voters also represent a growing portion of the electorate, their relatively high turnout rate will no doubt increase their political influence. And third, the smallest decrease among the education subgroups occurred among the most highly educated. The result was that the turnout differential between the lowest and highest educational groups actually increased between 1964 and 1976.

The turnout rates that we have discussed do not describe a politically active electorate, at least as far as electoral politics is concerned. The absolute levels of turnout that appear so dismal in comparison to other countries are not quite so distressing when differing registration requirements and turnout measurement procedures are taken into account. But the variations in turnout by type of election and among different social groups indicate that electoral politics fails to engage a substantial part of the electorate, and that part is disproportionately at the lower end of the socioeconomic scale. The argument that elections provide an effective direct linkage between voters and candidates may perhaps be correct, but it is correct only for those who participate, and those who participate are not representative of the entire electorate.

98   PARTIES AND THE ELECTORATE

Campaign Activities. The available data relating to other forms of political participation also provide little evidence of a more active and involved electorate. For most citizens, voting continues to be the only form of political activity. As more demanding and time-consuming types of political activity are considered—such as belonging to a political club or organization, or contributing funds to parties or candidates during an election campaign—the level of participation drops sharply. As one study concluded, "Activities that require the investment of more than trivial amounts of time and energy as well as those that have a short time referent (such as a single election) tend to be performed by no more than 10-15 percent of the citizens."[9]

This situation has not changed much over the years. Table 4.3 shows the extent of popular participation in several campaign-related activities over two decades. With the exception of "talking to other people in order to influence their votes," none of these activities is performed by more than a small fraction of the electorate in 1956, 1974, or 1976. Moreover, this is the only activity in which there has been a conspicuous increase, and despite the nondemanding nature of this form of participation, it still does not engage much more than a third of the electorate.

Attention to Politics. Since the 1950s, the electorate's use of the various sources of campaign information has changed. The most dramatic shift has occurred, of course, in the use of television. When asked whether they followed the national campaign in the different communications media, 89 percent of the respondents in a 1976 national election study reported they they were attentive to campaign coverage on television (see Table 4.4). This compared to about one-half of the respondents in 1952. Much of this shift, however, occurred between 1952 and 1956, with a more gradual increase after that.

The proportion of the electorate following the election in newspapers has varied only slightly over this period, with almost three-fourths of the respondents following the campaign in newspapers in 1976. As might be anticipated, the use of radio has dropped significantly, although as with television, most of the change occurred during the 1950s. Finally, magazine usage dropped between 1952 and 1956 but has increased since that time.

The change in sources of campaign information has had no long-term effect on the electorate's interest in presidential campaigns or on its concern about their outcome. There was a drop in campaign interest in 1956, but the percentages of respondents who were "very much interested" in the campaign were roughly equal in 1952, 1964, and 1976. Since 1956, however, there has been a decrease in the percentage of those who reported being least interested. With respect to the party outcome, however, there has been a drop in electorate interest since 1964. Approximately two-thirds of the electorate cared a good deal which party won in 1952, 1956, and 1964, but this declined to less than 60 percent in 1976.

[9] Sidney Verba and Norman H. Nie, *Participation in America* (New York: Harper & Row, Publishers, 1972), p. 32.

TABLE 4.3 Extent of Mass Political Participation in Campaign-Related Activities (Percentage of Electorate)

	1956	1964	1976
Attended meetings or rallies	7	9	6
Displayed campaign button or car sticker	16	17	8
Talked to people to influence vote	28	31	37
Did other work for party or candidates	3	5	5

Source: Center for Political Studies of the Institute for Social Research, University of Michigan. Data made available through the Inter-University Consortium for Political and Social Research.

TABLE 4.4 Attention to Sources of Campaign Information and Interest in Campaign (Percentage of Electorate)

	1952	1956	1964	1976
Attentive to Campaign:				
In newspapers	79	69	79	73
On radio	70	45	48	45
In magazines	40	31	39	48
On television	51	74	89	89
Interest in Campaign:				
Very much interested	37	30	38	37
Not much interested	29	31	25	21
Interest in Outcome:				
Cares a good deal which party wins	68	65	69	58
Don't care very much	32	35	31	42

Source: Center for Political Studies of the Institute for Social Research, University of Michigan. Data made available through the Inter-University Consortium for Political and Social Research.

The way in which the public follows politics has changed with the widespread use of television. This change has not been reflected, however, in increased turnout or heightened interest in campaigns or election outcomes. There are variations in these factors from election to election, and this suggests that the electorate's response is affected by the particular candidates and issues of an election. There has been no long-term upward shift in the mass electorate's interest and involvement, and a very large part of the citizenry continues to be relatively uninvolved even when we consider the most basic political act, voting.

PARTISAN IDENTIFICATION: THE WEAKENING OF PARTY LOYALTIES

Research on the American electorate during the 1950s stressed the importance of party identification for political behavior. The concept of party identification is used to define an individual's psychological attachment or allegiance to a party.

TABLE 4.5 Measuring Party Identification: Questions Used by the Center for Political Studies, University of Michigan

"Generally speaking, do you usually think of yourself as a Republican, a Democrat, an Independent, or what?"

(If Republican or Democrat) "Would you call yourself a strong (Republican/Democrat) or not very strong (Republican/Democrat)?"

(If Independent) "Do you think of yourself as closer to the Republican or to the Democratic party?"

These questions provide the following categories:

Strong Democrat	
Weak Democrat	*Democrat*
Independent Leaning Democrat	
Independent	*Independent*
Independent Leaning Republican	
Weak Republican	
Strong Republican	*Republican*

(One of the most widely used sets of questions that measures the direction and intensity of this attachment is shown in Table 4.5). Party identification is believed to have substantial and wide-ranging effects on individual voting behavior as well as general political perceptions and other types of political participation.[10]

Data on party identification became widely available during the 1940s. From that time through the mid-1960s, there were some shifts in the relative proportions of Democratic and Republican identifiers, with the general trend among the electorate favoring the Democratic party. The level of Independent identification, however, was quite stable. It fluctuated in a narrow range between 20 and 25 percent of the electorate. Since the mid-1960s, however, the level of Independent identification has increased sharply, and it now represents over one-third of the electorate (see Figure 4.1). Independent identification exceeds by a considerable extent Republican identification, although it remains below the level of Democratic identification.

Several related trends are also worth noting. First, the increase in Independent identification has been accompanied by an equivalent decrease in the proportion of strong partisans—that is, strong Democrats and strong Republicans—in the electorate (see Table 4.6). In the 1950s, strong partisans accounted for 37 percent of the electorate, only slightly below the percentage of weak partisans. By 1968, the proportion of strong partisans had dropped to 30 percent, equal to the growing number of Independents. But while the Independent increase has continued over the past decade, the proportion of strong partisans has shrunk and now accounts for only about one-fourth of the electorate.

[10]Campbell, et al., *The American Voter*, chap. 5.

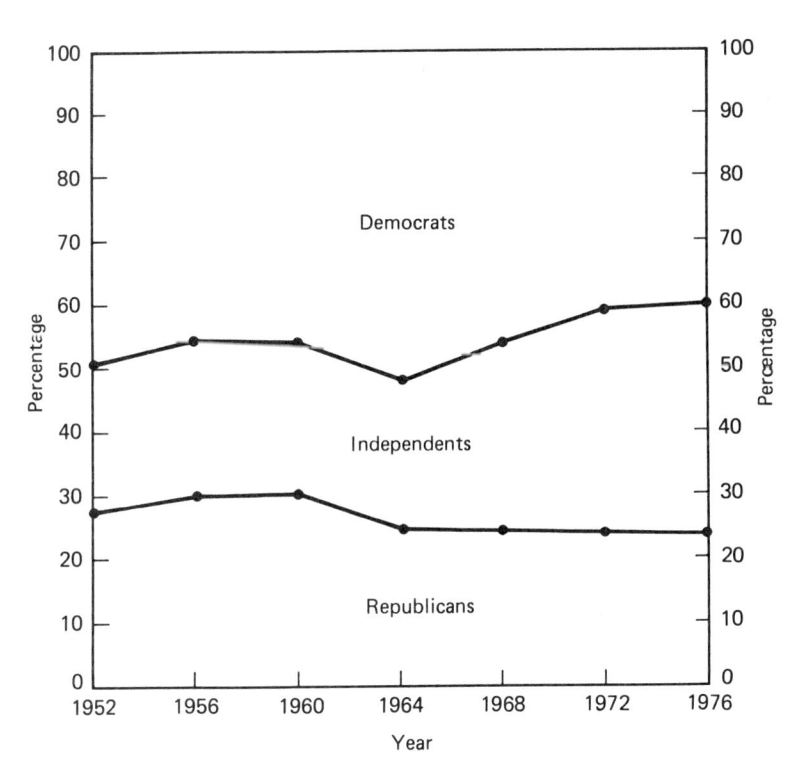

FIGURE 4.1 Party Identification Trend, 1952-1976. *Source:* Center for Political Studies of the Institute for Social Research, University of Michigan. Data made available through the Inter-University Consortium for Political and Social Resarch.

TABLE 4.6 Strong Partisans, Weak Partisans, and Independent Identifiers, 1952-1976 (Percentage of Electorate)

	Independents	Weak Partisans[a]	Strong Partisans[b]
1952	23	40	37
1956	24	39	37
1960	24	40	37
1964	23	39	38
1968	30	41	30
1972	35	39	25
1976	36	40	24

Note: Row percentages do not always equal 100 percent due to rounding.

[a] Includes Weak Republican and Weak Democratic identifiers.

[b] Includes Strong Republican and Strong Democratic identifiers.

Source: Center for Political Studies of the Institute for Social Research, University of Michigan. Data made available through the Inter-University Consortium for Political and Social Research.

TABLE 4.7 Composition of Independent Identification Category, 1952-1976 (Percentage of Electorate)

	Independent Leaning Democrat	"Pure" Independent	Independent Leaning Republican	Total
1952	10.0	6.0	7.3	23.3
1956	6.6	9.2	8.6	24.4
1960	6.5	10.1	6.9	23.5
1964	9.4	7.9	5.7	23.0
1968	10.0	10.7	8.8	29.5
1972	11.3	13.3	10.6	35.2
1976	11.9	14.7	9.8	36.4

Source: Center for Political Studies of the Institute for Social Research, University of Michigan. Data made available through the Inter-University Consortium for Political and Social Research.

Second, the types or categories of Independent identification have changed. The questions shown in Table 4.5 provide a three-part categorization of Independents—those who "lean" toward the Democratic party, those who "lean" toward the Republican party, and the "pure" Independents who profess complete neutrality. As Table 4.7 indicates, approximately two-thirds of the overall increase in Independent identification is attributable to the growth of the "pure" Independent category. Since 1968, this has been the single largest category and now accounts for almost 15 percent of the entire electorate.

Third, the weakening of party ties that is reflected in the rise of Independent identification is underscored by the decline of partisan voting among party identifiers. They are more likely to split their voting tickets and less likely to support their party's candidates consistently from election to election. Between 1952 and 1966, for example, the proportion of the electorate that reported having supported the same party in all presidential elections dropped from 68 percent to 48 percent.[11] During the 1950s, defection rates among strong partisans were extremely low. Well under 5 percent of the strong Democratic and strong Republican identifiers reported voting against their respective party's candidates in national elections. Between 1962 and 1970, these average defection rates nearly doubled. Among weak partisans, defection rates also rose by several percentage points to 22.4 percent for weak Democrats and 19.6 percent for weak Republicans.[12] The extent of consistent partisan voting, then, decreased among identifiers in both parties at roughly equal rates.

Split-ticket voting has also become quite prevalent. At the state and local level, the portion of the electorate reporting straight ticket voting dropped from 73.7 percent in 1952 to less than 40 percent in 1974 (see Table 4.8). At the na-

---

[11] Walter Dean Burnham, *Critical Elections and the Mainsprings of American Politics* (New York: W. W. Norton and Company, Inc., 1970), p. 120.

[12] Miller and Levitin, *Leadership and Change*, p. 37. Also see Nie, Verba, and Petrocik, *The Changing American Voter*, pp. 50-51.

TABLE 4.8 Straight Ticket Voting for State and Local Offices, 1952-1974 (Percentage Reporting Straight Ticket Vote)

1952	74
1956	71
1960	73
1964	60
1968	52
1972	42
1974	39

Source: Center for Political Studies of the Institute for Social Research, University of Michigan. Data made available through the Inter-University Consortium for Political and Social Research.

tional level, "split results" have increased markedly as a result of split-ticket voting. Split results occur when a congressional district's vote favors one party's candidate for president and the other party's candidate for the U.S. House. Thus, if a party's candidates for these offices either both win or both lose in a congressional district, there is no split result. The incidence of split results is useful in assessing the partisan integration of voting behavior—that is, the extent to which party loyalties or party cues consolidate a voter's choices for different offices. Over the past two decades, split results have become increasingly frequent. During the first half of this century, split results usually occurred in less than one-sixth of all congressional districts. From the mid-1950s through the mid-1960s, this figure had roughly doubled to between one-fourth and one-third of all districts.[13]

The changes in party identification and party voting have had a decided impact on national politics, especially presidential elections. Party strength in presidential races has fluctuated widely over the past several decades, with "landslides" following "squeakers" in no apparent pattern. At the congressional level, partisan voting and therefore party strength have been much more stable. But since this strongly favors the Democrats, the result is usually a divided government when the Republicans hold the White House.

The currents of "antipartisanship" are apparent in other ways besides party identification and voting. Between 1952 and 1972, for example, the use of party as an evaluative standard in politics decreased markedly. In 1952, about one-half of the electorate spontaneously cited party as a reason for liking or disliking a candidate. An additional 12 percent reported evaluating both candidates in terms of party. Since then, the proportion evaluating at least one candidate in party terms has declined gradually, with the only exception occurring in 1968. In 1972, only 24 percent of the electorate mentioned party as a criterion for evaluating one of the candidates, and only 2 percent mentioned it for both candidates. Thus, while well over half of the electorate responded to a party cue in 1952, only about one-

[13] Burnham, *Critical Elections*, pp. 108-9.

fourth noted a similar reliance by 1972. Strikingly, this decline has occurred among party identifiers as well as Independents. In 1972, Democratic and Republican identifiers were only slightly, indeed almost indistinguishably, different from the general electorate in their use of party as a standard to evaluate the candidates.[14]

Open-ended questions asking respondents to evaluate the parties by explaining what they like and dislike about them provide another means for assessing party support in the electorate. In 1952, approximately two-thirds of the electorate perceived one of the parties in positive terms (that is, their comments were on balance favorable about one party and neutral or negative about the other). An additional 5 percent of the electorate was positively inclined toward both parties. Less than one-third of the electorate, then, could be characterized as "nonsupporters" of the party system due to their lack of a favorable view of either party. After alternating decreases and increases in this percentage between 1952 and 1960, it has gradually risen to encompass slightly over one-half of the electorate. The positive evaluations of parties that characterized more than two-thirds of the electorate as recently as 1960 are now confined to a minority of the electorate.[15]

The weakening of party loyalties appears to be a long-term trend. In part, it can be attributed to a changing electorate encompassing new voters who entered the voting age population during the 1960s and 1970s and who have been much more likely to identify themselves as Independents initially than those who entered the electorate during the 1950s. In 1968 and 1972, for example, almost one-half of the new voters were Independents, as compared to roughly one-fourth of the new voters in 1952. Moreover, these younger voters are also likely to be weaker identifiers when they do profess a partisan attachment.[16] Other types of partisan erosion, however, have been characteristic of the general electorate, not just its more recent additions. Split-ticket voting has increased, party evaluations have become more negative, and the relevance of party as an evaluative standard has decreased among older voters as well as younger voters. What we can say, however, is that the young tend to be most strongly antiparty.[17]

Party identification, then, has become less important as a guide to voting behavior and considerably weaker as a cue for voters. These changes together with the increase in Independent identification suggest an electorate that is "nonpartisan" or "antiparty" in many important respects. But it is also important to remember that the electorate's "freedom" from party ties depends upon the visibility and salience of elections. It is much more pronounced in presidential than congressional elections, and it is greater in some presidential elections (such as 1972) than in

---

[14] Nie, Verba, and Petrocik, *The Changing American Voter*, pp. 55-57.
[15] Ibid., pp. 57-58.
[16] Ibid., pp. 62-65.
[17] Ibid., pp. 62-70.

others (such as 1976).[18] Party is far from being irrelevant for the electorate, but it is certainly not the compelling force that it once was, especially in presidential elections.

PARTISAN IDENTIFICATION: INTERPARTY DIFFERENCES

The early voting studies provided a number of important generalizations about the nature of partisan loyalties.[19] Party identification was characterized as a stable, long-term commitment that was heavily influenced by the family. Most individuals, in other words, "inherited" their parents' party loyalties and were unlikely to change those loyalties.

There were also important demographic differences, especially social class distinctions, between Republicans and Democrats. Republican identifiers were drawn most heavily from the upper socioeconomic strata while Democratic strength was concentrated among those at the lower end of the socioeconomic scale. The class distinctions that were so much a part of the New Deal party system continued to be a key characteristic of party politics through the 1950s. This was particularly true outside the South, where, as one study found, "northern white Protestants of high socioeconomic status appeared as the most Republican cohort; while low status northern Catholics were the most Democratic group" whether one considered presidential voting, congressional voting, or party identification.[20]

The relationship between socioeconomic status and party identification was not as sharp in the United States as in some other western democracies.[21] There was, to be sure, a degree of heterogeneity in both parties that blurred to some extent the lines of social class division. Nevertheless, there were still important class distinctions between the party electorates.

There was, however, no significant relationship between party loyalties and issue preferences. Only a small fraction of the electorate could be considered ideologically oriented under even the most generous definition.[22] For the general electorate, issue differences between Republicans and Democrats were usually quite

---

[18] See Miller and Levitin, *Leadership and Change,* chaps. 5, 7.

[19] The discussion that follows is drawn primarily from Campbell, et al., *The American Voter,* chaps. 5-8. See also the discussion in Gerald M. Pomper, "From Confusion to Clarity: Issues and American Voters, 1965-1968," *American Political Science Review,* 66 (June 1972), 415-28.

[20] Ladd and Hadley, *Transformations of the American Party System,* p. 122.

[21] See Robert R. Alford, *Party and Society: The Anglo-American Democracies* (Chicago: Rand McNally, 1963), chap. 8.

[22] See Nie, Verba, and Petrocik, *The Changing American Voter,* p. 19. During the 1950s, only 2½ percent of the electorate could be categorized as ideologues using the measures employed by the Survey Research Center. See Campbell, et al., *The American Voter,* p. 131.

limited, even with respect to economic policy questions that were considered to be at the core of partisan politics. In comparing party activists and other political elites, researchers typically found definite and consistent interparty differences, but these faded and sometimes disappeared when the mass electorate was considered.[23]

The voting studies of the 1950s also found that party identifiers did not perceive clear differences in what the parties stood for or in what they had accomplished.[24] Assessments of party performance were rarely related to specific legislative issues, nor did most identifiers see a broader differentiation between the parties in liberal-conservative terms.

The party electorates, then, viewed politics in fairly simple terms. Perhaps 10-15 percent of the electorate could be described as at least ideologically sensitive or aware, while the remainder responded to the parties (and their candidates) in terms of the "nature of the times," or how the parties treated certain groups, or simply in terms of habitual loyalties.[25] Thus, in addition to the electorate's relatively low degree of political involvement, there was little to suggest sharp or widespread ideological divisions:

> When we examine the attitudes and beliefs of the electorate as a whole over the broad range of policy questions—welfare legislation, foreign policy, federal economic programs, minority rights, civil liberties—we do not find coherent patterns of belief. The common tendency to characterize large blocs of the electorate in such terms as "liberal" or "conservative" greatly exaggerates the actual amount of consistent patterning one finds.... It is also apparent ... that there is a great deal of uncertainty and confusion in the public mind as to what specific policies the election of one party over the other would imply.... We have, then, the portrait of an electorate almost wholly without detailed information about ... government. A substantial portion of the public is able to respond in a discrete manner to issues that *might* be the subject of legislative or administrative action. Yet it knows little about what government has done on these issues or what the parties propose to do.[26]

Over the past two decades, this view of the American electorate has been repeatedly challenged. It has been argued, for example, that the political issues and candidates of the 1960s have changed the electorate's basic responses to politics. According to this view, political attitudes are more coherent than during the 1950s, and voters are more likely to evaluate candidates and parties and also to vote on the

---

[23] For a dated but important analysis of interparty differences, see Herbert McClosky, Paul J. Hoffman, and Rosemary O'Hara, "Issue Conflict and Consensus among Party Leaders and Followers," *American Political Science Review,* 54 (June 1960), 406-27.

[24] See Pomper, "From Confusion to Clarity."

[25] Campbell, et al., *The American Voter,* pp. 129-44.

[26] Angus Campbell, et al., *The American Voter* (New York: John Wiley & Sons, Inc., 1960), p. 543.

basis of issue positions.[27] The remainder of this section, then, will examine the major changes in the party electorates and will assess their implications.

Social Class

There have been some important shifts in the relationship between social characteristics and party identification. Several recent studies, for example, have pointed to an "inversion" of the traditional relationship between social class and party loyalties. A "new" middle class has emerged that is characterized by high levels of education and heavy representation in professional and managerial ranks, and unlike the older, business-oriented middle class, it is not solidly Republican and conservative.[28] As one study suggests:

> Over the last decade, a decisive inversion has taken place in the relationship established during the New Deal of class to sociopolitical commitments. The high social strata now consistently provide a greater measure of support for liberal programs and candidacies than do the lower strata. . . .
>
> What we now call liberalism frequently makes the old New Deal majority contributors rather than beneficiaries. Lower-status whites more often feel threatened than encouraged by current extensions of equalitarianism. . . . The high socioeconomic cohorts, which had such a distinctive business coloration in the 1930s (and earlier) have changed their social and political character—notably through the growth of the professional stratum.[29]

The linkage between social status and party identification has also been affected by the rise in Independent identification. Traditionally, one of the strongest Republican groups in the electorate was composed of northern, white, upper-status Protestants. Between 1952 and 1972, Republican identification in this group dropped from 56 percent to 41 percent. Democratic identification, however, remained virtually constant.[30] There was, however, an increase in Independent identification. By 1972, Independent identifiers equalled the proportion of Republican identifiers. This served to weaken the class-party relationship.

In the South, the class basis for parties did not develop during the New Deal because both upper status and lower status groups were solidly Democratic. Since the late 1950s, however, there has been a very sharp decline among high status southern whites in terms of Democratic identification. Between 1958 and 1972,

---

[27] See especially Pomper, "From Confusion to Clarity," and Nie, Verba, and Petrocik, *The Changing American Voter,* chaps. 7-9. There have been a number of critiques suggesting that methodological changes account for a good deal of the supposed change in the electorate's issue responsiveness and ideological awareness. See, for example, John H. Kessel, "Comment: The Issues in Issue Voting," *American Political Science Review,* 66 (June 1972), 459-65.

[28] Ladd and Hadley, *Transformations of the American Party System,* pp. 217-31.

[29] Ibid., pp. 227-28.

[30] Nie, Verba, and Petrocik, *The Changing American Voter,* p. 225.

for example, it dropped from 85 percent to 44 percent. Republican identification, however, did not increase commensurately. It did go up during this period from 4 percent to 18 percent, but Independent identification went from 13 percent to 39 percent. By 1972, the number of Independents was only slightly less than the number of Democrats among high status native southern whites.[31]

Since the 1950s, most groups have changed their preference (if they changed) to Independent identification rather than to either of the major parties. The major exceptions appear to be blacks and middle and lower status, northern, white Protestants. Other groups—such as Catholics, Jews, and especially the high status groups we have discussed—have become weaker in terms of their traditional affiliation but have moved towards Independent status rather than towards the other party.[32]

Many of the class and other social group differences between the parties have become more blurred over time. As Table 4.9 indicates, there are still some class differences. Republican identification, for example, is higher than Democratic identification in only one income group—those with annual incomes of over $25,000. In the lower income and educational categories, and among those in lower status occupations (skilled or unskilled blue-collar workers), the proportion of Democratic identifiers is roughly 2-3 times the level of Republican identification. An even more striking feature of these socioeconomic classifications, however, is the high degree of Independent identification at all levels. The high proportion of Independents weakens, and in some instances eradicates, the relationship between social class and party identification.

The breakdowns in Table 4.9 also illustrate the relative weakness of the Republican party. In only one case—the highest income category noted above—is the proportion of Republican identifiers in any category higher than either the Democratic or Independent percentages. Thus, Democrats outnumber Republicans in all but one educational category (college graduate), but the Independent identification level is the single highest in this instance. Democrats also exceed Republicans in every occupational category, as in fact do Independents with the single exception of the farmer category. Republicans are similarly disadvantaged in the sex, race, age, and religion distributions, although their weaknesses here do vary slightly: they are better represented among Protestants than among Jews or Catholics, more prevalent among older than younger voters, and much more heavily represented among whites than among blacks.

Another way to examine social class differences is to see how individuals categorize themselves in terms of several social class types. Table 4.10 presents a comparison of the relationship between *subjective* social class and party identification in 1956 and 1976. The degree of Independent identification in each social class category has increased sharply, with Independents representing one-third or more of all identifiers in each of the categories. The proportion of strong identifiers in

[31] Ibid., pp. 221-25.
[32] Ibid., pp. 226-35.

TABLE 4.9 Social Characteristics and Party Identification, 1976

	Strong Democrat	Weak Democrat	Independent	Weak Republican	Strong Republican
Education					
0-8 years	24.2%	31.3%	23.6%	14.2%	6.8%
9-12 years	15.3	25.7	38.0	13.7	7.3
Some college	9.9	20.6	43.3	14.9	10.2
College graduate	6.2	19.6	38.9	16.3	19.0
Advanced degree	12.9	23.9	37.6	14.2	11.3
Income					
$0-4999	22.0	28.8	29.0	11.3	8.8
$5000-9999	18.1	30.0	30.7	14.5	6.7
$10,000-14,999	13.7	23.3	43.0	12.6	7.4
$15,000-19,999	10.8	25.7	45.7	11.8	6.0
$20,000-24,999	9.5	21.8	39.6	19.7	9.3
$25,000 and over	10.4	15.5	35.1	20.0	19.0
Occupation					
Professional	10.8	22.9	38.4	17.4	10.5
Manager, official	12.6	17.4	42.0	14.0	14.0
Clerical, sales	13.2	22.8	38.5	14.6	11.0
Skilled, semiskilled	19.9	25.7	38.2	12.2	3.9
Unskilled, service	18.6	30.1	31.4	12.8	7.1
Farmer	20.6	23.5	20.6	22.1	13.2
Sex					
Male	14.5	22.5	42.5	13.3	7.2
Female	15.3	27.1	32.0	15.3	10.3

TABLE 4.9 Continued

	Strong Democrat	Weak Democrat	Independent	Weak Republican	Strong Republican
Race					
White	12.7%	23.3%	37.9%	16.1%	10.1%
Black	34.9	36.5	24.1	2.8	1.7
Other	4.7	45.3	38.7	9.4	1.9
Age					
Less than 25 years	9.4	25.9	46.4	12.7	5.5
25-29 years	9.7	26.3	48.8	11.5	3.6
30-39 years	10.6	23.7	43.3	15.1	7.2
40-49 years	14.9	24.3	34.8	16.7	9.3
50 years and over	20.8	25.4	25.7	15.1	12.9
Religion					
Protestant	14.4	22.8	34.1	17.7	11.1
Catholic	17.6	32.2	34.9	9.1	6.1
Jewish	24.4	31.1	37.0	4.4	3.0
Other	6.8	10.2	77.4	2.3	3.4

Note: Row percentages do not always equal 100 percent due to rounding.

Source: Center for Political Studies of the Institute for Social Research, University of Michigan. Data made available through the Inter-University Consortium for Political and Social Research.

TABLE 4.10 Subjective Social Class and Partisanship, 1956 and 1976[a]

	Strong Democrat	Weak Democrat	Independent	Weak Republican	Strong Republican
1956:					
Average-working	24.6%	26.9%	23.9%	13.5%	11.2%
Upper-working	28.4	19.9	23.4	13.5	14.9
Average-middle	16.6	19.6	27.5	15.8	20.6
Upper-middle	14.0	25.4	18.4	17.5	24.6
1976:					
Average-working	18.4	28.0	35.3	13.4	4.9
Upper-working	16.7	27.6	35.4	13.2	7.1
Average-middle	11.2	23.5	37.9	15.9	11.5
Upper-middle	11.2	17.6	34.0	16.3	21.0

Note: Row percentages do not always equal 100 percent due to rounding.

[a]Subjective social class is ascertained by asking: "There's been some talk these days about different social classes. Most people say they belong either to the middle class or to the working class. Do you ever think of yourself as belonging in one of these classes?" (If yes) "Which one?" (If no) "Well, if you had to make a choice, would you call yourself middle class or working class?" Respondents are then asked: "Would you say that you are about average middle class (or working class), or that you are in the upper part of the middle class (or working class)?"

Source: Center for Political Studies of the Institute for Social Research, University of Michigan. Data made available through the Inter-University Consortium for Political and Social Research.

both parties has decreased significantly also, although the losses are quite small in the upper-middle social class category. Two different types of changes appear to have occurred. Among those classifying themselves as average-working, upper-working, or average-middle class, increases in Independent identification have been matched by sharp drops in strong identification. The proportion of weak Democrats and weak Republicans in each of these categories has stayed constant (for Republicans) or actually increased (for Democrats). In the upper-middle category, however, the increase in Independents reflects a sharp decline in the proportion of weak Democrats and only a slight drop among strong partisans in either party.

Social class distinctions, as well as other demographic differences, did not disappear during the 1960s and 1970s. The rise in Independent identification and the overall decline in Republican strength, however, reduced many of the differences that had characterized the parties since the New Deal:

> The Democratic party has become more black, less southern, and has developed a larger "silk-stocking" component. The Republican party, in contrast, has become more southern, less black, less Catholic, and relatively less of a silk-stocking and Protestant party compared to the fifties. . . .
>
> By replacing white southerners with black supporters, the Democratic party has changed the balance of pressures it received from racial liberals and racial conservatives. But its continuing dependence as well on northern Catholics

and lower status Protestant whites implies continuing cross pressures if the racial issue continues to be a northern one.

The Republicans, on the other hand, have moved in a more consistently conservative direction.[33]

Attitudes and Beliefs

How differentiated the party electorates are with respect to political attitudes and beliefs represents an important aspect of party politics. The degree to which the parties are homogeneous in terms of social groups and are ideologically cohesive and distinct affects their electoral strategies, their issue positions, and the types of candidates they offer. Diverse and ideologically indistinct party electorates, which is what the American public has traditionally been split into, are compatible with centrist, election-oriented parties. Such electorates are less likely to respond favorably to highly ideological, issue-oriented parties. Recently, however, there have been analyses that suggest a heightened issue awareness and more widespread ideological coherence within the electorate. In this section, therefore, we will examine the party electorates in terms of attitudes and beliefs in order to assess these ostensible changes.

Of course, it may be that the differences are too subtle to be apparent in the types of data that we will use. As two nationally syndicated journalists, Jack Germond and Jules Witcover, explain, one must be especially attentive to matters of style.

Ideological Differences. The possible differences between the party electorates in terms of ideological conceptions are difficult to evaluate. One recent study suggests that the proportion of "ideologues" has risen significantly since the 1950s, if by the term ideologue one means citizens who refer to candidates or parties in such terms as *liberal conservative,* and so forth.[34] Another analysis concludes, however, that any heightened ideological awareness or issue consistency has been almost exclusively attributable to changes confined to about one-third of the electorate rather than to any broad change in electorate awareness.[35] It also suggests that the meaning of ideological distinctions such as liberal-conservative may be very different for different groups in the electorate.[36]

For our purposes, it is possible to focus on the ideological self-perceptions of the party electorates and their views of the parties rather than to deal with the complexities of conceptualization and ideological content. In effect, we will assume that the terms liberal and conservative have meaning for the electorate and simply look at whether the party electorates differ in responding to the labels. Since this

---

[33] Ibid., pp. 241-42.

[34] Ibid., chap. 7. See also Gerald M. Pomper, *Voter's Choice* (New York: Dodd, Mead & Company, 1975), chap. 8.

[35] See Miller and Levitin, *Leadership and Change,* chap. 6.

[36] Ibid., pp. 173-74.

JACK W. GERMOND and JULES WITCOVER

Vive la Difference

Washington

WITH JIMMY Carter in the White House, they are saying there's no difference between Republicans and Democrats, but it's not so. All you have to do is pay close attention.

Democrats wear striped shirts with funny designs within the stripes. Republicans prefer gray suits and navy blazers and blue shirts with button-down collars. Rural Republicans wear brown suits, and big city Democrats, white shoes.

Republicans are tall, except for Midwest Republicans who tend to be fat and bald. Democrats are short, unless they are women or Mo Udall.

Republicans and Democrats both practice law, but Republicans make more money at it, except in Washington. Democrats, especially liberals, eat a lot of prune Danish; Republicans prefer All-Bran and make a point of it.

Democrats make longer speeches than Republicans, but southern Republicans make the longest speeches of all. They are the most certain they have the One True Word.

More Republicans than Democrats smoke pipes, but Democrats usually smoke better cigars. People who get up at public meetings and complain about smokers are almost always Democrats.

Republicans drink Scotch and bourbon, in that order, and so do Democrats. But Liberal Democrats often drink things like vermouth on the rocks and white wine. Conservative Democrats drink beer.

Republicans are friendlier to individuals than Democrats, but less friendly to groups, particularly in the abstract.

Democrats love people with whom they don't have to spend much time.

Democrats imagine that Republicans have Republican sex lives, but they don't, necessarily. Gay Republicans rarely come out of the closet.

Republican women who are not named Nixon are more likely to have fur coats than Democratic women, who either can't afford them or tend to worry a lot about endangered species and think mink is ostentatious.

Democrats drive Volvos, if they are liberals, and Mercedes if they are conservative and rich. Republicans like Buicks.

Republican men wear shoes with heavy soles and wingtips, usually shined. Demorats don't believe the black-shoes-with-blue-suit rule. If a woman is wearing groundgripper shoes, she is either a liberal Democrat or a Conservative Republican. The one in the gray cardigan with the pearls is a Republican.

Republicans are more inclined to drink at lunch. Democrats always imagine they have something to do in the afternoon that requires a clear head, but they are usually wrong.

Republicans like steaks, and so do Democrats. Very earnest women who serve chicken casseroles over rice are usually liberals. Republicans eat a lot of filet of sole; Democrats a lot of pasta.

Democrats say they like reporters but they lie a lot. Republicans only tolerate reporters, except for Republican professionals who understand reporters really don't give a damn.

At the track Republicans sit in the clubhouse and Democrats in the grandstand. More Democrats than Republicans scream at jockeys who they suspect are crooked. People who go to horse shows are almost always Republicans, but Democrats go to polo matches and talk about the horses rather than the riders.

Republicans in big cities send their children to private school if they can afford it, and so do Democrats. But liberal Democrats always explain how many black kids there are in every class.

Both Republicans and Democrats who live in the suburbs are afraid to go downtown to dinner at night, but the Democrats never admit it. When Democrats flee the city for the suburbs, they always explain how it is really easier to get to work from there. It always takes 15 minutes.

Republicans and Democrats both like professional football, but Republicans like football coaches, too, because they suspect they are also Republicans. And they are usually right.

More Republicans than Democrats like baseball, but Republicans are Yankee fans more often while Democrats root for the Red Sox. Conservative Republicans like day games, and liberal Democrats rarely have too many beers at the ball park.

Republicans pay more attention to their lawns than Democrats, but Democrats talk a lot about trees.

Republicans like dogs and Democrats like cats, but nobody active in either party likes poodles. Democrats get very annoyed by German shepherds. —(c1977.)

Reprinted by permission of the Chicago Tribune—New York News Syndicate, Inc.

is not a very strenuous test of ideological awareness, it should overstate rather than understate the differences between the party electorates.

If we examine where individuals place themselves on a liberal-conservative scale, there are some noteworthy differences among the party identification categories. In Figure 4.2, the distributions for each category of party identification are shown on a seven-point liberal-conservative self-identification scale. The proportion of identifiers left-of-center is highest among strong Democrats and lowest among strong Republicans, as might be expected. In addition, the highest percentage of absolute centrists (indicated by the solid bar) is highest among Independents, and the proportion of right-of-center identifiers is highest among Republicans, especially strong Republicans. Thus, there does appear to be a somewhat different ideological "center of gravity" for Democrats, Republicans, and Independents. It

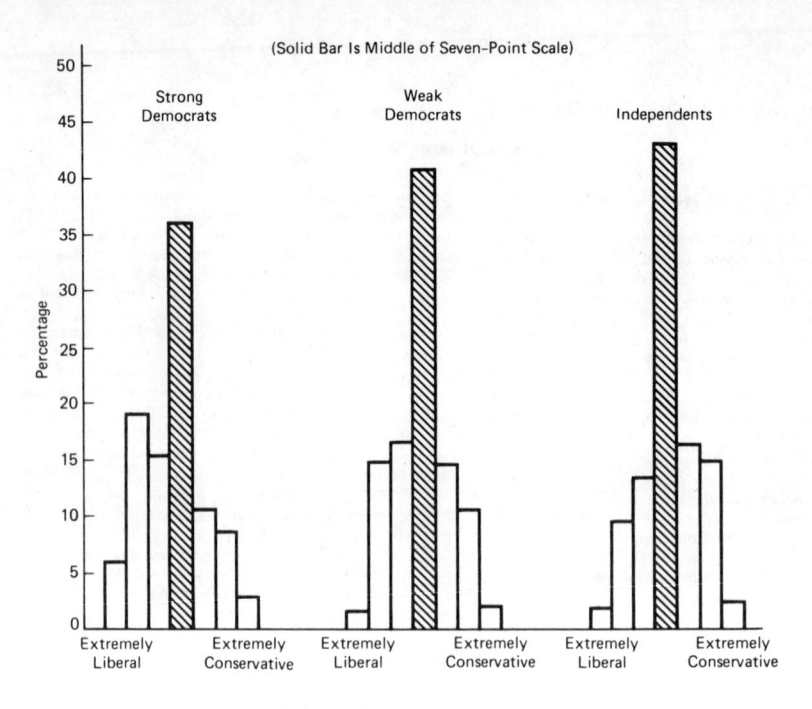

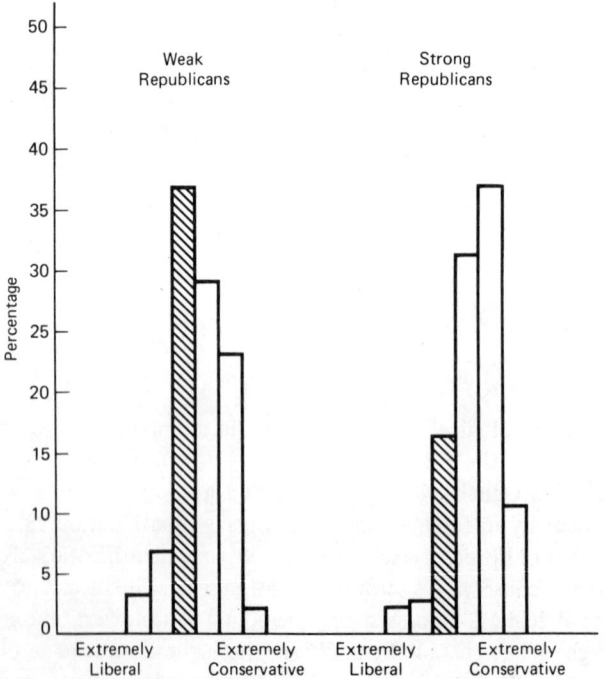

FIGURE 4.2 Ideological Self-Identification and Party Identification, 1976. *Source:* Center for Political Studies of the Institute for Social Research, University of Michigan. Data made available through the Inter-University Consortium for Political and Social Research.

TABLE 4.11 Perceptions of Democratic Party and Republican Party on Liberal-Conservative Scale by Party Identifiers, 1976 [a]

	Strong Democrats	Weak Democrats	Independents	Weak Republicans	Strong Republicans
Perceives Democrats as:					
Extremely liberal/liberal	40%	34%	36%	52%	69%
Moderate	49	56	59	45	30
Extremely conservative/conservative	12	10	6	3	1
Perceives Republicans as:					
Extremely liberal/liberal	8%	9%	7%	3%	1%
Moderate	38	48	59	60	65
Extremely conservative/conservative	55	43	35	37	34

Note: Column percentages do not always equal 100 percent due to rounding.

[a] The categories here are based on the seven-point ideological scale ranging from extremely liberal to extremely conservative. The extremely liberal/liberal category includes points 1 and 2 on the scale; moderate includes points 3, 4, and 5; and extremely conservative/conservative includes points 6 and 7.

Source: Center for Political Studies of the Institute for Social Research, University of Michigan. Data made available through the Inter-University Consortium for Political and Social Research.

should also be noted, however, that the center is the single highest self-placement point for every group of identifiers except strong Republicans. And if we define moderates as the middle three positions on the scale, we find that over 60 percent of the weak Democrats, Independents, and weak Republicans are accounted for. Even among strong Republicans, almost 50 percent are within this moderate classification.

This indicates, then, only a modest degree of ideological distinctiveness between the Republican and Democratic electorates. Perceptions of the ideological positions of the parties, however, are only a bit sharper (see Table 4.11). When asked to place the parties on the liberalism-conservatism scale, the tendency among both Republicans and Democrats was to place their respective parties near the center. This occurs among roughly half of the Democrats and almost two-thirds of the Republicans. Fifty-nine percent of the Independents see both parties as moderate. At the same time, a substantial proportion of each group of identifiers— ranging from 34 percent among weak Democrats to 69 percent among strong Republicans—perceives the Democratic party as extremely liberal or liberal, while the Republican party is perceived as extremely conservative or conservative by an almost equally sizeable proportion, ranging from 34 percent of the strong Republicans to 55 percent of the strong Democrats. For a significant portion of the electorate, then, the parties have clearly differentiated ideological orientations. For an even more sizeable segment, however, the parties are viewed as centrist.

Issue Preferences. As we have noted, one of the central concerns of political behavior studies is the extent of attitude consistency or attitude constraint within the electorate. During the Eisenhower era, citizen attitudes on various issues were not strongly related to their attitudes on other issues or to party identification. Recent investigations suggest, however, that there has been a significant increase in attitude consistency with respect not only to conventional political issues but also to the issues that emerged during the 1960s.[37] Moreover, this change does not reflect simply the rising educational level of the public but also appears to be the result of an increase in the numbers of persons interested in politics among whom the rise in attitude consistency has been especially pronounced.[38] Thus, the politicized part of the electorate appears to have increased, and this has heightened the potential impact of issues during elections. (It is still necessary to remember, however, that these "politicized" citizens do not account for a numerical majority of the electorate.)[39]

Here again, we will use limited comparisons to assess the interparty differences. We will not compare the relationships among attitudes on different issues but will simply look at the distributions within the several party identification groups on discrete issues.

In comparing the party electorates on the basis of different types of issues,

[37] Nie, Verba, and Petrocik, *The Changing American Voter*, chap. 8.
[38] Ibid., pp. 153-55.
[39] Miller and Levitin, *Leadership and Change*, pp. 69-73.

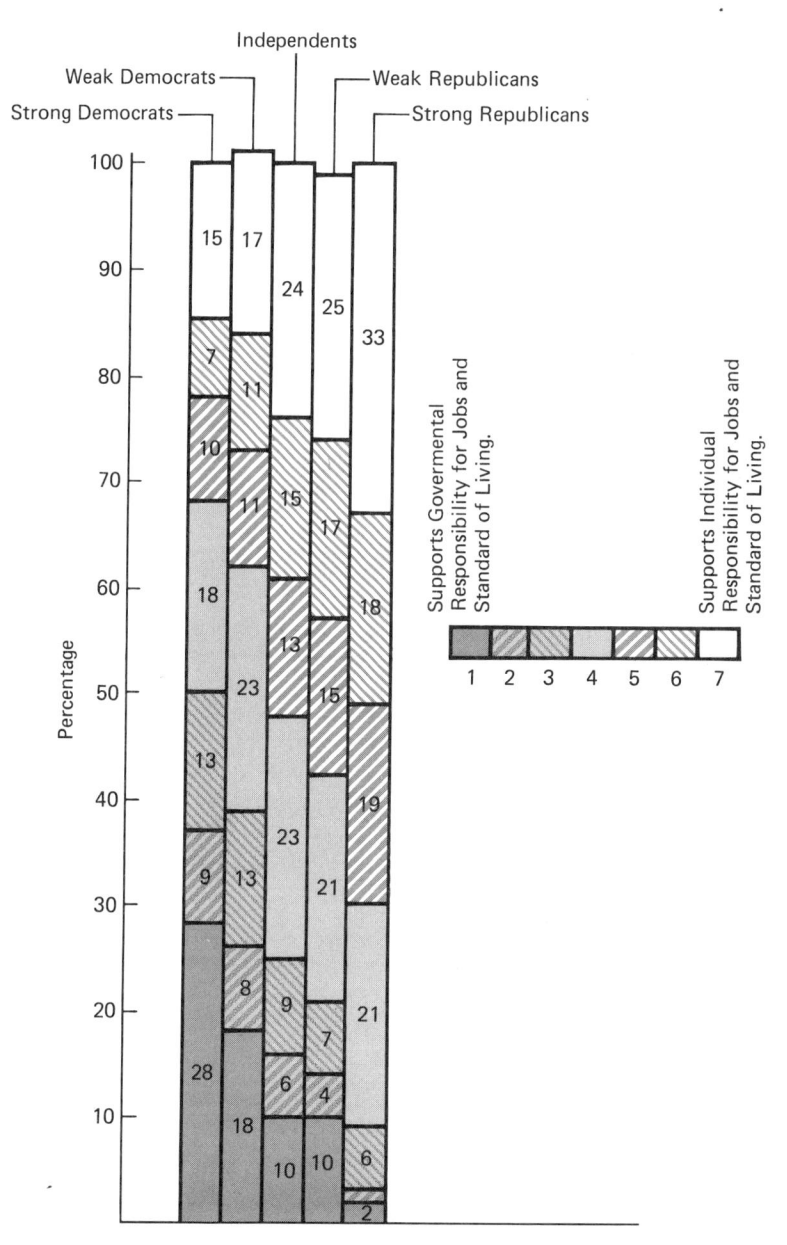

FIGURE 4.3 Views on Government vs. Private Responsibility for Jobs and Standard of Living, Among Party Identifiers, 1976. *Source:* Center for Political Studies of the Institute for Social Research, University of Michigan. Data made available through the Inter-University Consortium for Political and Social Research.

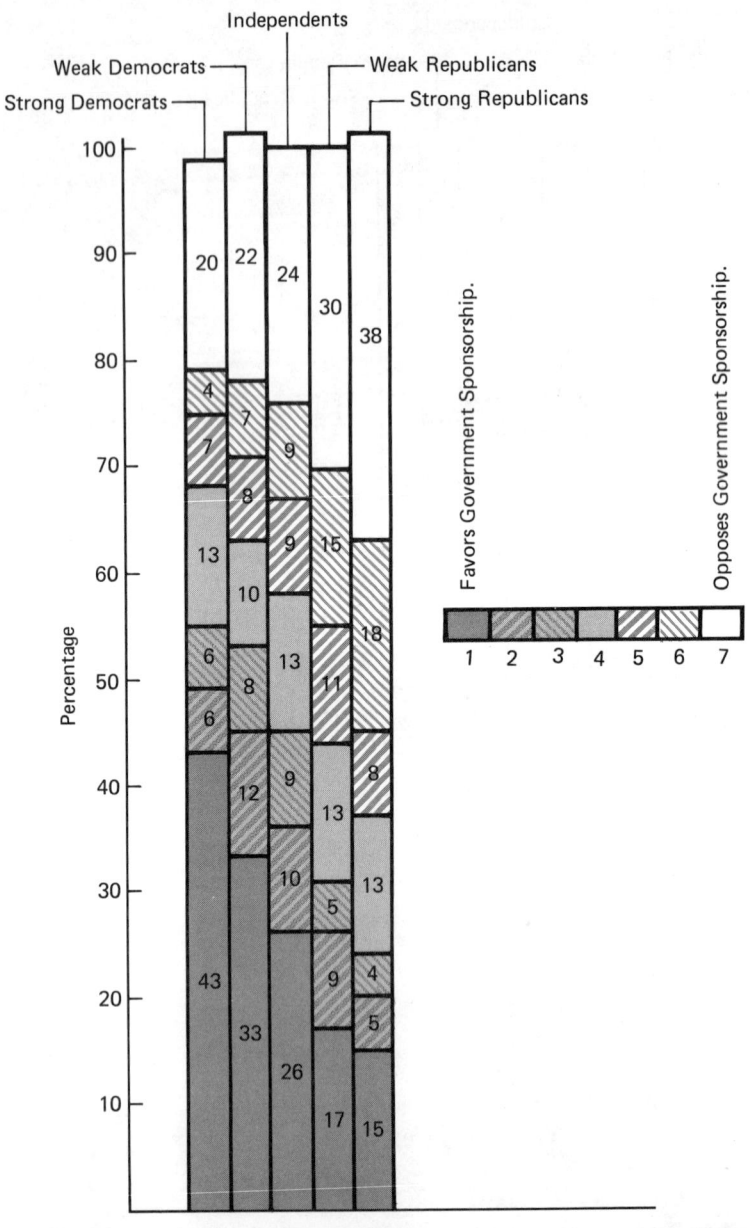

FIGURE 4.4 Views on Government Sponsorship of National Medical Insurance Plan, Among Party Identifiers, 1976. *Source:* Center for Political Studies of the Institute for Social Research, University of Michigan. Data made available through the Inter-University Consortium for Political and Social Research.

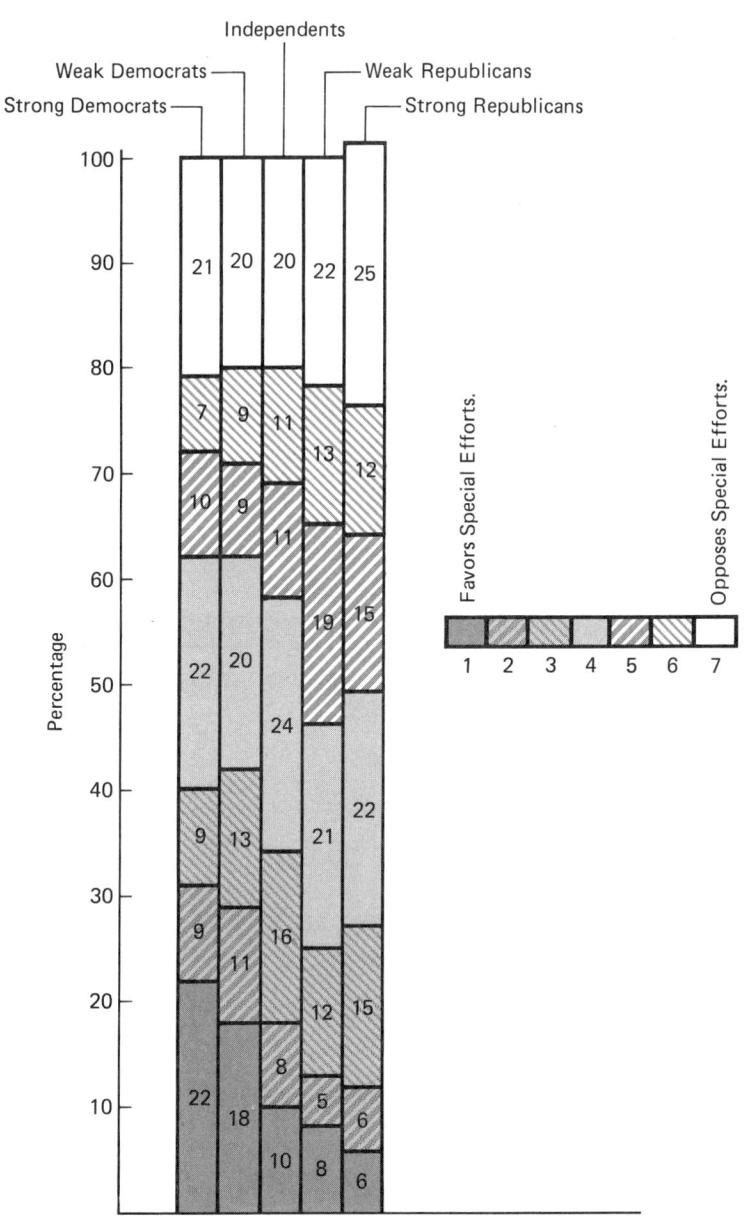

FIGURE 4.5 Views on Special Government Efforts to Aid Minorities, Among Party Identifiers, 1976. *Source:* Center for Political Studies of the Institute for Social Research, University of Michigan. Data made available through the Inter-University Consortium for Political and Social Research.

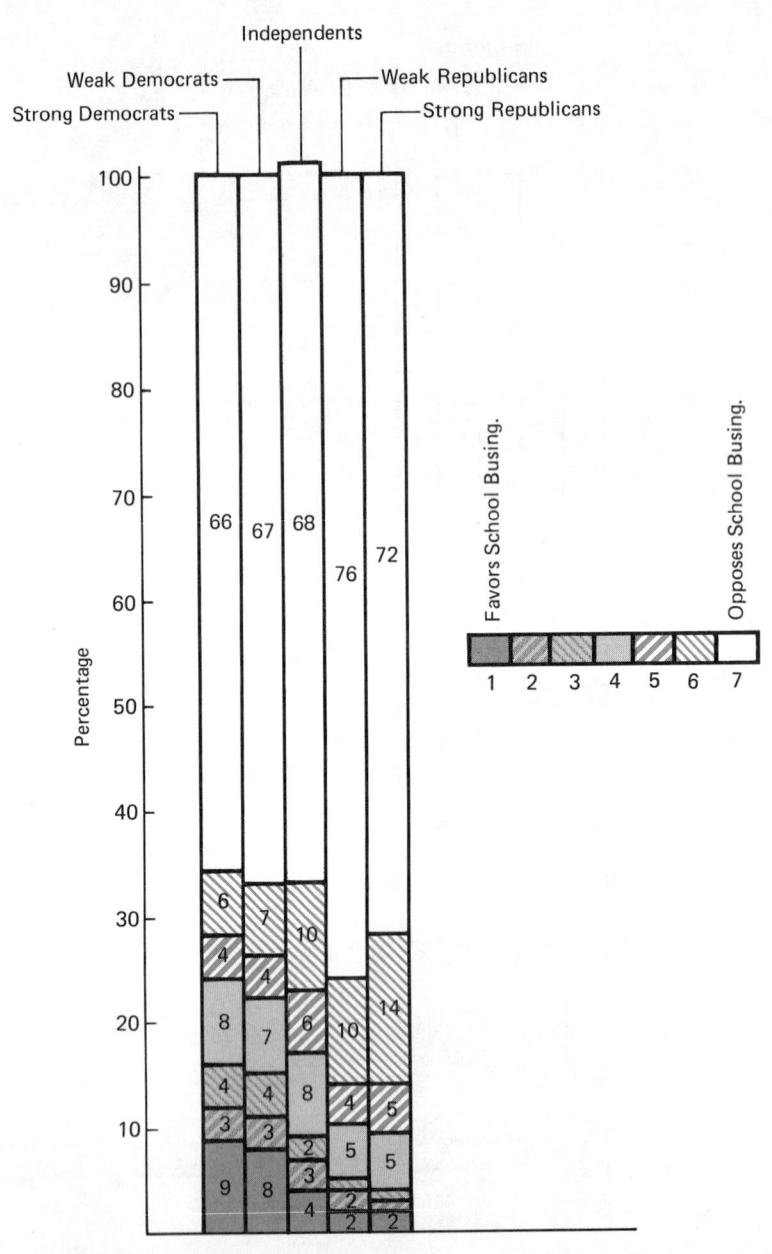

FIGURE 4.6 Views on School Busing, Among Party Identifiers, 1976. *Source:* Center for Political Studies of the Institute for Social Research, University of Michigan. Data made available through the Inter-University Consortium for Political and Social Research.

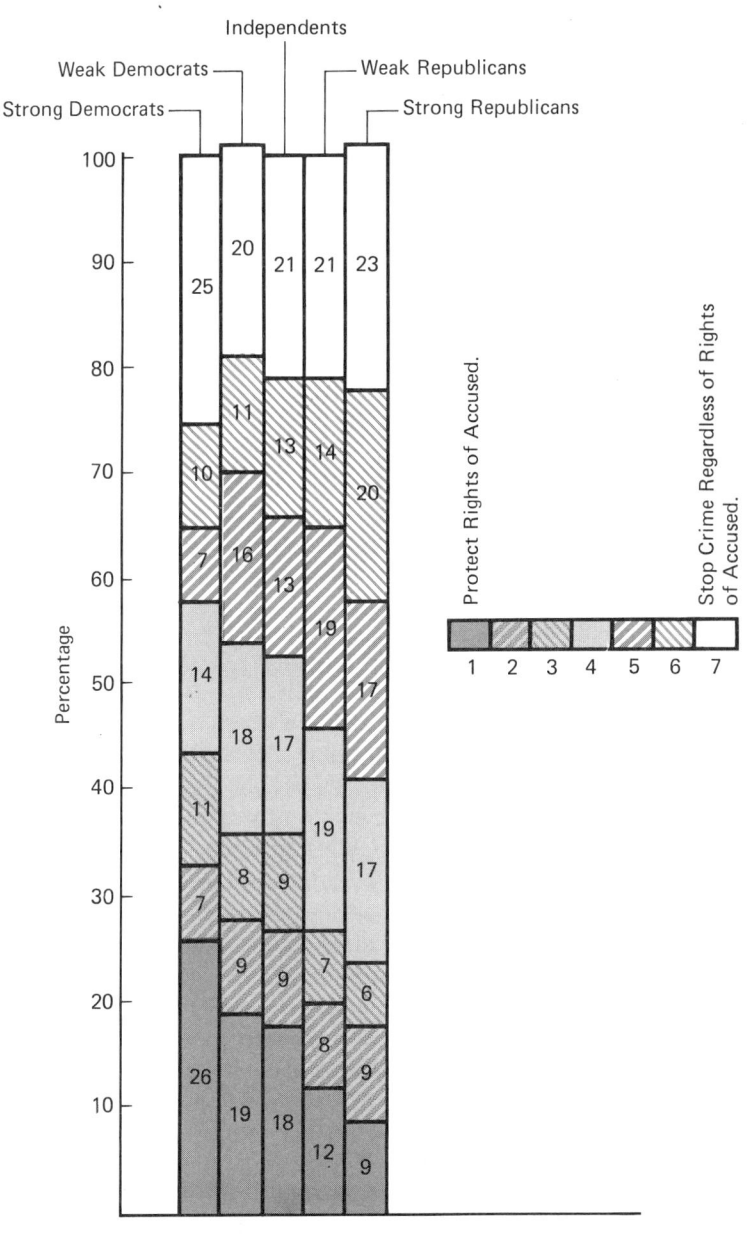

FIGURE 4.7 Views on Rights of Accused vs. Stopping Crime, Among Party Identifiers, 1976. *Source:* Center for Political Studies of the Institute for Social Research, University of Michigan. Data made available through the Inter-University Consortium for Political and Social Research.

the contrasts are not always clear or consistent. Figures 4.3-4.7, for example, show how party identifiers feel about several major issues, again using the seven-point scale. On the first two "economic issues"—the government's responsibility to insure jobs and a good standard of living for everyone and government sponsorship of a national health insurance plan—there are fairly clear differences among the groups of partisan identifiers. The groups which differ most from each other are the strong Democrats and strong Republicans. Strong Democrats are much more likely to take the most liberal or progovernment position on these issues, while strong Republicans evidence comparable levels of support for the most conservative position. Moreover, the transition from highly liberal to highly conservative is consistent and gradual as one moves from the strong Democrats through the intermediate categories to the strong Republicans.

The strong partisans, then, are relatively distinct on these issues. Even within these groups, however, there are substantial minorities with opposing positions. This is especially true among the strong Democrats, where 15 percent take the most conservative position on the jobs and standard of living question and 20 percent do so on national health insurance. And, of course, it is important to recall that the strong partisans account for only about one-fourth of the electorate. The bulk of the electorate consists of weak partisans and Independents, and the issue differences among these groups are much less distinct.

On special government efforts to assist minorities, the intraparty divisions are as interesting as the interparty ones, with the split among the strong Democratic identifiers being the sharpest. On the busing issue, there are really no significant differences. Democratic identifiers are more likely to favor busing than are Independents or Republicans, but this still represents only a very small minority of Democrats. Partisans and Independents are all strongly opposed to busing. Finally, in regard to the rights of the accused issue, there are limited interparty differences at the liberal end of the scale (26 percent of the strong Democrats as opposed to 9 percent of strong Republicans taking the most liberal position) but none at the conservative end. Indeed, strong Democrats have the highest percentages at both the extreme liberal and the extreme conservative positions. Similar, if less clearcut, splits occur within the other identification groups, suggesting again that intraparty differences may be as important as interparty divisions.

The range of issues examined here is obviously quite limited, but each issue is a significant one in national politics. The distributions on these issues indicate that the issue differences between the parties are not always clearcut. In addition, neither party's electorate is ideologically homogeneous, although the Republicans are somewhat more so than the Democrats. If we consider, then, the ideology scales and the issue scales, we find that the party electorates do differ. Democratic identifiers are more likely to be liberal, Republicans more likely to be conservative, and Independents to be in the center. This characterization, however, reflects differences of degree rather than highly cohesive and clearly differentiated party electorates. The lines shift within as well as between the party electorates as one moves from one issue to another, and the ideological predispositions of all identification groups are oriented toward the politically "moderate" categories. These patterns suggest a fluid electorate which, in terms of absolute members, is heavily concentrated in the political center.

INDEPENDENTS AND PARTISANS

The recent growth in Independent identification raises questions about the possible differences between Independents and partisans in terms of political interest and awareness. In contrasting these groups, the voting studies of the 1950s provided a less than flattering assessment of Independents. The Independents were, as a group, "relatively politically unconscious."[40] They were less knowledgeable about issues and candidates, less interested in campaigns and their outcomes, and less likely to make choices between candidates based on "discoverable evaluations of the elements of national politics."[41] Whatever the myths about the staunch objectivity of those who voted "for the man not the party," Independents were even further from the model of democratic citizenship than were partisan identifiers.

Since the mid-1960s, however, the increases in Independent identification have been especially pronounced among upper-status groups and younger voters, leading to speculation that the conventional differences between Independents and partisans have become blurred or nonexistent. It has been suggested, for example, that the "new Independents" are more likely than the "old Independents" to be able to analyze issues and campaigns and to make informed electoral choices.[42] In fact, there is evidence that Independents have become as politically knowledgeable and aware as partisans.[43] There are, however, additional similarities, as well as some differences, that should be taken into account in assessing the possible effects of these partisan changes in the electorate.

Political Participation. Turnout rates among Independents, although still well below those of strong partisans, are comparable to those of weak partisans. In a 1976 national election study, for example, almost two-thirds of the Independent identifiers reported having voted in all or most presidential elections since becoming eligible to vote. This compared to slightly more than two-thirds of the weak partisans and well over three-fourths of the strong partisans.[44]

This suggests that Independents are less concerned with electoral politics than are partisans, and this interpretation is borne out by the data reported in Table

---

[40] Burnham, *Critical Elections*, p. 127.

[41] Campbell, et al., *The American Voter*, p. 83.

[42] Pomper, *Voters' Choice*, pp. 31-35.

[43] Ibid., p. 32.

[44] These data are from the Center for Political Studies 1976 national election study; data made available through the Inter-University Consortium for Political and Social Research.

TABLE 4.12 Attitudes toward and Participation in Electoral (Campaign) Politics among Independents, Weak Partisans, and Strong Partisans, 1976

	Independents	Weak Partisans	Strong Partisans
Electoral Politcs			
Care a good deal about which party wins presidential elections	43%	57%	85%
·Very much interested in political campaigns	28	31	60
Voted in presidential preference primary	47	56	72
Worked for one of the candidates in primary	3	2	6
Attended political meetings or rallies	8	6	9
Talked to people in order to influence their votes	42	35	47
Made campaign contributions	3	4	10
Watched three or more televised debates	52	52	70

Source: Center for Political Studies of the Institute for Social Research, University of Michigan. Data made available through the Inter-University Consortium for Political and Social Research.

4.12. Strong partisans, as might be expected, are much more likely than weak partisans or Independents to care a great deal about which party wins the election. They are also more interested in political campaigns—28 percent of the Independents and 31 percent of the weak partisans say that they are very much interested in campaigns as opposed to 60 percent of the strong partisans. With respect to most of these activities, Independents and weak partisans are quite similar, but both are differentiated from strong partisans. Although some of the differences are fairly minor, as in the case of talking to others in order to influence their vote or attending political rallies, all are consistent with the argument that electoral politics is much more compelling an interest to strong partisans than to weak partisans and Independents.

When nonelectoral political activities are considered, however, this pattern changes (see Table 4.13). Independents participate in a variety of nonelectoral activities at both the national and local level at rates that are roughly equivalent to those of the strong partisans and generally above those of the weak partisans. There are variations among the specific activities and between the national and local level, but it is apparent from these distributions that Independents compare very favorably with partisans in terms of political participation that is not directly tied to electoral politics.

Political Efficacy, Citizen Duty, and Governmental Responsiveness. In the mid-1950s, Independents were not significantly different from partisans in their responses to questions concerning political efficacy. Indeed, the Independent was

TABLE 4.13 Reported Participation in Non-Electoral National and Local Politics among Independents, Weak Partisans, and Strong Partisans, 1976

	Independents	Weak Partisans	Strong Partisans
Non-Electoral Politics (National)			
Write "letters to editor" about national problem	5.2%	2.2%	4.7%
Join with others about national problem	8.1	6.5	11.8
Communicate with a national leader	17.2	13.3	21.1
Sign a petition	12.3	11.3	11.2
Demonstrate or protest	2.1	1.5	1.6
Non-Electoral Politics (Local)			
Attend city council or school board meetings	18.2	17.3	20.0
Write "letter to editor" of local paper	6.0	3.8	4.1
Join with others about local problem	22.3	19.3	22.9
Communicate with local officials	20.2	17.1	20.6
Sign a petition	24.6	20.1	18.1
Demonstrate or protest	1.9	1.5	1.6

Source: Center for Political Studies of the Institute for Social Research, University of Michigan. Data made available through the Inter-University Consortium for Political and Social Research.

slightly less likely than his partisan counterpart to believe that he had no influence on what the government did, that voting was the only way to influence government, or that public officials did not care about his opinions (see Table 4.14). Since that time, the level of inefficacious responses has risen dramatically among Independents and partisans. The most startling increase has occurred in regard to the statement, "I don't think public officials care much what people like me think." In 1956, 23 percent of the Independents and roughly one-fourth of the partisans agreed with this statement. By 1976, the proportion agreeing had risen to well over half of the Independents and weak partisans and to just under one-half of the strong partisans. Thus, from having the lowest level of cynicism about public officials' motives during the Eisenhower era, Independents had become the most cynical by the mid-1970s. On the remaining questions relating to political efficacy, the differences between Independents and weak partisans have remained quite small. The decline in political efficacy has been slightly less among strong partisans, so they now tend to appear at least a bit more favorably disposed to their place in the political process than do Independents or weak partisans. The central points, however, are that (1) Independents are not significantly different from partisans in terms of their views on political efficacy; and (2) negative perceptions about politics have become much more prevalent among all identification groups.

Strong partisans are more likely than weak partisans or Independents to re-

TABLE 4.14 Political Efficacy among Partisans and Independents, 1956 and 1976 (Percentage of Group Taking Stated Position)

	Independents	Weak Partisans	Strong Partisans
"People like me don't have any say about what the government does."			
Agree: 1956	22	29	28
Agree: 1976	44	42	39
"Sometimes politics and government seem so complicated that a person like me can't really understand what's going on."			
Agree: 1956	60	69	58
Agree: 1976	72	77	66
"I don't think public officials care much what people like me think."			
Agree: 1956	23	26	26
Agree: 1976	57	53	49
"Voting is the only way that people like me can have any say about how the government runs things."			
Agree: 1956	71	75	75
Agree: 1976	53	58	61
"Generally speaking, those we elect to Congress lose touch with the people pretty quickly."			
Not Asked 1956	–	–	–
Agree: 1976	77	71	66
"Parties are only interested in people's votes but not in their opinions."			
Not Asked 1956	–	–	–
Agree: 1976	67	65	56

Source: Center for Political Studies of the Institute for Social Research, University of Michigan. Data made available through the Inter-University Consortium for Political and Social Research.

gard voting as an important civic duty regardless of the circumstances of an election (see Table 4.15). The strong partisans are also less inclined to agree that local elections are not worth bothering about. The only issue that clearly distinguishes the identification groups, however, is the one that deals with whether a person should vote in an election when he does not feel that the outcome is important. The Independents are almost evenly split on this issue; weak partisans are slightly in favor of voting even if one does not care about the outcome. Almost two-thirds of the strong partisans, however, think that one should vote under these circumstances. There appears to be, therefore, a more deeply ingrained sense of citizen duty among strong partisans when it comes to electoral politics, and this no doubt affects the differences in turnout among identification groups.

TABLE 4.15 Attitudes toward Voting and Citizen Duty, 1976
(Percentage of Group Disagreeing with Statement)

	Independents	Weak Partisans	Strong Partisans
"It isn't so important to vote when you know your party doesn't have a chance to win."	91	92	94
"So many other people vote in the national elections that it doesn't matter much to me whether I vote or not."	88	89	96
"If a person doesn't care how an election turns out, he shouldn't vote in it."	48	54	63
"A good many local elections aren't important enough to bother with."	85	85	91

Source: Center for Political Studies of the Institute for Social Research, University of Michigan. Data made available through the Inter-University Consortium for Political and Social Research.

TABLE 4.16 General Political Assessments among Independents and Partisans, 1976[a]

"How much do you feel that you and your friends are well-represented in our political system?"

	Independents	Weak Partisans	Strong Partisans
Poorly Represented	26%	17%	16%
Moderately Represented	66	70	64
Well Represented	9	13	21

"To what extent would you say that the leading politicians in the United States have had good intentions?"

	Independents	Weak Partisans	Strong Partisans
Minimal Extent	9%	6%	8%
Moderate Extent	64	65	61
Considerable Extent	27	29	31

Note: Column percentages do not always equal 100 percent due to rounding.

[a]Responses to these questions are along a seven-point scale ranging from "none" to "a great deal." The categories used here aggregate responses by combining points 1 and 2 as "poorly represented" (and "minimal extent"), 3, 4, and 5 as "moderately represented" (and "moderate extent"); and 6 and 7 as "well represented" (and "considerable extent").

Source: Center for Political Studies of the Institute for Social Research, University of Michigan. Data made available through the Inter-University Consortium for Political and Social Research.

Independents are not very different from partisans when it comes to analyzing the intentions of politicians (see Table 4.16). Less than 10 percent of each group believes that politicians have rarely, if ever, had good intentions. Most of the identifiers fall into the middle category, while 27 percent of the Independents, 29 percent of the weak partisans, and 31 percent of the strong partisans have a very favorable assessment of politicians' intentions. But as Table 4.16 also indicates, the Independent identifier is more likely than the weak or strong partisan to feel that he and his friends are not well represented in the political system.

On considering perceptions of governmental responsiveness, however, we again find only slight differences between Independents and partisans (see Table 4.17). There is virtually no difference in their assessments of how attentive the government is to public opinion (about two-thirds of the Independents, weak partisans, and strong partisans think it is attentive some or most of the time) or of the effectiveness of elections in making government attentive (roughly 90 percent think that elections are helpful), or of the attentiveness of members of Congress. Partisans

TABLE 4.17 Assessments of Governmental and Institutional Responsiveness among Independents, Weak Partisans, and Strong Partisans, 1976

	Independents	Weak Partisans	Strong Partisans
Government attention to what the people think:			
A good deal	11%	11%	12%
Some	58	56	54
Not much	32	34	34
Parties help to make government attentive to what the people think:			
A good deal	14	19	24
Some	56	55	55
Not much	30	27	21
Elections make government attentive to what the people think:			
A good deal	50	54	58
Some	39	36	34
Not much	12	11	8
Congressmen attentive to their constituents:			
A good deal	17	20	21
Some	58	60	57
Not much	25	21	22

Note: Column percentages do not always equal 100 percent due to rounding.

Source: Center for Political Studies of the Institute for Social Research, University of Michigan. Data made available through the Inter-University Consortium for Political and Social Research.

are slightly more positive than Independents in their evaluations of parties as increasing governmental responsiveness, and the strong partisans are more likely to respond in this fashion than are weak partisans. These disparities are far from overwhelming, but they do suggest that Independents are less convinced than partisans that political parties are an effective linkage between the public and government.

The distinctions between Independents and partisans, then, are few. Indeed, Independents and weak partisans are often more similar to each other than either is to strong partisans. The important differences may lie in the relative emphasis placed on electoral politics. Independents and weak partisans (who together account for some three-fourths of all identifiers) are less interested in and concerned about political campaigns, and their voting participation rates are below those of strong partisans. When one moves away from electoral politics (and parties), the differences among the identification groups tend to blur. Certainly, Independents and weak partisans are not appreciably more negative than strong partisans on questions of political efficacy or assessments of governmental responsiveness. But they are decidedly different from strong partisans in their responses to the parties. As Table 4.18 indicates, over 60 percent of the Independents believe that there are no important differences between the parties, and almost half of the weak partisans agree with this assessment. Three-fourths of the strong partisans, however, believe that there are important differences. These distinctions, moreover, exist even though there is considerable agreement among the identification groups that one of the parties is more conservative than the other. Almost two-thirds of the Independents agree that there is a liberal-conservative distinction between the parties, but there is a much smaller proportion that considers this distinction important.

TABLE 4.18 Perceptions of Inter-Party Differences among Independents, Weak Partisans, and Strong Partisans, 1976

	Independents	Weak Partisans	Strong Partisans
Important differences between Republican and Democratic parties:			
Yes	39%	53%	75%
No	61	47	25
One of the parties is more conservative than the other at the national level:			
Yes	64	74	82
No	36	26	18

Source: Center for Political Studies at the Institute for Social Research, University of Michigan. Data made available through the Inter-University Consortium for Political and Social Research.

THE IMPACT OF PARTISAN CHANGE

The ties between today's electorate and the parties are much weaker and more tenuous than during the 1950s. In particular, party has greatly diminished as a guide for voters, and short-term electoral forces, such as issues and candidates, have become considerably more potent. Of course, this pattern of change has been evidenced primarily in presidential politics. At the congressional level, the Democratic majority has been remarkably stable, reflecting the party's advantage in terms of party identification within the electorate and the relative insulation of congressional races from short-term electoral forces.

The corresponding instability of presidential election results suggests that issues and candidates can have significant and unpredictable effects on electoral outcomes. As new issues, such as Vietnam, racial conflict, and social concerns, arose during the 1960s and early 1970s, voters responded to them by not only developing opinions but also by evaluating the parties and the candidates in terms of the issue positions they took.[45] Thus, the 1972 presidential election "was the first election in the more than two decades for which survey data are available wherein issues were a relatively more important determinant of the vote choice than parties or candidates for a substantial proportion of the electorate."[46] The impact of issues, however, is highly variable, depending on what the issues are, how they relate to traditional partisan alignments, and the manner in which they are presented. Since the mid-1960s, there has been an increased tendency for party identifiers to vote on the basis of their personal issue preferences when they perceive a conflict between those preferences and their party affiliation.[47] Together with the growing body of Independents who vote in accord with their issue positions, they make up an electorate that is more responsive to electoral appeals based on issues.[48]

While discussions of short-term forces often tend to emphasize issues, it is also necessary to recognize the effects that candidate evaluations may have on the vote. In the same way that the effects of issues are gauged, the influence that candidates have can be measured by employing normal vote analysis. A "normal vote" is an estimate of the election result based on the distribution of party identification in the electorate. It takes into account different rates of voting turnout for the several groups of party identifiers, defection rates of identifiers, and the likely vote division of Independents. The hypothetical result is what would occur if voters responded only to party rather than to issues or candidates.[49]

---

[45] Nie, Verba, and Petrocik, *The Changing American Voter*, p. 348.

[46] Miller and Levitin, *Leadership and Change*, p. 166.

[47] Nie, Verba, and Petrocik, *The Changing American Voter*, p. 348.

[48] Ibid., pp. 299-300.

[49] For a detailed description of the normal vote concept, see Philip E. Converse, "The Concept of a Normal Vote," in *Elections and the Political Order*, ed. Angus Campbell, et al., (New York: John Wiley & Sons, 1966), pp. 9-39.

The normal vote estimates since the early 1950s have favored the Democratic party, since the party has clear advantage over the Republicans in terms of party identifiers. (At the congressional level, actual election results have been remarkably close to the normal vote estimates, reflecting, as noted above, the stable impact of party on voter choice.) The presidential election results have deviated substantially from the normal vote estimates in most cases. and these deviations have usually been a result of the electorate's candidate evaluations. In 1952 and 1956, Eisenhower's personal appeal deflected the normal vote sufficiently to produce a Republican victory. In 1960, Richard Nixon's appeal as a candidate, as well as the impact of the Catholic issue, cut into expected Democratic strength. Whatever the retrospective assessments might be, Nixon was evaluated more favorably than Kennedy. Indeed, with the exception of 1964 when Johnson was more favorably perceived than Goldwater, Republican candidates for president have been higher on candidate affect measures than their Democratic opponents in every election since 1952.[50]

The particular candidates in a race may also have a tremendous effect on the ultimate impact of issues. This does not simply depend on whether they differ and by how much with respect to certain issues but also on their effectiveness in convincing voters to associate them with particular issue positions. Whatever the objective realities about the differences between the candidates, voters' perceptions will determine the effects of those differences. As one analysis concluded about the 1972 election, "Whatever the 'real' match between the policy preferences of Senator McGovern and the New Liberals, many of the New Liberals were unpersuaded that his positions [rather than Nixon's] better matched their own issue concerns."[51]

The changes in the partisan composition of the electorate—especially the increase in Independent identification and decrease in strong partisanship—have magnified the importance of short-term electoral forces in presidential elections and increased the unpredictability of those elections. The potential influence of issues has increased greatly with the emergence of new types of concerns as well as changes in the electorate's responsiveness to issues. How either party can capitalize on this is unclear. While the Democrats are the majority party and while their rank-and-file members tend to be liberal, there are significant intraparty splits on many key issues. A Democratic candidate who takes clear and consistently liberal positions risks both large defections from his own party and the real possibility of losing the bulk of moderate Independents to a Republican better able to establish himself as centrist.

A Republican candidate, on the other hand, has a more ideologically homogeneous party. Since his party is a decided minority, however, he must appeal also

---

[50] Miller and Levitin, *Leadership and Change,* p. 43.

[51] Ibid., p. 151.

to Independents and potential Democratic defectors. Yet a clear and consistently conservative ideological appeal would probably reduce the likelihood of putting together such a coalition.

There appears to be, then, a decided lack of continuity in the contemporary electorate's response to politics, at least at the presidential level. With changes from election to election in the candidates and issues, stable coalitions have not been built around either the parties or their standard-bearers. Most important, it appears highly unlikely that a specific candidate will be able to translate personal support into lasting support for his party, as Franklin Roosevelt did in the 1930s.

The prospects for partisan realignment in the near future therefore appear to be rather dim. It is probable that party loyalties will continue to dominate congressional elections. At that level, the party system is well entrenched, if not especially competitive. Presidential politics, on the other hand, seems to promise continual "individualistic voting choice between ad hoc electoral organizations mediated by television...."[52] And as the authors of this assessment concede, it is hard to say what effects such a system would have on "such fundamental political values as effectiveness of decisions, responsiveness to the public, and continuity of an open political process."[53]

SUMMARY

Controversies concerning the performance of the American party system often focus on its alleged lack of "real choices" for voters. Critics charge that the Democratic and Republican parties are too heavily oriented towards winning elections and are not sufficiently programmatic. Therefore, the parties do not provide the choices between policy alternatives that would allow the electorate to make meaningful electoral decisions. In rebuttal, it has been argued that the electorate is not sufficiently attentive or informed to be able to respond appropriately to ideologically distinctive parties.

While this debate has gone on for decades, it has acquired new prominence in recent years. Some political analysts have claimed that the American electorate today is more skilled, aware, and attentive than its 1950s counterpart. They suggest, moreover, that these changes require a "new politics," with distinctive and disciplined parties. The actual contrasts between the American voter of the 1970s and 1950s, however, appear to be relatively modest.

The electorate of the 1950s, for example, was only peripherally involved in politics. For most citizens, political information was limited, interest in politics moderate, and participation beyond voting quite rare. Over the past two decades,

---

[52] Nie, Verba, and Petrocik, *The Changing American Voter*, p. 354.
[53] Ibid., p. 355.

television has changed the way in which the public receives its political information. Access to a direct and immediate form of national political communication, however, has not increased the electorate's interest or involvement in politics.

There have been, however, marked changes in the public's response to the parties. Identification with the two parties has declined, as Independent identification has risen dramatically. In addition, the proportion of strong partisan identifiers has dropped. Split-ticket voting has increased at the national and state levels. Party evaluations have become more negative, and voters are less reliant on parties as guides to evaluating candidates. Party is still an important element in voting choice, but issues and candidates now appear to have a greater impact on voter decisions than they did two decades ago, at least in highly visible and salient elections.

There has not been, however, any sharp change in the electorate's ideological awareness. During the 1950s, issue differences between Democratic and Republican identifiers were limited. The party electorates, moreover, did not have clear perceptions of what the parties stood for or what they had accomplished. While there has been some sharpening of the ideological divisions within the electorates, these broad outlines still apply. There is only a modest degree of difference in the ideological self-perceptions of Democrats and Republicans, as well as in their perceptions of interparty differences. Distinctions between the party electorates in terms of issue preferences are not consistent. Neither party electorate is ideologically homogeneous, although the ideological "center of gravity" is somewhat liberal among Democrats, centrist among Independents, and conservative among Republicans. These are, however, differences of degree. The electorate is concentrated in the political center.

The differences between partisans and Independents have largely disappeared. Independents are, in many respects, similar to weak partisans. Both groups are less involved in electoral politics than strong partisans. There are, however, no significant differences among the groups in their views on political efficacy. Independents and weak partisans can be distinguished from strong partisans in their assessments of the parties. The strong partisans are more likely to perceive interparty differences and to believe that these differences are important.

The electorate of the 1970s is less firmly committed to parties than the electorate of the 1950s and more responsive to electoral appeals based on issues or candidate evaluations. This responsiveness, however, is chiefly confined to presidential elections, which have become increasingly susceptible to sharp swings in party support. The prospects for significant partisan realignment appear to be dim, since there is no particular continuity to the electorate's behavior in presidential politics.

five

The Party Elites: Inter-Party Differences

One of the most common (if not necessarily accurate) criticisms of the American party system is that the differences between the Democratic and Republican parties are few and superficial. The parties do not, it is argued, take clear and distinctive policy positions that would provide voters with a "real choice." Moreover, once a party gains power, it is unable to govern effectively. The party lacks coherence as a governing body, with the result that it cannot deliver what it advocates. Beset with similar internal splits, the party out of power cannot act as a responsible opposition, formulating alternatives that voters can judge at the next election.

The "Tweedledee vs. Tweedledum" characterization of American parties is not new nor is it confined to certain groups. In the early nineteenth century, Alexis de Tocqueville asserted that the "great parties" of the Jeffersonian age had been replaced by "minor parties" motivated by selfish gain. According to Tocqueville, the leaders of the great parties were primarily concerned with principles, while the minor parties were animated simply by the desire for power. Since there was no disagreement over fundamental questions, the differences between the parties were "mere differences of hue." In one of his more widely quoted lines, Tocqueville stated that "society is convulsed by great parties, by minor ones it is agitated; it is torn by the former, by the latter it is degraded; and if these sometimes save it by a salutary perturbation, those invariably disturb it to no good end."[1] Thus,

---

[1] Alexis de Tocqueville, *Democracy in America, Volume I,* trans. Henry Reeve (New York: Schocken Books, 1961), p. 197.

"America has already lost the great parties which once divided the nation; and if her happiness is considerably increased, her morality has suffered by their extinction."[2]

From the elegant critics like Tocqueville (who also recognized that there were positive benefits when parties were not divided on fundamental, moral questions), we move to the formulations of today. Senator Barry Goldwater, the Republican presidential nominee in 1964, defended his candidacy by stating it was time to provide the electorate with "a choice, not an echo." Four years later, George Wallace ran as the nominee of the American Independent party and scornfully noted that there was "not a dime's worth of difference" between the Republicans and Democrats. In 1968, the McCarthy "movement," and in 1972, the more successful McGovern "movement" promised a "politics of conscience." At least according to those who were participants, sophisticated idealism would transform the party into an instrument of social change. After Ronald Reagan lost the 1976 Republican presidential nomination, some of his supporters revived the decades-old rhetoric of the Republican right that called for two new parties, one liberal and one conservative, based on principles.

Academic critics and reformers have also been active in detailing the weaknesses and deficiencies of the major parties. One of their most persistent debates has involved the relative merits of a *responsible party system.*[3] Under such a system, the party and its candidates would appeal to the electorate on the basis of a common program. The voter would evaluate the past performance and legislative records of the parties, assess their proposed programs, and finally select candidates on the basis of national party programs. Whichever party then gained a popular majority would be able to use its control of the government to enact the program that it had advocated.

Responsible parties offer, at least in theory, an efficient instrument for converting popular preferences into government policy. Indeed, the proponents of responsible parties believe that such parties are uniquely qualified to perform this linkage function. Parties are able both to advocate policy proposals and, unlike other groups, to present voters with a relatively direct and accessible method for responding to these proposals—that is, the candidates who run under the party labels. Thus, responsible parties would strengthen popular control of the policy-making process, since elections would serve as programmatic mandates.

Many liberals and conservatives, academics and politicians, and even, as we found in chapter 4, a large segment of the electorate believe that the major parties do not stand upon significant, competing principles. Before one can assess the possible benefits or shortcomings of this type of party system, it is necessary to see whether the general characterization is accurate. This chapter, therefore, will

---

[2]Ibid.

[3]See Austin Ranney, *The Doctrine of Responsible Party Government* (Urbana, Ill.: University of Illinois Press, 1962).

examine the differences between the party elites as a means of analyzing interparty differences.

One of the difficulties in evaluating interparty differences is the lack of consensus on what factors should be considered. Since we have previously stressed the importance of parties as linkages between the public and government, our focus will be on several related factors that affect this linkage function:

1. the differences between the parties as expressed in official policy statements, presidential initiatives, and legislative records;
2. interparty policy differences as reflected in the competing candidates who run under the party labels; and
3. interparty policy differences between party activists within the party organizations.

OFFICIAL POLICY DIFFERENCES

The Democratic and Republican parties do not issue policy manifestoes or other statements of party doctrine that are regarded as binding on party candidates or officeholders, to say nothing of officials or party organizations within the states. For the party that controls the White House, the president is acknowledged as head of the party, and his policy positions are regarded as the official ones of the national party. This does not mean, however, that members of the president's party in Congress or elsewhere are obliged to support his position. The party out of power typically lacks even the pretense of definitive policy statements. Rather, separate efforts at explaining where the party stands on a given issue may involve the congressional party leaders, national committee, past and potential presidential candidates, and other self-designated party spokesmen.

The concept of a tightly reasoned party doctrine expressing the collective judgment of the various sectors and levels of the political party has not been considered feasible, or some would even argue necessary, in the American party system. There are, nevertheless, important differences between the parties. These may vary over time and from issue to issue, but there are certain guides that one can utilize in ascertaining interparty differences.

Party Platforms

The party platform adopted by each party's national convention every four years is sometimes treated by political commentators as a meaningless joke. Of course, there is mindless rhetoric in a platform, and it is a bit discomforting to find that grown men and women need as much self-justification and self-congratulation as the typical platform contains. Nor is it terribly clear how one should respond to the statement that "the people are skeptical of platforms filled with political platitudes," as the Democratic platform felt compelled to announce in 1972.

The party platform is primarily, of course, a campaign document. It is especially important in reflecting the areas of agreement among the numerous interests and constituencies represented in the party. As the Democratic platform battles in 1968 and 1972 or the Republican convention divisions in 1976 suggest, spokesmen for these interests and constituencies take the language, as well as the substance, of the platform planks very seriously. Even if not widely read by the electorate, the platform may be important, since it can indicate "program initiatives made by parties in anticipation of voter needs and demands. The electorate's choice of a party would then become a choice of policies as well."[4]

If the platform is to be considered as a significant statement of party policy, however, it must meet certain standards of specificity and voter relevance. Fortunately, there has been an excellent and thorough examination of what the parties pledge in their platforms and, equally important, what happens to these pledges after the election. Using a method known as "content analysis," Gerald Pomper has analyzed the Democratic and Republican platforms from 1944 to 1968.[5] He found that only about one-sixth of all platform statements were rhetorical, while evaluations of past party performance and future policy initiatives accounted for most of the platform content during this period. These evaluations and initiatives were often quite specific in terms of actual policy.[6]

As Table 5.1 shows, party pledges also tend to be distinctive. Similar or bipartisan pledges are contained in the platform, but they are considerably less prevalent than pledges made by one or the other party. In addition, approximately one-tenth of the pledges represent conflicting positions taken by the parties. Of course, the degree of distinctiveness varies over time and by policy area. Bipartisan pledges are much more frequent in the areas of civil rights and foreign policy than on economic, labor, and welfare issues. This suggests that there are limits to partisan conflict on certain types of issues, as well as contrasting approaches to domestic social welfare policies that are related to traditional bases of party electoral strength.

While comparable analyses of more recent platforms are not available, there have been sharp interparty differences on some of the most highly publicized issues of the 1970s. Table 5.2, for example, shows that the 1972 Republican and Democratic platforms contained conflicting pledges on a number of major issues. There was a bipartisan pledge supporting the Equal Rights Amendment, as well as one-party pledges relating to right-to-work laws and the legalization of marijuana. Further, neither platform dealt with abortion. On the remaining issues, however, the contrasts were clear and unmistakable. As one objective source concluded after the conventions, "The politicians of both major parties have predicted that

---

[4]Gerald M. Pomper, "Controls and Influence in American Elections (Even 1968)," *American Behavioral Scientist*, 13 (November/December 1969), 218.

[5]Gerald M. Pomper, *Elections in America* (New York: Dodd, Mead & Company, 1968). The technique is explained on pp. 149-78 and 274-79.

[6]Ibid., p. 159.

TABLE 5.1 Party Platform Pledges—Similarities and Differences

	N	One-Party Pledge Only	Bipartisan Pledges	Conflicting Pledges
Election Year				
1944	102	70%	28%	2%
1948	124	51	42	7
1952	205	52	29	19
1956	302	61	34	5
1960	464	51	39	10
1964	202	70	19	11
Policy Topic				
Foreign	216	47	47	6
Defense	84	65	33	2
Economic	177	62	22	16
Labor	84	42	33	25
Agriculture	150	56	33	11
Resources	185	63	26	11
Welfare	255	60	27	13
Government	136	76	24	0
Civil Rights	113	40	60	0
All pledges	1,399	57	33	10
Total N	1,399	799	464	136

Source: Reprinted by permission of Dodd, Mead & Company, Inc. from *Elections in America* by Gerald M. Pomper. Copyright © 1968 by Dodd, Mead & Company, Inc.

Note: Rows add horizontally to 100 percent for the three right-hand columns.

election year 1972 will offer the American voters a real choice. And judging by the Republican and Democratic platforms, that is true."[7]

In the 1976 campaign, the ideological contrasts appeared, at least in comparison to 1972, muted. There were, however, Democratic and Republican platform differences on a number of major issues—busing, gun control, welfare and tax reform, right-to-work laws, national health insurance, and abortion (see Table 5.3). As the actual platform statements indicate, the degree of distinctiveness varied from issue to issue. The abortion language, for example, was almost painfully delicate as each party sought to handle this emotional and controversial issue. There were, as in the past, one-party pledges (on amnesty and school prayer), and the bipartisan support of the Equal Rights Amendment was continued.

Since the platforms, then, contain a meaningful degree of specificity, provide evaluations of past party performance, and deal extensively with future policy initiatives, they do present voters with a reasonable and meaningful opportunity to judge interparty differences. Moreover, the platforms focus on matters that can be readily understood by voters whose interest and information is otherwise limited

---

[7]*Congressional Quarterly Almanac*, vol. 28, 92d Congress, 2nd Session (Washington, D.C.: Congressional Quarterly, Inc., 1972), p. 1057.

TABLE 5.2 Platform Contrasts, 1972

	Republicans	Democrats
Busing:	Opposed busing to achieve racial balance in schools.	"Transportation of students is another tool to accomplish desegregation. It must continue to be available . . ."
Gun Control:	Opposed gun control laws—"safeguard the right of responsible citizens to collect, own, and use firearms for legitimate purposes."	Supported ban on sale of handguns.
Amnesty:	Opposed amnesty for war resisters.	Favored amnesty for war resisters.
Vietnam:	"We have not abandoned an ally to aggression, not turned our back on their brave defense against brutal invasion, not consigned them to the bloodbath that would follow Communist conquest."	"Immediate and complete withdrawal of all U.S. forces in Indo-China."
Equal Rights Amendment:	Supported ratification.	Supported ratification.
School Prayer:	Supported voluntary school prayer.	No platform statement.
Section 14(b) of Taft-Hartley Act (the "Right-to-Work" Provision):	No platform statement.	Endorsed repeal.
Marijuana:	Opposed legalization.	No platform statement.
Welfare:	"We flatly oppose programs or policies which embrace the principle of a government guaranteed income."	Supported government-guaranteed income "substantially more than the poverty level."
Tax Reform:	Support of reform that "more equitably spreads the tax burden and avoids incentive-destroying tax levels."	Favored a "more equitable distribution of income" through tax reform.
National Health Insurance:	Opposed "nationalized compulsory health insurance."	Favored federally-financed and administered system of universal, comprehensive national health insurance.
Abortion:	No platform statement.	No platform statement.

TABLE 5.3 Platform Contrasts, 1976

	Republicans	*Democrats*
Busing:	"We oppose forced busing to achieve racial balance in our schools." Favored constitutional amendment forbidding assignment to schools on the basis of race.	"Mandatory transportation of students beyond their neighborhoods for the purpose of desegregation remains a judicial tool of last resort."
Gun Control:	"We oppose federal registration of firearms."	"Ways must be found to curtail the availability of [handguns]."
Amnesty:	No platform statement.	Pledged "full and complete pardon" for war resisters and case-by-case treatment of deserters.
Asia:	"United States troops will be maintained in Korea so long as there exists the possibility of renewed aggression from North Korea."	Supported withdrawal of U.S. troops and nuclear weapons in Korea.
Equal Rights Amendment:	Supported ratification.	Supported ratification.
School Prayer:	Supported constitutional amendment to allow voluntary school prayer.	No platform statement.
Section 14(b) of Taft-Hartley Act (the "Right-to-Work" Provision):	Opposed repeal.	Supported repeal.
Welfare:	Opposed "federalizing the welfare system," as well as the "guaranteed annual income concept."	Supported system of "income maintenance, substantially financed by federal government."
Tax Reform:	"While the best tax reform is tax reduction, we recognize the need for structural tax adjustments to help the working men and women."	"The Internal Revenue Code offers massive tax welfare to the wealthiest income groups . . . and higher taxes for the average citizen."
National Health Insurance:	Opposed "compulsory national health insurance."	Supported "comprehensive national health insurance with universal and mandatory coverage."
Abortion:	Supported constitutional amendment to restore "protection of the right to life for unborn children."	Opposed constitutional amendment to "overturn the Supreme Court decision in this area."

—namely, the policy successes and failures of the incumbents and the group benefits each party promises in the future.[8]

Finally, Pomper's study found that platform pledges were usually carried out by the parties. He states that "moreover, and contrary to the conventional wisdom, these platform pledges are redeemed. Legislative or executive action directly fulfills more than half of the planks, and some definite action is taken in nearly three-fourths of the cases. Achievement is even greater for the party in the White House."[9]

In this context, the ambiguities and generalities of the platforms can be seen as attempts to cope with intraparty divisions. As V. O. Key explained, "All this is not to glorify obfuscation, but merely to suggest that the platform is conditioned by the political system as a whole. . . . No simpler way exists to destroy an electoral coalition than for its majority to insist on precise, forthright and advanced policy positions unacceptable to other elements of the coalition."[10] The platform defines the boundaries of intraparty agreement, and it does so with sufficient clarity to differentiate the parties and the interests they represent.

Amendments and Modifications. Once a platform has been adopted and the nomination decided, the presidential candidate has broad discretion in deciding which platform themes will be stressed and how they will be presented and interpreted. Occasionally, the candidate's prerogatives extend to actually amending or modifying the platform. V. O. Key describes, for example, how the Democrat's 1904 presidential candidate, Alton B. Parker, informed the convention that he was unwilling to accept the platform's silence on the gold standard and the free coinage of silver. The convention agreed that since the platform did not deal with this issue, Parker could freely state his views on it. In 1928, the Democrats pledged that their nominee would faithfully enforce the Eighteenth Amendment. Alfred E. Smith, after being nominated by the convention, told the delegates that he believed major changes were necessary in dealing with prohibition.[11] When the candidate's personal views conflict with the platform, it is also possible, of course, for him to deal with the conflict by ignoring the issue entirely.

Campaign strategy may also affect the extent to which issue differences are stressed. As Polsby and Wildavsky have suggested, "The contents of election campaigns appear to be largely opportunistic." In addition to other strategic issues, candidates must decide "what kinds of appeals shall they make to what voting groups? How specific or general shall they be in their policy proposals?"[12] Democratic candidates, for example, may attempt to capitalize upon their greater elec-

---

[8]Pomper, *Elections in America*, p. 176.

[9]Ibid., p. 202.

[10]V. O. Key, Jr., *Politics, Parties, and Pressure Groups*, 5th ed. (New York: Thomas Y. Crowell Company, 1964), p. 421.

[11]Ibid., p. 422.

[12]Nelson W. Polsby and Aaron Wildavsky, *Presidential Elections*, 4th ed. (New York: Charles Scribner's Sons, 1976), pp. 164-65.

toral strength by emphasizing partisan themes and stressing the economic policy differences between the parties. Their Republican opponents, in order to overcome their minority party status, may attempt to deemphasize the electoral influence of party cues by directing attention to the personal qualifications of the candidates or to downplay economic policy differences in order to exploit their party's relatively favorable image in the realm of foreign affairs.[13]

The extent to which the electorate perceives interparty policy distinctions, then, is affected by several factors: (1) how salient certain types of issues are during an election; (2) the objective differences between the parties; and (3) the manner in which the competing candidates handle these issue differences in terms of focus and emphasis. It is also clear that voters may see the issue distances between the candidates as distinct from the issue distances between the parties. When the parties nominate highly ideological candidates, as the Republicans did in 1964 and the Democrats did in 1972, the electorate may react strongly to the candidates' issue differences while not markedly altering its perception of broader interparty differences.[14]

The party platform, then, is a meaningful statement of principles and issue positions. It is also a reasonably accurate guide to what party officeholders will attempt to accomplish in the future. If the party wins the presidency, it stands a much better chance of realizing these objectives. But there are also limits on the differences between the parties as expressed in their platforms. Congressional and other nonpresidential candidates are not bound by the platforms. Even presidential candidates are not rigidly bound. They retain necessary discretion in interpreting or modifying platform statements. Perhaps most important, the electorate does not simply base its presidential voting on party themes or platform issues. It also responds to the particular candidates by evaluating their competence and character.

The differences between the parties, moreover, are not always sharp or consistent over time. And given our conclusions about the party electorate in chapter 4, there is little reason to expect that the parties will take extreme and opposite positions. The parties must deal with their internal minorities as well as a large ideological center. The differences between their platforms may, as a consequence, often seem to be matters of "emphasis, degree, detail, or timing, but these are, in the main, the differences of American politics."[15]

Presidential Programs

The president's policy leadership responsibilities have expanded enormously during this century. The White House initiates many of the major legislative programs and proposals with which Congress deals, sets the terms of debate on crucial

---

[13] Ibid., pp. 160-74.

[14] On the use of proximity measures that indicate different placements by voters of candidates and parties on issue or ideological scales, see Warren E. Miller and Teresa E. Levitin, *Leadership and Change: Presidential Elections from 1952 to 1976* (Cambridge, Mass.: Winthrop Publishers, Inc., 1976), especially chap. 5.

[15] Key, *Politics, Parties, and Pressure Groups*, p. 421.

matters of public policy, and must attempt to develop public and congressional support for administration programs.[16] In addition, the president's administrative and budgetary responsibilities provide continuing opportunities to influence the scope and operation of executive agencies and their programs.[17]

For the party that controls the White House, there is a program that can be identified and assessed. The president, more than any other leader or group of leaders within the party, enjoys legitimacy in defining this program and bringing it to the attention of the electorate. The opportunities for doing so are readily available. The State of the Union message sets out the central legislative issues for the coming year and describes the general direction of the administration's programs. During the year, special messages and legislative "packages" are formulated to provide detailed policy initiatives for Congress. In just six months after his inauguration, for example, President Carter had sent Congress some two dozen special messages including major proposals for economic recovery, energy policy, election law and ethics reform, health care cost reductions, welfare system revision, social security financing adjustments, labor law changes, and executive reorganization.[18]

Shortly after Congress convenes each year, the president's economic report and budget are also presented. These are the official administration positions on economic management policy and program priorities. The budget has become an enormously influential document, because it directly affects a wide range of social, economic, and political goals. As a result, recent presidents have placed major emphasis on budgetary policy leadership, and this emphasis gives the public still another indicator of the way an administration defines itself in policy terms.

The president, therefore, has the institutional capabilities and direct access to the electorate that allow him to speak authoritatively for his party. (This also applies to governors, who usually serve as official spokesmen for their state parties. Single executives share a common advantage over other official party groups in asserting and achieving party leadership.) At the same time, we must recognize that there are certain ambiguities in the president's role as party leader.

First, many Americans are uncomfortable with the concept of a partisan president. The view that the inauguration converts a party nominee into the president of "all the people" has been widespread through much of our history. Responding to this belief, as well as to the practical necessity of maintaining popular approval, presidents may seek to cloak their policies in conciliatory rather than strongly partisan appeals.[19] It is generally agreed that the president's depend-

---

[16] See Stephen J. Wayne, *The Legislative Presidency* (New York: Harper & Row, 1978).

[17] See Dennis S. Ippolito, *The Budget and National Politics* (San Francisco: W. H. Freeman and Company, 1978), chap. 2. For the view that the president should emphasize these administrative duties to a greater extent than in the past, see Thomas E. Cronin, *The State of the Presidency* (Boston: Little, Brown and Company, 1975), pp. 250-58.

[18] For these and other special messages during the Carter administration's first year in office, see *Congressional Quarterly Almanac*, vol. 33, 95th Congress, 1st Session (Washington, D.C.: Congressional Quarterly, Inc., 1977), pp. 6E-64E.

[19] This point is discussed in David Broder, *The Party's Over* (New York: Harper & Row, 1971), pp. 64-77.

ence on public opinion is substantial; so long as his administration maintains a favorable public image, he can pursue his policy goals with some hope of success. The loss of public favor, however, inevitably impedes an administration's efforts to provide effective policy leadership. It is obvious from the distribution of party identification in the electorate that no president can maintain a high level of popularity by depending solely on his party's identifiers. Under such circumstances, a Democratic president who was viewed positively by *all* Democratic identifiers would still lack majority approval. A Republican president's problems in this regard are even more serious. In order to maintain a sufficiently broad appeal within the entire electorate, then, the president may be forced to personalize his policies and appeals rather than to frame them in stark, partisan terms.

A second difficulty arises from the president's dealings with Congress. Even when the same party controls both the legislative and executive branches, there is likely to be considerable intraparty conflict. Even though presidential programs may be acknowledged as party programs, this does not guarantee their support

TABLE 5.4 Presidential "Boxscores"—Presidential Programs Approved by Congress, 1954-1975*

Year	Party Controlling: White House	Congress	Presidential Proposals Submitted	Percent Approved by Congress
1954	Rep. (Eisenhower)	Rep.	232	65%
1955	Rep.	Dem.	207	46
1956	Rep.	Dem.	225	46
1957	Rep.	Dem.	206	37
1958	Rep.	Dem.	234	47
1959	Rep.	Dem.	228	41
1960	Rep.	Dem.	183	31
1961	Dem. (Kennedy)	Dem.	355	48
1962	Dem.	Dem.	298	45
1963	Dem.	Dem.	401	27
1964	Dem. (Johnson)	Dem.	217	58
1965	Dem.	Dem.	469	69
1966	Dem.	Dem.	371	56
1967	Dem.	Dem.	431	48
1968	Dem.	Dem.	414	56
1969	Rep. (Nixon)	Dem.	171	32
1970	Rep.	Dem.	210	46
1971	Rep.	Dem.	202	20
1972	Rep.	Dem.	116	44
1973	Rep.	Dem.	183	31
1974	Rep.	Dem.	97	34
1974	Rep. (Ford)	Dem.	64	36
1975	Rep.	Dem.	110	27

*These represent specific presidential legislative requests to Congress in each year.

Source: Data for 1954-1968 are from *Congress and the Nation*, Vol. II, 1965-1968 (Washington, D.C.: Congressional Quarterly Inc., 1969), p. 625. Data for 1969-1975 are from *Congressional Quarterly Weekly Report* (various years).

among the president's fellow partisans in Congress. As shown in Table 5.4, presidential success in terms of legislative leadership has not been especially high over the past two decades. Part of this stems from divided control of government. President Eisenhower, for example, had 65 percent of his proposals approved when his party held majorities in the House and Senate. When he was faced with a Democratic Congress for the remaining six years of his presidency, however, he failed to get congressional support for a majority of his proposals. Presidents Nixon and Ford faced opposition-controlled Congresses throughout their terms, and their legislative achievements were appropriately modest. Party control of both branches, however, produced a dismal legislative record under President Kennedy. Lyndon Johnson was more successful, although 1965 was the only year in which a truly exceptional record was achieved. These data indicate the lack of total harmony even when one party controls both the Presidency and Congress, as well as the absence of absolute stalemate even in the case of divided control.

There is a limit on how effectively a president can employ strict party appeals in Congress. He is often forced to construct supporting coalitions on an issue-by-issue basis. And while he can generally count on his fellow partisans to provide the bulk of his support on most issues, the lines between the parties begin to blur as minority defectors on both sides cross party lines. Moreover, there is little to suggest that any short-term changes in these relationships are imminent. Despite the high hopes for party cooperation after the Democrats captured the White House in 1976, President Carter's relations with Congress have been less than harmonious. Democrats in Congress have not directly challenged Carter as party leader, but neither have they equated party loyalty with support for administration programs.

A third obstacle in the way of partisan presidential leadership is the absence of a clearly defined and stable political opposition that can provide alternatives to presidential programs.[20] There is no institutionalized opposition within the out-party. Congressional party leaders, presidential aspirants, the national committee, and other party organization groups may attempt to fill this vacuum, but different constituencies and institutional jealousies generally sabotage these efforts. Even if the out-party could agree on a collective leadership group to serve as spokesman, it would then have to convince the public of the legitimacy of this effort. Whether this can be done is not clear. Past attempts by the opposition party to "answer" the president have enjoyed mixed success at best. Perhaps the most successful effort along these lines was the Democratic party's designation of Senator Edmund Muskie to provide a televised rebuttal to President Nixon on the evening preceding the 1970 congressional elections. Muskie's performance was considered to be extremely effective in countering Nixon's attacks on congressional Democrats, although there is no direct evidence that it had a substantial impact on actual voting. Other Democratic attempts to act as a "loyal opposition" during the Nixon

---

[20] See Dennis S. Ippolito, Thomas G. Walker, and Kenneth L. Kolson, *Public Opinion and Responsible Democracy* (Englewood Cliffs, N.J.: Prentice-Hall, 1976), pp. 280-82.

and Ford administrations did not elicit the type of public response that would lead one to conclude that the characteristic impotence of the out-party opposition had been overcome. The Republicans' performance as opposition party during the Carter presidency has not been especially promising either. Congressional Republicans have been frustrated in their attempts to develop coherent alternatives to Carter administration domestic programs. Only with respect to foreign policy and national security matters have there been signs of an emerging Republican consensus that could develop and articulate opposition-party themes with some possibility of success.

Presidential policies and programs provide useful guidelines for analyzing party politics, but the limiting conditions that we have discussed suggest that these guidelines are sometimes imprecise. The president's legislative program is not analogous to the governing party's program in a parliamentary system. The differences reflect, of course, the historical relationship between the president and Congress as well as public perceptions about the nature and purposes of presidential leadership. They also indicate significant contrasts between the American party system and parliamentary party systems. In terms of policy, it does make a difference whether a Democrat or a Republican holds the White House. But a president's ties to his party are sufficiently loose that he must maintain sources of support and influence outside the circle of his fellow partisans.

Legislative Records

The parties in Congress do not adopt platforms, nor do they ordinarily issue formal public pronouncements about their legislative records or intentions.[21] A party's congressional candidates do not, of course, run under the party platform. Once elected, members of Congress are not obligated to support their respective parties when legislative issues are decided. There are, however, major policy controversies that find many, if not all, congressional Democrats on one side and many, if not all, congressional Republicans on the other. A concurrence of views characterizes each of the parties in Congress, and it is this concurrence rather than sanctions or leadership control, that explains party voting among members of the House and Senate.

The differences between the parties, however, are not consistent within all policy areas. In some policy areas, such as social welfare, government regulation, economic management, and agricultural assistance, there have been significant and fairly stable interparty differences over the years.[22] On issues involving civil rights and civil liberties or foreign policy and national security considerations, these differences have usually been less important than bipartisan agreement or intraparty splits.[23]

---

[21] The organization and functions of the congressional parties are described in chapter 7.

[22] Aage R. Clausen, *How Congressmen Decide: A Policy Focus* (New York: St. Martin's Press, 1973), p. 93.

[23] Ibid.

The legislative records that congressional Democrats and congressional Republicans develop as parties are an important criterion for assessing interparty differences. Some insight into these records is provided by each party's response to especially controversial or significant issues. The *Congressional Quarterly,* for example, selects what it terms "key issues" during each session of Congress. Issues are judged by the extent to which they represent "a matter of major controversy, a test of presidential or political power, [and/or] a decision of potentially great impact on the nation and lives of Americans."[24]

Using this admittedly subjective approach makes it possible to analyze specific interparty differences on a reasonably limited number of issues. In 1977, for example, 16 "key issues" were identified in the House, and an equal number were selected in the Senate. These could be grouped into several general categories, such as energy and environment or defense and foreign policy. By examining these issues and how the parties voted on them, it is possible to provide a reasonably coherent and accurate summary of the legislative performance of each party.

Energy and Environment. On April 18, 1977 President Carter announced his administration's comprehensive energy program in a nationwide, televised address. In defending this complex package of more than 100 regulatory and tax measures, the president employed rather dramatic rhetoric, stating that "with the exception of preventing war, this [energy crisis] is the greatest challenge our country will face during our lifetime." The Democratic congressional leadership responded by making the passage of a national energy program the top legislative priority for 1977. Despite these concerted efforts, however, the Carter energy program did not clear Congress as scheduled, and it continued to be a major problem throughout the remainder of the Ninety-fifth Congress.

Several energy votes were key issues. In the House, which generally supported the Carter program, the president gained two important victories. A proposal to end federal regulation of natural gas prices was defeated 199 to 217. The House also refused to eliminate a proposed tax on domestic crude oil by a margin of 203-219. As shown in Table 5.5, the interparty divisions on these votes were very sharp. The Republicans voted almost as a bloc, while approximately three-fourths of the Democrats opposed them. Because of the Democratic party's roughly 2-1 majority in the House, it was able to withstand a considerable number of defections and still win the votes on these issues.

In the Senate, the administration's energy program suffered a reversal as a move to deregulate natural gas pricing succeeded by a vote of 50-46. Here again, the party majorities were on opposite sides, but there were sufficient Democratic defections to swing the outcome. Another rebuff to the administration occurred when the Senate refused to terminate the Clinch River breeder reactor project. The vote on this proposal was 48-49, as a large majority of Republicans joined with numerous Democratic defectors to support the breeder reactor project.

[24]*Congressional Quarterly Almanac,* vol. 33, p. 1B.

TABLE 5.5   Party Voting on "Key Issues," House and Senate, 1977 (95th Congress, 1st Session)

	Senate	House
Energy/Environment:	Deregulate natural gas (R 34-3; D 16-43). Terminate breeder reactor (R 6-27; D 32-22).	Deregulate natural gas (R 127-17; D 72-210). Eliminate crude oil tax (R 137-3; D 66-216). Relax automobile emissions standards (R 105-21; D 150-118). Delete water resources project funding (R 65-74; D 129-144).
Economy/Labor:	Permanent tax cuts (R 35-3; D 5-56). Social Security financing (R 2-29; D 39-12).	Tax rebates (R 140-1; D 54-218). Common-site picketing (R 14-129; D 191-88). Youth differential for minimum wage (R 130-12; D 80-199).
Defense/Foreign Policy:	Warnke nomination (R 10-28; D 48-12). Terminate neutron bomb production (R 10-28; D 28-30). Korean policy (R 21-15; D 58-0). Cuban policy (R 5-28; D 49-9).	Defense spending increases (R 119-20; D 106-164). Cancel production of B-1 bomber (R 33-103; D 169-96). Foreign aid and human rights (R 48-89; D 225-37).

TABLE 5.5 Continued

Senate	House
Congressional Reforms: Prohibit limitations on outside income (R 24-13; D 11-49). Financial disclosure statutory requirements (R 23-5; D 51-0). Relax limitations on franking privilege (R 25-12; D 21-35). Tighten limits on committee and subcommittee chairmanships (R 21-13; D 26-29). Public financing of congressional races—cloture vote (R 4-33; D 48-13).	Deletion of ethics code provision to increase office allowances, ban unofficial office accounts (R 126-15; D 61-220). Consideration of Commission on Administrative Review reform proposals (R 0-139; D 160-113).
Other: Reject waterway user fees (R 16-21; D 28-30). Lower wheat price supports (R 18-20; D 28-30). Restrict federal funding of abortions (R 17-15; D 45-12).	Maintain traditional formula for allocating community development funds (R 45-89; D 104-172). Limits on legal services corporation attorneys (R 106-16; D 72-182). Prohibit federal funding of abortions (R 98-21; D 103-34). Oil cargo preference (R 17-125; D 148-132).

Source: *Congressional Quarterly Almanac*, Vol. 33, 95th Congress, 1st Session (Washington, D.C.: Congressional Quarterly, Inc., 1977), pp. 1B-14B.

On two environmental issues, the House not only rejected the administration's recommendations but also displayed bipartisan majorities. By a margin of 255-139, the House voted to delay and to relax automobile emissions standards. It also rejected, by 194-218, attempts to delete funding for water resources projects. In both cases, a majority of Democrats was joined by a majority of Republicans, although there was a deep split among Democrats on both issues and among Republicans on the water projects vote.

Economy and Labor. There were several significant votes on economic policy in 1977. Both the House and Senate rejected permanent tax cuts sponsored by congressional Republicans. In the House, a move to substitute tax cuts for the administration's $50 tax rebate plan lost by 194-218, with the parties taking opposing positions. When the President later withdrew the rebate plan, Senate Republicans proposed major, permanent tax reductions. This was defeated on a strict party vote by 40-59.

Republicans in the Senate also moved to insure that future payroll taxes needed to support the Social Security system would conform to the traditional formula of equal payments by employers and employees. The Democratic majority was committed to shifting a greater share to the employer, but there were sufficient defections on this vote to produce a tie. The Republican proposal was then killed when Vice President Mondale cast the deciding vote.

Some of the most intensive lobbying efforts of the year surrounded two labor votes in the House. Since 1951, labor had sought legislative sanction for common-site picketing in the construction industry. (Common-site picketing would allow unions protesting against a single contractor to picket and attempt to shut down an entire site.) The Ninety-fourth Congress had passed such legislation, but it had been vetoed by President Ford. When President Carter announced that he would sign a similar bill, labor's success seemed assured. Business organizations mounted a drive to defeat the proposal, however, and the House finally voted against common-site picketing by 205-217. The party majorities were opposed, but numerous Democrats joined the almost-unanimous Republican bloc to defeat the measure. Later in the year, the House again divided sharply on a labor-related issue. A proposal to create a lower minimum wage for young workers was attacked by organized labor, which had also pushed for an increase in the minimum wage. This time the House supported labor's position, but by only one vote—210-211. Once again, the party majorities opposed each other, but there were enough Democratic defectors to keep the issue in doubt until the final vote.

Defense/Foreign Policy. Party splits also occurred on defense and foreign policy issues. President Carter's nomination of Paul C. Warnke to head the U.S. delegation to the Strategic Arms Limitation (SALT) talks aroused considerable negative reaction from senators who believed that Warnke would not take a sufficiently "hard line" during the negotiations. Indeed, the Senate Armed Services Committee voted to reject the nomination, but the full Senate approved it by a vote of 58-40, with the vote following party lines. However, this controversy suggested that ratification of any SALT treaty would not be easy.

The Senate's rejection of an attempt to terminate production of the neutron bomb underscored the divisions over defense policy. While most Republican senators opposed termination, Senate Democrats split almost evenly. On votes relating to U.S. policy initiatives in Korea and Cuba, the Democrats were able to achieve a high degree of unity, but only because the resolutions at issue were watered-down versions of earlier attempts to endorse administration policy. The president's troop withdrawal plan for Korea was endorsed by the Senate Foreign Relations Committee through a provision in the State Department authorization bill. When controversy threatened this endorsement, the Senate leadership sponsored a substitute provision that contained neutral language on the troop withdrawal plan and noted that U.S. policy should be arrived at by joint decision of the president and Congress. While the substitute passed overwhelmingly, a minority of Republicans who did not favor the troop withdrawal plan voted against it. A similar problem arose as negotiations with Cuba concerning diplomatic recognition and the U.S. trade embargo commenced. While some senators wished to give the administration maximum leeway in conducting these negotiations, others supported proposals to tie the negotiations to compensation for expropriated U.S. property in Cuba and to withdrawal of Cuban troops from Africa. The Senate leadership again intervened with a neutral provision, although this time the Republicans refused to accept the compromise.

House votes reflected a blurring of party lines on defense and foreign policy issues. An amendment to increase the defense-spending target in the House Budget Committee's budget resolution passed the House by 225-185, with over 100 Democrats joining the overwhelming majority of Republicans. When the administration canceled production of the B-1 bomber, the House, which had repeatedly backed the B-1 program, narrowly assented to this move by a vote of 202-199. This time 33 Republicans crossed party lines to support the president while 96 Democrats joined the Republican majority in opposing him. When the House voted to prohibit the use of U.S. funds by international banks to aid certain countries accused of human rights violations, the Carter administration attempted to delete the provision. Finally, a compromise was worked out that directed U.S. officials within the international banks to vote against such assistance; this language proved acceptable to most Democrats, although a majority of Republicans pressed for a stronger restriction.

Congressional Reforms. The Senate and House dealt at great length with ethics codes and other political "reform" legislation during 1977. As Table 5.5 indicates, Senate Democrats and Republicans were opposed on most of the key votes, although there was usually some crossing of party lines. There was strong bipartisan agreement on statutory financial disclosure requirements, but there was a very sharp split on public financing of congressional races. In this instance, the Republicans did not have enough votes to block passage of public financing legislation, but their filibuster was successful as 13 Democrats refused to vote cloture on the third and final attempt. On two other occasions—the proposal to remove limitations on outside income and the reduction of committee and subcommittee chairmanships that could be held by any one senator—the Republican majority swung behind measures sponsored by Democratic senators. On the second of these, there was a sufficient number of dissenting Democrats to form a successful coalition with the Republicans.

On the House side, the Republicans and Democrats differed also. A Republican attempt to eliminate increases in office allowances (as an incentive to ban unofficial office accounts used by many members) lost on a party vote. When a set of additional proposals relating to internal administration was offered under a rule barring amendments, Republicans voted unanimously against the rule and were joined by over 100 Democrats. Rejection of the special rule effectively killed the "reform" proposals.

Other Issues. Several other votes reflected the range of interparty differences and the variety of intraparty splits. In the Senate, for example, a bare majority in both parties banded together to defeat a measure to lower wheat price supports. Majorities on both sides of the aisle also supported the administration's imposition of waterway user fees to finance navigation improvements on inland waterways. On abortion, a slight majority of Republicans joined an overwhelming majority of Democrats in approving compromise restrictions on the federal funding of abortions.

A bipartisan majority in the House supported changes in funding formulas for community development funds. (The purpose of these changes was to provide additional assistance to cities in the Northeast and Midwest.) Another bipartisan majority emerged on a vote to outlaw federal funding of abortions. Republicans were unable to overcome the Democratic majority in the House when they sought to impose new limits on activities of legal services attorneys, but they won a major victory in defeating the Carter administration's oil cargo preference bill. On this latter vote, the Democrats split almost evenly, while the Republicans voted solidly against the legislation.

The legislative records of the congressional parties during 1977, then, were reasonably distinctive, if not always absolutely clear. The interparty differences varied from issue to issue. The degree of intraparty cohesion also fluctuated, although the Democrats usually had a more serious problem with defections than did the Republicans. And on some key votes, there was a bipartisan majority. What we find here reinforces Pomper's conclusions about party platforms. The majority party, if it also controls the White House, is able to deliver on many of its "promises." At the same time, the minority party also achieves a degree of success by joining on occasion with defectors from the majority party. Finally, some issues find the parties in agreement. The precise outlines of each congressional party's legislative record will no doubt change from year to year, but there is little question that there are substantial differences between these records.

ATTITUDINAL DIFFERENCES

Numerous studies have examined interparty differences by comparing the attitudes and policy preferences of activists and leaders within the Republican and Democratic parties. As one such study noted, "The party, in one sense, is what it believes—its attitudes and perspectives, at all echelons. And what the party leaders believe may certainly determine in large part the image it communicates to the public, and the success with which it mobilizes public support."[25] In general, the research on party elites indicates that they are ideologically distinctive. The attitudinal differences between Democrats and Republicans at the elite level tend to be more clearcut and consistent than at the level of the mass electorate. Leaders are not simply better informed and more involved; they are also likely "if liberal, to be more liberal, if conservative, to be more conservative."[26]

This suggests that, contrary to persistent critiques of the American party system, there are significant differences separating the parties and that these differences are primarily attributable to the parties' leadership strata. Despite the moderating tendencies of an electorally competitive two-party system, the party leaderships have managed to preserve relatively cohesive and stable ideological identities. Thus, "the observation that the two parties do not differ ideologically from one another may be due in large part to our failure to distinguish the party's organizational leaders from the party's electoral coalition."[27]

Even the party leaderships, however, are not ideological monoliths. There is a degree of ideological diversity within each party even at the elite level. Since interparty differences, as well as intraparty homogeneity, often vary among leadership levels or echelons within the party, it is helpful to examine specific elite groups in developing ideological "portraits" of the two parties.

Party Officials: National Convention Delegates. One leadership group that has received considerable attention consists of delegates to the Democratic and Republican national conventions. As one early study noted, conventions are an important context in which to examine party elites, since they are the "leading and most representative of the party organs, their delegates coming from every part of the United States and from every level of party and government activity."[28] Whether this assumption regarding representativeness still holds given the dramatic changes in delegate selection procedures is obviously questionable. Since delegates do choose the most visible and salient of all party nominees and do adopt the party

---

[25] Samuel J. Eldersveld, *Political Parties* (Chicago: Rand McNally, 1964), pp. 180-81.

[26] Jeane Kirkpatrick, *The New Presidential Elite* (New York: Russell Sage Foundation and The Twentieth Century Fund, 1976), p. 297.

[27] John W. Soule and James W. Clarke, "Issue Conflict and Consensus: A Comparative Study of Democratic and Republican Delegates to the 1968 National Conventions," *Journal of Politics,* 33 (February 1971), 89.

[28] Herbert McClosky, et al., "Issue Conflict and Consensus among Party Leaders and Followers," *American Political Science Review,* 54 (June 1960), 408.

platform, however, their ideological predispositions can have a substantial impact on party politics.

The first major study of convention delegates' issue preferences was conducted in the late 1950s.[29] In addition to comparing interparty differences between delegates to the 1956 Republican and Democratic conventions, this study also examined parallel differences between party identifiers in the electorate. The two dozen issues used to explore these differences were grouped into several broad categories—public ownership of resources, government regulation of the economy, equalitarianism and human welfare, tax policy, and foreign policy. Among the delegates, there were significant interparty differences on virtually all issues. Thus, the party leaderships were quite distinctive across all of these policy domains. The direction of these differences, moreover, conformed fairly closely to popular notions about the Democratic party's relative liberalism and the Republican party's relative conservatism.

The party electorates, however, were less clearly divided. On many issues, Democratic and Republican identifiers had similar attitudes. The interparty distinctions that did emerge were considerably smaller than, although they tended to parallel, the distinctions found among party leaders. A particularly interesting finding was that Republican leaders and followers differed from each other much more sharply than did Democratic leaders and followers. Democratic leaders were only slightly more liberal than their followers, while Republican leaders were substantially more conservative than their rank-and-file supporters. Indeed, over the broad range of issues that distinguished the party leaderships from each other, the Republican identifiers were closer to the Democratic leadership than to the leaders of their own party.

This study concluded that interparty differences at the leadership level were a "function not of chance but of systematic points of view."[30] There was little support for the "claim that the 'natural divisions' of the electorate are being smothered by party leaders. Not only do the leaders disagree more sharply than their respective followers, but the level of consensus among the electorate (with or without regard to party) is fairly high."[31]

More recent studies indicate that these conclusions are still accurate. In 1968, for example, there were substantial ideological distinctions between Democratic and Republican convention delegates.[32] Once again, Democrats were much more liberal than their Republican counterparts on most issues.[33] On domestic policy issues, 52 percent of the Democratic delegates and 11 percent of the Republicans

---

[29] Ibid., pp. 406-27.
[30] Ibid., p. 410.
[31] Ibid., p. 419.
[32] Soule and Clarke, "Issue and Conflict and Consensus," pp. 72-91.
[33] The only exception was Vietnam. This issue did not distinguish between the two parties. Ibid., p. 77.

could be categorized as liberal, while 58 percent of the Republicans and 21 percent of the Democrats could be categorized as conservative. Contrasts were less sharp on foreign policy issues, but interparty differences were still significant.[34] Moreover, these differences remained when variables such as education, income, religion, and region were taken into account.

In addition, there were Republican-Democratic differences in intraparty consensus (or homogeneity) and in the relationship between issue preferences and candidate preferences. The Democratic leadership, while predominantly liberal, was more fragmented and less homogeneous than the Republican leadership. This lack of consensus carried over into candidate nomination. Among Democratic delegates, the relationship between ideology and candidate preference was stronger than among Republicans. This had the effect of reinforcing ideological unity on the Republican side and sharpening intraparty conflicts among Democrats. As Soule and Clarke stated, "Republicans were better able to bury the ideological hatchet, so to speak, in nominating Richard Nixon."[35]

Interparty ideological differences were especially pronounced in 1972.[36] On a broad range of attitudinal measures—policy issues, attitudes toward groups, ideological self-classification—Republican and Democratic delegates took sharply contrasting positions (see Table 5.6). Moreover, the interparty differences between the party elites were in most instances considerably greater than those between Republican and Democratic party identifiers.

The Democratic convention in 1972 also reflected a serious intraparty split. McGovern delegates were much more liberal than delegates supporting other Democratic candidates. More important perhaps, their attitudes were dramatically different from those of the Democratic party's rank-and-file voters. As Table 5.7 shows, Republican delegates were much closer to their rank-and-file identifiers than McGovern delegates were to Democratic identifiers on almost all attitudinal measures. Indeed, Republican delegates and Democratic identifiers were more similar in their views than were McGovern delegates and Democratic identifiers. Thus, "1972 Democratic delegates were less representative of the views and values of voters than were delegates to the 'unreformed' Republican Convention, and the 'new' political type concentrated in the McGovern ranks were least representative of all."[37]

Which party's elite holds views that are fairly representative of its own identifiers as well as the broader electorate is obviously subject to change. In the 1950s, Republican delegates held views on a range of important issues that were much more conservative than those held by Republican identifiers. In 1972, the delegates who controlled the Democratic convention were extremely unrepresentative, in

[34] Ibid., pp. 76-79.
[35] Ibid., p. 91.
[36] Kirkpatrick, *The New Presidential Elite.*
[37] Ibid., p. 331.

TABLE 5.6 Attitudinal Differences between Party Elites and between Rank and File Identifiers, 1972[a]

	Republican vs. Democratic Identifiers	Republican vs. Democratic Delegates
Policy Issues:		
Welfare	18	95
Busing	21	117
Crime	14	100
Inflation	1	34
Abortion	10	18
Vietnam	1	113
Attitudes toward Groups:		
Welfare recipients	19	65
Political demonstrators	16	95
Police	5	34
Military	8	81
Blacks	17	8
Conservatives	42	105
Liberals	39	119
Union leaders	41	67
Business interests	34	80
Ideological Self-Classification:		
Liberal/Conservative	52	118

[a]The differences reported here are scores based on responses to issue and ideological self-classification scales and, for attitudes toward groups, on "feeling thermometers." The midpoint on a scale or thermometer is considered neutral, while remaining points are categorized as liberal/conservative or favorable/unfavorable. Thus, the difference score for party identifiers on the welfare policy scale, for example, is the percentage difference between Republicans and Democrats at the liberal end of the scale added to the corresponding percentage difference at the conservative end of the scale. The possible range for scores is 0 to 200.

Source: Adapted from Jeane Kirkpatrick, *The New Presidential Elite* (New York: Russell Sage Foundation and The Twentieth Century Fund, 1976), p. 318.

terms of ideology, of their party's electorate. Given the discrepancies between mass and elite opinion that have been repeatedly documented, these intraparty differences are not completely unexpected. There are problems, however, when a party elite is either unaware of these differences or refuses to be responsive to the views of the electorate in nominating candidates or adopting a platform. If the party elite is willing to compromise, the party's electoral prospects can be protected. The successful nominations of Eisenhower in 1952 and 1956, for example, suggest that Republican delegates were willing to subordinate their individual ideological preferences in the hope of expanding the party's popular appeal. The nominations of Goldwater by the Republicans in 1964 or McGovern by the Democrats in 1972, however, illustrate the ascendancy of ideological considerations among convention delegates. Either through ignorance or design, Goldwater dele-

TABLE 5.7 Attitudinal Differences between Party Elites and Rank and File Identifiers, 1972[a]

	McGovern Delegates vs. Democratic Identifiers	Republican Delegates vs. Republican Identifiers	Republican Delegates vs. Democratic Identifiers
Policy Issues:			
Welfare	110	1	19
Busing	147	12	9
Crime	107	7	21
Inflation	21	19	20
Abortion	89	40	50
Vietnam	109	35	34
Attitudes toward Groups:			
Welfare recipients	76	18	1
Political demonstrators	123	11	5
Police	33	13	18
Military	97	21	29
Blacks	34	43	26
Conservatives	89	1	41
Liberals	75	34	73
Union leaders	10	11	52
Business interests	57	11	45
Ideological Self-Classification:			
Liberal/Conservative	83	7	59

[a]The differences reported here are scores based on responses to issue and ideological self-classification scales and, for attitudes toward groups, on "feeling thermometers." The midpoint on a scale or thermometer is considered neutral, while remaining points are categorized as liberal/conservative or favorable/unfavorable. Thus, the difference score for party identifiers on the welfare policy scale, for example, is the percentage difference between Republicans and Democrats at the liberal end of the scale added to the corresponding percentage difference at the conservative end of the scale. The possible range for scores is 0 to 200.

Source: Adapted from Jeane Kirkpartrick, *The New Presidential Elite* (New York: Russell Sage Foundation and The Twentieth Century Fund, 1976), pp. 312, 319.

gates and McGovern delegates supported ideological candidacies that had little correspondence to the views of the electorate.

Interparty differences between convention delegates, as well as intraparty conflicts, are an important determinant of the ideological content of presidential politics. There is clear evidence that Republican and Democratic elites at this level are much more ideologically distinctive than are their respective party electorates. If the choices these elites finally present to the voters are moderate or ambiguous, the reason would appear to be that elites are appealing to an electorate whose views and values are similarly moderate and ambiguous.

Party Officials: State and Local Parties. Ideological differences between Republican and Democratic party activists at a variety of organizational levels have been investigated in a number of locales.[38] Most studies have indicated that party activists are differentiated in terms of ideology, with Democratic activists tending to be more liberal than Republican activists at the same organizational level and in the same locale. These differences also tend to be greater than those between the party electorates.

Among party activists in the Wayne County (Detroit) party organizations, for example, Eldersveld found "major ideological differences between the two parties' leadership structures, at all leadership levels."[39] The degree of interparty distinctiveness did vary slightly by organizational level, with the differences greatest between upper-echelon Republican and Democratic officials. Thus, the top Republican leaders were the most conservative group, while their Democratic counterparts were the most liberal group. Despite intraparty divisions on some issues that reduced ideological congruity within each party, Eldersveld concluded that the "party structure may be characterized as a group in ideological terms—the Republican structure predominantly conservative, the Democratic structure strongly liberal."[40]

Among voters, however, interparty divisions were quite limited. Many party identifiers—even those who reported extensive contacts by their respective party organizations—were uncertain about their party's ideological position.[41] Relatively few voters perceived party differences in issue terms.[42] And on specific issues, the attitudes of Republican and Democratic party identifiers were fairly similar.

Other, more limited studies have provided additional information about the ideological distinctiveness of party organizational elites. Even at the local level, the party activist is likely to share certain policy attitudes with other members of his party, to perceive issue differences between the parties, and to take policy and issue concerns into account when deciding to enter or to continue party work.[43]

Those who are active in the party organizations can therefore be contrasted with the mass electorate along several dimensions. The party activists tend to be better informed about policy issues. Their attitudes are more likely to be structured

---

[38] See Eldersveld, *Political Parties,* chap. 8; M. Margaret Conway and Frank B. Feigert, "Motivation, Incentive Systems, and the Political Party Organization," *American Political Science Review,* 62 (December 1968), 1169-83; Thomas A. Flinn and Frederick M. Wirt, "Local Party Leaders: Groups of Like Minded Men," *Midwest Journal of Political Science,* 9 (February 1965), 77-98; Robert S. Hirschfield, Bert E. Swanson, and Blanche D. Blank, "A Profile of Political Activists in Manhattan," *Western Political Quarterly,* 15 (September 1962), 489-506; Dennis S. Ippolito, "Political Perspectives of Suburban Party Leaders," *Social Science Quarterly,* 49 (March 1969), 800-815.

[39] Eldersveld, *Political Parties,* p. 218.

[40] Ibid., p. 529.

[41] Ibid., p. 490.

[42] Ibid., p. 196.

[43] Ippolito, "Political Perspectives of Surburban Party Leaders."

along a liberal-conservative continuum. Activists within one party are likely to differ, as a group, from activists in the opposite party to a much greater degree than the party electorates differ from each other.

This does not mean that we find wildly clashing ideologies at the elite level. There are many important issues that do not divide activists along party lines nor separate the activists from the party rank-and-file.[44] As a consequence, the major parties in the United States reflect high levels of consensus in their values and appeals. But there are also significant areas of interparty conflict that reflect the beliefs of competing party elites.

Party Candidates. The maintenance and articulation of reasonably coherent partisan ideologies also depends, of course, upon the competing party candidates for public office. Their contact with the electorate is more direct than that of the party organization. Moreover, candidates ordinarily have considerable discretion over the extent to which campaigns are issue-based and the degree to which these issues are debated within a partisan context.[45] While there are very few studies that compare large aggregates of party candidates—as opposed to case studies of particular races—there is limited evidence that party candidates do present the voters with ideologically meaningful choices.

Congressional candidates, for example, have been found to differ significantly, in the aggregate, by party. Fishel's study of approximately 300 congressional challengers in the 1964 election determined that "these party candidates constitute groups in ideological terms, although these 'communities of co-believers' are neither monolithic entitites nor ideological oligarchies."[46] When asked to classify themselves in terms of ideological orientation, a majority of Democratic challengers (50 percent) identified themselves as liberals while a majority of Republicans (53 percent) chose the conservative designation. (Only 8 percent of the Republicans identified themselves as liberals, while 1 percent of the Democrats picked the conservative label.) As Table 5.8 indicates, these self-identifications were strongly related to issue preferences. Democratic liberals and Republican conservatives took opposite sides when responding to a series of domestic policy issues.

There were also significant contrasts on most issues between moderates in the two parties. Slightly over one-third of the Democrats and Republicans classified their ideological orientation as "middle of the road." On the federal government's role with respect to minority and Negro rights, roughly one-fourth of the Democratic and Republican moderates agreed that more federal action was necessary (see Table 5.9). The remaining policy issues, however, reflected a clear split be-

---

[44] See Sidney Verba and Norman H. Nie, *Participation in America* (New York: Harper & Row, 1972), chap. 15.

[45] Candidates' perceptions of the relative importance of party, issues, and personal characteristics to voters are examined in John W. Kingdon, *Candidates for Office: Beliefs and Strategies* (New York: Random House, 1966).

[46] Jeff Fishel, "Party, Ideology, and the Congressional Challenger," *American Political Science Review,* 63 (December 1969), 1221.

TABLE 5.8 Issue Preferences of Liberal Democratic and Conservative Republican Congressional Challengers, 1964[a]

Percentages Responding that Federal Government Should "Do More"

Policy Issue:	Democratic Liberals	Republican Conservatives
Minority and Negro rights	57	19
Assist public education	79	8
Medical care for elderly	96	8
Programs to help poor	87	12
Programs to regulate labor unions	9	60
N =	(83)	(83)

[a] Ideological classification is based on self-identification. The question used was: "Next, we would like some idea about how you feel on certain policy issues being discussed around the country this year. On most issues, would you consider yourself liberal, middle of the road, conservative, or what?"

Source: Adapted from Jeff Fishel, "Party, Ideology, and the Congressional Challenger," *American Political Science Review*, 63 (December 1969), 1220.

TABLE 5.9 Issue Preferences of Moderate Democratic and Moderate Republican Congressional Challengers, 1964[a]

Percentages Responding that Federal Government Should "Do More"

Policy Issues:	Democratic Moderates	Republican Moderates
Minority and Negro rights	27	26
Assist public education	73	19
Medical care for elderly	73	28
Programs to help poor	60	19
Programs to regulate labor unions	12	56
N =	(57)	(56)

[a] Ideological classification is based on self-identification. The question used was: "Next, we would like some idea about how you feel on certain policy issues being discussed around the country this year. On most issues, would you consider yourself liberal, middle of the road, conservative, or what?"

Source: Adapted from Jeff Fishel, "Party, Ideology, and the Congressional Challenger," *American Political Science Review*, 63 (December 1969), 1220.

tween the party groups. The Democratic moderates were less supportive of conventional liberal positions than were Democratic liberals. Similarly, Republican moderates were less supportive of conventional conservative positions than were Republican conservatives. On most issues, the contrasts between moderates in the two parties were considerably greater than these intraparty differences.

A related study compared the attitudes of all U.S. House candidates in the

1966 election, incumbents as well as nonincumbents, using questions on foreign policy, civil rights, and domestic welfare issues.[47] The study focused on differences between competing candidates in the same district, since this choice constitutes a crucial test of effective ideological distinctions between the parties. It was found that "the Democratic candidates were almost invariably more liberal than their intradistrict Republican competitors."[48] Indeed, on an overall liberalism-conservatism scale based on responses to specific policy issues, only 19 Republicans were more liberal than their Democratic opponents.[49]

This finding was underscored by analyzing the ideological composition of several "hypothetical Congresses"—that is, the lineups in the House that would have occurred given different electoral outcomes in contested congressional districts. Table 5.10 shows the ideological makeup of the Congress that was elected and contrasts this with hypothetical Congresses. (The "most Democratic" Congress, for example, would simply include all Democratic candidates plus those Republicans who ran unopposed.) The hypothetical Democratic and liberal Congresses are almost identical in terms of ideological composition, as are the hypothetical Republican and conservative Congresses. The Democratic and Republican Congresses differed dramatically from each other (and, to a lesser extent, from the actual Congress) in ideological composition. The electorate was thus presented with substantively significant choices in this election, and it could have altered the ideological balance of power in Congress by focusing on the party label of candidates. According to Sullivan and O'Connor, "If our findings may be generalized to other elections, party may be said to provide a valid cue for the policy-oriented voter who does not have a thorough awareness of the issues or the policy positions of the candidates."[50] The party system, in sum, provides ordered choices on issue positions.

Party Officeholders. Finally, it is necessary to examine whether elected officials who have run under the party labels maintain relevant interparty differences. Does it make any difference that one party rather than the other gains a majority of seats in a state legislature or in Congress? Does it matter whether a Democrat or a Republican occupies the White House? Are the American parties capable of enacting their respective programs if the electorate provides them with control of government?

It is apparent, of course, that the American parties are not the programmatic, disciplined governing bodies that the admirers of European parliamentary parties

---

[47] John L. Sullivan and Robert E. O'Connor, "Electoral Choice and Popular Control of Public Policy: The Case of the 1966 House Elections," *American Political Science Review,* 66 (December 1972), 1256-68.

[48] Ibid., p. 1264.

[49] Ibid.

[50] Ibid.

TABLE 5.10 Ideological Composition, 90th Congress and Hypothetical Congress, Domestic Issue Scale

	Actual Congress Winners	Hypothetical Congress			
		Most[a] Democratic	Most[b] Republican	Most[c] Liberal	Most[d] Conservative
Liberal and moderate-liberal	160	290	32	290	32
Moderate	43	64	64	67	61
Conservative and moderate-conservative	232	81	339	78	342
	435	435	435	435	435

[a], [b]The "most Democratic" Congress includes all Democratic candidates plus Republicans who ran without opposition. The "most Republican" includes all Republicans plus Democrats who ran without opposition.

[c], [d]The "most liberal" and "most conservative" Congresses are composed of candidates having the lower or higher score, respectively, in each district on the domestic issue scale plus those candidates running unopposed.

Source: Adapted from John L. Sullivan and Robert E. O'Connor, "Electoral Choice and Popular Control of Public Policy: The Case of the 1966 House Elections," *American Political Science Review*, 66 (December 1972), 1260.

TABLE 5.11 Interest Group Ratings of U.S. Senators, 1976 (94th Congress, 2d Session)

	Average Support Scores— Liberal Interest Groups			Average Support Scores— Conservative Interest Groups	
	ADA	COPE	NFU	CCUS	ACA
Democratic	54%	74%	80%	16%	23%
Republican	26	32	43	57	63
Number of Issues	(20)	(20)	(12)	(9)	(27)

Note: ADA scores are the only ones that are lowered by failure to vote on an issue. The remaining groups calculate their scores based on actual votes (ACA), votes or pairs (COPE), or votes, pairs, or announcements in accordance with their positions (NFU and CCUS).

would like them to be. Compared to the Labor or Conservative parties in Britain, for example, the legislative parties in Congress are not very cohesive. As we indicated earlier in this chapter, some issues divide Congress along partisan lines, others create bipartisan majorities, and certain others fragment both parties. The outcome of a number of very important legislative issues, however, was clearly determined by the existing party balance in Congress.

There is, in fact, a very large body of literature demonstrating quite clearly that party is ultimately the most important determinant in legislative decision making. Party also influences, if less directly, executive and even judicial decision making. While the influence of the "party in government" will be covered in detail in chapter 7, some attention to liberal-conservative differences between Democratic and Republican officeholders might be helpful at this point.

A useful, if limited, method of assessing these differences compares interest group ratings of members of Congress. In recent years, liberal interest groups such as the ADA (Americans for Democratic Action), COPE (AFL-CIO Committee on Political Education), and the NFU (National Farmers Union), along with conservative organizations such as the CCUS (Chamber of Commerce of the United States) and ACA (Americans for Constitutional Action) have assigned ratings or scores to individual senators and representatives. These ratings are based on a legislator's support for each group's position on what it considers to be major issues. Since only floor votes are counted, these scores are only a partial measure of a member's performance, but they do provide a general indication of liberalism-conservatism across a broad range of issues. The ADA and ACA, for example, generally consider a mix of legislation—economic, defense, environmental—in compiling their scores. COPE usually focuses on votes affecting economic policy, job programs, and housing and energy legislation. The National Farmers Union is especially concerned with legislation affecting the small farmer, while the Chamber of Commerce tends to concentrate on economic policy and business-related issues.

Table 5.11 shows the average scores given by each interest group to Democratic and Republican senators during 1976. Not surprisingly, the results conform to our previous findings concerning party elites. While neither party group is ideologically homogeneous, the interparty differences are substantial. Even with southern Democrats included, the average support scores of Democratic senators indicate they are, as a group, much more liberal than Republicans. When ratings of liberal interest groups are used, average Democratic support scores are roughly twice as high as average Republican scores. For the conservative interest groups' positions, the average support scores among Republicans are approximately three times higher than Democratic scores.

Table 5.12 provides a further indication of the impact of party on ideology. In this instance, support scores of senators from the same state have been compared. When senators from the same state are of the same party, the average differences in support are fairly small, ranging from 14 percent (using CCUS and COPE ratings) to 23 percent (using ADA ratings). When they are from different

TABLE 5.12 Differences in Interest Group Ratings between U.S. Senators from the Same State, 1976

	colspan="3"	Average Differences in Support Scores—Liberal Interest Groups		Average Differences in Support Scores—Conservative Interest Groups
	ADA	COPE	NFU	CCUS	ACA
Senators from same state, same party	23%	16%	14%	14%	16%
Senators from same state, different parties	32%	44%	39%	49%	47%

parties, however, the disparities in support scores are considerably greater, ranging from 32 percent (using ADA ratings) to 49 percent (using CCUS ratings).

These interparty differences among officeholders are substantial. Even though there are some liberal Republicans and some conservative Democrats, the "average" Democrat is much more liberal than his Republican counterpart. For those who would prefer disciplined, responsible parties, these "substantial" differences may be inadequate. Yet what we have found elsewhere in the party system, particularly among the electorate, suggests that there are constraints on the ideological content of party politics. If the gap between mass opinion and elite behavior becomes too great, the parties risk electoral defeat, and this is a sanction that applies with special force to the party in government.

The "Issue Activists." Throughout this chapter, our emphasis has been on "official" party elites—that is, those who hold formal positions in the party organizations or in government. We have found fairly consistent ideological distinctions at the elite level, and the available comparisons indicate that these distinctions are typically greater than those characterizing the party electorates. There is, however, a portion of the electorate that does appear to be sharply differentiated ideologically, and its impact on the parties is probably disproportionately great relative to its size.

Ladd and Hadley, for example, report that increasing polarization has occurred between college-educated Democrats and Republicans.[51] They argue that formal education and ideological thinking go hand in hand—"higher education correlates significantly with an ability and inclination to evaluate politics in terms of systematic issue concerns—or, to put it differently, to view politics ideologically."[52] Comparing college-educated Democrats and Republicans to each other and to their respective party electorates, Ladd and Hadley found a consistent pattern from the 1940s through the early 1960s. The college-educated within each party were more conservative than their respective party rank-and-files on economic matters but more liberal on civil rights and civil liberties issues and more internationalist with respect to foreign policy matters. The differences between college-educated Democrats and Republicans on these issues, however, were similar to those between the party electorates.

Since the mid-1960s, however, two significant trends have developed. First, there has been a marked increase in attitudinal differences between college-educated Republicans and Democrats, particularly when compared to the corresponding differences between their respective party electorates. Second, these college-educated groups, or cohorts, have become more polarized, with college-educated Democrats becoming much more liberal than Democrats generally and college-educated Republicans becoming more conservative than the Republican rank-and-file. Indeed, Ladd and Hadley have found that "in many cases they [the college-

---

[51] Everett Carll Ladd, Jr. and Charles D. Hadley, *Transformations of the American Party System,* 2nd ed. (New York: W. W. Norton & Company, 1978), pp. 349-59.

[52] Ibid., p. 349.

educated cohorts] occupy opposite sides of a question where majorities of both Republican and Democratic supporters at large are on the same side."[53] These cases include not only economic and social welfare legislation but also civil rights and civil liberties issues.

A more focused examination of issue differences within the party electorates is possible when relatively inactive voters are distinguished from those who are more active in politics.[54] While the latter are not party elites in the sense of holding formal party positions or elected public office, they do represent an important stratum within the party. The ordinary voter's participation in politics rarely goes beyond the act of voting. The "activists," however, are more involved in campaign politics. They are more likely than the average citizen to contribute money and time during elections, to attend party caucuses, and to take part in primary campaigns and vote in primary elections. In terms of numbers, the activists are a small minority within each party, but as a result of their participation and involvement, their influence on party elites is likely to be disproportionately great. It is therefore important to contrast their attitudes with those of the ordinary party supporters.

Table 5.13 shows the liberal-conservative balances within each party. Among Democrats, the changes have been dramatic. In 1956, there was little difference in issue preferences among Democrats. The proportion of liberals among Democratic activists (20 percent) was only slightly higher than the proportion of conservatives (17 percent). The corresponding proportions among all Democrats were 15 percent (liberal) and 10 percent (conservative). Since 1960, however, the proportion of Democratic activists at the liberal extreme has increased at a much faster rate than it has among Democratic identifiers. There has been a widening split between liberal and conservative Democratic activists and between liberal activists and Democratic identifiers. The Democratic activist group has become much more liberal than the Democratic electorate. Moreover, the proportion of conservatives among Democratic identifiers has actually increased (from 10 percent in 1956 to 17 percent in 1972). While this is slightly below the increase in the proportion of liberal identifiers, the liberal-conservative balance within the electorate has been maintained. At the activist level, however, no such balance exists.

Among Republicans, activists are more conservative than party supporters generally, but the differences between them have narrowed. In 1956, the proportion of conservative activists was 16 percentage points higher than the proportion of conservative identifiers. By 1972, this difference had almost been halved. In addition, the conservative-liberal balance among identifiers and among activists in 1972 was roughly the same as in 1956.

The Democratic and Republican activists are more sharply differentiated from each other than are their respective party's supporters. Moreover, neither

---

[53] Ibid., pp. 353-54.

[54] Norman H. Nie, Sidney Verba, and John R. Petrocik, *The Changing American Voter* (Cambridge, Mass.: Harvard University Press, 1976), pp. 201-205.

TABLE 5.13 Proportions of Democratic and Republican Activists and Identifiers at "Most Liberal" and "Most Conservative" Ends of Issue Scales, 1956-1972

	Republican Activists[a]		All Republicans	
	Prop. Liberal	Prop. Conservative	Prop. Liberal	Prop. Conservative
1956	8%	34%	9%	18%
1960	10	28	8	17
1964	5	54	7	34
1968	5	34	8	27
1972	8	32	11	23
Change	0%	−2%	+2%	+5%

	Democratic Activists[b]		All Democrats	
	Prop. Liberal	Prop. Conservative	Prop. Liberal	Prop. Conservative
1956	20%	17%	15%	10%
1960	21	14	15	13
1964	35	15	28	13
1968	45	12	33	13
1972	43	13	26	17
Change	+23%	−4%	+11%	+7%

[a, b] Defined as persons who engage in two or more of the six campaign activities about which the Survey Research Center asks. These include displaying campaign buttons or stickers; attending political meetings or rallies; belonging to a political club or organization; working for parties or candidates; giving money, buying tickets, or otherwise helping candidates; and talking to people about how they should vote.

Source: Adapted from Norman H. Nie, Sidney Verba, and John R. Petrocik, *The Changing American Voter* (Cambridge, Mass.: Harvard University Press, 1976), p. 203.

group is representative of its party's identifiers in terms of political attitudes, although Democratic activists have replaced their Republican counterparts as the less representative group. As we suggested earlier, because activists do participate more frequently and extensively than ordinary citizens, they are likely to have a disproportionately high level of influence on electoral politics. Recent moves to encourage greater public participation in party affairs, especially in presidential nominating processes, heighten the potential for activist influence.

If political elites wish to be sensitive to mass opinion, they must be cautious in responding to issue activists. As a major study of participation has pointed out, "The political leader who thought he was learning about the attitudes of the public by observing the preferences of those activists around him, or the preferences of the citizens who come forward to contact him, or of the citizens who write letters to the press would be receiving an inaccurate impression of the population as a whole."[55]

Of course, party elites are also more ideologically distinctive than party supporters and are consequently unrepresentative of the citizenry parties. But the elites operate within traditions and constraints that encourage them to sacrifice their personal ideological predispositions in the interest of electoral success. Issue activists lack any accountability to the electorate at large, since electoral failure does not affect them directly as it does the party organization or the party in government.

If issue activists have become a persistent feature of party politics, and there is every indication that they have, the parties face serious internal conflicts and electoral problems. The party linkage provides a mechanism for aggregating mass preferences and converting them into electoral decisions. In order for this linkage to operate, the parties must be responsive to the electorate. The American electorate is not devoid of ideology, but it is not sharply divided along ideological lines. The tendencies are moderate and centrist. Segments of the electorate, however, are active and ideological. In responding to these issue activists, the parties run the risk of nominating candidates and taking issue positions that rupture rather than strengthen the ties between them and the mass of their supporters.

SUMMARY

American parties have been repeatedly criticized for not providing the voters with "real choices." According to this critique, party candidates do not present clear and distinctive policy positions during elections. Once elected, a party's officeholders are unable to act cohesively to implement a coherent party program. The party out of power fails to articulate programmatic alternatives that the electorate can assess. Because the parties are not "responsible" electing and governing bodies,

---

[55] Verba and Nie, *Participation in America*, p. 284.

voters are unable to perceive substantial differences between the Republican and Democratic parties.

Comparisons of Democratic and Republican party elites lend very little support to these charges, however. Official policy differences between the parties—as expressed in platforms, presidential programs, and congressional legislative records—are substantial and stable in many instances. The parties are not sharply divided from each other on all issues, nor is internal agreement within each party consistent from one issue to the next. Official policy differences do not reflect highly ideological parties of the left and the right, but they *do* reflect parties that disagree on many important and specific issues that characterize American politics. The differences are not trivial, and information on them is available to voters who pay even limited attention to what the parties say and do.

There are also reasonably sharp attitudinal differences between party elites. Democratic party officials, party candidates, and officeholders are different from their Republican counterparts in their policy preferences and broad political attitudes. The party elites do not constitute ideological monoliths. They do have different ideological centers of gravity, with Democratic elites predominantly liberal and Republican elites predominantly conservative.

The differences between the party elites, moreover, are substantially greater than those between their respective party electorates. If the ideological content of American politics is normally muted, this appears to reflect the party system's accommodation to its electorate. The party elites often choose compromise and consensus appeals in order to win elections. A potential difficulty in this traditional accommodationist role has been the increasing proportion of issue activists in the electorate. While these groups are still a small minority, they are more influential then their numbers indicate, and they are as ideologically distinctive as the party elites. This presents the danger that party elites will mistakenly assume that these issue activists are representative of the general electorate and will consequently articulate ideological appeals that will be unacceptable to most voters.

six

The Party in Politics: Nominations and Elections

The political party linkage between the public and government is directly tied to the nomination-election process. The aggregating function that the party performs for the mass electorate—in which various interests are brought together behind a limited number of choices for political leadership positions—depends upon the party's ability to recruit and nominate candidates for public office who are reasonably well committeed to its policies and values and who are also sufficiently appealing to the electorate to be competitive.

Party control of nominations is therefore crucial if the aggregating function is to be performed effectively. In the interests of winning elections and thereby maintaining the strength and vitality of the party, organizational officials must take into account a candidate's ability to bring together the diverse interests within the party. In addition, since the party's interests are long-term, candidates must be chosen who can govern effectively once elected. This does not guarantee, of course, that strong candidates will always be chosen. It does mean that the electorate can exercise very strong sanctions against the party if its candidates are unappealing or incompetent.

If the party cannot control nominations, the potential for accountability through elections is considerably reduced. The electorate can still impose sanctions against individual candidates or incumbents, but it will not have the opportunity to respond to the relatively stable and ordered long-term choices that the party provides. The party organization's role as recruiter and nominator of candidates thus provides an opportunity for coherence in electorate decision making that is otherwise very difficult to achieve.

In most democracies, the nomination-election process is considered the direct responsibility of the leadership within the party organization. These leaders control the choice of party candidates and exercise considerable influence on the conduct of election campaigns. The American party system is dramatically different. As a matter of law, nominations for Congress as well as for most state and local offices are, in virtually all the states, open to mass participation through the peculiarly American device of the direct primary. Presidential nominations, while still made formally by party conventions, have been increasingly determined by mass participation in delegate selection procedures. As a result of technological change and, to a lesser extent, legal regulation, the parties have also lost much of their control over the conduct of election campaigns.

The influence of the American parties on electoral politics has been seriously undermined. The resourceful candidate for public office can create a personal organization, raise funds independently, hire professional pollsters and campaign consultants, and appeal directly to the electorate through television or other media. Able to gain nomination and election "outside" the party, such a candidate is immune from organizational entreaties or discipline, even after election. And this, of course, considerably weakens the party in government.

American electoral politics has been radically influenced by attempts at democratization. In many instances, democratic "reforms" have been aimed at weakening party leadership and strengthening direct linkages between the mass public and the political leadership. Whether these direct linkages can replace parties as effective organizers of public opinion and aggregates of mass interests is one of the central issues in contemporary party politics.

NOMINATING PRACTICES: AN OVERVIEW

There continues to be some variety among the states in terms of nominating practices and procedures, although the direct primary is clearly the most prevalent method for nominating candidates for Congress, for state offices, and for many positions at the local level. Unlike democratic party systems elsewhere, the American parties are subject to substantial legal regulation that limits each party's authority over how candidates are to be nominated and who will be allowed to participate in making nominating decisions. A review of the evolution of nominating practices at the state and national levels will provide an insight into the forces that have shaped contemporary nominating activities.

The Caucus and the Convention

During the colonial period, parties had not yet taken organizational shape, and nominating procedures were usually informal. Outside the New England colonies, members of the lower houses of the colonial legislature were typically the only directly elected officials. There were no formal nominating procedures for these offices. Office seekers simply announced their candidacies, presumably after consultation with other local notables. Since the number of elective offices was small, the franchise limited, and deference to a ruling class well established, self-announcement for legislative candidacies continued throughout this period.[1]

In the New England colonies, however, the original charters usually required the election of governors and both houses of the legislatures. The method of nomination was also specified in some instances. Candidates for the upper house, for example, were usually designated by the voters in each town. The legislature would then review the list of nominees, adding or subtracting names, before the candidates were presented to all of the voters.[2] In addition, the town meeting form of local government in the New England colonies required the election of numerous local officials. While candidates for these offices were often nominated in open town meetings or county meetings, small groups of leaders frequently met in advance for the purpose of making initial selections. John Adams' diary describes a February 1763 meeting of a Boston leadership group or "caucus" that evokes the archetypal "smoke-filled room":

> Boston—February—This day learned that the Caucus Club meets at certain times in the garret of Tom Dawes, the adjutant of the Boston Regulars. He has a large house, and he has a movable partition in his garret which he takes down, and the whole club meets in one room. There they smoke tobacco till you cannot see from one end of the garret to the other. There they drink flip, I suppose, and there they choose a moderator, who puts questions to the vote regularly; *and selectmen, assessors, collectors, wardens, firewards, and representatives are regularly chosen before they are chosen in the town.*[3]

State Legislative Caucus. The state and national constitutions adopted after the Revolution soon led to the establishment of party nominations. While legislative candidacies were still handled by personal announcements, more formal procedures were required to deal with statewide candidacies, such as governor and lieutenant governor, and later with national candidates for president and vice president. In order to provide prospective candidates with some indication of potential support by the party, consultation with party leaders was necessary. Calling a statewide or national meeting for this purpose, however, was impractical given the rigors and hazards of travel.

In the absence of a general party conference, the legislative parties assumed the responsibility for nominating statewide candidates. Members of the same party in both houses of the state legislature would meet, make their selections, and announce them to the voters by means of a proclamation which they signed in-

---

[1] M. Ostrogorski, *Democracy and the Party System in the United States* (New York: The Macmillan Company, 1910), pp. 4-5.

[2] Theodore W. Cousens, *Politics and Political Organizations in America* (New York: The Macmillan Company, 1942), pp. 340-41.

[3] Quoted ibid., p. 341. (Italics added.)

dividually. By the mid-1790s, the legislative caucus was the settled practice (and formal title) of nomination in all of the states.[4]

Since the legislative caucuses initially included only members of the party in the legislature, there were objections that this left unrepresented those districts where the party was in a minority. A number of states moved to remedy this by allowing party members in unrepresented districts to elect delegates to the caucus. This "mixed caucus" or "mongrel caucus" signaled the beginning of party attempts to adapt to pressures for greater representativeness and public participation.

The Congressional Caucus. A parallel method of nomination developed at the national level. During the 1790s, Federalist members of Congress had established the practice of meeting as a group to determine party policy on important issues. By 1800, they extended the responsibilities of the caucus to include the nomination of candidates for president and vice president. While the Republicans in Congress denounced this as antidemocratic arrogance, they followed the Federalist lead in nominating their national candidates by secret caucus. In 1804, secrecy was dropped by the Republicans, and the caucus' assumption of the nominating function was treated as settled.[5] While the Federalists resisted open legislative caucus nomination, their decline as an electoral force left the Republican congressional caucus with the effective authority to choose the president and vice president by the second decade of the nineteenth century.

The absence of two-party competition, however, put a severe strain on the caucus system. With no interparty competition, the Republicans began breaking up into factions. Moreover, the legitimacy of the caucus as a nominating body was increasingly attacked as antidemocratic and unrepresentative. In 1824, most congressional Republicans refused to attend the nominating caucus. Although a presidential candidate, William H. Crawford, was still nominated, competing candidacies had already been announced by state legislatures and other party gatherings. Crawford's subsequent defeat signaled, for all practical purposes, the end of the caucus system.

The Convention System. After a period of turmoil and uncertainty in party politics, the newly formed national parties—the National Republicans (Whigs) and Democratic Republicans (Democrats)—adopted the convention system of nominations. This system had first been employed in New Jersey and Delaware in 1804, when the Republicans in those states allowed party voters to elect delegates to a nominating convention. These delegates, representing the party electorate, then nominated the party's candidates for state offices.[6] Over the next two decades, state nominating conventions became prevalent in the eastern states, and by the 1850s, the convention system was firmly established throughout the country.

[4] Ostrogorski, *Democracy and the Party System*, pp. 6-7.
[5] Ibid., pp. 7-8.
[6] Cousens, *Politics and Political Organizations*, p. 343.

At the national level, the first presidential nominations by national conventions were made for the 1832 election. In 1831 a short-lived minor party, the Anti-Masons, held a national convention composed of delegates chosen by state and local party organizations for the purpose of nominating a presidential candidate and issuing a platform. Later that year, followers of Henry Clay organized a national convention to nominate Clay for president. Andrew Jackson's party, the Democratic Republicans, held its convention in the spring of 1832. When the present Republican party was founded in 1854, it also adopted the convention system.

The general organization of the national conventions remained largely unchanged until the first decade of the twentieth century. The national conventions of each party determined the apportionment of delegates among the states, although each state party was allowed to decide how its delegates would be chosen. In a few states, the state party committees and governors appointed the delegation. More frequently, however, national convention delegates were chosen by state party conventions.[7] These conventions, in turn, were usually composed of delegates from county party conventions that had been selected by party members meeting in precinct caucuses, conventions, or primaries.[8]

Party conventions at the local, state, and national levels were chiefly concerned with nominations. The day-to-day activities of the parties and the management of election campaigns became the responsibilities of permanent party committees. As party organizations developed at the state and local level, they often attempted to dominate party conventions in order to control party nominations. By the latter part of the nineteenth century, this resulted in widespread charges of fraud and abuse. Even when accomplished by legitimate means, organizational control of nominations was attacked as antidemocratic. In addition, many jurisdictions, most notably in the South, had become one-party areas, so that the majority party nomination was tantamount to election. This increased the pressures to expand public participation in party nominations.

The Direct Primary

The perceived abuses of the convention system and of party politics generally led to state regulation of party affairs. State intervention into nominating procedures took the form of mandating direct primaries for the nomination of candidates. Direct primaries, in which party voters selected nominees for public office in much the same way that they finally chose between candidates in the general election, had been used in scattered counties for several decades.[9] During the 1890s, South Carolina and Georgia instituted, by party rules, direct primary nominations for statewide and local offices. In 1903, Wisconsin adopted the first

[7] Ostrogorski, *Democracy and the Party System*, pp. 26-27.

[8] V. O. Key, Jr., *Politics, Parties, and Pressure Groups*, 5th ed. (New York: Thomas Y. Crowell Company, 1964), p. 373.

[9] Ostrogorski, *Democracy and the Party System*, pp. 342-43.

direct primary law. Other states soon followed, and by 1915, the direct primary was being used in 43 states.[10]

The primary system has remained fairly well entrenched over the past half-century. Occasionally, states have abandoned the primary for particular state offices. There has also been considerable fluctuation in the numbers of states using presidential preference primaries to choose delegates to the national nominating conventions. During the past decade, presidential preference primaries have proliferated, and there is once again serious discussion about replacing the national conventions with a national presidential primary. At present, however, the presidency is one of the very few major offices for which nominations are still made by convention.

Types of Primaries: Participation. There remain some important differences among the states with respect to primary procedures. A basic distinction is between open primaries and closed primaries, each of which defines voter qualifications for participating in a primary. The states with *open* primaries—Idaho, Michigan, Minnesota, Montana, North Dakota, Utah, Vermont, and Wisconsin—allow any qualified voter to participate in a party primary without designating a party affiliation or preference.[11] The voter receives every party's ballot (or uses a consolidated format), and choice as to which party primary to participate in is made in the voting booth. The voter is allowed to participate in only one party primary, and is restricted to choosing among that party's candidates for different offices.

A variant of the open primary is the *blanket primary*. Used in Alaska, Louisiana, and Washington, the voter has access to any party's primary without designating preference of affiliation.[12] Moreover, the voter can choose from among one party's candidates for one office and from another party's candidates for a different office; the only restriction is that the voter is limited to one party nomination per office.

The remaining states employ the *closed primary*. Here, the voter must designate a party affiliation or preference and has access only to that party's ballot. Most states using the closed primary provide for initial party registration of voters; others simply allow the voter to state a preference at the time of the primary. Those states with party registration usually require that any registration change be accomplished within a specified period before the election, usually one to three months. (The states are not allowed to prohibit a voter who changes party registration from participating in his new party's primary for a certain length of time or number of elections.)

The differences between open and closed primaries are not always clearcut. Although the open primary states are distinguished by a rather extraordinary sensitivity to the feelings of primary voters, which presumably extend to embarrassment

---

[10] Cousens, *Politics and Political Organizations*, p. 350.

[11] *Book of the States, 1978-1979* (Lexington, Ky.: The Council of State Governments, 1978), p. 241.

[12] Ibid.

at having to acknowledge association with a party, the looseness of procedures in some closed primary states allows a voter to participate in the primary of his or her choice at the time of election. The contrast between these approaches and the party registration requirements of the more rigorous closed primary states suggests the range of opinions about who can legitimately participate in making nominations for the party. At one extreme, few or no restrictions (beyond the general qualifications for voting) are defended on the grounds that voters should be able to participate freely in primaries. Openness and participation are, according to this thinking, more important than party loyalty or other party-related considerations. An opposing argument is that only those who are willing to accept at least some formal association with a party should be allowed to choose the candidates for that party. Without restrictions, opposition party loyalists can cross over to another party's primary if it presents more interesting contests. And while there is only limited evidence that voters shift primaries in an organized attempt to nominate a weak opposition candidate, there have been such instances in the past. In 1966, for example, Republicans in Georgia "raided" the Democratic primary and helped to nominate Lester G. Maddox who they thought would be a weak gubernatorial candidate. Maddox subsequently ran behind the Republican candidate in the general election, but since neither candidate received a majority, the election went to the Democratic-controlled legislature which chose Maddox. Crossovers and raiding aside, however, the closed primary advocates argue that *party* nominations are the exclusive responsibility of party supporters. They believe that the general electorate can exercise its judgment after the parties have chosen their nominees.

Types of Primaries: Procedures. There are additional variations among the states in the specific method of nomination for state offices. Some three-fourths of the states employ the primary for nominating all major statewide officials. A number of these allow the parties to make preprimary endorsements of candidates, although some allow only informal endorsements. Six states allow either the primary or convention method of nomination. Most major party candidates in these states, however, are selected in primaries (although parties may sometimes attempt to avoid potentially divisive primaries, as Virginia Democrats did in 1978 when they decided to nominate their U.S. Senate candidate by convention rather than primary). New York allows the state central committees to nominate candidates, although serious intraparty splits almost always result in primary challenges. Finally, some states mix conventions and primaries. In Connecticut and Utah, a primary is held only if the losing candidate at the party's nominating convention receives a specified minimum of the convention vote. In Iowa and South Dakota, there is a postprimary convention to make nominations if none of the primary candidates receives a specified minimum of the primary vote. Colorado employs preprimary designation assemblies.[13]

A number of southern and border states, moreover, require a run-off primary if no candidate receives 50 percent of the vote in the initial primary. The run-off

[13] Ibid.,

in such cases is between the two candidates receiving the most votes in the initial primary. While this run-off device has been adopted in some localities outside the South, such as New York City, most nonsouthern jurisdictions simply require pluralities for nomination. In one-party areas, the run-off device provides some insurance that the eventual winners will need to develop support beyond a minority faction within the dominant party.

Also, it should be noted that in numerous local jurisdictions, primaries as well as general elections are nonpartisan. In these areas, a procedure similar to the run-off is often employed. The two candidates with the highest numbers of votes qualify to run against each other in the general election. Of course, just how nonpartisan these candidacies are—beyond the lack of party designation on the ballot—is sometimes unclear. In some areas, the nonpartisan tradition is taken seriously. Elsewhere, candidates and party groups may cooperate openly, even if formal affiliations or endorsements are precluded.

Effects of Primaries. The widespread use of the direct primary method of nomination is a major decentralizing force affecting the party system. The national parties have minimal influence over congressional nominations in the states. What role they do play in elections for the House and Senate is usually limited to supporting the party candidates in the general election. Moreover, the influence of state party organizations on presidential nominations has no doubt been weakened by the proliferation of presidential preference primaries and open delegate selection procedures in the states. The ties between the national and state parties are tenuous in numerous respects, and the characteristics of the nomination process represent a formidable obstacle to the strengthening of these ties.

Within the states, the impact of the direct primary has not been uniform. A few state parties have retained substantial control over nominations, particularly where preprimary endorsements are allowed and primaries are closed.[14] Similarly, local party organizations in some jurisdictions have been able to dictate the naming of candidates despite formal nomination by primary. It is possible, then, for strong party organizations to survive direct primaries. The crucial point, however, is that strong parties exist in spite of, not because of, direct primaries.

The primary method of nomination can have some obvious negative effects on the party. First, a party that cannot control nominations finds it difficult to create balanced tickets—that is, a slate of candidates for various offices who reflect the ethnic, religious, or ideological diversity of the party's supporters. Thus, the party's electoral appeal may be weakened. Second, primaries can be costly and divisive. While it is not clear that serious primary contests have a systematic impact on the outcomes of general elections, a particularly bitter and divisive intraparty contest is not likely to enhance a party's electoral prospects.[15] The losing candi-

---

[14] See Malcolm E. Jewell and David M. Olson, *American State Political Parties and Elections* (Homewood, Ill.: The Dorsey Press, 1978), pp. 131-37.

[15] See ibid., pp. 173-76.

date's supporters may defect to the other party or simply sit out the election. If the two parties are competitive, this could be decisive.

Third, the party's primary electorate may be very different from that of the general election.[16] Turnout in primaries is usually well below general election turnout, so it is possible for unrepresentative minorities to control a party's nomination. Here again, clear evidence on systematic patterns is lacking, but the realities of primary turnout represent an open invitation to ideological or other minorities within a party. And, as we have suggested, the party organization's assessment of potential nominees necessarily takes into account their ability to win. Primary voters, while perhaps not oblivious to this consideration, are more likely to support a candidate that they *personally* find more appealing or ideologically compatible.

Finally, primaries make it difficult to enforce party responsibility. The party does represent a mechanism for offering reasonably coherent and stable choices to the electorate through its candidates. It also has a vested interest in overseeing the activities of its candidates once they are elected. While primaries may have an undeniable appeal in terms of democratic control, it is worth asking whether they can reasonably be expected—given the involvement and the knowledge of most voters—to provide sufficient coherence or accountability.

ELECTIONS: AN OVERVIEW

Parties in the United States have been directly affected by various technological innovations in political campaigning. Today's major electoral contests typically involve the extensive (and expensive) utilization of media advertising (especially television), public opinion polling, and direct mass mailing. There is widespread agreement that the parties' role in electoral politics has been weakened as a consequence of these changes in campaign technology. Candidates are able to appeal directly to a mass electorate, thereby reducing dependence on the party as an active intermediary. Professional campaign consultants provide candidates with independent sources of expertise in the mobilization of electoral support. And nonparty political organizations, notably interest groups, provide financial and other resourcs to candidates, further limiting party control of electoral politics.

It is not inconceivable that the American parties could have adapted reasonably well to changes in campaign technology. Parties in other western democracies, for example, appear to have made the transition to television, polls, and the like with minimal disruptions of their electoral control. The legal framework within which American parties operate, however, lessens the possibility of successful adaptation. As we have seen, the direct primary allows candidates without party organization backing to compete for the party nomination. With modern

---

[16] See Austin Ranney, "The Representativeness of Primary Electorates," *Midwest Journal of Political Science,* 12 (May 1962), 224-38; "Turnout and Representation in Presidential Primary Elections," *American Political Science Review,* 66 (March 1972), 21-37.

campaign techniques, candidates have a much greater opportunity for mobilizing electoral support independently during the primary as well as the general election. In examining the party in politics, then, it is important to take into account federal and state regulations affecting such matters as campaign finance, electoral procedures, and even the qualifications for voting. The first of these, campaign finance legislation, is an example of reform that has serious, and generally negative, implications for the parties.

Campaign Finance Legislation

During the 1960s, the costs of political campaigns increased sharply. In 1952, for example, total campaign costs for all elective offices in the United States were estimated at $140 million. By 1964, costs had risen to $200 million, an increase of less than 50 percent over the twelve-year period. Four years later, however, costs were estimated at $300 million, and in 1972, they climbed to $400 million, with the Nixon and McGovern presidential campaigns alone accounting for approximately one-fourth of this total. Thus, in less than a decade, the costs of running for office had doubled. Part of this increase was attributable to economic and political factors, such as inflation and the growing number of presidential primaries. Nevertheless, there were very substantial, real increases in campaign spending, and these were especially noticeable in the area of broadcast media advertising.[17]

The growth of total costs, moreover, was thought by many observers to invite campaign-financing abuses and governmental corruption. According to this view, candidates must depend on a few major contributors, either wealthy individuals or organized interests, in order to raise large sums quickly and easily. This dependence could encourage the successful candidate to protect the interests of these contributors once in office. In addition, even if this dependence is more imagined than real, it can lead to public cynicism about the motives and autonomy of elected officials.

By the late 1960s, then, campaign finance had become a serious national issue. In addition to growing concern about the influence of money in politics, there was also a question of partisan advantage. The Democratic party was heavily indebted after the 1968 campaign, while the Republicans were in excellent financial shape. And since the Republicans had traditionally been able to outspend the Democrats in elections, restrictions on campaign spending had a special appeal for the Democratic party. Congressional Democrats therefore pressed campaign finance legislation in 1970 and 1971. While President Nixon vetoed a 1970 bill that limited spending on broadcast advertising, Republicans in Congress were sensitive to the potential dangers of opposing this type of "reform." In 1971, Congress passed legislation limiting spending on all media as well as a plan for public financing of presidential elections. The Nixon administration accepted the first, and after Congress

---

[17]*Congress and the Nation,* vol. 3, 1969-1972 (Washington, D.C.: Congressional Quarterly, Inc., 1973), p. 398.

agreed to delay implementation of public financing until after the 1972 election, the president signed the second as well. The subsequent unfolding of the Watergate scandals in 1973 and 1974 provided a major impetus for additional regulation of campaign finance. The serious abuses in campaign contributions and spending practices associated with the Nixon reelection campaign organization resulted in passage of comprehensive regulatory legislation in 1974 and, after the Supreme Court found portions of the 1974 law to be unconstitutional, to additional legislation in 1976. A review of the current and proposed federal legislation in this area, as well as the outlines of state regulation, will suggest some important effects on the party system.

The 1971 Campaign Finance Laws. Prior to 1971, the basic federal legislation covering political campaigns was the Federal Corrupt Practices Act. It set expenditure limits for House ($2500) and Senate ($10,000) candidates, prohibited campaign contributions by corporations and national banks, and required the filing of reports on campaign finances. In 1940, an amendment to the Hatch Act set a contribution limit of $5000 annually for individuals and a spending limit of $3 million for political committees operating in two or more states. In 1947, a permanent ban was enacted that prohibited labor union contributions to political campaigns from their general funds. There were, however, major loopholes in these laws. Candidates could easily evade the spending limits by establishing multiple committees. Filing requirements were loose and generally unenforced. And corporations and labor unions set up political action committees using voluntary contributions to escape the contribution prohibitions.

In 1966, Congress enacted a tax checkoff plan to provide federal subsidies to presidential election campaigns. Under this plan, individual taxpayers could earmark $1 of their tax due in any year to a Presidential Election Campaign Fund which would then disburse its receipts on a proportional basis to the political parties that qualified. (In order to qualify, a party had to receive a minimum of five million votes in the preceding presidential election.) Congress failed to pass the necessary implementing legislation for this plan the following year, however, and the public financing plans of future years were aimed at the candidates rather than the parties.

The Federal Election Campaign Act of 1971 set spending limits on media advertising for all federal candidates. Candidates were restricted to spending no more than 10 cents per eligible voter on all advertising and to a maximum of 60 percent of this total amount on broadcast media. The law required that any contribution or expenditure of $100 or more be reported, and it also limited the amount that a candidate or his family could contribute to his own campaign ($50,000 for president or vice president, $35,000 for senator, and $25,000 for representative). Despite these restrictions, a number of loopholes soon became apparent during the 1972 elections. Prior to official announcements of candidacy, candidates could accept contributions and spend money without being subject to the media advertising limitations. Individual contributors could avoid federal gift taxes on political contributions by making donations of less than $3000 each to numerous political committees set up by a single candidate. Sources of loans did not have to be reported, and family members could make loans in addition to the maximum contribution allowed to support a candidate in the family. Finally, since no independent commission was established to monitor and enforce the law, close scrutiny of the voluminous campaign finance reports was virtually impossible.

In 1971, Congress again enacted a plan for public financing of presidential election campaigns. Like the 1966 plan, it provided for a $1 tax checkoff for individual taxpayers, with the accumulated monies to be distributed to major party candidates. The maximum amount for each candidate was set at 15 cents multiplied by the voting age population. Candidates were restricted to this spending limit if they chose public financing, and they could not accept private contributions unless the funds available from the income tax checkoff were less than this spending limit. This legislation did not go into effect, however, until January 1, 1973.

1974 Legislation. The campaign abuses of 1972 forced Congress to consider once again regulatory legislation. On October 10, 1974, Congress cleared the Federal Election Campaign Amendments, which were far more comprehensive than the 1971 law. The 1974 legislation established new limits on contributions and expenditures, set up a new plan for public financing of presidential elections and partial financing of primaries, set strict disclosure and reporting requirements, and created a Federal Election Commission for monitoring and enforcement.

The 1974 law had several features of particular importance to political parties. First, it channeled public funds for presidential primaries and general elections to the candidates, not the parties. Together with the changes in delegate selection procedures and the proliferation of presidential primaries during the early 1970s, this further loosened the ties between the parties and their presidential candidates. Second, it limited the amounts that national party organizations could contribute to congressional campaigns. Third, the law made it extremely difficult for minor parties and minor party candidates to qualify for public financing. In effect, the law helped candidates seeking major party nominations while discouraging third-party or independent candidacies.

The Federal Election Campaign Amendments of 1974 took effect on January 1, 1975. On January 2, the constitutionality of this legislation was challenged in a suit filed by then Senator James L. Buckley of New York, former Senator Eugene McCarthy (who had run for president in 1968 and would run again as an independent candidate in 1976), and several minor parties and civil liberties groups. The challenges asserted that the limits on contributions and expenditures violated First Amendment guarantees of free expression and that the public financing provisions discriminated against minor parties.

Although the U.S. Court of Appeals for the District of Columbia upheld the 1974 amendments in their entirety, a subsequent appeal to the United States

Supreme Court resulted in the invalidation of several key provisions.[18] On January 30, 1976, the Supreme Court in a long and divided opinion held that the contribution limits for individuals and groups, as well as the disclosure requirements for contributions and expenditures, were valid. It also upheld the plan for public financing of presidential primaries and general elections.

The Court struck down as unconstitutional, however, the campaign spending limits for House and Senate candidates (and for presidential and vice-presidential candidates who did not accept public financing). Restrictions on independent expenditures made on behalf of a candidate were held invalid, as were limitations on how much of the candidate's own money could be spent. Finally, the Court stated that the appointment procedure for the Federal Election Commission was unconstitutional, since the commission exercised executive powers but had members who were appointed by Congress. The Court held that in order for the commission to exercise the executive, administrative, and enforcement functions it was given under law, all commission members had to be appointed by the president. Congress was given a 30-day deadline to reconstitute the commission.

1976 Legislation. In response to the Supreme Court's decision, Congress changed the Federal Election Commission to a six-member panel nominated by the president and confirmed by the Senate. It also made a number of other changes in the 1974 law. The definition of independent expenditures on behalf of a candidate (limits on which had been invalidated) was tightened to insure that such expenditures would be truly independent. Disclosure requirements for corporate and union political action committees were tightened to include communications to stockholders or members advocating the election or defeat of candidates. Specific contribution limits were set for both individual and group contributions to national parties and political committees. (The Republican and Democratic National Committees and Senatorial Campaign Committees were limited to a total of $17,500 in contributions to any Senate candidate.) In addition, regulations on fundraising and expenditures by political action committees were tightened.

With the exception of minor provisions establishing cut-off procedures and reimbursement requirements for presidential candidates, the public financing plan was left intact. As it operated for the 1976 presidential campaign, it provided that candidates could qualify for up to $5 million in matching funds for the primaries. In order to be eligible, candidates had to raise at least $5,000 in each of 20 states from donations of $250 or less. Federal funds would then be available to match these individual contributions of $250 or less. The purpose of this limitation was to encourage small contributions, since a minimum of 20,000 contributors would be necessary to generate federal matching grants of $5 million.

During the general election, the Democratic and Republican nominees automatically qualified for full public financing amounting to approximately $22

---

[18] *Buckley v. Valeo*, 424 U.S. 1 (1976).

million for each national ticket. Candidates who opted for public financing, as both Carter and Ford did in 1976, were not allowed to accept private contributions and were subject to the expenditure limit of the maximum federal grant. (Since the size of the grant depends on the size of the voting age population, it will increase slightly for the 1980 presidential election.)

Congressional Election Financing. Attempts to extend public financing to congressional elections have thus far been unsuccessful. In 1973 and 1974, the Senate approved public financing plans, but the House rejected both plans. In 1977, President Carter made public financing of congressional elections part of his election "reform" package, but even with strong administration support, the legislation was blocked by a Senate filibuster. In the House, a public finance plan did not even survive committee scrutiny.

Proponents of public financing were especially upset by interest group spending in the 1976 congressional races. Total congressional campaign contributions reported by interest groups in 1976 were $22.6 million, an increase of more than $10 million over 1974.[19] This suggested to some that interest groups had simply shifted their attention to congressional elections when public financing reduced their role in presidential elections. Public financing, it was claimed, was necessary to eliminate influence buying from congressional elections. Opponents, however, suggested that public financing was a thinly disguised attempt to provide a partisan advantage for Democrats as well as a general advantage for incumbents. Congressional Republicans, for example, have charged that public financing would actually protect the huge Democratic majorities in Congress.

In addition to questions about partisan advantage and accountability, the general effects of public financing on the party system must be considered. As with presidential public financing, a congressional public financing scheme would no doubt further separate candidates (and officeholders) from the parties. If extended to congressional primary elections, public financing would presumably encourage more candidacies and limit even further the party's influence over nominations. During general elections, public financing would provide candidates with considerable independence from the party and would probably preclude cooperative activities between congressional candidates and privately financed candidates on the party ticket. Such cooperative activity appears to have been reduced by reporting and disclosure requirements already, but public financing would introduce an even greater degree of formal disassociation among party candidates.[20]

Whether public financing of campaigns for national office will reduce the influence of organized interests is not at all clear, especially since groups such as organized labor can provide many "in-kind" services for candidates, including

---

[19] *Congressional Quarterly Almanac*, vol. 33, 1977 (Washington, D.C.: Congressional Quarterly, Inc., 1977), p. 804.

[20] Xandra Kayden, *Campaign Organization* (Lexington, Mass.: D.C. Heath and Company, 1978), pp. 172-73.

volunteers, registration and vote campaigns, and polling and canvassing operations. Whether it will substantially reduce the costs of nonpresidential elections is also questionable. Although these and other effects of public financing may be difficult to predict, it is fairly clear that current and proposed plans will not materially strengthen the parties and, in fact, may contribute to their decline as active intermediaries between candidates and the electorate.

State Regulation. Attempts to regulate campaign finances have not been confined to the national government. Responding to many of the same concerns about actual or potential abuse, the states have become very active in this area. Since the early 1970s, approximately two-thirds of the states have passed major campaign finance legislation. In 1974 alone, 24 states passed new laws. Since the federal legislation preempts any state regulations applying to congressional races, state laws affect only state and, where applicable, local offices.

The regulatory efforts at the state level parallel the general scope of federal campaign finance laws. Most states have adopted disclosure and reporting requirements for candidates, political committees, and parties. These usually extend to campaign contributions and expenditures during both primary and general elections for statewide offices and state legislative seats. Many states have also enacted laws that prohibit contributions by corporations or unions, restrict the amounts and sources of other contributions, and also impose restrictions on types of expenditures as well as total campaign spending. Of course, some of these restrictions, such as the limitations on independent expenditures on behalf of a candidate and campaign spending limits, have been rendered ineffective as a result of *Buckely v. Valeo*. A majority of the states have also followed the federal lead by establishing independent commissions or boards to administer and enforce their campaign finance laws.

A few states have instituted limited public financing of elections, funded by voluntary income tax checkoffs and tax surcharges. Unlike the federal plan, however, state monies are usually channeled through the parties. In several states (Idaho, Iowa, Kentucky, Rhode Island, and Utah), public funds provided to the parties can be used to finance partywide activities, such as registration and vote campaigns, or to support candidates in specific races. In several other states, the parties are required to allocate designated amounts from public funds for different offices and activities.[21] New Jersey is the only state with major public financing, having provided $2.1 million in matching funds to Democratic and Republican gubernatorial candidates in 1977.[22] While the amounts available to the parties have thus far been fairly limited, public financing plans that give the parties a central and discretionary role appear preferable from the standpoint of the party organization.

Money and Politics. Much of the attention paid to electoral politics in recent years has been directed toward the influence of money in politics. Unfortunately,

---

[21] Jewell and Olson, *American State Political Parties and Elections*, p. 211.
[22] *Book of the States, 1978-1979*, p. 230.

there is little hard evidence that illuminates this relationship. Campaigns do require money, frequently large amounts of money, but the outcomes of elections are affected by numerous factors, not just spending. It is also not clear what campaign contributions "buy" apart from the access that most organized groups would enjoy anyway. "Special interests" will not disappear because of campaign finance regulation, even though their role in directly financing elections will be restricted.

Legislation aimed at curbing fraud or abuse, particularly through disclosure and reporting requirements, may prove to be helpful. Public financing, however, poses a serious threat to the parties, at least in the form that it now takes in presidential politics. One can legitimately ask, for example, exactly to whom, given the average citizen's interest in and knowledge about politics, the publicly financed candidate will be accountable once elected. Who will mobilize voters behind a coherent and stable program of public policy? Public financing of candidates assumes that intermediaries between the public and government are unnecessary or even harmful. For those who see the parties as important linkages for the great mass of voters, this argument is hardly convincing.

Electoral Procedures

There is a fair degree of uniformity in the electoral rules and procedures used in the states. A number of important issues (for example, the use of secret ballots) have been settled for quite some time. Others, such as the form of ballot used or the election system for a particular office, occasionally become the subject of political debate. While electoral rules and procedures do not always have clear and direct effects on the parties, they do represent the framework within which the parties operate.

Ballot Form. During the colonial period and the early years of the republic, oral voting was the common practice. Voters would appear before election officials and simply announce their choices. This system gradually gave way to printed ballots prepared by the parties or their candidates. Since the parties usually provided distinctively colored ballots, this change yielded little improvement in secrecy. Toward the end of the nineteenth century, a majority of states moved toward secret or Australian ballots, prepared by public authorities and marked in the privacy of the voting booths. Secret ballots are now used throughout the United States, although most jurisdictions employ automated systems such as voting machines or computer punch cards instead of printed paper ballots.

Nevertheless, there is still some variation in the ballot format used. A majority of states use the party-column ballot. A party's candidates for all offices are listed in a vertical column. A parallel column then lists the opposition party's candidates for these offices. The office-block ballot which groups candidates by the office being sought is used in the remaining states. (Since the order in which the candidates' names are listed may have an impact on some voters, the states use several methods or ordering names: alphabetical listing, drawing lots, rotating the order based on a certain percentage of ballots or from one precint or voting district to another, or listing the incumbent first.)

The party-column ballot facilitates straight-ticket voting, especially when the voter can vote the entire ticket by using a single mark or lever. Approximately one-half of the states use a ballot format that allows the voter to vote for all candidates of the same party in this fashion,[23] and most of these states have party-column ballots. The rationale behind the office-block ballot is that it will encourage the citizen to consider the candidates for each office separately, and there is some evidence that this format actually does decrease straight party voting. (It also appears to increase "roll-off," as citizens fail to vote for minor offices near the end of the ballot.)[24]

Election System. The system of electing statewide officers is similar in most states. The candidate with a plurality of votes is elected. Georgia and Vermont, however, require an absolute majority for election; in the absence of such a majority, the choice goes to the state legislature.[25] A majority of states also use single-member constituencies and plurality election to choose their state legislators. (Single-member districts, as well as plurality election, are also used for the U.S. House of Representatives.)

Multimember districts are used in some states, although here again the plurality principle determines the winners among the several candidates running for the seats within a district. Whatever the type of district, the state's freedom to draw district boundaries has been sharply limited by the federal courts. The states are now obliged to insure population equality among legislative districts. And while the reapportionment cases have not eliminated all forms of gerrymandering (that is, the drawing of district lines to gain partisan advantage), at least in its more subtle forms, they have removed much of the discretion that the states enjoyed until the early 1960s.[26]

Proportional representation and other alternatives to single-member, plurality election have been used very rarely in the states. This has probably discouraged minor parties from entering elections. Although this bolsters the two-party system, the major parties' leverage over candidates and officeholders is limited by their lack of control over nominations.

Tinkering with election systems is not confined to the states. For several

---

[23] Ibid., p. 242.

[24] Jack L. Walker, "Ballot Forms and Voter Fatigue: An Analysis of the Office Block and Party Column Ballots," *Midwest Journal of Political Science*, 10 (August 1966), 448-63.

[25] Jewell and Olson, *American State Political Parties and Elections*, p. 179.

[26] Federal court jurisdiction was extended to legislative apportionment in the states in *Baker v. Carr*, 369 U.S. 186 (1962). Population equality among congressional districts in a state was required by the Supreme Court in *Westberry v. Sanders*, 376 U.S. 1 (1964). The one-man one-vote rule for state legislative apportionment was enunciated in *Reynolds v. Sims*, 377 U.S. 533 (1964).

decades, there has been sporadic debate about various changes in the electoral college system of choosing the president. The proposals have run the gamut from minimal to wholesale change—with the simple elimination of the individual electors on the one extreme to the replacement of the electoral college with direct election at the other. The latter was proposed by President Carter in 1977, and Senator Birch Bayh (D-Indiana) has sponsored a constitutional amendment that would abolish the electoral college and award the presidency to the candidate receiving the highest popular vote. In order to be elected, however, the top candidate would need to draw a minimum of 40 percent of the total vote. Otherwise, a runoff election would be held between the top two candidates. Senate opposition to such a change, however, has been extremely strong, and there is a serious question about obtaining ratification by three-fourths of the states even if two-thirds of the Senate and House should approve a direct vote amendment.

Ballot Access. The parties are directly affected by state laws that regulate access to primary and general election ballots. States requiring filing fees for candidates have been forced to provide alternative means of qualification for indigents.[27] States that require petitions signed by a minimum number of registered voters for minor party or nonparty candidates who wish to be listed on the general election ballot must not establish unreasonable or discriminatory standards in terms of the numbers of signatures needed or the time period allowed to collect those signatures.[28] The states are allowed, however, to limit ballot access. The United States Supreme Court has upheld, for example, state laws that prohibit a candidate from seeking ballot listing as an independent if that candidate voted in the immediately preceding primary or was registered as a party member within one year prior to the primary.[29] The Court has also upheld laws that establish one-percent petition requirements for general election ballot access (that is, one percent of the voters in the previous election), that disqualify individuals who voted in the preceding primary election from signing such petitions, and that provide reasonable time limits for securing signatures.[30]

Registration and Elections

The size and composition of the electorate have a decided impact on the party system. As electorates expand and become more diverse, the parties must be able to broaden their appeals and adapt to different organizational requirements. Thus, it is of more than passing interest that the legally defined electorate has grown significantly since the mid-1960s. This recent growth is simply the latest of several major expansions in the eligible electorate that have moved the United

[27] *Lubin v. Parrish,* 415 U.S. 709 (1974).
[28] *Williams v. Rhodes,* 393 U.S. 23 (1968).
[29] *Storer v. Brown,* 415 U.S. 724 (1974).
[30] *American Party of Texas v. White,* 415 U.S. 767 (1974).

States toward universal adult suffrage; it also reflects a growing federal involvement in the definition of voter qualifications.

Property and Taxpaying Qualifications. The United States Constitution originally left the qualifications for voting to the states, requiring only that a state apply the same standards for voting in national elections as it did in elections for the largest branch of its state legislature. The common practice among the states was initially to restrict the franchise to property-owning, taxpaying white males. Even though these requirements were, at least in some jurisdictions, not especially stringent, there was strong opposition to relaxing or eliminating such standards in many states. Nevertheless, property and taxpaying qualifications were gradually lifted in the states and were largely eliminated by the middle of the nineteenth century. With the final abolition of poll taxes in the 1960s, the last remnant of this category of qualifications disappeared.

Race and Sex Qualifications. With the exception of a few New England states, the suffrage extension of the early nineteenth century affected only white males. The struggle to enfranchise blacks after the Civil War was, of course, long and arduous. Only in recent years has nondiscrimination in voter qualification been effectively enforced throughout the United States. Woman suffrage, while generating conflict and controversy, was more easily resolved.

The first federal effort aimed at establishing voting rights for blacks was the Reconstruction Act of 1867 that applied only to the former Confederate states. The Fifteenth Amendment, ratified in 1870, prohibited any state from denying the right to vote on the basis of race. But the exercise of black suffrage in the southern states where the overwhelming majority of blacks resided was dependent on active federal enforcement, and this effectively came to an end during the 1870s. There followed the adoption of numerous voter qualification devices by southern states to accomplish legal disenfranchisement of blacks. These included poll taxes, literacy and understanding tests, good character tests, grandfather clauses, and white primaries.[31] In some areas, coercion and intimidation achieved the same ends. While the U.S. Supreme Court ultimately overturned some of the more blatantly discriminatory devices, it was unable to reverse the wholesale cessation of black voting

---

[31] The poll tax was usually a one-dollar or two-dollar payment required prior to voting. While the amount was small, the tax was sometimes cumulative (if it had not been paid in prior elections), and potential voters were often required to present their receipt for taxes paid on election day. Literacy and understanding tests were often coupled, requiring the would-be registrant to read and interpret portions of a state's constitution to the local voting official. The grandfather clause allowed those who could vote, or whose ancestors could vote, prior to adoption of the Fifteenth Amendment, to register without passing literacy tests or meeting other qualifications. The discriminatory intent and potential of each of these was clear. Even clearer was the white primary, which simply limited participation in direct primaries to whites. Since the Democratic primary was the effective election in the southern states, this precluded blacks who voted in the general election from having any electoral impact.

in much of the South. It was not until the late 1950s that Congress finally commenced active intervention to secure the voting rights of blacks.

The woman suffrage movement was, during its initial stages, associated with the abolitionist movement in some areas, but its success with respect to voting rights was more immediate than was the case for blacks. Initial attempts to extend the franchise to women were concentrated at the state level, and by the middle of the nineteenth century, a number of states had extended a limited franchise that allowed women to vote in school elections. It was not until 1890, however, that the full franchise was extended by any state. Wyoming was the first state to do so, and several western states quickly followed Wyoming's lead. Thereafter, state-by-state progress became much more difficult. By 1914, less than a dozen states had acted favorably, and the suffrage movement shifted its emphasis to the constitutional amendment route. For the next several years, protests, demonstrations, and arrests dramatized the controversy. Finally, in 1919, Congress approved the Nineteenth Amendment and submitted it to the states for ratification. In August of the following year, the necessary three-fourths of the states had ratified the amendment, thus eliminating voter qualifications in the states that discriminated against women.

For the next several decades, federal action in the area of voting rights was largely restricted to the federal courts, which attempted to deal with racial discrimination. From the 1920s through the 1940s, for example, the Supreme Court wrestled with the problem of white primaries. Not until 1944 did the Court find that the right to vote in party primaries enjoyed constitutional protection.[32] This decision had a considerable impact on black voting in some southern states, but in the "Deep South" states, black registration and voting were still severely restricted. Prior to 1957, discrimination suits were handled by private litigation, a slow and costly process. In 1957, however, Congress enacted the first of a series of civil rights acts designed to reach those areas where serious discrimination existed. For example, the 1957 law authorized the attorney general to institute court suits to provide injunctive relief. In 1960, legislation was approved that authorized the appointment of federal voting referees in jurisdictions where discrimination had been proved. The 1964 Civil Rights Act attempted to curb the use of literacy tests and required fair administration of such tests.

The most significant and effective legislative action, however, was the 1965 Voting Rights Act. This law contained an automatic triggering device—if a state (or county) had a literacy test or similar test in effect as of November 1, 1964 *and* less than 50 percent of its potential voters were registered or had voted in the 1964 presidential election, the state (or county) was subject to other provisions in the act. Literacy tests were automatically suspended. Federal voting examiners were authorized to supervise registration and voting procedures. Any new state or local

---

[32] *Smith v. Allwright,* 321 U.S. 649 (1944).

legislation affecting elections and voting required approval by the Attorney General or by the Washington, D.C. Federal District Court. Finally, states had to prove nondiscrimination for a five-year period in order to obtain a federal court waiver of the 1965 act's provisions.

In some areas, the effects of the 1965 law were quite dramatic. During the 1960s, black registration in the southern states doubled, from 29 percent to 58 percent. This was only slightly below registration for whites. In Mississippi, where black registration in 1960 was approximately 5 percent, it increased to almost 60 percent by 1971. In Alabama and South Carolina, where black registration had been less than 15 percent, it increased to 55 percent and 46 percent, respectively, by the end of the decade. Elsewhere, black registration had been much higher prior to 1965, so the gains were less striking, but the overall impact of federal action was quite apparent.[33] Subsequent extensions of the 1965 Voting Rights Act in 1970 and 1975 have broadened its scope, but the basic protections of black voting rights remain.

Age Qualifications. Until 1970, all but a few states set the minimum voting age at 21 years. As part of the 1970 Voting Rights Act, however, Congress granted the right to vote in federal, state, and local elections to citizens between the ages of 18 and 21 in all of the states. A court test of the law resulted in the Supreme Court's holding that Congress could lower the minimum voting age by statute for federal elections but did not have the authority to lower it for state and local elections.[34] Congress then proceeded to approve a constitutional amendment to remedy this exclusion. The Twenty-sixth Amendment was promptly ratified by the states and was in effect for the 1972 elections. Its immediate consequence was to add approximately 11 million potential voters to the voting age population.

Residence Requirements. Prior to 1970, most states had substantial residence requirements that had to be met before a citizen was allowed to vote. These requirements generally included minimum length of residence in the state (usually 1 year), in a county (usually 90 days), and in a voting district (usually 30 days). The 1970 Voting Rights Act prohibited state residence requirements of more than 30 days for voting in federal elections, and this was upheld by the Supreme Court.[35] Two years later, the Supreme Court invalidated a Tennessee law that set a one-year residence requirement for voting in state and local elections.[36] In a later case, the Court upheld a 50-day residence requirement but indicated that longer require-

---

[33] U.S. Bureau of the Census, *Statistical Abstract of the United States: 1973* (Washington, D.C.: Government Printing Office, 1973). This includes Alabama, Arkansas, Florida, Georgia, Louisiana, Mississippi, North Carolina, South Carolina, Tennessee, Texas, and Virginia.

[34] *Oregon v. Mitchell, Texas v. Mitchell, U.S. v. Idaho, U.S. v. Alabama*, 400 U.S. 112 (1970).

[35] Ibid.

[36] *Dunn v. Blumstein*, 405 U.S. 330 (1972).

ments would be constitutionally suspect.[37] Currently, 19 states have no residence requirements, while most of the remaining states have 30-day requirements.[38]

Registration and Turnout. Federal government initiatives have substantially increased the eligible electorate. The legal and extralegal barriers to voting by major population groups have been largely eliminated. In 1975, for example, Congress extended coverage of the Voting Rights Act to language minorities. In voting jurisdictions where more than 5 percent of the citizens were of a single language minority, where election materials were printed only in English, and where less than 50 percent of the voting age citizens had been registered for or voted in the 1972 presidential election, federal supervision of election laws and procedures was required. In addition, where the illiteracy rate in English of such a language minority was greater than the national illiteracy rate, bilingual election materials were required.

Despite these federal efforts, voting turnout has declined in recent years. Turnout in the United States is relatively low in comparison to other democracies. The 1976 presidential election turnout, for example, was 54 percent, the lowest level since 1948. This was some 30-40 percentage points lower than the turnout in recent parliamentary elections in countries such as Australia, Italy, West Germany, and France.[39] Turnout also varies substantially by type of election. It is some 15-20 percentage points higher in presidential elections than in off-year congressional elections.[40] In most states, turnout in state and local elections is also well below presidential turnout. Finally, registration and voting are related to factors such as education, income, and race. Citizens in the higher income and education brackets are more likely to be registered than are those at the bottom of the socioeconomic ladder. If registered, they are also more likely to vote.[41]

There has been speculation that at least some of the disparity in voter participation rates among various social groups might be eliminated by easing registration requirements in the states. This is based on the contention that more difficult requirements have a disproportionately discouraging effect on the poor and less educated. In response to these and related criticisms, a number of states have sought to make registration easier. Almost one-half now allow registration by mail. Minnesota and Wisconsin have even dispensed with required pre-election registration by allowing election day registration at the polls.[42]

---

[37] Residence requirements of 50 days were found acceptable in *Burns v. Fortson*, 410 U.S. 686 (1973), and *Marston v. Lewis*, 410 U.S. 679 (1973).

[38] *Book of the States, 1978-1979*, p. 235.

[39] Dennis S. Ippolito, Thomas G. Walker, and Kenneth L. Kolson, *Public Opinion and Responsible Democracy* (Englewood Cliffs, N.J.: Prentice-Hall, Inc., 1976), p. 213.

[40] Ibid., p. 214.

[41] See U.S. Bureau of the Census, Current Population Reports, Series P-20, no. 322, "Voting and Registration in the Election of November 1976," (Washington, D.C.: Government Printing Office, 1978).

[42] *Book of the States, 1978-1979*, p. 235.

Easier registration does not, of course, guarantee higher turnout. In 1976, for example, 20 states had registration rates of 75 percent or more, compared to a national average of 70.5 percent. However, while the turnout rate for registered voters in all states averaged 77.7 percent for the 1976 presidential election, only four of the high registration rate states (Colorado, Connecticut, Utah, and Wisconsin) had equivalent or higher turnout rates among registered voters.

In 1977, however, the Carter administration sponsored the Universal Voter Registration Act, patterned after Minnesota's system, to ease registration requirements in all states. As originally written, it required each state to provide election day registration in federal elections. This was a more far-reaching proposal than the postcard registration plans that had been advocated previously, and it generated intense opposition from those who believed it would increase voter fraud. It also was received less than enthusiastically by many Republicans who viewed it as a potential boon for Democrats, since the bulk of nonregistered citizens fall into predominantly Democratic socioeconomic groups. As attacks on the administration's plan became more heated, its sponsors agreed to make the system optional for each state. This failed to quiet the criticism, however, and the bill never reached the floor.

The Election System. It is difficult to generalize about the many factors that have been reviewed here. Some, such as campaign finance regulations, affect the parties and party system to a much greater extent than others. It is apparent, however, that considerable change has occurred in the electoral rules and procedures within which the parties operate, and few, if any, of these are designed to increase the discretion or importance of party organizations.

PRESIDENTIAL NOMINATIONS AND ELECTIONS

The changes in presidential electoral politics have been the most visible and probably the most significant ones as far as the party system is concerned. As we noted earlier, the electorate in presidential campaigns has become much less dependent on party labels and party cues. In addition, the process of selecting presidential nominees has been altered dramatically over the past decade, with even more far-reaching changes currently being debated. Finally, presidential elections have now incorporated the profound advances in campaign tactics and organization that accompany the use of television and polling to mobilize a large and diverse electorate. The party's role in selecting presidential nominees and organizing their campaign was, at one time, of central importance. This role is now shared with, if not completely lost to, self-selected candidates and their personal organizations, interest groups, professional campaign consultants and managers, activist ideologues, and other nonparty institutions. Whether these individuals and groups can coalesce interests and mediate between the public and government effectively is a major unresolved issue in contemporary politics.

Nominating the President

At a recent conference on American party politics, one commentator explained the traditional function of the presidential nominating process:

> The function of nominating a Presidential candidate by the two major parties through the mechanism of the national convention used to provide an occasion for bringing together a lot of people with strong, active interest in the forthcoming election, in continuing governance, and continuing prospects for party organizations and candidates out in the states—to attempt to accommodate with one another with some kind of aggregate decision responsive to our electoral college arithmetic. The decision took note of the likely sets of party loyalists in states, interests in states, to produce enough popular majorities in enough states to produce a majority in the electoral college. The popular phrase "brokered-convention" is not a very accurate expression. What the brokers were engaged in was, among other things, trying to think out that electoral college arithmetic across the states to the advantage of their nominee or the disadvantage of the other; trying to put together two sets of electoral political coalitions. . . .[43]

Since 1968, however, the number of states holding presidential primaries has almost doubled, and the percentage of convention votes cast by delegates selected or bound by primaries has also doubled, to approximately 70 percent at both the Democratic and Republican conventions.[44] These changes in delegate selection procedures are principally directed toward such goals as popular participation, representativeness, and openness in the presidential nominating process. They do not, in all likelihood, enhance the party's ability to perform the traditional function of aggregating and accommodating interests.

Delegate Selection. Presidential primaries first appeared around the turn of the century. By 1916, over half of the states had adopted some form of primary system for selecting delegates to the national nominating conventions. This method, however, was gradually abandoned in a number of states, and by 1968, only 16 states (and the District of Columbia) still held presidential primaries. These states accounted for approximately 37 percent of the votes at the Democratic convention and 34 percent of the votes at the Republican convention in 1968.[45] All states enjoyed substantial discretion, however, as to the methods employed in selecting delegates, and the rules governing caucuses or conventions to choose delegates in

---

[43] Statement of Richard E. Neustadt, in *Voters, Primaries, and Parties, Selections from a Conference on American Politics,* ed. Jonathan Moore and Albert C. Pierce (Cambridge, Mass.: Institute of Government, John Fitzgerald Kennedy School of Government, 1976), pp. 32-33.

[44] *Congressional Quarterly Weekly Report,* 34, no. 5 (January 31, 1976), 225-42. Austin Ranney, *Participation in American Presidential Nominations, 1976* (Washington, D.C.: American Enterprise Institute for Public Policy Research, 1977), p. 6.

[45] Ranney, *Participation in American Presidential Nominations, 1976.*

nonprimary states were, with limited exceptions, considered to be the appropriate responsibilities of the state parties.

In the aftermath of its 1968 election defeat, the Democratic party launched a "reform" movement that still continues. The McGovern-Fraser Commission on Party Structure and Delegate Selection established the guidelines for delegate selection to the 1972 convention. The "Mikulski Commission" and midterm charter conference set new rules for 1976. On June 9, 1978, the Democratic National Committee adopted further changes recommended by the "Winograd Commission" for the 1980 convention. (The Republicans have moved more slowly and less comprehensively than the Democrats in their attempts to "democratize" delegate-selection procedures in the states. Republican state parties enjoy greater discretion than their Democratic counterparts.)

Current Democratic party rules require the state parties to insure "full, timely, and equal opportunity" for voters to participate. This can be accomplished through primaries (now used by the majority of states) or through precinct, district, and state caucuses and conventions. Much of the controversy and debate about accompanying party rules has concerned the following:

1. Composition of state delegations. The 1972 Democratic convention had quotas for women, blacks, and youth. In 1976, quotas as such were eliminated, but "affirmative action" was required to insure representation of these groups. For 1980, there is a general requirement that state delegations contain equal numbers of men and women. In addition, rules for the 1980 convention increase the size of state delegations by 10 percent to accommodate state party officials and elected officials.
2. "Winner-take-all" primaries, caucuses, and conventions. Proportional representation is now required in delegate selection at all levels. In 1976, however, delegates could still be elected at the congressional district level on a winner-take-all basis. The use of this so-called loophole primary to escape proportional representation requirements has been prohibited for 1980. For 1980, however, the threshold required to receive a proportionate share of delegates has been increased slightly, on the grounds that the proportional representation requirements would otherwise encourage minor or splinter candidacies and make it more difficult to achieve a party consensus.
3. Participation in delegate-selection process. Open, crossover primaries are now banned under party rules. There is no way to insure that only "real" Democrats participate, however, since numerous states do not require prior party registration to vote in primaries.
4. Length of process. This has been shortened from a maximum of six months for the 1976 convention to three months for 1980. Each state is to commence its delegate-selection process within a period extending from mid-March to mid-June.

Popular Participation. While attention has focused on these frequently esoteric questions, the impact of party reform on popular participation has been somewhat overlooked. The results have not been exactly overwhelming, however, in either the primary states or the nonprimary states. In 1976, for example, almost 29 million votes were cast in all of the presidential primaries. While this was an impressive total, it represented only about 28 percent of the voting age population and well under one-half of the registered voters in these states.[46]

Participation rates among the primary states differed greatly—from lows of slightly over 10 percent (of the voting age population) in New Jersey and Rhode Island to a high of 44 percent in Oregon. These interstate disparities are substantial, and they appear to be only marginally related to such factors as registration requirements, binding vs. advisory primaries,[47] or proportional representation requirements for selecting delegates.[48] Thus, states with less stringent registration requirements did not have significantly higher primary turnout rates than states with more stringent rules. Turnout rates for binding primaries and nonbinding or advisory primaries were similar. Proportional representation requirements also did not appear to encourage participation. In addition, while turnout rates were higher in closed-primary states than in open-primary states, the rates were not significantly affected by when the primary was held (early or late in the nominating "season") or by the closeness of primary contests.[49]

Perhaps most telling are comparisons between prereform and postreform primary turnout rates. According to a recent study, the mean turnout rate in competitive presidential state primaries was more than 10 percent higher during the period 1948-1968 than it was in 1976.[50] Although the primaries have proliferated since 1968, they have not broadened their participatory base. They continue to draw only about one-half of the presidential general election turnout rate and in this respect are no different from primaries for other offices. The public may support primaries as the preferred, "democratic" way to make presidential nominations, but only a minority of the public actually takes advantage of the opportunity to participate.

If the primaries have not provided overwhelming evidence of public interest and involvement, participation in alternative delegate-selection procedures has been even more limited. The Democratic party, for example, has issued rules requiring public access to the local party caucuses that commence the delegate-selection process in nonprimary states. In 1976, 21 states held precinct caucuses, the first and potentially most participatory round leading up to the state conventions. The available data, while imprecise, indicate that the average turnout rate for Demo-

---

[46] Ibid., p. 20. Figures do not include New York, where no statewide data are available, or Washington, D.C., which did not have a Republican primary. Also, statewide voter registration figures for Ohio and Wisconsin are not available.

[47] In 1976, seven states (Illinois, Nebraska, New Hampshire, New Jersey, Pennsylvania, Vermont, and West Virginia) had an "advisory" presidential preference poll and separate delegate selection. In three states (Georgia, Maryland, and Montana), preference poll results were binding in one party only. In the remaining primary states, presidential preference primary results were binding.

[48] Ranney, *Participation in American Presidential Nominations, 1976*, pp. 27-29.

[49] Ibid., pp. 26-34.

[50] Ibid., p. 24.

cratic caucuses in these states was less than 2 percent of the voting age population.[51] Thus, while some 700,000 activists attended caucuses, they composed only a tiny fraction of the potential electorate or of Democratic voters in these states.

Whether these levels of participation insure more representativeness in delegate-selection procedures is questionable. As one moves from presidential general election turnout to presidential primary turnout to caucus turnout, popular participation drops dramatically. This makes it possible for organized or highly activist minorities to exert a disproportionate influence in the delegate-selection process. Also, as we noted earlier, the shift of influence away from state parties toward an undefined public involves a shift in perspective. The parties must be responsive to voters in terms of providing attractive and competent candidates. Their short-term success and long-term survival require that they choose nominees intelligently, if not perfectly. Primary voters and precinct activists deal with different questions, notably how they personally feel about a prospective candidate.

The Convention. The national nominating conventions meet in July or August, although convention committees—rules, credentials, permanent organization, and resolutions (platform)—meet well in advance to prepare their reports and recommendations. The out-party traditionally holds its convention first, presumably to gain maximum publicity for its nominees. The usual order of business at the Republican and Democratic conventions is to settle procedural issues (rules, credentials, and organization), to adopt the platform, and then to nominate the presidential and vice-presidential candidates. Following both conventions, there is a short break until Labor Day, when the presidential campaign begins in earnest.

The extraordinary amount of television coverage now devoted to the party conventions usually conveys a high degree of drama and uncertainty. In fact, the importance of conventions as decision-making bodies has declined significantly. There has not been a genuine draft in either party since the Democrats nominated Adlai Stevenson in 1952. There has not been a "dark horse" of any consequence since Wendell Wilkie captured the Republican nomination in 1940. George McGovern and Jimmy Carter kicked off their candidacies with little fanfare, but by the end of the primary season, each was firmly established as the leading candidate. Neither candidate, moreover, had much initial support from party regulars, although Carter was able to pick up this support as his candidacy achieved success in the primaries. The pattern is clear. Since 1952, when the Democrats took three ballots to nominate Stevenson, all Democratic and Republican nominations have been decided on the first ballot (see Table 6.1). This is especially impressive since only four nominees (Eisenhower, Nixon, Ford and Johnson) have been incumbents.

What drama there has been at recent conventions has been confined to: (1) whether the leading candidate could successfully hold his delegates through credentials challenges, platform fights, and opposition raids; and (2) whether the losers and winners could effect a durable, if not necessarily enthusiastic, alliance for the

[51] Ibid., p. 16.

TABLE 6.1　Presidential Nominations, 1932-1976

Year	Democratic Nominee	Number of Ballots	Republican Nominee	Number of Ballots
1932	Roosevelt	4	*Hoover	1
1936	*Roosevelt	1	Landon	1
1940	*Roosevelt	1	Wilkie	8
1944	*Roosevelt	1	Dewey	1
1948	*Truman	1	Dewey	3
1952	Stevenson	3	Eisenhower	1
1956	Stevenson	1	*Eisenhower	1
1960	Kennedy	1	Nixon	1
1964	*Johnson	1	Goldwater	1
1968	Humphrey	1	Nixon	1
1972	McGovern	1	*Nixon	1
1976	Carter	1	*Ford	1

*Incumbent President.

election. As the first-ballot nominations indicate, none of the preconvention leaders has been displaced during the actual convention. Tension has existed during platform fights, as at the Democratic convention in 1968 or Republican convention in 1976, but the eventual nominee has managed to control these and related conflicts. Reconciliation is sometimes more difficult. In 1964, the Goldwater forces managed to antagonize their opponents sufficiently so that the party was more divided after the convention than before. In 1968, Hubert Humphrey was unable to placate antiwar Democrats at the convention and started his campaign with a split party. He eventually managed to pull part of the opposition behind his candidacy, but some Democrats chose to sit out the election. The 1972 Democratic convention was also unsuccessful in resolving intraparty splits. Organized labor, party regulars, and southern conservatives could not strongly support McGovern's candidacy. And, as in 1964, the intraparty split was serious enough to produce an electoral disaster. The convention is not unimportant, of course, but its significance often lies in reflecting the degree of party harmony (or discord) and the nature of a candidate's probable coalition, rather than in seriously deliberating the choice of nominees.

The changes in the deliberative and decision-making functions of the national conventions reflect the decreased role of state party leaders who control their delegations and can negotiate with candidates and other organizations.[52] Most delegates today are committed to a candidate for one or more ballots. Delegate-selection processes and convention rules further inhibit the emergence of strong delegation leaders. Candidates who wish to compete effectively for the nomination must do their "negotiating" well in advance of the convention within the states. It is not necessary, as both McGovern and Carter proved, for a candidate to have the support of state party organizations and leaders. The delegate-selection process in both

[52] Nelson W. Polsby and Aaron Widavsky, *Presidential Elections*, 4th ed. (New York: Charles Scribner's Sons, 1976), p. 128.

primary and nonprimary states allows groups of activists outside the party to exercise considerable and sometimes dominant influence over a state's delegation. The decreased influence of state party leaders and organizations has been more evident within the Democratic party than the Republican, but neither party has been immune to this change.

While the delegations are still designated by state, candidate loyalties or other types of commitments are, for increasing numbers of delegates, the essential spurs to activism. The demographic caucuses that have been so much in evidence at recent Democratic conventions—such as the women's caucus and the black caucus— often appear to be more responsive to group causes and interests than to the state parties or even the national party. In a similar fashion, the ideologically motivated convention activists tend to be intensely concerned with platform statements and candidates' issue positions. The idea that there are legitimate state party interests to be represented at the conventions has almost disappeared, at least on the Democratic side, with the "nationalizing" of the presidential nomination process.

The convention now takes place at the end of a nominating campaign dominated by mass media (especially television) coverage and numerous public polls that present "trial heats" between different sets of candidates. Decisions concerning which primaries to enter, which issues to emphasize, and which direction the campaign should take are important matters for individual candidates, but the framework within which the campaign takes place necessitates a constant emphasis on primaries. Unless there is no candidate with sufficient strength to gain first-ballot nomination, candidates have no need to meet and bargain with party leaders at the convention. Under the current rules, moreover, the bargaining during a brokered convention is likely to be between candidates heading party factions rather than individual candidates and groups of influential party leaders. As Polsby and Wildavsky conclude, the nominating process today focuses on candidates and their followings, not on parties.

> Over the long run, as mass communications media continue or possibly increase their saturation coverage of early events in the election year, successful candidates (at least of the party out of office) increasingly will have to have access to large sums of money . . . , a large personal organization, and an extra measure of skill and attractiveness on the hustings and over television. In these circumstances, other resources—such as the high regard of party leaders— would come to be less important. Thus, early candidacy, opulent private financing . . . , and strong personal organizations such as characterized the Kennedy, Goldwater, Nixon, and McGovern preconvention campaigns can overcome strong misgivings on the part of party leaders. . . . If out-party candidates in the future follow similar strategies, the national convention as a decision-making body may go into eclipse.[53]

Future Changes. There is little likelihood that the nominating process will be changed in ways that would benefit state parties and party leaders, at least in any

---

[53] Ibid., p. 152.

immediate way. The current enthusiasm is in the direction of organizing and extending the present system. There have been proposals to organize the numerous state primaries into a series of regional primaries. Within a region, states would hold their presidential primaries on the same day.

A more dramatic change is contained in proposals for a national presidential primary. While the specifics vary from one plan to another, most would require that a candidate achieve a minimum of 40 percent of the primary vote in his party for nomination. If no candidate received this minimum, a runoff would be required. While the national primary is, for its advocates, the next logical step in making presidential nominations more open and participatory, there is no particular reason to suspect that national primary turnout will be proportionately any higher than state primary turnout has been in the past. The problem of representativeness among the primary electorate will remain. Candidate followings will further displace the parties as electorate mobilizers. Perhaps most important, active intermediation by parties in presidential nominating politics will likely disappear.

Electing the President

The essential tasks of a presidential campaign do not differ markedly from other campaigns. A campaign organization is needed to plan and supervise campaign operations. Potential supporters in the electorate must be identified. Appropriate strategies must be devised to communicate effectively with these supporters. Finally, the vote must be activated on election day.

The presidential campaign organizations of recent elections contain impressive rosters of political specialists—media consultants, pollsters, issue advisers, field organizers, advance men—headed by this or that master strategists. The most elaborate and expensive campaign in history was the 1972 Nixon reelection effort. The president's campaign organization (Committee for the Re-Election of the President) had a $50 million budget, several hundred staff members and thousands of volunteers, and special divisions to handle advertising, finance, direct mail and telephone appeals, special groups (ethnic, racial, and interest groups), and campaign security.[54] There was also no question that the exclusive concern of this campaign operation was to reelect Richard Nixon, not to provide assistance for other Republican candidates. Nixon's victory in 1972 was intended to be, and indeed was, a personal victory rather than a party victory.

While the Nixon organization was unusual for reasons beyond size and expense, its narrow focus was not atypical of candidate organizations. In 1976, for example, President Carter's campaign relied heavily on the personal organizations that he had built up in the states during the primaries. It also received considerable assistance in voter mobilization from the interest groups that normally support Democratic candidates, most importantly organized labor. The Carter campaign did

[54] Robert Agranoff, *The Management of Election Campaigns* (Boston: Holbrook Press, Inc., 1976), p. 182.

make use of regular Democratic party organizations, but the separation between the presidential race and other party contests was clear.

Of course, the major emphasis in presidential campaigns now involves utilization of television. This includes not only political advertising but also news coverage. Candidates crisscross the country, delivering speeches, primarily to stimulate coverage on the evening television news. They also spend millions of dollars to produce and run commercials that can reach, if not necessarily influence, a mass audience. Since people depend more on television for political information than they do on other sources, and since they consider television news to be especially reliable, this emphasis is understandable.[55] When candidates can reach the electorate directly, however, the party simply functions as one of a number of auxiliary organizations that assist the candidate in performing specific tasks, such as registration and vote drives.

Many party effects on the candidate are indirect. Democratic candidates, for example, tend to benefit when economic domestic issues are salient during a campaign. Republican candidates, who must confront an electorate that is skeptical about their party's record in domestic affairs, enjoy an initial advantage when foreign policy issues are dominant. Similarly, the constituencies for each party are reasonably clear, and a candidate must attempt to preserve his party's natural base, do reasonably well among Independents if a Democrat and extremely well if a Republican, and also if a Republican, gain considerable defectors from the opposition party. Whether they like it or not, the party candidates are linked to the successes, failures, and constituencies associated with each of their parties.

Beyond these very general limits, what a presidential candidate does during the campaign is, within the bounds of reason, up to him and his advisers. He may use some party leaders in the campaign, although the party does not finance, plan, or run the campaign. Of course, much of what is done will be dictated by events and circumstances during the campaign, by what the opposition party candidate does or does not do, and by practical limits on resources and knowledge.

The central point, however, is that the parties have limited *direct* control over presidential campaigns, just as they have limited direct control over the nomination. As a result, a successful candidate will be unlikely to view his party as having been conspicuously responsible for his election. And this diminishes the likelihood that he and other elected officials in the party will recognize a mutual dependence on and responsibility to the party once they are in office.

NONPRESIDENTIAL ELECTIONS

While the contest for the presidency is the most dramatic and important election for most of the electorate, the parties cannot ignore electoral politics at other levels. Indeed, the strength of state parties is ordinarily measured by their competitiveness

---

[55] See Walter DeVries, "American Perceptions of Parties, Institutions, and Politicians," in *Voters, Primaries, and Parties,* p. 21.

in statewide, state legislative, and congressional elections. A number of trends in nonpresidential politics parallel those that we have examined at the presidential level. In particular, the political party's monopoly over the resources and expertise associated with campaigns has declined as personal candidate organizations and interest groups have become increasingly influential in electoral politics.

Nominations

Party control over nominations is affected by a number of factors. As discussed earlier in this chapter, state electoral laws have a significant impact. Where preprimary nominations or endorsements are allowed, for example, the state parties can often control nominations for major state offices, such as governor. Open primaries, easy ballot access, and prohibitions against organizational endorsements make it extremely difficult for the party to maintain dominant influence during the nomination process.

In general, the state parties are unable to centralize control of nominations for a wide variety of offices. Nominations for state legislative seats, as well as for local offices, are controlled locally.[56] A similar lack of state party influence also characterizes nominations for the U.S. House. Where state parties are heavily involved in nominating politics—and there are numerous states where they are not— their attention is usually directed toward statewide offices. Thus, the degree of centralization characterizing party nominations is minimal in both state and national politics.[57]

The major problem facing the state parties is the direct primary. The primary method of making nominations was, and is, intended to increase the public's control of nominations at the expense of party "bosses," party "machines," and party organizations generally. While primaries have doubtless made life difficult for the parties, it is not clear that public control has thereby been enhanced. With the exception of one-party Democratic states in the South, for example, primary election turnout has usually been much lower than general election turnout, with turnout rates for primaries often in the 20-30 percent range. One study of turnout for gubernatorial and Senate races during the 1960s found that in competitive, two-party states, primary turnout rates for both these races were less than 30 percent, while general election turnout was over 60 percent.[58] Just as in presidential primaries, only a minority of the electorate participated in choosing nominees for even these major offices.

Disparities in turnout have not disappeared. In Table 6.2 turnout rates are shown for recent gubernatorial elections. These are calculated in terms of registered

[56] Austin Ranney, "Parties in State Politics," in *Politics in the American States*, 2nd ed., ed. Herbert Jacob and Kenneth N. Vines (Boston: Little, Brown and Company, 1971), p. 98.

[57] Ibid., p. 99.

[58] Ibid., p. 98. See also Jewell and Olson, *American State Political Parties and Elections*, pp. 139-63.

TABLE 6.2 Primary and General Election Turnout, Gubernatorial Elections, 1974

	Voting Age Population— Percent Registered	Registered Voters— Primary Turnout	Registered Voters— General Election Turnout
Alabama	75%	46%	33%
Alaska	82	49	57
Arizona	62	36	62
Arkansas	70	59	55
California	68	52	63
Colorado	71	29	68
Connecticut	74	NA	71
Delaware (1972)	71	15	78
Florida	62	23	51
Georgia	65	43	45
Hawaii	60	66	73
Idaho	85	26	59
Illinois (1972)	77	32	75
Indiana (1972)	82	NA	72
Iowa	51	26	91
Kansas	71	50	69
Kentucky (1975)	64	30	48
Louisiana (1975)	70	NA	25
Maine	90	29	58
Maryland	63	29	55
Massachusetts	72	35	63
Michigan	79	22	56
Minnesota	73	24	70
Mississippi (1975)	NA	NA	NA
Missouri (1972)	NA	NA	NA
Montana (1972)	77	58	82
Nebraska	74	36	57
Nevada	62	93	76
New Hampshire	77	15	54
New Jersey (1973)	69	24	59
New Mexico	69	40	65
New York	66	77	64
North Carolina (1972)	63	42	64
North Dakota (1972)	NA	NA	NA
Ohio	61	40	69
Oklahoma	71	59	60
Oregon	72	49	67
Pennsylvania	66	24	66
Rhode Island	74	NA	63
South Carolina	55	42	52
South Dakota	87	40	69
Tennessee	68	46	53
Texas	66	31	32
Utah (1972)	83	NA	77
Vermont	84	24	53
Virginia (1973)	62	NA	51
Washington (1972)	80	46	75
West Virginia (1972)	83	49	73
Wisconsin	NA	NA	NA
Wyoming	76	55	69

voters rather than the total voting age populaton, so that we are dealing with that segment of the public that is sufficiently involved and interested in politics to register. Even within this group, general election turnout is usually much higher than primary election turnout, with the average difference in turnout rates equaling approximately 25 percent. In the few states where primary turnout is higher, the average difference is less than half this amount. Especially striking is the fact that only about one-fifth of the states for which figures are available achieve primary turnout rates of 50 percent or higher, while only about 10 percent of the states fail to reach this level in their general elections.

Primary nominations for major state offices, as well as for Congress, are typically decided by a relatively small minority within the electorate. The limited evidence we have about primary electorates shows that they differ from the general electorate in several respects. Primary election voters are disproportionately drawn from upper socioeconomic groups and tend to be more interested in and knowledgeable about politics. However, they do not tend to be more strongly identified with the parties.[59] This suggests that primary voters are unlikely to pick a strong *party candidate*. Their attraction to candidates will be based instead on subjective reactions to candidates' personalities, issue positions, or competence.

The frequency and competitiveness of primary contests are also affected by such factors as incumbency, party strength, and party endorsements. Primaries involving incumbents tend to draw fewer challengers than do primaries without incumbents, and when incumbent challenges do occur, they tend to be disproportionately noncompetitive. Incumbency appears to discourage serious primary competition, especially outside the one-party states of the South.[60]

Primary competition is more likely to occur within dominant parties than within weaker parties. Contested primaries, with two or more "serious" candidates, are more frequent within the electorally stronger party in a district or state.[61] In one-party states, where the majority party primary determines the election for most offices, primaries on the majority side are almost always sharply contested, while the minority party often encounters trouble in finding a sufficient number of candidates to fill its slate.

Of special interest is the finding that primary contests are less frequent and less competitive in states that have preprimary nominations and formal or informal party endorsements.[62] This suggests that parties can discourage challenges if electoral laws support an active party organizational role in the nomination process. It does not mean that nominations are tightly controlled under all circumstances, but rather that where a party is allowed to recruit and support nominees, its choice is

---

[59] These findings are drawn from studies in Wisconsin. See Ranney, *Parties in State Politics*, p. 97.

[60] Jewell and Olson, *American State Political Parties and Elections*, pp. 132-39.

[61] Ibid.

[62] Ibid.

likely to prevail unless challengers are willing to mount extensive and expensive primary campaigns.

The range of supportable generalizations about the political party's role in making nominations is limited. We do know that parties in some states are more heavily involved and influential than parties in other states. We also find that electoral laws are important determinants of party involvement and influence. And it appears that centralized control of nominations for offices at different levels within the states is quite rare. The number of offices and the frequency of elections require that parties focus their efforts on the particularly significant races. The direct primary, however, is a potential obstacle that the party must confront when attempting to control candidacies for even these offices.

Elections

For competitive, major offices, the party organization may be able to perform important tasks for a candidate. It can provide assistance in raising funds, planning campaign strategy, and mobilizing the electorate. Huckshorn reports, for example, that parties in some states direct all their resources toward a single statewide race, such as governor or U.S. Senator. Others emphasize activities such as voter registration, public relations, and issue development designed to provide a party-oriented campaign that can benefit all of the party's candidates. In some states, however, the party has no substantial role in campaigning. Personal candidate organizations dominate campaigning in these areas.[63]

Party involvement in election campaigns thus varies from state to state and from office to office. In many states, candidates for virtually all offices are on their own. Party candidates run individual campaigns, using personal organizations and raising their own funds. In most states, there are from six to twelve separate statewide offices alone on the ballot, and this encourages further decentralization in election campaigns:

> It is by no means uncommon for a particularly popular incumbent to win re-election even when his fellow partisans are being defeated. Such a man has every reason to play up his own experience and qualifications and play down his party connections with other candidates on the ticket. So usually only weak or little-known candidates talk much about the party ticket or seek joint campaign appearances with their fellow candidates.[64]

Elections in the states, moreover, have not been immune to the technological changes in campaign politics that have transformed presidential elections. Candidates for major offices in the states are increasing their use of professional campaign management, polling, and television. The costs of gubernatorial and U.S. Senate

[63] Robert J. Huckshorn, *Party Leadership in the States* (University of Massachusetts Press, 1976), pp. 117-18.

[64] Ranney, "Parties in State Politics," pp. 100-101.

elections now sometimes reach several million dollars in the larger, more populous states. In 1976, for example, 10 candidates for the U.S. Senate (of the 33 seats that were up for reelection) spent more than $1 million, with H. John Heinz III of Pennsylvania being the top spender with expenditures reported at over $3 million. At the other extreme, William Proxmire (D-Wisconsin) won reelection with total reported expenditures of $697, and roughly half of the Senate candidates spent less than $500,000 on their campaigns. Of some additional interest is the fact that higher spending did not guarantee victory. In 15 of the 31 contested races (candidates in West Virginia and Mississippi ran unopposed), the winning candidate spent less than the loser.[65] For the U.S. House, there were 15 candidates who spent $250,000 or more in the primary and general elections. Eight of these candidates lost. However, the majority of congressional campaigns were small, low-budget operations, with most of the large expenditure totals concentrated in a relatively small number of campaigns.[66]

These spending differentials suggest the wide variety of campaign approaches in the states, as candidates attempt to accommodate the available resources to the general legal and political environment of their state or district as well as to the particular characteristics of their specific races. Such factors as party competition, incumbency, and money affect the type of campaign that is necessary and possible. All races, even for major offices, do not require extensive use of television, polling, or other expensive campaign tools. All candidates who might need these campaign tools cannot necessarily afford them.

There are, of course, certain tasks that must be performed in most campaigns (or at least those that are contested)—creating an organization, raising funds, and developing strategies for mobilizing voters. How elaborate and expensive these efforts are depends on some of the variables discussed above. The organizational structure and functions that might be required for an important and competitive statewide or congressional race are shown in Table 6.3. The first stage is to recruit personnel who can direct the fulltime operation of the campaign. Of these, the campaign director or manager is the key official, since it is his responsibility to plan and implement campaign strategy and to supervise other organizational officals. Within the organizational structure, there are several divisions that have specific responsibilities, such as fund raising or advertising.

The organization's objective, of course, is to mobilize the electorate behind the candidate. In order to accomplish this task, it is necessary to identify current and potential supporters, communicate effectively with these supporters to reinforce their predispositions, and finally to insure that these supporters actually vote. The identification and communication functions have been transformed by changes in campaign technology. Public opinion surveys are now used by candidates to

[65] *Congressional Quarterly Almanac,* 1977, p. 44-A.
[66] Ibid., p. 32-A.

TABLE 6.3 Campaign Organization and Functions

Campaign Organization: Key Positions
  Campaign director
  Finance chairman
  Communications director
  Research director
  Field supervisor
  Legal counsel

Campaign Organization: Key Divisions
  Research (issues, voting records, media monitoring)
  Volunteers (recruitment, organization, supervision)
  Fund raising (direct mail, door-to-door, dinners)
  Finance (budget planning, expenditure control, audits and reports)
  Advertising (literature, commercials, media planning, news coverage)

Functions: Identifying Voters
  Demographic analysis
  Polling
  Canvassing

Functions: Communicating with Voters
  Rallies, meetings (scheduling, advance work)
  Broadcast media (speeches, commercials)
  News coverage (news relations, advances)
  Campaign material distribution (door-to-door, direct mail)
  Endorsements (outside speakers, groups)

Functions: Getting Out the Vote
  Registration drives
  Election day activities (poll workers, transportation, telephone banks)

assess their strengths and weaknesses (along with those of the opposition), to determine what types of issues are most salient for specific groups of voters, to ascertain where advertising and reinforcement are most needed, and to identify trends during the campaign. Increasingly, public opinion polling has provided vital information to candidates and their campaign directors. The advertising and other communications tasks for the campaign have also become highly professionalized. Market research, for example, must be used to assess the demographic characteristics of audiences reached by various media outlets. The results of public opinion surveys must be used to develop a plan for broadcast and other media. Media consultants must plan and produce materials to be used. Since television is the most effective means for reaching a massive audience directly, it has become a staple of modern campaigns. But since it must be used correctly (some candidates simply do not come across well on television), professional help is a necessity. While other media are less dramatic and immediate, they are also important for full coverage of the campaign. Publicity must be coordinated, press releases prepared, and advertising materials distributed.

Technological innovations have probably had their smallest impact on "getting out the vote" activities. The final work of getting voters to the polls on election day requires volunteers to make telephone calls and knock on doors to remind people to vote, to provide transportation or other assistance where necessary, to serve as poll watchers, and to do whatever else is necessary to produce the maximum number of favorable votes. This is where traditional party organizations often excelled, and it is where many are still active.

Whether campaigns are this organized or expensive, the fact is that most party organizations do not have the resources, the expertise, or the control necessary to dominate election campaigns. Candidates who are not dependent on the party organization for nomination are unlikely to submit to the organization during the campaign. Professional campaign consultants, personal organizations, citizens groups, and interest groups can be used to organize and conduct the campaign. Surveys can be used to identify the voters. Television can be used to reach them directly. Party organizations can help, but how and where they help are usually up to the candidate. All too frequently, it is the party that needs the candidate rather than the candidate who needs the party.

SUMMARY

Electoral politics in the United States has been dramatically altered by legal regulation and technological change, usually to the detriment of party organizations. In addition, attempts at democratization have further weakened the party's influence over its own candidates. These changes make it difficult for the party to serve as an active and effective intermediary between the public and elective political leadership.

Perhaps the most conspicuous disadvantage of the American parties in comparison with other democratic party systems is their inability to control nominations. The direct primary is now used for virtually all important offices in the states, and it has become, in its presidential preference variant, the means for selecting most delegates to the national nominating conventions. The primary is a major decentralizing force within the party system. National and state party organizations cannot simply pick those candidates who will have the greatest voter appeal and who will advance the interests and programs for which the party stands once in office. Instead, loosely defined party electorates must be allowed to participate in the nomination process. Although actual participation in primaries at all levels has been extremely low, creating an ever-present danger of unrepresentative minorities dictating the party's nominations, there is little likelihood that "democratic reforms" will be reversed. And this may make it increasingly difficult for the parties to aggregate electoral interests effectively and promote compromise and consensus within the political system.

In addition, the parties are not treated, as they are elsewhere, as essentially private associations. Federal and state regulations of campaign finance, electoral procedures, and internal party affairs have in many instances been explicitly aimed at limiting the discretion and influence of party organizations. Whether parties would indeed be less responsive to the needs and interests of voters if these regulations did not exist is an issue that has been ignored by reform advocates.[67]

In addition to losing both its legal right to designate nominees and its status as a reasonably private political enterprise, the party has also suffered from technological obsolescence. Modern campaigning has changed the tools and the assumptions of electoral politics. Campaigning is personalized, appeals to voters are direct, and candidates are not dependent on or beholden to party organizations. The resources and knowledge that define electoral politics are no longer monopolized by the parties. They are available to candidates from other sources.

Nominations and election campaigns, then, have become less susceptible to party organizational influence. Nonparty organizations and specific candidates have assumed increased importance as the party's sphere of influence has shrunk. Electoral politics is "open" to more groups and to different techniques and approaches today. Whether an entrepreneurial politics that emphasizes individual candidates is suited to effective government is a question that should trouble those who applaud the decline of the parties.

---

[67]For an instructive discussion of this point, see E. E. Schattschneider, *Party Government* (New York: Farrar and Rinehart, 1940).

seven

The Party in Politics: Governing

Once elected to public office, political party members assume the tasks of organizing the government and enacting public policy choices. How well the parties accomplish these obligations determines the level of popular support for the government and the degree of success the political structure will have in coping with the problems facing the nation. Under the doctrine of responsible political parties, we expect the elected members of a party to make a concerted effort to implement party supported public policy programs. A special responsibility is borne by the majority party because it enjoys sufficient numbers to decide matters of public policy as long as it is able to maintain unity among its members. Of course, there are a number of factors that work against the emergence of responsible political parties. A government based upon federalism, a division of authority resulting from the separation of powers doctrine, the lack of meaningful rewards and punishments for use by party officials, and competing pressures applied by various constituencies work against the ideal of strong political parties capable of implementing party based government programs. The extent to which political parties are able to organize the government and control the flow of public policy will be the central concern of this chapter.

In the legislature, party control of the governing apparatus reaches perhaps its most effective level. While there are numerous pressures placed on American representatives to the law-making bodies, political party affiliation remains the most consistent and dependable predictor of a legislator's policy choices. The organization of the legislature and the selection of its leaders are almost exclusively based upon political party considerations. While geographical, ideological, constituent and other factors regularly split the members, political party continues to be the dominant variable in the legislative equation.

In the executive branch, too, political party is an important factor. The president (or the governor at the state level) retains a great deal of control over the administrative machinery of the government. This includes the important power to appoint individuals to fill political positions within the executive branch. These policy-making offices are overwhelmingly staffed by members of the chief executive's political party. A change in party control of the White House or the Governor's mansion normally signals a wholesale turnover in key executive branch officials. Because political party affiliation generally determines the pool from which potential governmental appointees are drawn, it is an important factor in the administrative process. Members of the same party will normally share similar views on many public policy issues. But perhaps more important to the shaping of the executive branch are the personal qualities and priorities of the chief executive. Commitment to the goals and modes of operation of the incumbent can be more significant than loyalty to the political party. The impact of the chief executive's personality can shape the administrative wing of the government beyond the form imposed by political party control.

The judiciary is designed to be the least political of the three branches of government. At the federal level, judges are appointed by the president and confirmed by the U.S. Senate. At the state level, a number of formal selection systems are used, with varying degrees of participation by political party organizations. Whatever selection system is employed, however, party affiliation becomes a key factor in the judicial recruitment process. The party that controls the selection authority will show a preference for judicial candidates of the same political persuasion. Once on the court, there are no formal party organizations or caucuses to influence the way in which judges decide cases assigned them. Yet the political experiences which a judge carries with him to the bench may well have an impact on the manner in which he evaluates the claims of parties who bring their disputes before the judiciary for settlement. This may especially be the case when such claims involve matters of public policy.

In each of the three branches, then, political party can be a significant factor in the personnel, organization, and performance of the government. The role of the political party in our nation's basic governmental institutions will be of primary interest in the following pages.

POLITICAL PARTIES AND THE LEGISLATURE

The legislatures of the United States are clearly organized according to the political party affiliations of their members. Legislative leaders are identified with their political parties, members commonly meet in party-defined formal and informal organizations, and seats on legislative committees are frequently determined by the relative strengths of the major political parties within the legislative chamber. The majority party within the legislature normally advances a legislative program. Members of the same political party as the chief executive organize to advance his proposals through the legislature. However, in spite of this relatively high degree of party-centered activity, American legislators exhibit rather modest levels of party cohesion. The result has been that American legislative parties fall short of the unified, well disciplined party delegations in the legislatures of several European nations.

Legislative Leaders

The leaders of American legislatures are essentially party leaders. Members of the majority and minority parties within a legislative chamber select from their ranks individuals who will fulfill partisan leadership functions. These responsibilities commonly include organizing party members, participating in the selection of legislators to sit on the various legislative committees, providing information and other services for party members, and scheduling legislative business. The efficiency and effectiveness of the legislature is to a large measure dependent upon how well the leadership carries out these responsibilities.

United States House of Representatives. The United States Constitution stipulates one specific officer of the lower chamber of Congress, the Speaker of the House.[1] The members of the House have complete freedom in selecting a Speaker. There are no constitutional requirements for filling the position. The Speaker does not even have to be an elected member of the House, although from the very beginning the representatives have followed the tradition of restricting this position to currently sitting legislators. It is clear that the framers of the Constitution intended the Speaker to be the presiding officer of the House and to be an active leader of the chamber rather than simply a neutral moderator of chamber debate.[2] However, the Constitution defines no specific powers to be exercised by the Speaker, and the authority wielded by the holder of that office has been determined through tradition and internal agreement.

The importance of the Speaker's position has undergone considerable modification as the House has evoked through the years. The office has been sufficiently flexible to allow each Speaker to make the position as powerful and active as the personality and informal influence of the incumbent would allow it to be. The first individuals to hold this position were relatively weak, although from the very beginning the Speaker was empowered to preside over House business, decide parliamentary points, appoint committees, and vote in cases of an equally divided

---

[1] *United States Constitution,* Article I, section 2.

[2] See Mary P. Follett, *The Speaker of the House* (New York: Longmans, Green and Company, 1896).

chamber. It was not until 1811 when Henry Clay was elected Speaker during his first term in the House that the position began to emerge as a powerful political office which could be used to advance a legislative program. From Clay's tenure until contemporary times the Speaker's office has been associated with the partisan politics of the chamber's majority party. Clay explicitly rejected the role of objective moderator by frequently engaging in partisan debate, using party considerations in committee appointments, voting on all issues, and developing strategies for enactment of his party's legislative priorities. While the power of the Speakership was to fluctuate over the years, it never returned to the relatively weak status associated with the office prior to Clay's service.

The Speaker's position grew in both power and partisanship during the years following the Civil War. Speakers such as James G. Blaine (R-Maine), John Carlisle (D-Kentucky), Thomas B. "Czar" Reed (R-Maine), and Charles Crisp (D-Georgia) used their influence to convert the office into a dominant force in the House. These legislative leaders cultivated procedural powers which allowed them to impose their wills on an often unsupportive chamber and to block any obstructionist strategies attempted by the minority party. The dominance of the Speaker's position rose to its greatest level under the 1903 to 1911 tenure of Joseph G. Cannon, a Republican from Illinois. Cannon exercised his power in an arbitrary and often abusive manner. He rewarded his supporters and would take whatever actions were necessary to block those who were not his allies from attaining any measure of effectiveness within the House. He built upon Speaker Crisp's use of the Rules Committee as an instrument of political power and guided the actions of this committee to assist him in reaching his personal and partisan goals. In 1910, however, a group of Republican rebels broke from Cannon's influence and joined forces with Democratic legislators. The resulting coalition was of sufficient size to strip Cannon of much of his power and to reform the Speaker's office into a much less powerful position. Under the new rules, the Speaker could no longer appoint committees, was prohibited from serving on the Rules Committee, and had his absolute power of floor recognition severely reduced.

Following the 1910 revolt, the Speaker of the House remained an important figure, but his powers were balanced by various party committees and other party leaders. The modern role of the Speaker began to evolve during this period. During the tenure of Nicholas Longworth (R-Ohio) from 1925 to 1931, the Speaker's office began to reemerge as a focal point of political power. Longworth had well-honed skills of political persuasion and was able to form a solid, working relationship with other leaders in the House. Longworth was followed in this office by Sam Rayburn (D-Texas), who is generally regarded as the most influential Speaker of the modern era. Rayburn was extraordinarily successful at leading his Democratic colleagues. Using informal persuasion and effective bargaining techniques, Rayburn became a master of the legislative process, obtaining House acceptance of both foreign and domestic policy programs.[3] The men who filled the Speaker's position after Rayburn, John McCormack (D-Massachusetts), Carl Albert (D-Oklahoma), and Thomas O'Neill (D-Massachusetts), generally followed the role developed by Rayburn. No substantial growth in the power of the position has occurred during the past two decades.

Like many governmental positions, the power of the Speaker's office is largely determined by the personal qualities of the incumbent. Bargaining, persuasion, and informal influence frequently dictate the degree of power the Speaker will enjoy. Legislative skills and personal attributes significantly affect the level of support the Speaker will attract from his fellow party members and how well he is able to use that support to forge a legislative program. In addition to his informal influence, the Speaker is granted certain formal powers. Chief among these are the responsibility to preside over the House deliberations, to refer bills to appropriate committees, to appoint members of certain special committees, and to decide parliamentary questions. In addition, the members of the Democratic Party have allowed the Speaker, when he is a Democrat, to name the Democratic members of the House Rules Committee, to chair the Democratic Policy and Steering Committee, and to have considerable influence in assigning members to the standing committees. Most important, however, is the fact that the Speaker of the House is the leader of the majority party and that position carries substantial political influence.

Assisting the Speaker in organizing and directing the members of the majority party is the majority floor leader. This position was not formally recognized until 1899 and was considered a dual assignment along with the chairmanship of the Ways and Means Committee until 1911. In recent decades the majority leader's primary duties have centered on cooperating with the Speaker in developing both the majority party's legislative program and the legislative strategy necessary to gain enactment of that program. He guides bills through floor action and has considerable influence over the scheduling of House business. In essence, the majority leader is the second ranking official of the majority party in the House with primary responsibilities for managing floor action of specific interest to the party.

The House minority party also has a designated floor leader, a position that was formally established in 1883. Today the minority leader assumes many of the same responsibilities as the majority party's floor leader. The minority leader organizes and manages the minority party forces on the House floor. He leads in the development of minority party strategy and cooperates in the development of the minority's legislative program. When the minority leader is of the same political party as the president, he normally becomes the chief executive's primary spokesman in the House. The powers of the minority leader are based largely upon indi-

---

[3] See Randall B. Ripley, *Party Leaders in the House of Representatives* (Washington: The Brookings Institution, 1967). On congressional leadership generally, see Robert L. Peabody, *Leadership in Congress* (Boston: Little, Brown and Company, 1976).

vidual ability and informal authority. The minority leader has no formal role in legislative scheduling or other important House matters.

The members of each party in the House also designate a party whip who acts as the floor leader's assistant.[4] Specifically, the party whip has organizational and information gathering responsibilities. The whip maintains information on the whereabouts of each legislator belonging to the party, encourages party members to be present when important votes are taken, and assists the floor leader in attempting to influence legislators to vote in accordance with the party's position on important issues. An additional function of the whip is to poll members of the party to ascertain their positions on pending legislation. This information is particularly valuable to the floor leaders for developing strategy and scheduling legislative action. The whips for both the Democratic and Republican delegations in the House are supported in their tasks by a group of assistant whips. The assistants (normally numbering about 15) are assigned responsibility for covering specific regional or state delegations. The assistant whips serve an important function as a communications link between the leadership and the rank-and-file legislators.

Party leaders are selected at the beginning of each Congress. The members of each legislative party meet in a party caucus or conference to designate their leaders for the upcoming two-year period. Each party nominates a candidate for the office of Speaker of the House. Later, during an official meeting of the House, a Speaker is elected from those nominated by the opposing parties. The formal election of the Speaker is customarily a straight party-line vote. Consequently, the Speaker of the House is always the leader of the majority party. Floor leaders and whips are selected by the party delegations without a formal vote by the entire House membership. The minority party's candidate for Speaker normally becomes the minority floor leader. The whips and floor leaders are selected by majority vote of the party members.

Leadership in the House has been exceptionally stable over the past several decades. Since 1940 the Democrats have had but four party leaders: Sam Rayburn, John McCormack, Carl Albert, and Thomas O'Neill. During this period, the leadership of the House Democrats changed only due to death or retirement. Although there were occasional challenges to the reelection of various leaders (normally mounted by liberal representatives), the postwar leaders have been quite successful in maintaining their support. Furthermore, the Democratic leadership has commonly advanced up the leadership ladder. Speakers Rayburn and McCormack served as the party's floor leader before being elevated to the highest leadership post. Speakers Albert and O'Neill advanced from whip to floor leader and finally to the Speaker's position. House Republicans also have displayed leadership stability, although the history of the party has exhibited two major leadership struggles during the past

---

[4] See Randall B. Ripley, "The Party Whip Organizations in the United States House of Representatives," *American Political Science Review*, 57 (September 1964), 561-576.

TABLE 7.1 Party Leaders in the U.S. House of Representatives, 1945-1980

Years	Speaker of the House	Majority Leader	Minority Leader
1945-46	Sam Rayburn (D-Tex.)	John McCormack (D-Mass.)	Joseph Martin (R-Mass.)
1947-48	Joseph Martin (R-Mass.)	Charles Halleck (R-Ind.)	Sam Rayburn (D-Tex.)
1949-50	Sam Rayburn (D-Tex.)	John McCormack (D-Mass.)	Joseph Martin (R-Mass.)
1951-52	Sam Rayburn (D-Tex.)	John McCormack (D-Mass.)	Joseph Martin (R-Mass.)
1953-54	Joseph Martin (R-Mass.)	Charles Halleck (R-Ind.)	Sam Rayburn (D-Tex.)
1955-56	Sam Rayburn (D-Tex.)	John McCormack (D-Mass.)	Joseph Martin (R-Mass.)
1957-58	Sam Rayburn (D-Tex.)	John McCormack (D-Mass.)	Joseph Martin (R-Mass.)
1959-60	Sam Rayburn (D-Tex.)	John McCormack (D-Mass.)	Charles Halleck (R-Ind.)
1961-62	Sam Rayburn (D-Tex.)[1]	John McCormack (D-Mass.)	Charles Halleck (R-Ind.)
1963-64	John McCormack (D-Mass.)	Carl Albert (D-Okla.)	Charles Halleck (R-Ind.)
1965-66	John McCormack (D-Mass.)	Carl Albert (D-Okla.)	Gerald Ford (R-Mich.)
1967-68	John McCormack (D-Mass.)	Carl Albert (D-Okla.)	Gerald Ford (R-Mich.)
1969-70	John McCormack (D-Mass.)	Carl Albert (D-Okla.)	Gerald Ford (R-Mich.)
1971-72	Carl Albert (D-Okla.)	Hale Boggs (D-La.)	Gerald Ford (R-Mich.)
1973-74	Carl Albert (D-Okla.)	Thomas O'Neill (D-Mass.)	Gerald Ford (R-Mich.)[2]
1975-76	Carl Albert (D-Okla.)	Thomas O'Neill (D-Mass.)	John Rhodes (R-Ariz.)
1977-78	Thomas O'Neill (D-Mass.)	Jim Wright (D-Tex.)	John Rhodes (R-Ariz.)
1979-80	Thomas O'Neill (D-Mass.)	Jim Wright (D-Tex.)	John Rhodes (R-Ariz.)

[1] Sam Rayburn died in November of 1961. John McCormack was promoted by the Democrats from majority leader to Speaker of the House and Carl Albert was elected majority leader replacing McCormack.

[2] Gerald Ford resigned his seat in the United States House in December of 1973 in order to accept President Nixon's nomination to become vice president of the United States. John Rhodes was elected by the Republicans to assume the position vacated by Ford.

four decades.[5] Joseph Martin led the Republican delegation for twenty years beginning in 1939. In 1959, however, the Republican members of the House, after experiencing a bitter intraparty battle, replaced Martin with the younger and more conservative Charles Halleck of Indiana. Halleck quickly offended large numbers of Republicans and was himself the target of a successful rebellion in 1965. At that time the members of the Republican delegation selected Gerald R. Ford of Michigan to be minority leader. Ford served in that post until 1973 when he resigned his House seat to accept Richard Nixon's nomination to be vice president. With the exception of the Martin and Halleck defeats, House members appear to have been generally satisfied with the performances of those selected to lead the party delegations.

United States Senate. The Constitution designates two officers of the United States Senate and allows the upper chamber to select additional officials as necessary.[6] The two designated officials are the vice president of the United States and the president pro tempore of the Senate. Both positions have failed to become meaningful seats of power. The Constitution gives the United States vice president the responsibility of being the president of the Senate. As such, the vice president is empowered to preside over the Senate and vote in those situations when the chamber is equally divided. Over the years the vice president has become increasingly removed from his Senate duties. He is likely to be found presiding over the Senate only on those ceremonial occasions which command his presence or when a tie vote is probable on an issue of particular concern to the president. The vice president has always been viewed by the members of the Senate as an outsider from the executive branch, and the chamber has refused to allow power to gravitate into his hands.

The Constitution directs the Senate to select a president pro tempore to preside over the chamber when the vice president is absent. In this capacity the president pro tempore recognizes speakers, renders decisions on parliamentary points, enforces order and the rules of the Senate during debate, and administers oaths. Because he is a properly elected senator, the president pro tempore may vote on every issue coming before the chamber. During recent years the position has become largely an honorary one and is not associated with significant legislative power. It is now customary for the Senate to select the most senior member of the majority party to fill this post.

Prior to this century, formal leadership positions of substantial authority were not recognized. Leadership was exerted by powerful individuals who were able to attract support because of their personal qualities. In 1911, however, the Senate began formal designation of party floor leaders. This was the result of a number of

---

[5] See Robert L. Peabody, "Party Leadership Change in the United States House of Representatives," *American Political Science Review,* 61 (September 1967), 675-693.

[6] Article I, section 3.

factors in institutional development, including the growing influence of political parties in the chamber and the enlarging of the Senate due to the increased number of states. The majority and minority floor leaders hold the greatest amount of power in the Senate. Neither position, however, has developed authority comparable to the office of Speaker of the House. Because the Senate is less than one-fourth the size of the House, rigid leadership structures have not been necessary. Both floor leaders are selected by the Senate members of their respective political parties. Since there are relatively few formal powers attached to these positions, the floor leaders hold powers largely because of the support given them by their party colleagues, and their influence is based primarily upon what their personal qualities and political support is able to attract. The majority floor leader is particularly important in the Senate because he has developed over the years the power to exert controls over legislative scheduling and the flow of Senate business.

Assisting the floor leaders are the party whips. The whips in the Senate serve much the same function as their counterparts in the House of Representatives. However, whip organizations have been far less successful in the Senate.[7] The Senate does not demand the same tight organization that is required in the House, and therefore, well-functioning whip organizations are not essential to the successful operation of the party delegations. When a whip and his assistants do operate in an effective manner, such as occurred during Senator Robert Byrd's (D-West Virginia) 1971-1976 tenure, the legislative party functions in a much more potent manner.

Similar to patterns that have emerged in the House, Senate leadership has been quite stable over the past decades. Death and retirement are the two most common reasons for leadership change. Between 1953 and 1976, Senate Democrats had but two leaders. Lyndon Johnson (D-Texas) led the party from 1953 to 1960, resigning the post only to accept the vice presidency under John Kennedy. Johnson's years as floor leader have often been used to illustrate strong and effective legislative leadership.[8] Mike Mansfield (D-Montana) was promoted by the party from whip to majority leader in 1961 and retained that post until his retirement in 1976.[9] During the same 1953-1976 period Senate Republicans had three floor leaders. From 1953 until 1958, William Knowland of California headed the Republican Senate forces. When Knowland did not return to the Senate following the 1958 elections, the Republicans elevated Everett Dirksen of Illinois from the whip position to the office of minority floor leader. Dirksen served in that capacity until his death in 1969, after which he was replaced by Senator Hugh Scott of Pennsylvania, who had served as minority whip. In 1977, with the retirements of Senators Mansfield and Scott, both parties installed new floor leaders. The Democrats elevated Robert

---

[7] Randall B. Ripley, *Power in the Senate* (New York: St. Martin's Press, 1969), esp. ch. 4.

[8] Ralph Huitt, "Democratic Party Leadership in the Senate," *American Political Science Review,* 55 (June 1961), 333-344.

[9] John G. Stewart, "Two Strategies of Leadership: Johnson and Mansfield," in *Congressional Behavior,* ed. Nelson W. Polsby (New York: Random House, 1970).

Byrd from the whip position. The Republicans, rejecting the opportunity to promote whip Robert Griffin of Michigan, selected Tennessee's Howard Baker, a man who had previously challenged Senator Scott without success.

The whip positions of both parties have generally enjoyed similar stability. Only during the 1969-1971 period was there substantial dissatisfaction demonstrated by Democratic senators over the performance of the incumbent whip. In 1969, Senator Edward Kennedy of Massachusetts successfully challenged incumbent whip Russell Long of Louisiana. Long was vulnerable to a reelection defeat because

TABLE 7.2   Party Leaders in the U.S. Senate, 1945-1980

Years	Majority Leader	Minority Leader
1945-46	Alben Barkley (D-Ky.)	Wallace White (R-Maine)
1947-48	Wallace White (R-Maine)	Alben Barkley (D-Ky.)
1949-50	Scott Lucas (D-Ill.)	Kenneth Wherry (R-Nebr.)
1951-52	Ernest McFarland (D-Ariz.)	Kenneth Wherry (R-Nebr.)[1]
		Styles Bridges (R-N.H.)
1953-54	Robert Taft (R-Ohio)[2]	Lyndon Johnson (D-Tex.)
	William Knowland (R-Calif.)	
1955-56	Lyndon Johnson (D-Tex.)	William Knowland (R-Calif.)
1957-58	Lyndon Johnson (D-Tex.)	William Knowland (R-Calif.)
1959-60	Lyndon Johnson (D-Tex.)	Everett Dirksen (R-Ill.)
1961-62	Mike Mansfield (D-Mont.)	Everett Dirksen (R-Ill.)
1963-64	Mike Mansfield (D-Mont.)	Everett Dirksen (R-Ill.)
1965-66	Mike Mansfield (D-Mont.)	Everett Dirksen (R-Ill.)
1967-68	Mike Mansfield (D-Mont.)	Everett Dirksen (R-Ill.)
1969-70	Mike Mansfield (D-Mont.)	Everett Dirksen (R-Ill.)[3]
		Hugh Scott (R-Pa.)
1971-72	Mike Mansfield (D-Mont.)	Hugh Scott (R-Pa.)
1973-74	Mike Mansfield (D-Mont.)	Hugh Scott (R-Pa.)
1975-76	Mike Mansfield (D-Mont.)	Hugh Scott (R-Pa.)
1977-78	Robert Byrd (D-W.Va.)	Howard Baker (R-Tenn.)
1979-80	Robert Byrd (D-W.Va.)	Howard Baker (R-Tenn.)

[1] Senator Wheery died in November, 1951. Republicans elected Senator Bridges to replace him.

[2] Senator Taft died in July, 1953. Republicans elected Senator Knowland to replace him.

[3] Senator Dirksen died in September, 1969. Republicans elected Senator Scott to replace him.

of his failure to support several important legislative proposals backed by the Democratic administration. Kennedy's tenure was also to be short-lived, and in 1971, he was defeated by Senator Robert Byrd. Democratic senators had been disappointed by Kennedy's failure to devote himself to the daily administrative tasks and legislative detail work required of the whip. Leadership in the Senate has been generally characterized by stability, and leaders, once in office, have been quite successful in maintaining the allegiance of members of their own party.

State Legislatures. The leadership structure in the state legislatures generally follows the model established by the United States Congress.[10] In the lower house the presiding officer is known as the Speaker of the House. In most states the Speaker is a powerful individual, often exerting even more influence in the lower house than his federal counterpart. It is common for state Speakers to be empowered to preside over debate, refer bills to committees, appoint legislators to committees, vote on all legislative questions, interpret the rules of the house, and administer the staff and resources of the chamber. The states follow the federal custom of the Speaker leading the majority party. The political position of the Speaker as leader of the chamber's most numerous party, coupled with the powers granted the presiding officer by the formal rules of the state legislature, make the state Speaker one of the most politically powerful offices in American state government. Most state legislatures have relatively high turnover rates which increase the Speaker's influence in intralegislative politics and decrease the likelihood of his being challenged by competitors for power.

At the state senatorial level, the lieutenant-governor is designated as the presiding officer in a majority of states. This position is often more powerful than the role of vice president of the United States as presiding officer of the U.S. Senate. The lieutenant-governor is normally given certain formal powers associated with his obligations to manage the state senate while it is in session. In some states he is even given the power to appoint legislators to committees. However, the lieutenant-governor is commonly viewed as an outsider by members of the state legislature, in much the same way that the vice president is viewed by the federal legislature. He is considered a member of the executive department of the government and, therefore, is often not well accepted by state senators. For this reason, the lieutenant-governor must share his power with other leaders or committees in the chamber. The role of the lieutenant-governor is also diminished whenever he belongs to the political party which does not hold a majority of state senate seats. In those states which do not have a lieutenant-governor as the presiding officer of the senate, the upper house elects a presiding official from its own number. Normally this position is filled by the leader of the majority party. In such states the presiding officer can be an exceptionally powerful individual with authority comparable to the position of Speaker in the lower house.

Both the upper and lower chambers of the state legislatures have floor leaders who perform the same variety of functions as the party leaders in the U.S. House and Senate. These party leaders have primary responsibility for organizing members of their own party, encouraging party unity, and managing the flow of business on the floor of the legislature. If the floor leader is of the same political party as the governor, he may have responsibility for managing the governor's proposals through-

---

[10] For a very good discussion of state legislative leaders, see Malcolm E. Jewell and Samuel C. Patterson, *The Legislative Process in the United States,* 3rd ed. (New York: Random House, 1977), ch. 6.

out the legislative process. The importance of the majority and minority party leaders is especially significant in those states which have sharp two-party competition within the legislature. In such cases, how well the leaders manage and administer the party's members and legislative platforms will often determine which party will successfully control the state's policy-making process. In one-party states and in those legislatures in which the minority party is badly outnumbered, the role of the party leader is less significant.

State legislatures display a great variety of methods of leadership selection. In many states the selection of leaders proceeds according to the federal model of party members electing legislative officers. Normally this is the case in the selection of the Speaker or the presiding officer of the senate. Floor leaders, however, may be elected by party members or, in some states, appointed by the presiding officer. In still other states, the governor has an important role in the selection of floor leaders for his political party. There are similar variations in leadership tenure. While congressional leaders can normally count on reelection every two years, this is not the case at the state level. State legislative leaders generally exhibit much lower levels of stability than in the federal legislature.[11] Several state legislatures even impose the tradition of regular rotation of leaders and very short terms of office. Of course, the method of selection and the length of the leader's term of office may have a significant impact on the amount of power the leader is able to exercise.

Party Committees

American legislatures often have partisan-based committees which serve special functions in the law-making process. The most common party committee is the party caucus. The caucus is an organization composed of all the members of the same political party who have been elected to a particular legislative chamber. In addition to the caucus, parties may have policy committees, steering committees, and informal groups which function within the legislative setting. Some of these party-based organizations have significant influence on the policy-making process, while others are relatively weak and ineffective.

Party Caucus. A party caucus is the meeting of the legislative members of a political party. The primary purpose of the caucus is to bring together in formal session the members of a political party to reach agreement on the party's legislative program and to plan strategy for maneuvering the program through the legislative process.[12] The congressional party caucus has a long history, dating back

---

[11] Douglas Camp Chaffey and Malcolm E. Jewell, "Selection and Tenure of State Legislative Party Leaders: A Comparative Analysis," *Journal of Politics,* 34 (November 1974), 1278-1286.

[12] For a discussion of the party caucus, see Jewell and Patterson, *The Legislative Process in the United States,* ch. 7; *Guide to Congress,* 2nd ed. (Washington: Congressional Quarterly, Inc., 1976).

to the very beginning of the institution. The importance of the party caucus has fluctuated widely during the history of the national legislature. During certain periods, it was the legislative party's primary means of organizing and mobilizing support. During other years, caucus meetings were rarely called. The use of the caucus has largely depended upon the leadership methods of the party's legislative officials.

The Democratic caucus in the United States House has undergone substantial revision in recent years. Following World War II, the Democrats made relatively little use of the caucus. This decision was made primarily by Speaker Sam Rayburn, who, faced with a party that was often bitterly divided by ideological and regional factions, believed the party leadership could be more effective by working with individual representatives than by bringing all of the Democrats together. However, in the 1970s the Democratic caucus underwent a considerable revamping.

Prompted primarily by members of the liberal wing of the party, the Democrats began making more frequent use of regular caucus meetings. Between 1971 and 1975, the Democratic caucus devoted considerable resources to a study of reforming the procedures that governed the House committee system. Following these studies and deliberations, the Democratic caucus imposed dramatic changes in the way in which the standing committee system operated with respect to the Democratic membership. First, the caucus eroded the power of Democratic committee chairmen by establishing a Democratic caucus for each committee consisting of the party members of each committee. These committee caucuses were given powers to decide questions of subcommittee jurisdiction, budget, staffing, and the selection of subcommittee chairmen. Such powers had previously been exercised by the committee chairman alone. Second, the Democratic caucus imposed new procedures for the selection of committee members and committee chairmen. Under the revised procedures, the newly formed House Democratic Policy and Steering Committee was given the power to nominate Democratic members of the various standing committees and to recommend committee chairmen. These recommendations were to be made to the Democratic caucus which would have final authority to ratify them by secret ballot. Under old guidelines, the Democratic members of the Ways and Means Committee decided questions of committee assignments, and committee chairmen were determined exclusively on the basis of seniority. Third, the caucus passed new rules opening the legislative process by commanding that certain committee meetings previously held in secret be opened to the public and by dictating that all Democratic legislators be given at least one major committee assignment. These changes prompted a greater distribution of power among Democratic members and gave a new importance to the Democratic caucus.

Along with these procedural reforms the Democratic caucus began discussing policy issues. Deliberations on specific legislative questions, however, met significant opposition, and this aspect of the revamped caucus has not yet developed substantially. Opposition came primarily from ranking members of the various standing committees who felt that the caucus was beginning to intrude on the jurisdictions of the standing committees, as well as from more conservative representatives. Until 1975, the Democratic caucus held the power to bind all Democrats to support caucus decisions on the floor of the House. This power, which could be invoked by a two-thirds vote of the participating caucus members, was rarely used but was quite controversial nonetheless. Bowing to this criticism, the caucus revised the rule and provided for the binding power to be used only on questions such as the selection of the Speaker and other House officers, and not on issues of public policy.

The House Republican caucus (officially known as the Republican "conference") has not been used as extensively in recent years as its Democratic counterpart. In addition to selecting Republican nominees for House leadership positions, the Republicans have used the conference as a vehicle for communication between the party leadership and the rank-and-file members. Leaders brief the Republican members on numerous issues and procedural matters. Legislative strategy and issue positions are discussed, but votes are rarely taken on matters of substantive policy. The Republican conference has never adopted a rule that binds members to the decisions of the caucus. The conference meets regularly and has been an important method of building unity within the Republican membership.

In the United States Senate, both Democrats and Republicans have caucus organizations which are known as party conferences. Both parties use the conference as a method of increasing communication and distributing information to members. Legislative strategy and policy issues are discussed in the conferences, but neither party has applied rules that bind members to support conference positions on the floor of the Senate. Meetings of the party conferences give the leadership an opportunity to communicate directly with rank-and-file members and allow the junior senators to have a voice in party affairs within the chamber.

Party caucuses are used with varying degrees of success in state legislatures. Not all state assemblies have adopted the use of party caucus meetings, though many of those which have done so have found that the caucus can be an effective mechanism for organizing the legislative party. Because state legislatures are often faced with high membership turnover and short legislative sessions, a way to distribute information rapidly to party members, to organize legislative strategy, and to answer member questions about substance and procedure is needed. The caucus meets this need quite adequately. In those states which use the party caucus, meetings are held regularly throughout the legislative session.

Policy and Steering Committees. Congress has commonly used policy and steering committees to aid the party leaders in the development of legislative policies and strategy. In comparison to the party caucus, the policy and steering committees are relatively small groups and therefore more manageable than the caucus. How extensively these committees are used depends greatly on the preferred manner of operation of the party leaders. Therefore, the significance of such committees has undergone substantial variation over the years. The use of policy and steering committees has been primarily a congressional phenomenon. Such groups have not emerged in any meaningful way at the state legislative level.

The current version of the House Democratic Steering and Policy Committee was created in 1973, after the party had experimented with various policy committee formats. Prior to the 1970s, the Democratic House leadership had given little attention to policy committees. The current Democratic Steering and Policy Committee was established by the Democratic caucus as another means of opening the party apparatus to increased participation. The committee is composed of the Speaker of the House (when Democrats are in the majority), the floor leader, the caucus chairman, a number of regionally elected representatives, and an additional number of legislators appointed by the Speaker. In recent years the committee has worked toward the development of legislative programs. However, its most significant power is the authority to recommend to the full caucus nominees for committee chairmanships and committee membership assignments.

The Republican Policy Committee in the House is used as an organ for articulating party positions on a wide variety of legislative issues. The committee is composed of a broadly representative group of Republican legislators: the Republican leadership, representatives from various geographical regions, at-large representatives, and legislators representing the junior members of the Republican House delegation. The committee meets frequently to discuss various legislative policy issues and to consider the positions taken by the Democratic members of the House. The Policy Committee regularly issues statements explaining the stand taken by it on these matters. Republican House members are urged to support the committee's positions, which are considered statements of the preferences of the House Republican Party. Because the Republicans have found themselves in the role of the minority party in recent decades, the statements of the Policy Committee have frequently been used to register the views of the loyal opposition.

The House Republican Policy Committee does not possess the committee assignment power enjoyed by the Democratic Steering and Policy Committee. Instead, the committee assignment power is exercised by a special Committee on Committees. This nominating committee is composed of the Republican floor leader and a representative from every state that has a Republican legislator. The recommendations of the Committee on Committees are referred to the House Republican Conference for final approval.

In the Senate, both Democrats and Republicans have established policy committees. The Democratic Policy Committee is used to advise the floor leader on legislative strategy, scheduling, and the management of party business. On occasion the committee has taken positions on policy issues and has made recommendations to the Democratic caucus. How extensively this committee is used depends upon the philosophy of the floor leader. The Republicans use their Policy Committee as a means of communicating information from the leadership to the other members of the party. In addition, the Policy Committee members study various legislative issues and make recommendations to the party caucus and the floor leader.

The committee assignment power in the Senate is divorced from the party policy committees. The Democrats have a Steering Committee which possesses the power to nominate Democratic members for committee assignments. This committee is composed of a number of Democratic members appointed by the floor leader. Members of the committee serve for as long as they are in the Senate. The Republicans have a Committee on Committees which is entrusted with the committee assignment responsibility. The Republican committee is appointed by the party leadership. Service on the committee is restricted to a two-year term. Both Democratic and Republican committee assignment recommendations must be approved by the full party conference.

Informal Legislative Groups. In addition to formal party organizations, legislatures often have informal groupings of delegates with shared interests or similar policy goals. While many of these groups are open to members of both political parties (such as the Congressional Women's Caucus or the Black Caucus), others are distinctly party oriented. The establishment and growth of these informal groups are more frequently found at the federal level than in state legislatures.

The most notable example of an informal, partisan-based legislative organization is the Democratic Study Group.[13] This association was formed in 1959 by a group of liberal Democrats. For the most part, the founders of the group were younger representatives from the North, Midwest, and West. Upon entering Congress, these newly elected legislators found the power base of the legislative party in the firm control of conservative and Southern members. Devoted to the research and study of public policy issues, the Democratic Study Group was formed as an alternative to the formal party structure. The group has become quite powerful, and it now speaks for the liberal wing of the House Democrats. The group retains a staff which spends a portion of its time studying bills and issuing reports to group members on pending legislation. The Democratic Study Group has been in the forefront of attempts to reform the procedures of the House generally and of the Democratic caucus in particular. In addition, it has attempted to develop research efforts centering on policy alternatives. In recent years the Democratic Study Group has broadened its appeal and now has several members from the southern region of the country, as well as from its traditional power base in the North, Midwest, and West. Association membership is voluntary, and the group carries no procedures for binding the members to any group decisions. The organization began with a membership list of 80 legislators. Since that time its membership has

---

[13] Arthur J. Stevens, Jr., Arthur H. Miller, and Thomas E. Mann, "Mobilization of Liberal Strength in the House, 1950-1970: The Democratic Study Group," *American Political Science Review,* 68 (June 1974), 667-681; Kenneth Kofmehl, "The Institutionalization of a Voting Bloc," *Western Political Quarterly,* 17 (June 1964), 256-272.

grown substantially along with the general growth in Democratic representation in the House. In 1976, the Democratic Study Group reached a membership high of an estimated 226 members.

The Republican answer to the Democratic Study Group is the Republican Wednesday Group. The Wednesday Group was formed in 1963 as an association devoted to developing Republican policy alternatives. Its membership has traditionally come from the more liberal elements of the Republican House delegation. The group has never developed into an organization as strong as the Democratic Study Group, but it has been instrumental in providing constructive opposition alternatives to the proposals of the Democratic majority. The group has a small staff which conducts clerical and research tasks. The regular Wednesday meetings of the group provide an opportunity for the moderate-to-liberal membership to discuss common problems and share legislative ideas. Relative to the Democratic Study Group, the Republican Wednesday Group is quite small, with a membership of between 25 and 40 in recent sessions of Congress.

In addition to these organizations, the House has several other informal discussion and research groups (such as the conservative Republican Chowder and Marching Society and the liberal House Democratic Research Organization), which serve as clubs for members who share philosophical and public policy views. Also significant are the party caucuses of the various state delegations. Although several state delegations have too few members to form effective party organizations and other state party delegations are severely split, some states have developed effective party caucuses.

In the United States Senate, attempts to develop informal party organizations have generally failed. The primary reason for their lack of success is that the size of the Senate makes such associations unnecessary. The upper house has developed sufficient collegiality so that informally structured groups have not been required to bring together senators with shared policy concerns.

Party Unity in Legislative Decision Making

For a legislative party to have maximum effectiveness it must be able to enforce party unity in legislative decision making. Several European political parties have been able to reach this goal. Legislators in these countries are expected to vote according to the party line position. Legislators who fail to support the party may be subject to party disciplinary procedures. The cohesiveness displayed by these parties allows the political party to campaign on the merits of a legislative platform. The electorate may vote for party members with the confidence that the legislator will support the party's programs. This confidence is rarely misplaced. Voting cohesion statistics in the British parliament, for example, demonstrate high rates of party unity behavior. It is indeed infrequent for a legislator to desert his party's position. Such behavior on the part of the legislative party is a mark of the responsible party system of government. Legislative parties in the United States generally have failed to measure up to this standard.

Party Cohesion. The organizational structure of the American legislature focuses on political party as the primary distinguishing factor among legislators. Party leaders emphasize partisan unity; committee seats and other legislative rewards are granted on the basis of party membership; information and communications are distributed through party committees and caucuses; even seating in the legislature is arranged according to party affiliation. In addition, the chief executive submits a legislative program that is customarily based on party platform pledges made during the previous election campaign. Legislators are usually lifelong members of a particular political party and have been elected to office after running on a party label and being supported by party machinery. Local party members maintain communications with their legislators. Given such reinforcement, we might expect party unity in American legislatures to be exceedingly high. However, this has not proven to be the case.

A number of factors have contributed to the relatively modest degree of party cohesion in American legislative chambers. Legislators run for political office with a considerable level of independence. American legislative candidates do not campaign on unified, binding tickets with other nominees of the same party. Candidates are not strictly bound to support party platforms, and ideological commitment to the goals of the party is not required. Some candidates may successfully gain a legislative office without receiving the blessings of party officials. Furthermore, legislative candidates are elected by local constituencies and are members of local party organizations. American political parties, being broad-based electoral organizations, manifest substantial variation from locality to locality and region to region. A rural Mississippi Democrat may be a much different political animal than a New York City Democrat. All things being equal, legislators have a general loyalty to their political parties. But in American politics, all things are rarely equal. Constituency pressures, interest group influence, and philosophical beliefs often rival party considerations in commanding the allegiance of the legislator. For the majority of legislators, the primary concern is gaining reelection. Following the party line in legislative voting may well assist the legislator in his drive to be returned by his constituency. But when constituency and reelection considerations conflict with party, party is likely to be deserted. However, in spite of all these competing pressures and intraparty differences, political party affiliation remains the most consistently revealing clue to the way in which a legislator will vote on public policy issues.

The degree of party cohesion exhibited by American legislative parties depends upon the criterion one uses to measure party unity voting. In its absolute form, party cohesion would be manifested by 100 percent of the members of the majority party being opposed by 100 percent of the members of the minority party. Such party line votes are exceptionally rare and would be expected only on such party-oriented issues as the selection of the Speaker of the House and other legislative leaders. Given the context of American legislative politics, party unity votes are normally defined as those issues on which a majority of one political party takes a position opposite that of a majority of the other political party. In

TABLE 7.3　Party Unity Votes,[1] U.S. Congress, 1967-1977

Year	Senate	House
1977	42%	42%
1976	37	36
1975	48	48
1974	44	29
1973	40	42
1972	36	27
1971	42	38
1970	35	27
1969	36	31
1968	32	35
1967	35	36

[1] Party unity votes are defined as the number of votes in which a majority of voting Democrats opposed a majority of voting Republicans expressed as percentage of all recorded votes.

Source: *Congressional Quarterly Almanac* (Washington: Congressional Quarterly, Inc., various years).

such cases where most of the members of one party oppose most of the members of the other party, we have political party-based voting behavior.

In the United States Congress, the level of party cohesion is modest. Table 7.3 presents data concerning the frequency of party unity votes in the United States Senate and the House of Representatives. The information summarized in this table indicates the number of party unity votes expressed as a percentage of all recorded votes in each chamber of Congress. During the period 1967 to 1977, party cohesiveness manifested itself at an average rate of 39 percent in the Senate and 36 percent in the House. While there are year-to-year fluctuations in the percentage of party unity votes in Congress, the range of variation is not particularly great. Rarely does the incidence of votes in which one party opposes the other party drop below 30 percent or exceed 45 percent.

Of course, the percentage of times the majority of one party opposes the majority of the other party does not reveal a perfectly accurate account of the extent of party cohesiveness. On a large number of recorded votes there is relatively little disagreement or controversy. There are many minor issues requiring recorded votes on which we would expect general unanimity. Not every issue is one which splits the parties. On what variety of issue, then, do we find party opposition occurring? If we exclude questions related to the selection of legislative leaders, party cohesiveness reveals itself most prominently when the legislature deliberates on recommendations from the president and on issues over which there are socioeconomic class differences.[14]

[14] Jewell and Patterson, *The Legislative Process in the United States*, ch. 16.

At both the federal and state levels, the president presents legislative proposals to the law-making body. These proposals are almost always perceived by the legislature in partisan terms. Members of the chief executive's party regularly fall in line behind the proposals of the unofficial leader of the party. Members of the opposing political party often immediately react against the president's or governor's recommendations. While the responses of the legislators are not uniform and while there are frequent defections, party cohesiveness tends to occur with a fair degree of regularity on votes concerning the chief executive's legislative program.

Since party affiliation among the general public tends to divide roughly along socioeconomic lines, it is not surprising that relatively cohesive and unified parties present themselves when domestic economic and social welfare issues are debated in the legislature. While there may be numerous exceptions to this general rule, the Republican party has tended to support business interests, the middle and upper socioeconomic classes, and the free enterprise ethic, and has tended to have somewhat negative views on expansion of the welfare state. The Democrats, on the other hand, have generally supported policies beneficial to the interests of organized labor, the lower and working economic classes, and racial and ethnic minorities, and they have taken a favorable posture on using the legislative power to improve the lot of the economically disadvantaged through expansion of social welfare programs. When legislative proposals that will have an impact on these economic concerns are brought before an American legislature, there is a relatively high likelihood that a majority of Democratic legislators will find themselves opposed by a majority of Republican representatives.

An important question regarding the strength of a legislative party is how much loyalty the party can command on those issues that prompt partisan division. A strong party organization within a legislature should be able to attract high levels of support in the form of unified party voting when the chips are down and a confrontation with the opposing party is imminent. One way to analyze this question is to examine the level of party unity voting within a legislature when such issues arise. In Table 7.4, average party unity scores are presented for both political parties in the United States Senate and House for the years 1970-1977. These scores, calculated from the *Congressional Quarterly,* represent the average percentage of time a legislator votes with his own party on those issues over which the two parties find themselves divided. The data reveal some interesting facts regarding party unity voting in Congress during the 1970s. First, taking both houses into account, the average support enjoyed by the two major parties is relatively even. Democrats commanded an average support score of 63 percent and Republicans 64 percent. Second, the degree of party unity voting is moderate. The scores indicate that in a typical session of Congress during this period the legislative party could expect defections from about one-third of its members when it squared off against the opposing party. Such desertion rates on party-oriented issues would be unheard of in parliamentary systems. Third, party unity voting tends to fluctuate from year-to-year. Table 7.4 does not reveal any significant trends toward either a substantial

TABLE 7.4 Party Unity Voting,[1] U.S. Congress, 1970-1977

	Democrats	Republicans
1977		
Senate	63%	66%
House	68	71
1976		
Senate	62	61
House	66	67
1975		
Senate	68	64
House	69	72
1974		
Senate	63	59
House	62	63
1973		
Senate	69	64
House	68	68
1972		
Senate	57	61
House	58	66
1971		
Senate	64	63
House	61	67
1970		
Senate	55	56
House	58	60

[1] Party unity voting figures illustrate the percentage of time the average Democrat and the average Republican voted with his party majority in disagreement with the other party's majority.

Source: *Congressional Quarterly Almanac* (Washington: Congressional Quarterly, Inc., various years).

increase or decrease in party cohesion. Fourth, over the eight-year period represented, Democrats and Republicans have supported their parties at almost identical levels in the Senate; in the House, Republicans have been slightly more cohesive than the Democrats.

The degree of support members of Congress give to their own political parties displays a good deal of regional variation. Table 7.5 illustrates the party support levels by region for four recent sessions of Congress. The data reveal several interesting patterns in the distribution of party support. In every session examined for both the House and the Senate, the lowest levels of support are exhibited by southern Democrats. The tendency for southern Democrats to deviate from the party line position is not a recent phenomenon. The North-South division in the congressional Democratic party is one of long standing. In the House, the highest levels of party unity are earned by southern Republicans; in the Senate, the southern Republicans and the northern Democrats exercise the highest degree of party unity voting. For both the Democratic and Republican parties the areas of party unity

TABLE 7.5 Party Unity Voting,[1] U.S. Congress: Sectional Differences

	Senate	House
1977		
Northern Democrats	72%	75%
Southern Democrats	41	51
Northern Republicans	63	69
Southern Republicans	78	81
1975		
Northern Democrats	78	79
Southern Democrats	43	48
Northern Republicans	59	69
Southern Republicans	85	81
1973		
Northern Democrats	79	77
Southern Democrats	44	50
Northern Republicans	60	66
Southern Republicans	78	79
1971		
Northern Democrats	72	72
Southern Democrats	49	40
Northern Republicans	61	66
Southern Republicans	71	76

[1] Party unity voting figures illustrate the percentage of time the average Democrat and the average Republican voted with his party majority in disagreement with the other party's majority.

Source: *Congressional Quarterly Almanac* (Washington: Congressional Quarterly, Inc., various years).

weakness are obvious. The Democrats are faced with rather substantial defections from southern senators and representatives. These southern legislators represent generally conservative constituencies that do not favor the more liberal positions of the Democratic mainstream which is controlled by the northern wing of the party. For the Republicans, defections most commonly come from legislators representing the northern states. Northern Republicans with weak party unity scores tend to come from metropolitan districts which have a more liberal constituency than the typical Republican stronghold.

The level of support given by a representative to the positions taken by his legislative party is often heavily dependent upon the nature of the legislator's constituency.[15] Generally a legislator will demonstrate high support for his party's

[15] See, for example, Morris P. Fiorina, *Representation, Roll Calls, and Constituencies* (Lexington, Mass.: Lexington Books, 1974); Frank J. Sorauf, *Party and Representation* (New York: Atherton, 1963); Duncan MacRae, Jr., *Issues and Parties in Legislative Voting* (New York: Harper and Row, 1970); W. Wayne Shannon, *Party, Constituency and Congressional Voting* (Baton Rouge, La.: Louisiana State University Press, 1968); Julius Turner, *Party and Constituency: Pressures on Congress*, rev. ed., ed. Edward V. Schneider (Baltimore: Johns Hopkins University Press, 1970).

legislative program if the district he represents contains an electorate that is typical of the kinds of people who traditionally support the party. For example, a Democrat who represents a northern, metropolitan, working class district that contains a high proportion of minority citizens and has traditionally supported liberal public policy alternatives will normally engage in legislative voting behavior that is highly supportive of the Democratic party's programs. The more a congressman's district differs from this typical Democratic support source, the more likely he will be to desert the party on roll call votes. A southern Democrat who represents a white, rural, conservative community, therefore, can be expected to take positions contrary to those of his legislative party leaders with a fair degree of regularity.

Another constituency factor which has an impact on party support is the competitiveness of the district. A legislator who is in firm control of his district, who has no substantial opposition likely to challenge him, and who is a member of the political party that clearly dominates his district will often have relatively high party support scores. Because reelection probabilities are high, such a congressman can afford to respond to the demands of his party even if it means occasionally turning his back on the positions favored by some of his constituents. On the other hand, a legislator who represents a highly competitive district cannot afford to vote the party line position if doing so means the loss of significant support from his constituency. Since reelection is often of utmost concern to politicians, such a legislator is likely to place constituency demands ahead of party. The legislative parties are fully aware of these realities. When a congressman informs a party leader that he cannot vote in accordance with the wishes of his legislative party because of constituency demands, the leadership will, under normal circumstances, release the legislator from any expected loyalty obligations.

A final factor worthy of mention here is the legislator's own personal philosophy or conscience. There are occasions in which the legislator will defect from his party's position on a given piece of proposed public policy legislation simply because the legislator believes the proposal to be a bad one. This situation arises most frequently when the issue under consideration touches on matters of religion, morals, or ethical standards. The norms of most American legislative chambers, both state and federal, condone a legislator's bolting from the party position because of matters of conscience.

When Cohesion Dissolves. Because American parties have never evolved into rigidly unified political organizations, it is generally expected that on many issues a legislative party will experience sizeable defections from the position preferred by the leadership. In addition, there are situations in which the leadership of both major political parties will cooperate and combine efforts in order to obtain the adoption of a particular public policy. These situations are uncommon in nations with well disciplined legislative party organizations, but in the United States, defections and interparty cooperation are not particularly unusual events. At the federal level, two manifestations of this abandonment of party unity are worthy

TABLE 7.6 Bipartisan Voting,[1] U.S. Congress, 1968-1977

Year	Senate	House
1977	58%	58%
1976	63	64
1975	52	52
1974	56	71
1973	60	58
1972	64	73
1971	58	62
1970	65	73
1969	64	69
1968	68	65

[1] Bipartisan voting is the number of times a majority of voting Democrats and a majority of voting Republicans vote in agreement, expressed as a percentage of total recorded votes.

Source: *Congressional Quarterly Almanac* (Washington: Congressional Quarterly, Inc., various years).

of discussion: the phenomenon of bipartisan voting and the strength of the conservative coalition.

The term *bipartisan voting* refers to legislative actions on which a majority of Democrats and a majority of Republicans support the same position. As Table 7.6 clearly indicates, bipartisan voting is not an unusual event in Congress. In fact, bipartisan votes are the rule rather than the exception. However, many votes upon which both parties are in general agreement are noncontroversial minor issues upon which reasonable individuals might be expected to agree regardless of partisan loyalties.

Because regional and ideological splits frequently divide a legislative party, cooperation between the parties is occasionally necessary if an important public policy is to be enacted. During the past three decades, there have been two areas in which bipartisan cooperation has been especially significant. First, Congress has often demonstrated bipartisan cooperation in the area of foreign policy. American foreign policy since the end of World War II has quite often been the product of cooperation between the leaders of the Democratic and Republican parties. Second, the parties have often found it necessary to cooperate in the area of civil rights policy. The Democratic party has generally advocated strong civil rights laws and, when doing so, has experienced almost uniform defections from the southern wing of the party. In order to fashion sufficient majorities to pass such significant pieces of legislation as the Civil Rights Acts of 1957, 1960, 1964, and the Voting Rights Act of 1965, the Democrats have had to seek cooperation from northern Republicans who similarly favored the expansion of civil rights legislation.

The *conservative coalition* is a term which refers to the alliance between southern Democrats and Republicans. The conservative coalition is an extremely potent force in Congress. While the Democratic party in recent years has had rather substantial majorities, the legislative party has been frequently unable to enact important pieces of legislation. The reason for this failure is usually found in the defection of southern Democrats from the liberal policies of the northern wing of the party and the cooperation of those defecting Democrats with congressional Republicans. The glue which holds this coalition together is the common ideological positions held by the Republicans and the Democrats from the South. The southern Democrats have been of insufficient numbers to take control of their own legislative party and the Republicans have been hopelessly outnumbered by the Democrats. Therefore, these two groups have found that the only way to impede the passage of liberal legislation backed by northern Democrats is to combine voting strengths.

Table 7.7 provides information on the activity of the conservative coalition since 1961. It is clear that the coalition is an extremely important voting bloc in congressional policy making. A majority of southern Democrats and a majority of Republicans join forces in opposition to a majority of northern Democrats in almost one-quarter of the votes taken in a typical session of Congress. If we were to examine the presence of the conservative coalition on only those votes over which

TABLE 7.7 Conservative Coalition Voting,[1] U.S. Congress, 1961-1977

Year	Conservative Coalition Votes as a % of Total Votes, Both Houses	Conservative Coalition Victories as a % of All Conservative Coalition Votes, Both Houses
1977	26%	68%
1976	24	58
1975	28	50
1974	24	59
1973	23	61
1972	27	69
1971	30	83
1970	22	66
1969	27	68
1968	24	73
1967	20	63
1966	25	45
1965	24	33
1964	15	51
1963	17	50
1962	14	62
1961	28	55

[1] A conservative coalition vote is defined as any vote in the Senate or House on which a majority of voting southern Democrats and a majority of voting Republicans oppose a majority of voting northern democrats.

Source: *Congressional Quarterly Almanac*, (Washington: Congressional Quarterly, Inc., 1977), p. 16-B.

there was substantial disagreement, we would find the southern Democrat/Republican alliance in well over one-half of the recorded tallies. Furthermore, the conservative coalition has an excellent record of success. While there is considerable year-to-year fluctuation, the 17-year period ending in 1977 indicates that the coalition was victorious in 60 percent of the votes in which it was present. Clearly the conservative coalition has been the primary impediment to the Democratic party's enactment of a comprehensive, liberal legislative program. The coalition first emerged with southern defections from the Democratic ranks in reaction to the liberal policies promoted by Franklin Roosevelt. The coalition has endured since the New Deal days and continues to be a viable voting bloc today.

Political Parties and Legislative Policy Making

Political party affiliation is the single most important element in the organization of the American legislature. Leadership is based upon party membership strength, formal and informal groups are organized with party restricted memberships, committee seats are assigned by party committees and leaders, and the entire atmosphere of a legislative chamber is charged with partisan loyalties. In spite of this rather pervasive party environment, however, the legislative party is rarely capable of maintaining high rates of unity. Defections from party positions are common, bipartisan voting is a regular occurrence, and nonparty-based voting blocs, such as the congressional conservative coalition, are frequently experienced. Therefore, while political party is an exceptionally important factor in the legislative policy-making process, American political parties have not developed the strength or cohesion necessary to qualify as engaging in responsible party government of the variety found in many European nations.

POLITICAL PARTIES AND THE EXECUTIVE BRANCH

At both state and federal levels, the chief executive is the most visible government official. The president and the state governors perform many of the same functions. As the head of the executive branch, these officials are responsible for executing the laws passed by the legislature, administering the daily business of the government, promoting legislative proposals, and serving as the primary spokesman for the nation or state. The chief executive is also a partisan political official. He is perceived as the leader of his political party. The members of the chief executive's political organization expect him to provide direction for the party's development and to promote within the executive branch the policies advocated by the party. In earlier sections of this chapter we asked how well the political parties were able to organize and impose party policy choices within the legislative branch. We now need to ask a similar question of party control of the executive department of government.

The Chief Executive as Party Leader

The president and the various state governors have distinct responsibilities as leaders of their political parties.[16] Americans expect their chief executives not only to be the head of the executive branch, but also to lead the political party. As the highest ranking official within the nation or the state, the president and the governors are relied upon to set the tone and priorities of the political party's activities. The fortunes of a political party often rise or fall on the way in which the chief executive carries out his governmental and party duties.

A chief executive is expected to lend support to the party organization. Having won a state or nationwide election, the chief executive is the only official who can lay claim to legitimate leadership of the party in all sections of the polity. Presidents and governors may or may not be comfortable in this role. Some actively provide party leadership, while others allow this power to be delegated to subordinates. At the national level and in most states, the chief executive directly or indirectly controls the selection of the party chairman and other key personnel in the party organization. Effective appointments of quality people to head the formal party organization can be greatly beneficial to the future successes of the party machinery.

The actions of the chief executive must support faithful party members. Patronage, while not as great a source of rewards as it was in decades past, can be effectively distributed to party regulars as compensation for past service to the party and as encouragement for future labors in behalf of the organization. Benefits may take the form of government employment, the awarding of contracts, and the support of policies that help those who have shown loyalty to the party in the past. Furthermore, the president and the governors must also pay attention to government officials who are members of the same political party. This attention shores up the natural support which the president or governor will normally receive from fellow party regulars. When an executive fails to support the party organization and the party's lower-ranking officials, he may well begin to lose the support of his own power base. Such was the fate of Lyndon Johnson who became too preoccupied with the war in Vietnam to devote sufficient attention to Democratic congressmen who had been loyal to him in previous years. Richard Nixon made a similar fatal error when he refused to support certain Republican members of Congress for reelection and went so far as to give informal endorsements to select Democratic candidates. When both Johnson and Nixon later needed the support of their party at crucial times, they found that formerly loyal party members had deserted them.

The executive's responsibility as party leader includes an influential role in the electoral process. A popular governor or president can often be a substantial

---

[16] See Thomas E. Cronin, *The State of the Presidency* (Boston: Little, Brown and Company, 1975), pp. 253-254; Clinton Rossiter, *The American Presidency*, 2nd ed. (New York: Harvest Books, 1960); James MacGregor Burns, *The Deadlock of Democracy* (Englewood Cliffs, N.J.: Prentice-Hall, Inc., 1963).

benefit to other members of the party running for public office. When the chief executive is running for reelection, he may well have a "coattail effect," with fellow party members running for lower offices being swept to victory along with the chief executive's winning electoral tide. While there is considerable scholarly debate over the actual degree of impact the "coattail effect" may have,[17] there is little doubt that party members running for lower political office prefer to have the party ticket headed by a popular, attractive chief executive seeking reelection. In addition to providing leadership to the party's slate of candidates, the chief executive can often increase the likelihood of party members winning public office by aiding their campaigns through personal appearances, policy support, and organizational assistance. The level of influence the president or governor may exert on state or local campaigns is extremely difficult to measure. Yet the head of the executive branch is also perceived by the voters as the head of the party and so gives the party an image in the eyes of the public. It is within the context of this image that party members must run for lower state and federal offices.

The Chief Executive as Leader of the Administration

At the federal level the party that controls the White House controls the executive branch. A similar situation exists in the various state governments. Unlike the legislative branch in which there is a majority and minority party, there is no room in the executive branch for minority opposition. Apart from his vice presidential running mate, the president is the only executive branch official who is elected. All other political officials under the president are appointed directly by him or indirectly through his political subordinates. Since the executive branch has no party caucus, steering committee, or other partisan agency in charge of organizing it for political party purposes, the president has exclusive authority to set the partisan tone of the administrative department of government. For some presidents, party considerations have been of paramount importance in conducting the affairs of the executive branch. For others, party interests have been of secondary significance. The degree of partisanship within the executive branch is determined largely by the personality and philosophies of the incumbent.

Through his appointment power, the president can impose a great deal of party control over the executive branch. It is customary for the incoming president to remove any holdover officials from the previous opposition party administration and replace them with members of the president's own choosing. This appointment power not only serves as a patronage tool to reward the party faithful, but it also allows the president to fill key governmental positions with persons committed to the goals of the party. By carefully selecting individuals to assist him in the exercise of executive power, the president normally extends and solidifies his party's control over the administration of the federal government.

[17] See, for example, Milton C. Cummings, *Congressmen and the Electorate* (New York: Free Press, 1966).

TABLE 7.8 Presidential Cabinet Appointments, 1933-1978

President	Party	Years	% Democrats	% Republicans	% Independents
Roosevelt	Dem.	1933-45	92%	8%	0%
Truman[1]	Dem.	1945-53	85	8	8
Eisenhower	Rep.	1953-61	10	90	0
Kennedy	Dem.	1961-63	85	15	0
Johnson[1]	Dem.	1963-69	88	13	0
Nixon	Rep.	1969-74	6	90	3
Ford[1]	Rep.	1974-77	24	71	6
Carter	Dem.	1977-	92	8	0

[1] Presidents Truman, Johnson, and Ford assumed the presidency due to the death or resignation of their predecessors. Cabinet officials in office at the time Truman, Johnson, and Ford were elevated to the presidency were not considered appointments of these newly installed presidents unless they were retained in their positions for at least one full year.

In making such appointments, presidents have been overwhelmingly preferential to members of their own political party. While few presidents will go so far as to preclude the possibility of an appointment being given to the opposition party, no chief executive has been particularly generous in bestowing such positions on political rivals. Among the key appointments which a president must make are the selections of individuals to administer the various cabinet departments. It is through the cabinet positions that the largest share of policy administration takes place. Cabinet appointments often provide an excellent indication of the degree of party control imposed on the executive branch.[18] Table 7.8 summarizes the extent of such partisanship in the selection of cabinet secretaries under the last eight presidents. On the average, recent presidents have only appointed members of the opposing party to approximately 11 percent of the cabinet seats. This token acknowledgment of the opposition party frees the administration from having a blatantly partisan public image that may lead to a negative reaction in the minds of the citizenry. However, those opposition party members who are brought into the cabinet are almost always individuals whose political philosophies conform to the president's.

Although the president has broad discretion over appointments made in the executive branch, this power is not without limit. Furthermore, it is a power which has been generally decreasing over the years. The most important limitation on the president's appointment power has been the growth of civil service and other merit system coverage of federal employees. In the nineteenth century, particularly after the presidency of Andrew Jackson, all federal government employment was considered political patronage distributed by the president to his party supporters. Today, the president has appointment power over fewer offices than some governors exercise. Federal civilian employment approaches three million individuals.

[18] See William F. Mullen, *Presidential Power and Politics* (New York: St. Martin's Press, 1976), p. 185.

The president exercises appointment power over fewer than three thousand of them. While presidential appointment still extends to the most important and politically significant federal offices, the proportion of federal positions falling under the authority of the chief executive has decreased.

The nature of contemporary administrative positions has also restricted the role of partisanship. Today, because many executive responsibilities require technical ability and professionalism, none of the executive agencies can be successfully run by party hacks who are in office only as a reward for party service. For example, the position of postmaster general was traditionally reserved for a person who had labored long and well for the party. This was especially true of the Democrats who used the position as a particularly attractive patronage reward. The demands of running the postal service, however, have radically changed in recent years. Automation, unionization of workers, economic inefficiencies, and other factors have forced the government to remove the postal service from partisan politics. Increasingly, executive department positions are requiring professionalism and technical expertise which must be given equal consideration with party loyalties.

For some offices, the president may be prohibited from nominating individuals from his own political party. The federal regulatory agencies, for example, have been considered too important to be dominated by partisan political considerations. Therefore, Congress has stipulated that only a certain number of seats on such commissions can be held by members of the same political party. This limitation effectively removes the possibility that the president can use his appointment powers to engineer a situation in which his political party totally dominates a regulatory agency.

The president, of course, must share his appointment powers with other important individuals. Because most of his nominations must be approved by the U.S. Senate, the president customarily consults with key senators to insure that important individuals in the upper house are not offended by an appointment. Often the president will be forced to alter his nomination plans in order to appoint individuals who are acceptable to the Senate and thus capable of achieving confirmation. Key party officials must also be consulted to avoid the possibility of appointing persons who are unacceptable to the party organization. And finally, the president may have to consult with leading interest group leaders. The Democrats, for example, would not nominate a person for secretary of labor without first consulting the president of the AFL-CIO and other major unions.

The nomination of party members to various administrative positions does not guarantee that they will behave in a manner consistent with party-dictated policy. In fact, the president may have difficulty keeping his administration unified and cohesive as an executive party. Unfortunately, the degree of party unity in the executive branch is difficult to measure. There are no roll call votes of administrators as there are in the Congress. There do exist a number of forces which work against the implementation of a unified partisan administration of the administrative branch of government. First, although the president may have direct control over the White House staff and other personnel working immediately under him, appointees scattered in the various agencies are somewhat difficult to control. There is no whip organization or other party-based official with the responsibility for promoting the party in the executive branch. The president may have too many pressing obligations to devote sufficient time and effort to maintaining party discipline in the administration. Second, the vast majority of federal employees are prohibited from participating in active party politics. Legislation such as the Hatch Act makes attempts to politicize the bureaucracy unlawful. These restraints, imposed because of the abuses under the old spoils system of government, make it difficult to promote party loyalty in the executive branch. Third, agency personnel frequently become loyal to the clientele groups with which they work, and this loyalty often competes with party loyalty. As we shall see in subsequent discussions of interest groups, pressure organizations often "capture" administrative agencies and their officials. Agency administrators are frequently more interested in pleasing the interest groups with which they work than they are in imposing party-supported policy. As a consequence of these factors, the political party in the federal executive branch may become only a secondary force. What party cohesion exists can normally be attributed to the internal values of the personnel administering the government rather than to the organizational activities of the party.

The Chief Executive as a Legislative Leader

The political party reaches its greatest potential influence when it captures control of both the executive and legislative branches. In contemporary politics we expect the president or governor to prepare policy proposals for legislative consideration. If those legislative programs are acted upon by a legislature dominated by the chief executive's political party, the principles of the party should have a high probability of being enacted into formal public policy. This potential strength, however, becomes a reality only when the legislative party remains united and there is policy agreement between the party in the legislature and the party in the executive branch. When the president or governor is faced with a legislature that is dominated by the opposition party, the probability of party-based policy being adopted is severely reduced. To be successful under such conditions, the chief executive must work closely with the minority party leaders of the legislature and attract sufficient defections from the majority party. For party government to be successful, the chief executive must propose policies consistent with party principles, and the legislative party must remain sufficiently unified to dispose of such policy proposals in a favorable fashion. An examination of the recent experiences of the president and Congress will provide an indication of how successful American parties have been when using the combined strengths of the political party within the legislative and executive departments.

Figure 7.1 illustrates the level of success enjoyed by the presidents from 1953 through 1978. The table highlights the percentage of congressional victories earned

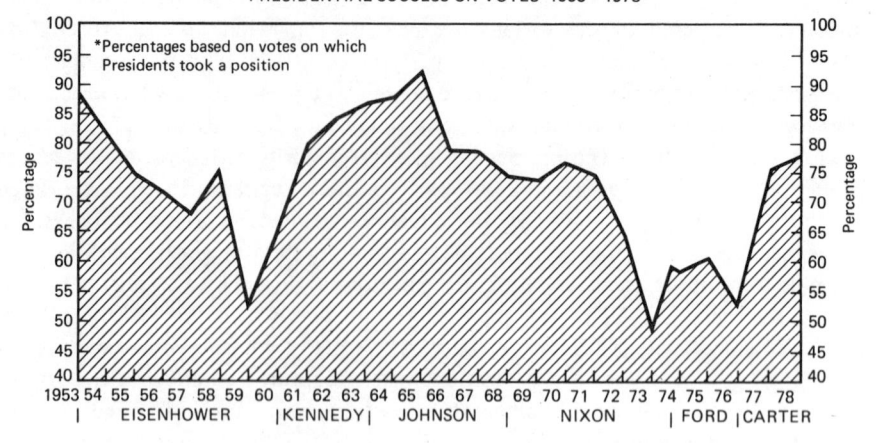

FIGURE 7-1 Presidential Success on Votes 1953-1978. *Source: Congressional Quarterly Weekly Report,* 36 (December 9, 1978), p. 3408

by the president based upon those votes on which the president took a public position. Perhaps most noticeable about the legislative success records of the presidents is the extreme variation over the years. The greatest success rates earned by a president during the 26-year period under study occurred in 1953, when Eisenhower convinced Congress to accept his position 89 percent of the time, and 1965, when Lyndon Johnson obtained the support of Congress on 93 percent of his recommendations. In both cases, the president had been swept into office the previous November with large electoral majorities and enjoyed the cooperation of congressional majorities of his own political party. The two years of lowest congressional support for the president's program were 1959, when a Democratic-controlled Congress supported only 52 percent of "lame duck" Republican president Dwight Eisenhower's legislative recommendations, and 1973, when Republican Richard Nixon, embroiled in the Watergate controversy, won the support of the Democratic Congress only 50.6 percent of the time.

It is clear that during periods of unified party control of the executive and legislative branches, the president enjoys far greater success than during years in which the opposing party controls the legislature. Table 7.9 presents more specific data on this phenomenon. Over the 26-year period beginning with Eisenhower's first term in 1953, four presidents (Eisenhower, Kennedy, Johnson, and Carter) experienced control of both branches of government by members of the same political party. The average annual success rate compiled by these presidents during periods of unified party control was 83 percent. The lowest rate of success under these conditions was Lyndon Johnson's 75 percent in 1968, a year which saw many liberal Democrats desert the president because of his Vietnam War policy.

During periods of divided control (when one party controlled the White House and the other dominated the legislature), the success rate of the president

TABLE 7.9 Congressional Support for the President:[1] Unified and Divided Control of the Government, 1953-1977

Presidential Support during Years Congress and Presidency were Controlled by the Same Political Party:

President	Year	Support Score
Eisenhower (Rep.)	1953	89.0%
	1954[2]	82.8
Kennedy (Dem.)	1961	81.0
	1962	85.4
	1963	87.1
Johnson (Dem.)	1964	88.0
	1965	93.0
	1966	79.0
	1967	79.0
	1968	75.0
Carter (Dem.)	1977	75.4
	1978	78.3

Presidential Support during Years Congress and the Presidency were Controlled by Different Political Parties:

Eisenhower (Rep.)	1955	75.0%
	1956	70.0
	1957	68.0
	1958	76.0
	1959	52.0
	1960	65.0
Nixon (Rep.)	1969	74.0
	1970	77.0
	1971	75.0
	1972	66.0
	1973	50.6
	1974	59.6
Ford (Rep.)	1974	58.2
	1975	61.0
	1976	53.8

[1] Congressional support is defined as the percentage of presidential victories in Congress on votes where the president took clear-cut positions.

[2] During 1954, the Republicans controlled the House, but in the Senate, due to the death of Senator Taft, the Democrats held 48 seats, the Republicans 47, and 1 seat was held by an Independent.

Source: *Congressional Quarterly Weekly Report,* 36 (December 9, 1978), p. 3407.

declines substantially. Three Republican presidents were forced to contend with Democratic majorities in Congress. Eisenhower, Nixon, and Ford compiled an average annual success rate of only 65.4 percent. Faced with dominating majorities from the opposing party, presidents simply are unable to impose the policy choices of their party. The highest level of legislative success attained by any president under conditions of divided government control during the quarter century studied was Richard Nixon's 77 percent in 1970; the lowest was Nixon's 50.6 percent in 1973. Clearly, if a political party is to have any reasonable chance of imposing comprehensive party-supported policy on the nation, the party organization must capture both the White House and the Congress.

Whether the president is confronted with a Congress dominated by the opposition or by his own party members, it is important for the chief executive to maintain the support of his own party in Congress. If his party has a majority in Congress, strong cohesion will insure major legislative victories. When his party controls a minority, party unity is essential if the president is to have any likelihood at all of seeing the enactment of his legislative program. Table 7.10 shows the levels of support that recent presidents have received from their fellow partisans in Congress. Neither party has been able to achieve particularly high levels of support. During Democratic administrations, the average support scores of Democrats in the House and Senate have ranged from a low of 48 percent to a high of 74 percent.

TABLE 7.10 Support of Members of Congress for Presidents of Their Own Political Party, 1962-1978[1]

Democratic Support for Democratic Presidents:

President	Year	Senate	House
Kennedy	1962	63%	72%
	1963	63	72
Johnson	1964	61	74
	1965	64	74
	1966	57	63
	1967	61	69
	1968	48	64
Carter	1977	70	63
	1978	66	60

Republican Support for Republican Presidents:

Presdident	Year	Senate	House
Nixon	1969	66%	57%
	1970	60	66
	1971	64	72
	1972	66	64
	1973	61	62
	1974	57	65
Ford	1974	55	51
	1975	68	63
	1976	62	63

[1] Support is defined as the percentage of time a member of Congress voted in accord with the president's positions, based upon all those votes upon which the president took a position.

Source: *Congressional Quarterly Almanac* (Washington: Congressional Quarterly, Inc., various years); *Congressional Quarterly Weekly Report,* 36 (December 9, 1978), p. 3409.

Republican presidents Nixon and Ford did not fare substantially better than their Democratic counterparts.

The presidential support scores presented here indicate the problems that chief executives face in attempting to provide legislative leadership. Even when the president's party controls Congress, as has been the case with presidents Kennedy, Johnson, and Carter, he may be unable to obtain the support of sufficient numbers of his own party's members to pass his legislative proposals and therefore must attempt to develop support within the opposition party. When the president faces an opposition party-controlled Congress, as did presidents Nixon and Ford, the opportunities for legislative leadership are even more limited.

POLITICAL PARTIES AND THE JUDICIARY

The judicial branch is normally classified as the least political of the three departments of government. For many, the goal of objective justice is inconsistent with party politics. Our national political culture dictates that the one branch of government which should be free of partisan taint is the judiciary. Americans seem to accept the role of party politics in the legislative and executive branch, but the idea that justice should be administered according to one's political party affiliation is not well received. For these reasons, a number of protections against overt party activity in the judicial process have been imposed on the court system either by law or by tradition. The separation of the courts from politics can be seen in some of the provisions governing the federal court system. Under the United States Constitution, for example, judges are appointed to office by the president and confirmed by the Senate. This procedure removes federal judgeships from partisan election campaigns and splits the selection authority between the executive and legislative branches so that a federal judge need not owe allegiance to any one political official or faction. Federal judges serve for terms of "good behavior," which in practice means for as long as the judge shall live and desire to continue in office. Impeachment, the official method of judicial removal, is a very rare event. This form of job security removes from federal judges the task of running for reelection, thereby insulating judges to a certain degree from the partisan trends that have such an impact on officers of the legislative and executive branches. The legislature cannot reduce the salaries of judges while they are in office. This protection frees the judiciary from fears of economic sanctions imposed by partisan-based congressional majorities that disagree with a judge's decision. However, the many provisions designed to remove the courts from partisan politics have not been totally successful, and political parties still play a major role in the activities of the judicial branch.

The Structure of the American Court System

At both the federal and state levels, the structure of the judicial branch has been largely determined by partisan considerations. Questions such as the number of courts to be established, the location of newly created courts, the powers to be exercised by the courts, and the number of judgeships necessary to staff the courts are partisan issues. Since the judiciary has substantial powers to make public policy through its rulings, the political parties have a stake in the shaping of a court system that will favor their respective party fortunes. Furthermore, judgeships are often viewed as patronage positions, and each political party attempts to be in control of the selection process when new judgeships are created so that party faithful may be rewarded.

The political nature of such questions was firmly established shortly after the founding of the American republic. When the Federalist party of presidents Washington and Adams correctly predicted that its days of dominating national electoral politics were at an end, it attempted to retain control of the judicial branch by creating new courts and packing the existing ones with Federalist appointees. For example, immediately prior to the ascension to power of the Jeffersonians, the Federalist-dominated Congress created sixteen circuit court judgeships, and President Adams quickly appointed Federalist judges to staff the new court positions. This blatantly partisan move was countered by the Jeffersonian-controlled Congress that was swept into office in the 1800 elections. The Jeffersonians promptly repealed the act which created the new judgeships and thereby blocked one of the attempts by the Federalists to retain control of the judicial branch.[19] Following this repeal, circuit courts were not to be reestablished on a permanent basis until 1891.

The tradition of partisan conflict over the contours of the judiciary continues in the contemporary era. In recent years, for example, the responsibilities of certain federal judicial circuits have grown beyond reasonable limits. This has been particularly true of the caseloads borne by the Fifth Judicial Circuit, which has jurisdiction over the states in the Deep South, and the Ninth Judicial Circuit, which has jurisdiction over the Pacific Coast region. Administrative considerations in both cases point to the advisability of splitting each of these two unwieldy jurisdictions into two separate circuits. However, Congress has been unable to arrive at a formula for doing so because of partisan and regional battles over the proper manner to impose such change. Similar partisan conflict over the creation of judgeships is commonplace. During the 1950s, for example, it was clear that the federal courts had become significantly understaffed. New judgeships were needed to cope with the rising caseloads. Congress, however, was dominated by Democratic majorities who refused to create new judicial positions while Republican Dwight Eisenhower was in the presidency. However, almost immediately after Democrat John Kennedy assumed the presidency in 1961, Congress began serious action which led to the creation of more than 100 new judgeships. An identical situation emerged in the 1970s. The federal courts had again become understaffed, but Congress—controlled by Democrats—balked at expanding the number of judgeships while Richard Nixon and Gerald Ford were in the White House. However, when Democrat Jimmy Carter

[19] Alfred H. Kelly and Winfred A. Harbison, *The American Constitution* (New York: W. W. Norton, 1970).

became president, Congress took the necessary action and created 152 additional federal judgeships.

Judicial Selection

Partisanship plays an important role in the selection of both federal and state judges. The party that controls the selection process always favors members of its own organization in recruiting judicial personnel for two basic reasons. First, judgeships can be used as a form of patronage; and second, members of the same political party are likely to hold public policy views that are acceptable to the party organization.

The federal selection system for judges is officially a two-step process.[20] The president nominates an individual to fill a particular judicial vacancy; the United States senate then approves the president's choice. This simple two-stage process, however, often masks the many activities that surround judicial appointments. When the president embarks on a search to fill a vacant judgeship, a number of people must be consulted. This is particularly true in the appointment of lower court judges who serve in a particular state or region. The president must consult party leaders for their suggestions and views on possible candidates. A president will normally not appoint a person who is unacceptable to the party organization in the state in which the new judge will serve. The president must negotiate with the senators from the state in which the new judge will serve if they are of the same political party as the president. These senators have the power to block confirmation of the president's choice when it is referred to the Senate, and therefore the chief executive must be careful to choose potential judges who are acceptable to the relevant senators. So pervasive is the power of the state's senators that frequently the president simply appoints an individual suggested by the senators unless the president finds the recommended person to be unacceptable. The influence exerted by a state's senators is particularly powerful at the district court level because appointed judges serve within the boundaries of a particular state. At the Supreme Court level, where justices serve the nation as a whole, this senatorial influence loses its potency.

During the Senate confirmation process, partisanship is also quite important. If the majority party in the Senate is of the same political party as the president, judicial nominations normally proceed quite swiftly. Minority party senators may attempt to stall confirmation, but Senate approval is rarely in doubt. However, when the Senate and the White House are controlled by different parties, rejection of the president's choice becomes a realistic possibility. Normally, the Senate will allow the president to obtain the judges he wants, but the senators will scrutinize the backgrounds and records of opposition party nominations much more carefully than they would nominations submitted by a president of their own political

---

[20] See Harold W. Chase, *Federal Judges: The Appointing Process* (Minneapolis: University of Minnesota Press, 1973).

TABLE 7.11 Presidential Appointments to the Lower Federal Courts, 1933-1977

President	Party	Years	Democratic Judges	Republican Judges
Roosevelt	Dem.	1933-45	188	6
Truman	Dem.	1945-53	116	9
Eisenhower	Rep.	1953-61	9	165
Kennedy	Dem.	1961-63	111	11
Johnson	Dem.	1963-69	159	9
Nixon	Rep.	1969-74	15	198
Ford	Rep.	1974-77	12	52
Carter	Dem.	1977-	26	0

party. For example, four nominations to the United States Supreme Court have been rejected in this century.[21] Three of these, Hoover's appointment of John Parker and Nixon's nominations of Clement Haynesworth and G. Harrold Carswell, were Republican nominees rejected by a Democratic Senate. Only in the case of Lyndon Johnson's nomination of Abe Fortas to be chief justice did the Senate reject a Supreme Court nomination when the president was of the same political party as the dominant membership of the Senate. In the Fortas situation, the exploitation of Fortas' alleged judicial improprieties by the conservative coalition was chiefly responsible for the rejection of the nomination.

The end result of the selection process is an overwhelming preference for individuals who share the president's political party membership. At the Supreme Court level, more than 90 percent of all the justices have been of the same political party as the appointing president. This tradition was begun by President Washington who had the opportunity to submit eleven Supreme Court nominations. Each one was a member of Washington's Federalist party. The first opposition party nomination to serve on the Court came with President Tyler's naming of Justice Samuel Nelson in 1845 and did not happen again until 1863 when President Lincoln chose Justice Stephen Field. Similar party preferences are shown in the appointment of judges to the lower federal courts. Table 7.11 summarizes the nominations of presidents Roosevelt through Carter. The clear conclusion is that party membership normally plays a major role in judicial selection. Although President Carter pledged to remove the significant influence of partisanship in judicial selection and impose selection on the basis of merit alone, his first appointments to the federal courts have indicated a continued reliance on party members as the primary pool of potential federal judges. We are not likely to see a decrease in the role played by partisanship in judicial selection in the foreseeable future.

The states use a variety of selection systems to fill court vacancies. Five distinct recruitment processes are used, with some states employing different selec-

---

[21] Henry J. Abraham, *Justices and Presidents* (New York: Oxford University Press, 1974).

TABLE 7.12 Primary Methods of State Judicial Selection[1]

Partisan Elections	Nonpartisan Elections	Merit Selection	Gubernatorial Appointment	Legislative Appointment
Alabama	Arizona	Alaska	Delaware	Connecticut[2]
Arkansas	California	Arizona	Hawaii	Rhode Island
Georgia	Florida	California	Maine	South Carolina
Illinois	Idaho	Colorado	Maryland	Virginia
Indiana	Kansas	Florida	Massachusetts	
Louisiana	Kentucky	Idaho	New Hampshire	
Mississippi	Michigan	Indiana	New Jersey	
Missouri	Minnesota	Iowa	Rhode Island	
New Mexico	Montana	Kansas		
New York	Nevada	Missouri		
North Carolina	North Dakota	Nebraska		
Pennsylvania	Ohio	Oklahoma		
Tennessee	Oklahoma	Tennessee		
Texas	Oregon	Utah		
West Virginia	South Dakota	Vermont		
	Washington	Wyoming		
	Wisconsin			

[1] Several states employ more than one selection system method. Where multiple selection systems are used for major appellate and trial court judges, the state is listed more than once.

[2] In Connecticut the legislature is the official agency for judicial selection. However, the legislature selects judges from nominees submitted by the governor.

Source: *Book of the States, 1978-1979* (Lexington, Kentucky: Council of State Governments, 1978).

tion systems at the various levels of the state judiciary. Table 7.12 indicates the selection systems that have been adopted by the fifty states.

Among the five systems currently in use, three include active political party involvement. Fifteen states rely on partisan elections to select judges. In these states judges are political party candidates in the same fashion as individuals who run for governor or the state legislature. Party activity is significant in the outcome of such electoral races. The system of partisan elections is most common in the South. It is a product of the Jacksonian era which emphasized partisanship in the selection of all public officials. Eight states use gubernatorial appointment to select their judges. (In addition, most states allow the governor to appoint judges when a vacancy occurs before the official end of a judicial term.) With the exception of Hawaii, states employing this system are located on the Atlantic Coast. These states, which adopted their governmental structures during the formation of the federal government, generally follow the same procedures that exist for naming judges in the federal courts. Four states rely on the legislature to select judges. These states are all among the original thirteen and can trace their selection philosophies back to colonial times. Under each system, party politics plays a role. Whether it is the party in the electorate, the executive party, or the legislative party, partisanship is important.

Many states, however, have moved to reduce the role played by party politics in the selection of judges. These reform states have modified their selection procedures to eliminate the possible corrupting influences of the political parties. Two such systems have been employed. First, 17 states use nonpartisan elections to choose judges. This system retains the concept of popular control over individuals who assume places on the bench but removes the formal activity of the political parties. The process is designed to take the focus off the candidate's party affiliation and place it on his qualifications and record. However, some studies of politics in nonpartisan election states have indicated that party organizations remain very active in the process.[22] Second, 16 states now use some form of merit selection. Merit selection (commonly known as the Missouri Plan) combines what proponents see as the strengths of the other selection systems. Under the most frequently used version of such a plan, a "blue ribbon panel" of experts is established to nominate persons for judicial vacancies. These panels normally have representatives from the bench, bar, and public serving on them. Usually the panel will submit three nominees for each vacancy. Upon submission of the nominees, the governor appoints one person from the approved list. The governor's choice serves for a probationary period (usually one year) after which the public must vote on whether or not to retain him in the judgeship. If he is retained, the judge will serve for a full term of office. While comprehensive studies of the merit selection system are not numerous, indications are that formal partisan politics are reduced under this system although not completely eliminated.[23] The nonpartisan election and merit selection plans are predominately found in the states west of the Mississippi where judicial reform has been an important issue. However, in recent years several Eastern states have reformed their selection systems by adopting one of these two plans.

Partisan Politics and Judicial Policy Making

The judiciary has no formal party organization. There is no majority or minority leader, no whips, no caucuses. There are no attempts to promote a program of partisan-based public policies. Any such attempts to organize the courts would be unacceptable to the American concept of equal justice. The party exists in its least identifiable form within the judiciary. Therefore, it is not surprising that we rarely hear discussions of responsible party government for the judicial branch.

This is not to say, however, that party considerations do not exist among the judges who sit on American courts. After all, individuals selected to conduct the government's judicial business normally attain the bench after having engaged in partisan political activities for many years. Because of the activity of the party in

---

[22] See, for example, S. Sidney Ulmer, "The Political Party Variable in the Michigan Supreme Court," *Journal of Public Law*, 11 (1962), 352-362.

[23] Richard A. Watson and Rondal G. Downing, *The Politics of Bench and Bar* (New York: John Wiley and Sons, 1969).

the selection of judges, most candidates for the bench have substantial records of prior political party service. The experiences of a lifetime are not erased when an individual slips into his judicial robes for the first time. The judge takes his place on the bench with the same philosophies and values that first attracted him to the political party of his choice and which years of party experiences and contacts helped to shape. Because the political orientations of Republican and Democratic judges tend to be different, it would not be surprising to find those differences reflected in judicial decision making.

A substantial amount of scholarly research has been devoted to studying the impact of party on judicial decisions. Early work found definite evidence of partisan differences.[24] This was especially the case in decisions involving socioeconomic issues that traditionally split the two parties. In disputes between labor and management, for example, Democratic judges were found to have a much greater tendency to support the working class than were Republican judges. Other studies demonstrated a tendency for Democrats, to a greater extent than Republicans, to support the government in business regulation and taxation cases; the defendant in criminal cases; tenants, debtors, and consumers in battles with landlords, creditors, businesses; and the individual in civil liberties cases. Later research, however, has established that these tendencies are far from universal.[25] The impact of political party affiliation on judicial decision making varies according to the individual judge, the political environment of the state in which the judge serves, and the nature of the cases coming before the court. Except for those state judges who must rely on party support at reelection time, there is little necessity for the judge to please party constituents in the decisions rendered. The American judge depends most heavily on his own scholarship and personal value system. But we must recognize that a judge's view of the law and his own values may have been influenced by his political party affiliations.

SUMMARY

Once elected, American political parties are entrusted with the responsibility of organizing the government and are expected to enact the policies to which they pledged their support during the election campaign. For the most part, we must classify the success of the parties in carrying out these responsibilities as modest.

---

[24] Ulmer, "The Political Party Variable . . . "; Stuart Nagel, "Political Party Affiliation and Judges' Decisions," *American Political Science Review*, 55 (December 1961), 843-850; Sheldon Goldman, "Voting Behavior on the United States Courts of Appeals, 1961-1964," *American Political Science Review*, 60 (June 1966), 374-383.

[25] David W. Adamany, "The Political Party Variable in Judges' Voting: Conceptual Notes and a Case Study," *American Political Science Review*, 63 (March 1969), 57-73; Edward N. Beiser and Jonathan J. Silberman, "The Political Party Variable: Workmen's Compensation Cases in the New York Court of Appeals," *Polity*, 3 (Summer 1971), 521-531.

In the legislative branch, the political parties actively organize into party units. The leadership of the legislature is party based. Elected presiding officers, such as the Speaker of the U.S. House of Representatives, are partisan leaders rather than neutral moderators of chamber debate. Each party in the legislature has a floor leader who is active in promoting party unity and organizing party forces. In Congress and in some state legislatures there are whip organizations which further work toward the promotion of party legislative programs. Party cohesion in the legislature exists only at moderate levels. In Congress, the Democratic party has been plagued by defections from its southern ranks. The Republicans have had difficulty maintaining consistent support from their more liberal, northern representatives. Issues upon which the majority of one party opposes the majority of the other party are common but do not comprise the majority of votes taken in Congress. Bipartisan voting and cooperation is quite frequent, and interparty voting alliances, such as the conservative coalition, undermine responsible party government in the national legislature.

In the executive branch, party plays an important role, but comprehensive party-based programs are not frequently enacted. The most common evidence of party influence in the executive branch is in the appointment of administrative officials. The chief executive shows a definite preference for members of his own political party in choosing individuals to fill key policy positions. These persons may well have greater loyalty to the incumbent, however, than they are willing to give to the party. In addition, administrative officials often develop loyalties to the interest groups with whom they come into daily contact, and this further detracts from party allegiances. For a party to be successful at implementing partisan policies, party leaders of the executive and legislative branches must cooperate. The executive branch must be able to attract a unified legislative party to support its programs if the party is to be truly capable of running the government according to its campaign pledges. History has shown, however, that a unified legislative and executive party is not a common event. Legislative party support for the chief executive's proposals can only be classified as moderate.

The judicial branch is the least involved in partisan politics. There is no partisan organization of the courts as there is in the legislature or the executive branch. However, party politics still plays a major role in the court system. The size, shape, and powers of the judiciary are determined by the political branches of the government, and these issues have historically been filled with partisan clashes. Appointments of judges to the federal courts have clearly been partisan choices. At the state level, there are several different selection methods, but most of them allow for some form of partisan political activity. It is difficult to measure the extent of party influence in judicial policy making. There are indications that party affiliation does influence to some extent the type of decisions that judges hand down. The nature of party influence in the judiciary, however, comes from the internal values and philosophies of the judge rather than reinforcement by party organizations.

eight

Party Conflicts and the Future of the Party System

The American party system faces an uncertain future in several important respects. Internal conflicts over party goals and procedures continue to split both parties. The loss of party influence in the electoral process affects all sectors of the party by reducing their common purpose. Competitive two-party politics is minimal below the presidential level because of the serious electoral weaknesses of the Republican party. Attacks on the parties and their performance continue, while new "reforms" are proposed that would further weaken the parties.

The parties are still pervasive in American politics, but by most standards they have lost much of their power. They must confront strong, and in many instances contradictory, demands by issue activists, candidates, party regulars, and political leaders. For the parties, the central issues are quite clear. Can they reassert their influence on the selection of political leadership? Can they strengthen their ability to organize government? Can they regain their custody of such important functions as aggregating mass preferences and mobilizing the electorate? Reviewing the current conflicts and tensions within the parties provides some guidelines for assessing the future of the American parties.

PARTY STRUCTURE

The three sectors of the party—the party in government, the party electorate, and the party organization—have traditionally coexisted within a loose web of common interests and reciprocal obligations. Over the past decade, changes in each of these sectors of the party have weakened this web considerably. Short-term considerations now tend to dominate the party in government and the party in the electorate, reducing the party organization's ability to mediate between them. A shared understanding of what the parties can provide and why they are important to each sector now appears to be rather dim.

The Party in Government

For the party in government, the party serves as an organizational mechanism. For elected officials, it also serves electoral purposes. The effectiveness of the party in government, in terms of reinforcement and internal discipline, is dependent on the party's value during elections. If candidates need parties to gain election, they are likely to be responsive to party considerations once in office. Where parties are not perceived as essential or even particularly helpful for electoral purposes, their strength as governing institutions is bound to decline. In examining the party in government, therefore, it is helpful to see how candidate interests and officeholder interest converge.

Party Candidates. The direct primary has, of course, freed candidates from dependence on the party organization for nomination. Even presidential nominations, which are formally made by party conventions, are now divorced from state party organization control. While the primary has existed for more than half a century, however, its negative effects on the party have become more pronounced with the advent of media campaigns and the "professionalization" of other aspects of campaign politics.

Television and other media provide candidates with independent access to the electorate. Public opinion surveys allow candidates to monitor voter concerns and preferences. Interest groups and personal campaign organizations can carry out the voter mobilization activities traditionally performed by the party organizations. The party's usefulness to candidates is reduced sharply by these alternatives during primaries as well as general elections. Several decades ago, party organizational efforts were the best available means for mobilizing a primary electorate. The alternative means were limited in number and difficult to employ. Today, however, candidates in party primaries need not depend on party organizational assistance even in those limited areas where it is still available.

Lack of control over nominations also makes it difficult to discipline incumbents who do not support party interests or party policies. As noted previously, national party organizations cannot exercise any serious sanctions over members of Congress. Because of the primary and the characteristics of modern campaigning, state and local party organizations also face formidable practical obstacles if they attempt to deny renomination. Incumbency is an enormous advantage during primaries, and this serves as a limited immunity for party officeholders.

There is another side to this that should also be mentioned. Just as the party organization's lack of control over nominations reduces its effective sanctions, this lack of control also limits the rewards. An incumbent who does support party interests and who has the backing of the party organization may still be confronted with primary challenges. The party cannot deny renomination, but neither can it guarantee renomination. In either case, the party's ties to its candidates are weakened.

The candidate for public office has one real and immediate concern—success at the polls. This remains the same during primaries and general elections. What happens to other party candidates may be of more than passing interest, but it becomes crucial only when an individual's election prospects are linked to the fortunes of other party candidates. Changes in campaign technology and increases in split-ticket voting have weakened, if not eliminated, this link for most candidates. Direct appeals to the electorate are now possible, and these have the advantages (to the candidate) of independence and immediacy. These appeals are especially well suited for emphasizing personal style and personal characteristics, thus further removing a candidate from the remainder of his party's ticket.

Since the electorate is now less dependent on party cues and less likely to vote a straight-party ticket, personalized candidacies have greater prospects of success. In national elections, for example, presidential coattails no longer seem to be of much concern to members of Congress. This is especially true for congressional Democrats. Since there is no real prospect that the Republican party can compete successfully for most Democratic seats, most notably in the House, presidential election impact on congressional elections is limited. The Carter administration's problems with the Democratic-controlled Congress no doubt reflect a number of factors, but among the most important is the perception that Carter's success or failure will have no serious electoral repercussions for most Democratic incumbents.

Candidate attitudes toward parties are predictably pragmatic and based on self-interest. If the party organization controlled nominations and monopolized the resources and expertise relating to electoral politics, candidates would have no choice but to accept party restrictions on their autonomy. Since the party organizations do not control the avenues to office, especially major offices, there is no reason for candidates to acknowledge any dependence either during the campaign or once in office.

Party candidates, then, are relatively independent of party organizations. Candidates do need the party labels, and they also need the party's base of electoral support. But they can capture the label and exploit the electoral support through personalized candidacies. Jimmy Carter showed how this strategy worked at the presidential level in 1976. The same method is also available to congressional candidates and to candidates for state and local office. The parties dominate the elections, but the parties are defined by their candidates.

Party Officeholders. The party's lack of influence in leadership selection is mirrored by its lack of success in organizing government. In one sense, the president's role as national party leader and spokesman might be interpreted as a sign that presidential-party ties are strong. As we have seen, the president controls the national committee of his party, his program is considered to be the party's program, and he is the acknowledged leader of his party. At the same time, the national committee is simply used or ignored by most presidents according to their personal reelection needs. The president's program is not assured of partisan support in Congress. The president's role as party leader is usually an empty one, since no recent president has made any serious attempt to strengthen his party's organization and resources at the state and local level.

The emergence of parties in the United States was based on the need to organize government, by providing a link between the constitutionally separated President and Congress and by serving as a means to choose legislative leadership and structure legislative decision making. The debate over responsible parties during recent decades has usually focused on the party's weakness in effecting this intragovernmental organization. Party cohesion in Congress, for example, has traditionally been modest at best. Partisan linkages between the president and Congress have usually been quite weak, and presidents have found it difficult to gain consistent support for their programs even when their parties have controlled Congress.

Under present circumstances, the concept of responsible parties appears to be even less relevant than in the past. The party majorities stand on opposite sides of many important issues, but there are substantial minorities on both sides of the aisle that shift back and forth. The huge Democratic majorities have not produced significant increases in party cohesion, despite the fact that the current Democratic contingent has a proportionately smaller southern bloc than was the case 15 or 20 years ago. The supposedly greater ideological congruence within the party, however, has thus far failed to produce stronger and more effective organization.

The president's ability to develop sustained support for his programs from a defined congressional coalition thus appears to be limited. The president and members of his party do not have ties to a common national party organization. The president has his national committee; members of Congress have their party campaign organizations. Both sides have personal organizations in the states. The electorate's willingness to split congressional voting from presidential voting loosens the electoral bond of a common constituency. Indeed, members of Congress may now be especially susceptible to interest group pressures in their districts or states, because presidential or party support no longer provides substantial electoral protection. Thus, a president's fellow partisans may refuse to support him when special interest pressure is most intense—which is, of course, when their support is most necessary—if they fear electoral repercussions.

Unable to rely on party, presidents must depend on their popular standing and public appeals to influence Congress. As a long-term strategy, however, this has been extremely ineffective. Most presidents have been unable to maintain high levels of popularity very long, so that even when image and reputation work with Congress, they do not work for very long. Presumably, there is a need for continuity and durability in presidential leadership, and it is difficult to see how this type of leadership can be achieved without a reasonably strong and cohesive governing party. One does not have to be a proponent of responsible parties to see the need for meaningful parties in government. As David Broder, a respected political journalist, has suggested, the current weakness of the party in government might prove serious:

> I think the trend, at least for the foreseeable future, is likely to be one toward greater entrepreneurial politics and a much more volatile political system . . . . I think the likeliest outcome is that there will be at some point a genuine crisis of control of the Presidential office, with some entrepreneurial individual who has achieved that office facing a crisis in which government has to govern, and discovering himself without the resources of a party, straining the Constitution much more dramatically than Mr. Nixon did. At that point, it may be that people will decide that they are safer and more effectively governed under a party system . . . . [1]

There are available alternatives to parties in the conduct of electoral politics, although such alternatives may not be attractive, but there is none that is remotely comparable in terms of organizing government. Officeholders have been responsible for many of the statutory and other restrictions that have weakened the parties. Their independence from party control has thereby been increased, but they may find that their ability to govern effectively has been reduced.

The Party Electorate

We have seen that there has been a definite erosion of support for the parties within the mass electorate. The proportion of the total electorate that identifies with the parties has shrunk, and over one-third of the electorate now classifies itself as independent. Even among those who do identify with the parties, the incidence of strong identification has dropped. Finally, generalized public attitudes toward the parties and their performance in the political system have become more negative.

Voter behavior also reflects the declining significance of parties. Split-ticket voting has increased in national and state elections, with especially dramatic results in concurrent presidential and congressional elections. Voters have become less reliant on party labels for voting cues, less willing to allow parties to screen candidates, and less interested in the partisan consequences of voting decisions.

The electorate's changed response to parties has produced conflicting assessments and interpretations. As discussed previously, some analysts have predicted partisan realignments, others have forecast the ultimate demise of parties, and still others have suggested that the current malaise is only temporary.

[1] Statement of David Broder, in *Voters, Primaries and Parties, Selections from a Conference on American Politics,* ed. Johnathan Moore and Albert C. Pierce (Cambridge, Mass.: Institute of Government, John Fitzgerald Kennedy School of Government, 1976), pp. 41-42.

In order to assess these interpretations, one needs satisfactory explanations for the erosion of party loyalties and support in the electorate. But there are no simple explanations. Demographic factors, for example, have contributed to the erosion, as the relative size of the younger age voting group has increased sharply. This group is more likely to be independent of party and cynical about politics, as well as less participatory, when compared to older groups in the electorate.[2]

Also important has been the emergence of major cross-cutting issues during the past two decades which do not fit existing party divisions and do not result in distinctive party responses. Thus, such divisive issues as the Vietnam war, civil rights and race relations, and the pace and extent of social change have not conformed to the traditional, largely economic-based divisions between the Republican and Democratic parties. The parties, like most other societal institutions, have not responded very coherently to these issues. And while the more convulsive issues have diminished or disappeared, some believe that the parties' inability to structure these conflicts effectively has led to electorate disenchantment.

Another interpretation that should be considered focuses on the interplay between social change and technology. According to this view, voters are now better educated, more affluent, and have more leisure time than in the past. They also have ready access to a national communications network for political information. The electorate today is less dependent on the party for information and guidance. Not surprisingly, it is also less likely to feel strong attachments to the party.

Each of these interpretations appears to have some validity. Less plausible are arguments that the decline of parties has occurred because the Democratic and Republican parties are not ideologically distinctive. Although there has been an increase in issue consistency and ideological awareness within the electorate, the simple fact is that most voters are not ideologues. Democratic and Republican party elites are separated from each other by sharper and more consistent ideological differences than are their party electorates. Moreover, most voters prefer the current party arrangement to one consisting of a liberal party and a conservative party. Indeed, according to the Gallup organization, over two-thirds of those who have an opinion on this issue do not favor party realignment.[3]

It should also be emphasized that the decline in party voting has largely occurred in highly visible and salient elections, most notably presidential elections. Party-based voting for Congress remains quite high, as does voting for legislative offices in the states. A presidential candidate's judgment and personal characteristics are not irrelevant considerations, so it is understandable that voters attempt to assess these qualities. Whether voters will ever be sufficiently interested to attempt similar assessments of candidates for other offices is questionable.

[2] Robert M. Teeter, "What Is the Electorate Telling Us," in *Voters, Primaries, and Parties*, p. 5.

[3] *Gallup Opinion Index*, Report No. 116 (February 1975), pp. 14-19.

Many voters still depend on parties, of course, and some voters depend more than others. Partisan attachments differ, as does knowledge about candidates and issues in various elections. The traditional party system has been based on domestic economic issues. These issues had a muted impact during the late 1960s and early 1970s, but if they become highly salient again, which appears probable, the relevance of party cues for voters should increase. The parties are unlikely to command the voter loyalties they once did, but they can be, and often are, important determinants of voter choice.

A related observation in this context is that "democratizing reforms" have not materially affected participation rates in the electorate. Although these reforms have increased the influence of nonparty groups in the presidential nominating process, there is no evidence that these groups are more representative of the party electorates or more responsive to electorate preferences and interests than were prereform decision-making bodies. Here again, the supposed remedy for electorate disaffection from the parties applies in reality to a distinct minority. What the parties have gained, if anything, by being more open is unclear. What they have lost is control over their own affairs.

Party Organization

The decline of the party machine is no doubt irreversible, brought on by social and economic change, legal regulation, public distrust, and officeholder antagonism. The process of change, however, has not been discriminating. As the bosses and machines disappeared, general party organization also suffered important reverses. The party organizations today cannot command the loyalties of committed electorates, nor can they exercise significant influence over party candidates or officeholders. In some areas, the organizations have been reformed into oblivion.

The party organizations face continuing troubles on several fronts. They find it difficult to compete with nonparty organizations for resources and especially for volunteers. Single-cause groups and specific candidates provide alternative and apparently attractive participatory opportunities for many activists. Those activists that the parties manage to attract have increased internal pressures for internal democracy and ideological consistency. Most party organizations suffer from high turnover, many lack strong leadership and discipline, and virtually all have become less effective in dealing with voters and candidates.

There has also been little progress in strengthening ties between national, state, and local party organizations. The centralizing aspects of national party regulation of delegate selection procedures in the states are obvious, but their primary effect has been to divorce presidential nominating politics from state and local party influence. It is unlikely that this type of centralization will significantly alter the diffusion of electoral responsibility that has traditionally characterized the party system.

The most serious problem that the party organizations must confront, however, is one of legal regulation that limits their authority. The direct primary is the obvious example. It is also the most significant restriction on party authority. The party organization is the sector of the party structure that has primary responsibility for aggregating mass preferences in a reasonably coherent fashion over time, not just for one election or for one candidate. The only way this can be accomplished is for the organization to play a major role in recruiting and screening potential candidates. By limiting or abolishing the organization's control over nominations, however, the direct primary and related legislation also restrict the recruiting and screening functions.

One cannot realistically expect that the states will abolish primaries and return to the parties responsibility for their own affairs. What might be possible is an easing of present regulatory efforts. States can allow preprimary conventions and formal endorsements. This type of change would not guarantee organizational control over nominations, but it would at least place the parties on an equal footing with other organized groups that seek to influence party nominations. The states and the Congress might also begin to consider the impact of other electoral changes or reforms on the parties. Public financing of candidates, for example, has been hailed by many as a reform, but if monies are provided directly to candidates, the parties will be further weakened. Channeling limited public financing through the parties, on the other hand, would at least avoid additional damage.

The party organization's claim to greater authority and responsibility rests on solid ground. Primaries do not result in popular majorities choosing preferred candidates. On the contrary, primary electorates are minorities, often unrepresentative minorities, and this is true for presidential preference primaries as well as for state and local primaries. Primary electorates cannot reasonably be expected to understand or assess a candidate's ability to bring together the groups and interests within the party. Consideration of electability, fitness to govern, representativeness, and ideological acceptability are best employed by those who have a continuing stake in the party and its electoral success, who can combine short-term and long-term perspectives. Party leaders can do this, but primary electorates cannot.

Party organizations in the United States will never dominate the other sectors of the party. Improving their present position through marginal changes and a clearer perception of the party's legitimate role in politics will not revive machines or bosses or lead to European-style party bureaucracies. What these changes can do is help the parties plan more effectively, nominate stronger candidates, and provide more coherence to the electorate's decisions.

PARTY GOALS

The competing interests of the various sectors of the party are reflected in the continuing intraparty conflicts over party goals. Despite attempts at democratization, small minorities, or elites, control what the parties do and what interests they represent. The competing elites that are most relevant today include entrepreneurial candidates for major offices (and their followings), party regulars, and issue activists.

The points of conflict tend to be concentrated within the sphere of presidential politics, but they also extend to party governance and broad issues of party ideology.

The Presidency

The office of the presidency is the great electoral prize of American politics. To most Americans, it is not simply another partisan office. The president is expected to provide personal and moral leadership for "all the people," not just those who voted for him. The president does have, however, the unique resources to lead his national party. He can build electoral and legislative coalitions, define party policy, and help to strengthen the party at all levels.

In the past, presidents were reasonably successful in building executive-led coalitions. Although the "presidential party" faced opposition from dissident party blocs in Congress and the electorate, there was at least some continuity in the policies and leadership provided by the Democratic presidents and presidential candidates and by their Republican counterparts. This continuity was a result of state party leaders, elected officials, and national party notables who were able to act as brokers and compromisers in selecting the leader of the presidential party. As one party scholar noted, "The national convention shows the presidential party in its full splendor and power .... All in all, the presidential party controls the convention as fully as the congressional party controls Congress."[4] Within this context, certain assumptions were clear—electability was critical, influence was centralized, and a defined segment of the party was responsible for the candidates that were produced.

These assumptions are no longer valid. The recent changes in delegate selection procedures have weakened the state parties, as have the major interest groups in each party's constituency (especially organized labor on the Democratic side). The nominating process is now open to entrepreneurial candidacies, heavy media utilization, and temporary activist groups. Many functions that the established sectors of the party once performed are now handled by communications media. Television news, for example, screens the candidates and determines which ones are serious, who is leading, and who has the "momentum." During the long primary campaign, polls and television gauge voter reactions and monitor candidate performance. There is no established group within the party that is responsible for making the choice and is later held accountable for that choice.

The Democratic party reforms have been much more extensive than the Republican changes, and their impact has been obvious. In 1972 and 1976, the presidential nomination was captured by two "outsiders." The McGovern candidacy was a disaster. But even the successful Carter candidacy illustrates the problems of the current system of presidential nominations. Carter, of course, was not widely

---

[4] James MacGregor Burns, *The Deadlock of Democracy* (Englewood Cliffs, N.J.: Prentice-Hall, Inc., 1963), p. 250.

known when the nominating process commenced. After respectable showings in the early caucus and primary states, especially Florida where he defeated George Wallace, he quickly became an established candidate in a crowded field. As others dropped out, Carter emerged as the front-runner, and despite several defeats near the end of the primary season, he was sufficiently far ahead to gain an easy convention victory.

When the Democratic convention was over, the Democrats were a united party. The Republicans were saddled with Watergate. Their appointed president, Gerald Ford, had to go through a bitter nomination fight. He was not perceived as an especially strong candidate, his party was in the minority, and his tenure as president had few major policy successes. At the close of the Democratic convention, Carter led by more than 30 percentage points in the public opinion polls.

The scenario seemed clear. A popular majority party candidate had emerged from the primaries. The party was ready for a huge victory. As it turned out, there was a huge victory in the congressional races, but Carter's final edge over Ford was extremely narrow. There had been no campaign disasters. Indeed, the campaign was, by all accounts, exceedingly dull, and the low turnout suggested these accounts were accurate.

What happened to Carter? First, it was never clear that Carter was an especially strong candidate in terms of broad voter appeal. Primary turnout in most states was light, and while Carter received almost 40 percent of the total votes in the Democratic primaries, this amounted to slightly over six million votes in more than two dozen primaries. Second, Carter's large early leads in a number of primaries dwindled as primary day approached, suggesting that his support was not very deep. When challenged late in the process by another newcomer, Governor Brown of California, Carter did quite poorly. Third, Carter's "outsider" candidacy was more effective in distinguishing him from other candidates in the primary than it was in communicating his credentials and qualifications for the presidency.

The Democratic nominee in 1976, then, was the choice of primary electorate and caucus participants who represented in terms of numbers a minority of all participating Democrats, slightly under 10 percent of all registered voters and approximately 5 percent of the voting age population. This was better than any other candidate on the Democratic side, but it was not the kind of verdict to erase all doubts about a political unknown. Indeed, Carter's nomination suggested to some that a party nomination system has been established "which is extraordinarily contemptuous of the notion that leaders are to be 'brought along,' tried and seasoned gradually, rather than suddenly tossed upon the national stage."[5]

Of equal relevance, the Carter presidency has not dispelled these doubts. Inexperience has proved troublesome, as the president and his advisers have found it difficult to grasp the reins of power firmly. Critics have questioned not only

---

[5] Everett Carll Ladd, Jr. and Charles D. Hadley, *Transformations of the American Party System,* 2nd ed. (New York: W. W. Norton and Company, Inc., 1978), p. 369.

administration policies but also presidential strength and competence. The Carter nomination did not establish or reinforce party ties that could be translated into strong supporting coalitions in Congress. The president's legislative success record during his first two years, for example, was not impressive. Moreover, Mr. Carter's drop in the presidential popularity polls has been dramatic, indicating that the public has been deeply dissatisfied with the presidential leadership. Early in 1978, after little more than a year in office, there was widespread speculation that President Carter might be facing serious renomination problems to say nothing of reelection. It was even suggested that the latest round of delegate selection process changes had been pushed by the administration in order to make it more difficult for presidential challengers in 1980. (A measure of how much things have changed is that no one seemed to be willing to argue that a party *should* make it difficult to challenge an incumbent president.)

These problems extend far beyond the nominating process, of course. During his campaign and immediately after his election, however, Jimmy Carter did emphasize the ineffectiveness of divided government. Democratic control of the White House and Congress has muted the rhetoric accompanying executive-legislative conflict, but it has not materially reduced that conflict. And this is rather remarkable given the overwhelming Democratic majorities in both chambers.

It is necessary to emphasize that the chief executive's ability to compel legislative support for his programs has always been quite limited. The president's party leadership role does not allow him to command automatically the support of his legislative party. But while the political party's capacity to combine what the Constitution separates has always been limited, it appears that the current debilities are greater than in the past. The "presidential party" never dominated national politics, but it was highly influential. It now has been shattered, especially within the Democratic party, with the result being that presidents will find it much more difficult to govern.

Party Governance

The contemporary attacks on the party system allege, among other criticisms, that it has been insufficiently responsive to public interests and preferences. The preferred remedy has usually been more open and participatory parties. To a certain extent, the recent approaches are different from those employed during the Progressive era, which was the last sustained effort at "party reform." The Progressives were explicitly attempting to bypass or destroy parties by strengthening direct links between the public and elected officials and also by establishing direct democratic decision-making procedures such as the referendum and initiative.

The modern reformers have not adopted the emphatic antiparty theme of the Progressives. Although they do share the Progressive-inspired belief that the cure for democracy's ills is more democracy, they have attempted to extend this prescription to the internal affairs of the parties. According to the reformers, their aim is to strengthen parties by making them internally democratic, accessible to their supporters, and principled and consistent. These changes would presumably increase public respect for the parties and improve the political process.

The reformist thrust of the past decade is therefore based on the alleged lack of party responsiveness to mass opinion and mass preferences. Is this allegation well founded? There is obviously no easy, unambiguous answer. It is not even clear what objective criteria we should use in dealing with the question. Should the parties be judged by the quality of the leadership choices they present to the public, by the positions they take on issues, by their performance in governing? Of course they should, but this means that to judge their responsiveness, one must also judge the responsiveness of the political system.

If we assume that responsiveness is a problem (and that is a debatable assumption), is it susceptible to the cures of democratization and participation? There is a great deal of evidence to suggest that it is not. Participatory reforms, such as the referendum and the direct primary, have not elicited high levels of public participation. They typically attract only a minority, whether measured in terms of the voting age population or the less rigorous yardstick of the registered voter population. If the visibility and salience of an electoral decision are high and if the mass public is interested and involved, then one should reasonably expect participation rates in primaries, for example, to equal the rates in general elections. This has not occurred in the case of presidential primaries, and there is no reason to expect that it ever will, given the mass public's approach to politics.

It is clear that participatory reforms assist minorities. Moreover, these are not disadvantaged minorities, but rather those individuals with the educational and income levels that provide the resources and time to participate in politics. Most important, these minorities are not necessarily representative of the party electorates or the mass public in terms of issue preferences. Indeed, the limited available evidence suggests that such representativeness is highly unlikely.

If the issue truly is responsiveness, then one might simply ask how participatory reforms that increase the influence of policy minorities can possibly make the parties more responsive. These minorities are totally unaccountable for the decisions they make. If they determine the nomination of an unappealing or incompetent candidate, they have no official status that can be challenged. As we have repeatedly discussed, the parties and their leaders have definite incentives to provide the electorate with what it wants. They stand to suffer directly if they make a mistake in assessing the electorate's wants. The institutional setting within which the parties operate therefore encourages, if it does not guarantee, responsiveness, and it provides encouragement through self-interest. Is the self-interest of the primary voter similarly engaged so that he or she supports a candidate based upon what the rest of the electorate wants or rather upon individual predilections and interests? The primary voter is not necessarily less virtuous or less intelligent or less concerned than the party official, but there is a fundamental difference in how primary electorates and party organizations evaluate potential candidates.

This suggests that the ultimate effect of intraparty reform is to increase the likelihood that a party will be "captured" temporarily by a policy minority that will dictate a disastrous candidacy for the party. What makes a candidacy disastrous is, among other things, massive rejection by the electorate. In addition, and perhaps more important, democratizing reforms reduce party responsiveness to precisely those groups for whom the party has been the principal, and perhaps the only, institutional resource:

> Political parties, with all their well-known human and structural shortcomings, are the only devices . . . which with some effectiveness can generate countervailing collective power on behalf of the many individually powerless against the relatively few who are individually—or organizationally—powerful. Their disappearance could only entail the unchallenged ascendancy of the latter unless new structures of collective power were developed to replace them and unless conditions in the social structure and the political culture were such that they could be effectively used. This contingency, despite recent publicity for the term "participatory democracy," seems precisely what is not likely to occur.... [6]

Whatever the theoretical advantages of a highly participatory society, most citizens are unable or unwilling or simply not desirous of doing more than voting at fairly regular intervals in general elections for major offices. In the real world in which the American parties operate, democratizing reforms do not and cannot mobilize the mass electorate. They can and do increase the influence of small and unrepresentative minorities. Good intentions cannot change the fact that democratizing reforms do not operate very democratically.

The debate over party governance often tends to ignore this basic relationship between the parties and the mass electorate. Restricting participation to those who have served the party, been loyal to its candidates and platforms, regardless of personal viewpoint, and have earned the right to make decisions for the party through being chosen by others in the party does not conflict with the goals of democratic government:

> If the party is described as a political enterprise conducted by a group of working politicians *supported* by partisan voters who approve of the party but are merely partisans (not members of a fictitious association), the parties would seem less wicked.... Will the parties be less responsive to the needs of the voters if their private character is generally recognized? Probably not. The parties do not need laws to make them sensitive to the wishes of the voters any more than we need laws compelling merchants to please their customers. The sovereignty of the voter consists in his freedom of choice just as the sovereignty of the consumer in the economic system consists in his freedom to trade in a competitive market. This is enough; little can be added to it by inventing an imaginary membership in a fictitious party

[6] Walter Dean Burnham, *Critical Elections and the Mainsprings of American Politics* (New York: W. W. Norton and Company, Inc., 1970), p. 133.

association. Democracy is not to be found *in* the parties but *between* the parties.[7]

Party Ideology

A substantial degree of conflict within the parties over rules and procedures is in reality conflict over how sharp interparty policy differences should be and how dramatically these should be expressed to the electorate. It has long been argued that the two major parties are not sufficiently distinctive in their policy positions and that this lack of distinctiveness frustrates voters. This position is sometimes extended to suggest that many people do not vote because they do not perceive a real choice between the parties or their candidates.

It is difficult to sustain these charges. The parties do take different positions on many important policy issues, and they do enact their platforms. The party electorates are not ideologically coherent or even very ideological at all. What ideological content there is in party politics tends to be supplied by the party elites.

In at least a certain context, however, the charges have some limited validity. The American parties do not disagree on all matters of public policy. There is widespread agreement on fundamental principles. The party that wins the election does not proceed to enact radical changes in all existing public policies. The losing party and its supporters are not totally without influence until the next election. All of this reflects the generally incremental nature of political change in the United States. Even incremental changes can be profound over the long term, but we generally find the parties searching for short-term advantages at the margins of this or that policy.

The party system in the United States does not usually provide the electorate with radically different choices. This does not suggest a clever conspiracy by party elites but rather an accommodation to a diverse and ideologically moderate electorate. The parties are accommodationist in their appeals, because they wish to win elections and to govern. They can best accomplish this by supporting popular policies and by governing effectively.

Within the parties, however, there has been increasing pressure from purists or amateurs who are dissatisfied with the lack of coherent, distinctive, and uncompromising platforms and party programs. These individuals also tend to support candidates who will champion these programs regardless of the electoral consequences. For the purist, the party and its candidates should not be deflected from the proper ideological course in order to pursue some temporary and ultimately meaningless electoral advantage.

The American parties have been reluctant in the past to pursue the holy grail of ideological orthodoxy. For party regulars, the occasional flirtations with extreme appeals have been sufficiently enlightening about the types of choices the electorate

---

[7] E. E. Schattschneider, *Party Government* (New York: Farrar and Rinehart, 1940), pp. 59-60. Italics in original.

wants to make. For issue activists in the electorate and in the party organizations, however, the lessons of 1964 and 1972 are perceived quite differently. They continue to pressure both parties—the left-of-center activists in the Democratic party and their right-of-center counterparts in the Republican party—to carve out distinctive positions, stress interparty differences, and *force* the electorate to make a meaningful choice.

It also helps to recognize that the issue activist's attraction to a politics of principle is not entirely selfless. Issue activists tend to have high levels of education and high incomes. Their formal training increases their effectiveness in debating issues and ideas, and their economic positions allow them to devote considerable time to the "politics of ideas."[8] At the lofty level of principled abstractions, there is no need to worry about how the less intelligent or perceptive might respond to this or that issue. And since the issue activists do not receive any material benefits from their participation or feel any great personal loyalty to their party, they do not risk any personal loss if the "party of principle" encounters a hostile electorate.

The Democratic and Republican parties are not, by the standards of American politics, identical, nor have they been identical in the past. There is an inevitable tension within major parties over the balance between electoral and programmatic goals. The American parties have usually resolved this balance in favor of electoral goals, in large part because of the nature of the American electorate. The ideological awareness of the mass electorate has not substantially increased in recent years. By responding to internal and external pressures for ideological distinctiveness, both parties run the risk of rejection by overwhelming popular majorities. Since these pressures tend to focus on presidential candidates and national party platforms, it is possible that presidential party politics will continue to be volatile and will become increasingly detached from the rest of the party system.

CONFLICT AND CHANGE

The declining influence of the American parties is only partially a result of social and technological change. It also represents the weakening of party organization through legal regulations and restrictions that have, in many instances, been based upon misconceptions about party functions and democratic politics. The parties today are dominated by candidates and officeholders, and they tend to be extremely responsive to the demands of issue activists. The results of party decline are clear in the process of leadership selection, electorate mobilization, and government.

The decline is not irreversible, but for the time being, parties are not able to compete effectively with other political organizations that have strong and stable leadership as well as considerable political resources. In Part Two, we will examine interest groups and the influence that they now exercise in the political process, influence that has been gained at the expense of the parties.

[8] On this point, see Ladd and Hadley, *Transformations of the Party System,* pp. 333-42.

part TWO

INTEREST GROUPS

nine

Interest Groups as Political Organizations

The influential role played by interest groups in the governmental process has been a continuing phenomenon since the founding of the American republic. Public policy has always been at least partially determined by the communication of interest group preferences to governmental officials. It is difficult, if not impossible, to identify any major governmental action which has been taken without significant lobby group participation. Normally, interest group activity is substantial and widespread. Acting as advocates in behalf of their memberships, competing interest groups often clash in their efforts to influence governmental decision making. Such activity has been a common occurrence at every stage in our historical development and has flourished from the highest reaches of the federal government to the most obscure councils of local administration.

The freedom to organize with others who have shared interests in order to articulate those concerns to the government is clearly protected by the First Amendment to the United States Constitution. Americans are guaranteed the right to peaceful association and assembly and to petition the government for redress of grievances. These liberties form the basis for interest group participation in the political process. Americans are free to join with others in both political and nonpolitical organizations. Any infringement on these rights would be considered a serious violation of First Amendment freedoms.

Given the long history of pervasive interest group activity and the constitutional provisions guaranteeing the rights of political association, it is perhaps surprising that Americans generally hold interest groups in low regard. A negative attitude toward interest groups has become an established characteristic of the American political culture. From the earliest days of our nation's formation, respected leaders have warned against the power of organizations representing narrow self-interests. During the debate over ratification of the Constitution, James Madison called such organized interests (known as "factions" in the language of that day) a "dangerous vice" and argued that one of the primary attributes of a well-ordered government was the ability "to break and control the violence of faction."[1] Throughout the years, interest groups have commonly been portrayed in the press and characterized from the political stump as corrupt, dishonest organizations of the monied classes, controlling government for their own benefit and against the best interests of the American people. At various points in our history, such economic interests as the railroads, oil companies, arms manufacturers, industrial combines, and large labor unions were accused of being the secret powers behind government decision making. Held in even greater contempt have been the paid representatives of such groups, known since the early 1800s as "lobbyists," who are often pictured as fat, cigar-smoking power brokers, at home in smoke-filled rooms, devoid of ethics, and masters of bribery. The vocabulary used to identify and describe the participants in this process is less than flattering. Terms such as "pressure groups," "special interests," "lobby groups," "lobbyists," or "agents of special interests" conjure up rather unbecoming images.

In spite of this long history of ill will toward interest groups (admittedly supported by occasional scandals and proven misconduct), the lobby organization is an integral part of the American political process. As long as our governmental system remains structurally the same as it is today, interest groups will continue to play an important role in policy making. Madison himself was quick to note that special interests could not be removed without destroying essential liberty.[2] Given the significant activity of interest groups in American politics, it is crucial to understand their nature and function as well as the positive and negative contributions they make to the operation of the American republic.

THE NATURE AND FUNCTION OF INTEREST GROUPS

Before examining in greater detail the political activities of organized interests in the United States, it is important to review some of their essential characteristics, as well as the elements which define interest groups, the tendency of Americans to join voluntary associations, and the extent of group participation in the United States.

[1] James Madison, "Federalist No. 10," in *The Federalist Papers* (New York: New American Library, 1961).
[2] Madison, "Federalist No. 10."

The Nature and Role of Interest Groups

While most Americans have a general understanding of the term *interest group,* some attention should be given to the components of the concept.[3] First, the word *interest* denotes a conscious desire for a particular result or condition. The desired end may be a material object or a more abstract philosophical goal. This special interest is shared by the membership of a pressure group. It allows many persons, perhaps of otherwise diverse backgrounds and circumstances, to join under a single association. This shared interest is the adhesive which binds the group together. There are almost no limits to the variety of interests around which groups have formed. The shared concern may be a single issue, such as the repeal of capital punishment laws, or a very broad interest, such as promoting "conservative causes." The interest may be associated with a person's employment, religion, recreational activity, philosophical beliefs, political views, racial or ethnic identification, sex, age, or goals for the nation. For almost any attitude toward matters relating to public policy, there quite probably exists a group composed of similarly minded individuals. An interest group, then, can be defined at least in part by the fact that its membership is based upon a common interest or desire.

Second, an interest group is a collection of individuals. Each member has exercised his or her freedom of association by joining together with other like-minded or similarly situated persons. Interest groups are normally voluntary associations composed of persons who freely agreed to enter the organization. The central purpose of the association is to further the commonly held interest of the group by employing various methods of collective action. An interest group is comprised of persons who share similar concerns and who feel sufficiently strongly about those concerns to take the actions necessary to join with others.

Third, an interest group is an aggregate of persons who come together to achieve goals that they are incapable of achieving on their own. Therefore, interest groups attempt to further their ends by making demands on persons or groups outside their own membership, and for this reason, they play an important part within a society. Interest groups, then, are more than merely self-help associations. They are organized, goal-oriented associations seeking certain valued goods for their membership which they hope to obtain by making certain demands on society.

Fourth, an interest group is a political organization. It is political because it attempts to obtain public policies favorable to its membership by petitioning governmental officials for the desired action. The government is the target of these efforts because only the government has the necessary power and authority to satisfy the group's political aims. If, for example, domestic steel producers wish a

---

[3] For related discussions of interest group definitions, see David B. Truman, *The Government Process,* 2nd ed. (New York: Alfred A. Knopf, 1971), pp. 33-39; L. Harmon Zeigler and G. Wayne Peak, *Interest Groups in American Society,* 2nd ed. (Englewood Cliffs, N.J.: Prentice-Hall, Inc., 1972), pp. 1-4; and Carol S. Greenwald, *Group Power* (New York: Praeger Publishers, 1977), pp. 14-19.

high tariff placed on inexpensive foreign steel imports, the producers must petition the government because it is the only agency capable of granting the desired end.

An interest group, then, is an organized collection of individuals who are bound together by shared attitudes or concerns and who make demands on political institutions in order to realize goals which they are unable to achieve on their own.

This definition sharply distinguishes interest groups from other voluntary associations. There are obviously many collections of individuals who come together out of some mutual interest or concern. Bridge and garden clubs, for example, are organized groups of persons with shared interests relating to their particular favored pastime. They are not, however, interest groups. They come together to meet certain needs for shared information and organized activities, but they are capable of meeting these needs within their own organizations. They do not engage in making demands on the government in order to achieve their goals. A group of homemakers who join together out of a shared concern over increased food prices do not fit the definition of an interest group until their activities go beyond holding meetings to discuss the issue and exchange cost-cutting suggestions. However, once the group attempts to pressure governmental officials into doing something about the high price of food, it is an interest group rather than a voluntary association.

While it is essential that an organization make demands on the nation's political institutions in order to be considered an interest group, this need not be the only, or even the primary, activity of the association. In fact, few interest groups are exclusively devoted to lobbying the government. The vast majority of such organizations engage in a wide variety of activities which have little or nothing to do with political action. The labor unions, for example, constitute one of the most powerful and effective lobbies in Washington, yet only a very small proportion of union activities are directed at governmental officials; instead, unions devote the bulk of their time and resources to providing various services for their members. In fact, these membership services may well be the most important activities in which an interest group engages. Such services provide immediate, tangible benefits for the membership and are quite necessary for the maintenance of the organization. Our definition only requires that a portion of the group's activities be devoted to communication with the government—even if that activity constitutes but a small fraction of the overall organization efforts. Such governmental communication may be direct, as when the organization employs representatives to contact political officials, or it may be indirect, as when the group attempts to influence public opinion to support its preferred policy positions. Attempts to convince the government to adopt policy favorable to the group's interest may be directed at any level of government (federal, state, or local) and at any division of government (the legislature, the executive, or the courts). Whatever form it may take, a pressure group, by definition, expends some of its energy attempting to convince government to respond to its interests.

By this point it should be obvious that there are essential differences between interest groups and political parties. While both exist for the purpose of exerting a degree of control over the government, their purposes and strategies are different. First, political parties strive to control the government by placing members of their own organization in official positions. This requires that the party take the lead in the electoral process. Political parties exist in order to elect their representatives to governmental positions. These elected officials can then exert legitimate influence and authority to have additional party members placed in appointive positions. The ultimate goal of a political party is to dominate the government by placing large numbers of party members in positions of political responsibility. Interest groups, on the other hand, have no commitment to electing members of their organizations to positions of public trust. Instead, pressure groups are normally interested only in controlling the public policy decisions of government. While interest groups regularly participate in the electoral process by supporting candidates with funds and organizational assistance, the motive for such support is only to contribute to the election of persons sympathetic to the groups' interests.

A second major difference between parties and pressure groups deals with the scope of their interests. Political parties, because they seek to control the entire government, must have a very broad array of interests and activities. Major parties commonly take positions on all the issues and problems with which modern government must deal. The party, if it is to be successful in the governing function, must be capable of coping with each of the problem areas facing the country. Interest groups, however, normally have much narrower spheres of concern. By definition, pressure groups confine their activities to those specialized areas of public policy which directly or indirectly affect their membership. For example, the Consumer Federation of America restricts its lobbying activities to those matters relevant to the American consumer; the Citizens Committee for the Right to Keep and Bear Arms is interested only in matters relating to firearms control; and the American Coalition limits the scope of its activities to promoting a reduction in the number of foreign peoples allowed to immigrate to the United States. An interest group is not concerned with the wide panorama of issues facing government, but only in those public policy areas relevant to the shared attitudes and activities of the organization's membership. Its purpose is to influence governmental policy in order to satisfy the needs of the group which it cannot satisfy on its own.

Like political parties, interest groups play an integral role in linking the government and the citizenry. Interest groups afford individuals the opportunity to join with other persons to express their shared views to governmental officials. Such organized efforts are often more effective than individual activities. For example, an individual who is interested in the quality of the environment may become a more informed and effective supporter of the ecology movement by joining an interest group like the Sierra Club. As a member of an environmental organization, the citizen pools his economic support (association dues) and his energies with other persons having similar interests. The interest group is then able to provide staff personnel who are responsible for expressing the interests of the organization's membership to the various agencies of government. Thus, the group has linked the citizen to the government. The government has received communication and information from the citizen. Similarly, the staff of the interest group is able to inform the membership of positions taken by governmental officials and of current political activities which relate to the interests of the group. Hence, the group can operate as a vehicle for communication from the government to the citizen. By joining with others, the citizen is able to express his views and receive information from the nation's political institutions. Usually this communications flow is much more efficient than an individual could attain on his own. A person acting on his own behalf rarely has sufficient time and resources to accomplish what the group can. Job, family, and other obligations do not allow most people to become as active in their special areas of concern as they might wish to be. The interest group provides an opportunity for the concerned individual to engage in effective relations with the government. It links the citizen with the government and represents the interests of the citizen-members before the relevant political agencies.

American Culture and Participation in Groups

It has been noted by observers of American society that the United States is a nation of joiners. One of the first writers to note this tendency was Alexis de Tocqueville, a nineteenth century French political commentator, who wrote after a visit to the United States:

> Americans of all ages, all conditions and all dispositions constantly form associations. They have not only commercial and manufacturing companies in which all take part but associations of a thousand other kinds,—religious, moral, serious, futile, extensive or restricted, enormous or diminutive. The Americans make associations to give entertainments, to found establishments for education, ... to send missionaries to the antipodes.... Wherever, at the head of some new undertaking, you see the Government in France, or a man of rank in England, in the United States you will be sure to find an association.[4]

"In America," Tocqueville noted, "there is no limit to freedom of association for political ends."

While recent empirical studies have indicated that perhaps Tocqueville was overstating the case to a certain extent, Americans clearly have exhibited a propensity for creating and maintaining voluntary associations. Studies comparing the United States with other nations have generally concluded that the tendency to join organizations in America is stronger than in most other countries.[5] In the

---

[4] Alexis de Tocqueville, *Democracy in America, Vol II*, ed. trans. by Henry Reeve (New York: Schocken, 1961), 128-129.

[5] See, for example, Gabriel A. Almond and Sidney Verba, *The Civic Culture* (Princeton, N.J.: Princeton University Press, 1963). See also James Q. Wilson, *Political Organizations* (New York: Basic Books, 1973), ch. 5.

United States there is a proliferation of voluntary organizations. No matter what one's interests or concerns might be, there is quite probably an association of persons with similar leanings. The various interests represented by these organizations run the gamut of almost every conceivable philosophical position, area of concern, and preferred activity. Table 9.1 illustrates the extent to which associations can be found in the United States and the distribution of interests represented by these organizations. It should be noted that the more than thirteen thousand associations summarized in Table 9.1 are those organizations with a national scope and membership. If local voluntary organizations were added, the resulting total would be increased exponentially. In addition to the sheer number of associations represented in Table 9.1, the distribution of these organizations is of interest. The data clearly reveal the predominant position of organizations devoted to business interests. The tendency of the commercial sector of the United States to organize for mutual benefit has a long tradition, and this variety of association has historically been far more common than groups based upon any other single interest. It should be kept in mind that not all of the organizations represented here meet our definition of interest groups since some are merely private organizations which do not make demands on our political institutions. Nonetheless, the information provided indicates the extent and scope of voluntary associations within the American society.

The existence of a multitude of voluntary groups devoted to thousands of

TABLE 9.1 Voluntary Associations of National Scope in the United States

Type of Organization	Number	Percent
Business, Trade or Commercial	2,914	22.3
Cultural	1,259	9.6
Health and Medical	1,173	9.0
Scientific, Engineering, Technical	898	6.9
Educational	873	6.7
Public Affairs	855	6.5
Social Welfare	789	6.0
Religious	742	5.7
Hobby	700	5.4
Agricultural	613	4.7
Legal, Governmental, Military	460	3.5
Fraternal, Nationality, Ethnic	459	3.5
Athletic, Sports	452	3.5
Greek Letter Societies	321	2.5
Labor	233	1.8
Veteran, Patriotic	211	1.6
Chamber of Commerce	111	0.8
Totals	13,063	100.0

Source: Margaret Fisk (editor), *Encyclopedia of Associations*—Vol. 1 (Detroit: Gale Research Company, 11th edition, 1977).

different causes and concerns supports the conclusion that Americans have a propensity to affiliate within a group framework. However, the mere existence of vast numbers of organizations does not tell us why groups form, what proportion of the population assume membership in groups, how many citizens are active in the associations to which they belong, why people join groups, or to what extent political activity takes place within groups. These questions are obviously significant ones if we wish to gain a proper understanding of the role of groups in the American political process.

To answer the question of why groups form, we may begin with the proposition advanced by Aristotle that man is a social animal. Human beings prefer social interaction to individual isolation. But this tendency to band together does not sufficiently explain America's great attraction to group affiliation. Some additional factor must be present, particularly with respect to the formation of organizations active in the political process. Truman and others have argued that politically oriented groups tend to be created when the existing order of things is disturbed, when the political environment is thrown out of balance.[6]

Many factors may cause a disruption in the equilibrium of the political environment, prompting individuals to band together in a group structure. First, groups often are created in response to an existing crisis. The war in Vietnam, for example, was seen by many as a particularly menacing situation. The growing United States participation in the war gave rise to scores of antiwar groups devoted to ending the bloodshed in Southeast Asia. Second, organizations commonly come into existence as part of a more general social movement. Examples are the great growth in civil rights groups associated with the rise in social integration and awareness among black Americans, and the expansion in the number of labor unions associated with the rising importance of the American worker. Third, the perceived threat of some future danger often triggers the creation of a group. Ecologically oriented groups were formed in response to the perceived threat of a deteriorating environment. The Ku Klux Klan was spawned from a fear that the future existence of a white, Christian America was being threatened by various ethnic and racial minorities. Business organizations have often been created in reaction to a fear of future government regulation. Fourth, certain groups come into existence because competing interests have organized. For instance, the National Association of Manufacturers grew largely in response to the organization of the labor union movement.[7] Fifth, groups may be formed in order to protect favored positions supported by the status quo. Greenwald, for example, reports that in the year of the 1974 oil crisis, more than 50 petroleum interests registered as lobby groups, obviously intent on preserving favorable governmental regulation of the

[6] Truman, *The Governmental Process*, ch. 4. See also, Robert Salisbury, "An Exchange Theory of Interest Groups," *Midwest Journal of Political Science*, 13 (February 1969), 1-32.

[7] Joseph G. Rayback, *A History of American Labor* (New York: Free Press, 1966); Truman, *The Governmental Process*, pp. 81-86.

oil companies.[8] Finally, government regulation itself can promote group formation. When government officially recognized the right of collective bargaining, it promoted significant growth in the number of labor unions. Government welfare regulations encouraged organizations of welfare recipients to form. Recent election law reforms have prompted an explosion of political action groups. Each of the above situations, occurring either individually or in combination, causes a sufficient disturbance in the political environment to encourage the formation and growth of politically oriented groups.

While the American constitutional framework and the nation's relatively open political environment encourage group formation of all varieties, not all citizens share the general tendency to join organizations. However, most Americans do hold memberships in one or more voluntary associations. Almond and Verba, in a study of political participation in five nations published in 1963, found that 57 percent of American citizens were members of voluntary associations.[9] A later research project conducted by Verba and Nie reported evidence of 62 percent of the nation belonging to various groups, with 39 percent holding multiple memberships.[10] And in 1976, Robert Salisbury made available research results showing that 74.5 percent of Americans held group affiliations, with 48.8 percent having joined more than one association.[11] While these findings vary to a certain extent, it is clear that well over half and perhaps as many as three-fourths of the American people are affiliated with organizations.

Most of these groups do not have political objectives as their central reason for existing. However, many of the seemingly nonpolitical groups do in fact harbor political activity. Verba and Nie provided an indication of this in their study of participation in the United States when they examined the kinds of groups Americans joined and whether political discussion took place within these organizations. The results of this research can be seen in Table 9.2. According to the Verba and Nie findings, the most common variety of group affiliations are found in labor unions, school associations, and fraternal organizations. This is not a particularly surprising finding given the emphasis Americans place on their jobs, the education of their children, and various community affairs. What is surprising, however, is the degree of political activity within the typical organizations to which Americans belong. In eight of the fifteen kinds of organizations studied, a majority of members reported political discussion occurring within the confines of the group. Even within organizations devoted to sporting activities, the least political of all groups studied, one-fifth of the members reported political discussion taking place. Clearly, when

---

[8] Greenwald, *Group Power*, p. 29.

[9] Almond and Verba, *The Civic Culture*.

[10] Sidney Verba and Norman H. Nie, *Participation in America* (New York: Harper and Row, 1972), p. 176.

[11] Robert Salisbury, "Overlapping Memberships, Organizational Interactions, and Interest Group Theory" (Paper presented at the annual meeting of the American Political Science Association, 1976).

TABLE 9.2 The Types of Organizations to Which Individuals Belong

Type of Organization	Percentage of the population who report membership	Percentage of members who report that political discussion takes place in the organization
Political groups such as Democratic or Republican clubs, and political action groups such as voters' leagues	8	97
School service groups such as PTA or school alumni groups	17	54
Service clubs such as Lions, Rotary, Zonta, Jr. Chamber of Commerce	6	64
Youth groups such as Boy Scouts, Girl Scouts	7	36
Veterans' groups such as American Legion	7	56
Farm organizations such as Farmer's Union, Farm Bureau, Grange	4	61
Nationality groups such as Sons of Norway, Hibernian Society	2	57
Church-related groups such as Bible Study Group or Holy Name Society	6	40
Fraternal groups such as Elks, Eagles, Masons and their women's auxiliaries	15	33
Professional or academic societies such as American Dental Association, Phi Beta Kappa	7	57
Trade unions	17	44
School fraternities and sororities such as Sigma Chi, Delta Gamma	3	37
Literary, art, discussion, or study clubs such as book-review clubs, theater groups	4	56
Hobby or garden clubs such as stamp or coin clubs, flower clubs, pet clubs	5	35
Sports clubs, bowling leagues, etc.	12	20

Source: Sidney Verba and Norman H. Nie, *Participation in America* (New York: Harper and Row, 1972), pp. 178-179.

individuals come together for whatever purpose, there is a tendency at some point for the membership to focus on political matters. This tendency is obviously stronger if the group's primary concerns are affected by what occurs in the political arena.

Studies of participation in group activities have generally concluded that organizational membership tends to be an upperclass phenomenon. Joiners are usually higher on the socioeconomic ladder than nonjoiners. In comparing those who hold memberships with those who do not, we consistently find that social status indicators separate the two groups of individuals.[12] The tendency to join voluntary associations increases with advances in income, education, and occupational status. Joiners are more often male than female, white than black, Jewish or Protestant than Catholic, and older than younger. Furthermore, those who have roots in the community (defined as being married, having children, owning homes, and voting regularly) more often participate in group activities than those without such community ties. Individuals with these favored socioeconomic and community characteristics not only are more likely to join organizations, but they are also more apt to be active members. These factors point to a final observation of considerable importance. Those groups whose members or potential members are drawn from the higher socioeconomic classes will be more easily organized and enjoy a greater likelihood of long-range maintenance than groups with members from the lower socioeconomic classes.

Even though we are able to identify the types of persons who are likely to join voluntary organizations, we have yet to discuss why they join. What kinds of incentives exist to attract individuals to join groups? Economist Mancur Olson has argued that it makes little sense for persons to join groups that attempt to advance the interests of a particular segment of the population.[13] This is especially the case if the group is successful at improving the lot of all persons similarly situated, whether or not they hold membership in the group. For example, if the National Association for the Advancement of Colored People is successful at prompting Congress to enact a civil rights bill, the legal protections for all black Americans will generally improve. The bill will not help only the members of the NAACP. Similarly, if farm organizations successfully encourage the government to increase agricultural price supports, such a change will affect all producers of the designated commodities, not just members of the politically active groups. Therefore, Olson would ask, why should a person join an organization, pay membership dues, and expend time and energy in group activities if he is able to enjoy the fruits of the group's labor without being a member?

The answer to the question is that the group may be able to provide certain benefits which only the membership is able to enjoy and that participation itself

---

[12] See Verba and Nie, *Participation in America*; Wilson, *Political Organizations*; and Greenwald, *Group Power*.

[13] Mancur Olson, Jr., *The Logic of Collective Action* (Cambridge, Mass.: Harvard University Press, 1965).

may provide certain intangible benefits. James Q. Wilson and his colleague Peter Clark have identified three classes of benefits which group membership may offer: material benefits, solidary benefits, and purposive benefits.[14] These benefits provide the basic incentives for group membership. They attract individuals to join groups, and they serve as inducements to maintain membership within such organizations.

Material incentives are tangible rewards that have a monetary value. Labor unions are an example of groups that distribute tangible material incentives to their memberships. It is obvious that unions are able to use the collective bargaining procedure to gain increased wages and salaries for members of the group. Other material benefits may take the form of health insurance coverage, retirement plans, life insurance, legal aid, and disability benefits. Many voluntary associations have arrangements whereby members receive discount travel privileges, the use of organizational facilities, and discounts on certain products or services. Material incentives are very powerful incentives for group membership. Many persons join groups for the material benefits with little or no knowledge of the organization's political activities. For example, older Americans might join the American Association of Retired Persons just to be eligible to purchase prescription medicines from the group's discount pharmacy, while the Association uses membership dues to advance a comprehensive program to improve the plight of senior citizens, including lobbying governmental agencies. Similarly, an individual may join an environmental group in order to receive publications on wildlife and wilderness areas. The group may then use that person's name, along with other members, to indicate to legislators the number of persons committed to environmental protection. The group may also use the new member's dues to support lawsuits to force an improvement in environmental quality. The importance of material benefits is that they are tangible and have economic worth. Individuals are attracted to the group because it can provide the member with better or less expensive goods and services than the person is able to obtain as a nonmember. The most effective of such material incentives are benefits which are available only to the membership of the group. For example, when a union negotiates a wage settlement for workers in a given industry, the benefits are exclusive to the members covered by the labor contract. We should not forget, however, that such groups also provide material benefits with general applicability. If a labor union successfully lobbies Congress to pass a higher minimum wage law, the benefits of the law affect all persons working at the lowest salary levels, not just members of the union.

Solidary incentives are intangible benefits attached to group membership, such as the sociability and prestige associated with certain groups. People often join

---

[14] See Peter B. Clark and James Q. Wilson, "Incentive Systems: A Theory of Organizations," *Administrative Science Quarterly*, 6 (September 1961), 219-266; and Wilson, *Political Organizations*. See also William P. Browne, "Benefits and Membership: A Reappraisal of Interest Group Activity," *Western Political Quarterly*, 29 (June 1976), 258-273.

fraternal organizations such as the Elks or the Odd Fellows in order to have fun and enjoy the company of other people. Others join ethnic, religious, or occupation-based social groups in order to socialize with persons of similar interests or backgrounds. Still others will affiliate with groups such as the Junior League, a yacht club, or a country club not only to share social relationships with others, but to gain the prestige attached to the mere status of being accepted as a member of the group. In addition to these general solidary benefits connected with group memberships, certain specific solidary benefits may be associated with group affiliation. These benefits are related to a person's performance or status within the group. The group may recognize certain members by bestowing honors on them, electing them to office, conferring a particular level of membership, or entrusting them with certain responsibilities. These special rewards are additional degrees of prestige which the member may enjoy as part of affiliating with the group, and they can be powerful inducement to join and maintain membership in the group.

Purposive incentives are intangible rewards that provide the member with the satisfaction that he is part of a worthwhile cause. The cause promoted by the group may be any goal, ideology or philosophical position with which the member desires to be identified. Unlike solidary incentives, which are largely based on a desire to be seen favorably by others, purposive benefits are primarily internal and are connected to an individual's self-image. A person may join and work for the American Heart Association or the American Cancer Society because he believes these organizations engage in worthy activities and he wants to play a part in the improvement of the nation's health standards. Another individual may feel good about himself because he is working with others in an organization to reduce cruelty to animals or to slow down the arms race. Still another person may join a communist action group in order to be associated with the struggle to change the world order. In each case, the primary benefit to the member rests on the individual's evaluation that he or she is involved in a worthwhile, meaningful activity. The member may not receive any material benefits, enjoy new social relationships, or be perceived as having increased prestige, but the knowledge that he is taking part in a favorably evaluated collective effort is incentive enough to join and be active within the group.

People, therefore, join organizations for many different reasons. The specific organizational characteristics that motivate a person to join a group can be broadly categorized as satisfying some material, solidary, or purposive need. It should also be noted that these incentives are not mutually exclusive. Many groups offer attractive material rewards, pleasant social interaction, *and* a common interest in working toward worthwhile goals. None of these incentives for group affiliation is necessarily political, and in fact, relatively few people join groups for purely political reasons. This, however, does not mean that the group refrains from political activity. In order to attain the goals and objectives that many groups have set for themselves, some political activity is often necessary. At the point at which a group enters the sphere of politics, it ceases to be a simple voluntary association and becomes an interest group.

CONTEMPORARY AMERICAN INTEREST GROUPS

During the past two decades, the number of groups engaged in attempts to influence government policy has grown rapidly. Not only have interest groups mushroomed in terms of absolute numbers, but the variety of interests and concerns represented by such organizations has increased significantly. Prior to the 1960s, business, labor, and agricultural interests constituted the primary pressure groups with significant influence in the formulation of public policy. Today, while these interests remain viable and active, several other categories of political organizations have entered the process, often competing with the traditional groups for power and influence. A review of some of the more significant interest group movements currently active in political affairs will illustrate the complex nature of interest representation in contemporary American politics.

Business Interests

Groups representing various aspects of the business and commerce sector of American society have a long tradition in American politics. From the earliest operations of the federal government, economic interests made their policy preferences known to governmental decision makers. In fact, it has been argued that even the Constitutional Convention itself was heavily dominated by persons representing particular economic interests.[15] During the early years, of course, business interests were not typically organized into associations that would meet our definition of a formal interest group. Nonetheless, representatives of the business community were quite capable of influencing government in order to advance their own particular interests. During the period following the Civil War, business influence in national politics reached its highest peak. First railroad interests and then other commercial concerns became dominant forces in the formulation of public policy. Commercial enterprises maintained a warm relationship with the controlling Republican party, enabling them to protect their favorable position which included relative freedom from adverse government regulation. During the period from the end of the Civil War to the New Deal era ushered in by Franklin Roosevelt, the business community was able to exert pressure on the government without substantial opposition from countervailing interests. Although populist and agrarian movements were occasionally successful, business was generally able to convince government to foster free enterprise policies.

[15] See, for example, Charles Beard, *An Economic Interpretation of the Constitution* (New York: Macmillan, 1913).

Contemporary interest groups representing business concerns do not enjoy the relative dominance which such organizations had in years past. The rise of labor unions, consumer groups, environmental organizations, and public interest associations has provided substantial opposition to the business point of view. Business groups remain strong and quite active in governmental lobbying. They represent more economic assets than any other variety of pressure organization. But their success rate in recent years has been somewhat uneven. Although business is far more regulated and perhaps more heavily taxed than in previous generations, it has been reasonably successful in blocking attempts to enact radical changes in the American economic system. Furthermore, many segments of the business sector have welcomed various kinds of regulation which would have been considered intolerable by the "captains of industry" during the laissez faire years of American economic history.

One factor which should be stressed is that the American business community and the many interest groups which represent it are not homogeneous in their views on public policy. Furthermore, business concerns sometimes have fundamentally differing interests. It is difficult to speak of a business point of view on most issues because the business community is not a monolithic, single-minded entity. A policy good for the airlines, for example, might mean economic hardship for the rail industry or the interests involved in highway construction. A policy responsive to the needs of the natural gas industry might jeopardize the future of the coal companies. For this reason, business groups often conflict with each other as much as they do with their rivals in the labor, consumer, and environmentalist movements.

Business interests can be generally classified into three very different types of associations. First, there are several interest groups that represent business and industry generally. Second, there are trade associations that work to advance the status of members of a particular industry. And third, there are corporations that attempt to attain governmental policy favorable to their own specific needs.

The general business associations are umbrella organizations designed to represent commercial interests in the broadest sense. These groups articulate to governmental decision makers the business viewpoint on broad issues of public policy. Because of the varied interests represented, umbrella organizations may find it somewhat difficult to take stands on specific, concrete issues. Due to the diversity of interests and opinions within the business community, there are few governmental policies upon which all segments of industry can agree. This condition obviously limits the effectiveness of the general business interest groups.[16] At times they are unable to take hard positions on specific issues without risking the dissatisfaction of large segments of their membership.

Two traditional organizations have sought to become a voice for the business

[16] See, for example, Raymond A. Bauer, Ithiel de Sola Pool, and Lewis Anthony Dexter, *American Business and Public Policy* (New York: Atherton Press, 1967).

community. The oldest of these, the National Association of Manufacturers (NAM), was formed in 1895 to advance the interests of the nation's producers of manufactured goods.[17] NAM's membership is comprised of some thirteen thousand companies, representing less than one-third of the nation's manufacturers. Most of the member firms are of moderate size, employing less than five hundred persons each. However, some of the nation's industrial giants (General Motors, duPont, U.S. Steel, IBM, Standard Oil, and RCA, for example) also hold membership, giving rise to the criticism that the organization is dominated by big business. Throughout much of its history, NAM has taken extremely conservative positions on most issues relevant to business and has assumed a particularly hard line with respect to the labor movement. This overly conservative approach caused both a decline in membership growth and a loss of lobbying effectiveness. In recent years, however, the association has regained much of its viability by moderating its position on public policy issues, although it maintains a distinctly conservative posture.

The second traditional voice of the commercial sector has been the Chamber of Commerce of the United States. The Chamber is a federation of state and local chambers of commerce, trade associations, and other business concerns, formed in 1912 to promote the interests of the business community. The economic elements represented by the Chamber are even more diverse than those for whom the National Association of Manufacturers speaks. Therefore, it is restricted to lobbying for general business principles such as "free enterprise" and for measures capable of spurring economic growth; it can do relatively little to assist specific industries or corporations. The Chamber, however, does maintain a relatively large staff of one thousand and engages in extensive research and publishing activities promoting the general interests of commercial concerns.

In addition to these two traditional business organizations and several other less-established ones, a relatively recent organization, the Business Roundtable, has developed into a very effective voice for American business.[18] The Roundtable was formally organized in 1974 in order to establish a prestigious association of business advocates. The membership of the Roundtable is restricted to the chief executive officers of the nation's largest business concerns. Currently 180 of these highly placed business executives constitute the organization's members. These individuals head such giant industrial firms as Coca-Cola, Allied Chemical, Procter and Gamble, Firestone, General Motors, and Sears. The Roundtable is unique and particularly effective because its members are individually active in organizational affairs as well as in the actual process of lobbying governmental officials. Substitutes and representatives are not used. This strategy improves access to political decision-

---

[17]For a discussion of the National Association of Manufacturers, see Andrew J. Glass, "Washington Pressures/NAM's New Look Is Toward the Goal of Business Unity," *National Journal,* 6 (January 5, 1974), 15-23. See also Philip H. Burch, Jr., "The NAM as an Interest Group," *Politics and Society,* 4 (Fall 1973), 97-130.

[18]See *Congressional Quarterly Weekly Report,* 35 (September 17, 1977), 1964-1968.

makers and therefore increases effectiveness. Although a congressman might well avoid holding a private discussion with an unknown lobbyist for the business community, it is doubtful that he would refuse to grant an appointment requested by the head of General Motors. The Roundtable has already posted fairly sizeable legislative victories in matters relating to consumer protection, energy, taxes, and government regulation of business.

Trade associations differ from the general business interest groups in that they represent only a single industry or, quite often, only a small portion of a particular industry. All major industries have at least one trade association to provide collective efforts on behalf of the industry's participants. These trade associations provide numerous services for their members, including the promotion of the group's interests in the political process. Groups such as the American Hotel and Motel Association, American Trucking Association, National Cable Television Association, and the National Association of Greeting Card Publishers are examples of trade associations devoted to improving the economic conditions surrounding a particular industry. There is almost no end to the number of trade associations in the United States. There are, for example, 54 trade associations representing various components of the periodical publishing industry, 29 associations active in the hardware industry, 15 organizations for stationery producers, and 6 groups composed of businesses that manufacture screws. Obviously, not all of these groups regularly engage in political lobbying. However, many are exceptionally active and quite effective.

Trade associations differ from other interest groups in at least two important ways: first, their memberships consist primarily of corporations rather than individuals, and second, their memberships are usually relatively small. These two characteristics have an important bearing on the way in which these groups operate in interest group politics. Their corporate membership generally guarantees significant financial backing, allowing for substantial funding should the membership decide that increased activity in the political process is necessary. The small membership factor allows the organizations to take firm stands on specific issues. Unlike the broad, multimember groups representing industry generally, trade associations are not often plagued with a division of opinion within their ranks. Since the interests of the membership are quite similar, if not identical, the association does not normally have to worry about offending important segments of the membership whenever it takes a stand on an issue affecting the industry.

Finally, we should add a note about the activity of corporations in the political process. Whether corporations should be considered interest groups is a debatable point. Certainly they are not organizations in the same sense as a trade association or a general business group. However, they often engage in interest group politics in behalf of their own corporate interests. There are at least four reasons why corporations may decide on independent political action. First, if the corporation is involved in many different industries, specific trade associations would be unable adequately to represent the firm's interests. Second, the corpora-

TABLE 9.3 Examples of Business Interest Groups

Organization	Date Founded	Staff	Membership
General Business Assocations:			
Chamber of Commerce of the United States	1912	1,000	3,600 commercial associations and 56,000 business firms and individuals
National Association of Manufacturers	1895	200	13,000 manufacturers
Business Roundtable	1974	*	180 corporate chief executives
Trade Associations:			
American Insurance Association	1964	327	127 insurance companies
American Petroleum Institute	1919	500	8,000 oil industry concerns
Association of American Railroads	1934	480	243 rail companies
National Beer Wholesalers' Association	1938	6	2,100 beer wholesalers
National Pest Control Association	1933	17	2,500 pest control firms
Shipbuilders' Council of America	1921	10	50 marine vessel construction companies

*data unavailable.
Source: Margaret Fisk (ed.), *Encyclopedia of Associations* (Detroit: Gale Research, 11th edition, 1977).

tion may simply want to provide additional efforts in behalf of certain industry goals, thus working to reinforce the efforts of the trade associations. Third, the trade associations may be taking positions not totally compatible with the corporation's best interests, thus prompting the firm to speak out for the specific positions it favors. And fourth, the business may have unique problems or situations not common to other firms active in the same industry. For any of these reasons, specific corporations may attempt to influence the making of public policy. In recent years, such well-known companies as Allied Chemical, Chase Manhattan Bank, General Electric, and Ford Motor Company have been active in attempts to influence the making of public policy.

Business interest groups have historically participated in the political process by promoting governmental policies consistent with the advancement of the business community. These groups are formed primarily to provide material benefits for their members. They form the largest and most numerous of all the categories of pressure groups. Business interests do not always obtain the policies that they prefer, but they can always be counted on to be active in the political process whenever commercial interests may be affected by government action.

Labor Interests

Labor organizations have traditionally served as countervailing interest groups, providing the political arena with general opposition to many positions taken by the business community. Like the business-oriented groups, labor associations can trace their origins to the earliest years of the American republic.[19] However, labor unions were never as strong as the business associations until the twentieth century. Prior to that time, labor organizations had difficulty developing strong, effective unions. The history of the labor movement during the 1800s demonstrates the difficulties associated with obtaining unity among the American workers. While certain local labor organizations were effective and relatively strong, attempts to organize into national groups largely resulted in failure. Associations such as the National Labor Union (1866-1872) and the Knights of Labor (1869-1917) represented efforts to create broadly diversified organizations of workers with a national membership. These associations ultimately failed due to a lack of consensus on group goals and the difficulties associated with satisfying a diverse membership.

However, in 1886 the American Federation of Labor was born. The AFL became the first broad-based, national labor organization to be successful in terms of organization, political effectiveness, and the ability to survive and grow. The AFL was a federation of small labor unions, generally representing the skilled trades. Each member union had its own governing procedures and retained autonomy over internal matters. This federated structure contributed to the initial success of the AFL. By maintaining the smaller craft unions as units, the workers continued to associate primarily with members of their own trade. This strategy had the advantages of retaining worker identity with a specific occupational group and allowing member unions to provide selective benefits for the members of the various craft occupations. The combined strength of the federated member unions gave organized labor a considerable amount of power, which could be focused on those issues affecting the general rights and conditions of the American worker. The AFL underwent dramatic growth in its early years, gaining a national membership of 1,675,000 by 1904. This figure represented more than 80 percent of all organized workers in the United States at that time.[20]

As the mass production industries grew during the 1900s, a movement for a national labor union of unskilled workers began. By the 1930s, many industrial workers had formed labor organizations associated with a particular industry. Auto workers, mine workers, and steel workers, for example, had unions representing relatively unskilled industrial workers. However, there was no umbrella organization for the industrial workers like the AFL provided for the craft unions. This void

---

[19] For a discussion of the origins of the labor movement, see Harry Millis and Royal E. Montgomery, *Organized Labor* (New York: McGraw-Hill, 1945).

[20] See Harwood Childs, *Labor and Capital in National Politics* (Columbus, Ohio: Ohio State University Press, 1930).

gave birth to the Congress of Industrial Organizations, which, like the AFL, was organized on a confederate principle. The CIO was even more politically active than the AFL. It worked for the adoption of such measures as a minimum wage law, social security, and a more activist social welfare role to be adopted by the federal government.

The role of labor unions in the United States has been significantly enhanced by the passage of various pieces of labor legislation. Perhaps the most important of these was the National Labor Relations Act of 1935. This law gave formal recognition to labor unions and guaranteed certain rights of collective bargaining. Official recognition of organized labor proved to be of inestimable importance to the labor movement. It not only gave unions a legitimate status, but it also was designed to prevent unfair actions on the part of businesses opposed to unionization and collective negotiations. The effect of this legislation was to trigger a massive increase in union membership. Additional legislation, usually passed while Congress was under the control of the Democratic party, further established the role of labor unions.

In 1955, the AFL and the CIO merged into a single national labor organization. The new association, known as the AFL-CIO, retained the federated nature of its parent groups. Individual unions associated with the AFL-CIO maintain a certain degree of independence and autonomy over internal matters, while the combination of the various unions into a single national entity allows labor to speak with a very loud voice on issues of mutual concern. Today, the AFL-CIO is by far the largest labor organization in the United States. It consists of some 110 member labor unions representing more than 14 million workers. Its member unions are among the largest individual organizations in the country.

Not all national labor unions are affiliated with the AFL-CIO. The United Autoworkers Union, for example, left the AFL-CIO in 1968 in a dispute over policy differences and because of the incompatibility of George Meany of the AFL-CIO and the late United Auto Workers president Walter Reuther. The International Brotherhood of Teamsters remains independent of the AFL-CIO after having been removed from the umbrella organization in 1957 because of internal corruption and charges of ties with organized crime. But the vast majority of American labor unions maintain membership in the AFL-CIO, making it a powerful influence in national political affairs.

The days of massive increases in union membership have generally come to a close. A majority of the nation's large industries have union representation of workers, and only minimal growth in unionization is expected in these basic industries. However, labor organizations continue to expand, although at a less rapid pace than in previous years, into segments of the economy which have traditionally stayed outside the unionization movement. Agricultural workers, teachers, hospital employees, and government workers have recently undergone considerable courting by union organizers. In many instances, these efforts have been remarkably successful. For example, between 1968 and 1974, union membership in the private sector increased 3.7 percent (to a total of 18.8 million workers), but during the same time

TABLE 9.4 Examples of Labor Interest Groups

Organization	Date Founded	Staff	Membership
American Federation of Labor/ Congress of Industrial Workers	1955	600	110 national labor unions, representing 14,300,000 workers
American Postal Workers Union	1971	250	300,000
United Steelworkers of America	1936	830	1,400,000
International Brotherhood of Teamsters	1903	*	2,000,000
International Woodworkers of America	1937	15	100,000
National Football League Players Association	1956	8	1,100
Writers Guild of America	1954	36	3,650

*data unavailable.
Source: Margaret Fisk (ed.), *Encyclopedia of Associations* (Detroit: Gale Research, 11th edition, 1977).

frame, unionized government employees increased 38.3 percent. The largest growth occurred at the state and local government level which witnessed an increase of 28.9 percent in union membership.[21]

While business organizations back their demands on the government with economic power, labor unions use numbers as political currency. Labor organizations form some of the nation's largest associations with the numbers of organized workers in the millions. Such individual unions as the Teamsters, Steelworkers, Auto Workers, and Electrical Workers have between one and two million members. The Carpenters, Communications Workers, Retail Clerks, Building Trades, Meatcutters, and State, County and Municipal Workers unions all have memberships in excess of one half million. These large numbers of organized workers constitute a potent political force. As organized individuals they represent millions of votes, large sums of political contributions, and organized campaign assistance. With this caliber of support, labor union representatives are able to obtain access to governmental decision makers and have organized labor's policy preferences heard.

Organized labor membership, of course, is only partially voluntary. Much of its membership rests on a form of coercion since union affiliation is a requirement for working in certain establishments. Nonetheless, labor unions have been able to maintain their organizations by delivering material benefits and certain solidary rewards to the membership. Many of these benefits have come through various kinds of political action which has influenced public policy. There is little doubt that the labor movement has obtained significant gains through pressure group

[21] Neal R. Peirce, "Employment Report/Public Employee Unions Show Rise in Membership, Militancy," *National Journal*, 7 (August 30, 1975), 1239-1249.

politics, but the growth of that political power has leveled off in recent years due to the continued activity of the business lobbies, the increasing effectiveness of public interest groups, and the general decline in the rate of growth in union membership.

Agricultural Interests

Historically, agricultural areas have often been the spawning ground for new political movements. In the United States and in other societies, discontent among the agricultural producers has often been the beginning of fundamental changes. This is largely because the agricultural community sees itself as a distinct societal entity both economically and culturally. Farmers view their role as being crucial to the welfare of the nation because the country's food supplies depend upon their expertise. Often the farm interests perceive themselves as being unappreciated, undersupported, and misunderstood by the business and labor interests which have had such significant influence on governmental policy. Farmers also see themselves as being vulnerable to economic conditions, governmental economic and agricultural policies, and the positions of large banks and lending institutions. The agricultural producer is also susceptible to crop failure, the uncertainties of weather conditions, and the often unexpected attack of agricultural pests. This general vulnerability shared by all farmers has often motivated the agricultural sector of society to join in interest group associations seeking public policies which will improve the success and profitability of the American farm enterprise.

The first major agricultural organization in the United States was the National Grange, created in 1867. The group began with a membership of seven men devoted to expanding the educational experiences of farmers. The Grange, however, grew rapidly, particularly in the 1870s when the financial conditions of individual farmers were especially desperate. At the height of its growth, the Grange had a membership of 750,000 farmers with its primary strength found in the agricultural states of the Midwest. During the late 1800s, the Grange movement worked to improve the plight of the farmers, especially with respect to the railroad industry and other economic monopolies on whom the farmers found themselves dependent. However, the Grange always considered itself first an educational and social association. During most of its history it has purposefully refrained from active involvement in politics. Today, the National Grange remains a major agricultural organization, with a membership of 600,000 farmers. But it is also one of the least militant and activist farm organizations, taking only moderate stands on political issues.

The second national farmers' group of consequence was the National Farmers Union which came into being in 1902. The Farmers Union was born in response to a need for an organization to represent low income farmers. This general bias toward the less economically advantaged agricultural producer continues today. The primary goal of the Union has been to promote policies and conditions which will decrease some of the uncertainties in the production of agricultural products.

By doing so, the Union hopes to lessen the amount of risk involved in farm investment. This goal is particularly salient to the low income farmer who is unable to lose too many "gambles" in his crop production. The Union is committed to the farming way of life and to the small independent agricultural producer. It is clearly not oriented toward the large corporate farming establishment. This organization is one of the few agricultural groups that maintains favorable relations with labor. It has taken several positions consistent with the goals of organized labor and has even worked for the interests of the migrant farmers. Among the large, national farm organizations, the Farmers Union is usually depicted as the most radical. It has been quite active in promoting public policies which strike at established economic powers such as the banks, the transportation industry, and large agribusiness operations. It has championed low interest financing of farm production costs and effective agricultural price supports. Today, the Farmers Union enjoys a membership of 250,000 farmers with most of its support coming from the grain producers of the Great Plains states.

The largest of the national farm organizations today is the American Farm Bureau Federation. The Farm Bureau has a membership in excess of two and one-half million individuals. It was originally formed in 1919, and from the very beginning, the group had excellent relationships with government. This was largely because of its links with the Department of Agriculture and especially its close ties with local agricultural extension agents. The Bureau is clearly the most powerful and established of the large multicrop organizations, a strength that can be attributed to both its size and its friendly relations with the government. For many years, the government has listened to the Farm Bureau as the voice of the American farmer. Many, however, have challenged the assumption that the Farm Bureau provided adequate representation for the American agricultural community. Over the

TABLE 9.5   Examples of Agricultural Interest Groups

Organization	Date Founded	Staff	Membership
General Agricultural Organizations:			
National Grange	1867	26	600,000
National Farmers Union	1902	30	250,000
American Farm Bureau Federation	1919	60	2,505,258
Specific Commodity Organizations:			
American National Cattlemen's Association	1898	20	300,000
National Association of Wheat Growers	1950	*	79,000
National Potato Council	1948	3	13,500
National Turkey Federation	1939	10	3,000

*data unavailable.
Source: Margaret Fisk (ed.), *Encyclopedia of Associations* (Detroit: Gale Research, 11th edition, 1977).

past several decades the Bureau has become increasingly dominated by the larger, more economically secure farming operations. This association with the corporate approach to farming has caused the group to take positions that have been increasingly criticized by the smaller, family farm operators. In recent years, for example, the Farm Bureau has taken a position against the price support programs and has campaigned for a greater reliance on the "free enterprise" approach to agriculture. This, of course, has put the Bureau at odds with groups such as the National Farmers Union which supports the role of the government in assisting the agricultural producers. In spite of its opponents, the Farm Bureau remains the most effective of the general purpose farming organizations. It is very difficult for any piece of proposed agricultural legislation to be enacted over the vigorous opposition of the Farm Bureau.

Although other smaller organizations exist, these three national farm groups are the major voices of the American farmer. While each would like to be the true representative of the farming community, the groups have differing sources of strength and support. The Grange, the least political of the groups, finds most of its strength confined to the New England, Pacific Coast, and Mid-Atlantic areas and is particularly popular among dairy farmers. The Farmers Union derives most of its support from low income, family farmers located in the Plains states. It enjoys particular support among small grain farmers. The American Farm Bureau Federation, the most establishment-oriented group, has a membership concentrated among the cotton farmers of the South and the corn producers of the Midwest. Its appeal is clearly geared toward the more prosperous elements of the farming community. Therefore, each of the major organizations can be seen as having particular regional, commodity, and economic class constituencies.

Discontent among American farmers over both government agricultural policy and the activities of the various large farm organizations has been relatively common. Within recent years this feeling has sharpened, particularly among the smaller farm producers. Plagued by difficult weather conditions, undependable foreign and domestic markets, and an alarming 100 percent increase in national farm debt between 1974 and 1977, many farmers became increasingly disenchanted with the status of the American producer of farm commodities. These particular farmers were opposed to the positions taken by the American Farm Bureau Federation and were not particularly impressed by the activities of the National Farmers Union. Out of these conditions rose the newly formed American Agricultural Movement. The AAM began capturing the nation's attention in 1977 and 1978 when it called for a national farmers' strike which was to continue until the government adopted an agricultural policy that included 100 percent of parity price guarantees. The group urged farmers to stop buying farm equipment, stop producing, and stop marketing until its demands were met. The strike itself had only marginal effectiveness, but the AAM, which had the goal of developing into a national, commoditywide organization of farmers, demonstrated that the current agricultural interest groups left a void in group representation of farming interests.

In addition to the large, multipurpose farm organizations, there exist hundreds of smaller commodity-specific groups. These groups are the agricultural equivalent of the trade associations within the business community. There are associations operating today in behalf of the interests of almost every conceivable agricultural crop of commodity. There are organizations for corn producers, wool growers, asparagus producers, mushroom growers, hog farmers, and poultry producers. The nut industry alone has special organizations devoted to the interests of producers of almonds, walnuts, pecans, peanuts, and macadamia nuts. The list of such crop-oriented groups is quite lengthy. While such organizations are normally small in size and may appear at first glance to be rather inconsequential, they are often extremely effective. Small, single purpose groups can often succeed where the larger organizations fail. The crop-specific organizations hold the advantage of speaking with a single voice for a particular commodity. Rarely are there major divisions within such organizations because the membership is exceedingly homogeneous. These groups also are not likely to have major opposition. If, for example, the potato producers want a particular piece of legislation passed that has very little applicability to any interest outside the potato industry, they are likely to have their way. It is somewhat doubtful even in this era of increasing protest activity and public interest consciousness that any group would actively attack the request of the potato farmers. Through this variety of interest group activity, the potato farmers are able to achieve a favorable piece of legislation. Taken independently, the governmental action may be rather minor, but when combined with similar requests made by hundreds of other special purpose interest groups, a large volume of public policy is influenced.

Agricultural interest groups have a long history and continue to be quite viable today. Along with business and labor groups, agricultural organizations combine to constitute the three largest and most well-established interest group movements in the United States. Agricultural interest groups continue to be effective by working to provide both material and solidary benefits to their members. While a degree of discontent currently exists within certain segments of the farming community, it is not likely to cause radical changes in the manner in which agricultural interests are organized.

Professional Interests

Some of the most active and effective interest groups are those which can be classified as professional associations. These organizations are comprised of practitioners of the various learned professions. Today, every commonly recognized profession has an association to work for the advancement of the individuals engaged in that activity. Most of these professional societies have exceptionally long histories, dating back to the mid-1800s. Many of them were originally formed to provide a channel for information and opinions about subjects relevant to the practice of a particular profession.

Quite early, however, professional groups became involved in governmental policy relating to the practice of the profession. All states have specific licensing procedures and standards for designating persons qualified to practice a particular profession. Dentists, pharmacists, physicians, accountants, and lawyers, for example, must meet certain levels of competence before being allowed to engage in their chosen vocation. Because the professions are careers that require long years of study, the typical state government official is ill equipped to judge the qualifications of individuals requesting state approval to practice a given profession. For this reason the states have generally allowed the various professional associations to have a substantial voice in setting state standards for professional licensing, proposing procedures to determine when such qualifications are met, and judging the fitness of both new applicants and continuing practitioners of the art. The organized bar associations of the various states, for example, are given a substantial role in the administration of bar examinations, the setting of ethical and competence standards for the practice of law, and the disciplining of lawyers who fail to abide by the established codes of professional conduct.

The role of professional organizations relative to governmental policy grew gradually. Professional associations began by advising governmental institutions about all phases of professional practice. In many states these associations became powerful voices for the members of their organizations and had substantial influence over governmental regulation of matters relating to the activities of the profession. Often, because of the status of the profession and the well-organized effort operating on behalf of its practitioners, the society could almost dictate the state's regulations. Opposition was somewhat uncommon. Today, however, the situation has changed. The advent of public interest groups and consumer organizations of various kinds ushered in an era in which members of the professions are not able to enjoy such an overwhelming influence on governmental policy. Opposition to positions taken by bar associations, medical societies, and other professional groups is now commonplace and often quite successful. In recent years, traditional regulations initiated and supported by the professional societies have been successfully defeated by the activities of opposition interest groups. Examples are the minimum fee schedules promoted by the bar associations, the ban on publication of prescription prices long defended by associations of pharmacists, and the prohibition against the advertising of legal services by attorneys. The rise of opposing interest groups, as well as the ever increasing role of government regulation, has caused the political activity of professional societies to increase sharply. Contemporary professional associations now spend substantial resources in their lobbying activities. The American Medical Association and the American Bar Association provide interesting illustrations of the growth and expanding activity of the professional society as a pressure group.

The American Medical Association was formally created in 1847.[22] Like many such professional societies, the AMA did not grow very rapidly and did not

---

[22] See Oliver Garceau, *The Political Life of the American Medical Association* (Cambridge, Mass.: Harvard University Press, 1941).

TABLE 9.6 Examples of Professional Interest Groups

Organization	Date Founded	Staff	Membership
American Bar Association	1878	475	210,000
American Chiropractic Association	1963	55	10,147
American Dental Association	1859	370	125,000
American Institute of Certified Public Accountants	1887	390	120,000
American Medical Association	1847	860	179,900
American Nurses Association	1896	150	198,000
American Society of Civil Engineers	1852	115	72,194
American Veterinary Medical Association	1863	40	26,000

Source: Margaret Fisk (ed.), *Encyclopedia of Associations* (Detroit: Gale Research, 11th edition, 1977).

develop a significant role in politics until the 1900s. By 1912, however, the association had attracted the membership of one-half of the nation's physicians. This membership level gave the Association a legitimate claim to being the voice of the American medical doctor. Since that time, the AMA has continued to hold the allegiance of a majority of American physicians.

The AMA retains a high degree of control over the practice of medicine in the United States. It not only has substantial influence over the establishment of medical standards, but it is also instrumental in shaping the operations of the nation's medical education system. The organization serves as a distributor of valuable information regarding the status of the nation's health and the diagnosis and treatment of disease. It provides opportunities for the continuing education of physicians and is a source of reports on new developments in the medical field. The society has a voice in the development and operation of the nation's medical facilities and the standards of competence required of those who practice in them.

In addition to these purely medical activities, the AMA has become increasingly engaged in political affairs. The central public issue which has served as a rallying point for political action within the American Medical Association has been the question of socialized medicine. Government control of the medical profession has long been opposed by the AMA. Since the 1930s when proposals for national health care insurance were first discussed seriously, the AMA has taken the lead in opposing any proposition that might take the nation closer to government domination of the medical field. The AMA has doggedly fought every major proposal which would lead to a change in the relatively independent status of the individual medical practitioner. Significant campaigns were launched against government-provided medical care in the 1950s and 1960s. During most of this time, the AMA succeeded in fending off the efforts of reformers, but the cost was quite high. The association raised and spent millions of dollars in its crusade to save the nation from socialized medical care. Mass appeals were made to the American public, while more private means of pressure were placed on individual legislators. Finally in 1965, the AMA lost a key battle when the United States Congress passed the Medicare Program after the Kennedy and Johnson administrations had taken the initiative in supporting the legislation. Since passage of Medicare, the government has become increasingly involved in the regulation and control of American medical practice. At each stage, the organized medical profession has voiced protest. Following the election of Jimmy Carter in 1976 and the Democratic administration's renewed emphasis on a national health insurance plan, the AMA was again active in efforts to stop what it perceived as the nation's march to government control of the health care system.

Government health insurance plans are not the only issue over which the AMA has become active. Today the federal government has numerous programs and policies related to health, each of which affects various aspects of the medical profession, and the organized physicians have consistently voiced their opinions on the development and implementation of these policies. In many instances, the AMA has been quite successful in convincing governmental officials to shape public policy according to the preferences of the Association.

The AMA has been an effective voice in behalf of its membership. For the most part, that voice has had a distinctly conservative ring. At times the controlling councils of the Association have taken positions more conservative than would be preferred by certain segments of the medical profession, resulting in a general decline in the Association's membership. Fearing that the society was losing its attractiveness among practicing physicians, the AMA took actions that have recently reversed the downward trend in membership. Although the group at one point represented almost three-quarters of the nation's doctors, in recent years the organization has battled to stay above the 50 percent figure. Whether the AMA will continue to enjoy its position as the voice of the medical profession will largely depend on how successful it is in maintaining adequate membership rolls. This can only be attained by providing the necessary benefits to the American physician.

The American Bar Association initiated operations in 1878. This is considered to be a relatively late development considering the prominence of the legal profession from the very earliest years of the nation's history. In the beginning the ABA, like its medical counterpart, was primarily interested in patrolling entry into the profession and trying to improve professional education. Today these efforts continue. The ABA actively supervises the development of standards for admission into the legal profession and has significant authority, through the state and local bar associations, to discipline attorneys who veer from accepted standards of professional conduct. The Association provides numerous educational services, including the accreditation of law schools and the publication of numerous journals and books that contribute to the continuing education of the American lawyer.

Unlike the American Medical Association, the ABA has had difficulty recruiting a substantial proportion of American attorneys into its ranks. During most of its history, the organization has enlisted the membership of far less than half of the legal profession. Only recently has the Association begun attracting members in sufficient numbers to give it a valid claim as the representative of the legal community. This general lack of success in recruitment is in part due to the substantial diversity among American lawyers. The various specialties of the law often set lawyer against lawyer. Criminal defense lawyers have different attitudes and needs than government prosecuting attorneys. Personal injury plaintiff attorneys often conflict with lawyers specializing in the defense of such suits. Attorneys with large firms are in a much different position than solo practitioners. The ABA has had a difficult time representing all of these diverse interests. It has most frequently articulated the positions favored by attorneys employed by large law firms engaged in the practice of corporation law. This has led to an historic lack of support from attorneys engaged in private and trial practice.

In its political activities the ABA has devoted itself primarily to improving the legal system. This has taken two distinct forms. First, the Association has been quite active in promoting reforms in the legal codes of the various states and also at the federal level. The organization has divided itself into several sections, each responsible for the study of a particular area of the law. These sections identify problem areas in their legal specialties and recommend revisions to improve the way in which the law functions. The ABA has often been criticized for being too conservative in its approach to law reform and for favoring the positions supported by the large corporations. Second, the organization has worked to improve the judicial process. One of its most significant activities in this regard has been to advise the president and members of the United States Senate on the qualifications of persons considered for the federal bench. The ABA has established a permanent committee to investigate potential nominees for federal judgeships and to make the findings known to the appropriate governmental authorities. The group has exercised substantial influence over the federal courts through this evaluation process. In addition, the ABA from time to time makes recommendations on ways to streamline the judicial system.

Professional associations are frequently quite successful in interest group politics. Their influence is important because the professions control some of the most important services available to the American public. How government regulates such activities as the delivery of health care and the distribution of justice has a great impact on the standard of life enjoyed by American citizens. The political activity of such groups, then, has a direct effect on the daily lives of Americans. The professional societies have been relatively effective in pressure group politics for a number of reasons. First, most such groups represent a large segment of the profession, and therefore speak with considerable authority. Second, the professions represent areas of knowledge not readily or completely understood by nonprofessionals. Therefore, government officials are likely to defer to the expertise of the professional association on matters relating to the practice of that profession. Third, the professional societies are comprised generally of high status, well-educated, economically privileged persons. This endows the societies with a very favorable image as well as a reservoir of high quality talent from which to draw. And fourth, the professional societies normally have access to substantial economic resources which may be used to promote the goals of the group. The real key to the success of such groups, however, is the maintenance of high membership rates. For such a group to be consistently effective, it must be able to speak as the representative of the profession, and only earning the allegiance of the members of the profession permits such an advantage. In order to achieve this goal, the professional associations must provide an attractive array of incentives, normally consisting of both material and solidary benefits.

Special Situation Interests

The previously discussed business, labor, agricultural, and professional interest groups have one major factor in common. They are all organized around the manner in which their members earn a livelihood. They are all economic groups. However, there exist hundreds of voluntary associations which are based upon common concerns of a nonoccupational nature. Many of these we may categorize as special situation interest groups. Special situation groups are organizations whose members share a common characteristic that is usually based on a common life experience or genetically controlled trait. Obviously these groups are quite diverse. Some are well-established and effective in interest group politics. Others are of recent vintage, with marginal memberships and questionable viability. But all such groups are significant, if not in terms of governmental influence, then because they provide a combination of material, solidary, and purposive benefits to their respective memberships. They also have the interesting attribute of having memberships which often cut across occupational, educational, economic, and geographic boundaries, uniting people who otherwise have little reason to associate.

The veterans groups are a class of organizations that falls under the special situation category. These groups are comprised of individuals who have shared the common experience of serving in the nation's military. Veterans organizations have commonly been created following United States participation in wartime hostilities. They date back to loosely organized associations of veterans of the Revolutionary War. Today, the two largest military organizations are the Veterans of Foreign Wars, founded in 1913 in the aftermath of the Spanish-American War, and the American Legion, which was organized after the First World War in 1919. Both of these organizations are devoted to providing services for those who have served in the military, and both have been remarkably successful at replenishing their membership rolls following World War II, the Korean War, and the war in Vietnam. Together, the two represent more than 4.5 million veterans. These groups combined with other veterans associations have been quite effective in prompting government to bestow benefits on those who have been active in the military forces. They apply political pressure on government officials concerning a wide array of programs and policies affecting veterans. They are influential in Congress and especially with the Veterans Administration. In addition to the material benefits which such organizations are capable of eliciting from the government, the veterans associations sponsor a wide range of social programs for their members and a number of charitable activities for worthwhile causes.

There are dozens of interest groups whose members share a particular ethnic, racial, or nationality characteristic. Some of these organizations have been exceptionally effective in promoting their members' interests before governmental bodies. Groups representing black Americans, such as the National Association for the Advancement of Colored People and the Congress of Racial Equality, have caused massive changes in governmental policy over the years by effectively lobbying all three branches of government at the federal, state, and local levels and by using the electoral process to full advantage. It is hard to identify other interest groups which have had such a remarkably effective record in shaping public policy over the last thirty years. Another extremely influential class of pressure groups are those representing Jewish Americans. Organizations such as the American Israel Public Affairs Committee, the American Jewish Committee, the American Jewish Congress, and B'nai B'rith have made enormous inroads in affecting United States domestic policy as it relates to Jewish Americans, as well as influencing American foreign relations pertaining to the Middle East.

Other ethnic, racial, and nationality groups are far less effective and have far fewer political goals. Some are designed primarily to combat perceived discrimination against a specific ethnic group. The Italian American Civil Rights League, for example, is dedicated to eradicating the belief that there exists an Italian-American underworld of organized crime. Others, such as the Committee for a Free Estonia and the Supreme Committee for Liberation of Lithuania, work in behalf of nations long since forgotten by many and have a limited appeal. Still other organizations are simply devoted to preserving the heritage, culture, language, and history of specific nationalities and ethnic groups. All of these groups provide social benefits for the membership. Some also provide purposive and material incentives for joining.

In spite of the spirit of church and state separation invoked in the First Amendment, religious groups have been quite active in interest group politics. Church groups, composed of individuals with similar religious leanings, have been involved in pressure tactics at both the state and federal levels. They have expressed views on such broad issues as world peace, hunger, and social welfare, as well as on specific proposals affecting church operations (e.g., aid to parochial schools). Church organizations, of course, spend the bulk of their resources on nonpolitical matters. However, when government engages in policies which directly affect religious principles or the freedom of religious worship, religious organizations have not been reticent to enter the political arena. Large organizations, such as the National Council of Churches and the United States Catholic Conference, command a great deal of political respect. These groups not only have substantial resources, but they also represent large numbers of individuals. Smaller organizations and religious denominations have been equally active in attempts to influence public policy on matters concerning the church. The Church of Jesus Christ of Latter Day Saints has long worked to reduce governmental interference in areas it feels best left to the control of the churches. The Jehovah's Witnesses have an extended tradition of using the courts as a means of protecting religious freedom from governmental encroachment. Church groups primarily offer purposive incentives for joining and maintaining membership in their organizations. People become active in church groups in order to contribute toward certain higher goals associated with the religious principles of the specific church under whose auspices the group is formed.

Another special situation interest concerns the aging process. Senior citizens groups during the last two decades have become increasingly active in politics.[23] Regardless of geography, religion, economic status or educational background, senior citizens are faced with common problems and concerns. This mutual interest has prompted the formation of several associations devoted to the advocacy of policies favorable to citizens in their later years. The largest of these organizations is the American Association of Retired Persons, founded in 1958, which commands the allegiance of 7,500,000 members. The AARP has now joined forces with the 500,000 member National Retired Teachers Association to create an even larger and more effective organization. The AARP/NRTA directs its attention primarily to providing its members with services and information. It is not exclusively a political organization, although presenting the concerns of senior citizens to governmental agencies through direct and indirect methods has always occurred. A more political group, the National Council of Senior Citizens, was created in 1961. Its birth was largely due to the new spirit of social awareness ushered into the country in 1960 with the election of President John Kennedy. The specific issue that commanded the council's attention during its early years was the Medicare proposal which was finally enacted in 1965. The council has continued its activity, however, on behalf of senior citizens, generally advocating the adoption of liberal governmental policies designed to improve the lot of aging Americans. In 1970, an even more politically oriented group was launched by elderly Americans. This group, known as the Gray Panthers, gained over eight thousand membership commitments during its first five years of existence. Molded in the spirit of the antiwar movement of the 1960s and the women's liberation movement of the 1970s, the group is devoted to the elimination of all forms of "age-ism" in American society. Its tactics have been much more activist in nature than those used by the more traditional senior citizen interest groups. The growth of groups concerned with the problems of older Americans is inevitable. Individuals are living longer today than ever before; they are remaining active in their later years like they never have in the past; and demographic projections have spotlighted a consistently growing percentage of Americans

---

[23] See, for example, Henry J. Pratt, "Old Age Associations in National Politics," *Annals of the American Academy of Political and Social Science*, 414 (September 1974), 106-119.

in the post-60 age group. All this points to increasing political activism among older Americans.

During the last two decades, this nation has also seen a tremendous rate of growth among those groups focusing on gender-based concerns. Women's groups have a rich historical tradition in the United States, as exemplified by the temperance and suffrage movements. However, these earlier models of gender-oriented associations were somewhat primitive compared to the diversity, membership, and overall strength of contemporary organizations. Groups such as the National Organization for Women, the National Women's Political Caucus, the Women's Lobby, the Women's Equity Action League, and the Women's Action Alliance have promoted a rebirth of political activity designed to eliminate sex-based discrimination and improve societal conditions as they relate to female Americans. The majority of these groups have formed since the mid-1960s. They have enjoyed remarkable growth in a relatively short period of time, and they have provided their members with a considerable number of political victories at the election polls, in state and federal legislative chambers, and in the courts. These early political accomplishments encouraged increased participation and organization among women interested in altering the status of female Americans. The battle over the Equal Rights Amendment has given these groups a rallying point upon which to concentrate efforts and maintain enthusiasm.

Groups have also formed in reaction to the women's liberation organizations. Many of these associations formed in response to the struggle over ratification of the Equal Rights Amendment in order to demonstrate that not all female Americans supported a change in the traditional system of sex role expectations. For the most part, these groups remained smaller in both numbers of organizations and size of membership than the female rights groups. They have also remained somewhat less effective in terms of overall political accomplishments, although they recorded a number of political successes during the ERA ratification process. The League of Housewives organization is an example of a group offering general opposition to the feminist movement. In addition, organizations such as the Men's Rights Association and the Fathers United for Equal Rights have recently begun appearing as advocates of interests and concerns unique to males.

A final pressure group category which can be classified as a special situation interest involves organizations of welfare recipients. Members of these organizations are persons who share the common experience of receiving government welfare assistance. Organizations of welfare recipients were born during the 1960s. The Kennedy and Johnson administrations brought into existence a wide array of new or revitalized public assistance programs, which in turn increased the number of welfare recipients. Furthermore, the new programs called for increased public involvement. The recipients themselves were encouraged to play an active role in policies relating to public assistance. These kinds of incentives spawned various organizations concerned with the rights of those receiving public welfare. The largest and most successful of these groups has been the National Welfare Rights

TABLE 9.7 Examples of Special Situation Interest Groups

Organization	Date Founded	Staff	Membership
Veterans Organizations:			
American Legion	1919	378	2,700,000
Disabled American Veterans	1921	835	510,000
Veterans of Foreign Wars	1913	250	1,800,000
Ethnic, Racial, and Nationality Groups:			
National Association for the Advancement of Colored People	1909	125	450,673
American Jewish Committee	1906	350	42,000
Japanese American Citizens League	1930	15	30,000
United American Croats	1946	12	5,000
National Congress of American Indians	1944	8	150 tribes representing 350,000 Indians
Religious Groups:			
National Council of Churches	1950	407	30 Protestant & Eastern Orthodox denominations
United States Catholic Conference	1919	350	U.S. Catholic bishops
Senior Citizens Groups:			
American Association of Retired Persons	1958	150	7,500,000
National Retired Teachers Association	1947	629	500,000
National Council of Senior Citizens	1961	90	3,000,000
Gender Groups:			
National Federation of Business and Professional Women's Clubs	1919	50	170,000
National Women's Political Caucus	1971	8	30,000
League of Housewives	1970	*	6,000
Men's Rights Association	1971	3	3,000
Welfare Rights Groups:			
National Welfare Rights Organization	1966	20	125,000

*data unavailable.
Source: Margaret Fisk (ed.), *Encyclopedia of Associations* (Detroit: Gale Research, 11th edition, 1977).

Organization which came into being in 1966. This organization attempts to promote public policies which will insure adequate income, dignity, justice, and democracy for those who find themselves on the welfare rolls. For the most part, the welfare recipient groups have found it extremely difficult to maintain their viability following the period during the 1960s in which a war on poverty was a national priority. Many of the original groups have disappeared and new associations have not formed to take the place of the groups that failed.

Special situation interest groups are very diverse in terms of size, traditions, power, and successes. Some have mastered the intricacies of interest group politics, while others have led only marginal existences. Yet the groups continue to form and grow. One of the enduring phenomena of American politics has been that whenever a group of people find themselves in the same situation and facing common problems, they will quite likely form an organization designed to promote their interests.

Public Interests

Working to influence governmental policy for the best interests of all the American people has been a developing phenomenon in recent political history.[24] An increasing number of organizations have come into being not for the purposes of advancing the interests of a particular economic or social group, but out of the recognition that certain policies would be beneficial to all citizens. This phenomenon has altered the general notion of interest groups which heretofore have been associated with narrow concerns and a desire to promote only the fortunes of the groups' membership. Lobbying in the public interest means attempting to influence public policy in behalf of the common good. Public interest groups are those that seek "a collective good, the achievement of which will not selectively and materially benefit the membership or activists of the organization."[25]

Categorizing groups as public interest organizations is not a particularly easy task. There may be legitimate debate over whether or not a group is pursuing policies that will benefit the nation as a whole. A group dedicated to clean air, for example, will likely classify itself as working in the public interest. However, the president of a steel company or a pulp mill operator might see the group in an entirely different light. Nonetheless, certain causes can be generally categorized as being in the public interest. These are organizations devoted to attaining goals which benefit large portions of the population generally and whose members would not enjoy significant individual rewards if their objectives were met. The motives of the members of these groups are for the most part unselfish with few, if any, material benefits associated with membership.

Good government groups constitute one important category of public interest organizations. Civic-minded people joining together for improvement of the functioning of government is not a new phenomenon. At the local level, this variety of interest group has existed for many decades throughout the United States. But in

---

[24] Jeffrey M. Berry, *Lobbying for the People* (Princeton, N.J.: Princeton University Press, 1977); and Peter H. Schuck, "Public Interest Groups and the Political Process," *Public Administration Review,* 37 (March/April 1977), 132-140.

[25] Berry, *Lobbying for the People,* p. 7.

recent years such groups have achieved national stature and have begun exerting substantial influence on the federal government. One of the oldest public interest groups working to achieve an improved governmental process is the League of Women Voters. The League was formed in 1920 as an outgrowth of the suffrage movement. Over the years, however, the group has grown far beyond an exclusive concentration on female voting rights. The League consists of volunteers who are interested in making the political process more open and the American voter better educated. Activities of the League have been conducted at the local, state, and national levels. Organized into some thirteen hundred chapters, the League clarifies issues of public concern and educates the voters regarding candidates for public office. The League of Women Voters, for example, was the sponsoring organization for the 1976 nationally televised Presidential Election Campaign Debates between Jimmy Carter and Gerald Ford.

Two of the more recent entries in the government-oriented public interest group category are Ralph Nader's Center for the Study of Responsive Law and John Gardner's Common Cause. Both groups burst onto the national scene in 1968. The Nader organization has a wide variety of activities with one of the more significant ones involving monitoring the actions of Congress. Common Cause sees its role as working for the improved accountability of government. The group has been a significant force in reforming election laws, limiting certain kinds of campaign contributions, making more information available to the American public regarding government activities, and tightening ethical standards applicable to governmental officials.

Consumer groups constitute another variety of public interest organization. Because all citizens can be classified as consumers, these associations feel they are working in behalf of the general interest of the entire nation. Consumer groups normally work in one of two ways. First, public education efforts inform the citizenry about their rights as consumers and the relative merits of various kinds of competing consumer products. Second, direct political action places pressure on the government to enact policies favorable to the interests of consumers. The Consumers Union of the United States, supported by almost two million persons, is illustrative of an organization concentrating on the first strategy. The Union, while not rejecting direct political involvement, engages in a wide variety of product quality testing programs and makes the results available to the public. The group also distributes information on governmental actions affecting consumers and has a large public education program to increase citizens' knowledge of their rights as consumers. The Consumer Federation of America, on the other hand, concentrates its efforts on promoting consumer rights before governmental bodies. It supports administrative regulations favorable to consumers and lobbies Congress for passage of consumer-oriented legislation.

Groups devoted to the improvement of environmental quality are also considered to operate in the public interest. Most individuals would not take issue with the general principle that such objectives as clean air, pure water, and the reasonable preservation of certain wilderness areas and animal species are in the public interest. The stands taken by various interest groups on certain conservation issues sometimes evoke opposition as being unreasonable and extreme, but the general goals of such groups are usually considered to be in the best interests of the society as a whole. The Nature Conservancy, Sierra Club, Friends of the Earth, and National Wildlife Federation are examples of prominent interest groups devoted to improving the world's environment and preserving certain natural phenomena. Conservation groups have been active in disseminating environmental information to the American public, presenting the case for environmental protection before legislative and executive bodies, and initiating legal actions in behalf of conservation causes. While they often come in direct conflict with powerful business and labor groups, environmental organizations have earned a credible record of success in pressure group politics.

Still another category of public interest organization is the civil liberty group. The most prominent of the national civil liberties groups is the American Civil Liberties Union. This organization, born in 1920, has taken as its responsibility the defense of American civil rights. The ACLU has been active in representing persons whose rights have been violated by the government. The group is not particularly concerned with what a given individual might represent or with what he or she may have been charged. If basic liberties have been infringed, the ACLU has taken action against the violation. In doing so, the group has worked in behalf of murderers, rapists, pornographers, communists, Nazis, and other types of individuals not normally held in high esteem, which sometimes results in adverse public reactions. The ACLU firmly holds that only by opposing infringement of every person's rights can the general system of civil liberties for all Americans be preserved.

Public interest groups offer no substantial material benefits. Incentives to join such groups are often purposive benefits. Individuals who affiliate with such

TABLE 9.8 Examples of Public Interest Groups

Organization	Date Founded	Staff	Membership
Consumers Union of the United States	1936	350	2,000,000
Common Cause	1968	85	275,000
People's Lobby	1968	*	20,000
Consumer Federation of America	1967	7	220 consumer associations
League of Women Voters	1920	90	145,000
American Civil Liberties Union	1920	330	275,000
Sierra Club	1892	120	162,000
Water Pollution Control Federation	1928	40	25,000

*data unavailable.
Source: Margaret Fisk (ed.), *Encyclopedia of Associations* (Detroit: Gale Research, 11th edition, 1977).

groups do so because they enjoy being associated with what they consider to be a worthwhile cause and contributing to an effort which has general benefits.

Cause Interests

In contemporary American politics there exists a large number of interest groups whose members are united around a particular cause. Cause groups are found in two varieties. The first type consists of groups devoted to a particular ideological persuasion. These interest groups may take positions on a wide variety of public policy issues, but the positions are consistent with a particular political philosophy. Many of these groups call for fundamental changes in the way in which the government operates; others are less extreme in their approach. But all share the characteristic of being wedded to a particular ideology. Unlike the ideologically based minor political parties, these philosophically oriented interest groups do not nominate candidates for public office, but concentrate on convincing governmental officials and the American public that their ideological positions should be adopted.

Among the ideological interest groups, those at the conservative end of the political spectrum are prominent in terms of being adequately financed and firmly established. Some of these organizations, such as the John Birch Society and the Church League of America, place considerable emphasis on an anticommunist philosophy and devote a substantial portion of their resources to exposing communist subversion. The Committee for Constitutional Government and We, The People are conservative organizations that are pledged to defend the free enterprise economic system. Still other groups, such as the American Conservative Union and the Liberty Lobby, promote a general conservative philosophy which applies to a wide range of issues. On the liberal side of the political spectrum, the Americans for Democratic Action, created in 1947, is the most influential. The ADA promotes a wide range of policies, both foreign and domestic, which have a liberal philosophical base. The organization makes its positions known directly to governmental agencies and also urges the major political parties to adopt its views on specific issues. The group has had considerable success in dealing with members of the Democratic party.

The second variety of cause group encompasses those organizations that are devoted to the accomplishment of a single political goal. Their efforts are focused on convincing government to support a particular public policy. Many of these groups share certain characteristics with the public interest groups, in that the members have little or nothing to gain materially from their activities and the primary beneficiaries of the group's efforts may well be individuals who are not members. However, these cause groups differ from the public interest groups in that the policies they promote have a relatively narrow application and will not benefit all Americans in a general sense.

Almost any cause which could possibly command any support whatsoever is likely somewhere to have a group promoting it. In recent years, cause groups representing the various sides of the abortion issue have provided an excellent illustration of specific issue organizations operating in the political arena. There are several associations committed to preserving the right of women to terminate unwanted pregnancies without governmental interference. On the opposing side are numerous local and national groups devoted to protecting the lives of the unborn by restricting the free choice of pregnant women to undergo an abortion procedure. These opposing interest groups have no major concern other than the abortion issue. They are issue-specific cause groups. Over the last several years they have battled at the local, state, and federal levels in an attempt to convince governmental officials and the general public to adopt their respective positions. The abortion issue, of course, is just one of many public policy controversies over which cause groups have lobbied governmental institutions. On many issues there are groups on both sides of the controversy, each presenting government and the public with arguments and information in behalf of their respective positions. There are groups for abolition of the death penalty and groups for the restoration of the death penalty; organizations for censorship of obscene materials and organizations devoted to removing censorship; associations promoting the rights of nonsmokers and those urging government protection of smokers' rights; groups in favor of legalized gambling and groups opposed.

In comparison with other categories of interest groups, the cause groups have small memberships. Americans have never been attracted to ideological groups in any great numbers. They have instead shown a preference for pragmatic political organizations as demonstrated by the two major political parties. For this reason the philosophically based groups have remained in existence but have rarely achieved

TABLE 9.9 Examples of Cause Interest Groups

Organization	Date Founded	Staff	Membership
Ideological Causes:			
Liberty Lobby	1955	35	25,000
John Birch Society	1958	*	90,000
Committee to Restore the Constitution	1970	5	100,000
Americans for Democratic Action	1947	20	65,000
Specific Issue Causes:			
Citizens Committee for the Right to Keep and Bear Arms	1971	4	60,000
National Organization for Reform of Marijuana Laws	1970	6	13,000
National Abortion Rights Action League	1969	4	10,000
Citizens Against Legalized Murder	1966	*	6,000
Morality in Media	1962	6	42,000
Citizens League Against the Sonic Boom	1967	3	3,400

*data unavailable.

Source: Margaret Fisk (ed.), *Encyclopedia of Associations* (Detroit: Gale Research, 11th edition, 1977).

memberships in excess of 100,000 people. The issue-specific cause groups are also quite small in overall membership. This is largely due to the fact that such groups only attract persons who have particularly intense feelings about a very narrow issue. Unless a person places an unusually high priority on a particular policy, it is unlikely that he or she will join an issue-specific cause group. This is especially the case when the group offers no substantial material benefits. Members of cause groups generally affiliate because of a sincere belief that the ideology advocated is an important one or that the specific issue promoted is worthwhile. The incentives, therefore, are largely purposive.

Governmental Interests

Not all entities that attempt to influence governmental policy are associated with the private sector. A substantial amount of lobbying is done on behalf of other governmental interests. Government lobbies represent every political sector from local communities to foreign nations. Some government interests are organized into associations in much the same way that private interests are, while other governments approach political decision makers independently without the benefit of combining forces with similar entities.

Among the most active governmental organizations attempting to influence national public policy are those associations representing state and local government interests.[26] Although some state and local government associations, like the National Municipal League and the National Governors Conference, date back to the turn of the century, most governmental organizations trace their beginnings to the New Deal era. The national administration of Franklin Roosevelt greatly expanded the role of the federal government and the expenditures for various kinds of domestic programs. Many of these new policies significantly affected state and local governments. Therefore, it became increasingly clear that state and local governments would benefit by organizing in interest group fashion to articulate their needs and opinions to the federal government. Local governments today are represented by such groups as the National League of Cities, the National Association of Counties, and the United States Conference of Mayors. These organizations meet on a regular basis to discuss mutual problems and recommend policies to improve the conditions of local units of government. Many of these proposals are directed at the federal government. State governments are represented by groups such as the Council of State Governments and the National Governors Conference. In addition, there are special organizations consisting of state attorneys general, state lieutenant governors, state chief justices, state budget officers, and a host of similar associations devoted to the problems and interests of a specific state governmental function. The organizations representing state and local government entities are often quite active in placing pressure on the national executive and legislative branches to enact policies

---

[26] Donald H. Haider, *When Governments Come to Washington* (New York: Free Press, 1974).

TABLE 9.10 Examples of Domestic Government Interest Groups

Organization	Date Founded	Staff	Membership
Council of State Governments	1925	100	56 state government entities
National League of Cities	1924	12	15,000 municipalities
National Association of Counties	1935	130	1,525 counties
United States Conference of Mayors	1932	13	750
National Governors Conference	1908	*	54
Conference of Chief Justices	1949	*	53
National Association of State Budget Officers	1945	4	54
National Municipal League	1894	20	6,500 civic officials and organizations

*data unavailable.
Source: Margaret Fisk (ed.), *Encyclopedia of Associations* (Detroit: Gale Research, 11th edition, 1977).

beneficial to their interests. Often billions of dollars in funding are at stake. This was the case, for example, in the long battle for revenue sharing that was finally passed by Congress in the 1972 State and Local Fiscal Assistance Act.[27] Faced in recent years with a declining tax base and mounting social problems, the cities have been particularly vigilant in approaching the federal government for improved programs to alleviate urban blight.

Often ignored in discussions of lobbying and interest groups is the growing phenomenon of the federal government being pressured by its own agencies.[28] The most typical activity of this kind occurs when various departments of the executive branch lobby the legislative branch. In such instances, the executive departments are behaving in much the same manner as an interest group. The department attempts to influence legislative policy in the same way that the AFL-CIO or the National Farmers Union would. The federal government in essence lobbies the federal government.

The lobbying activities of the federal government's own agencies are more extensive than is often realized. Every cabinet level department, most executive agencies, and many offices and bureaus have congressional relations divisions.[29] These are staffed with personnel whose duty is to engage in "liaison" activities

[27] See Samuel H. Beer, "The Adoption of General Revenue Sharing: A Case Study in Public Sector Politics," *Public Policy*, 24 (Spring 1976), 127-195.

[28] See, for example, Abraham Holtzman, *Legislative Liaison: Executive Leadership in Congress* (Chicago: Rand McNally and Company, 1970).

[29] See, for example, *Congressional Quarterly Weekly Report*, 36 (March 4, 1978), 579-586.

with the legislative branch. The executive branch employs an estimated 675 persons whose primary duties include maintaining favorable relationships with Congress. The cost of these activities has been conservatively estimated at some $15 million annually, with the bulk of the money committed to the salaries of those engaged in such liaison activities.[30] In addition, substantial sums of money have been spent on improving agency relationships with the general public. While Congress attempted to limit such activities in 1919 with passage of the Lobbying with Appropriated Moneys Act, lobbying by administrative agencies continues without being significantly restrained.[31]

In the late 1970s, Congress conducted investigations into the activities of South Korean agents involved with various federal government officials. The publicity surrounding the scandal included charges of illegal payoffs and other unethical practices. The Korean controversy was not the first major investigation of alleged improprieties by foreign representatives. In the past, similar investigations were initiated into the activities of the China lobby, the international sugar lobby, and the influence of Nazi agents in the American governmental process. These events serve as a reminder that foreign interests (either foreign governments or major foreign business concerns) regularly engage in attempts to influence United States public policy through various lobbying techniques.[32] As such, these parties behave in a manner similar to domestic interest groups.

The United States has a significant impact on almost every other nation in the world. The policies adopted by the American government regarding foreign aid, trade, defense, arms sales, and foreign affairs affect the economic development, political stability, and security of many countries. For this reason, foreign interests find it advantageous to lobby the United States government. Almost every nation engages in this activity to a certain extent. For some countries, major lobbying efforts involve direct contact with governmental officials as well as public relations efforts to improve the nation's image among the American people. In order to provide some control over the activities of foreign lobbyists, Congress passed the Foreign Agents Registration Act in 1938. This statute has been amended on several occasions, most recently in 1966. The act calls for foreign representatives to register with the United States Attorney General and regularly disclose information regarding activities intended to influence American policy making. The law, however, has had only a marginal impact on foreign interests promoting their objectives among governmental officials. Following the completion of the investigation into the Korean lobbying scandal, it is likely that Congress will attempt to revise the law once again to increase control over foreign influence in national policy making.

[30] *Congressional Quarterly Weekly Report,* 36 (March 4, 1978), 579-586.
[31] Richard L. Engstrom and Thomas G. Walker, "Statutory Restraints on Administrative Lobbying—'Legal Fiction,'" *Journal of Public Law,* 19 (1970), 89-103.
[32] *Congressional Quarterly Weekly Report,* 35 (April 2, 1977), 695-705.

THE INTERNAL STRUCTURE OF INTEREST GROUPS

The previous section of this chapter reviewed typical American pressure groups according to the type of interest upon which the organization was built. These interests ranged from groups devoted exclusively to materialistic concerns to those whose motives were primarily philosophical. Certain groups are engaged in struggles to change a broad range of political and social characteristics, while others focus on a single, rather isolated cause. Many pressure groups are especially interested in enhancing the welfare of their members, while others claim to be working in behalf of the general welfare. Contemporary American interest groups are often quite complex organizations with many characteristics that make them difficult to categorize with any precision. There may be some difference of opinion, for example, as to whether a particular group is a cause group, a public interest association, or even a special situation interest group. In addition to the type of interest represented, pressure groups can be differentiated according to various internal characteristics. Classifications based upon the internal structure may be no more precise than those based upon the central interests of the group, but they do illustrate some of the important characteristics which may have a substantial bearing on the power and influence of a pressure group.

Range of Represented Interests

One of the most important characteristics of an interest group is the range of interests which the group represents. Some pressure groups concern themselves with a single interest. For example, the National Rice Growers Association represents the interests of some fifteen hundred rice producers. The group has but one type of member, farmers engaged in the growing of rice. In this case, the product upon which the group focuses is held constant (rice) and so is the activity of the membership related to that product (farming). Issue-specific cause groups provide additional examples of interest organizations whose primary concerns are quite narrow. Groups concentrating on issues such as capital punishment, a return to the gold standard, prayer in public schools, or abortion reform do not have a host of constituent interests to please; they have but one.

Other interest groups may represent a substantially broader constituency. This may occur in spite of the fact that the group confines itself to a single activity or societal division. For example, the National Association of Wholesalers-Distributors and the American Retail Federation each represent a particular type of commercial activity. While the activity is held constant, in this case wholesaling or retailing, such significant factors as product line, size of operation, and geographical location are not. Not all wholesalers and retailers have identical positions on various public policy questions. They may not all have the same interests because of differences in situation. Similarly, the International Brotherhood of Teamsters may represent workers, but the labor interests represented may range from truck drivers to teachers.

A final category of pressure group represents the broadest possible range of constituencies. The Chamber of Commerce of the United States is typical of this variety of interest group. The Chamber attempts to speak for all those engaged in commerce. Here nothing is held constant except an affiliation with the American business system. The Chamber has an underlying membership of approximately five million businesses and individuals. The components of this membership are so diverse that they rarely reach a consensus on any issue of substance. The interests included within the group are always dissimilar in significant respects and can be quite hostile to each other.

The range of represented interests is important to the effectiveness of the pressure group. The narrower the interests represented, the greater likelihood that the group will be able to take strong, unified stands on issues of importance to the organization's membership. There is normally a relatively low level of internal conflict regarding the appropriate position to assume. Organizations representing a broad base, on the other hand, may rarely be able to take positions on controversial issues without risking substantial dissatisfaction among certain segments of the group's membership. A broadly constructed commercial organization, for example, will not often please both domestic producers and importers on any issue having a direct impact on federal trade policies. While the broadly based interest group may have a certain degree of prestige because of its size and scope, its internal conflicts may sharply reduce its effectiveness. The narrowly focused group, on the other hand, may not take positions on a wide array of issues, but when a position is assumed by the group, it will normally be a strongly held one.

Organizational Structure

American interest groups are organized in two basic ways. Many pressure groups are federations of smaller constituent groups. We have discussed a number of such groups in this chapter. The Consumer Federation of America, for example, has a membership of some 220 smaller consumer organizations. These member organizations represent various national, regional, state, and local interests. The AFL-CIO membership consists of 110 national labor unions. In turn, each of these national unions consists of hundreds of local unions. The National Federation of Business and Professional Women's Clubs is comprised of 53 regional and 3,800 local groups. Pressure associations organized in a federal structure normally allow the constituent groups a considerable degree of autonomy in pursuing courses of action and setting policies tailored to the individual needs of the member organizations. The central organization, however, has the authority to establish standards for the member organizations and to speak in their behalf.

Other interest groups have a unitary structure. A unitary interest group is distinguished by direct membership in the central organization. For example, a person engaged in farming soybeans may directly join the Soybean Growers of America. Similarly, a manufacturer may take membership in the National Association of Manufacturers. In unitary organizations, the individual member is directly linked to the central organization. This, of course, differs greatly from the federated group whose individual members can only join the central organization by holding membership in one of its constituent associations.

The organizational structure of the group has a substantial influence on its efficiency and flexibility. A federated organization normally has a governing framework of considerable complexity. The various constituent organizations are generally given certain representational considerations, and the group's hierarchy may veer substantially from the pattern preferred by persons placing a high priority on efficiency. However, federated organizations do enjoy considerable flexibility. A national organization made up of various state organizations, for example, can allow its member associations to solve problems specific to an individual state or region without having to engage the resources and machinery of the entire national association. A unitary group does not have the advantage of such flexibility. However, a unitary group has no intervening associations with which to deal, since the individual members are directly a part of the central group. For this reason, the organizational structure of a unitary group is much simpler and the hierarchy of authority much more direct.

Change versus the Status Quo

Interest groups are often categorized as either favoring change or opposing it. Some interest groups have called for radical changes in our society. For example, the Students for a Democratic Society received a great deal of publicity during the 1960s as a group committed to promoting a new society free from such evils as poverty, exploitation, racism, and war. The SDS did not accomplish these goals; instead, it split into various factions (Weathermen, Worker Student Alliance, and Revolutionary Youth Movement) which ultimately went underground or totally disappeared. The John Birch Society represents a group calling for widespread changes in the way in which American society operates and is governed, although the change advocated is based upon what members see as a return to fundamental American principles. Other groups may simply be calling for change in a particular condition or policy.

Some interests are in agreement with the status quo and work to defend the current state of public policy against any attempts to change it. Those who are prospering under the current system and have a stake in it obviously do not want it radically changed. For many years, the petroleum industry organized to intercept those groups seeking a change in government energy policy. The oil companies received excellent tax advantages, for example, which various reform-oriented interest groups wished to have changed. General business interests have recently combined forces to repel attacks made by consumer groups who have urged government to give more rights to consumers, to place greater obligations on business, and to create a national cabinet level consumer agency to promote the interests of the public.

A group defending the status quo generally has an advantage over a group advocating change. The American governmental system places heavy burdens on those working for change. Before new policies can be adopted, they must negotiate numerous obstacles. If a proposal is defeated at any point in the process, it dies. Those wishing to impose change, therefore, must win a series of victories and lose none. Those preferring the status quo need only defeat the reformers at one point. In addition, the advocates of the status quo are typically in positions of greater power and have at their command more extensive resources. Nonetheless, change does occur, though often gradually and rarely with ease, and the system remains sufficiently open to accommodate pressure group activity aimed at altering established policy.

Political Currency

The political goal of an interest group is to influence public policy in a direction favorable to the views of the organization's membership. Obviously not all pressure groups have earned the same degree of success in obtaining their goals. Some have been extremely effective in influencing government decision making, while others have been relative failures. A good portion of an association's success in the political arena is attributable to its resources. These resources are a form of political currency which can be spent on various pressure group strategies and activities. Like monetary currency, political power comes in many different forms and denominations. The political assets that an organization has at its disposal depend on many different group characteristics.

One of the most obvious bases of political power is membership size. If an interest group represents a large number of individuals, it has substantial clout. Members of interest groups are likely to have a high probability of voting participation, and numbers of voters comprise a political currency that all governmental officials understand. Political officeholders are much more likely to respond to the demands of large membership groups than to those with limited memberships. The national labor unions, for example, back their petitions to the government with large masses of voters.

Of course, sheer size alone is not enough to sway the attitudes of public officials. An effective interest group is one which has not only large numbers of members, but also the ability to mobilize these members. Mobilizing the membership depends upon the organizational capabilities of the group. A well-organized interest group whose members are committed to the group's goals can very likely mobilize its membership to political action. This degree of cohesiveness is often necessary for an interest group to be truly successful. An example of such a group is the National Rifle Association. The NRA membership consists of more than one million persons interested in sporting activities that include the use of firearms. The association is well organized and is particularly committed to blocking attempts to impose what it considers unreasonable controls on the possession and use of guns. Whenever the Congress has attempted to pass gun control legislation of any significance, the NRA has been able to mobilize a large proportion of its membership in protest. So effective has the NRA been in employing this form of political pressure that it has an extremely high success rate of defeating or weakening gun control bills. Congressmen, particularly those in the West where the NRA membership is the strongest, realize that the organization can mobilize its membership to call for the defeat of gun control legislation and that those same members are quite willing to vote against uncooperative incumbents at the next election.

Another factor which determines the political impact of group size is the distribution of the group's membership. At the federal level, groups that can boast of a nationwide membership normally have more influence than organizations whose membership is largely concentrated in a single region of the country. Agricultural organizations, for example, have their greatest influence over governmental officials responsible for representing the agricultural regions of the country and may have little or no influence over representatives from industrial areas. On the other hand, groups such as those representing government employees can make legitimate demands on a much wider range of officials because government employees are found in every constituency in the country.

Numbers, of course, do not represent the only form of political power. Another extremely important base of influence is economic resources. Economic assets come in two politically relevant forms. The first is the amount of money an interest group is willing to spend to further its political goals. If the group has access to large sums of money and is willing to commit that money to its political objectives, the group is likely to be quite successful. In spite of recent legislation imposing new restrictions on political spending, interest groups have a wide variety of opportunities to spend money to influence the government. Such expenditures may take the form of campaign contributions distributed through various political action committees, information distribution activities, and even large-scale public relations campaigns in behalf of their specific goals. Such expenditures can indirectly influence governmental officials by molding public opinion or can directly influence government through legitimate communications to officeholders.

Another form of economic power is based upon the economic assets of the group's membership. If the group represents important economic forces in society, it will have an excellent chance of being heard; on the other hand, a group representing only minor economic concerns will have a more difficult time in attempting to influence the government. For example, the nation's petroleum industry is an absolutely essential one for the well-being of the nation. Because the industry represents huge economic assets and controls a resource that is crucial to the country's economy, the oil industry is able to wield a good deal of political power. While petroleum interests have not always been victorious in the political sector, they have always been able to gain access to governmental policymakers, and their success rate has generally been quite high.

The prestige of its membership can often contribute to an interest group's political power. The professional associations have always been able to take advantage of their prestigious position in society. One of the reasons that the American

Medical Association has been so successful as an interest group is that it speaks for one of the most respected professions in American society. The Business Roundtable is another example of how prestige can increase the power of a group. The Roundtable represents the underlying economic assets of the largest corporations in the country. That in itself is a substantial base for political power. But what accentuates that power is that the Roundtable membership consists of the chief executive officers of these major corporations who each carry immense prestige of their own.

The philosophy of the group can have a substantial bearing on the political influence of the organization. Americans are not a particularly ideologically disposed nation. Therefore, the more ideologically inflexible the group is, the less political power it is likely to have. Extreme philosophies do not translate into political influence within the customary avenues of political activity. Most politicians do not want to be identified with groups such as the John Birch Society for fear of offending the broad middle range of the American electorate. For this reason, groups advocating extreme right or left wing philosophies have a difficult time obtaining access to government decision makers.

Finally, the political power of an interest group can be materially affected by the quality of the group's leadership, which can enhance the other resources available to the group. The daily operations of the interest group are directed by the leadership. This includes responsibility for the formal organizational apparatus, the activities of the staff, and the administrative and policy positions of the association. The day-to-day administrative operation of the interest group is essential to its overall effectiveness and influences its vitality, the loyalty members have to the organization, and the attractiveness of the association to potential members. A large portion of an interest group's obligations centers on distributing information to the membership regarding organizational activities and common problems facing the members. The communications process is controlled by the organizational leadership and how well it is managed often determines the extent to which members feel they have received the appropriate material, solidary, or purposive benefits attached to group affiliation. A successful interest group which has a long history of effectiveness can almost always boast of having had quality leaders. The competent interest group leader is able to satisfy the membership with an efficient use of resources, a well-organized staff, an effective communications network, and a successful use of the political process. In short, an effective leader is one who assumes responsibility for the pooled resources provided by the membership and exercises that responsibility in such a way as to bring the group closer to its organizational goals.

Interest Group Decision Making

Decision-making procedures employed within interest groups are by no means uniform. The specific procedures followed depend to a great extent on the size of the group, the organizational hierarchy, and the structure of the association. In some organizations, a very small number of leaders assume responsibility for group decisions. In other associations, the membership participates either directly or indirectly in the decision-making process. In unitary groups, organizational policies are determined at the national level alone, whereas in federated interest groups, the decisional responsibilities are divided between the national organization and the various local or regional units.

While the specific procedures vary from group to group, the key persons involved in making group decisions are those in leadership capacities. The distinction between leaders and followers is an important one in understanding decision making within voluntary associations. In his classic treatment of political parties, Robert Michels points out that in all voluntary organizations there is a natural tendency for the group to divide into leaders and followers.[33] He calls this process the "iron law of oligarchy" and argues that it invariably diminishes the role played by the rank-and-file members. The leadership of an interest group has almost exclusive authority to make the day-to-day administrative decisions. There is little if any membership involvement in this function. The leadership also generally has control over the major policy decisions of the interest group. The membership may share in this process to a certain extent, but the key participants are the leaders. Even when the membership has a vote on policy decisions, such as whether a labor union should strike or accept a contract offer, the rank-and-file are only responding to leadership recommendations. On relatively few occasions does the membership reject the leadership position. One example of such an action, however, occurred in 1978 when the members of the coal miners union rejected a contract settlement negotiated by the union's national leadership.

How widespread the decision-making responsibility is distributed depends upon the complexity of the organization. Interest groups with a relatively simple structure may well concentrate decision-making power in the hands of a very small number of persons. On the other hand, the large federated groups with highly complex leadership hierarchies distribute decision-making authority among a wide range of leaders. Often the manner in which decision-making authority is allocated has a substantial impact on what the interest group does and how the political process is effected. For example, in 1972 the national leadership of the AFL-CIO refused to endorse either Richard Nixon or George McGovern for the presidency. This decision, made at the national level, had the impact of denying substantial union monies and organizational efforts to either presidential candidate. This obviously was injurious to the McGovern campaign since the AFL-CIO support had traditionally favored Democratic party candidates. However, the federated structure of the union allowed affiliated unions to take independent positions on the campaign. A number of such unions rejected the neutrality decision of the national organization and endorsed presidential candidates. The affiliated unions who supported McGovern outnumbered those who supported Nixon three to one.

[33] Robert Michels, *Political Parties,* trans. Eden and Cedar Paul (New York: Free Press, 1962).

The distinction between leadership and membership in the decisional process is important because the leaders are often quite different from the rank-and-file members. This is particularly true when the interest group is comprised of members from the lower socioeconomic groups. Full-time interest group leaders by necessity are managers. They must have the capacity to administer staff, resources, budgets, and other administrative responsibilities. These tasks call for persons who have sufficient education and training to assume leadership roles. As the interest group becomes larger and more complex, the gap between leaders and members normally becomes wider. No better example can be provided than that of the labor unions. The large national unions have leaders who have become more and more similar to the union's natural foe, management. The style of life, occupational responsibilities, available resources, and other aspects of a leadership position distinguish it from the union membership. It may well be difficult for a worker to identify with a national union leader who wears three-piece suits and whose annual income may exceed $100,000. George Meany, for example, can trace his working life back to a time when he earned his living as a plumber. But the longtime head of the AFL-CIO now lives a much different life than the plumbers and other laborers he represents.

The division between leaders and members does not necessarily mean that the leaders are at odds with the membership. In fact, regardless of the extent of the leadership/membership gap, interest group decision makers can be quite in touch with the needs and feelings of the rank and file. If the leadership is responsive to the opinions and needs of the membership, then it is capable of providing quality direction and maintaining the loyalty of the membership. However, when the leadership makes policy decisions which are clearly out of step with membership values, serious damage can be done to the organization. An excellent illustration is provided by the American Civil Liberties Union activities in 1977-1978. The ACLU is the nation's most prominent defender of constitutional rights. In 1977, the members of the American Nazi Party announced plans to hold a parade in Skokie, Illinois. Almost half of Skokie's residents are Jewish, and the city is home for approximately seven thousand survivors of Nazi concentration camps. Legal action was taken to prevent the parade on the grounds that it would lead to possible violence. The ACLU, however, decided to defend the right of the Nazis to conduct their march. The ACLU held the position that the Nazis were entitled to the same First Amendment protections as other Americans. The legal maneuverings surrounding this issue lasted well over a year. The decision by the ACLU was extremely unpopular with a large segment of the organization's membership, of which approximately 25 percent are Jews. Following the association's decision to support the Nazis, thirty thousand ACLU members withdrew from the organization and took with them $500,000 in annual financial support.[34] In this instance, the leadership of an interest group took a position clearly out of line with the thinking of a

---

[34] "Why the ACLU Defends Nazis," *U.S. News and World Report,* 84 (April 3, 1978), 49.

large segment of its membership, and as a consequence, the association suffered a rather serious setback.

The ACLU example also illustrates typical member reaction when the leadership of an interest group takes positions of which the member does not approve. An individual joins an interest group for certain material, solidary, or purposive benefits. When those benefits are no longer forthcoming because of actions taken by the leadership, the member is much more likely to withdraw from the group than to wage internal battles to change the organization's position. Occasionally when large segments of an interest group's membership become dissatisfied, they will withdraw from the group and form a new organization with goals and positions more consistent with their views than the old association. It is a relatively infrequent event when groups from within the interest organization successfully challenge the decisions of the leadership. Normally the leadership is able to retain effective control over the interest group. However, groups that have regularly scheduled, open elections for leadership positions occasionally experience strong campaigns from insurgent factions. In recent decades, for example, there have been several notable challenges in national labor union elections. These usually occurred when portions of the union membership strongly believed that the leadership was corrupt or had lost touch with the needs of the working members. By and large, however, the leadership in most interest groups remains relatively stable and secure.

SUMMARY

Interest groups have been a fixture in American politics since the very beginning of the Republic. Protected by First Amendment rights of assembly and petition, citizens of the United States have regularly exercised their freedom of association by joining political organizations. These groups play an important role in linking the citizen to his government and in the shaping of public policy.

An interest group is an organized collection of individuals who are bound together by shared attitudes or concerns and who make demands on political institutions in order to realize goals which they are unable to achieve on their own. Such organizations pressure government through direct communications with political officials or indirectly by means of molding public opinion.

Individuals are attracted to groups by various incentives. Some interest groups provide material benefits to their members in the form of increased income possibilities, protected employment rights, use of group-controlled facilities, or discount purchasing arrangements. Other groups attract members by offering solidary benefits which include socializing and sharing in the prestige of group membership. Still other groups offer purposive benefits that give the member a feeling of satisfaction for being part of a worthwhile cause.

Contemporary American pressure groups can be classified according to the interests upon which the groups are based. The most powerful interest groups are those based upon economic considerations. Business, labor, agricultural, and professional groups are centered on the way in which the members earn their economic livelihood. The special situation groups are based upon commonly shared traits or life experiences. The public interest lobbies promote what they see as being policies beneficial to the general citizenry. Cause organizations work in behalf of an ideological program or a particular political goal. Governmental interests, representing local, state, federal, and foreign political entities, are also active in the lobbying process.

Interest groups differ substantially in terms of internal structure. The range of represented interests, organizational structure, and degree of advocacy of change influence the role a pressure group plays. The effectiveness of an interest group is dependent upon such factors as the size, distribution and degree of mobilization of membership, economic assets, prestige, philosophy, and leadership. Although there is a significant variation in the way in which decision-making occurs within interest groups, the leadership normally remains in firm control of the organization.

ten

Indirect Lobbying: Interest Groups and the Public

The process by which an interest group attempts to influence public policy is commonly known as *lobbying*. The term was coined in the early 1800s to describe the activities of people who sought governmental favors by approaching political officeholders in the lobbies of public buildings. As the term evolved, it became descriptive of the process by which interest group representatives (known as *lobbyists*) made contact with persons in political power to argue in support of the group's objectives. Today, however, the term *lobbying* is used in a much broader sense to include any attempt by pressure groups to influence governmental decisions. Direct lobbying occurs when an interest group or its representatives make direct contact with government officials. Indirect lobbying, on the other hand, refers to interest group activities designed to influence public policy without direct interaction with persons in political positions. Both methods can be quite effective.

Indirect lobbying includes the ways in which interest groups use the public to advance their goals. Organizations commonly try to influence government by influencing the citizenry. Pressure groups attempt to mold public opinion to support organizational positions, to mobilize citizens to contact political officials urging adoption of specific interest group-favored policies, and to convince the electorate to select public officials sympathetic to group goals. In this chapter we will examine the techniques and strategies of indirect lobbying, reserving chapter 11 for a discussion of lobbying efforts requiring direct contact.

INTEREST GROUPS AND PUBLIC OPINION

Interest groups have long realized the importance of public opinion in pressure group politics. Public officials react much more sympathetically to the demands of an interest organization if the advocated policies are in accord with the wishes of the people. Conversely, it is very difficult for an interest group to attain its policy objectives if a vocal majority of the citizenry opposes the group's policy positions. For this reason, interest groups often commit large sums of money and organizational resources to campaigns intended to cultivate public opinion.

The History and Purposes of Grass-Roots Lobbying

The modern techniques of influencing public opinion can be traced back to the turn of the century. One of the interest groups most responsible for developing opinion manipulation strategies was the Anti-Saloon League of America.[1] The Anti-Saloon League was born in the 1890s in Ohio. It was a single purpose interest group with its primary support coming from the Protestant church. Its goal was simple and straightforward: it wanted alcoholic beverages removed from American society. The ultimate goal was legally imposed temperance. The Anti-Saloon League was not the only group devoted to the elimination of "John Barleycorn" from the American scene, but it became the most powerful and effective group advocating that cause.

Perhaps the most important factor in the success of the Anti-Saloon League was that its tactics were so innovative. It did not confine its activities to the traditional methods of contacting public officials. Instead, it developed a series of strategies which in refined form are commonly used today. The Anti-Saloon League organized itself in a federated structure. It was a national organization consisting of many state and local chapters. This structure gave the League the ability to make national demands on federal government and yet allow its state organizations to work for prohibition in the various state capitals.

The League realized the importance of gaining the support of the public. It was convinced that unless the citizenry was enlisted in the war against alcoholic beverages, our political institutions would not pass laws imposing prohibition. For this reason, the League developed a wide variety of tactics designed to attract public support. First, it founded its own printing operation which gave it the capability to publish its own journal, *American Issue,* as well as propaganda pamphlets urging adoption of prohibition. The primary purpose of the publishing house was to mold public opinion.

Second, the League was not above using prejudice as an agent in its attempt

---

[1] For a classic study of the Anti-Saloon League as a pressure group see Peter H. Odegard, *Pressure Politics: The Story of the Anti-Saloon League* (New York: Columbia University Press, 1928).

to convince the public of the evils of drink. The League's publications played to the anti-Catholic biases of large segments of the Protestant populace at that time by tying the "wet movement" to certain Catholic leaders. Similarly, during World War I the Anti-Saloon League made effective use of the fact that many American brewers were of German heritage, thereby attempting to associate supporters of alcoholic drink with the nation's wartime enemies. The League even used the racial prejudice of rural Southern whites as a weapon.[2] Racially based propaganda efforts had a degree of success. In the South, the League appealed to the same class of persons that the Ku Klux Klan had success in attracting.

Third, the League relied on the fear of moral and social decay to attract support. Liquor was portrayed as the great destroyer of American society. The publications of the League constantly argued that alcohol was the primary cause of crime, suicide, financial ruin, insanity, broken homes, and prostitution. Anyone who opposed prohibition was classified as being in concert with gamblers, prize fighters, bums, corrupt politicians, thugs, anarchists, low-class foreigners, burglars, counterfeiters, toughs, and vote sellers.

Fourth, the League's use of statistical information was somewhat novel. While the presentation was often biased and inaccurate, the reliance on statistical data added a great deal to the effectiveness of the campaign. Much of this statistical information was based upon the economics of prohibition. The League did such things as compare the economic development of dry states against that of wet states to demonstrate that states with prohibition were far more economically advanced. This implied that alcohol in a society retarded economic development. The League also published statistics showing the amount of waste associated with the consumption of liquor, and it presented statistical studies demonstrating the economic advantage of converting existing breweries to factories producing more positive products. These statistical studies provided an arsenal of information to be used by the prohibitionists.

Finally, the Anti-Saloon League developed methods of holding politicians accountable for their stands on the prohibition question. The publications of the League included information on the positions and votes of elected representatives on the question of legalized liquor. The publication of this information was often coupled with recommendations as to which of several competing candidates most deserved the support of League members. The League was thereby urging the public to support only those candidates who were willing to advocate the goals of the organization.

The Anti-Saloon League was quite successful in its drive to have prohibition imposed on the United States. Its efforts, along with those of other organizations, contributed to pressuring Congress in 1917 to propose the Eighteenth Amendment which was ratified in 1919 and became effective in 1920. This amendment made prohibition a national public policy. Having won its ultimate victory, the Anti-

---

[2] See Odegard, *Pressure Politics*, p. 62.

Saloon League withered away. In 1933, however, prohibition was repealed. By the 1930s, times had changed, and the League never reemerged as a major political force.

The tactics used by the Anti-Saloon League to marshal support among the populace were primitive, crude, and even offensive by today's standards. However, they helped develop the contemporary public relations methods used extensively by interest groups to mold public opinion. The Anti-Saloon League's use of its own printing operation today takes the form of television, radio, and print media campaigns. The blatant manipulation of fear and prejudice exemplified in the League's publications has been replaced today by more subtle techniques developed in the advertising field. The crude use of statistical information developed by the League has evolved into modernized, computer-assisted research operations conducted by many large interest groups. The publication of voting records of public officials and the endorsement of candidates, still in rudimentary form at the time of the League, are now commonly exercised interest group tactics. Although the Anti-Saloon League was not totally responsible for the initiation and development of all of these early forms of interest group activity, their successful use of these tactics ushered in the modern era of interest group concern with public opinion.

The development of various technological advances and the mass communication network in contemporary society have greatly contributed to the use of public opinion cultivation techniques by pressure groups. Information can be widely disseminated to alter the direction and intensity of public opinion. Computer-operated mass mailing techniques allow an interest group to place its message in the hands of receptive segments of society at a reasonable cost. Sophisticated psychologically based advertising messages are now far more effective than any public relations methods of generations past. Americans are now bombarded daily with slogans, jingles, and rhymes designed to encourage public support of interest group causes. Clearly the development of modern methods to influence public opinion has prompted one of the most fundamental changes in interest group politics. During each of the past several decades, more and more attention and resources have been committed to this variety of interest group activity.

The molding of public opinion has two basic objectives, one long range and one short range.[3] The long-range objective is to promote a generally favorable image for the interest group and its basic cause. Public relations campaigns tailored to this goal seek to develop a reservoir of good will in the minds of the citizenry that can be drawn upon when political battles over specific issues occur. The short-range objective is to convince the public to support the interest group's position on a particular issue that is currently a matter of controversy or subject to governmental action. The long-range objective is based on a strategy to create passive support among the people for the interest group. The short-range objective uses strategies

[3] V. O. Key, Jr., *Politics, Parties and Pressure Groups,* 5th ed. (New York: Thomas Y. Crowell, 1964), pp. 130-131.

designed to mobilize the citizenry to work for the adoption (or defeat) of specific public policy proposals.

Interest Groups and the Political Climate

Interest group attempts to manipulate the political climate form perhaps the greatest era of growth in pressure group politics today. While lobby organizations certainly have not forgotten direct contact with public officials as a method of obtaining group goals, many groups have placed increasing emphasis on public image building. The theory behind this approach is that effective lobbying must begin *before* a particular issue of importance becomes a current political question. Politics is now seen by interest groups as a much more complex process than it was decades ago. No longer is a visit to a key senator enough to win significant victories for a pressure organization. Today, politics is a more open process than it was generations ago. Competition among interest groups is also much more intense. Success cannot be left to last minute pressure tactics. Just as the political parties have learned that elections are won by long-range planning and organization, so too have interest groups discovered that major policy successes are much more likely to come after long-term efforts.

If the people are to support specific interest group positions when they are acted upon by the government, the interest group must have laid the proper groundwork months, and perhaps years, earlier. Influencing the political climate is essentially a process of image building. The interest group will often engage in large-scale attempts to present a positive, constructive image in the minds of the public. Often this is done quite subtly and quite successfully through the use of modern public relations techniques. If the public is convinced that the interest group is a worthy organization and the general interest advocated merits support, the pressure group will generally have a relatively successful record of accomplishments. In the following pages, several examples of such image-building tactics will be presented.

A common technique in public relations campaigns is for the interest group to present facts and information to the citizenry. This essentially becomes a mass education program, designed to bring certain information to the public's attention to which it might not otherwise have access. The message which the interest group pays to have distributed to the public obviously consists of material favorable to the pressure organization's cause. The advertising of the American Medical Association reprinted in this chapter is an example of an interest group disseminating information to the public in order to build its image. In this example, the AMA presents statistics to convince the reader that the medical profession is producing sufficient numbers of physicians and that the delivery of health care in this country has never been better. The advertisement attempts to counter many charges made by critics of the medical profession: 1) that medical schools are not educating enough health care professionals to service America's medical needs; 2) that black Americans are not receiving the same calibre of medical attention that whites are receiving; 3) that Americans are generally dissatisfied with the health care they

IS THERE A DOCTOR SHORTAGE?

For awhile there certainly was. In the 1960's, all of a sudden, doctors' offices were literally swamped. Our medical care system became overloaded almost overnight.

Many factors contributed to this tremendous demand on our doctors and hospitals. The rise in population. The passage of Medicaid and Medicare. The increase in our over-65 population whose medical needs are greatest, and the rise in people with health care insurance (from 123,000,000 in 1960 to 170,000,000 in 1974).

But today we have succeeded in doubling the output of our medical schools. This has produced a 34% increase in the total number of physicians practicing in this country. A recent University of Chicago study reveals that whereas in 1963 only 49% of black Americans saw a physician, by 1976 74% saw a physician, only two percentage points below the 76% for whites. Eighty-eight percent of Americans, according to this study, are generally satisfied with the health care they receive.

Of continuing concern to your doctor is maintaining the quality of care he provides. Your doctor, through his American Medical Association, is active in insuring our high standards of medical training through a major role in the accreditation of medical schools and graduate facilities. To help him renew his capabilities and knowledge, the A.M.A. keeps him up-to-date with a dozen publications and sponsors over 35 major national and regional conferences yearly. When it comes to your health, your doctor has a partner, too.

American Medical Association, 535 North Dearborn Street, Chicago, Illinois 60610.

Your Doctor's Your Partner
Help your doctor help you

receive; and 4) that the AMA has not been sufficiently active in improving the quality of post-graduate educational experiences available to physicians. The statistical evidence is presented in a clear and straightforward manner. The advertisement is a convincing one and helps build the image of the medical profession in the citizen's mind. The next time that the reader of this advertisement hears someone attack the medical profession on any of the counts listed above, he or she may well be less receptive to such criticism. At least that is the intention behind the AMA advertising campaign.

Similar campaigns are commonly waged by other interest groups. We frequently are confronted with interest group-generated information designed to improve the image of the organization's cause. The tobacco industry, for example, readily distributes information on the economic impact of America's tobacco farmers and processors. Interstate trucking firms frequently adorn their vehicles with information regarding the amount of taxes paid for the privilege of operating on the public highways. The pharmaceutical industry is eager to distribute information showing the tremendous costs involved in developing new drugs and satisfying government regulations for testing them before they can be given marketing approval. The petroleum producers often use advertising tactics to present information regarding the cost of exploration and production. These campaigns are intended to build the image of the particular industry, to create a fund of good will. By doing so, the interest groups hope to counteract frequently heard arguments in favor of prohibiting tobacco products, further regulating the trucking or pharmaceutical industry, or restricting the "obscene profits" of the oil companies.

The advertising campaigns of interest groups also frequently use fear and concern as methods of building public support. Fear, of course, is used in a much more subtle, and more effective, manner than in the past. The public relations strategy is to stir within the listener or reader a sense of alarm about an impending emergency. The recipient of the interest group's message is induced to fear that unless action is taken, some unpleasant event will surely take place.

Reprinted in this chapter is an example of an interest group message that relies, at least in part, on feelings of concern and urgency. Here the World Wildlife Fund, an organization dedicated to the preservation of endangered species and their habitats, presents to the reader the case of the sea otter. The photograph and accompanying prose depict the sea otter as a harmless, lovable creature. The tone of the advertisement immediately changes, however, as the World Wildlife Fund informs the reader of the threat that oil pollution poses to the very existence of the otter. To increase the believability of the message, the Fund includes the endorsement of a famous actor. Associating a well-known or trusted individual with an organization's mass media campaign is used by many groups to increase the effectiveness of their communications. The overall message of this advertisement is expertly conveyed: unless we do something soon, the sea otter may become extinct. The reader is induced into feeling concern that this fine animal may, in fact, vanish. The final impact of this advertisement is to improve the image of the environmental cause and the specific interest group promoting the cause.

"Take a long, long look at one of the sea's most charming creatures – it could be your last chance"

John Forsythe, host, "The World of Survival"

This is a sea otter. You can find small numbers of them off the coasts of California, Alaska and around the Kurile Islands and the Kamchatka Peninsula in the northern Pacific.

Their endearing habits include floating on their backs, cuddling their young, and breaking open shellfish against a stone balanced on their bellies. They sleep anchored to beds of kelp.

Earlier this century sea otters were snatched from imminent extinction at the hands of hunters who collected their magnificent fur. That is why a few hundred otters now live off the California coast.

A new menace

Today they face a new menace—oil pollution. Their life depends on their fur coats, because they have no fatty layer to insulate them against cold.

Air, trapped in the fur, serves as insulation. But if oil mats the fur, there's no insulation and the otter freezes to death.

World Wildlife Fund is campaigning to save the life and resources of the seas — for our own sakes and those of our children.

You can help

Send for our free information kit or send your tax-deductible contribution to: World Wildlife Fund, Department CTB
1610 Connecticut Ave., N.W.
Washington, D.C. 20009

THE SEAS MUST LIVE

World Wildlife Fund

"Just because I work for an oil company doesn't mean I like dirty beaches."

"Some of my friends actually seem to think that anybody who works for an oil company likes dead birds and dirty beaches," says Gulf Drilling Superintendent Bob Eslinger.

"Of course, I don't, any more than you do. But I like having a car and a warm house for my family. And those things take energy.

"I honestly think you can have both energy and a good environment, if you try to do things right. And a lot of things are being done right.

Three out of 20,000

"For instance, since the early 1940's, the oil industry drilled 20,000 oil and gas wells in the Gulf of Mexico—and has had only three major oil spills in all that time. That's a pretty good record. And in each case, after a year's time, you'd never know there had been an oil spill.

We're finding ways

"I'm proud of my company—Gulf Oil—because I know firsthand a lot of the things Gulf does, and the precautions we take, to get the energy and preserve the environment. Like relandscaping old surface mines. And helping industry find ways to eliminate pollution.

"Probably you can't expect oil companies and environmentalists ever to agree completely. But you don't need complete agreement to make something work.

"Gulf and the other oil companies are making a lot of things work to get the energy we need and protect the environment. It's a tremendous challenge, and I think we're handling it pretty well."

Gulf people: meeting the challenge.

"I think you can have both energy and a good environment, if you try to do things right."

Gulf Oil Corporation

Interest groups often find that they must engage in public relations campaigns in order to reestablish their credibility. Since the oil embargo imposed by the Arab petroleum producers in 1973, the American oil industry has experienced a noticeable decline in public favor. Environmental groups charged that oil companies were ruining our ecology; politicians attacked the industry for taking excessive profits; competing groups accused the companies of corrupt practices and withholding supply to increase prices. In general, it has not been a good time for the American petroleum producers. In order to counteract this negative image, the industry's companies engaged in massive advertising campaigns to educate the public about the status of the oil industry. An example of the petroleum producers' continuing efforts to upgrade the image of the industry is reprinted here. In this case, an advertisement sponsored by the Gulf Oil Company defends the industry against attacks made by environmentalists. In the words of a company employee, the industry communicates that it is interested in clean beaches and unpolluted shores. However, the featured employee assumes a position of moderation, obviously requesting the reader to be reasonable when considering proposals to regulate the industry. He invokes the image of his family protected in a home against the outside elements. Almost by implication the reader may conjure up the image of the same family freezing to death if the oil companies are frustrated in their attempts to produce more energy. The advertisement then reviews some of the notable environmentally positive accomplishments the industry has achieved and closes with a portrait of the oil companies and the environmental groups working hand in hand for a better world. The intention of the advertisement is clearly to improve the public status of the industry. The company attacks the negative image which the environmental groups have promoted and attempts to replace that unfavorable reputation with the image of the oil industry as a friend of the environment as well as being responsive to the energy needs of our society.

Other pressure group communications stress the worth of the interest group itself. Included here is an example of such a message in the form of an advertisement published by the National Rifle Association. The presentation lists several of the many benefits of NRA membership. In addition to certain material benefits, such as free publications and insurance, the organization links itself to various worthwhile activities including promotion of gun safety programs and support for the United States Olympics shooting team. The Association also presents itself as an effective defender of the fundamental right to keep and bear arms. Through its Institute for Legislative Action, the NRA engages in political action to protect the rights of the firearms owner. The communication is an explicit appeal for membership. The presentation describes the NRA in a very favorable light, emphasizing the positive contributions of the organization and the benefits of membership. The goal of the advertisement is to promote the image of the Association and to attract new members through the production of a favorable reputation. By image building and increasing membership, the NRA will be in a much stronger position when it next decides it must attack proposed gun control legislation.

18 good reasons why you should be an NRA Member!

I'm an NRA Member because a hunting buddy explained why I should belong. He was right, and I'm getting a lot out of it. But maybe no one ever invited *you* to join. Well, I'm asking you now, and here are 18 reasons why you should mail in the Membership Application—today!

1 A monthly subscription to your choice of either *The American Hunter* or the *American Rifleman*.

2 $300 FREE firearms insurance and the chance to buy additional coverage at low group rates.

3 The NRA Institute for Legislative Action is battling for *your* rights as a firearms owner.

4 You're supporting the U.S. Shooting Teams in the Olympics, World Championships and other prestigious competitions.

5 Participate in our shooting tournament programs.

6 Our Firearms Information and Hunter's Information services stand ready to answer your questions on firearms, equipment, ballistics, reloading, game, seasons and regulations.

7 Through NRA shooting and hunting clubs, meet other gun owners and get involved in events going on in your state.

8 Win attractive awards for your outstanding game trophies.

9 Shoot courses of fire that will develop a hunters shooting skills!

10 Become an NRA certified Hunter Safety, Rifle, Pistol or Shotgun Instructor.

11 Get free information and special bulletins.

12 Buy authoritative, low-cost NRA publications that focus on range plans, firearms, hunting and competitive shooting.

13 As a Member, qualify for our in-hospital income plan.

14 Get help from our Affiliates Department and our Field Staff in organizing your own club and in setting-up or renovating shooting ranges.

15 Support NRA junior programs —programs for youngsters of every level of ability, from future World Champions to tomorrow's hunters and shooters.

16 Our Hunter Safety Courses, and Hunter Seminars programs have been pioneered and developed by the NRA especially for hunters.

17 Each year, attend the NRA Annual Meetings and Firearm Exhibit.

18 And when you join now, you'll receive the convenient pocket-size whetstone—perfect for sharpening knives, cutlery—even fish hooks!

Sign me up! Send me my FREE whetstone, my membership credentials, and my first issue of (your choice of either)

☐ *The American Hunter* 1079C
☐ *The American Rifleman* 1019C

Name_____
Address_____
City_____
State_____Zip_____

Check enclosed ☐ 1 Year $15
☐ 3 Years $40 ☐ 5 Years $60

Bill my:
☐ Visa   ☐ Master Charge
#_____
exp. date_____
Signature_____

National Rifle Association
1600 Rhode Island Ave., N.W.
Washington, D.C. 20036

TABLE 10.1 Public Relations Resources of the Federal Agencies

	Public Relations Staff	1977 P. R. Budget (in millions)
Department of Defense	1740	$24.0
Department of State	204	5.1
Department of Health, Education and Welfare	396	22.9
Department of the Treasury	252	4.3
Department of Interior	195	1.0
Department of Commerce	170	5.2
Department of Agriculture	763	24.7
Department of Labor	200	6.5
Department of Housing and Urban Development	39	1.2
Department of Transportation	300	9.1

Source: *National Journal*, 9 (July 23, 1977), 1142.

The four examples of interest group-generated advertising examined in this chapter are typical of communications efforts by pressure groups designed to improve the political climate relevant to their own public policy concerns. But private interests are not the only ones which engage in public relations work to promote their policy objectives among the citizens. Governmental interests are also quite active in this form of indirect lobbying. Foreign governments, for example, spend massive amounts of money in public relations activities to promote their image among the American people and thereby to promote indirectly their interests before the United States government.

The federal government itself engages in widespread public relations activities.[4] Each of the major departments of the executive branch, for example, has public affairs offices. The presumed responsibility of these divisions is to educate the people relative to the activities of the various agencies and departments. In practice, a good portion of the public affairs office activity focuses on promoting the image and interests of the bureau. The goal of this activity is clear. If an agency receives a great deal of public support, if its programs are popular and well received, it is likely to do well when its authorization and appropriations proposals come before Congress. An elected representative will not vote to delete from the federal budget a program which his constituents favor. In many departments, such public affairs activities work to preserve the department itself, as well as its programs, and serve as a promotion of the administration's activities. Taken as a whole, the amount of federal dollars spent for such public affairs operations is considerable. Table 10.1 lists examples of the staff and budget of the public affairs offices in several governmental departments for a recent fiscal year. Neither the numbers of people involved in public affairs activities nor the amount of funds being expended are inconsequential. It is relatively clear that some form of public education relating to govern-

[4] See Dom Bonafede, "The Selling of the Government—Flackery and Public Service," *National Journal*, 9 (July 23, 1977), 1140-1145.

ment activities is important, but it is difficult to separate the activities that are purely educational in nature from those which are little more than thinly masked lobbying efforts. Critics of such executive lobbying activities have charged that it makes little sense for units of the federal government to spend millions of dollars in taxpayer money to lobby other departments of the federal government. In spite of this fact, the public affairs budgets for the various governmental departments continue to increase every year.

Most interest groups today, both public and private, engage in some form of public relations activities. For some groups, such as the major industry groups and the labor unions, these efforts are massive. Pressure groups today engage in public relations campaigns in much the same way that a company does when it launches a new product. The staff of these organizations maintain a continuous stream of press releases, information statements, and position papers from their respective research departments to the media as well as to relevant individuals and groups. Smaller interest groups with the necessary economic resources use such public relations tactics to enlarge the numbers of people sympathetic to their causes.[5] The mass membership interest groups use modern media techniques to attract even larger numbers to the organization. The messages and information that are distributed by the interest groups are obviously biased to a certain degree. Facts favorable to an interest group's cause are widely distributed, while the statistics that are detrimental are not publicized. Pressure groups are often charged by competing interests with presenting half-truths and using statistics in such a manner that the truth is distorted beyond recognition. These charges are certainly accurate in a number of cases. An interest group must be careful not to defeat its efforts by distributing materials which are so inaccurate that they destroy the credibility of the group.

For many interest groups today, cultivating public opinion has become a high priority activity. In spite of its expense and lack of immediate payoffs, image building is extremely important. It helps mold the political climate. If the interest group has accomplished this task well, it will have a much easier time when it is attempting to have the government approve or reject a specific public policy proposal. Image building gives an interest group access. An organization which approaches public policy makers with a decidedly favorable public image will have little trouble having its positions heard. However, a group which has earned a negative reputation among the people will have a much more difficult time attempting to convince government officials to consider its petitions. Furthermore, a group which has developed a reservoir of good will among the citizenry may well be able to mobilize those citizens in its behalf when the group requires public support on specific issues before government agencies.

[5] Carol S. Greenwald, *Group Power: Lobbying and Public Policy* (New York: Praeger, 1977), p. 93.

Grass-Roots Lobbying on Specific Policy Issues

In addition to image-building techniques, interest groups often take their message to the public in order to mobilize citizens with respect to specific policy issues pending before government decision makers. Although some of the same types of public relations tactics are used, the objective of this strategy is much different. When interest groups attempt to mold the political climate, they are not trying to elicit any active response on the part of the public. All the pressure organization hopes to attain is a feeling of good will among the citizens for the interest group and its advocated cause. However, when a proposal that is particularly salient to the interest group comes before government agencies, the interest group must do more than simply influence the attitudes of the people; it must move the citizens to action. The group hopes to motivate people sympathetic to its cause to communicate their views with those in public office. This is called *grass-roots lobbying*. The ultimate goal is that such a show of strength from the people will convince the decision makers to act in accordance with the preferences of the interest group. When competently managed, this interest group strategy can be exceptionally effective.

Interest groups have become engaged in grass-roots lobbying much more extensively in recent years than they have in the past. Almost every major controversial proposal coming before Congress prompts interest groups to encourage members of the public to contact their representatives and let them know how the constituents feel about the proposed legislation. Improvements in public relations technology and the refining of mass mailing techniques allow a well-prepared interest group to contact citizens favorable to the group's cause and mobilize those individuals to contact members of Congress within a very short period of time. In recent years campaigns over such issues as abortion, the Panama Canal Treaty, the labor law reform bill, the consumer protection bill, and the cargo preference bill prompted massive citizen reaction, most of it encouraged by the interested pressure groups.

The theory behind such grass-roots lobbying is that elected representatives will take into account the will of the people when deciding how to vote on specific pieces of legislation. The impact of citizen contact is particularly significant when the citizens are members of the representative's constituency. However, if it is to be successful, such a campaign must be conducted in expert fashion. Congressmen respond favorably to demands that are well reasoned, firmly held, and expressed through the citizen's own initiative. Members of law-making bodies are not particularly impressed with citizen response that has been blatantly incited by interest groups in some artificial manner. If an interest group can enlist citizens to write individual, rational letters to government officeholders in large numbers, the strategy will be quite effective. On the other hand, if the interest group distributes preprinted post cards which call for no more citizen effort than a signature, the campaign will often have little impact. Members of the legislative body must be convinced of the sincerity and honesty of the letters and telegrams written by constituents. James Deakin's analysis of lobbying techniques noted:

> As the results of grassroots lobbying campaigns show, the voice of the voter, when orchestrated by the lobbyist into a mighty symphony of pressure, can sound as loud in the ear of a legislator as the purring tones of the campaign contributor.[6]

While many contemporary interest groups are involved in grass-roots lobbying efforts, the National Rifle Association is generally conceded as being the most effective organization at mobilizing the public to contact government officials. The NRA has a membership in excess of one million and a staff of approximately three hundred. Since 1871 it has championed the cause of target shooters, hunters, gun collectors and others interested in activities relating to firearms. The Association sees one of its duties as surveying the activities of the government and informing its membership of any pending political action which may have an impact on those interested in lawful firearms ownership. The NRA has taken upon itself the guardianship of the Second Amendment's right "to keep and bear arms." When government considers legislation to restrict the use of firearms, the NRA quickly notifies its membership of the proposed action and urges members to contact their congressmen. Mobilizing the citizenry has been effectively employed by the NRA. In spite of opposing public opinion and the damaging impact of several political assassinations, the Association has been able to defeat several pieces of proposed legislation and water down other bills to the extent that their provisions had little significance.

The nation's first major piece of gun control legislation was the 1934 National Firearms Act. This particular law was designed to curtail the use of machine guns, sawed-off shotguns, and other "gangster" weapons. Since that time, various efforts have been mounted to control handguns, long guns, and ammunition. Proposals have called for the prohibition of such weapons, registration, bans on interstate shipments, control of mail-order weapons, and restrictions on the sale of ammunition. In the face of each of these various proposals, the NRA has been active in behalf of those who want to protect the right to bear arms.

For example, from 1963 to 1964, following the assassination of President John Kennedy by Lee Harvey Oswald with a mail-order firearm, Senator Thomas Dodd of Connecticut spearheaded a major drive to curtail the flow of firearms through the U.S. mails. Dodd had long been interested in gun control legislation, and the assassination gave great impetus to his proposal. In the final months of 1963, the publicity surrounding the death of the president prompted a flood of pro-gun control mail to Congress. The NRA was politically astute enough to wait until the initial reaction to the assassination had settled down. The activity of the organization even indicated that it might support a reasonable piece of gun control legislation. With the initial shock of the killing waning, the NRA and other gun-

---

[6] James Deakin, *The Lobbyists* (Washington: Public Affairs Press, 1966), p. 101.

oriented groups began informing their supporters about the pending legislation and urging constituents to contact their representatives. One congressional staff member reported that until December of 1963, mail was running three or four hundred to one in favor of the proposed law, but by February of 1964, the tide had completely shifted and ran ten thousand to one opposed.[7] By the summer of 1964, the bill had died in committee.

In 1968, the gun control advocates made another significant push to have Congress enact meaningful firearms legislation. This time the NRA was unable to stop the legislation, which became known as the Gun Control Act of 1968. However, the final version of that piece of legislation, which prohibited mail-order firearms and interstate gun transactions, was not as strong as its advocates had wished it to be. A great contributing factor to the weaking of the bill has been attributed to the letter-writing campaign incited by the National Rifle Association. The 1968 measure was proposed in Congress following the assassinations of Senator Robert Kennedy and civil rights leader Martin Luther King, Jr. The bill had large-scale public support and the vigorous backing of President Lyndon Johnson, and despite the famed lobbying tactics of the NRA, these forces proved to be even more powerful.

In 1972 and again in 1976, the controversy over gun control gained the public's attention once more when gun control advocates called for the restriction of the sale of "Saturday night specials," cheap handguns used in many killings, armed robberies, and assaults. In both years, however, the efforts of the NRA and other pro-firearms groups were sufficient enough to defeat the proposed legislation. In 1972, the legislation passed the Senate but was defeated in the House of Representatives; in 1976, gun control supporters were unable even to have the bill reported out of the House Judiciary Committee.

The history of the past three decades has shown that the National Rifle Association has been more than equal to the task of warding off attempts to control the use of firearms. The primary strategy employed so effectively by the organization is grass-roots lobbying, encouraging constituents to contact legislators. The Association has become a master at mobilizing citizens who support its cause to take the time and effort to register their feelings with appropriate government officials. The NRA boasts that it can flood Congress with 500,000 pieces of mail virtually overnight in opposition to any gun control proposals.[8] It accomplishes this goal by constant monitoring of congressional activity and swiftly contacting its membership when necessary. For example, on February 26, 1976 the NRA sent the following Mailgram to its members:

> The House Judiciary Committee is moving quickly for final approval of HR 11193. The Federal Firearms Act of 1976. Contrary to what the media has reported, HR 11193 is one of the strongest antigun bills ever to be considered

[7] Carl Bakal, *The Right to Bear Arms* (New York: McGraw-Hill Book Company, 1966), p. 199.

[8] Bakal, *The Right to Bear Arms*, p. 128.

by Congress. The bill would outlaw 3/4 of all hand guns now manufactured or imported and ban the sale of guns inherited or already in private hands. The bill's restrictions on dealers would severely limit availability of all long guns as well as ammunition. The Committee will meet on the second. Contact your Congressman.[9]

The result of this mailgram was that Congress was flooded with calls, letters, and telegrams. Five days after the NRA had sent its Mailgram, the House Judiciary Committee met and killed the proposed legislation in a 17-16 vote to recommit the bill to a subcommittee. There is little doubt that the carefully timed, expertly executed action by the NRA doomed the gun control bill.

One of the primary reasons that the National Rifle Association is so effective in its use of grass-roots lobbying techniques is that the pro-gun citizens hold their attitudes with great intensity. Those committed to protecting the right to keep and bear arms consider gun control a major public policy. NRA members will often go to great lengths to express their views and to withdraw support from representatives who do not heed the voice of the American hunter and sportsman. Congressmen are quite aware that no matter how much a pro-gun citizen might favor the activities and philosophy of an incumbent, a wrong vote on gun control can turn a supporter into a diehard opponent at reelection time. Those who have felt the wrath of pro-gun forces have occasionally described them as being fanatics. The communications of the pro-gun forces often indicate the intensity of their attitudes. Robert Sherrill reports that one pro-gun-control politician with an Italian name received the following letter from an anti-gun-control citizen:

> You dirty wop. You should go back to your Italy and Mafia. How did you get in this country anyway? I bet you are the type who has no gun in his house to protect himself and would let any housebreaker come in and help himself to anything, even your wife, and then you would pray for a humble spirit to bear it. God help America with such as you in office. Were your parents ever married?[10]

The National Rifle Association must be credited with having nearly perfected the use of grass-roots lobbying. Public opinion has been against their cause; assassinations and assaults on people such as President John Kennedy, Martin Luther King, George Wallace, Robert Kennedy, and Senator John Stennis have fueled the fires of the gun control forces; and key political leaders have implored Congress to impose effective gun control measures. Yet throughout the past several decades, the NRA and its supporters have effectively blocked all strong gun control regulation. The Association has attained a level of grass-roots lobbying effectiveness which other interest groups have not been able to reach.

[9] Quoted in *Congressional Quarterly Weekly Report,* 34 (March 6, 1976), 517.

[10] Quoted in Robert Sherrill, *The Saturday Night Special* (New York: Charterhouse Books, 1973), p. 196. Reprinted by permission of The David McKay Company, Inc., 750 Third Avenue, New York, New York 10017.

Interest Groups and Public Opinion:
Legal Regulation

The regulation of grass-roots lobbying and image-building techniques to alter the political climate is of questionable constitutionality. It is clear that the First Amendment rights of speech, press, assembly, and petition protect the freedom of individuals and groups to make their positions known to the public and to advocate political action. Prohibiting this kind of political expression is clearly repugnant to the Bill of Rights. However, this does not necessarily mean that all limitations on this variety of lobbying activity are unconstitutional.

Congress first passed a major lobbying regulation bill in 1946, which became known as the Federal Regulation of Lobbying Act. The main thrust of that piece of legislation was to require that individuals and groups seeking to influence legislation in Congress register with the House and Senate and file quarterly financial reports.[11] The 1946 act defined lobbying as any attempt "to influence, directly or indirectly, the passage or defeat of any legislation by the Congress of the United States." The intention of this statute was clearly to bring both direct and indirect lobbying under the registration and disclosure provisions of the act.[12] In 1954, in the case of *United States v. Harriss*, the United States Supreme Court upheld the validity of the 1946 act after it was challenged as being in violation of the First Amendment.[13] In doing so, however, the Court found fault with the regulation of indirect lobbying. The wording of the legislation pertaining to grass-roots lobbying attempts, in view of the Court's majority, was too vague. This narrow construction of the 1946 act had the impact of keeping interest group attempts to influence public opinion generally outside the purview of existing lobbying statutes. For this reason, grass-roots lobbying has occurred almost without significant legal burdens.

Between the years 1946 and 1978, there were no major pieces of legislation directly regulating lobbying activities. However, numerous attempts were made to improve the law and impose stronger regulation of activities designed to influence the government.[14] None was successful. The inadequacies of the 1946 act became more and more apparent. Reformers were particularly concerned with the fact that the 1946 legislation did not cover grass-roots lobbying and did not regulate activities designed to influence governmental agencies other than Congress.

A major drive to reform lobbying regulations was initiated in 1977-1978. The most controversial portion of the proposed legislation was that it would have brought grass-roots lobbying under federal regulation.[15] Reformers held such

---

[11] Hope Eastman, *Lobbying: A Constitutionally Protected Right* (Washington: American Enterprise Institute for Public Policy Research, 1977).

[12] Greenwald, *Group Power*, p. 91.

[13] *United States v. Harriss*, 347 U.S. 612 (1954).

[14] See Richard E. Cohen, "The Short Life of Lobbying Reform," *National Journal*, 12 (November 12, 1977), 1775.

[15] *Congressional Quarterly Weekly Report*, 35 (May 21, 1977), 993-994.

regulation to be essential given the vast growth in grass-roots lobbying techniques since the passage of the 1949 act.[16] Although this new regulatory bill passed the House in 1978, it did not survive Senate action. Undoubtedly, however, similar reform measures will continue to be introduced in the national legislature over the next several years.

Any provisions regulating grass-roots lobbying will quite probably be subjected to a court challenge on the grounds that they violate First Amendment freedoms. Court challenge may prove to be a substantial hurdle. On April 26, 1978, the United States Supreme Court declared unconstitutional a Massachusetts state law which prohibited corporations from spending funds to influence people's attitudes on public referendum measures.[17] The case involved state legal action taken against a bank which had publicized its views in opposition to a tax reform referendum which was to be voted on by the people of Massachusetts. By so ruling, the Supreme Court extended First Amendment protections to corporations. This and other decisions in recent years have demonstrated that the Supreme Court looks very critically at restrictions on freedom of expression.

In addition to statutes applying directly to lobbying, interest groups that operate as nonprofit educational groups with tax-exempt status must be particularly careful about engaging in activities designed to influence legislation. Tax-exempt status carries with it a prohibition against lobbying. If a nonprofit tax-exempt group violates this prohibition, the favorable tax status can be revoked. Environmental groups have had difficulties with this particular form of regulation. Since their primary purpose is to educate people about environmental problems, such groups are not technically lobby organizations as defined by law, although influencing public policy by "educating" people is certainly one of their aims. When an environmental group engages in large-scale "educational campaigns," it must be very careful not to be charged with lobbying. In 1966, for example, the government stripped the Sierra Club of its tax-exempt status after the organization distributed a series of advertisements protesting the construction of a water control project in the Grand Canyon area.[18]

A related provision of the tax code prohibits corporations and trade associations from deducting as a business expense funds used for grass-roots lobbying. The same prohibition does not extend to the direct lobbying of governmental officials. Therefore, if a company or trade association spends funds to testify before a congressional committee in support of or in opposition to a piece of pending legislation of direct interest to the company or association, the expenditures are tax deductible as a business expense. However, if the same corporation or trade

---

[16] See *Congressional Quarterly Weekly Report*, 36 (April 22, 1978), 955-956; *Congressional Quarterly Weekly Report*, 36 (April 29, 1978), 1027-1028; and *Congressional Quarterly Weekly Report*, 36 (May 6, 1978), 1119-1121.

[17] See *First National Bank of Boston v. Bellotti*, 98 S. Ct. 1407 (1978).

[18] See Greenwald, *Group Power*, p. 112.

association publishes magazine advertisements urging the public to support or oppose the same piece of proposed legislation, the expenditures are not tax deductible.[19] This particular tax code provision has been subject to both abuse and confusion as to its correct interpretation when applied to actual corporate expenditures. In 1977 and 1978, a subcommittee of the House Committee on Government Operations launched a major investigation into the grass-roots lobbying activities of 74 trade associations and their tax returns relative to lobbying expenditures (see Table 10.2). Investigations such as this will undoubtedly provide additional information about the extent of corporate grass-roots lobbying and may lead to a modification in the laws governing such communications with the public.

Legal controls over interest group attempts to influence public opinion are not very substantial. Attempts to strengthen such regulation have thus far failed. It is relatively safe to conclude, therefore, that image building and grass-roots lobbying will continue to flourish as a major form of interest group politics.

INTEREST GROUPS AND ELECTIONS

American interest groups regularly become involved in electoral politics. While they do not nominate members of their own organizations to run for political office, interest groups commonly take actions necessary to convince the public to elect persons to political office who are sympathetic to group-supported policies. The ultimate goal of the interest group is to contribute to the election of persons who, upon taking office, will grant access to interest group representatives. At the very least, an interest group hopes to avoid the election of persons who will turn a deaf ear to communications originated by the organization.

Interest group participation in elections is widespread. Americans in any four year cycle elect more than a half million persons to public office at the federal, state, and local levels. Interest groups take an active part in a large number of these political races, and at the federal level there is hardly an election that does not attract interest group attention of some kind. Pressure organizations are active in party primaries and nominating conventions, in the formulation of the party platforms, in the financing of campaigns, in the organization and staffing of electoral races, and in mobilizing the electorate to vote in favor of interest group-endorsed candidates. In order to influence elections, interest groups commonly work directly with their own memberships, through the political parties, or with the public at large. By participating in the selection of public officials, interest groups lay the foundation for future direct lobbying of officeholders.

Engaging in electoral politics is not a simple task for an interest group. In recent years, Congress has imposed increasingly complicated regulations which restrict or proscribe certain electoral activities. These regulations have depressed the

---

[19] Jean Conley, "Push Comes to Shove on Trade Association Lobbying," *National Journal*, 12 (October 22, 1977), 1646-1648.

TABLE 10.2 Trade Associations Under Congressional Investigation for Grass Roots Lobbying Activities, 1977-78

American Association of Advertising Agencies
American Bakers Association
American Council of Life Insurance
American Farm Bureau Federation
American Hotel and Motel Association
American Iron and Steel Institute
American Management Associations
American Meat Institute
American Mining Congress
American National Cattlemen's Association
American Petroleum Institute
American Pharmaceutical Association
American Public Power Association
American Trucking Associations
Associated General Contractors of America
Association of Home Appliance Manufacturers
Atomic Industrial Forum Inc.
The Council for Tobacco Research—USA Inc.
Council of Better Business Bureaus Inc.
Distilled Spirits Council of the United States Inc.
Edison Electric Institute
Electronic Industries Association
Electronic Manufacturers Association
Food Marketing Institute
General Federation of Women's Clubs
Glass Packaging Institute Inc.
Grocery Manufacturers of America Inc.
The Heritage Foundation
Independent Bankers Association of America
Independent Insurance Agents of America Inc.
Independent Petroleum Association of America
Livestock Marketing Association
Motion Picture Association of America
Motor Vehicle Manufacturers Association of the United States Inc.
National Air Transportation Association
National Association of Chain Drug Stores
National Association of Electric Companies
National Association of Food Chains
National Association of Home Builders
National Association of Manufacturers
National Association of Mutual Savings Banks
National Association of Realtors
National Association of Retail Druggists
National Association of Retail Grocers of the U.S.
National Association of Security Dealers Inc.
National Automobile Dealers Association
National Cable Television Association Inc.
National Canners Association
National Coal Association
National Confectioners Association of the U.S. Inc.
National Cotton Council of America
National Council of Farmer Cooperatives
National Electrical Manufacturers Association
National Forest Products Association
National LP-Gas Association
National Rifle Association of America
National Soft Drink Association
North American Telephone Association
Pharmaceutical Manufacturers Association
Portland Cement Association
Professional Insurance Agents Association
The Proprietary Association
Recording Industry Association of America
Rubber Manufacturers Association
Sheet Metal and Air Conditioning Contractors; National Association Inc.
Soap and Detergent Association
Society of the Plastics Industry
Supermarket Institute Inc.
Tobacco Institute Inc.
Transportation Association of America
United Fresh Fruit and Vegetable Association
U.S. Independent Telephone Association
U.S. League of Savings Associations
Wine Institute

Source: *National Journal*, 12 (October 22, 1977), 1647.

amount of activity of some interest groups, while encouraging the participation of others. For example, corporations and labor unions have long been prohibited from direct participation in electoral partisan politics, yet the law allows such groups to participate indirectly. Other regulations, such as the federal tax code, discourage tax-exempt, nonprofit organizations from becoming involved in the electoral process. If a tax-exempt educational or charity interest group is found in violation of these restrictions, a voiding of the favorable tax status may result. The most common pressure groups involved in electoral politics are the economic interests (business, labor, professional organizations, and agricultural groups). These associations have the economic assets, the membership size, and the political savvy to use the electoral process to their own benefit. Furthermore, they have been able to capitalize on the legal regulation of electoral campaigns to increase their role in the political process.

The Legal Regulation of Interest Groups in Electoral Politics

Prior to the 1970s, legal regulation of interest group involvement in the federal electoral process was relatively ineffective. The rules pertaining to pressure group activities were somewhat minimal, easily evaded, and rarely enforced. The primary emphasis of these statutes was placed on campaign contribution activities of pressure groups. The Federal Corrupt Practices Act of 1925 included a specific prohibition against campaign contributions made from the coffers of corporations. This provision was an extension of a similar ban first imposed in 1907. During World War II, Congress passed a prohibition against labor unions making contributions to political campaigns. This temporary ban was made permanent with the passage of the Taft-Hartley Act in 1947. These statutes generally barred corporations and unions from making campaign contributions to candidates or their committees and also prohibited direct expenditures by the corporation or union in behalf of a candidate. Such a restriction on the use of corporation or union funds applied to all federal elections at the primary and general election stages. However, there was no prohibition in any act of Congress barring corporation officers or union members from voluntarily contributing their own funds to a political campaign. In 1939, Congress passed an additional piece of legislation that had an impact on interest group participation in electoral politics. This statute, known as the Hatch Act, prohibited any person or group from contributing more than $5,000 per calendar year toward the election of any political candidate. However, each of these laws had exceptions and loopholes large enough to place only minimal restrictions on the amount of freedom interest groups had in electoral participation.

With a generally growing tide of public opinion in favor of strengthening the nation's election laws, Congress passed in 1971 the Federal Election Campaign Act. The primary importance of this legislation was to limit certain kinds of campaign expenditures and to call for much more expanded and strict record keeping and disclosure of political contributions. Any contribution of more than $100 was required to be disclosed publicly along with the name, address, and occupation of the person making the contribution. It was hoped that such disclosure and spending limitations would open the process to public scrutiny and, at a minimum, reveal to the public those persons or interests who were engaged in large contributions to political candidates.

Like previous legislation, however, the 1971 act was filled with loopholes and legitimate means of avoiding the spirit of the law. In addition, there was no effective means of enforcing the provisions of the act. Nevertheless, the 1971 Federal Election Campaign Act had a significant impact on the 1972 federal elections. Partially because of the disclosure requirements imposed by the act, the public became aware of the many abuses occurring within the nation's electoral process. The campaign of 1972, of course, was also the period of the famous Watergate break-in and subsequent investigations which further opened the electoral process to public examination.[20] The result of these disclosures prompted the public, as well as many political figures, to criticize openly the way in which the electoral system had been misused and to call for significant reform.

The campaign contribution disclosures following the 1972 presidential election confirmed what many citizens had believed for a long time: that big money interests dominated the election system through large campaign contributions. While most persons realized that wealthy individuals, often connected to business or industrial interests, made generous amounts of funds available to candidates for the presidency, few had any idea of the actual size of these contributions. Table 10.3 lists the major contributors to the presidential campaigns of both Democratic and Republican nominees. The size of the contributions is somewhat staggering, as are the names of the contributors which indicate the linkage between individuals making such contributions and large business interests. Leading the list of wealthy benefactors was W. Clement Stone, chairman of Combined Insurance Company of America, who provided Richard Nixon with more than two million dollars in campaign finances. Second on Nixon's list was Richard Mellon Scaife, heir to the Mellon family financial and petroleum empire, who contributed one million dollars. John Mulcahy, third largest contributor to the Nixon race with gifts of more than $600,000 was tied to drug and steel industry interests. On the Democratic side, the contributions are of much smaller size but still amount to massive sums of money. McGovern's top contributor was Stewart Mott, a General Motors fortune heir, with more than $400,000 in campaign assistance, followed by Max Palevsky, involved in the computer industry, with almost a third of a million dollars in contributions.

It was obvious from such figures that limitations in individual campaign contributions were ineffective. All of the above amounts were legal contributions made in various ways to avoid violation of federal election requirements.

---

[20] See Lester A. Sobel, ed., *Money and Politics: Contributions, Campaign Abuses and the Law* (New York: Facts on File, Inc., 1974); David W. Adamany and George E. Agree, *Political Money* (Baltimore: Johns Hopkins University Press, 1975).

TABLE 10.3 Leading Individual Contributors to the 1972 Presidential Election Campaign

Nixon	Amount	McGovern[a]	Amount
W. Clement Stone	$2,051,643.45	Stewart R. Mott	$407,747.50
Richard Mellon Scaife	1,000,000.00	Max Palevsky[b]	319,365.00
John A. Mulcahy	624,558.97	Anne and Martin Peretz	275,016.44
Arthur Watson	303,000.00	Alejandro Zaffaroni	206,752.76
Ruth and George Farkas	300,000.00	Nicholas Noyes	205,000.00
John J. Louis, Jr.	283,360.22	Danield Noyes	199,317.11
John Rollins	265,523.50	Alan and Shane Davis	158,872.25
Roy Carver	263,323.77	Richard Saloman	137,752.02
Sam Schulman	262,574.56	Joan Palevsky	118,616.86
Daniel Terra	255,000.00	Miles Rubin	108,000.00
Walter Annenberg	254,000.00	Bruce Allen	100,000.00
John Safer	251,000.00	John Lewis	100,000.00
Kent Smith	251,000.00	Henry Kimelman	82,533.99
Leon Hess	250,000.00	Albrecht Saalfield	82,000.00
Saul Steinberg	250,000.00	Diana and Salim Lewis	74,950.00
Jack Massey	249,999.96	Howard Metzenbaum	72,416.98
Max Fisher	249,773.05	Abner Levine	69,452.53
Ray Kroc	237,000.00	Alva Ted Bonda	67,454.73
Jack Dreyfus	231,000.00	Carol Bernstein	63,926.03
F.L. Cappeart	213,000.00	Robert Meyerhoff	63,486.52
Raymond Guest	200,000.00	Frank Lautenberg	57,955.48

[a]Includes loan amounts that were converted.
[b]Includes contributions from 1970.
Reprinted by permission of the publisher, from Herbert E. Alexander, *Financing the 1972 Election* (Lexington, Mass.: Lexington Books, D.C. Heath and Company, Copyright 1976, D.C. Heath and Company).

In addition to the massive contributions made by wealthy individuals, Americans learned of large campaign pledges offered to Richard Nixon by corporate interests. Two of the most publicized incidents surrounded the activities of the Associated Milk Producers, Inc., a dairy industry cooperative, and the giant ITT corporation. Investigations into corporate financing of the 1972 election uncovered a promise of some two million dollars to the Nixon campaign by the dairymen's group. The dairy industry, of course, was not making pledges for such large amounts without hoping that the president would initiate public policy alternatives that would benefit dairy interests. The group was particularly concerned with the milk price support program, government-subsidized milk for school lunches, and protection for domestic producers of dairy products. Following the campaign pledge, the Nixon administration took steps to support the industry in each of these areas of concern. The ITT corporation, a large multi-industry company, offered to underwrite the 1972 Republic National Convention with a contribution of $400,000. The contribution was to be handled through an ITT subsidiary, the Sheraton Hotels Company, and the money would permit the Nixon people to hold the convention in San Diego, an area of the country which had a long history of support for Nixon's political career. Once again, the contribution was not made in an altogether charitable fashion. The ITT corporation had been facing stiff opposition from the Justice Department's antitrust division relating to several of its acquisitions, especially its purchase of the giant Hartford Insurance Corporation. According to several reports, two months after the company made its pledge, it reached a compromise with the Justice Department which allowed it to retain control of Hartford Insurance while divesting itself of several relatively insignificant companies. However, after the public became aware of these activities, the Republicans decided to move the convention to Miami, and the Nixon forces were unable to accept the pledged contribution.

Incidents such as the Associated Milk Producers case and the ITT campaign pledge made the public aware that in return for campaign financing, interest groups were able to influence public officials to make certain public policy adjustments in their favor. In short, economic interests were buying public policy decisions. Similarly, disclosures of campaign contributions revealed that political offices were frequently distributed to those persons who most generously made funds available to winning candidates. The most frequently abused political office, which had become "purchasable" through large campaign gifts, was that of ambassador. For many years, certain highly sought after ambassadorships had been distributed according to the degree of campaign support received by the winning presidential candidate. Although this practice was certainly nothing new when Richard Nixon came to office, he continued it during a time when the public was becoming increasingly concerned with the lack of ethical standards in governmental decision making. Table 10.4 provides information regarding Nixon's granting of ambassadorship appointments to persons who had made large campaign contributions to his 1972 reelection bid. Clearly, a sizable campaign donation was more persuasive in gaining consideration for an attractive European ambassadorship than were skills and experience in the national foreign service.

The ITT and dairy cooperative incidents also brought to the attention of the public that bans on corporate giving to political campaigns were clearly not effective. A large number of corporations were violating the legal prohibition against the use of company monies as campaign gifts. Further investigation showed that highly placed officials in the Nixon election effort had placed pressure on corporate executives to make such contributions. The total of these gifts to the Nixon reelection campaign was substantial.[21] Table 10.5 presents information on 21 corporations that were prosecuted for violating the election campaign finance laws. Each of these companies or their officials were found guilty of one or more counts of violating federal laws. In most instances, relatively small fines were handed down as penalties. The largest fine imposed as a sentence on a corporation was a $35,000 penalty levied against the Associated Milk Producers.

---

[21] See Herbert Alexander, *Financing the 1972 Election* (New York: Lexington Books, D.C. Heath, 1976).

TABLE 10.4 Ambassadors and Money

Ambassadors and persons seeking ambassadorships often have made large contributions to presidential campaigns. After his 1972 re-election, President Nixon appointed 13 more non-career ambassadors, eight of whom had donated a minimum of $25,000 each and $706,000 in aggregate to his campaign. This led to charges that the Nixon administration was brokering ambassadorships.

According to the Senate Watergate Committee report, over $1.8-million in presidential campaign contributions was attributable, in whole or in part, to persons holding ambassadorial appointments from Nixon. The report said further that about 30 per cent of all foreign envoy posts were held in July 1974 by non-career appointees. The largest concentration was in Western Europe, where there was also a high concentration of persons contributing $100,000 or more.

While White House officials maintained they told persons seeking ambassadorships that no *quid pro quo* could follow contributions, the Senate Watergate Committee report concluded that "at the very least, a number of persons saw the making of a contribution as a means of obtaining the recognition needed to be actively considered."

A list of nine U.S. ambassadors to Western Europe and their contributions to Nixon's 1972 re-election campaign follows:

Country	Ambassador	Contribution
Great Britain	Walter H. Annenberg	$ 250,000
Switzerland	Shelby Davis	100,000
Luxembourg	Ruth L. Farkas	300,000
Belgium	Leonard K. Firestone	112,600
Netherlands	Kingdon Gould	100,900
Austria	John F. Humes	100,000
France	John N. Irwin II	50,500
France	Arthur K. Watson	300,000
Ireland	John D. Moore	10,442
Total		$1,324,442

Source: Congressional Quarterly, *Dollar Politics* (1974), vol. 2., p. 15.

Information such as this, along with the Watergate break-in and its related cover-up, gave rise to national support for reform of the federal election laws. Much of the criticism of the way in which elections were conducted centered on the activities of various economic interests, represented either by individuals, corporations, or interest groups. Congress, feeling the impact of public opinion, hurriedly constructed a reform bill and moved to prompt its passage before the 1974 congressional elections. By supporting large-scale reform, members of Congress hoped to disassociate themselves from past abuses of the election system and to be seen by their constituents as promoters of reform.

The 1974 act was technically a series of amendments to the 1971 Federal

TABLE 10.5 1972 Presidential Campaign: Illegal Corporate Contributions Prosecuted

Company	Candidate(s)	Total Contributions
American Airlines	Nixon	$ 55,000
American Ship Building	Nixon	25,000
Ashland Petroleum	Nixon	100,000
Associated Milk Producers	Nixon, Mills, Humphrey	155,000
Braniff Airways	Nixon	40,000
Carnation	Nixon	7,900
Diamond International	Nixon, Muskie	6,000
Greyhound	Nixon, McGovern	16,040
Goodyear Tire and Rubber	Nixon	40,000
Gulf Oil	Nixon, Mills, Jackson	125,000
HMS Electric Corporation	Nixon	5,000
LBC & W, Inc.	Nixon	10,000
Lehigh Valley Cooperative Farmers	Nixon	50,000
Minnesota Mining and Manufacturing	Nixon, Humphrey, Mills	32,000
National By-Products, Inc.	Nixon	3,000
Northrup Corporation	Nixon	150,000
Phillips Corporation	Nixon	100,000
Ratrie, Robbins, & Schweitzer, Inc.	Nixon	5,000
Singer Company	Nixon	10,000
Time Oil Company	Nixon, Jackson	7,600
Valentine, Sherman, & Assoc.	Humphrey	25,000 (in services)
	Total	$958,540

Reprinted by permission of the publisher, from Herbert E. Alexander, *Financing the 1972 Election* (Lexington, Mass.: Lexington Books, D.C. Heath and Company, Copyright 1976, D.C. Heath and Company).

Election Campaign Act. These amendments called for significant changes in the way in which federal campaigns would be conducted. First, the 1974 legislation called for public financing of presidential election campaigns through a system of federal grants to candidates, matching money already raised by the candidates themselves. Second, the new legislation required regularly filed disclosure of campaign contributions and expenditures. Third, the act created the Federal Election Commission to enforce the election laws. Fourth, limits were placed on individual and committee campaign contributions. Individuals could contribute no more than $1,000 to a candidate or that candidate's authorized committee, and no person could contribute more than $25,000 in total contributions in any one calendar year. Registered multicandidate political committees were restricted to $5,000 contribution maximums to any one candidate per election, with no limitation on total contributions. Fifth, candidates for federal office were limited as to the amount of personal funds that could be used in an individual's run for public office. Sixth, a $1,000 limitation was placed on persons spending money in behalf of a candidate but doing so independently of the candidate or his authorized committee. Seventh, total spending ceilings were imposed on campaigns for federal office.

The 1974 legislation obviously was designed to reduce the influence of wealthy individuals and groups in the political process. No longer were large campaign contributions possible, no longer could wealthy candidates commit large portions of their personal fortunes to a political race. The ceilings imposed on total campaign expenditures were intended to keep campaign financing from increasing beyond control. The Federal Election Commission was designed to place some teeth in the enforcement of campaign legislation. Many of the loopholes in earlier pieces of election legislation were closed.

As is often the case when comprehensive legislation is passed, court suits immediately were filed challenging the validity of the 1974 modifications in the Federal Election Campaign Act. In the 1976 decision of *Buckley v. Valeo*,[22] the United States Supreme Court provided a definitive answer to questions relating to the constitutionality of the 1974 provisions. Large portions of the legislation met the Court's approval. The Court ruled that the public financing of presidential election campaigns was constitutionally valid, that individuals and groups could be limited in the amount of funds they contributed to candidates or their committees, and that the disclosure provisions were permissible. In addition, the Court upheld the concept and powers of the Federal Election Commission but found fault with the selection process for the commissioners. However, the Court also struck down several provisions of the act. The Court ruled that it was constitutionally impermissible to place ceilings on total campaign expenditures or to restrict a candidate from contributing his own personal funds to his campaign. However, the Court held that Congress was within its power to make these two restrictions a requirement for those persons who elected to accept federal funds to finance their races. The Court also struck down the limitations placed on independent expenditures (i.e., spending in behalf of a candidate but carried out completely independent of the candidate or his authorized committees). In short, the Court upheld those portions of the legislation which dealt with preserving the integrity of the election process but struck down restrictions on the freedom of individuals or groups to express their own views regarding candidates in an election.

Following the decision by the Supreme Court, the Congress passed additional modifications to the act in 1976 in order to bring the legislation in line with the Court's ruling and to eliminate some of the deficiencies in the act which had already become apparent. The 1976 amendments to the 1971 Federal Election Campaign Act represent the final version of the reform legislation. The following points are important areas of regulation under the new statute, court decisions, and related laws which have particular relevance to interest group participation in the election process:

1. Corporations and labor unions remain prohibited from using corporate assets or labor union funds for campaign contributions.
2. Corporations, labor unions, and other groups may establish special political

---

[22] *Buckley v. Valeo*, 424 U.S. 1 (1976).

action committees which may solicit voluntary contributions for use as campaign contributions.
3. Individuals may contribute no more than $1,000 per election to any candidate or that candidate's authorized committees. No person may contribute more than $25,000 in combined political contributions in any one calendar year.
4. Political action committees established by interest groups for the purpose of supporting several candidates may contribute to each candidate or that candidate's authorized campaign committees no more than $5,000 per election.
5. Individuals and political action committees may spend unlimited amounts of money in support of candidates if the expenditures are made totally independent of the candidate and that candidate's authorized campaign committees.
6. Interest groups, including labor unions and corporations, may spend unlimited amounts of money for internal communications (i.e., communications to their own memberships) including such communications that support or oppose candidates for public office.
7. Interest groups may spend unlimited funds for nonpartisan electoral activities such as get-out-the-vote drives.

The original reform movement that began after the disclosures of campaign activities in the 1972 elections had as one of its prime goals a reduction in the influence exerted by wealthy individuals and economic interest groups. To a certain extent, the legislation passed in 1974 and modified by court decisions and the 1976 amendments moved toward accomplishing this goal. It has been particularly effective in reducing the role played by wealthy individual campaign contributors who can no longer contribute hundreds of thousands and even millions of dollars to a political campaign. However, the current state of the law leaves considerable room for interest group participation in the electoral process. Although the new laws change the rules of the game to a certain degree and may modify the ways in which pressure groups support or oppose candidates for federal office, interest group participation remains vigorous nevertheless.

Political Action Committees

Political action committees (PACs) have become the primary vehicle for interest group participation in the electoral process, particularly as it relates to the making of campaign contributions. Political action committees were originally authorized in the 1925 Federal Corrupt Practices Act.[23] The creation of political action committees has become a method by which corporations and labor unions can safely avoid the federal ban on the use of union dues or corporate assets as campaign contributions. Labor unions have a long history of effective use of political action committees. The most commonly recognized labor union PAC is the AFL-CIO's Committee on Political Education (COPE), which has long been an extremely active and influential conduit for labor contributions and organizational support for

---

[23] Greenwald, *Group Power*, p. 150.

political candidates. Corporations have lagged behind labor in the establishment and successful use of political action committees.

The campaign reform laws passed between 1971 and 1976 gave increased vitality to the use of political action committees. Under the current status of election campaign legislation, PACs may be established by unions, corporations, and other interest groups. A political action committee is established under the authority of the parent body. Union or corporation funds may be employed to create the political action committee, to administer the committee, and to solicit funds for the committee. However, no corporate assets or union dues may be used as campaign contributions. Any monies to be used for campaign contributions must be voluntarily given to the political action committee. The funds of the parent body must be kept completely separate from the funds of the PAC itself.

Labor union PACs may at any time solicit voluntary contributions from union members. Corporate PACs may solicit at any time voluntary contributions from company officers, management personnel, and shareholders. In addition, twice each year both union and corporate political action committees may request voluntary contributions from all employees of the company. These requests, however, must be made by mail, and the contributions must remain anonymous. Individual contributions to a political action committee are restricted to a $5,000 limitation per year. The individual who makes contributions to political action committees must also remain within the $25,000 limitation in total annual contributions to all candidates for federal office.

A key provision in these funding regulations is the requirement that all contributions to a political action committee must be voluntarily given. Obviously fears have arisen that corporations and unions will put pressure on employees and members to contribute a portion of their earnings to a political action committee. In order to prevent abuses, the Federal Election Commission has created certain guidelines for the solicitation of contributions from employees:

1. no superior should solicit funds from a subordinate;
2. the solicitor should inform the employee of the political purpose of the fund to which the employee is asked to contribute; and
3. the solicitor should inform the employee of his or her right to refuse to contribute without fear of reprisals of any kind.[24]

The voluntary contribution requirements, of course, is subject to abuse. In December of 1977, for example, the Federal Election Commission in response to complaints filed suit against the National Education Association charging that the NEA and 18 of its state affiliates had violated federal election laws by requiring that teachers donate funds to the NEA political action committees.[25]

If a political action committee has certain characteristics, it is considered a

[24] *Congressional Quarterly Weekly Report,* 34 (January 10, 1976), 48.
[25] *Congressional Quarterly Weekly Report,* 36 (January 28, 1978), 196.

multi-candidate political action committee as defined by the federal election laws. In order to so qualify, a PAC must have at least 50 contributors, have been registered for at least six months, and contribute to five or more candidates for public office. Upon meeting such qualifications, the political action committee may contribute up to $5,000 per election to a candidate or that candidate's authorized committees. Under the provisions of the campaign finance laws, any primary election, runoff election, special election, or general election is considered a separate "election." However, the combined presidential primary elections in the various states are considered a single election for the purposes of campaign finance limitations.

Until 1975, the labor unions' use of political action committees far exceeded that of business. The primary reason for this was that while both business and labor were authorized to create PACs, any corporation or union holding federal government contracts was barred from establishing a political action committee. This provision effectively limited PAC creation by most major corporations. In the early 1970s, however, labor unions received substantial federal manpower contracts which curtailed union use of political action committees. In order to continue to make political contributions through the political action committees, labor lobbied Congress to remove the regulation barring government contractors from creating and administering PACs. Congress responded to the demands of labor in a provision of the 1974 amendments to the Federal Election Campaign Act. While this pleased labor, it also had the impact of removing the last remaining restraint against full use of political action committees by corporations. However, the corporate world remained suspicious of the legality of creating political action committees until November of 1975 when the Federal Election Commission handed down an opinion reaffirming the right of corporations to administer political action committees. This ruling, known as the Sun Oil Company decision, provided full notice to the business community that it could freely engage in these election-related activities.[26] As a result, the number of corporate political action committees began growing at a rapid rate. As Table 10.6 indicates, labor's dominance over business in the creation of political action committees has reversed itself dramatically with corporate PACs now far outnumbering labor political action committees. Labor, however, still holds a clear advantage over business with respect to the use of political action committees. The unions have far more experience in this form of interest group politics and have been able to achieve greater success in the use of these political funds. As business grows in its experience, however, the balance of power and the competition between business and labor will sharpen considerably.

Campaign Contributions

In spite of the campaign reform laws formulated to curtail the contributions of special interests, pressure groups still have numerous ways to contribute to political races. The federal legislation has not significantly slowed interest group

[26] *Congressional Quarterly Weekly Report,* 34 (January 10, 1976), 46-49.

TABLE 10.6 Growth of Political Action Committees

Parent Interest	Dec., 1974	Nov., 1975*	May, 1976	Dec., 1976	Dec., 1977
Corporate	89	139	294	433	538
Labor	201	226	246	224	216
Others	318	357	452	489	544
Total	608	722	992	1,146	1,298

*Date of Sun Oil Company ruling by the Federal Election Commission.
Source: Federal Election Commission: see also *Congressional Quarterly Weekly Report*, 36 (April 8, 1978), 849-854.

activity. To the contrary, interest organizations recently have been involved in direct political campaign contributions to a greater extent than ever before.

The new laws, however, have made some modifications in the pattern of interest group expenditures. Because of the limitation on contributions to individual candidates, interest groups can no longer commit the bulk of their campaign funds to small numbers of candidates. For example, if a corporate PAC has at its disposal $20,000 for campaign contributions, it can commit no more than $5,000 of that amount to any one candidate in any one election. The political action committee may be desperately interested in the nomination of a particular presidential candidate, but the contribution limitation prohibits it from spending its entire $20,000 fund on that particular person's race. Prior to the passage of the 1974 legislation, an interest group was not effectively restricted in this manner. The impact of the contribution ceiling has been to broaden the distribution of campaign contributions by interest groups. Rather than donating large amounts to a select few candidates, interest groups are now giving smaller amounts of direct contributions to more candidates. This has also prompted interest groups to place greater emphasis on congressional races, helping to decrease the disproportionate attention given to presidential candidates.

The increased activity by interest groups in supporting candidates for federal office and the new attention being paid to congressional races can be seen by comparing interest group contributions made to congressional candidates for the 1974 and 1976 campaigns. Table 10.7 provides the information on such contributions for the major categories of pressure groups. The contributions summarized in this table include all direct contributions made and disclosed by interest groups for these particular elections. A number of trends are revealed in this comparison. First, the overall amount of dollars contributed by pressure groups to congressional campaigns almost doubled between 1974 and 1976. Second, contributions by every category of interest group have increased. Third, while labor still remains the largest source of interest group funds for congressional candidates, business groups have shown the greatest increase in giving. In comparing the two elections, corporate contributions increased almost threefold, reflecting the increased emphasis business has placed on becoming involved in electoral politics and making greater use of political action committees. It is clear that interest group giving has never been

TABLE 10.7   Interest Group Congressional Campaign Contributions

Group Classification	1974	1976
Agricultural	$ 361,040	$ 1,534,447
Business	2,506,946	7,091,375
Health Professions	1,936,487	2,694,910
Legal Profession	–	241,280
Labor	6,315,488	8,206,578
Ideological	723,410	1,503,394
Other	682,215	1,299,928
Total	$12,525,586	$22,571,912

Source: Common Cause; *Congressional Quarterly Weekly Report*, 35 (April 16, 1977), 710.

more pronounced, that the base of recipients of interest group funds is increasing, and that congressional races are receiving increased pressure group attention.

While the information included in Table 10.7 provides interesting data regarding the general activities of interest groups, it does not reveal which specific interest groups are the most prominent direct contributors to political campaigns. Table 10.8 indicates the 12 largest interest group contributors to the 1976 congressional campaign races. The specific special interest groups included on this list represent some interesting trends in campaign finance. First on the list is the political action committee of the American Medical Association. The AMA created the American Medical Political Action Committee (AMPAC) in 1961 in order to have a political arm which would be free to engage in electoral politics. AMPAC, since its very inception, has been one of the most active interest group committees in making contributions to candidates for congressional office. It has consistently been at or

TABLE 10.8   Major Interest Group Congressional Campaign Contributors in 1976

	Total Contributions
1. American Medical Associations	$1,790,879
2. Dairy committees	1,362,159
3. AFL-CIO COPEs	996,910
4. Maritime-related unions	979,691
5. United Auto Workers	845,939
6. Coal, oil and natural gas interests	809,508
7. National Education Associations	752,272
8. National Association of Realtors	605,973
9. Financial institutions	529,193
10. Intl. Assn. of Machinists	519,157
11. United Steelworkers of America	463,033
12. American Dental Associations	409,835

Source: Common Cause; *Congressional Quarterly Weekly Report*, 35 (April 16, 1977), 710.

TABLE 10.9   Leading Corporate PACs in 1976 Elections
(Contributions made in 1975 and 1976)

		Contributions to Federal Candidates
1.	Nonpartisan Political Support Committee (General Electric Co.)	$109,235
2.	United Technologies Corporation Political Action Committee (United Technologies Corp.)	90,500
3.	Political Awareness Fund (Union Oil Company of California)	86,190
4.	Texaco Employees Political Involvement Committee (Texaco, Inc.)	83,300
5.	Chrysler Nonpartisan Political Support Committee (Chrysler Corp.)	71,825
6.	American Family Political Action Committee (American Family Corp.)	71,550
7.	Nonpartisan Committee for Good Government (Coca-Cola Company)	68,200
8.	Southern Railway Tax Eligible Good Government Fund (Southern Railway Company)	66,830
9.	North Western Officers Trust Account (Chicago Northwestern Transportation)	64,900
10.	Hanson Fund (Tacoma Fund)	62,500

Source: Federal Election Commission; *Congressional Quarterly Weekly Report*, 36 (April 8, 1978), 850.

near the top in the rankings of large special interest contributors to political campaigns, regularly contributing well over a million dollars in election years. Coupled with the twelfth-ranked American Dental Association, the AMA provides the vast majority of health profession contributions to political campaigns. Second on the list of large contributors is the dairy industry, continuing its record of increasing activity in political affairs. Six of the top twelve positions are occupied by labor unions and their political action committees. The three business interests which made the top twelve list represent the energy, real estate, and banking industries. Table 10.9 further elucidates the activity of business interests by ranking the top ten corporate PACs in making direct campaign contributions to the 1976 congressional races.

The material just presented reviews interest group campaign contributions made directly to a candidate or a candidate's authorized committee. These contributions include cash donations as well as goods and services which have a monetary value. However, direct contributions are not the only kinds of campaign assistance that an interest group may provide candidates for federal office. There are a large number of indirect contributions which are not limited by federal election laws, but which can be of great benefit to a candidate seeking political office.[27] The labor unions have been particularly active in providing these indirect contributions and services to endorsed candidates. The $8.2 million in direct campaign contributions made to congressional candidates in 1976 by labor groups was only a small part of the total assistance provided by unions to their favorite electoral hopefuls. Indirect contributions have allowed labor's influence in the electoral process to surpass that of business in spite of the corporate world's renewed interest in election campaigns.

First, labor's endorsement of a political candidate often brings with it voluntary campaign assistance from union members. These individual volunteers offer their time and efforts to a political campaign or a specific candidate. They are mobilized primarily by the enthusiasm the union displays for selected political office seekers. By providing volunteer workers, the unions make a very important indirect political contribution. Business interests are not able to mobilize management or shareholders to participate in volunteer election activities to the extent that labor is able to do so.

Second, an interest group may engage in communications with its membership on political matters. The funds expended on such internal communications are not limited by the federal election laws. Only if such communications efforts specifically support or oppose candidates must such activities be reported to the Federal Election Commission. Labor takes excellent advantage of this provision of the law. For example, in 1976 unions reported expenses of almost $2 million for promoting partisan causes among their members, with more than half of this amount used to promote the Carter/Mondale presidential ticket. These internal communications to union members promote candidates for political office in much the same way as general campaign advertising, but because the union is communicating to its own members, the expenses are not limited by federal spending ceilings. This kind of communication allows labor to influence millions of union members. Corporations have the same opportunity, but few take advantage of it for fear that endorsements of political candidates communicated to shareholders with corporate assets would not be well received by the owners of company stock. Only four corporations reported such communications to the Federal Election Commission for the 1976 elections. All of the funds expended by corporations for such internal partisan communications were used to promote the candidacy of Gerald Ford. In addition to labor and corporations, one membership group, the National Rifle Association, reported committing funds to internal communications for the purpose of promoting political candidates. The NRA concentrated on communicating to its membership the group's endorsement of congressional candidates with acceptable positions on gun control, although it also allocated some

---

[27] See Michael J. Malbin, "Labor, Business and Money—A Post Election Analysis," *National Journal*, 12 (March 19, 1977), 412-417.

$13,000 to support Gerald Ford's presidential reelection effort. The information regarding interest group expenditures for internal partisan communications is summarized in Table 10.10.

TABLE 10.10 Communicating on Political Matters

Labor unions and corporations must report how much they spend to communicate with their own members or stockholders and administrative employees if the communications, as their principal purpose, directly advocated the election or defeat of specific candidates.

Following are lists of all unions whose reported communications costs exceeded $10,000 in 1976 and of all organizations that spent on internal communications on behalf of President Ford.

Most of the union spending was on behalf of the Carter-Mondale ticket, and such spending is listed separately. In most instances where unions sent materials to their members advocating the election of more than one candidate, their reports allocated the expenses among the candidates. In a few cases, *National Journal* allocated the spending, based on what appeared to be the common practice.

According to these figures, labor reported spending $26 on behalf of Carter for every dollar anybody spent on behalf of Ford for internal communications, counting only those communications required to be reported.

All reports were filed 30 days after the election except for a few (indicated by asterisks) that were filed 10 days before the election. The Federal Election Commission did not notify groups affected by the reporting requirement until last September. As a result, some spending that falls within the legal requirements may have gone unreported. —**Compiled by Sarah Jacobs**

	Total	Carter
Labor for Carter		
AFL-CIO	$400,557.90	$315,981.67
United Auto Workers	289,139.12	240,688.48
Building Construction Trades Department		
AFL-CIO	177,508.85	41,974.58
Communications Workers of America	120,423.69	106,813.64
Pennsylvania AFL-CIO	101,056.24	9,430.93
Active Ballot Club-Retail Clerks		
International Association	97,097.98	69,889.97
Ohio AFL-CIO	69,448.00	38,326.00
Michigan AFL-CIO*	45,720.79	—
Indiana AFL-CIO	42,034.16	4,045.98
American Federation of State, County		
and Municipal Employees	41,014.64	24,170.47
Maryland and D.C. AFL-CIO	34,972.33	3,281.39
New Jersey AFL-CIO*	29,943.00	26,858.00
Texas AFL-CIO	25,196.20	12,946.16
Tennessee State Labor Council*	23,622.42	9,462.61
United Steelworkers of America	23,696.61	15,678.99
Service Employees International Union	20,556.85	—
California Labor Federation, AFL-CIO	17,850.17	11,903.52

TABLE 10.10 (continued)

Colorado COPE	15,269.36	–
Buffalo AFL-CIO Council	14,683.35	6,412.94
International Association of Bridge, Structural and Ornamental Iron Workers*	13,494.05	13,494.05
Machinists Non-Partisan Political League*	13,959.66	7,666.64
South Carolina Labor Council	13,466.28	6,342.97
International Ladies' Garment Workers' Union	12,571.75	5,342.64
Council 13, AFSCME, AFL-CIO	12,567.00	6,283.00
Los Angeles County Federation of Labor, AFL-CIO	12,187.50	3,046.87
Rhode Island AFL-CIO	10,307.37	7,124.00
Cleveland AFL-CIO	10,265.66	7,699.25
Others	187,877.66	63,446.18
Total	$1,901,703.40	$1,051,897.23
Organization for Ford	Total	Ford
National Rifle Association Institute for Legislative Action	$101,528.57	$13,204.92
Libbey-Owens-Ford Co.	13,096.38	13,096.38
Dresser Industries Inc.	5,245.00	5,245.00
Cooper Industries Inc.	5,079.40	5,079.40
PepsiCo. Inc.*	4,485.15	4,485.15
Total	$129,434.50	$41,110.85

Source: *National Journal,* 12 (March 19, 1977), 415.

Third, there are no limitations on funds spent by interest groups for nonpartisan political activities. Labor unions have been quite active over the years in voter registration drives and in encouraging people to vote on election day. Unions regularly provide transportation service to the polls in an effort to "get out the vote." On its face, these nonpartisan political efforts are neutral, but in practice the impact disproportionately favors union-supported candidates. Occasionally, the Federal Election Commission has received complaints that such union activities have not conformed to nonpartisan guidelines but have been blatantly biased in favor of those persons endorsed by labor.[28] Once again, business interests have not taken advantage of similar opportunities.

The impact of these indirect campaign contributions is substantial. Labor's endorsement of Jimmy Carter for the presidency in 1976 was a mammoth boon to his chances for election. Not only did the various COPE and other union political action committees contribute directly to the Carter candidacy, but the union provided indirect contributions and services of great value. Labor unions are said to have sent out 75 million pieces of mail during the 1976 campaign, made 10 million

[28] *Congressional Quarterly Weekly Report,* 36 (January 28, 1978), 193-197.

telephone calls, and administered a $2 million computer operation. The monetary value of labor's indirect methods of support for Carter have been estimated at between 8.5 and 11 million dollars.

Interest groups allocate campaign funds and indirect contributions in a number of ways. However, the primary rule applied by all interest groups is to commit campaign assistance where it will do the most good. Some interest groups, usually those with a unitary structure, rely on the national leadership of the organization to determine to what political races the interest group will channel its funds and other assistance. Other associations, especially those with a federated structure, allow local and regional chapters substantial influence in selecting races for interest group involvement.

Some interest groups have a particular affinity to one of the two major political parties. The most obvious example of this is labor's generally warm relationship with the Democratic party.[29] In the 1976 elections, 96.5 percent of union contributions went to Democratic candidates. Business interests are normally regarded as favoring Republican party candidates, but business interest groups do not support Republicans to the extent that labor contributes to Democratic candidates. In 1976, corporate and business-related PAC contributions were destined for Republican candidates 58.9 percent of the time.[30] Ideological groups, such as the Conservative Victory Fund, also have strong ties to particular political parties.

For many interest groups, there is a tendency to support incumbents. If a member of Congress has performed well according to the standards of the interest group, the organization will often try to assist in that individual's reelection. For example, approximately two-thirds of all business and labor interest group contributions in 1976 went to incumbents. Campaign contributions to incumbent congressmen represent a relatively safe investment. More than 90 percent of all incumbent congressmen standing for reelection are returned to Congress. An interest group that contributes to these returning congressmen's campaigns will normally be able to attain a degree of success.

Some interest groups concentrate on political races that are close. The logic of this strategy is to put money where it will have the greatest impact. If a favored incumbent is running a close race for reelection, a pressure group may focus attention on that race to do what it can to have the representative returned. Conversely, if an incumbent who has been hostile to interest group positions is having difficulty retaining his or her seat, a lobby organization might provide as much assistance as possible to the incumbent's opponent in an attempt to tip the scales of the election to a candidate more in line with the goals of the group.

Often an interest group will allocate funds and campaign assistance for candidates who occupy key positions in the policy-making process. This is particularly important when the occupied position is of special relevance to the policy area of

[29] *Congressional Quarterly Weekly Report*, 36 (January 28, 1978), 193-197.
[30] *Congressional Quarterly Weekly Report*, 36 (April 8, 1978), 849.

immediate concern to the interest group. For example, in 1976 the third largest recipient of labor union contributions was Senator Harrison Williams of New Jersey with direct donations of almost $15,000 from various union political action committees. Senator Williams is chairman of the Senate Committee that has jurisdiction over labor matters. The National Education Association in 1976 contributed to the campaigns of 25 of the 37 members of the House Committee on Education and Labor. Dairy groups made donations to 23 members of the House Committee on Agriculture. Twenty-nine of the 37 members of the House Ways and Means Committee, which has jurisdiction over federal taxation policy, received campaign gifts from the American Medical Association's political action committees. The maritime industry labor unions contributed to the campaign funds of 30 members of the House Committee on Merchant Marine and Fisheries. Each of these contributions represents the commitment of resources to political campaigns which have special meaning to the pressure group because the winner of the election will have substantial influence in the making of federal policy of interest to the organization. Contributions to the winning candidate can mean a political officeholder who will be sympathetic to the interests of the pressure group and who will grant access to representatives of the organization.

Ratings and Endorsements

In addition to campaign contributions and election services of various kinds, interest groups engage in other activities which may have an impact on the electoral process. One such activity is the rating of incumbent federal officials. More than 50 pressure organizations currently issue ratings of members of Congress. These ratings indicate how well the representative or senator is performing according to the policy objectives of the interest group. The most common method of issuing such ratings is for the interest group to identify a number of key issues upon which Congress voted. These key issues are normally public policy questions over which the interest group is particularly concerned. Each member of Congress is then rated on a 0 to 100 scale based on the percentage of times the representative voted in accordance with the policy wishes of the interest group.

The impact of interest group ratings is not well established, but for the most part, they appear to have relatively low significance. Occasionally, however, an interest group's rating may become an issue in an incumbent congressman's reelection campaign. At the very least, such ratings provide information to group members as to which members of Congress are performing particularly well or especially poorly in the eyes of the interest group. This information may well change an interest group member's attitude about an incumbent and perhaps even alter some votes. How a congressman reacts to ratings by interest groups depends upon the interest group and the nature of the constituency represented. Each year the Consumer Federation of America issues its list of "Consumer Heros" and "Consumer Zeros." Few members of Congress want to return to their home districts at reelection time and have to explain to their constituents why they were branded a

"Zero" on consumer issues. Similarly, representatives prefer to avoid being rated poorly by environmental groups, good government organizations, and similar movements which represent public interest concerns that may be popular in the home district. However, it is important for some members of Congress to be rated low by certain groups. A member of Congress from a conservative district hopes for low rating by groups such as COPE or the Americans for Democratic Action. To be judged favorably by labor and liberal groups may be quite difficult to defend in an election campaign and may be seized upon as an issue by the incumbent's opponent.

In addition to ratings issued by interest groups, such organizations may also publicize endorsements of candidates during election years. These endorsements may be merely public announcements of support, or they may carry with them campaign contributions and organizational assistance. The importance of such endorsements depends upon the degree of influence which the interest group is able to deliver along with its public proclamation of support. Table 10.11 summarizes the endorsement activity of six prominent interest group organizations which regularly issue public support for political candidates. Obviously an endorsement does not guarantee a victory for the supported candidate. However, if an interest group is able to accompany its endorsement with direct campaign contributions, volunteer campaign workers, indirect contributions, and a membership that will follow the lead of the interest group's leaders, then the public support is indeed important.

Some interest groups not only issue endorsements of political candidates, but also publicly announce those incumbents which the interest group urges the voters to turn out of office. Occasionally these announcements of opposition are more significant than endorsements. Each election year, for example, the Washington-based lobby, Environmental Action, Inc., issues its "Dirty Dozen" list. This list includes the names of the twelve congressmen standing for reelection whose records on environmental issues are particularly poor according to the interest group's

TABLE 10.11 1976 Interest Group Congressional Campaign Endorsements

Interest Group	House Endorsements	% Victories	Senate Endorsements	% Victories
Americans for Democratic Action (Liberal)	86	78%	20	70%
AFL-CIO/COPE (Labor)	362	71%	28	68%
United Auto Workers (Labor)	327	76%	31	61%
Business-Industry Political Action Committee (Business)	105	43%	18	56%
Americans for Constitutional Action (Conservative)	153	79%	10	50%
National Conservative Political Action Committee (Conservative)	193	63%	13	62%

Source: *Congressional Quarterly Weekly Report,* 34 (November 6, 1976), 3136-3144.

analysis. Listing on the Dirty Dozen slate carries more with it than a simple public criticism from the environmental group. A Dirty Dozen candidate is targeted for defeat by the environmental movement supporters. Environmental Action sends campaign organizers into the districts of the targeted members of Congress to launch attacks on the incumbent for his or her stands on ecology policy. Of the twelve members of Congress included on the 1976 "Dirty Dozen" list, three were defeated, while others won reelection by narrow margins. A similar strategy has recently been adopted by the anti-abortion interest groups. These organizations identified five incumbent senators (Robert Packwood of Oregon, Birch Bayh of Indiana, John Culver of Iowa, George McGovern of South Dakota, and Frank Church of Idaho) as especially deserving defeat in the 1980 elections.

Occasionally an interest group will go to extraordinary lengths to bring about the defeat of a candidate for public office who has especially displeased the group. This was the case in 1970 when the pro-gun forces invested considerable effort to purge gun control advocates from Congress. High on the list of candidates marked for defeat were Senators Thomas Dodd of Connecticut and Joseph Tydings of Maryland, both Democrats. The gun lobbies and supporting organizations raised substantial funds, printed campaign literature, purchased advertising space, and acquired media time to urge voters to reject Tydings and Dodd. The effort was ultimately successful. Both Dodd and Tydings lost their reelection bids, with the Tydings vote being exceptionally close. There were obviously many issues and events which affected these two key elections, but gun lobby action certainly did not help either candidate's chance of being returned to the Senate.

Interest Groups in Electoral Politics

While interest groups play an important role in the American electoral process, they do not control election outcomes. Without doubt, the contributions of pressure groups in the form of financial donations, endorsements, indirect services, and volunteer campaign workers can give a candidate a considerable boost. On occasion, the assistance which an interest group provides can tip the balance in an election. But this is a far cry from concluding that interest groups circumvent the public will and decide elections behind the scenes. There are several factors which limit interest group domination of the electoral process.

First, interest groups normally do not have the power to deliver massive numbers of voters in support of an endorsed candidate on election day.[31] Interest group members are often a very diverse lot. They respond at election time to a complex set of factors. The recommendations of the leadership of an interest group may be one such factor, but in all probability it will not be the dominating one. The interest group of which an individual is a member may represent only one of several interests and concerns held by the individual. Furthermore, many persons hold

---

[31] See L. Harmon Zeigler and G. Wayne Peak, *Interest Groups in American Society*, 2nd ed. (Englewood Cliffs, N.J.: Prentice-Hall, Inc., 1972), pp. 122-128.

memberships in several different groups, the leaders of which may not be uniform in election recommendations. As indicated in chapter 9, interest group members tend to be from the higher socioeconomic classes than nonmembers and therefore less susceptible to following blindly the wishes of interest group leaders. The labor unions commit the most resources in attempting to deliver their members at election time to vote for union-endorsed candidates. Compared to other interest groups, labor has been quite successful in this regard. But labor, even with all its resources and organization, suffers large numbers of members who do not vote according to the directions of the union leadership. An interest group may well be able to deliver substantial numbers of votes, but an interest group's membership is not a single-minded, totally dependent entity which will automatically respond in unison upon receiving directions from the leadership.

Second, the contributions that interest groups make to political candidates do not automatically determine election outcomes. It is important to keep in mind that in a competitive election, interest groups contribute funds and services to both major candidates. A liberal Democrat may receive assistance from unions, ideologically liberal interest groups, and certain special situation and single-issue-oriented groups. A conservative Republican opponent may receive similar sums of money and services from business organizations and conservative ideology groups, as well as certain special situation and single-issue-oriented associations. While interest groups may be making massive contributions in the aggregate, the contributions offset each other. Although it is true that interest group support has tended to favor incumbents over challengers, the system remains sufficiently open for incumbents to be defeated by strong opponents. Interest group funds may provide disproportionate assistance to incumbents, but not of sufficient magnitude to insure reelection.

Third, recent federal legislation has restrained the impact of interest group participation to a certain extent. The limitations on direct contributions, disclosure requirements, and other provisions reduce the likelihood that an interest group can "buy" an election. Although the current laws, contrary to their original intent, encourage interest group activity in the election process, they do impose obstacles to the outright domination of an election by a single interest group. Pressure organizations have become increasingly involved in the electoral process, but the involvement is quite widespread and is not sufficiently concentrated in single races to prompt the conclusion that special interests determine who shall sit in public office.

Fourth, much of what an interest group contributes to the electoral process improves the way in which the country selects its representatives and leaders. Direct and indirect contributions are used to give candidates and issues improved publicity among the citizenry. Because of interest group efforts, more voters become better informed about the candidates and public policy concerns associated with the election. Ratings and endorsements improve the visibility of candidates. Political education drives, voter registration campaigns, and election day "get out the vote" efforts, often funded or administered by interest groups, hopefully contribute to wider political participation among the citizenry and help produce a more informed electorate.

Interest groups, of course, do not become involved in election politics for totally unselfish, civic betterment motives. Such activity is designed to help the organization attain its goals. Group activity may produce public officeholders who are sympathetic to organizational interests, or it may contribute to the defeat of candidates who are hostile to group objectives. Interest groups realize that they cannot purchase a president or congressman with campaign contributions. However, by actively supporting a winning candidate, the interest group does hope to guarantee that the elected public official will open his door to interest group representatives when the organization wishes to communicate with government officials. Groups know that they cannot buy a congressman's vote, particularly votes on major issues. A representative responds to a number of demands and expectations when he casts a vote—party considerations, constituency needs, personal judgment, expert opinions, and other factors. The position of an interest group may be one of the factors considered, but it is rarely the dominant factor except on very narrow policy issues which have little impact on anyone save the interest group itself.

SUMMARY

Over the past several decades, American interest groups have accelerated their indirect lobbying efforts. No longer do pressure organizations focus exclusively on direct contact with public officials. Instead, substantial resources are committed to influencing the public. Two important strategies are followed by interest groups. First, special interests often attempt to influence public opinion. The goal is to mold public attitudes in such a way that the citizenry generally supports the interest group and its cause. Second, interest groups are active in attempts to have the public elect individuals to political office who will favor the group's goals. Through these two strategies, the interest organization hopes to improve the access it has to elected public officials.

In conducting campaigns to influence public opinion, an interest group normally has one of two objectives in mind. First, the interest group may be trying to improve the image of the group among the nation's citizenry. In this fashion, the group hopes to influence the political climate. If successful, the organization will be seen by the public in a favorable light and will be creditably evaluated. Second, the interest group may be attempting to convince the public to support or oppose specific proposals. The objective here is not to induce a passive, favorable image, but to motivate the citizen to accept the positions of the interest group on a specific public policy issue and to communicate his or her views to appropriate public officials. The techniques and strategies used by contemporary interest groups to influence public opinion in both these ways has become increasingly sophisticated and effective.

American interest groups have regularly become involved in electoral politics. Since the early 1900s, legislators have been somewhat concerned about excessive campaign involvement by labor unions and corporations. Laws have been passed to prohibit union and corporation assets from being used as campaign contributions. Internal revenue regulations have also restricted electoral politics activity for certain kinds of interest groups. Federal law, however, allows interest groups to establish political arms, known as political action committees, which may solicit funds to be used for campaign contributions. Election reform legislation passed in the mid-1970s altered various campaign finance practices. These new regulations limit the size of direct contributions and impose strict disclosure requirements. However, several forms of indirect campaign support are not restricted under the new laws. While these laws originally sought to reduce interest group activity in electoral politics, they have not accomplished this goal. In fact, interest groups have never been more active in supporting candidates for federal office than in the most recent elections. By supporting candidates who successfully attain public office, an interest group hopes to improve its access to government decision makers.

eleven

Direct Lobbying: Interest Groups and Government

Interest groups commonly commit a large portion of their resources to direct lobbying activities. These efforts focus on public policy strategies that rely on direct contact between interest group representatives and government officials; this allows the interest group to articulate its demands and present supporting information for its positions. This form of lobbying has a long history and remains today one of the most viable methods whereby pressure organizations can have an input to the public policy-making process.

Traditionally, direct lobbying has been associated with attempts to convince the legislative branch to enact laws favorable to interest group members. In recent years this traditional process has become even larger and more complex. The great growth in interest groups has caused a substantial increase in legislative branch lobbying, with almost every major interest group engaging in direct lobbying contacts with members of Congress or their congressional staffs. Interest groups provide much of the information upon which congressional decisions are based. Many of the bills introduced in Congress were originally drafted by interest group research staffs. Pressure organizations are regularly given an opportunity to inform Congress of the impact that pending legislation would have on group members. Lobbyists provide many useful services for the legislature, and the majority of the legislators have favorable relationships with lobbyists and the organizations they represent.

A rapidly growing area of interest group involvement in the governmental process has been direct lobbying of the executive branch. As the complexity of our society has grown, Congress has delegated increasingly large amounts of rule-making power to the executive branch and the independent regulatory agencies. Because of the vast power the executive branch has in shaping the contours of public policy, interest groups have found it particularly important to maintain access to governmental decision makers in the bureaucracy. Often the application and enforcement of the law has a much greater impact on an interest group than passage of the actual law itself. For this reason, interest groups are finding it especially fruitful to continue direct contact with executive personnel.

Interest groups have always been aware of the power of the judicial branch of the government. Certain interest groups have traditionally devoted considerable resources to lobbying the government by taking litigation to the court system. Groups that have relied heavily on the judicial branch include the American Civil Liberties Union and the National Association for the Advancement of Colored People. Other groups have historically used the courts when other methods of lobbying have failed. In contemporary times, however, more and more pressure organizations are taking advantage of the powers of the courts. Persuasive legal arguments are often able to accomplish as much or even more than the traditional lobbying of the executive and legislative branches.

The increasing activity of interest groups in direct lobbying strategies has placed the government under more pressure from a greater number of sources than ever before. The growth in the number of "public interest" groups has offset the increased activities of the economic organizations, thus preventing the dominance of any one particular special interest. The development of such countervailing interest movements has been one of the most important phenomena in pressure group politics.

LOBBYING THE LEGISLATIVE BRANCH

Interest groups approach Congress and the various state legislatures in order to obtain special favors for group members. These special favors take the form of public policy choices that will benefit the groups' members or assist the groups in reaching their announced objectives. Legislative lobbying has developed from a fairly crude process of soliciting special treatment during the early years of our nation's development to a refined, professional activity in contemporary times. In the process of articulating member interests to the legislative branch, interest groups provide many valuable services to the nation's lawmakers.

The Regulation of Legislative Lobbying

The history of lobbying the federal legislative branch has not been entirely free of corruption and abuse. Moreover, specific incidents of misbehavior on the part of lobbyists or legislators have been of sufficient seriousness for Congress to have an interest in the regulation of pressure group politics. As in other areas of interest group regulation, lawmakers must walk a fine line between constitutional guarantees of freedom of speech, association, and petition, and the right of the government to protect itself against corrupting influences. For the most part, Congress has failed to pass legislation that effectively regulates the activities of pressure organizations and yet allows free and open opportunities for groups to express their policy preferences before the legislative branch, despite numerous attempts to create such a legal code. Specific regulations were passed restricting the activities of foreign lobbyists and representatives of the shipping and utility industries, but no comprehensive lobby bill was enacted until 1946.

The Federal Regulation of Lobbying Act was passed in 1946 as part of a general legislative program to reform the operations of the United States Congress.[1] Congress elected to cope with the lobbying issue by requiring registration and disclosure rather than attempting to restrict or prohibit various lobbying activities. This strategy was taken in order to avoid First Amendment violations and to construct a bill that was capable of being enacted. More severe restrictions placed on the lobbying process would have surely had difficulty passing both houses of Congress. The 1946 law required that any person who was hired by another person or group for the principal purpose of influencing legislative actions register with the clerk of the United States House of Representatives and the secretary of the United States Senate. Furthermore, such lobbyists were instructed to file financial reports four times a year disclosing the nature of their activities. In addition, all organizations which raised and spent funds for the purpose of influencing legislation were required under the act to provide financial disclosure statements.

The 1946 legislation was not effectively drafted, and a number of loopholes minimized the impact of the regulation. The language used in the act was exceedingly vague, allowing for a wide array of interpretations as to the meaning of the statute. There was very little explicit language in the law that defined exactly what kinds of activities qualified as "lobbying" under the meaning of the legislation. Certain activities were exempt. For example, the act specifically exempted testifying before congressional committees from the criteria that defined attempts to influence legislation. Later, by interpretation this exemption was extended to persons who assisted in the preparation of testimony to be delivered at congressional hearings. Since presenting evidence to legislative committees is a principal activity of interest group lobbyists, this exemption seriously reduced the applicability of the statute. Another glaring weakness in the statute was that it failed to provide a meaningful mechanism for enforcement of the act's provisions. Without a method of effective enforcement, the law had minimal impact. During the first 30 years of the statute's existence, the Justice Department was only called upon to prosecute violators of the law five times.

The constitutionality of the 1946 Federal Regulation of Lobbying Act was

---

[1] For a general review of the 1946 Act, see *Guide to Congress,* 2nd ed. (Washington: Congressional Quarterly, 1976), pp. 670-674.

upheld by the United States Supreme Court in the case of *United States v. Harriss* in 1954.[2] While the Court held that the act was a valid piece of legislation and not in conflict with the First Amendment, the justices construed the statute in very narrow terms and found certain portions of the act to be invalid. For example, the Court struck down provisions of the statute dealing with indirect lobbying techniques. It also interpreted the statute as not applying to persons who engaged in lobbying activities but whose "principal purpose" was not influencing legislation. Such narrow construction reduced the applicability of an already less than fully comprehensive piece of legislation. In the final analysis, the 1946 regulations were vague, filled with loopholes, and largely unenforceable.

In spite of general dissatisfaction with the Federal Regulation of Lobbying Act, Congress has been unsuccessful at enacting a meaningful substitute. On numerous occasions, members of Congress have introduced legislation designed to replace the 1946 statute, and such proposals have sometimes gained the support of congressional subcommittees or full committees. There have even been occasions when one of the houses of Congress has passed a bill revising the 1946 act, including a 1978 attempt.[3] However, the legislature has been unsuccessful at reaching a final agreement on an effective regulatory reform.

Legislative Lobbyists

Interest group representatives who lobby the legislative branch share a primary task: to present effectively their organizations' positions on public policy issues so that legislative enactments are favorable to the groups' interests. In spite of this common purpose, there is considerable variation in the operations, tactics, resources, and support available for lobbying efforts. Some lobbyists represent several small interest groups which individually cannot afford to employ a full-time staff. Other lobbyists may be only one of many legislative liaison staff members employed by a single interest group. Small ideological or single issue groups may provide their representatives with little staff assistance and research support. Large labor unions and business pressure organizations are capable of placing full research, clerical, and staff resources at the disposal of the group's lobbyists. But whatever the degree of support available to the lobbyist, he shares with all other lobbyists the experiences of a career devoted to advocating the preferred policies of a "special interest."

Lobbying is rarely an individual's career goal.[4] It is not an occupation that requires a distinct educational background. No college or university offers career training leading to a degree in legislative lobbying. College and professional school

---

[2] 347 U.S. 612 (1954).

[3] For a review of this legislation see *Congressional Quarterly Weekly Report,* 36 (May 6, 1978), 1119-1121.

[4] For a classic examination of the backgrounds of lobbyists at the federal level, see Lester W. Milbrath, *The Washington Lobbyists* (Chicago: Rand McNally, 1963).

graduates do not normally seek a position as a lobbyist immediately following graduation. Lobbying is not a high status career choice in the eyes of most Americans. The activities of an interest group representative remain viewed with skepticism in our society. For these reasons, individuals recruited to become lobbyists customarily enter the lobbying profession after spending a considerable portion of their lives in other professional pursuits. Lobbying tends to be a person's second or third career rather than one to which a person commits himself immediately after completing his formal education.

Interest groups seek persons for lobbying positions who have certain attributes which qualify them to represent the organization's interests before governmental bodies. Training and experience in four basic areas are looked upon favorably by most interest groups.[5] First, interest groups prefer to recruit individuals with knowledge of the legislative and political process. The law-making procedures which govern the flow of business in Congress can be quite complex. A lobbyist who understands the intricacies of the process can often use such knowledge to his organization's advantage in planning and executing legislative strategy. Second, knowledge of the law and legal processes can be an important attribute in conducting the business of a lobbyist. One of the primary functions of the legislature is the formulation of the nation's laws. Interest groups often participate in the drafting of legal statutes, and their representatives must be able to work with legal concepts and understand the way in which public policy is formulated through the enactment of statutes. Third, a quality lobbyist is one who is well schooled in the subject matter of central concern to the interest group. Legislators often rely on interest group representatives to provide detailed information about substantive issues related to the purposes of the organization. For a lobbyist to perform as a credible spokesman for group interests, he must be knowledgeable in the organization's subject area. Fourth, the representative needs to have experience and talents in the area of public relations. Much of what a lobbyist does involves using a variety of techniques to promote the group's interests as favorably as possible and to enhance the impact of the group's message.

Obviously, few lobbyists can boast of knowledge and experience in all of these areas. However, such strengths provide a very good basis for a career as a lobbyist. Various interest groups, of course, place primary emphasis on qualities that are particularly pertinent to the group's individual situation and needs. For example, large pressure groups especially favor lobbyists with experience in the legislative and political process. Corporations generally have a tendency to select persons with legal abilities. Interest groups focusing on narrow interests or on issues of a technical nature prefer lobbyists who are well schooled in the subject matter. All interest groups are attracted to individuals who are able to maintain good relationships with others and deal effectively in social situations.

[5] Milbrath, *The Washington Lobbyists*, pp. 61-71.

Lobbyists in Washington represent a wide variety of career patterns and training. The most common educational background among lobbyists is law school training; the most frequent career experiences among lobbyists are governmental service, the practice of law, and business. Many lobbyists entered the activity after spending a period of their lives working for the executive branch. With their knowledge of the political process and the substantive area, these individuals often become very effective lobbyists. Quite successful records have also been earned by former members of Congress who remain in Washington as lobbyists upon completing their governmental service. While relatively few former representatives enter into full-time lobbying, those who do have the advantage of an excellent knowledge of the legislative process, established contacts among members of the house in which they served, and the limited floor privileges given to a previous member of Congress.

For the most part, lobbyists share a common social background with legislators. Lobbyists are generally individuals who have been reared in middle or upper-middle class homes, have received the advantage of college and perhaps professional school educations, and have enjoyed above-average annual incomes. Reflective of the fact that lobbying is rarely a first career choice, group representatives are normally persons in their middle years. Except for those lobbyists who represent civil rights or women's rights groups, group representatives are generally white, male, and of Protestant religious affiliation. A lobbyist's political party membership is often closely related to the variety of interest he is representing. This occurs both through a process of self-selection, with individuals being attracted to causes which they have politically favored over the years, and because interest groups often have ties to specific political parties and prefer to select representatives from these familiar political groups. Labor unions and civil rights groups, for example, are generally represented by lobbyists with Democratic party affiliations. Corporate interests are much more likely to have Republicans in their employ. Furthermore, lobbyists generally possess a personal commitment to the goals of the interest group.[6]

The number of persons involved in lobbying at the federal legislative level is not well determined. The previously mentioned inadequacies of the 1946 Federal Regulation of Lobbying Act are such that relatively few of those individuals actually involved in influencing legislation are specifically required to register with the House and Senate officials. In 1974, approximately 1,000 persons or groups registered with the government under the provisions of the 1946 act. Greenwald, however, estimated in 1977 that more than 5,000 persons were engaged in legislative lobbying at the federal level.[7] A great proportion of these group agents are not registered as lobbyists.

---

[6] Milbrath, *The Washington Lobbyists*, pp. 109-114.
[7] Carol S. Greenwald, *Group Power* (New York: Praeger, 1977), p. 191.

Lobbyists and the Legislative Process

The legislative process in the United States involves complex procedures which must be followed if a proposed law is to be enacted. Bills must be introduced in the House and Senate, survive subcommittee and full committee deliberation, and then receive the approval of the full house after floor action. Should the final action by the second house result in a version of the bill that is different from that of the first, the proposed law must have its differences resolved in a conference committee made up of representatives from both chambers. The resulting product of the conference committee deliberations must then receive the approval of both houses. Should a bill survive this process, it is still subject to presidential veto.

The procedures employed by the United States Congress make it relatively difficult for a proposed law to be enacted. To complete the process successfully, a bill must receive approval at each stage in the process. Should the proposed law be rejected at any one of these stages, it does not become part of the federal legal code. For this reason the legislative process works to the advantage of those groups who support the status quo. It is much easier to defeat a bill than it is to obtain its passage. An interest group supporting a change in public policy must be able to shepherd the proposal through each stage of the process successfully. A group urging defeat of the proposal needs only to block the proposed law at a single stage.

Interest groups participate fully in each of the various stages of the legislative process. Bills which have only minimal interest to pressure groups may attract little, if any, activity by lobbyists. However, controversial measures with far-reaching ramifications are sure to attract substantial interest group participation. In such situations, competing interest groups may vie for congressional approval at each of the various stages of the process. The many decision-making stages in the legislative process create multiple access points for interest group participation in legislative policy formation.

Interest group activity in the initiation stage has undergone substantial expansion over the past several years. Lobby organizations have always participated in drafting bills, particularly pieces of proposed legislation with specific applicability to interest group members. Traditionally, however, pressure organizations have been oriented more toward maintaining the status quo than toward working for social change. In the past it was more common to witness an interest group working to stop a piece of proposed legislation than it was to see a group committed to drafting bills that would alter legislative policy. This condition was largely due to the dominance of the business interests which clearly supported the current status of federal regulatory action and which generally assumed a defensive posture on proposals recommending major changes. However, the rise of public interest groups and citizen lobbies has meant that the pressure organizations are more involved in promoting the initiation of legislation than ever before. Change-oriented interest groups now exist in sufficient numbers and have the necessary strength to be responsible for the initial drafting of a substantial portion of bills introduced each year. Perhaps as many as one half of the bills introduced in Congress are written in part by interest groups.[8]

At the bill drafting stage, interest group representatives work closely with members of Congress who share the interest organization's commitment to particular policy goals. Labor union lobbyists, for example, maintain close ties with prolabor representatives. Union legislative proposals are discussed with members of Congress usually affiliated with the Democratic party, and agreements are reached as to the proper form of the bill and the appropriate legislative strategies to follow. This cooperation between the interest group and the lawmakers also frequently includes members of the executive branch. This is almost always the case when an administration favorable to labor goals occupies the White House. A member of Congress then sponsors the proposed legislation that the interest group is working to have enacted. Although labor unions are especially active in cooperating with legislators in devising a legislative program, other organizations representing a wide array of interests become actively involved in the legislative initiation stage as well. The procedure at this stage of the process is quite uniform. Lobbyists devote their time and attention to those legislators who hold similar views on policy matters. Legislator and lobbyist often cooperate as colleagues working toward a shared goal. Interest groups at this point in the process contribute ideas, information, and research to the drafting of appropriate public policy legislation.

Thousands of bills are introduced in each session of Congress, yet relatively few receive the careful attention of congressional committees. The decision as to which bills will attract the committee's resources and be given priority in committee deliberations is made by the committee chairman. In making such decisions, the head of the committee relies on the recommendations of committee staff, respected advisers, and senior members of the committee, as well as his own political judgment. In order to increase the likelihood that favored bills will receive the committee's study and opposed bills will be ignored, interest groups devote considerable resources to maintaining access to committee chairmen, senior staff members, and other important members of the committee. When a proposal of substantial concern is relegated to a committee, the interest group wants to have the opportunity to express its views to those members of the committee with influence in the decision-making process.

The legislative process places a premium on specialization. Members of Congress are expected to become experts in substantive legislative areas. This expertise is developed through the committee system, with members of committees and subcommittees attaining high levels of competence and knowledge in specific areas of governmental business. Congress relies on this expertise which, in turn, gives rise to a certain degree of committee and subcommittee autonomy. The House and Senate will quite often bow to the expertise of members of a committee or subcommittee

---

[8] See James Deakin, *The Lobbyists* (Washington: Public Affairs Press, 1966).

when they bring forth recommendations within their areas of expertise. Because of this reciprocity norm and the general value placed on the development of expertise, the recommendations of a subcommittee may become law with little controversy. The division of labor that operates in both houses of Congress frequently allows each chamber to defer to its committees and subcommittees. This is particularly true when the recommendations deal with subject matter clearly within the committee's expertise and have relatively narrow applicability. Of course, some committees and subcommittees enjoy more respect and autonomy than others. These specialization and division of labor processes, therefore, create a series of "subgovernments" which wield tremendous amounts of power over substantive policy areas.

Because legislative power in Congress is clearly divided along substantive lines, interest groups often do not have to retain close ties with every committee and subcommittee in each of the two chambers. Instead, the interest groups are able to concentrate their efforts on the one or two committees which have substantive jurisdiction over the areas of legislative action that are of particular concern to the group. The narrower the scope of the interest group's goals, the fewer committees the group must cultivate. Labor organizations, for example, will place primary interest on maintaining friendly relations with the staff and members of the Senate Human Resources Committee and the House Committee on Education and Labor, which have jurisdiction over legislation of particular relevance to the union movement. However, because the goals of organized labor go far beyond issues pertaining only to unionization itself, labor finds it important to maintain access to committees with responsibility over legislation closely related to these other union goals. An interest group with reasonably narrow interests may well be able to accomplish its legislative goals by working almost exclusively with the staff and members of a single subcommittee in each house. Table 11.1 contains examples of relationships between certain agricultural interest groups and the subcommittees

TABLE 11.1 Agricultural Interest Groups and Subcommittees of Primary Importance in the U.S. House of Representatives

Interest Group	Commodity Interest	House Subcommittee
National Cotton Council	Cotton	Subcommittee on Cotton
Soybean Council of America	Soybeans	Subcommittee on Oilseeds and Rice
Tobacco Institute	Tobacco	Subcommittee on Tobacco
National Milk Producers	Dairy Products	Subcommittee on Dairy and Poultry Products
National Association of Wheat Growers	Wheat	Subcommittee on Livestock and Grains
National Broiler Council	Poultry Products	Subcommittee on Dairy and Poultry Products
National Wool Growers Association	Sheep and Wool	Subcommittee on Livestock and Grains

Adapted from: Randall B. Ripley and Grace A. Franklin, *Congress, the Bureaucracy, and Public Policy* (Homewood, Illinois: The Dorsey Press, 1976), p. 78.

in the U.S. House of Representatives with which they have developed special relationships. Almost every congressional committee and subcommittee has interest groups and lobbyists with which they must regularly deal. These regular contacts tend to develop into solid relationships over the years. By maintaining these relationships with committee members and staff, the interest groups are assured of access to the committee or subcommittee whenever necessary.

One of the most important activities of the lobbyist in his relations with congressional committees is the presentation of research results and information on pending committee action. The legislative process at the subcommittee and committee stages demands quality information. At this point in the process, legislators determine whether or not legislation is necessary and, if so, what kind of legislation should be proposed to the full chamber. Committees analyze the submitted bills and modify them until they become, in the view of the committee members, workable and acceptable. In determining the need for legislation and arriving at conclusions as to the specifics of legislation to be recommended, committee members must have input from those who are to be affected by the legislation. Interest groups provide a large portion of the data that is used by the committee to evaluate legislative proposals. For this reason, interest group representatives regularly make available to committee members and staff personnel the results of research projects dealing with subjects under the committee's jurisdiction. These research reports are written in a fashion supportive of the group's policy objectives, but to maintain credibility with the committee, the information provided must be of sound quality. Often such material presents only one side of the legislative arguments surrounding a particular bill. Legislators generally expect group-generated research to be slanted to a certain degree, but the interest group risks a loss of access if it presents material that is inaccurate.

Lobbyists generally consider the presentation of arguments to members of Congress as an important interest group tactic. However, such communications may be made in varying contexts. The most favorably evaluated method of presenting the interest group's position involves direct communication between a lobbyist and a legislator. Most interest group representatives feel that a face-to-face exchange offers the lobbyists the most effective atmosphere for presenting an effective argument that the legislator will thoughtfully consider. Direct presentations to staff members can also be effective, especially when the lobbyist is able to make his presentation directly to important and trusted members of the committee staff who are relied upon extensively by the leadership of the committee. Written communications are often employed when direct personal contact is not possible, although lobbyists for the most part regard this method of communication to be less effective. With written communications there can be no guarantee that the legislator will pay the report any heed, there is no opportunity to evaluate the congressman's reaction, and there is no possibility of responding to questions and insuring that the legislator has a full appreciation of the interest group's position.

Special mention should be made of the formal presentation of opinion and information at subcommittee and committee hearings. It is customary for legislative committees to schedule days for interested parties to express their positions on business currently before the committee. At times, the committee will invite specific parties or group representatives to give testimony in order to receive the considered opinions of experts in the area under scrutiny. Often some of the most knowledgeable experts are interest group representatives. At other times, the committees will solicit the view of groups and individuals on both sides of a particular issue for the purpose of giving these segments of society a chance to be heard and also to evaluate the legislative proposal from the point of view of those who will be most directly affected by it. Frequently, however, legislative committee hearings are only formal proceedings that committees feel compelled to schedule. The attendance of congressmen at such hearings is normally quite poor. It is not uncommon for such hearings to be held with only one member of the committee or subcommittee present at any one point in time. Nonetheless, interest groups respond to public hearings enthusiastically. Lobbyists who are experienced Washington veterans realize that the presentation of arguments and information at legislative hearings has limited impact, but few interest groups are willing to forego the opportunity of expressing the group's position at any meeting. Even if the legislators themselves pay only minimal attention to hearing testimony, such events are often covered by the media, and there is always the possibility that the interest group may receive press coverage of their viewpoints.

Table 11.2 lists the participants at subcommittee hearings on three recent legislative proposals. The interest groups included presented written or oral arguments defending their positions on the pending legislation. The list conveys the degree of interest group activity involved in the formal consideration of three very different pieces of legislative action. First, the Senate hearings on the Labor Reform Act of 1977 demonstrates the large numbers of interest groups that attempt to have their views heard by the government on an important piece of legislation. The bill was designed to make some rather fundamental changes in labor law and was seen by many as having the impact of tipping the delicate balance of power between labor and management decidedly in favor of the unions. This appraisal of the bill should not be too surprising since the proposed act was drafted with the help of labor supporters, and had the backing of the Democratic administration and the support of liberal members of the Democratic party in Congress. The list of participants in the hearings is indicative of the variety of groups which appear before governmental bodies whenever a change is proposed that would affect labor-management relations. Groups sending witnesses to argue for the proposed law came primarily from the union movement. Almost every important union joined the campaign to win congressional support for the act. The union representatives were joined by a sprinkling of lobbyists representing liberal civil rights and religious groups. Important support was provided by the Carter administration which lobbied for the bill through the efforts of Secretary of Labor Marshall and other administration officials. Opposing the bill were numerous representatives of business and

TABLE 11.2 Interest Group Participants in Congressional Committee Hearings: Three Examples

I. U.S. Senate Subcommittee on Labor of the Human Resources Committee: Hearings on the Labor Reform Act of 1977

Supporting the Legislation	*Opposing the Legislation*
U.S. Department of Labor	Aerospace Industries Association
National Labor Relations Board	American Council on Education
Amalgamated Clothing Workers Union	American Farm Bureau Federation
United Brotherhood of Carpenters	American Iron and Steel Institute
United Steelworkers	American Mining Congress
National Council of Negro Women	American Newspaper Publishers Association
NAACP	Ashland Oil
A. Philip Randolph Institute	Association of General Merchandise Chains
United Paperworkers Union	J.P. Stevens and Company
United Furniture Workers Union	American Trucking Association
Retail Clerks International Union	Building Service Contractors Association
Service Employees Union	Council of Construction Employers
International Ladies' Garment Workers	Burlington Industries
National Union of Hospital Employees	Dresser Industries
International Typographical Union	Electronic Industries Association
The Newspaper Guild	Federal-Mogul Corporation
National Football League Players Association	General Telephone Corporation
AFL-CIO	Independent Armored Car Operators Association
United Auto Workers	Independent Business Association
International Union of Machinists	International Harvester
Rhode Island Workers Union	National Association of Chain Drug Stores
United Electrical Workers Union	National Association of Plumbing, Heating and Cooling Contractors
Distributive Workers of America	National Electrical Manufacturers Association
International Union of Allied Industrial Workers	National Labor Management Foundation
Amalgamated Meatcutters	National Restaurant Association
American Nurses Association	New Jersey Business and Industry Association
Bakery and Confectioner Workers	National Right to Work Committee
Coalition for a Democratic Majority	Associated Builders and Contractors
Coalition of Labor Union Women	American Bankers Association
AFL-CIO Professional Employees Union	Associated General Contractors
Actors' Equity Association	Bituminous Coal Operators Association
American Federation of Musicians	National Crushed Stone Association
International Union of Electrical Workers	National Industrial Council
National Women's Political Caucus	National Association of Manufacturers
International Brotherhood of Painters	U.S. Chamber of Commerce
Synagogue Council of America	Small Business Legislative Council
United Paperworkers International	Printing Industries of America
U.S. Catholic Conference	American Paper Institute
Southerners for Economic Justice	Southern Furniture Manufacturers Association
International Longshoremen's Union	American Retail Federation
	National Retail Merchants Association
	National Association of Retail Grocers

TABLE 11.2 Continued

Supporting the Legislation	Opposing the Legislation
	National Small Business Association
	Western States Meat Packers Association
	Nisei Farmers League
	American Hospital Association
	PPG Industries, Inc.
	Whirlpool Corporation

II. U.S. House Subcommittee on Civil and Constitutional Rights of the Judiciary Committee: Hearings on Anti-Abortion Constitutional Amendment (1976)

Supporting the Amendment	Opposing the Amendment
National Conference of Catholic Bishops	New York Federation of Reform Synagogues
U.S. Catholic Conference	Rockefeller Foundation
State of Missouri	U.S. Commission on Civil Rights
Social Concerns Committee of the Lutheran Church/Missouri Synod	United Methodist Church
	Religious Coalition for Abortion Rights
National Rights to Life Committee	Planned Parenthood
State of Pennsylvania	American Association of University Women
Ohio Right to Life Society	
American Citizens Concerned for Life, Inc.	American Baptist Churches
Alternatives to Abortion International	Americans United for Separation of Church and State
Wisconsin Citizens Concerned for Life	Jewish Community Council of Greater Washington
	Lehigh Valley Abortion Rights Association
	Church of the Brethren
	American Jewish Congress

III. U.S. House Subcommittee on Indian Affairs and Public Lands of the Interior and Insular Affairs Committee: Hearings on the Endangered American Wilderness Act (1977)

Supporting the Legislation	Opposing the Legislation
Citizens for America's Endangered Wilderness	Southern Oregon Resource Alliance
Sierra Club	Territorial Statesmen, Inc.
Wilderness Society	Western Timber Association
Friends of the Earth	Louisiana-Pacific
National Audubon Society	American Forest Products Co.
Oregon Natural Areas Committee	Sierra Forest Products Co.
Lone Peak Wilderness Committee	Homestake Mining Co.
New Mexico Wilderness Study Committee	Blue Mountain Resource Council
	Northwest Timber Association
Colorado Open Space Council	Northwest Pine Association
Sitka Conservation Society	Willamette Industries, Inc.
Mountain Wilderness Association	Inland Forest Resources Council
Federation of Western Outdoor Clubs	Burlington Northern Railroad
	St. Regis Paper Company
California Wilderness Coalition	National Forest Products Association
	Federal Timber Purchasers Association
	American Plywood Association
	Kennecott Copper
	North West Mining Association
	Associated Oregon Loggers

other large employers. Large umbrella organizations such as the National Association of Manufacturers and the U.S. Chamber of Commerce were joined by lobbyists representing trade associations, industry councils, and corporations.

The second issue presented in Table 11.2 is a prolife constitutional amendment proposal upon which the House Judiciary Committee's subcommittee on Civil and Constitutional Rights held hearings in 1976. The proposed amendment would have had the impact of reversing the 1973 United States Supreme Court ruling which struck down state laws restricting the right of women to obtain abortions. Proponents of the amendment were represented at the hearings by lobbyists employed by Catholic religious groups, right-to-life single issue interest groups, and certain states that argued in favor of their authority to regulate in this area. Opposing the amendment were lobbyists from Jewish groups, certain Protestant churches, women's groups, and various liberal agencies and foundations.

The third example shown in Table 11.2 involves hearings on the Endangered American Wilderness Act held in 1977 by a subcommittee of the House panel on Interior and Insular Affairs. The confrontation at these hearings was largely part of the ongoing struggle between environmental groups committed to preserving the wilderness areas and trade associations and corporations involved in the economic development of the nation's natural resources.

Once a bill has been referred from a legislative committee to the floor of the chamber, the activity of interest groups involved in the proposed legislation takes a somewhat different approach. With the bill being drafted and modified, the central concern shifts toward gaining the acceptance or the defeat of the bill, depending upon the position taken by the particular interest group. As in all other stages of the process, lobbyists generally confine their efforts to working with legislators who are already supporting the group's position on the bill. Interest groups cooperate with these legislators by providing them with the necessary information to promote the cause among fellow legislators and to refute attacks on their position. Lobbyists also often help devise proper legislative strategies to promote the desired action on the proposed statute. It is not uncommon for lobbyists also to make direct contacts with members of Congress to argue in behalf of the organization's position on the bill. In doing so, lobbyists generally restrict their activities to those members of Congress with whom they already have friendly relations. Emphasis is placed on reinforcing those legislators already favoring the group's position and on winning over those representatives who are undecided. Lobbyists devote almost no attention to opposition legislators or those with whom they have had considerable difficulty in the past.

Interest groups, therefore, are participants in a wide range of legislative activities. Lobbyists maintain relationships with congressional representatives and key staff personnel, engage in the drafting of legislation, present their views to subcommittee and committee members in a variety of ways, and attempt to influence the outcome of action on the floor. Interest groups take active positions not only on legislation affecting their memberships, but on related matters such as important resolutions and Senate confirmation of key government nominations.

The Roles and Activities of Legislative Lobbyists

How a lobbyist allocates his time and resources depends upon a number of factors.[9] Lobbyists who occupy but one position on a staff of representatives of a single interest group may have specialized duties assigned through a division of labor among the group's lobbying staff. Those lobbyists who are the sole representatives of a single organization may have much broader responsibilities. Still other lobbyists who are spokesmen for more than one interest group may have very diversified duties. Responsibilities may also vary according to the type of group represented. A large mass membership group may require lobbyists to devote their attention to different matters than would a corporation. An ideological interest group may place different demands on its representatives than would a professional association. In spite of these differences, lobbyists share a great number of common responsibilities, although they may allocate their time and efforts to these duties differently, depending upon the demands of their employing group and their own personal styles.

All lobbyists spend a good deal of time working in their own offices. The office serves as the lobbyist's communications headquarters. He devotes considerable time and effort to written correspondence and telephone communications which are directed to and received from congressional representatives, legislative staff members, members and officers of the interest group, and influential people who may be able to aid the lobbyist in the conduct of his duties. For many lobbyists, communications with representatives of other interest groups that support similar public policy positions are extremely important. Such alliance-building techniques can be crucial to winning congressional approval of interest group objectives. In addition to these communications activities, the lobbyist may also be required to direct an office staff and supervise research activities. Finally, the lobbyist may be required to devote a segment of his day to reading and research in order to keep pace with events important to his organization's interests and to keep abreast of congressional business so that he is well informed of the often rapidly changing conditions on Capitol Hill.

While lobbyists are commonly depicted as spending most of their time making direct contacts with members of Congress, a surprisingly small portion of a lobbyist's day is actually devoted to this duty. National legislators obviously cannot spend their days in continuous discussions with agents of the special interests. Members of Congress realize that relationships with interest groups can be important, but other responsibilities may be more demanding. A quality lobbyist, therefore, realizes that direct contact is a relatively rare event. Lobbyists do not want to abuse whatever access they might develop with a particular legislator. Therefore, interest group representatives do not normally make demands on a legislator's time unless such communications are particularly important. A legislator who recognizes that a lobbyist is considerate of the lawmaker's time will appreciate this fact and will

[9]Milbrath, *The Washington Lobbyists,* ch. 6.

often be more inclined to grant a personal meeting with the lobbyist when it is requested. A study by Lester Milbrath revealed that a majority of lobbyists spend less than 5 percent of their time calling on members of Congress.[10] Lobbyists representing mass membership groups with power at the polls and those interest group representatives who are active in partisan politics tend to devote more of their time to direct contact with legislators than other lobbyists.

Individuals employed by interest groups spend a good bit of time engaged in various forms of grass-roots lobbying. Some lobbyists are public relations experts who are heavily involved in planning and executing mass media promotions of the group's cause. Other lobbyists find it profitable to communicate with key members of a legislator's constituency. For example, a lobbyist for the drug industry may expend considerable effort encouraging individual pharmaceutical companies to communicate with legislators who represent districts encompassing company plants and offices. Agricultural interest group lobbyists may regularly urge farmers to contact their representatives in Congress. By working through such intermediaries, interest groups can often influence members of Congress. Where a group representative may have difficulty gaining access to a legislator, a major constituent of that congressman may be warmly welcomed.

Entertaining, often in lavish fashion, has been customarily associated with the role of a lobbyist in American political folklore. In truth, however, lobbyists spend a very small portion of their time sponsoring social engagements and parties. There is a certain degree of social responsibility attached to the job, as there is with any professional occupation, but entertaining is significantly overrated by the public as a method of lobbying. The degree of entertaining, however, does vary considerably according to the personal traits of the lobbyist. Those lobbyists who are particularly skilled at social interactions rely on this technique more than those who are less comfortable in such situations. For the most part, the entertaining that does occur is designed primarily as an access-maintenance strategy rather than as a forum for conducting business.

The amount of time allotted to these various lobbying activities is at least partially determined by the way in which the lobbyist perceives his job. Lobbyists view their role in different ways, and these various role orientations have an impact on how a lobbyist carries out his duties and orders his priorities. Jewell and Patterson discuss five basic role orientations which are commonly held by lobbyists: contact man, campaign organizer, informant, watchdog, and strategist.[11]

The lobbyist who perceives himself as a contact man places primary emphasis on maintaining personal contacts with legislators and key staff members. He devotes a substantial amount of time to patrolling the halls of government buildings, speaking to significant participants in the legislative process. He feels that he can best

---

[10] Milbrath, *The Washington Lobbyists*, p. 117.

[11] Malcolm E. Jewell and Samuel C. Patterson, *The Legislative Process in the United States*, 3rd ed. (New York: Random House, 1977), pp. 286-290.

work in behalf of his organization by direct personal associations with legislators. If a problem needs to be dealt with, the contact man is likely to handle it by entering into direct discussions with the persons involved. As we have previously indicated, a lobbyist's responsibilities require direct contact work at some point, and most lobbyists value the effectiveness of the direct lobbying technique. The lobbyist who assumes the contact man role orientation, however, places personal contacts very high on his list of priority activities. Labor lobbyists have been found to be particularly prone to accept this particular role orientation, whereas corporate representatives have tended to shy away from this perception of the job.

The campaign organizer, according to Jewell and Patterson, sees his duties as revolving primarily around the planning and execution of grass-roots support for the organization's public policy objectives. Although he may engage in direct contact with legislators, the emphasis is placed on gaining mass public support for interest-group-supported positions. This kind of lobbyist feels that if the legislator becomes convinced that his constituents support a particular policy, he will usually bow to the wishes of those who elected him. Consequently, the campaign organizer devotes much of his lobbying efforts to public relations work. Such group representatives make extensive use of the media and often orchestrate full-scale public relations campaigns to sell the organization's positions to the public at large. Television, radio, magazines, newspapers, pamphlets, and direct mail techniques are all used by the campaign organizer to promote public support. Such efforts obviously carry a substantial price tag and can only be effectively used by interest groups with significant financial backing.

The informant role places a high priority on the distribution of information to congressional representatives and staff. The activities of an informant center on research and dissemination of factual material. Lobbyists of this variety spend a good portion of their time testifying at congressional committee hearings and distributing research reports to individual congressmen and committee staff personnel. The purpose of the informant's efforts is to keep Congress abreast of certain conditions and situations facing members of the interest group he represents. It is assumed that by having this knowledge, members of Congress will reach decisions that are generally favorable to the interest group. The informant does not engage to any great extent in grass-roots lobbying efforts or personal contact advocacy.

The watchdog role orientation is held by lobbyists who are careful students of the legislative process. They perceive their job as developing accurate and current information on everything the legislature is doing that might be of interest to the pressure group represented. The watchdog is a keen observer of the legislative process and is always alert for the slightest activity which might signal legislative action of concern to his employer. When such activity is discovered, the watchdog reports back to the interest group he represents. The watchdog orientation is common among interest groups that are generally satisfied with the status quo. If a particular group is prospering under the current scheme of things, its lobbyist does not have to engage in overt pressuring activities. Instead, the lobbyist is instructed to maintain surveillance over the legislative scene and to inform the interest group of even the slightest activity which might ultimately upset the favorable status enjoyed by the group.

The final role orientation discussed by Jewell and Patterson is the strategist. This is a very specialized role and not assumed by many lobbyists. The job of a strategist is to map out legislative lobbying campaigns for other lobbyists. He is the "lobbyist's lobbyist." Interest group representatives come to him with a particular legislative objective in mind, and the strategist devises the means to help them attain their legislative goals.

Jewell and Patterson caution that these various lobbying role orientations are not mutually exclusive. At one time or another, almost all lobbyists engage in each of these activities. Certain situations call for different orientations. However, when a lobbyist takes on a particular role orientation, it tells us a great deal about how he sees his position, orders his priorities, and carries out his duties.

Alliances and Coalitions

Interest groups commonly enter into alliances and coalitions with other pressure organizations in order to promote mutually supported policy goals. For some organizations, such as the AFL-CIO, U.S. Chamber of Commerce, and the American Farm Bureau Federation, coalition behavior is a natural course of action because these federated organizations are, in essence, alliances themselves. Relatively few important pieces of legislation proceed through the legislative process without being affected by the efforts of cooperating interest organizations. The strategy of an interest group proceeding independently without coordinating activities with other organizations is, for the most part, a thing of the past. Only when a proposed bill is exceptionally narrow in scope and of potential significance only to the members of a single interest group will a pressure group proceed independently.

Some interest group alliances have become firmly established because they have been operative for a long period of time. The general cooperation between liberal ideological groups, civil rights organizations and organized labor unions, for example, has existed since the years of Franklin Roosevelt. All of these groups have generally taken progressive positions on domestic policy, and their mutual commitment to a more liberal public policy posture has brought them together on numerous occasions. This regular interaction has facilitated the organization of cooperative lobbying efforts, and the alliance has earned an enviable record of success over the years. Other groups have joined in temporary coalitions when their interests, while generally disparate, dictate a mutual position on a given legislative proposal. Such coalitions are often quite fragile due to the lack of established relationships between the groups and the overall incompatibility of their long-term goals. However, temporary coalitions of this variety can be reasonably successful in influencing the outcome of specific legislative deliberations.

Often alliances and coalitions are brought together out of economic considerations. One of the most powerful alliances of interest groups over the past several decades has been the "highway lobby," a term used to describe a wide range of transportation and construction interest groups with a large economic stake in the nation's highway policy. Each of these individual interests has an investment in the nation's highway construction program. The participants in this alliance include the petroleum industry and the automobile companies which have a stake in the purchase and use of cars and trucks; the construction companies, concrete producers, asphalt manufacturers, and heavy equipment producers which have an economic investment in highway construction; the banks and financial institutions which provide funds for construction and automobile purchasing; the bus and trucking industries which require excellent surface transportation systems in order to compete with rail and air travel; and the tourist industry which depends on automobile transportation. Working together, these interests have convinced Congress to establish the most comprehensive system of interstate highways in the world's history. Such a system has cost American taxpayers billions of dollars, which the public has generally been quite willing to pay, and has reaped large profits for the economic interest groups involved.

Other economically based cooperation occurs because of short term expedience, rather than any long-range similarity of interests. An example of such a temporary coalition occurred in 1977 in lobbying efforts on federally imposed auto emissions standards.[12] Originally these antipollution standards were mandated by clean air legislation to become effective in 1975. However, because of automobile company difficulties in developing the technology to remove substantial amounts of pollutants from auto emissions, the standards were temporarily lifted. In 1977, however, the automobile companies requested a longer extension until the year 1981. In this instance, the auto industry joined forces with labor union groups to push the extension legislation through Congress. If the standards had not been once again temporarily lifted, the automobile manufacturers would not have been able to produce cars without substantial increases in cost. And because various models of American cars were not sufficiently developed to meet federal clean air standards, production of certain autos would have had to be eliminated altogether. An immediate imposition of the standards, therefore, would have resulted in great economic loss for the manufacturers and a subsequent severe loss of jobs for labor unions representing workers in the automobile industry. Therefore, these two groups, labor and management, normally bitter rivals in legislative politics, entered into a successful lobbying coalition that served both of their purposes.

Interest groups representing similar ideological causes often find themselves working side by side. During the battle over Senate ratification of the Panama Canal Treaties in 1977, interest groups sharing a conservative political philosophy joined

---

[12] Dick Kirschten, "The Clean Air Conference—Something for Everybody," *National Journal*, 9 (August 13, 1977), 1261-1263.

forces to work for the defeat of the ratification resolution.[13] The cooperative venture included almost all of the major conservative ideological organizations that regularly take positions on governmental policy. Among these were the Conservative Caucus, the American Conservative Union, the Citizens for the Republic, the Committee for the Survival of a Free Congress, National Conservative Political Action Committee, American Security Council, and Council for National Defense. In addition to these established groups, the Emergency Coalition to Save the Panama Canal provided an umbrella structure for cooperating conservative political organizations. Although the efforts of these groups were ultimately unsuccessful, the forces against the treaty were far more effective working together than they would have been proceeding individually.

The philosophical differences between business and labor provide one of the most enduring and predictable divisions in American interest group politics. Issues that divide management and the unions often prompt the formation of cooperative efforts to engage in lobbying battles. Such conflicts involve not only economic issues, but also ideological arguments regarding what is seen as a delicate balance of power between labor and industry in America's economic system. In 1977, legislation allowing common site picketing by unions was introduced in Congress. This measure, sponsored by labor union interest groups and liberal Democrats, was seen by unions as an essential piece of labor legislation but was perceived by business as a policy which would damage the position of management. The lobbying over this bill pitted a coalition of almost every significant labor union against an alliance of more than one hundred corporations and business associations, led by the construction industry.[14] Similarly, the 1977 Labor Reform Act proposal prompted a labor/management conflict. Once again a coalition of labor unions, joined by certain civil rights and religious groups, worked against an alliance of corporations and trade associations in attempts to influence Congress. Massive spending for direct lobbying and for grass-roots campaigns accompanied the interest groups' political activities. Labor was estimated to have spent more than $2.5 million in support of the reform and business to have committed almost $5 million to kill it.[15] On both of these legislative matters, the business lobby was the victor.

If well coordinated and properly directed, interest group alliances can be particularly effective political forces. The advantage of such efforts lies not only in the pooling of resources with which to conduct a legislative lobbying campaign, but also the combined allies of the various interest groups in Congress. This is especially

---

[13] William J. Lanouette, "The Panama Canal Treaties—Playing in Peoria and the Senate," *National Journal*, 9 (October 8, 1977), 1556-1562; *Congressional Quarterly Weekly Report*, 36 (January 21, 1978), 135-137.

[14] *Congressional Quarterly Weekly Report*, 35 (March 26, 1977), 521-524.

[15] James W. Singer, "Labor and Business Heat Up the Senate Labor Law Reform Battle," *National Journal*, 10 (June 3, 1978), 884.

significant when a coalition of organizations encompasses a wide variety of special interests. An example of this combined lobbying power occurred in 1977 when a coalition of interest groups formed to defeat the Energy Transportation Security Act.[16] This piece of proposed legislation, popularly known as the Cargo Preference Bill, was an especially important proposal to the labor unions. The act, if passed, would have required that a certain percentage of all oil imported to the United States be carried in United States owned and operated ships. Leading the fight in support of the bill were the maritime unions, backed by assistance from organized labor generally and the U.S. shipping industry. Opposing the legislation was a broad-based coalition of interest groups, some of whom found themselves on the same side of a legislative issue for the first time in many years. Leading the opposition was the business community, represented primarily by the U.S. Chamber of Commerce and the oil companies. Also participating were certain public interest groups, such as the good-government-oriented League of Women Voters, Ralph Nader's Congress Watch, and Common Cause, along with several environmental groups and farm organizations. The strength of the coalition was in its diversity. Each group had special allies in Congress which the others did not. For example, the Chamber of Commerce concentrated its efforts on business-oriented Republican legislators. The League of Women Voters, Congress Watch, and Common Cause were able to focus on the liberal/reform-oriented representatives. Petroleum representatives relied on their strength with the delegates from the oil-producing states. Agricultural organizations lobbied the farm belt legislators, and the environmental interests contacted representatives with whom they had successfully dealt in the past. In addition, each of these groups was able to generate grass-roots activity within their own special memberships. The result was that the coalition against the Cargo Preference Bill covered a tremendously large number of members of Congress. Only those legislators who were staunch labor supporters or who had large shipping interests in their home constituencies were relatively immune from the coalition's efforts, and the bill was defeated. Although the members of the coalition had succeeded, the very construction of the alliance determined that it was to be a short-lived cooperative effort. The interests represented were simply too diverse to permit more than a single joint effort. The long-range objectives of the oil and environmental groups or the U.S. Chamber of Commerce and Ralph Nader's organizations, for example, conflicted too greatly to expect anything more than a single mutual effort.

If united efforts can bring success, it is conversely true that division within a particular class of pressure group can mean difficulties for the special interests involved. An illustration is provided by lobby organizations representing the hospital industry.[17] While one might expect the hospital industry to be represented by a

---

[16] *Congressional Quarterly Weekly Report*, 35 (October 1, 1977), 2071-2073; *Congressional Quarterly Weekly Report*, 35 (October 22, 1977), 2223-2224, 2270.

[17] See John K. Iglehart, "The Hospital Lobby is Suffering from Self-Inflicted Wounds," *National Journal*, 9 (October 1, 1977), 1526-1531.

single interest group, it is actually represented by several different lobby organizations. Eight are particularly significant: the American Hospital Association, Federation of American Hospitals, National Council of Community Hospitals, American Protestant Hospital Association, Catholic Hospital Association, Association of American Medical Colleges' Council of Teaching Hospitals, American Osteopathic Hospital Association, and the National Association of Private Psychiatric Hospitals. While each of these groups represents hospitals and their operators, they attract the support of different segments of the hospital industry. Memberships differ by profit vs. nonprofit status, religious affiliation, state vs. private ownership, and type of health care delivered. During the 1970s, the federal government was particularly concerned with the status of American medical care. The rising cost of hospital services was one of the primary areas of study by Congress and was of particular interest to liberal Democratic members. The hospital lobby, however, has been unable to unite in response to the various health care proposals introduced in the federal legislature. Because the industry itself has suffered division, the hospital associations sometimes have been unable to provide effective representation for their memberships.

The politics of interest group alliances is one of the most significant aspects of the legislative process. Temporary or semipermanent coalitions can be powerful forces, especially because they may well include legislators and members of the executive branch who may support the coalition's objectives. Frequently, interest group politics takes the form of conflicts between pressure group coalitions rather than individual special interest organizations. This is particularly true when the issues at stake are controversial or have a potentially widespread impact.

Interest Groups, Lobbyists and Legislative Politics

Interest groups and their lobbyist representatives are a fixed part of the legislative process. In one form or another, they have been part of the American legislative system from its very beginning. Constitutional guarantees of freedom of speech, assembly and petition insure that we will always have interest groups and lobbyists as part of the law-making process.

The presence of special interest groups in the national legislature should not be considered a particularly dangerous phenomenon. While lobbyists occasionally violate the law or otherwise cause legislative scandals to occur, these incidents are relatively rare given the number of lobbying activities that take place. Popular notions of interest groups that instruct their lobbyists to promote group goals among congressmen by staging lavish parties, distributing bribes, and providing female companionship are grossly exaggerated. While these indiscretions may take place on occasion, they are not the standard political format. Instead, lobbying can be considered a professional practice with an informal code of ethics similar to that of other professions. Most lobbyists are engaged in the legitimate articulation of group concerns before the legislative apparatus.

Members of the legislature generally have favorable attitudes toward interest groups and lobbyists. Relatively few representatives can be said to have distinctly negative views toward interest group participation in the legislative process.[18] Since the range of interests represented by pressure groups has expanded so rapidly over the past several years, few members of Congress now find themselves totally without interest group support for legislation in which they have a particular interest. Furthermore, representatives realize the contributions which interest groups regularly make to the legislative process. Interest groups are one of the primary sources of information available to legislators. A group's lobbyist may be one of the leading experts on the subject matter with which the group is concerned. With Congress generally needing more research and a larger investigative staff than it has at its command, the information provided by lobby organizations is often quite important. Of course, legislators must take into account the origin of the information and should perhaps consult more than one source to insure objectivity, but the fact remains that interest group research assists members of Congress in evaluating proposed legislation. Special interest groups also provide assistance in the drafting of bills, the planning of legislative strategy, and other activities of a representative's concern.

Perhaps most importantly, interest groups provide a link between the people and the national legislature. When an interest group's representatives contact members of Congress, they are speaking in behalf of a segment of the citizenry. The legislator is receiving a report on the feelings of a portion of the American people. Under a representative form of government, this is an especially important function. The opinions expressed by interest groups, as we have noted previously, are not representative of the American people generally, but only reflect the views of a given segment of the American society. In spite of this fact, interest group politics is an integral part of a system that allows the people to express their views to the lawmakers.

LOBBYING THE EXECUTIVE BRANCH

During the last forty years, there has been a significant increase in interest group activities pertaining to the executive branch of government. This growing attention on the nation's bureaucratic structure has occurred in response to the expanding role played by administrative agencies in America's system of governing. The administrative wing of the government no longer can be considered a group of civil servants whose job is simply to execute the laws passed by Congress. The bureaucracy today wields tremendous power and is involved in many more activities than in generations past.

The executive branch has become a major participant in the legislative process. The president today is expected to submit and promote legislative proposals. The nation and the Congress as well look to the president to supply a degree of legislative

[18] See Roger H. Davidson, *The Role of the Congressman* (New York: Pegasus, 1969).

leadership. Many of the proposals that are approved by the chief executive originate in the various bureaucratic agencies. It is important for interest groups to maintain contact with the executive agencies in order to have an input during the stage at which agencies begin to formulate legislative proposals.

Because of the complexity of American society, the legislature has granted increasing amounts of discretion to the administrative branch of government. It is now customary for the legislature to pass general laws and to allow the administrative bureaus to "fill in the gaps" in the law through the administrative process. Often the application of the law can be as important as the law itself. For this reason, pressure organizations have expanded their administrative lobbying efforts, insuring that they are given an opportunity to voice their opinions on matters related to the execution of congressionally passed laws.

The bureaucracy has also become one of the most significant sources of regulation. Numerous federal agencies have rule-making powers which permit the regulation of various segments of American society. Some of these agencies are incorporated into the political departments of the executive branch, while others have been established as independent regulatory agencies. These agencies annually enact more legislation (in the form of administrative regulations) than Congress passes through the legislative process. These regulatory acts often affect millions of dollars of economic assets as well as the way Americans conduct their daily lives. Because of the significant power of the federal regulators, interest groups have been active in lobbying efforts designed to influence agency decision making.

Lobbying the executive branch carries with it far fewer legal restrictions than attempts to influence the legislative branch. The 1946 Federal Regulation of Lobbying Act dealt only with Congress and had no applicability to interest group relations with the president or his administration. Those who lobby the bureaucracy are free from the registration and disclosure requirements imposed on persons involved in congressional lobbying. Those interested in reforming the lobby regulation laws have given a high priority to extending disclosure requirements to executive branch lobbying. Thus far, however, these reformist efforts have been unsuccessful.

The absence of registration requirements has resulted in a lack of systematic research on administrative lobbyists. We do know, however, that this brand of lobbying has existed for a long period of time and that it has been increasing over the past several decades commensurate with the growth in bureaucratic power. We also know that the economic interest groups have been extremely active in executive branch lobbying for many years and that they have expanded their efforts in this area. Furthermore, the economic pressure groups have been quite successful at influencing the policy made by agency personnel. Public interest groups, on the other hand, have had a general lack of success in dealing with the administrative agencies, and this has prompted the public interest lobbies to concentrate their efforts on the legislative and judicial branches.[19]

[19] Peter Woll, *American Bureaucracy*, 2nd ed. (New York: W. W. Norton, 1977), p. 202.

For an interest group to conduct a successful lobbying campaign to influence the government, the executive branch surely cannot be ignored. In many instances the administration is a much more important cog in the nation's policy-making wheel than is the legislature. The executive branch initiates policy proposals, administers the policy once enacted by Congress, applies the policy in concrete situations, and makes the rules which give the policy force and meaning. Unless an interest group is successful at convincing the executive branch to pursue activities acceptable to the organization, a victory in the halls of Congress can be a very shallow one indeed.

Interest Groups and the President

The president, as head of the federal executive branch, makes major policy decisions and sets priorities for the national bureaucracy. Executive proposals for changes in administrative structures, creation of new programs, development of new procedures, and funding of government activities must receive the support of the president before being referred to Congress for legislative action. The president is relied upon for supplying policy leadership, and his recommendations on matters of public policy are the most important to be considered by Congress. In recent decades the Congress has increasingly become a reactor to administrative proposals for legislation rather than developing policy initiation capabilities of its own. This has been especially true with respect to policies dealing with major national problems.

The modern presidency includes a number of advisory groups and staffs tied directly to the president. The White House staff, for example, is a key advisory group. Other influential groups are the Council of Economic Advisers, the National Security Council, and the Office of Management and Budget. These advisory groups, as well as others within the Executive Office of the President, are responsible for assisting the president in determining administration policy.

Interest group access to the president and his close advisers is fairly limited. The President himself has far too many demands upon his time and resources to allow interest groups regular access, and relatively few interest group leaders are in a position to make demands on a president's time. Occasionally an interest group that was instrumental in the president's election campaign will lay claim to White House access. Labor and civil rights leaders, for example, argued that they deserved such special contact rights following the election of Democratic candidate Jimmy Carter in 1976. However, even such specially privileged groups are not allowed access at will. Direct communications between the president and interest groups are usually initiated by the president.[20] Often such communications are instituted when the president is displeased with the policies of certain interests, such as when the steel industry increases prices to the extent that the president fears an escalation of the inflationary cycle.

[20] Greenwald, *Group Power*, p. 215.

In spite of the fact that access to the president is carefully controlled, provisions are usually made for significant interest groups to have special contacts within the White House staff. Members of the presidential staff are often assigned special liaison responsibilities with various interest groups. For example, one member of the staff may specialize in maintaining relations with the business community, while others work with civil rights groups, agricultural organizations, big city mayors, labor unions, and women's organizations. This system allows a certain degree of contact between the president's office and the interest group community.

Another point of access to the president which is employed regularly by interest groups is the advisory committee system.[21] In recent years, presidents have appointed committees to advise the executive branch on special concerns such as health, the status of women, environmental quality, juvenile delinquency, and a host of other subjects. Estimates have claimed that some three thousand such advisory panels are scattered throughout the executive branch. Many have been created by federal law, but most have been instituted by the president or his administrative officials. These committees advise the executive branch about current and potential problems and suggest possible solutions to these problems. Members of the commissions are normally public citizens rather than office holders. Interest groups, however, have been very adept at urging the creation of special advisory committees that might aid their causes as well as at maneuvering to have interest group members appointed to the commissions. These panels do not have a great deal of influence over public policy, but they do allow interests to have a means of expressing their concerns in the upper levels of the executive hierarchy.

One of the responsibilities of the president which is important to all interest groups is the appointment of administrative personnel. As the chief administrator of the federal bureaucracy, the president is empowered to make some twenty-five hundred top appointments to federal office. These appointments range from his own close advisers and heads of the major cabinet positions to less powerful political positions in the various departments of government. Because these appointments determine who will administer the individual governmental programs relevant to specific pressure organizations, interest groups have long been active in promoting acceptable people and opposing those whom they believe are unqualified to serve. Interest organizations are particularly desirous of presidential appointees who are committed to the federal programs that are beneficial to group members. Securing good appointments is a major interest group strategy.[22]

In making key appointments, the president will often consult important interest group officials to determine their feelings on potential nominees, especially when the interest group has played a substantial role in the election of the president. Several cabinet level positions have become closely associated with certain interest

[21] Greenwald, *Group Power*, p. 221-225.
[22] L. Harmon Zeigler and G. Wayne Peak, *Interest Groups in American Society*, 2nd ed. (Englewood Cliffs, N.J.: Prentice-Hall, Inc., 1972), pp. 168-174.

organizations, and it has become traditional for these groups to have a major voice in the selection of these department secretaries. Appointments for the Departments of Transportation, Labor, Commerce, and Agriculture are examples of nominations that are subject to interest group acceptability. How much influence an interest has often depends upon which political party controls the White House. Traditionally, the Democrats have given organized labor almost veto power over the selection of a secretary of labor, whereas under Republican administrations, labor has much less influence. If the interest group does not support the president's choice, representatives of the organization may oppose the confirmation of the appointment during Senate investigations of the nominee. For example, certain civil rights groups expressed displeasure at President Carter's appointment of Griffin Bell as attorney general of the United States, and some agricultural interest groups protested President Nixon's designation of Earl Butz as secretary of agriculture because he was associated with agri-business economic concerns. If a coalition of interest groups can mount a substantial campaign against a nominee, Senate rejection of the president's choice is possible, if not probable.

Interest groups, therefore, have an opportunity to express their concerns at the presidential level. However, lobbying politics at this level is distinctly different from legislative lobbying. The opportunities for direct contact with influential members of the executive branch at the presidential level are far more limited than at the congressional level. Interest groups may occasionally be successful at the presidential level, but the politics are much more difficult than attempting to influence other agencies of government.

Interest Groups and the Administrative Departments

Much of interest group lobbying of the executive branch concentrates on the various administrative departments. In the federal government there are now approximately two thousand departments, agencies, offices, and commissions with administrative responsibilities. Each of these agencies provides a point of access at which an interest group is able to articulate its particular opinions and concerns. Pressure organizations have well-developed methods of presenting their positions to these departments, particularly before those agencies with jurisdiction over subject areas of special concern to the individual interest group.

Federal agencies range in size from the mammoth Department of Health, Education, and Welfare, which administers several hundred government programs, to many tiny offices with relatively limited jurisdictions. While the power and prestige of the various administrative departments may vary considerably, each has a certain authority and may be significant to special interest groups. These administrative divisions have numerous powers. First, they are assigned the responsibility of executing congressionally authorized government programs. Second, they develop proposals for policy changes and legislative proposals which have special relevance to their area of jurisdiction. Third, they are engaged in developing program support from governmental and nongovernmental sources, especially among those segments of society affected by the programs. Fourth, they are engaged in research projects and evaluation studies of the policy areas in which they work. In each of these areas of activity, an administrative agency is capable of taking actions that may affect interest groups operating within the agency's policy sphere. This situation makes it almost mandatory for interest groups to engage in lobbying at the administrative agency level.

The activities of interest groups relative to administrative departments begin even before the agency is officially created. The history of many agencies indicates that it is the agitation of interest groups which often leads to the institution of executive departments.[23] When the pressure organizations in a given area of activity perceive a need for government involvement, they will commonly propose the establishment of a federal department to administer a particular government program to cope with the problem area. In recent years, for example, the consumer-oriented interest groups have lobbied heavily for the creation of a national consumer agency which would have the authority to take action in support of the interests of the American consumer. Similarly, it has been the goal of several feminist pressure groups to influence Congress to establish a cabinet level department dealing with the status of American women.

Once established, an administrative department may become closely associated with the interest groups that worked for its creation. The agency and the interest groups operating within its jurisdiction become bound together by mutual concerns and cooperative efforts and often work together on an almost daily basis. Cooperative efforts are quite frequently mutually beneficial undertakings. The interest groups affected by the agency are particularly committed to developing the best possible relationships with it. By maintaining access to officials of the department, the group is assured of a hearing when significant issues come before the agency. Furthermore, the interest group is able to present its views to the agency on how it feels a federal program might best be administered and what changes might be instituted to improve the effectiveness of the government activity. In order to establish and maintain such access, the interest group may provide various services for the agency. Pressure organizations have commonly provided research efforts, staff assistance, and political support. It is not unusual to find interest groups engaged in lobbying for programs favored by the agency, not only because the group may support the program, but also in order to establish good relationships with the agency.[24] Some interest groups become so closely attached to government administrative agencies that the distinction between the two begins to blur. An example of such a condition exists in the relationship between the Depart-

[23] Francis E. Rourke, *Bureaucracy, Politics and Public Policy*, 2nd ed. (Boston: Little, Brown and Company, 1976), p. 1-2.

[24] Randall B. Ripley, *American National Government and Public Policy* (New York: Free Press, 1974), pp. 99-100.

ment of Agriculture (particularly its agricultural extension service) and the American Farm Bureau Federation.

Most agencies have natural constituent clientele groups. For example, the Department of Commerce is closely associated with such groups as the U.S. Chamber of Commerce, the National Association of Manufacturers, and other representatives of private business. The Bureau of Mines and the coal industry have a long history of cooperation. The American Legion is almost synonymous with the Veteran's Administration, as is the Department of Labor and the organized unions. The administration of certain agricultural stabilization programs inside the Department of Agriculture have been closely linked with interest groups representing producers of specific commodities.

Administrative departments of government often become closely linked to certain special interest groups that can provide them with political support. The power of a government agency frequently depends upon the amount of support provided by its associated interest groups. If an agency is strongly backed by a powerful interest group, the agency will normally fare well in intra-executive branch politics as well as with the legislature.[25] Occasionally an interest group will campaign for a program which it particularly favors but is restrained from promoting because higher level administrators or perhaps the president himself does not support the program.[26] The agency may welcome interest group lobbying because it may contribute political support and administrative services. Some administrative departments, however, do not enjoy the support of powerful clientele organizations which may be enlisted to support the agency's interests. The clientele of the United States Bureau of Prisons, for example, are those persons incarcerated in federal penitentiaries. The support of convicts is obviously not the kind of clientele strength that can be converted into political or administrative power.[27] Similar problems face agencies that lose the support of their clientele groups, such as the Bureau of Indian Affairs which has largely been repudiated by major Indian organizations.

Because the success of a department may be dependent upon the amount of support it receives from its clientele groups, an agency will often pursue a strategy of identifying its clientele, developing services for the clientele, and then gradually expanding its clientele groups. The danger involved in this mode of operation is that the agency may well become "captured" by its clientele interest groups. The tendency for an interest group to assume a degree of control over the administrative agency becomes greatest when the agency has only a single interest constituency.[28] The Department of Labor and the Veterans Administration are examples of government agencies which verge on being dominated by the interest groups they serve. In

[25] Ripley, *American National Government and Public Policy*, p. 98.
[26] Rourke, *Bureaucracy, Politics and Public Policy*, p. 18.
[27] Aaron Wildavsky, *The Politics of the Budgetary Process*, 2nd ed. (Boston: Little, Brown and Company, 1974), p. 65.
[28] Rourke, *Bureaucracy, Politics and Public Policy*, p. 52.

such instances, the interest group has such open access that it has almost become a part of the government.

Interest Groups and the Regulatory Agencies

In addition to administrative agencies that have responsibility for managing federal programs, the bureaucracy includes certain departments that are empowered to formulate and apply government regulations. These agencies normally have jurisdiction over a specific kind of economic activity. The regulations are designed to promote competition, protect certain segments of the economy, and insure consumers, workers, and others against exploitation by powerful economic concerns.

At the present time, approximately 100 federal agencies have significant regulatory power. These agencies are found in two specific varieties. First, approximately one-fifth of the regulatory bodies are independent of the larger administrative departments. As such, they are intended to be less susceptible to political influence. The members of these regulatory commissions are appointed by the president and confirmed by the Senate. Officials have specific terms, established on a staggered basis so that no president will be able to appoint a majority of the commissioners during any one presidential term. The first of these agencies was the Interstate Commerce Commission, established in 1887 to regulate the railroad industry in the public interest. Other agencies, such as the Federal Communications Commission, Civil Aeronautics Board, Federal Trade Commission, and the Securities and Exchange Commission, are independent regulatory bodies with great amounts of power to regulate specific industries and activities.

The second variety of regulatory agency is established as part of the structure of a major administrative department. As such, these agencies are under a greater degree of control by the president and his administration. Examples of these agencies are the Department of Health, Education, and Welfare's Food and Drug Administration, the Department of Transportation's Federal Aviation Administration, the Commerce Department's Maritime Administration, and the Labor Department's Occupational Safety and Health Administration.

The regulatory agencies were established by Congress to assist in the implementation of national public policy standards. In each case, Congress enacted legislation that established policy goals and broad standards. The regulatory agencies were created to interpret and implement the congressionally established policy goals. The agency mechanism is used so that Congress does not have to devote its resources to writing detailed legislation covering economic activities in which it has little expertise. The national legislature sets broad standards for these various industries and assigns the detailed regulations to an agency that can devote itself to the specific industry or activity falling under its jurisdiction.

The regulatory agencies wield tremendous power. While theoretically they are given responsibility to "fill in the gaps" in congressionally enacted legislation, their impact is much greater. These agencies taken as a whole regulate huge segments of American society. The regulations passed have staggering economic consequences. The Food and Drug Administration, for example, is entrusted with licensing every drug before it can be sold on the market. The FDA, therefore, holds enormous power over the pharmaceutical companies since the granting of such a license can mean millions of dollars in sales to a company. The Federal Communications Commission determines who will operate radio and television stations and what standards must be followed in the broadcast industry. The Occupational Safety and Health Administration establishes standards for employee safety. Compliance with a simple regulation handed down by the OSHA can cost industry millions of dollars. The Consumer Product Safety Commission has the power to ban the sale of products which it finds to be in violation of federal safety regulations, which the Commission itself has the authority to impose. Forcing withdrawal of a product from the market may cost a corporation millions of dollars. Each of these agencies and the many other similar ones are established to regulate in the public interest and in accordance with the broad standards set by Congress. Yet these commissions have immense power over interest groups, especially economic pressure organizations. It should not be surprising, therefore, that interest groups have been active in lobbying efforts directed at these regulatory powers.[29]

Lobbying the regulatory agencies is similar to lobbying the administrative agencies. Pressure organizations concentrate on those regulatory bodies which have the authority to issue rules applicable to interest group members. Therefore, securities interests focus upon the Securities and Exchange Commission, broadcasters on the Federal Communications Commission, and the highway lobby on the Federal Highway Administration. Interest groups with very broad areas of concern may be required to conduct lobbying efforts on several different regulatory agencies. Organized labor, for example, has an interest in the rulings of the National Labor Relations Board, the Occupational Safety and Health Administration, the Bureau of Employment Security, and several other agencies dealing with areas of jurisdiction of interest to working Americans.

Lobbying the regulatory agencies occurs in both informal and formal settings. Representatives of groups affected by the regulating industry engage in a wide variety of activities designed to achieve and maintain access to regulatory personnel. These informal contacts may occur at social gatherings, industry-wide conventions which both the regulated and the regulators customarily attend, or during visits by group lobbyists to the offices of the members or staff of the regulating body. During such informal contacts, the generally accepted rules of conduct do not permit the discussion of specific cases pending before the agencies, but wide-ranging discussions about the regulated industry are common. For the most part, these contacts are designed not to influence specific matters before the commissions, but only to insure that the relationships between the interest group and the regulating

[29] Louis M. Kohlmeier, Jr., *The Regulators* (New York: Harper and Row, 1969).

agency are as friendly as possible. Such efforts are an investment in successful future dealings with the agency when significant issues are to be decided.

Another form of contact between interest group representatives and the regulating agencies occurs when the regulating commission holds nonpublic meetings to discuss specific cases or policy issues. Normally these meetings are relatively small and generally deal with rather insignificant cases. A form of informal adjudication, these meetings often dispose of minor complaints against the regulated groups for infractions of agency-imposed rules. Kohlmeier reports that some 100,000 items of business are disposed of each year by regulatory agencies using this informal procedure.[30] Similar meetings are often held when a regulating agency is considering the adoption of industry-wide regulations, in order for the commission to receive some preliminary input from the affected interests. During these informal meetings, the pressure groups representing the regulated industries have ample opportunity to articulate the positions of their organizations.

The regulatory agencies also conduct formal, public hearings. The 1946 Administrative Procedure Act imposes due process of law standards on important decision making by the regulatory agencies. The law requires the agencies to provide formal notice of all proposed regulations prior to their imposition. The act further mandates that formal hearings be held before the regulating agency enacts the proposed rules. All parties who wish to express their views regarding a proposed regulation have the right to be heard. Interest group representatives commonly exercise this right. When a regulation proposal is announced, it is standard practice for a large number of group lobbyists to present their organization's views on the proposal. These hearings provide the regulated interests with the opportunity to make formal presentations of their group's position, to submit the results of research efforts having relevance to the rule proposals, and to argue for acceptance, modification, or rejection of the regulation. While these hearings are important as a means of allowing full participation by those affected by the regulating agencies' actions, they have been criticized for permitting the regulated groups to delay the adoption of reasonable reforms in regulatory laws. The Administrative Procedure Act has also had the consequence of causing the regulatory commissions to proceed much more like a judicial tribunal than an administrative agency. This is particularly the case when a commission is considering charges that a regulated entity has engaged in major infractions of the agency's rules.

The regulatory agencies, then, are important points of access for interest groups. These agencies wield substantial power. They set national public policies relative to the economic activities under their jurisdiction. Their decisions affect billions of dollars in economic resources each year and significantly alter the lives of millions of people. Given these powers, it is not surprising that interest groups devote substantial efforts to influencing regulatory agency decisions.

[30] Kohlmeier, *The Regulators*, ch. 6.

Lobbyists and the Executive Branch

Although some lobbyists engage in both legislative and executive branch influence attempts, there are important differences between those interest group representatives who specialize in lobbying Congress and those who concentrate on the administrative arm of the federal government. Two characteristics of those lobbyists who represent clients before the executive branch are particularly worthy of mention here. First, interest groups tend to rely more on Washington-based law firms to represent them before the bureaucracy than they do in attempting to influence Congress. Second, many of the lobbyists representing private organizations were formerly officials in the executive branch and administered programs and imposed regulations on the very interests now employing them.

Many law firms in Washington specialize in practicing before the agencies of the federal government. Several large law firms, based in the nation's capitol, have developed reputations for producing spectacular results for their clients.[31] The lists of clients purchasing the services of these prestigious lawyers include many of the most significant economic interest groups. In representing such clients before administrative and regulatory agencies, the lawyers are acting as lobbyists through the practice of law. The more well known law firms specializing in this variety of practice, such as Covington and Burling, and Arnold and Porter, have not only legal connections which make them effective as attorneys, but also well-developed political contacts which provide them with access to individuals who wield governmental power. For this reason such lawyers are well equipped to represent interest group clients before the various governmental agencies.

In recent years there has been a large increase in the number of small law firms that have been established in Washington for the primary purpose of representing clients before specific governmental agencies.[32] The clients of these newer firms are quite often economic interests which need a spokesman to articulate their interests before specialized bureaucratic offices. A law firm, for example, may develop a specialization in communications law. Such a firm would often represent broadcast media clients before such government agencies as the Federal Communications Commission. Other specialized law firms might concentrate their efforts on the Food and Drug Administration and represent the pharmaceutical industry. These narrowly focused firms are often quite successful in behalf of their clients because they specialize in a particular bureaucratic agency and in a specific area of the law. Therefore, they have expertise over the legal regulations applicable to the field and are well versed in the intricacies of the special governmental agency that has responsibility over the relevant area of regulation.

The use of lawyers as lobbyists before the executive branch has increased with the dramatic rise in importance of administrative law. With government

---

[31] Joseph C. Goulden, *The Superlawyers* (New York: David McKay, 1972).

[32] James W. Singer, "Practicing Law in Washington—An American Growth Industry," *National Journal*, 10 (February 4, 1978), 172-179.

agencies now issuing far more regulations each year than Congress passes laws, interest groups must be represented by persons skilled in the administrative law field. Not only do the agencies have the power to write and impose regulations, but they also have the power to find persons and businesses in violation of those regulations. As such, the modern administrative and regulatory agency combines the legislative, executive, and judicial functions. The best representative to handle an organization's dealings with such agencies is often an attorney specializing in this rather unique variety of political/legal practice.

Interest group representatives who practice before the executive branch have often been described as participating in a "revolving door" recruitment pattern. This phrase describes the high incidence of former governmental employees who leave public service and take positions with the special interest organizations. Two basic patterns tend to emerge. The first usually involves young attorneys who join the federal government shortly after graduating from law school. While working for a particular governmental agency, they gain experience in the administration and regulation of programs which pertain to a particular kind of economic activity. After spending several years learning an area of regulatory law, these lawyers are often recruited away from the government by the very interests they have been working to regulate. For example, an attorney working for the Securities and Exchange Commission might be attracted by a large salary offer to take a position with a business concern operating in the securities field. His new position may very well include representing the securities industry in cases before the Securities and Exchange Commission. The regulator has become a representative for the regulated. The government has trained a new graduate from law school, only to see that person take his experience and training with him as he begins a new career working against the regulations he once labored to impose. In addition, he is often far more qualified in his new position than the young, recent law school graduate which the government hires to assume his former position. This revolving door pattern often puts the government at a quality and talent disadvantage in its regulatory proceedings against the special interest groups.

A second form of movement from government to private interests has a more political basis. Politically appointed officials in the executive branch often leave their positions with the federal government and assume new positions representing the interests of pressure organizations. This phenomenon occurs in its most dramatic form when there is a change in political party control of the White House, bringing with it a massive termination of relatively high-ranking administrative officials to make room for the new president's political appointees. Many of these officials who have lost their jobs for political reasons affiliate with private businesses or with interest groups who can benefit from their governmental experience. Table 11.3 provides examples of some of those individuals who have made the transition from government service to the service of private interests. The recently enacted Federal Ethics in Government Act, however, seeks to curtail high ranking administrative officials from accepting positions with organizations having dealings with

TABLE 11.3 Examples of Executive Branch Officials Who Have Taken Positions with the Special Interests

Official	Government Position	Special Interest Position
William Ruckelshaus	Administrator, Environmental Protection Agency	Vice President of Weyerhauser Paper Company having environmental regulation responsibilities
Theodore Byers	Director of Compliance Food and Drug Administration Bureau of Drugs	Pharmaceutical corporation employee
Dean Burch	Chairman, Federal Communications Commission	Washington lawyer specializing in communications law
James Needham	Securities and Exchange Commission	New York Stock Exchange
Alan Boyd	Secretary of Transportation	Illinois Central Railroad
Hamer Budge	Securities and Exchange Commission	President, Investor's Diversified Services
Clarence Palmby	Assistant Secretary of Agriculture	Vice President, Continental Grain Company
Nicholas Katzenbach	Attorney General	International Business Machines Corporation, having antitrust responsibilities
William Doub	Atomic Energy Commission	Lawyer in private practice specializing in nuclear regulatory law
Carl Bagge	Federal Power Commission	President, National Coal Association

Source: William J. Lanouette, "The Revolving Door—It's Tricky to Try to Stop It," *National Journal,* 9 (November 19, 1977), 1796-1803.

the government. The impact of this legislation, which became effective in July of 1979, is not yet certain. The revolving door, of course, also swings from the private interest groups to government employment, although such transitions are less frequent. President Carter's Secretary of Health, Education, and Welfare, Joseph Califano, for example, was formerly a lawyer representing the interests of drug companies before the administrative and regulatory agencies of the federal government.

Lobbying the executive branch completes the triangle between the interest groups, Congress, and the bureaucracy. Frequently, public policy is determined by negotiations which occur between bureau leaders, committee leaders, and interest group officials.[33] Through the development of consensus and agreement, these key

---

[33] Lewis C. Mainzer, *Political Bureaucracy* (Glenview, Illinois: Scott, Foresman and Company, 1973).

actors in the policy-making process work out responses to national problems which are acceptable to those participating.

LOBBYING THE JUDICIAL BRANCH

The judicial branch of the government, like the legislative and executive departments, has significant powers to affect the distribution of political and economic resources in our society. The courts are entrusted with the responsibility of interpreting the Constitution and determining the meaning and validity of laws passed by the legislature and the executive agencies. In handing down its rulings, the judicial branch delineates the legitimate bounds of government power, protects legal rights, and settles disputes which may involve millions of dollars in economic assets. Obviously, the decisions of the courts can significantly affect the interests of pressure group members. For this reason, the nation's interest groups allocate a substantial portion of their lobbying resources to attempts to influence the judicial branch.

The judicial branch, however, differs substantially from the legislative and executive agencies of government and requires lobbying efforts that are different from those used to influence the political branches.[34] Judges are expected to remain objective and relatively free from overt influence attempts. Direct access to federal judges is not normally considered acceptable behavior. Lobbyists for the business community, for example, cannot make an appointment with a judge to urge him to interpret the antitrust laws in a manner favorable to the nation's large corporations. Such direct contacts would be permissible in dealing with members of Congress and most administrative officials, but the judiciary has been constructed to remain relatively isolated from such blatant influence attempts.

The tactics used by interest groups in efforts to gain favorable policy outcomes from the judiciary include:

1. attempting to influence the selection process so that those staffing the courts are open to the positions advocated by the interest group;
2. participating as a "friend of the court" by supplying judges with formal legal arguments pertaining to pending cases; and
3. sponsoring court cases and supporting litigants in disputes that involve policies affecting members of the interest group.[35]

In carrying out these strategies, the interest groups normally rely on attorneys to act as "legal lobbyists." The pressure organization may use its own legal counsel

---

[34] See, for example, Clement E. Vose, "Litigation as a Form of Pressure Group Activity," *Annals of the American Academy of Political and Social Science,* 319 (September, 1958), 20-31; Nathan Hakman, "Lobbying the Supreme Court," in *The Federal Judicial System,* ed. Thomas P. Jahnige and Sheldon Goldman (New York: Holt, Rinehart and Winston, 1968), pp. 39-53.

[35] Ripley, *American Government and Public Policy,* pp. 100-101.

or may purchase the services of a law firm specializing in the field of law of interest to the group.[36]

Interest Group Use of the Courts

Not all interest groups use the courts as a method of attaining organizational objectives. Some pressure groups devote considerable resources to judicial lobbying, whereas others prefer to concentrate on the more traditional forms of executive and legislative branch influence activities. Using the courts as a method of gaining favorable public policy is a particularly good strategy for interest groups that lack political clout. Groups with small memberships, relatively low levels of economic influence, and generally unpopular causes often find the courts to be the most accessible branch of the government. An interest group need not convince the judiciary that it represents millions of votes or billions of dollars in economic assets to have the government hear its claims. All the interest group needs is a valid legal dispute and sufficient funds to support the attorneys who present the group's position. Often the courts are used as a last resort by groups that are defeated by more powerful interests in the legislative and executive branches. The National Association for the Advancement of Colored People, for example, developed highly successful judicial lobbying techniques because for many years the political branches of the government had turned a deaf ear to civil rights group demands.

Courts offer greater possibilities of success for those groups who wish to stop or delay the execution of a public policy than for those organizations that wish to see innovative policies adopted.[37] The judiciary is often seen by an interest group as providing protection from abuses by the other branches of the political system. An interesting example is provided by the legal victory won by a coalition of environmental groups in 1978 which culminated in the judiciary blocking the construction of a large multipurpose dam on the Little Tennessee River. Environmental interests had lost battles in Congress and the executive branch to halt construction activities on hydroelectric and floor control dams that might damage unique ecological settings and animal habitats. One of the federally funded projects of great concern to the environmentalists was the Tellico Dam on which construction had begun in 1967. The Friends of the Earth and other environmental organizations took their cause to court, hoping that the judicial system would order an end to the construction activities where Congress and the executive branch had failed to do so. The basis of their petition to the courts was that the Little Tennessee River was the home of a three-inch, tan-colored fish known as the snail darter. This member of the perch family was unknown to scientists until it was discovered in 1973, six years after construction of the dam had begun. There was ample evidence that completion of the dam would eliminate the only known habitat of the snail darter,

---

[36] For a discussion of group advocate attorneys, see Jonathan Casper, *Lawyers before the Warren Court* (Urbana, Illinois: University of Illinois Press, 1972).

[37] Herbert Jacob, *Justice in America*, 3rd ed. (Boston: Little, Brown and Company, 1978), p. 138.

TABLE 11.4 Interest Groups Active in Lobbying the Judicial Branch

Organization	Interest Advocated
American Bar Association	The legal profession; the administration of justice and legal reform
American Civil Liberties Union	Civil rights and civil liberties
AFL-CIO	Rights of labor unions and union members
American Jewish Congress	Separation of church and state; rights of religious minorities with special attention to the rights of Jewish Americans
American Legion	Veterans' rights; patriotic causes
Common Cause	Election campaign reform
Environmental Defense Fund	Environmental causes
Jehovah's Witnesses	Rights of religious minorities
National Association for the Advancement of Colored People	Civil rights with special attention to the rights of black Americans
Ralph Nader Organizations	Consumer interests
Sierra Club Legal Defense Fund	Environmental causes
Women's Rights Project	Sex discrimination

thus threatening it with extinction. Environmentalists filed suit to stop dam construction on the grounds that the Endangered Species Act prohibited the federal government from engaging in activities that would cause the loss of any species. This dispute between the environmental interest groups and the federal government was ultimately appealed to the United States Supreme Court. In June of 1978, the Court ruled in favor of the interest group position, holding that the Endangered Species Act would be violated if the dam were to continue to completion.[38] Therefore, the Court ordered the construction to stop. The environmental groups were therefore able to use the courts to achieve their desired goal. In this case the ecology organizations obtained a halt to a three-quarters completed dam which had already cost the taxpayers approximately $75 million in order to help preserve a threatened animal species. By using the judicial branch, the interest groups were able to achieve a result not obtainable from the other divisions of government.

Most of the organizations that have traditionally used the courts as a means of governmental lobbying have been reformist-oriented groups. The most conspicuous of these are the civil rights organizations which regularly rely on the judiciary to defend individuals from governmental abuse of constitutionally protected rights. Consumer groups, environmental organizations, religious associations, and labor unions have also frequently sought relief from the nation's judges. Table 11.4

---

[38] *Tennessee Valley Authority* v. *Hill*, 98 S. Ct. 2279 (1978).

outlines some of the organizations most active in lobbying the judicial branch and the basic interests advocated by these interest groups.

Judicial Selection

Interest groups commonly enter the politics of the judiciary by attempting to influence the selection of those persons who will occupy positions in the judiciary. At the federal level, judges are appointed by the president and must be confirmed by the Senate. This division of authority in the judicial selection process provides interest groups several points of access at which to influence the recruitment of judges. First, an interest group can lobby the Justice Department, which is normally entrusted with the responsibility of compiling a list of potential nominees and screening the backgrounds and qualifications of those under serious consideration. Second, a pressure group can attempt to influence the president, who must make the ultimate decision of whom to appoint to the bench. Third, an interested organization can approach the members and staff of the Senate Judiciary Committee, which is given the duty of investigating nominees and making a recommendation to the full Senate regarding confirmation. And fourth, the full Senate membership can be lobbied in an attempt to influence floor action on a nomination.

Interest groups often use all of these opportunities to exert some influence on the selection of federal judges. Obviously, interest groups want judges who will be sympathetic to the demands of the group members. When a vacancy occurs, interest groups often make suggestions to the president, members of the Justice Department, and key senators in an attempt to have influential officeholders seriously consider candidates favorable to the special interests. Once nominated, the pressure organizations can mount full campaigns in support of or in opposition to the nominated individual. The research departments of an interest organization might probe into a nominee's background, qualifications, political record, legal philosophy, and other attributes and make the results of the research known to the Senate. Interest group representatives will often appear before the Senate Judiciary Committee to present the group's position on the nominee. These interest group activities are especially intense when the president fills a vacancy on the United States Supreme Court.

Interest group views on a nominee can have a substantial impact on the nature of person who is finally sworn in as a federal judge. Often the president will consult with key interest group officials to receive an indication of organizational opinions on potential nominees. If the president receives serious negative evaluations, the considered individual may well be dropped from the list of potential nominees. When a president ignores the opposition of significant interest groups, the pressure organizations have been known to block confirmation. The four Supreme Court nominees who have failed to obtain confirmation in this century have all been able to blame a significant portion of their defeat on the actions of special interest groups. In 1930, President Hoover's selection of Judge John Parker of North Carolina was defeated in the Senate largely because of opposition from the labor unions. Justice Abe Fortas' nomination by President Johnson in 1968 was rejected in part because of the activities of a coalition of conservative interest groups. In 1969 and 1970, two Nixon appointees to the Court, Clement Haynsworth of South Carolina and G. Harrold Carswell of Florida, were denied confirmation after bitter attacks by labor unions, civil rights groups, and liberal ideological organizations.[39] It is clear that the views of powerful interest groups, like the labor unions, must be taken into account if the president wishes to have his nominees confirmed by the Senate without significant difficulty.

Of particular importance in the selection of federal judges is the activity of the American Bar Association. The ABA has an established Standing Committee on the Federal Judiciary which has as its primary responsibility the investigation of individuals receiving the consideration of the president for appointment to the federal bench.[40] The ABA committee carries out investigatory procedures into the qualifications of the potential judges. Upon completing this investigation, the committee issues a report to the president and also to the Senate Judiciary Committee, which rates the overall qualification of the individual to be a federal judge. This rating is important because it represents the judgment of the organized bar on the nominee's judicial ability. Presidents normally give the ABA rating considerable weight in deciding if a seriously considered individual is worthy of appointment. Occasionally, presidents have acted contrary to the advice given by the Committee on the Federal Judiciary, but the advice is almost always given a degree of consideration by the president and his advisers. The Senate Judiciary Committee also gives careful consideration to the ABA report. It is often one of the more important pieces of information used by the Senate in evaluating the nominees' fitness for office.

In becoming involved in the judicial selection process, interest groups hope to influence government by securing officeholders who have favorable positions on public policy questions. Interest organizations enter into the judicial recruitment process for the same reasons they become involved in legislative and executive election campaigns and attempt to influence presidential appointments to administrative posts. A public official who is sympathetic to the interests represented by an organization may assist the group in attaining its goals, whether that official sits in Congress, in an executive department, or on the federal bench.

"Friend of the Court" Activities

Interest groups often become aware of important court cases which may have an impact on their members. Although the interest group itself is not directly involved in the litigation as a party to the suit, the organization may still play a role in the decision of the case through *amicus curiae* ("friend of the court") participa-

---

[39] See Richard Harris, *Decision* (New York: E. P. Dutton, 1971).

[40] See Harold W. Chase, *Federal Judges* (Minneapolis: University of Minnesota Press, 1972); Joel Grossman, *Lawyers and Judges* (New York: John Wiley, 1965).

tion. By participating as a "friend of the court," the interest group can provide the members of the court hearing the case with written briefs and, on rare occasions, oral arguments which present the organization's views on the issues about to be decided. When an interest group participates *amicus curiae*, its duty is to provide the court with information or legal arguments which are not being presented by the actual litigants to the suit. Originally, *amicus* participations were designed to be neutral, with their principal purpose being to provide the court with information it would not otherwise have at its disposal. However, over the years *amicus curiae* have evolved into advocacy briefs with interest groups using this opportunity to voice their support of one or the other parties to the suit.[41] Interest group *amicus curiae* briefs often advise the court as to the possible consequences of the various alternatives facing the judges in deciding the case.

Participation as a "friend of the court" is normally restricted to those cases which have broad policy implications. No interest group is likely to devote resources to acting in an *amicus* capacity in a case whose outcome will affect only the litigants themselves. Because of this, "friend of the court" activities are normally found at the appellate level where court decisions have wide-ranging impact and constitute precedents for future court decisions. In theory, any person or organization can participate as a "friend of the court." In practice, however, these activities are confined to interest groups, state governments, and, of course, the federal government. There is no absolute right to engage in *amicus curiae* activities in a specific case. Rules of procedure normally place certain restrictions on such participations. At the Supreme Court level, a private group must receive the permission of all parties to the suit before having the right to proceed as *amicus curiae*. Should the group fail to receive such permission, the Supreme Court itself is empowered to grant the privilege.[42] However, the federal government and the state governments may act as a "friend of the court" without first receiving the permission of the justices. *Amicus curiae* briefs are now common occurrences at the Supreme Court level. In recent years, over half the cases decided by the Supreme Court with full opinions included some form of "friend of the court" activity.[43] Cases with important and far-reaching policy implications often attract substantial interest group activity. Table 11.5 lists the organizations and private individuals who participated in *amicus curiae* activities in the Supreme Court's decision in *Bakke* v. *Regents of the University of California*.[44] The *Bakke* case was a landmark decision in which a white male medical school applicant challenged the constitutionality of a university admissions policy which gave preferential consideration to racial minority

---

[41] Samuel Krislov, "The Amicus Curiae Brief: From Friendship to Advocacy," *Yale Law Journal*, 72 (1963), 694-721.

[42] George C. Piper, "Amicus Curiae Participation–At the Court's Discretion," *Kentucky Law Journal*, 55 (Summer 1967), 864-873.

[43] Jacob, *Justice in America*, p. 38.

[44] 98 S. Ct. 2733 (1978).

TABLE 11.5 Amicus Curiae Briefs Filed by Private Parties in the Case of *Allan Bakke* v. *the Board of Regents of the University of California*

In support of Allan Bakke:

American Federation of Teachers (A.F.L.-C.I.O.)
American Jewish Committee
American Jewish Congress
American Subcontractors Association
Anti-Defamation League of B'nai B'rith
Chamber of Commerce of the U.S.A.
Committee on Academic Nondiscrimination and Integrity
Conference of Pennsylvania State Police Lodges of the Fraternal Order of Police
Council of Supervisors and Administrators of the City of New York
Fraternal Order of Police
Ralph J. Galliano (unsuccessful white applicant to U. of Florida law school)
Hellenic Bar Association of Illinois
Timothy J. Hoy (student of Oberlin, planning to apply to law school this year)
International Conference of Police Associations
International Association of Chiefs of Police
Italian-American Foundation
Jewish Labor Committee
Jewish Rights Council
Mid-American Legal Foundation
National Advocates Society
National Jewish Commission on Law and Public Affairs
National Medical and Dental Association
Order of the Sons of Italy in America
Pacific Legal Foundation
Polish-American Affairs Council
Polish-American Educators Association
Polish American Congress
Queens Jewish Community Council
Ukrainian Congress Committee of America (Chicago Division)
UNICO National
Rep. Henry A. Waxman, Democrat of California
Young Americans for Freedom

In support of the University of California:

American Association of University Professors
American Bar Association
American Civil Liberties Union
American Civil Liberties Union of Northern California
American Civil Liberties Union of Southern California
American Coalition of Citizens with Disabilities
American Medical Student Association
Americans for Democratic Action
American Federation of State, County, and Municipal Employees (A.F.L.-C.I.O.)
American Indian Bar Association
American Indian Law Students Association
American Indian Law Center
American Public Health Association
Asian-American Bar Association of the Greater Bay Area
Aspira of America (national organization of Puerto Rican educators and students)
Association of American Law Schools
Association of American Medical Colleges
Association of Mexican American Educators
Bar Association of San Francisco
Black Law Students Association at U. of California at Berkeley
Black Law Students Union of Yale U. law school
Board of Governors of Rutgers, the State University of New Jersey
Children's Defense Fund
Cleveland State U. chapter of Black American Law Students Association
Columbia University
Council on Legal Education Opportunity
County of Santa Clara, Cal.
Fair Employment Practices Commission of the State of California
GI Forum
Harvard University
Howard University
Image
International Union of Electrical, Radio, and Machine Workers (A.F.L.-C.I.O.)
International Union, United Automobile, Aerospace, and Agricultural Implement Workers of America (U.A.W.)
Japanese American Citizens League

TABLE 11.5 Continued

Jerome A. Lackner, director of California Dep. of Health
La Raza National Lawyers Association
Law School Admissions Council
Lawyers' Committee for Civil Rights Under Law
League of United Latin American Citizens
Legal Services Corp.
Los Angeles County Bar Association
Los Angeles Mecha Central
Mexican American Legal Defense and Education Fund
Mexican-American Political Association
N.A.A.C.P. Legal Defense and Educational Fund
National Association for Equal Opportunity in Higher Education
National Association for the Advancement of Colored People
National Association of Equal Educational Opportunity
National Association of Minority Contractors
National Bar Association
National Council of Churches of Christ in the U.S.A.
National Council of La Raza
National Council of Negro Women
National Education Association
National Health Law Program
National Lawyers' Guild
National Legal Aid and Defender Association
National Employment Law Project
National Fund for Minority Engineering Students
National Medical Association
National Organization for Women
National Urban League
Native American Law Students of the U. of California at Davis
Native American Student Union of the U. of California at Davis
North Carolina Association of Black Lawyers
Puerto Rican Legal Defense and Education Fund
Rutgers Law School Alumni Association
Society of American Law Teachers
Stanford University
State of Washington and University of Washington
Student Bar Association of Rutgers School of Law–Newark
University of Pennsylvania
U.C.L.A. Black Law Students' Association
U.C.L.A. Black Law Alumni Association
Union of Women's Alliance to Gain Equality
Unitas
United Farm Workers of America (A.F.L.-C.I.O.)
United Mine Workers of America
U.S. National Student Association
John Vasconcellos (Democratic member of the California Assembly)
Marion J. Woods, director of California Dept. of Benefit Payments
Young Women's Christian Association

Others

Antioch School of Law–Urges that the case be sent back to lower court for rehearing.
Equal Employment Advisory Council–Urges Court to set guidelines for determining to what extent race or sex-conscious employment decisions are constitutional.
Price M. Cobbs and Ephraim Kahn, representing 22 doctors and medical educators–Takes position that Court should not have agreed to hear case because of inadequate lower court record.
National Association of Affirmative Action Officers–Urges that case be sent back to lower court for rehearing.
National Conference of Black Lawyers–Urges that the case be sent back to lower court for rehearing, but if decision is made, should be for U. of California.

Source: Appeared originally in *The Chronicle of Higher Education.* Copyright 1977 by Editorial Projects for Education, Inc.

candidates. The suit had important significance in the areas of racial discrimination law, affirmative action programs, and professional school admissions procedures. As such, it attracted an unusually large number of interest group *amicus curiae* participants.

Amicus curiae participation offers some important advantages to interest groups who wish to influence the direction of judicial policy making. It provides the pressure group with an opportunity to have an input to the policy-making process without having direct involvement in the case. "Friend of the court" activities are relatively inexpensive forms of lobbying. The cost of participating *amicus curiae* is only a fraction of the expense entailed in direct involvement in a court suit. The major disadvantage of *amicus* participation is that the group has absolutely no influence in the development of the case or the legal strategy employed by the litigants.

Litigation Sponsorship

In order to attain greater control over litigation involving group interests than *amicus curiae* participation permits, interest groups will often become directly involved in court suits. This involvement may take the form of interest group sponsorship and financing of a litigant whose dispute is already underway, or the interest group may seek a potential court suit before an actual dispute arises. In either case, the interest group normally provides the funds and the legal assistance to carry out the litigation. This form of judicial lobbying is more costly than *amicus* participation. If an important case is to be tried and appealed all the way to the United States Supreme Court, it may involve thousands of dollars in legal fees, printing costs, research services, and court expenses. The five court cases which comprised the component parts of the 1954 school segregation decision in *Brown v. Board of Education* cost between $200,000 and $250,000.[45] Similar litigation today would demand even greater funds due to the increases in legal costs and general inflationary trends. In spite of the relatively high costs of this activity, many interest groups find litigation sponsorship to be a reasonable lobbying technique. Only by exercising direct control over a case can an interest group be assured that the arguments and strategy are properly aligned with the interest group's goals.

Normally groups use litigation sponsorship as a means of testing the constitutionality of a particular public policy or of testing the interpretation of a specific law or administrative rule. Because litigation can be very expensive and time consuming, interest groups must exercise great care both in the selection of cases for sponsorship and in the planning and execution of those cases. The organization must find or create a legal dispute that offers a clear-cut presentation of the specific issue upon which the interest group wishes the courts to rule. The party to

---

[45] Stephen Wasby, *The Supreme Court in the Federal Judicial System* (New York: Holt, Rinehart and Winston, 1978), p. 130.

the suit sponsored by the group must meet the requirements of the "standing to sue" doctrine (i.e., having the proper involvement in the dispute in order to bring legal action) and other prerequisites in order to gain access to the courts.[46] Furthermore, the party must be willing to accept interest group control over the case and be generally committed to the policy objectives which the group hopes to obtain through the legal action. In addition, the pressure group must carefully select the jurisdiction in which the case is brought, the courts before which the case will be heard, and the timing of the case. One mistake in the execution of this legal strategy might well mean that the judiciary could avoid the specific issue the group wants litigated or that the group might lose the case in court. Being defeated in this form of interest group politics can be more costly than losing a bid to influence the legislative or executive branches of government. When an interest group fails to convince Congress to adopt a particular law in one session of Congress, the group can always renew its efforts at a later date. However, when an interest group loses an important test case before the United States Supreme Court, a precedent is set by the Court which may be applied in future cases at the Supreme Court and lower court levels. Once such a policy decision is made, it is most difficult to convince the Court to reverse itself.

Given the amount of control an interest group often exerts over a suit which it sponsors, the individual party to the dispute runs the risk of being forgotten. The fact that the pressure group has supplied the attorneys, research, and financial support of the lawsuit can occasionally result in the actual litigant having very little to say in the planning and execution of the case. When this occurs, the suit can no longer be said to belong to the person who may have suffered an injustice, instead, it has become for all practical purposes a vehicle for the interest group to attain its policy goals. It is not uncommon for the interest of the organization to come into conflict with the interests of the individual originally party to the dispute. For example, if a woman is dismissed from her job due to possible sexually discriminatory policies used by her employer, an interest group might come to her defense and sponsor litigation against the employer. The dismissed employee may be hoping to receive economic compensation for her loss of position. The interest group, on the other hand, may look at the suit as a means of prompting the judiciary to issue an important ruling on sex discrimination which can benefit other women in the work force. However, if the employer offers a generous monetary settlement before the courts issue a ruling on the case, a serious conflict may arise between the party to the suit and the sponsoring organization. To the dismissed woman, the monetary settlement is important. She may want to accept it rather than risk the unknowns of a court decision and the lengthy time necessary to litigate the issue. The interest group, on the other hand, may not want to accept the settlement because, for its purposes, it is necessary to obtain a policy ruling the courts. Such conflicts hold the potential of sabotaging an interest group lobbying effort

[46] Karen Orren, "Standing to Sue: Interest Group Conflict in the Federal Courts," *American Political Science Review*, 70 (September 1976), 723-741.

and also carry with them dangers of conflict of interest ethics violations. With well-honed skills for selecting appropriate cases for sponsorship, however, an interest group will avoid such situations before the organization devotes time, effort, and money to the preparation of a legal suit.

For the interest group that perfects this variety of lobbying, the benefits can be substantial. Litigation sponsorship is particularly effective for groups that wish to obtain a declaration of individual rights or to block possibly illegal or unconstitutional public policies. Some of the earliest practitioners of this variety of interest group politics developed well-earned reputations for being able to use the courts to obtain policy decisions beneficial to the group membership. The Jehovah's Witnesses, for example, were very active in litigation sponsorship between 1925 and 1950. During this period, they brought 50 major cases to the United States Supreme Court and were victorious in 45 of those suits. The legal strategies employed resulted in a great expansion of religious civil liberties.[47] The National Association for the Advancement of Colored People provides another example of a group which was able to score major victories in the courts that it was unable to obtain in the legislative or executive arenas. Between 1935 and 1961, current Supreme Court Justice Thurgood Marshall served as counsel for the Legal Defense Fund of the NAACP. During that period, he argued 32 cases before the Supreme Court and won 29, many of them classic decisions in the area of racial discrimination and civil rights law.

SUMMARY

Interest groups allocate substantial resources to activities that involve direct contact with governmental officials. Through the use of employed representatives, known as lobbyists, pressure organizations articulate their concerns directly to governmental decision makers in the legislative, executive and judicial branches. These lobbying activities have traditionally involved the legislature, but with increases in both bureaucratic and judicial power over the past forty years, interest groups have found it necessary to expand influence attempts focused on the administrative agencies and the courts.

Lobbying at the congressional level is regulated by the 1946 Federal Regulation of Lobbying Act which imposes registration and disclosure requirements on those persons whose principal purpose is to influence legislation. The act, however, is riddled with loopholes, and Congress has been attempting to improve the regulation with reform legislation. Lobbyists who concentrate on the legislative branch are very much like the legislators in terms of background and experience. Lobbyists engage in a number of activities, ranging from direct contact with legislators and staff members to testifying before legislative committees. Because of the specializa-

---

[47] Greenwald, *Group Power*, p. 287.

tion which occurs in Congress, interest groups are often able to concentrate their activities on a single committee. Lobbyists commonly engage in cooperative efforts with other interest group representatives when the organizations share legislative goals. These cooperative efforts can be short-lived coalitions of groups which have essentially different long-term goals, or they can be semipermanent alliances of organizations with shared long-term objectives. Lobbying provides information, staff assistance, and legislative ideas to the congressional process. Interest groups are generally viewed in a positive way by legislators.

With the growth in the complexity of American society, the executive branch has expanded its legislative, administrative, and regulatory powers. Congress expects legislative leadership from the president, and those few interest groups with access to the presidential level of the executive branch may have an important advantage in the legislative proposal formation stage. By necessity, access at this level is extremely limited. However, at the administrative and regulatory agency levels, interest groups have very little difficulty gaining access to important offices and commissions which have powers over the interests represented by the pressure groups. Lobby organizations have found that substantial benefits for their membership can be attained through proper relations with the various agencies of the executive branch. Occasionally the interest groups obtain such a degree of influence over the agencies lobbied that the agencies can be said to have been captured by the group. Lobbyists at this level are frequently attorneys specializing in the particular substantive area of the agency's jurisdiction or former employees of the executive branch who had regulatory responsibilities.

Lobbying the judicial branch can be as effective a strategy for an interest group to pursue as attempting to influence the legislative and executive branches. However, lobbying the courts must take a much different form than lobbying the more political branches of government. Interest groups devote their efforts to three major activities relative to the court system. First, they try to influence the judicial selection process in order to attain appointments of individuals who will be favorable to the interests of the respective groups. Second, pressure organizations participate as "friends of the court" by presenting legal arguments to the judiciary in law suits to which they are not a formal party. Third, interest groups sponsor litigation out of which they hope to obtain judicial policies beneficial to their membership.

twelve

Parties, Interest Groups, and American Politics

The American republic functions as a representative democracy. Political leadership is selected through a process of open and free elections. Once in office, the nation's governors are expected to take into account the preferences and opinions of the governed. America has long prided itself on its democratic traditions and its constitutional foundation which hold that the country's sovereignty ultimately rests in the hands of the people. The quality of the nation's leadership and the extent to which the people's views are incorporated into public policy depend to a substantial degree on the nature of public participation in the governmental process.

Americans exercise their participatory birthright in two basic ways. The first includes various acts of *individual political behavior*. The most common of these political activities is voting. In casting a ballot, the American citizen exerts his influence on the political process by designating his preferences among those persons offering themselves for election to positions of public trust. Participation in frequent and competitive elections affords the citizenry the authority to select leaders and to reward or punish those officials who wish to be returned to office. Widespread, intelligent participation in the electoral process is one of the cornerstones of a smoothly functioning representative democracy. Other forms of individual political participation are less institutionalized than the right to vote. They include informal political discussions, writing letters to public officials, and otherwise attempting to make one's views known to fellow citizens and directly to those in public office.

The second basic way in which Americans become involved in their government is through *collective action*. Within the American political tradition there are two institutionalized methods of collective political participation. The first revolves around the political party. American political parties seek to influence the government by electing their members to political office. In order to accomplish this goal, political parties attempt to mobilize the electorate to support candidates affiliated with the party organization. Once elected to office, party members strive to organize the government and enact public policies which reflect the party's political philosophies and goals. Interest groups serve as the second basic method of collective political participation. Pressure organizations are private groups that attempt to influence public policy. Such organizations do not usually seek to elect members of their own group to public office, but rather work to convince public officials to support group goals and objectives. For the most part, interest group activities focus on policies that would benefit the organization's membership. Interest group political involvement is thus aimed at achieving relevant values which are determined through the political process.

Individual and collective forms of political participation serve linkage functions in a democracy. Elections, political parties, and interest groups link the public to the nation's leadership. America's governmental institutions are only as responsive and responsible as the people make them through their acts of political participation. Informed and intelligent voting can place in political leadership positions individuals who are capable of responding to the needs and opinions of the citizenry. Political party participation serves the purposes of recruiting potential public officials, promoting coherent political discourse, and organizing the electorate to make political choices. Interest groups serve to transmit preferences and demands to government officials by expressing the political views of their members.

The American political system is directly affected by the operation of its formal linkage institutions, and political parties and interest groups are central participants in this linkage process. The purpose of this book has been to examine the roles, functions, and performance of these group participants in terms of the realities of democratic politics. While there is a considerable amount of reasoned debate about precisely what these realities are, it does appear that organized groups perform an important, if not always well understood, function in bringing public influence to bear upon the policy-making process. The crucial point is that the transmission of group influence can accomplish democratic ends. Group politics and democratic politics are not incompatible.

POLITICAL PARTIES

The selection of national, state, and local political leadership is profoundly affected by the nature and vitality of the party system. Through much of the past two centuries, the United States has had a relatively competitive two-party system, at least at the national level. Whenever one party or another has for a time managed to establish dominance, a viable opposition party has emerged to challenge this dominance. The two-party system has shaped the contours of American electoral politics and the way in which the public influences the governmental decision-making process. Although sociopolitical forces have periodically upset the balance of power between the two major parties, the party system has thus far shown considerable resilience. Beyond the very general pattern of two-party politics, however, it is important to recognize certain salient characteristics of the major American parties.

The contemporary political party organizations in the United States are relatively weak when compared to partisan organizations in many other advanced democracies. In the United States, for example, the party organizations are not hierarchically controlled. The federal system continues to divide party organization in much the same way that it traditionally divided government authority. The American parties are, as a result, highly decentralized. They are in many important respects loose associations of state and local organizations rather than strong national associations. Furthermore, state and local regulation of the parties tends to reinforce this decentralization. In sum, powerful and pervasive national party organizations that can dominate the party electorates and the party in government have not developed in the United States.

In addition, the major American parties place a primary emphasis on electoral success. Because they would usually rather win elections than impose ideological purity on the political system, the major parties design their platforms and appeals to embrace a majority of the electorate. For this reason, they are often criticized for failing to offer "real choices" to the voters. However, in spite of the fact that the parties are not ideologically homogeneous, they do differ significantly on many important public policy issues.

While electoral supporters of the two parties do not exhibit sharp and consistent ideological and policy positions, Republican and Democratic party elites do differ in a number of important respects. Party platforms, presidential programs, and legislative records demonstrate that the two major parties have distinctive public policy goals and approaches. These distinctions do not necessarily rival the ideological divisions found in certain other democratic party systems, but neither are they trivial.

Americans largely rely on the political parties to recruit and nominate candidates for public office. If it is to be successful, a political party must select candidates for office who can win elections. In order to carry out this function, the parties must exercise a good deal of control over the nomination process. Today, however, as we have repeatedly noted, the party has lost much of its authority over the selection of its own nominees. This has been a severe blow to party organizations. The loss of control has resulted from increasing legal restrictions on the party organizations and from technological changes that have affected the way in which election campaigns are conducted. Today a candidate can win a party's nomination through the direct primary system without support from the party organization. The resourceful political candidate can create a personal organization, raise funds, hire professional campaign consultants, and appeal directly to the public for votes. The party organizations can sometimes be bypassed completely. Parties no longer monopolize the campaign resources necessary to win elections, nor are they the sole mobilizers of the electorate.

Upon electing members to positions of public trust, the parties are expected to organize the government and enact public policies consistent with the pledges made to the electorate during the campaign. In the legislative branch, party activity is quite prominent. The leadership and organization of the legislative chamber closely follow political party divisions. However, in terms of legislative roll-call voting, highly cohesive parties are not the rule. On many issues the two major political parties do not take opposing sides. However, the more controversial a legislative proposal, the greater likelihood there is that the parties will take differing positions. This is especially the case when the legislature considers the proposals submitted by the chief executive or when legislative issues have socioeconomic class significance. In the executive branch of government, the party also has considerable influence. The chief executive enjoys important appointment powers. These powers extend to a wide variety of policy-making positions within the executive administration. Traditionally, presidents and governors have distributed the overwhelming majority of these appointments to members of their own political parties. Supported by these political appointees, the chief executive is able to advance the programmatic objectives of his party. In comparing Democratic and Republican administrations at the national level, clear policy program differences can be seen. Party influences are least evident in the operations of the judicial branch. However, even here party affiliation is a major factor in the selection of judges at both the state and federal levels; and while nonpartisanship largely controls the process of judicial decision making, some evidence of differences between the rulings of Democratic and Republican judges has been discovered.

INTEREST GROUPS

Interest groups are organized collections of individuals who are bound together by shared attitudes or concerns and who make demands on political institutions in order to realize goals which they are unable to achieve on their own. Interest organizations have played an important part in American public policy development throughout the nation's history. In spite of the public's generally negative views of interest groups, pressure organizations make several positive contributions to American politics. The most important function of the interest group lies in its role as a means by which citizens can express their opinions and needs to those elected to public office.

Supported by First Amendment guaranteed rights of political association and expression, American citizens have long used the interest organization as a method of promoting public policy preferences. Individuals are attracted to interest groups for a number of reasons. For many, a pressure group can be a means of obtaining certain material benefits. These benefits may include such tangible advantages as increased employment opportunities, favorable business regulation, or the use of group-controlled facilities. Other individuals are attracted to interest groups because they offer pleasant social experiences, and membership has a certain prestige attached to it. Still others join such voluntary associations in order to work for the attainment of some worthy cause.

Among American interest groups the most powerful are those which have organized for economic reasons. Business, labor, agricultural, and professional organizations have as their central goal the improvement of occupational opportunities and conditions. They are all based upon their members' chosen method of earning a living. Other groups are based upon their membership's common experiences or shared traits. Interest groups classified as public interest lobbies work for governmental policies which they believe will benefit the entire nation. Cause groups organize in behalf of an ideological position or for the attainment of a specific political goal. Governmental interests, representing local, state, federal, and foreign political entities, are also active in the lobbying process.

There is considerable variation in the internal characteristics of American interest groups. The range of interests represented, the organizational structure, and the degree of support for political change are important traits that can differ substantially depending on the particular interest group. Interest groups also differ significantly in terms of their effectiveness in the political process. Group size, economic resources, prestige, philosophy, degree of membership mobilization, and quality of leadership are contributing factors to the overall potency of an interest group.

Pressure groups play an important role in American politics. They serve as a method of political participation by pooling the resources of like-minded individuals to make collective expressions of concern to government officials. They promote political discourse by supporting public policies among the general citizenry as well as among political officials. They serve a communications function by informing government of the views of a portion of the citizenry and by keeping their memberships informed of governmental actions. They serve a representative function by speaking in behalf of various groups within society.

Traditionally, interest groups have been associated with lobbying efforts which allow group representatives to make direct contact with public officials in an attempt to convince them to support group goals. In recent years, however, interest groups have become increasingly involved in indirect lobbying efforts. Indirect lobbying attempts to influence government by convincing the public to support policies, programs, and candidates that would benefit group members. Such indirect efforts can be classified into two basic strategies. First, interest groups attempt to mold public opinion. They employ modern public relations tactics designed to improve their public image and to convince citizens to support specific policy goals which they advocate. Second, interest groups have been active in election campaign activities. Candidates are supported through campaign contributions, organizational assistance, and endorsements. The objective here is to promote the candidacies of persons who share group attitudes on salient issues.

Modern pressure organizations also remain committed to traditional direct lobbying efforts. Lobbyists are perhaps more involved in legislative branch lobbying than ever before, but they have also grown increasingly interested in executive and judicial branch lobbying. The great growth in the importance of the administrative and regulatory agencies has not gone unnoticed by America's special interests. As these governmental bodies have increased in power, interest group attempts to influence the policies made by these offices have correspondingly proliferated. In addition, the courts have become an important arena for interest group activity. Like the administrative branch of government, the judiciary has become increasingly involved in public policy making. This has prompted an acceleration of interest-group-generated litigation.

RECENT TRENDS AND FUTURE PROSPECTS

Recent political trends suggest that American political parties and interest groups are in a state of flux. The relative strengths of these important linkage institutions have been changing. Furthermore, it is clear that this process of change is not yet complete. Additional modifications in the American system of group politics are likely to occur. The way in which this evolutionary process develops will have a substantial impact on America's future policy decisions.

Growth and Viability

Political parties and interest groups have demonstrated conflicting recent trends with respect to organizational health and strength. While political parties have undergone substantial degeneration over the past two decades, interest groups have experienced dramatic growth both in numbers and vitality.

The decline in political party affiliation is among the most important changes in American party politics. Today's voters are far less likely to feel strong attachments to the two major political parties than did voters two decades ago. The decline in party attachments has been reflected in the recent growth in the ranks of political independents. Until the mid-1960s, independents comprised about one-fifth of the electorate. Now independents account for approximately one-third of the electorate, outnumbering Republican party identifiers. The decline in political party affiliation has reduced the importance of partisan identification in the electoral process. Straight party-ticket voting is not as common today as it was in years past. Voters are much more likely to respond to candidate personalities and campaign issues. For the Democrats and especially the Republicans to be successful, substantial numbers of independent voters must be attracted to party candidates.

There is little evidence from recent political events to suggest that political parties are on the verge of reversing this trend away from strong party attachments. However, there is also very little to indicate that the present two-party system is about to undergo substantial change. Minor political parties are not achieving significant success in attempting to grow to major status. The dominance of the two established parties is not being challenged by rival party organizations. Nor is there hard evidence to suggest that the major parties will undergo radical transformation. While there is periodic discussion of the formation of a new centrist political party from the moderate wings of the two established parties or the creation of more ideologically consistent liberal and conservative parties, such major changes do not appear likely in the near future. Instead, the present two-party system, albeit in a weakened form, shows every sign of continuing to play an active role in American politics.

In contrast to the troubles facing the political parties, interest groups have shown increased growth and activity. Perhaps the most significant change over the past three decades has been the proliferation of new interest groups. The traditional business, labor, agriculture, and professional interests have now been challenged by a new generation of special interest organizations representing causes never before advocated in pressure group politics. The civil rights movement, the war in Vietnam, the environmental campaign, the women's rights struggle, and other similar social movements and events have spawned hundreds of new politically oriented groups. Many of these groups have directly confronted the more powerful and wealthy traditional lobbies and have achieved some surprising victories. These successes have in turn encouraged the creation of even more interest groups and have also prompted the traditional economic interests to redouble their lobbying efforts. Today, the arena of interest group politics is no longer made up exclusively of secure, status-quo-oriented, economic organizations, and there is little to suggest that interest group politics will revert to being completely dominated by the economic groups alone.

The activities of lobby organizations have also grown and expanded. No longer are group influence attempts restricted largely to direct contact with legislators. Instead, interest groups have developed a complete arsenal of public relations techniques to influence the opinions of the public and to encourage people to take action in behalf of group causes. More interest organizations are involved in election campaigns than ever before, in spite of legislation designed to reduce the role of pressure groups in the selection of public officials. Moreover, lobbying efforts have expanded beyond the legislative branch to include a wide array of administrative agencies. Similarly, the nation's courts are increasingly used by pressure groups to achieve favored public policy rulings. The escalation of interest group activities in these areas shows no sign of abating in the near future.

Composition and Control

As a class, persons who join organizations tend to differ slightly from the general population. Joiners for the most part are better educated, more economically secure, and have higher status occupations than the average American citizen. For those who become active participants in organizational affairs, the socioeconomic gap between group affiliators and those who do not become associated with voluntary organizations is even greater. These general tendencies have not materially changed over the past several decades.

In interest group politics today, however, there is a slightly different type of person involved than was the rule 25 years ago. The great proliferation of public interest groups has introduced a new generation of interest group activists with different values and outlooks. Today, a member of a lobby group is less likely to be status quo oriented and less apt to be interested primarily in the economic condition of the group's membership. Capitol Hill is now being patrolled by lobbyists concerned with the environment, consumer rights, openness in government operations, and other values to which little attention was paid by interest groups decades ago.

For the political parties, change in the composition of the activist category of group membership has been even more pronounced. Years ago, both major political parties were strongly influenced by organizational leaders. These leaders, along with members of the party who held public office, determined most of what the party did on matters of policy and candidate selection. The backbone of the party was the organization worker, the individual who spent many hours over a period of several years working on behalf of the party at the precinct level. These party regulars made up the activist element of the political organization. They provided the labor force for the party leaders and were rewarded for their loyalties with patronage and preferment.

Since the 1960s, however, major changes have occurred. Local organization leaders have lost much of their influence within the party. The precinct, county, and state organizations no longer control party policy and the party's nominees for public office. Today, both policy and candidate selection responsibilities have gravitated into the hands of a new variety of political party participant. These new activists, unlike their predecessors, are not organizational workers with strong party machine allegiances, but are policy-oriented activists with relatively low levels of party organization loyalties. Alterations in the nomination process, particularly the widespread adoption of presidential primaries, have taken candidate selection away from the party regulars and have theoretically given it to members of the general electorate who claim party membership. Delegates to party conventions at all levels are now selected through much more "open" procedures than ever before. These reforms, designed to make party politics more broad-based, have resulted in allowing party policy and candidate selection decisions to be susceptible to control by well-organized groups of political activists having nominal membership in the party.

Today, groups of political activists, coalescing around particular candidates or issues, can use the direct primary and other reform procedures to seize control of the party decision-making apparatus. The party regulars no longer hold sufficient power to defeat such well-orchestrated attempts, and the general party membership within the electorate lacks sufficient interest to stop such movements. Unfortunately for the party organizations, these groups of policy-oriented activists are often not in touch with general public opinion. Therefore, when they control the party platform and candidate selection decisions, the results at election time can be disastrous for the party. As discussed previously, two examples are worthy of note. In 1964, the Republican national convention was controlled by Goldwater delegates who were selected through the well-designed efforts of the more conservative wing of the party. The nomination of Senator Goldwater, the adoption of a very conservative platform, and the rejection of many of the Republican party's more moderate organization members led to a national political campaign that was completely out of step with the nation's electorate. Goldwater and the Republicans were overwhelmingly defeated at the polls, and many political observers had serious questions about the ability of the party to survive such a serious rejection by the people. The Democratic party experienced a similar situation in 1972. Liberal activists used the new reform procedures to advance the candidacy of Senator George McGovern. The 1972 Democratic delegates interested in various liberal domestic and foreign policy causes nominated Senator McGovern, adopted a very liberal party platform, and generally rejected the party regulars who had for the most part supported former vice president Hubert Humphrey. The controlling activist element of the party in 1972 was out of touch with the electorate. The result was that the nation's majority party was only able to capture one state in the presidential contest.

While the Republican party has generally slowed its movement toward reforming its internal procedures, the Democrats have continued to open the party to those persons outside the formal party organization. This has resulted in persons interested in liberal special interests becoming increasingly active in Democratic party affairs. Surprisingly, many of these new Democratic activists now exercising power within the party are also activists within various interest group movements. In fact, the various lobby organizations have become increasingly active within the Democratic party, often at the expense of the party regulars. The Democratic party for several decades has had civil rights and labor union officials active within its ranks, but today other interest groups not previously active within the party are gaining more influence.

An excellent example of the consequence of this activity is provided by the Democratic party's 1978 midterm conference. This national meeting was designed to be a forerunner of the 1980 national convention. The influence of interest group representatives was quite pronounced at this midterm conference. Issue activist delegates dominated many segments of the conference's deliberations. A significant number of party regulars, who had been selected as delegates, did not even attend the meetings. The conference passed 23 resolutions of party policy dealing with national domestic policy. A majority of these resolutions were special-interest-supported policies. For example, delegates interested in civil rights for blacks and other minorities influenced the conference to endorse making Martin Luther King, Jr.'s birthday a national holiday, to support granting electoral votes to the District of Columbia, to increase enforcement of civil rights laws, to support black colleges, to aid bilingual education, and to promote single-member legislative districts. Labor union activists convinced the conference to support full implementation of the Humphrey-Hawkins full employment program and to call for labor law reform. Senior citizens advocates succeeded in passing a resolution calling for more government attention to conditions facing older Americans. Feminist representatives won conference endorsement of the Equal Rights Amendment and a resolution calling for more vigorous support of affirmative action programs. Liberal ideology interest representatives won party support of such causes as federal aid to urban areas, national health insurance, public financing of congressional elections, the elimination of tax loopholes for the wealthy, and the promotion of ecology sensitive energy sources.

Furthermore, the conference adopted new delegate selection procedures for the presidential nominating convention which called for one-half of the 1980 delegates to be female, a significant victory for women's rights advocates. In the final analysis, the 1978 midterm conference seemed to reflect the demands of special-cause-oriented interests within the party rather than the careful planning of a national policy platform. While there is certainly nothing wrong with the Democratic party being open to these various interests, it does point to one especially significant development. The Democratic party and, to a lesser extent, the Republican party are becoming increasingly responsive to the issue-oriented activist, leaving a substantially reduced role for the party regular and the nonactivist electorate. In so doing, each party runs a serious risk of falling into the hands of those whose ideology is not consistent with the mainstream of its own or of the nation's electorate. Moreover, by deemphasizing the role of the party regulars, the internal organization of the political party may become even more seriously weakened.

Regulation

The general movement toward increased government regulation of public affairs has not ignored political parties and interest groups. The political party over the past century has completely changed in terms of its legal status. Political organizations previously were considered private associations and generally outside the sphere of government regulation. Today, however, political parties are highly regulated at both the state and, to a lesser extent, federal levels. As we have seen, this increased regulation, while intended to encourage political participation and reduce corruption, has taken much of the strength away from the political party organizations. Unable to control many of its own decisions, the political party exercises much less independent authority and power in American politics. Future regulation remains well within the realm of the possible. National concern with corruption in government and a general distrust of political parties provide a degree of public support for increased regulation. Good government interest groups have also maintained their activity in support of further reforming the activities of the political parties. Should additional reforms be instituted through government regulation, they will quite probably be at the expense of the independent strength of the party organizations.

Interest groups have been able to avoid government regulation in recent years because the proponents of regulation have not been able to agree on what kind of regulation to impose or in what form to impose it. Furthermore, First Amendment rights of assembly, petition, and speech are significant obstacles blocking any sweeping reform of interest group activities. However, current conditions make it likely that increased regulation will in fact come about. Primary targets for such regulation are lobbying efforts that concentrate on the executive branch and grassroots campaigns designed to influence public opinion. New regulations are likely to be limited ones, calling for comprehensive registration of lobbying personnel and public disclosure of lobbying activities and expenditures. Constitutional guarantees and the overall strength of today's interest groups make more restrictive regulation highly unlikely.

Group Politics and the Democratic Linkage

Political parties and interest groups are the traditional mechanisms of linking the citizenry to the government through collective action. During much of the nation's history, political parties have enjoyed a more significant role in this regard than have interest groups. However, in recent years political parties have been weakened by a number of forces, while interest groups have become more influential. Pressure organizations today represent more than the status-quo-oriented economic concerns of previous years. More citizens are turning to interest group membership as a method of expressing themselves to the government. The successes of the civil rights groups and the antiwar organizations have encouraged the formation and activity of increased numbers of voluntary associations. Political parties, on the other hand, have continued to weaken as political organizations because of increased regulation and internal reforms. Today, major candidates for public office can ignore the party organization and still win major election victories. Many recent presidential campaigns have placed personal organizations far above formal party committees. This has further reduced the prestige and influence of the party organizations. Such a situation would not have been possible in years past when the parties had strong organizations and the authority to control party policy and candidate nomination decisions.

The increase in interest group numbers and activities and the corresponding weakening of the parties has already had a substantial impact on American public policy. The parties appear less capable of drafting and implementing comprehensive national policy programs. Interest groups, on the other hand, have been accelerating their demands on all three branches of government. Government has been responding to these increased demands with new legislation, administrative regulations, and court decisions that benefit special interest group members. Interest groups are now assuming a greater role in setting the national public policy agenda, and this has come in large part at the expense of the political parties. The result has often been fragmented, rather than comprehensive, national policies.

Both interest groups and political parties remain important vehicles for linking individual citizens with the government. Organized political groups, though marred by weaknesses and imperfections, remain an essential means by which the public can influence political institutions. At the same time, the decline of parties should be a source of concern for those who value governmental responsiveness to a mass electorate. It is unlikely that interest groups, regardless of their numbers and influence, can promote this type of responsiveness on a continuing basis, especially in a way that large segments of the electorate can comprehend. Given the limited political interest, involvement, and knowledge of a good portion of the electorate, electorally pragmatic parties are a necessary complement to ideologically focused and specialized interest groups. Their continued decline in the pursuit of a more participatory politics may result in a political process that is theoretically open but in practical terms inaccessible to much of the citizenry.

Index

Activists, most liberal and most conservative, 167
Adams, John, 30, 172, 244
Adams, John Quincy, 31
Administrative Procedure Act (1946), 395
AFL-CIO, 308, 381
　Committee on Political Education (COPE), 163, 348, 356, 359
Agriculture, Department of, 392
Agriculture, House Committee on, 358
Albert, Carl, 213, 214
Alien and Sedition Acts (1798), 30
Allan Bakke v. Board of Regents of University of California, 404
　friends of the court in, 405-6
Amateur's long-term impact, 16
Ambassadors and money, 345
American Agricultural Movement, (AAM), 291
American Association of Retired Persons (AARP), 279, 299
American Bar Association (ABA), 293, 295
American Cancer Society, 280
American Civil Liberties Union (ACLU), 304, 317, 365
American Conservative Union, 305, 383
American Dental Association, 353
American Farm Bureau Federation, 290, 381, 392

American Federation of Labor (AFL), 286. *See also* AFL-CIO
American Heart Association, 280
American Hospital Association, 385
American Hotel and Motel Association, 284
American Independent party, 56
American Israel Public Affairs Committee, 298
American Issue, 321
American Jewish Committee, 298
American Jewish Congress, 298
American Legion, 297, 392
American Medical Associaion (AMA), 293, 295, 314-15, 326, 352, 358
　advertising of, 324
American Medical Political Action Committee (AMPAC), 352
American Osteopathic Hospital Association, 385
American Protestant Hospital Association, 385
American Retail Federation, 310
American Security Council, 383
American Trucking Association, 284
Americans for Constitutional Action (ACA), 163
Americans for Democratic Action (ADA), 163, 305, 359
Anti-Saloon League of America, 321

423

424 INDEX

Associated Milk Producers, Inc., 343, 344
Association of American Medical Colleges' Council of Teaching Hospitals, 385
Attitudinal differences, 153-68
   national convention delegates, 153-57
   party candidates, 159-61
   party officeholders, 161-65
   party officials, state and local, 158-59

Bailey, John, 80
Baker, Howard, 218
Ballot access, 187
Ballot form, 185-86
Bayard, James A., 31
Bayh, Birch, 360
Bell, Griffin, 390
Bipartisan voting, 232
Black Caucus, 62, 224
Blaine, James G., 212
Blanket primary, 175
Bliss, Ray, 71, 80
B'nai B'rith, 298
Brock, Bill, 70
Broder, David, 255
Brown, Edmund G., Jr., 260
Brown v. Board of Education, 407
Bryant, William Jennings, 33, 51
Buckley, James, 79, 181
Buckley v. Valeo, 184
Burke, Edmund, 26
Burr, Aaron, 30
Business and Professional Women's Clubs, National Federation of, 311
Business interest groups, 281-85
   examples of, 285
Business Roundtable, 283, 284, 315
Butler, Paul, 71
Butz, Earl, 390
Byrd, Harry F., Jr., 49
Byrd, Robert, 217-18

Califano, Joseph, 398
Campaign activities, 98
   organization and functions, 206
   state regulation of, 184
Campaign contributions, 350-58
   congressional, 352
Campaign endorsements, by interest groups, 359
Campaign finance legislation, 179-85
   1971, 180-81
   1974, 181-82
   1976, 182-83
Campaign information, sources of, 99
Candidate independence, 13
Cannon, Joseph G., 212
Cargo Preference Bill, 384
Carlisle, John, 212

Carswell, G. Harrold, 246, 403
Carter, Jimmy, 56, 57, 62, 68, 143, 196, 197, 244, 253
   labor's endorsement of, 356
Catholic Hospital Association, 385
Caucus, 171-72
   black, 62, 224
   congressional, 173
   conservative, 383
   Democratic, 221
   party, 220-22
   state legislative, 172-73
Cause interest groups, examples of, 306
Cause interests, 305-7
Chamber of Commerce of the United States (CCUS), 163, 283, 311, 377, 381, 384, 392
Chambers, William, 27
Chief executive
   as administration leader, 236-39
   as legislative leader, 239-43
   as party leader, 235-36
Church, Frank, 360
Church of Jesus Christ of Latter Day Saints, 299
Church League of America, 305
Churches, National Council of, 298
Citizens Committee for the Right to Keep and Bear Arms, 272
Citizens for the Republic, 383
Civil Aeronautics Board, 393
Civil Rights Act(s)
   1957, 232
   1960, 232
   1964, 189, 232
Civil War, 33
Clark, Peter, 279
Clarke, James W., 155
Class distinctions, 105
Clay, Henry, 174, 212
Closed primaries, 175
Cohesion, party, 226-34
Collective action, 412
Commerce, Department of, 392
Committees, common party, 220-25
Common Cause, 17, 303, 384
Community Hospitals, National Council of, 385
Competition, 35-47
   in presidential elections, 40
Congress of Industrial Organizations (CIO), 287
Congressional challengers, issue preferences of, 160
Congressional elections, 40-43
   financing, 183
Congress of Racial Equality, 298
Congress Watch, 384

Conservative Caucus, 383
Conservative coalition, 232
Conservative party, 58
Conservative Victory Fund, 357
Constitutional Convention, 281
Constitutional Government, Committee for, 305
Consumer Federation of America, 272, 303, 311
Consumer Product Safety Commission, 394
Consumers Union of the United States, 303
Contemporary trends
    interest groups and, 16-20
    political parties and, 11-16
Controversial issues, 10
Conventions, national. *See* National conventions
Convention system, 173-75
Cook County Democratic Central Committee, 85
Coolidge, Calvin, 54
COPE. *See* AFL-CIO, Committee on Political Education
Corporate political power, 16
Counties, National Association of, 307
Courts, interest group use, 400-402
Court system, structure of, 243-45
Crawford, William H., 173
Crime, 121
Crisp, Charles, 212
Culver, John, 360
Curtis, Kenneth M., 68, 70

Daley, Richard, 85
Daley machine, 84-86
David, Paul T., 45
Davis, John W., 54
Debs, Eugene, 58
Delegate selection, 193
Delegates and Organization, Committee on, 66
Democratic Advisory Council, 71
Democratic caucus, 221
Democratic charter, 62, 74
Democratic Convention (1972), 15
Democratic government, institutional linkages and, 2-11
Democratic National Committee (DNC), 65, 66, 67, 70, 73, 194
Democratic National Congressional Committee, 72
Democratic National Convention (1972), 66
Democratic Party, first midterm conference of, 62
Democratic Republicans (Democrats), 173, 174
Democratic Senatorial Campaign Committee, 72

Democratic Study Group, 224, 225
Democratizing the parties, 32
Democrats vs. Republicans, 32-33
Direct primaries, 61, 174-75
Direct primary system of nominations, 13
Dirksen, Everett, 79, 217
Dixiecrat, 54, 55, 64
Dodd, Thomas, 334, 360
Domestic government interest groups, examples of, 308

Eagleton, Thomas, 67
Eastland, James O., 79
Economic Advisers, Council of, 388
Education and Labor, House Committee on, 372
Eighteenth Amendment, 322
Eisenhower, Dwight D., 145, 244
Eisenhower administration, 71
Eisenhower years, calm of, 95
Eldersveld, Samuel J., 90, 158
Elections, 3-4, 204-7
    interest groups and, 339-62
    registration and, 187-92
Election system, 186-87, 192
Electoral college, 187
Electoral procedures, 185-87
Electoral vote, by state
    1912, 53
    1948, 55
    1968, 57
Electorate partisanship, 12-13
Elites. *See* Party elites
Elks, 280
Emergency Coalition to Save the Panama Canal, 383
Employment Security, Bureau of, 394
Endangered American Wilderness Act, 377
Endangered Species Act, 401
Energy Transportation Security Act, 384
Equal Rights Amendment, 137, 138, 300
Executive branch, lobbyists and, 396

Farmer-Labor party, 58
Farmer's Alliance, 50
Fathers United for Equal Rights, 300
Federal agencies, public relations resources of, 331
Federal Aviation Administration, 393
Federal Communications Commission, 393, 394, 396
Federal Corrupt Practices Act (1925), 180, 341, 348
Federal Election Campaign Act (1971), 180, 341, 342, 346, 347
Federal Election Campaign Amendments (1970), 181-82

Federal Election Commission, creation, of, 181, 182, 346, 347, 349, 354
Federal Ethics in Government Act, 397
Federal Highway Administration, 395
Federalist revival, 31
Federalists, 27, 29
Federal Judiciary, Committee on, 403
Federal Regulation of Lobbying Act (1946), 20, 337, 366, 367, 369, 387
Federal Trade Commission, 393
Federation of American Hospitals, 385
Field, Samuel, 246
Fifteenth Amendment, 188
Fishel, Jeff, 159
Food and Drug Administration, 393, 394, 396
Ford, Gerald, 70, 71, 145, 216, 244, 260, 354, 355
Foreign Agents Registration Act (1938), 309
Fortas, Abe, 246, 403
Free Estonia, Committee for, 298
Friend of the court activities, 403
Friends of the Earth, 304, 400

Gardner, John, 17, 303
Germond, Jack, 112
Goldwater, Barry, 71, 131, 135
Goldwater campaign (1964), 15
Goodell, Charles, 79
Governing, 209-50
Governmental interests, 307
Government Operations, House Committee on, 339
Governor's Conference, Democratic, 73
Granger movement, 50
Grant, Ulysses S., 39
Grass-roots lobbying, 333
  regulation of, 337-39
  trade associations under investigation for, 340
Great depression, 34
Greenback party, 50
Greenwald, Carol S., 275
Greeting Card Publishers, National Association of, 284
Griffin, Robert, 218
Gun Control Act (1968), 335

Hadley, Charles D., 165
Halleck, Charles, 216
Hamilton, Alexander, 27, 31
Harding, Warren G., 53
Hartford Insurance Corporation, 344
Hatch Act, 180, 239, 341
Haynesworth, Clement, 246, 403
Health, Education and Welfare, Department of, 390

Heinz, H. John III, 205
Hoover, Herbert, 402
House Budget Committee, 151
House Democratic Research Organization, 225
House Judiciary Committee, 335
  subcommittee on Civil and Constitutional Rights, 377
House of Representatives, U.S., 211-16
  party leaders in, 215
House Republican caucus, 222
House Rules Committee, 213
House Ways and Means Committee, 358
Huckshorn, Robert J., 204
Hughes, Charles Evans, 53
Hume, David, 26

Ideological differences, 112-16
Independent identification category, composition of, 102
Independents and partisans, 122-29
  attitudes towards electoral politics, 124
  attitudes toward voting and citizen duty among, 127
  inter-party differences among, 129
  participation in non-electoral national and local politics, 125
  political assessments among, 127
  political efficacy among, 126
  political participation, 123
  responsiveness among, 128
Indian Affairs, Bureau of, 392
Instructed delegate, 8
Interest groups, 268-319, 385-86, 414-16
  active in lobbying the Judicial Branch, 401
  and administrative departments, 390-93
  agricultural, 389-92, 372
  alliances and coalitions, 381-85
  business, 281-85
  campaign endorsements by, 359
  cause, 305-7
  contemporary American, 381-409
  decision making, 315
  defined, 270-73
  development of, 17-18
  and elections and, 339-62
  in electoral politics, 360-62
  governmental, 307
  internal structure of, 310-18
  labor, 288
  liberal, 163
  lobbyists, legislative politics and, 385-86
  nature and function of, 269-81
  organizational structure of, 311
  participants in congressional committee hearings, 375-76
  political currency of, 313-15

Interest groups *(cont.)*
  president and, 388-90
  professional, 292, 294
  public, 302-4
  range of interests of, 310-11
  regulation of, 20
  regulatory agencies and, 393
  special situation, 297-302
  targets of, 18-19
Intermediate institutions, contributions of, 10-11
Interparty competition, classification of states by, 37
Interstate Commerce Commission, 393
Issue activist, 165
Issue preferences, 116-22
Italian American Civil Rights League, 298
ITT corporation, 343

Jackson, Andrew, 27, 31, 32, 174, 237
Jackson, Henry M., 79
Jefferson, Thomas, 27, 30
Jeffersonian Republicans, 27
Jehovah's Witnesses, 299, 409
Jewell, Malcolm, 380, 381
Jobs and standard of living, responsibility for, 117
John Birch Society, 305, 312, 315
Johnson, Lyndon, 131, 145, 217, 235
Johnson Administration, and public assistance programs, 300
Judicial selection, 245-48, 402-3
Justice, Department of, 344, 402

Kennedy, Edward, 78, 131, 218
Kennedy, John F., 145, 244, 299
  assassintion of, 334
Kennedy, Robert, assassination of, 335
Kennedy administration, and public assistance programs, 300
Key, V.O., 141
Key issues, 147
  voting on, 148-49
King, Martin Luther, Jr., 335
  assassination of, 335
Knights of Labor, 286
Knowland, William, 217
Kohlmeier, Louis M., 395
Ku Klux Klan, 54, 275, 322

Labor, Department of, 392
Labor interest groups, 286-89
  examples of, 288
Labor Reform Act (1977), 374
Labor unions, political influence of, 16
Ladd, Everett Carll, Jr., 165
LaFollette, Robert M., 53, 54
Language minorities and voting, 191

Leading corporate PACs in 1976 elections, 353
League of Housewives, 300
League of Women Voters, 303, 384
Legislation, party unity in, 225-34
Legislative Action, Institute for, 329
Legislative groups, informal, 224
Legislative leaders, 211
Legislative records, 146-52
  congressional reforms, 151-52
  defense/foreign policy, 150
  economy and labor, 150
  energy and environment, 147-50
  other issues, 152
Liberal party, 58
Liberation of Lithuania, Supreme Committee for, 298
Libertarian party, 58
Liberty Lobby, 305
Lieutenant-governor, 219
Lincoln, Abraham, 246
Literacy tests, 189
Litigation sponsorship, 407-9
Lobbying, 320
  direct, 364-410
  executive branch, 386-99
  grass roots, 321-24
  indirect, 320-63
  judicial branch, 399
  legislative branch, 365
  organizations, 18
  tactics, 19-20
Lobbying with Appropriated Moneys Act (1919), 309
Lobbyist(s)
  legislative, 367-81
  and the legislative process, 370-78
  ratings and endorsements, 358-60
Long, Russell, 218
Longworth, Nicholas, 212
Loyalty pledge, 64

McCarthy, Eugene, 89, 181
McCarthy movement, 135
McCormack, John, 213, 214
McGovern, George, 56, 65, 69, 89, 131, 196, 197, 316, 360
  campaign (1972), 15, 179
  candidacy, 259
McGovern-Fraser Commission on Party Structure and Delegate Selection, 194
Mc Govern movement, 135
Maddox, Lester, 176
Madison, James, 1, 3, 26, 27
Majority floor leaders, 213
Major and Third Party Voting, 49
Management and Budget, Office of, 388

428   INDEX

Mansfield, Mike, 217
Manufacturers, National Association of (NAM), 275, 283, 311, 377, 392
Maritime Administration, 393
Marshall, Thurgood, 409
Martin, Joseph, 216
Mass political participation in campaigns, 99
Mayor's Conference, Democratic, 73
Meany, George, 287, 317
Medicare program, 295
Men's Rights Association, 300
Merchant Marine and Fisheries, House Committee on, 358
Merit selection, 248
Michels, Robert, 316
Mikulski Commission, 194
Milbrath, Lester, 379
Mines, Bureau of, 392
Minorities, aid to, 119
Minor parties in presidential elections, 50, 58
Missouri Plan. *See* Merit selection
Money and politics, 184
Monocrats, 30
Mott, Stewart, 342
Mulcahy, John, 342
Multimember districts, 186
Muskie, Edmund, 145

Nader, Ralph, 17, 303, 384
National Association for the Advancement of Colored People (NAACP), 278, 298, 365, 400, 409
    Legal Defense Fund of, 409
National Cable Television Association, 284
National committees, 67-73
    national chairman, 69-73
    president and, 68
National Conservative Political Action Committee, 383
National conventions, 63-67
    delegate apportionment, 63-64
    party rules and procedures, 64-67
National Defense, Council for, 383
National Education Association, 349, 358
National elections, 38-43
National Farmers Union (NFU), 163, 289, 308
National Firearms Act (1934), 334
National Governors Conference, 307
National Grange, 289, 291
National groups, other, 73-74
National Labor Relations Act (1935), 287
National Labor Relations Board, 395
National Labor Union, 286
National League of Cities, 307
National Medical Insurance Plan, 118
National Municipal League, 307

National nominating conventions, 196
National organizations, 62-75
National Republican Congressional Committee, 72
National Republicans (WHIGS), 173
National Retired Teachers Association (NRTA), 299
National Rice Growers Association, 310
National Rifle Association (NRA), 313, 314, 329, 334, 335, 336, 354
National Security Council, 388
National Welfare Rights Organization, 300-301
National Wildlife Federation, 304
National Women's Political Caucus, 300
Nature Conservancy, 304
Nelson, Samuel, 246
Neutron bomb, 151
New Deal, 16, 34, 307
New Deal Politics, 34-35
New Liberals, 131
New politics, 14
Newspapers, 98
Nie, Norma, 276-77
Nineteenth Amendment, 189
Nixon, Richard, 71, 79, 131, 145, 236, 240, 244, 316
    administration, 70
    campaign, 179
Nofziger, Lyn, 68
Nominating practices, 171-78
Nomination-election process, 171-208
Nominations, 201-4
Nonpresidential elections, 200-207

Occupational Safety and Health Administration (OSHA), 393, 394
Odd Fellows, 280
Officials who have taken positions with special interests, 398
Olson, Mancur, 278
O'Neill, Thomas, 213, 214
One-party system, modified, 36
Open and closed primaries, differences between, 175
Open primaries, 175
Organizations, types of, 277
Oswald, Lee Harvey, 334

Packwood, Robert, 360
Palevsky, Max, 342
Panama Canal Treaties (1977)
    debate over, 8
    ratification of, 382
Parker, Alton B., 141
Parker, John, 246, 402
Participation groups, 273-81

INDEX 429

Parties
    cadre, 83
    and the electorate, 93-133
    mass membership, 83
Partisan identification
    attitudes and beliefs and, 112-22
    interparty differences, 105-22
    measuring, 100
    social class and, 107-12
    trends in, 101
    weakening of party loyalties, 99-105
Partisan politics and judicial policy making, 248-49
Partisanship in the United States, 245
    1896-1930, 47
    1932-1970, 48
    restricted role of, 238
Party control
    in the House and Senate, 41
    national, and power, 74-75
    of the Presidency and Congress, 39
Party elites, 134-69, 155-57
    and rank and file, differences between, 156-57
Party in the government, 27, 252-55
Party leaders in the Senate, 218
Party organization, 257-58
    incentives and, 84-90
    maintenance of, 83-91
    recruitment and, 90-91
    and responsibilities, 77
Party outside government, 29
Party platforms, 136-41
    amendments and modifications, 141-42
    pledges, 138
Party politics, 31
Party Structure and Delegate Selection, Commission on, 65
Party system, 25-59
    candidates and, 203, 252-53
    electorate and, 255-57
    goals, 260
    governance, 261-64
    ideology, 264-65
    loyalties, decline in, 12
    officeholders, 253-55
    origin and development of, 26-34
    structure, 251-58
    substantial changes in, 25
Party unity
    in legislation, 225-34
    in voting, 229, 230
Party whip, 214
Patronage, 236, 237
Patterson, Samuel, 380, 381
People's party. *See* Populist party
Pinckney, Charles, 30

Platform contrasts
    1972, 139
    1976, 140
Policy and steering committees, 213, 221, 222-24
Policy differences, official, 136-52
Political Action Committees (PACs), 348-50
    growth of, 351
Political activist, 14-15
Political behavior, individual, 411
Political climate, manipulation of, 324
Political influence, labor unions and, 16
Political interest groups, 6-9
Political interest and involvement, 95-99
Political matters, communicating on, 355-56
Political parties, 4-6, 412-14
    contemporary trends in, 11-16
    and the executive branch, 234-43
    influence on government, 45
    judiciary and, 243-49
    and the legislature, 210-34, 234
    structure, elements of, 60
Political party organization, 60-92
    distinctive features of, 61
Political spoils, 84-90
Politics
    attention to, 98
    electoral, 13-14
    money and, 184
    organizational, 14-16
Polsby, Nelson W., 141, 198
Pomper, Gerald, 137, 141
Popular participation, 194
Populist party, 50
Power, transfer of, 30-31
Presidency, 259-61
President
    congressional support, 241
    electing, 199-200
    partisan congressional support, 242
Presidential appointments
    to cabinet, 237
    to lower federal courts, 246
Presidential campaigns
    illegal corporate contribution prosecuted, 346
    party control over, 200
Presidential Election Campaign Fund, 180
Presidential elections, 39, 199-200
    campaign debates (1976), 303
    leading contributors to, 343
Presidential nominations and elections, 192-207
Presidential Nominations and Party Structure, Commission on, 66
Presidential preference primaries, 61
Presidential primaries, 193

Presidential programs, 142-46
  approved by Congress, 1954-1975, 144
Presidential success on votes, 240
President pro tempore of the Senate, 216
Primaries
  blanket, 175
  closet, 175
  direct, 61, 174-75
  effects of, 177-78
  open, 175
  presidential, 191
  procedures for, 176-77
  types of, 175
Prisons, Bureau of, 392
Private Psychiatric Hospitals, National Association of, 385
Professional interest groups, 292-97
  examples of, 294
Progressive movement, 33, 54
Progressive Political Action, Conference for, 54
Progressives, 51
Progressivism, impact of, 33-34
Prohibition party, 58
Proportional representation, 186
Proxmire, William, 205
Public Citizen, 17
Public interest groups, 17
  examples of, 304
Public interests, 302-4
Public opinion, molding of, 323
Public relations campaign, 324

Rayburn, Sam, 212, 214, 221
Reagan, Ronald, 70, 135
Reconstruction Act (1867), 188
Reed, Thomas B. "Czar," 212
Re-Election of the President, Committee for, 199
Registration and elections, 187-92
Republican Chowder and Marching Society, 225
Republican Committee on Committees, 224
Republican conference. See House Republican caucus
Republican-Federalist conflict, 29
Republican National Committee, 69, 72, 74
Republican Policy Committee, 223
Republican Senatorial Campaign Committee, 72
Republican Wednesday Group, 225
Republican Women, National Federation of, 74
Responsible party system, 135
Responsive Law, Center for the Study of, 303
Reuther, Walter, 287
Revolutionary Youth Movement, 312

Ribicoff, Abraham, 18
Ripon Society, 64
Rockefeller, Nelson, 78
Roosevelt, Franklin, 34, 132, 281, 307
Roosevelt, Theodore, 51
Rules Committee, 212

Scaife, Richard Mellon, 342
School busing, 120
Scott, Hugh, 217
Sectionalism, 33
Securities and Exchange Commission, 393, 394, 397
Senate, U.S., 216-18
  party leaders in, 218
Senate Armed Services Committee, 151
Senate Foreign Relations Committee, 151
Senate Human Resources Committee, 372
Senate Judiciary Committee, 403
Senate leadership, 217
Senior Citizens, National Council of, 299
Sherrill, Robert, 336
Shriver, Sargent, 67
Sierra Club, 272, 304, 338
Smith, Alfred E., 141
Social characteristics and party identification, 109-10
Socialist party, 58
Social status and party identification, linkage between, 107
Solid South, 36
Soule, John W., 155
South, secession of, 54
Soybean Growers of America, 311
Speaker of the House, 211-13
Special situation interest groups, 297-302
  examples of, 301
State and Local Fiscal Assistance Act (1972), 308
State and local organizations, 75-83
  county committees, 81
  interrelationships, 82
  legal structure, 76-78
  state chairman, 80-81
  state committees, 78-79
State chairman, responsibilities of, 81
State Governments, Council of, 307
State judicial selection, primary method of, 247
State legislative caucus, 172-73
State legislatures, 219-20
State party organizations, support of, 197
State party strength in presidential elections
  in 1868-1892, 44
  in 1896-1928, 45
  in 1932-1976, 46
State party systems, 43-47
State regulation of campaigns, 184

States' Rights Democratic party. *See* Dixiecrat
Statistical information, use of, 322
Stevenson, Adlai, 71, 196
Stone, W. Clement, 342
Strategic Arms Limitation (SALT) Talks, 150, 151
Strauss, Robert, 69
Students for a Democratic Society (SDS), 312
Study of Responsive Law, Center for, 17
Subjective social class and partisanship, 111
Survival of a Free Congress, Committee for, 383

Taft, William, 51, 52
Taft-Hartley Act (1947), 341
Television, 98
Tellico Dam, 400
Third party(ies), 47-58
 national, 49-57
 presidential voting, 51
Thomas, Norman, 58
Thurmond, Strom, 54
Thurmond-Fielding ticket, 55
Tipps, Paul, 68
Tocqueville, Alexis de, 134, 135, 273
Trends and prospects, 416-22
Truman, Harry S., 54, 71
Twenty-sixth amendment, 96, 190
Two-party system, requirements for competitive, 36
Two-party vote for the U.S. House, 41
Two-thirds rule, 35
Tydings, Joseph, 360
Tyler, John, 246

United Auto Workers, 287
United States Catholic Conference, 298
United States Conference of Mayors, 307
United States v. Harriss, 337, 367
Universal Voter Registration Act, 192

Verba, Sidney, 276-77
Veteran's Administration, 392
Veterans of Foreign Wars, 297
Vice-president, U.S. 216
Vietnam War, 96
Voluntary associations, voluntary, 274

Vote
 getting out the, 206
 switching, 93
Voter qualifications
 age, 190
 property and taxpaying, 185
 race and sex, 188
 residence requirements, 190
Voter registration, 191
Voters, black, 64
Voter turnout, 3, 95, 96, 97, 191
Voting, 95
 bipartisan, 232
 conservative coalition, 233
 language minorities and, 191
 party unity in, 229
 straight ticket, 103
 voter qualifications and, 188-90
Voting Rights Act (1965), 189, 232
Voting Rights Act (1970), 190, 191

Wallace, George C., 50, 56, 57, 135, 260
War of 1812, 31
Warnke, Paul C., 150
Washington, George, 246
Watergate, 180, 240, 345
Ways and Means Committee, 213, 221
Weathermen, 312
Westwood, Jean, 69
We the People, 305
White, John C., 70
Wholesalers Distributors, National Association of, 310
Wildavsky, Aaron, 141, 198
Wilkie, Wendell, 196
Williams, Harrison, 358
Wilson, James Q., 279
Wilson, Woodrow, 53
Winograd Commission, 194
Witcover, Jules, 112
Woman suffrage, 189
Women, National Organization for, 300
Women's Action Alliance, 300
Women's caucus, 62, 224
Women's Equity Action League, 300
Women's Lobby, 300
Workers Student Alliance, 312
Wright, Fielding, 54

Young Democratic Clubs of America, 74
Young Republican National Federation, 74

48110383

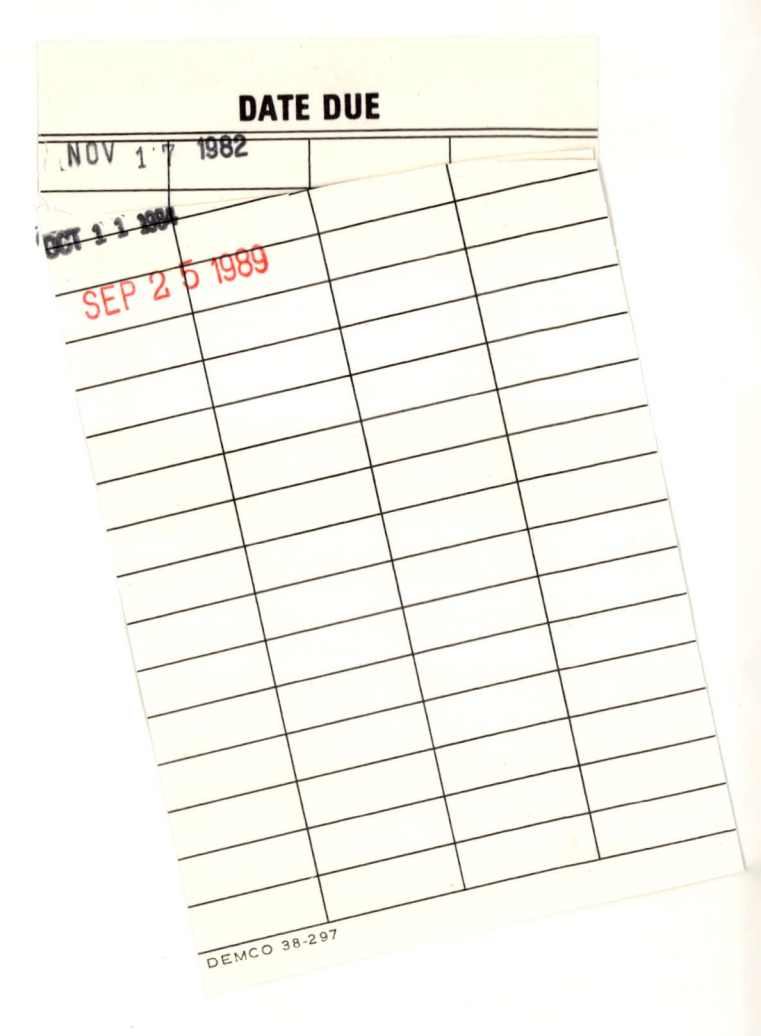

JK2261.I66

IPPOLITO   DENNIS S.

POLITICAL   PARTIES

INTEREST   GROUPS   AND

WITHDRAWN

DATE DUE

NOV 17 1982

OCT 11 1984

SEP 25 1989

DEMCO 38-297

MONTGOMERY COLLEGE LIBRARIES
germ, circ   JK 2261.I66
          Political par

0 0000 00196783 5